murach's C#

8TH EDITION

Anne Boehm

Joel Murach

MIKE MURACH & ASSOCIATES, INC.

3730 W Swift Ave. • Fresno, CA 93722

www.murach.com • murachbooks@murach.com

Editorial team

Authors: Anne Boehm
                                      Joel Murach

Contributors: Mary Delamater
                                      Nick Taggart

Production: Juliette Baylon

Books on programming languages

Murach's C#
Murach's C++ Programming
Murach's Python Programming
Murach's Java Programming
Murach's Visual Basic

Books on data analysis

Murach's R for Data Analysis
Murach's Python for Data Analysis

Books for web developers

Murach's HTML and CSS
Murach's JavaScript and jQuery
Murach's ASP.NET Core MVC
Murach's PHP and MySQL

Books for database programmers

Murach's SQL Server for Developers
Murach's MySQL
Murach's Oracle SQL and PL/SQL for Developers

For more on Murach books, please visit us at www.murach.com

10 9 8 7 6 5 4 3 2 1
ISBN: 978-1-943873-07-4

Contents

Contents

Expanded contents

Section 2 The C# language essentials

Chapter 4 How to work with numeric and string data

Chapter 5 How to code control structures

Section 4 Basic skills for working with data

Section 5 Database programming

Introduction

C# is an elegant, object-oriented language that uses syntax that's similar to C++ and Java. As a result, it provides an easy migration path for C++ and Java developers who want to leverage the power of the .NET platform. In addition, C# provides an opportunity for Visual Basic developers to learn a powerful language that's in the C++ family without leaving the comfort of the Visual Studio development environment.

If you're ready to add C# to your skill set, there's no better way to do that than with this book. It has helped thousands of programmers learn C# ever since the first edition came out in 2004. Now, this 8th edition has been updated throughout to make it easier than ever for you to gain the C# and Visual Studio skills that employers are looking for in today's application developers.

Who this book is for

This book is for anyone who wants to learn the C# programming language. To teach C#, this book shows how to develop professional Windows Forms applications using Visual Studio and .NET. Since Visual Studio makes it so easy to develop the user interface for a Windows Forms application, this is a great way to focus on learning the C# code that provides the functionality for the application.

This book works for complete beginners to experienced Java, C++, and Visual Basic programmers. To make that possible, this book uses a unique, topic-based approach that lets you set your own pace. For example, section 1 guides you through the basics of using Visual Studio and its Windows Forms designer to develop a desktop application with C#. Whether you're a Java or C++ programmer or a complete beginner, you can get up to speed quickly with this development environment by reading this section and doing the exercises at the end of each chapter. And if you're a Visual Basic programmer who is already comfortable with Visual Studio, you can skim this section.

Sections 2 and 3 use the same approach to teach the C# language. If you're familiar with another language in the C++ family, such as Java, you should be able to move through these sections quickly, focusing on the classes and methods that are available from .NET. Conversely, if you're already familiar with .NET, you can focus on the details of the C# syntax. And if you're new to both C# and .NET, you'll find that the material is broken down into manageable bites and organized in a logical sequence, so you can take as much time as you need to master one topic before moving on to the next. In each case, you're going to learn C# at a pace that's right for you.

What you'll learn in this book

Section 1 introduces the concepts and terms needed for working with the .NET platform, and it teaches the basics of working with Visual Studio. Here, you'll learn how to develop a simple Windows Forms application. To do that, you'll use the Form Designer to design a Windows form, and you'll use the Code Editor to write the C# code for the form.

Section 2 presents the data types, control structures, and other essential elements of the C# language as well as the core .NET classes that you'll use to develop Windows Forms applications. Along the way, you'll learn how to create professional applications. In chapter 7, for example, you'll learn data validation techniques that every developer should know.

Section 3 teaches the powerful object-oriented programming features of the C# language. Here, you'll learn how to create your own business and database classes, and you'll learn how to use the database classes to populate the business objects with data from files or a database. That, of course, is how applications work in the real world. Along the way, you'll learn how to use inheritance, polymorphism, interfaces, and much more.

Section 4 teaches some basic skills for working with data. That includes storing data in files. It also includes working with LINQ, a feature that lets you query most any data source using the C# language.

Section 5 teaches how to develop database applications. To start, it shows how to use Entity Framework (EF) Core to work with a database by mapping the objects of an application to the tables of a database. In most cases, this technique is considered a best practice. Then, it shows how to manually write ADO.NET code that directly accesses the database. This technique is useful if you need to customize your data access code. Finally, this section shows how to use the DataGridView control to display and update the data in a table, a critical skill for many database applications.

Why you'll learn faster and better with this book

Like all our books, this one has features that you won't find in competing books. That's why we believe that you'll learn faster and better with our book than with any other. Here are five of those features:

- This book shows you how to get the most from Visual Studio as you develop your applications. Since using the features of this IDE (integrated development environment) is one of the keys to development productivity, we illustrate the best use of Visual Studio throughout this book.

- The exercises for each chapter guide you through the development of the book applications and challenge you to apply what you've learned in new ways. Because you can download the starting points for these exercises from our website, you get the maximum amount of practice in a minimum of time. And because you can also download the solutions, you can check your work and correct any misconceptions right away.

- All of the examples presented in this book are drawn from realistic applications. This difference becomes especially apparent in the object-oriented programming section, where we present the use of business classes like customers, invoices, and products so you can see how object-oriented programming is used in the real world.

- To help you develop applications at a professional level, this book presents *complete* applications. That way, you can see the relationships between the C# code, objects, properties, methods, and events that an application requires, which is essential to your understanding.

- All of the information in this book is presented in our unique paired-page format, with the essential syntax, guidelines, and examples on the right page and the perspective and extra explanation on the left page. Programmers tell us that they love this format because they can learn new skills whenever they have a few minutes and because they can quickly find the information that they need when they use our books for reference.

What software you need

To develop the Windows Forms applications presented in this book, you must have a computer that's running Windows 10, Version 1607 or later. In other words, even though .NET 7 is cross-platform, you can't use macOS or Linux to develop Windows Forms applications like the ones shown in this book.

On your Windows computer, you need an edition of Visual Studio, and we recommend using Visual Studio Community. This edition of Visual Studio can be downloaded from Microsoft's website for free. However, if you already have another edition of Visual Studio installed on your computer such as Visual Studio Professional, you can use that edition instead if you prefer.

When you install Visual Studio, you can install all the other components you need to work with this book. This includes the compiler for the C# language, the .NET platform, and SQL Server Express LocalDB, which is an embedded version of the SQL Server database that's designed to make it easy for developers to test database applications.

Downloadable files that can help you learn

If you go to our website at www.murach.com, you can download all the files that you need for getting the most from this book. These files include:

- the applications presented in this book
- the starting points for the exercises that are at the end of each chapter
- the solutions to the exercises
- the database and files that are used by the applications and exercises

The code for the book applications is especially valuable because it lets you run the applications on your own computer, view the source code, experiment with the code, and copy and paste any of the source code into your own applications.

Support materials for trainers and instructors

If you're a college instructor or corporate trainer who would like to use this book as a course text, we offer a full set of the support materials you need for a turnkey course. That includes:

- instructional objectives
- extra exercises
- projects
- test banks
- PowerPoint slides

Instructors tell us that this is everything they need for a course without all the busywork that you get from other publishers.

To learn more about our instructor's materials, please go to our website at www.murachforinstructors.com if you're an instructor. If you're a trainer, please go to www.murach.com and click on the *Courseware for Trainers* link, or contact Kelly at 1-800-221-5528 or kelly@murach.com.

Please remember, though, that the primary component for a successful C# course is this book. Because your students will learn faster and more thoroughly when they use our book, they will have better questions and be better prepared for class. And, because our paired pages are so good for reference, your students will be able to review for tests and do their projects more efficiently.

2 companion books

If you need to learn how to develop web applications with C#, we recommend *Murach's ASP.NET Core MVC*. This book shows how to use the Model-View-Control (MVC) pattern to develop cross-platform web applications at a professional level.

Just about any business application you develop in C# needs to work with a database. Because of that, we recommend keeping a copy of *Murach's SQL Server for Developers* close at hand. Although most developers know some elementary SQL, they often stop there, never realizing all the power that SQL has to offer. But this book helps you learn how to use SQL to write powerful and complex queries. Beyond that, this book shows how to design and implement databases and how to use advanced features like stored procedures, triggers, and functions.

Please let us know how this book works for you

This is the 8th edition of our C# book. For each edition, we've added what we think are the most important new features of Visual Studio, .NET, and C#. But we've also tried to respond to the feedback that we've received and improve the content of the book.

Now that we're done with this book, we hope that we've succeeded in making it as easy as possible for you to master C#, no matter what your background. So if you have any comments about our book, we would appreciate hearing from you. If you like our book, please tell a friend. And good luck with your C# programming.

Anne Boehm, Author
anne@murach.com

Joel Murach, Author
joel@murach.com

Section 1

An introduction to Visual Studio

This section gets you started right by introducing the components that support C# programming. To start, chapter 1 introduces you to the .NET platform, the languages that work with the .NET platform, and the Visual Studio development environment. Then, chapter 2 shows you how to use Visual Studio to design a form for a Windows Forms app. Finally, chapter 3 shows you how to use Visual Studio to enter and edit the code that determines how the form works.

When you complete this section, you should have a general understanding of how to use Visual Studio to develop a Windows Forms app. You should also have the skills that you need for designing a Windows form and entering the code for it. Then, the next section of this book will teach you the essentials of the C# language.

1

How to get started with Visual Studio

This chapter gets you started with C# programming by introducing the .NET platform, the languages that work with the .NET platform, and the Visual Studio development environment. It also provides a quick tour of this development environment. Along the way, you'll learn all the concepts and terms that you need for developing .NET applications.

An introduction to .NET development

This section presents some concepts and terms that you should be familiar with before you begin developing .NET applications. Although this section focuses on C#, most of these concepts and terms also apply to the other .NET programming languages.

Platforms for .NET applications

This book teaches C# by showing how to use it to create *desktop apps*, also called *desktop applications*, that run on the .NET platform that's running on a Windows computer. For example, the top of figure 1-1 shows a desktop app that you'll learn to develop in this book. To do that, this book shows how to use the *Windows Forms* (or *WinForms*) platform because it provides a drag-and-drop designer that makes it easy to develop the user interface for an app. As a result, this book can focus on teaching the C# code that provides the functionality for these apps.

In a WinForms app, each *Windows form* (or just *form*) provides a user interface that lets the user interact with the app. In this figure, the app consists of a single form. Many apps, though, require more than one form. As part of the user interface, a Windows Forms app uses *controls* like the ones shown in this figure.

Besides WinForms, you can use two newer platforms to develop Windows desktop apps that run on .NET. *WPF* (*Windows Presentation Foundation*) provides a more modern user interface than Windows Forms apps. To define that user interface, it uses *XAML* (*Extensible Application Markup Language*).

UWP (*Universal Windows Platform*) provides an even more modern way to develop apps. Like WPF, UWP uses XAML to define the user interface. However, UWP provides a way to define a responsive user interface that supports various screen sizes for any Windows 10 or later device.

Besides desktop apps, you can use C# to create *web apps* that run on the .NET platform that's running on a server. Then, the C# code runs on a web server, but the user can display the user interface for the app in a web browser that's running on the user's computer.

If you want to develop a simple web app with C#, you can use *ASP.NET Web Forms*. Like the Windows Forms platform, the ASP.NET Web Forms platform provides a drag-and-drop designer that makes it easy to develop the *web forms* that define the pages of a web app. However, the ASP.NET Web Forms platform isn't available from the latest versions of .NET.

If you want to develop a more complex web app with C#, the more modern *ASP.NET Core MVC* and *ASP.NET Core Razor Pages* platforms are probably a better choice. The ASP.NET Core MVC platform uses the *MVC* (*Model-View-Controller*) pattern to structure code in a way that makes it easier to test, debug, and maintain apps. To learn more about this subject, we recommend a companion book, *Murach's ASP.NET Core MVC*. The ASP.NET Core Razor Pages platform is used to create page-focused web apps and is built on top of ASP.NET Core MVC.

A Windows desktop app

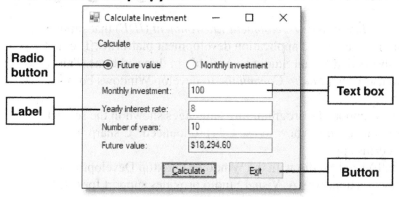

Three platforms for developing Windows desktop apps with .NET

Type	Description
Windows Forms (WinForms)	Provides a drag-and-drop designer that automatically generates the code that defines the user interface.
Windows Presentation Foundation (WPF)	Requires the programmer to write XAML (Extensible Application Markup Language) that defines the user interface, but provides an enhanced user experience.
Universal Windows Platform (UWP)	Requires the programmer to write XAML that defines the user interface, but provides a way to create responsive apps that support various screen sizes. Supported by any Windows 10 or later device.

Three platforms for developing web apps with .NET

Type	Description
ASP.NET Web Forms	Provides a drag-and-drop designer that automatically generates the code for the web forms that define the pages of the web app.
ASP.NET Core MVC	Requires the user to write code that uses the Model-View-Controller (MVC) design pattern to define the pages of the web app.
ASP.NET Core Razor Pages	Uses a model that's built on top of ASP.NET Core MVC and is used to create page-focused apps.

Description

- A *desktop app* is an application such as a word processor or a spreadsheet that runs directly on the user's computer.

- A *web app* is an application such as a website that runs on a web server. Then, the user can view the pages of a web app with a web browser.

- The user interface for an application typically contains *controls* like labels, text boxes, and buttons. These controls allow the user to interact with the application.

Figure 1-1   Platforms for .NET applications

Visual Studio and the .NET programming languages

Visual Studio is an *Integrated Development Environment* (*IDE*) that supports many programming languages and application development platforms. The first table in figure 1-2 shows that Visual Studio is available in three editions. This book shows how to use *Visual Studio Community* to develop Windows Forms apps.

All three editions support the programming languages shown in the second table. This book, of course, shows how to use C# (pronounced "C sharp") to develop Windows Forms apps.

When you install Visual Studio with the Windows Desktop Development workload as described in appendix A, Visual Studio provides support for C#. In addition, you can choose which versions of the *.NET Framework* (pronounced "dot net framework") or *.NET Core* you want to install. These are the versions you'll be able to target from the apps you create, as you'll see in the next chapter.

These .NET platforms provide a way to run applications written in C#. However, they can also run applications written in other .NET languages such as Visual Basic or F#. These languages are briefly described in the second table in this figure. Like C#, Visual Basic is an object-oriented language. By contrast, Visual F# is a newer language that provides functional programming in addition to object-oriented and procedural programming.

The Visual Studio Installer also lets you install *SQL Server Express LocalDB*. This version of the SQL Server database management system is designed for developers and doesn't require any setup. Because of that, it's ideal for testing database applications on your own computer.

The editions of Visual Studio described in this figure only run on Windows. However, you can run Visual Studio on macOS using a version known as Visual Studio for Mac. This version allows you to develop web apps such as ASP. NET Core MVC apps, but it doesn't provide a way to develop desktop apps for Windows like the Windows Forms apps presented in this book.

Visual Studio 2022 editions

Edition	Description
Community	A free edition that's appropriate for hobbyists, students, and individual developers building non-enterprise applications.
Professional	Designed for small teams of professionals building non-enterprise applications. Includes tools for analyzing code and collaborating with teams.
Enterprise	Designed for teams of any size who want to build complex, scalable enterprise applications.

.NET programming languages

Language	Description
C#	An object-oriented language with a syntax that's similar to C, C++, Java, and JavaScript.
Visual Basic	An object-oriented language with a syntax that's designed to be easy to learn and use.
F#	A language that combines functional, procedural, and object-oriented programming.

Description

- *Visual Studio* is an *Integrated Development Environment* (*IDE*) that supports many programming languages and application development platforms.

- When you install Visual Studio, you can choose the versions of the *.NET Framework* and *.NET Core* you want to install. These platforms provide a library of code that supports .NET programming languages such as C#.

- When you install Visual Studio, you can choose to install *SQL Server Express LocalDB*, a scaled back version of the Microsoft SQL Server database management system that's designed for developers.

- The editions of Visual Studio shown in this figure only run on Windows. There's a version of Visual Studio known as Visual Studio for Mac that runs on macOS, but it doesn't provide a way to develop desktop apps for Windows.

Figure 1-2   Visual Studio and the .NET programming languages

The .NET Framework and .NET Core

To describe how .NET works, figure 1-3 presents the main components of the .NET Framework and .NET Core. This shows that .NET Core works similarly to the .NET Framework. In fact, many of the code and techniques that are presented in this book work the same regardless of whether you use the .NET Framework or .NET Core.

The main difference between these platforms is that the .NET Framework is older and only supports Windows. On the other hand, .NET Core is newer and cross-platform. As a result, .NET Core can run on Windows, macOS, and Linux. Because Microsoft ended development of the .NET Framework at version 4.8, .NET Core is the future of .NET development.

In fact, starting with version 5, .NET Core is now just called .NET (no Core in the name). In this book, all applications are created using .NET 7, which was released in November of 2022. Because .NET combines the best features of the .NET Framework and previous versions of .NET Core, it provides an easy migration path for .NET Framework applications, and it provides a foundation for future development of the .NET platform.

Both the .NET Framework and .NET provide a set of *class libraries*. These class libraries consist of segments of pre-written code called *classes* that provide many of the functions that you need for developing .NET applications. For instance, the Windows Forms classes are used for developing Windows Forms apps. The ASP.NET and ASP.NET Core classes are used for developing Web Forms apps. The EF and EF Core classes are used for developing apps that access databases. And other classes let you manage security, access files, and perform many other functions.

The .NET Framework and .NET also provide a common infrastructure that applications written in a .NET language such as C# can use to run on various operating systems and hardware platforms. This infrastructure includes the Common Language Runtime, the .NET languages, and the compilers for those languages.

The *Common Language Runtime (CLR)* provides the services that are needed for executing any application that's developed with one of the .NET languages. This is possible because all the .NET languages compile to a common intermediate language, which you'll learn more about in figure 1-5. The CLR also provides the *Common Type System* that defines the data types that are used by all .NET languages. Because all the .NET applications are managed by the CLR, they are sometimes referred to as *managed applications*.

If you're new to programming, you might not understand this diagram completely, but that's all right. For now, all you need to understand is the general structure of the .NET Framework and .NET and the terms that have been presented so far. As you progress through this book, this diagram will make more sense, and you will become more familiar with each of the terms.

The .NET Framework and .NET Core (.NET)

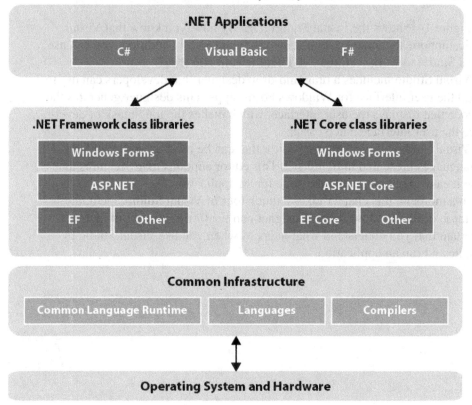

Description

- Windows Forms apps do not access the operating system or computer hardware directly. Instead, they use services of the .NET Framework or .NET Core (now just called .NET), which in turn access the operating system and hardware.

- The .NET Framework and .NET provide *class libraries* that contain pre-written code known as *classes* that are available to all of the .NET programming languages. These class libraries consist of thousands of classes, but you can create simple .NET applications once you learn how to use just a few of them.

- The .NET Framework and .NET use a common infrastructure that includes the *Common Language Runtime* (*CLR*), the languages, and the compilers.

- The CLR manages the execution of .NET programs by coordinating essential functions such as memory management, code execution, security, and other services. Because .NET applications are managed by the CLR, they are called *managed applications*.

- The *Common Type System* is a component of the CLR that ensures that all .NET applications use the same basic data types no matter what programming languages are used to develop the applications.

Figure 1-3   The .NET Framework and .NET Core

The Visual Studio IDE

Figure 1-4 shows the Visual Studio IDE. By now, you know that Visual Studio supports the languages presented in figure 1-2. In addition, you can use Visual Studio to work with the .NET Framework and .NET.

Visual Studio includes a drag-and-drop designer that developers can use to design the user interface for Windows Forms apps. This designer generates the C# code that displays the user interface, which makes the tough task of developing the user interface much easier.

Visual Studio also includes an editor that can be used to work with any of the languages presented in figure 1-2. This editor contains many features that make it easy to enter and edit the code for an application.

In a moment, this chapter takes a quick tour of Visual Studio, including a glimpse of the Windows Form Designer and the Code Editor. But first, it's important that you understand what happens when you use Visual Studio to compile and run an application.

The Visual Studio IDE

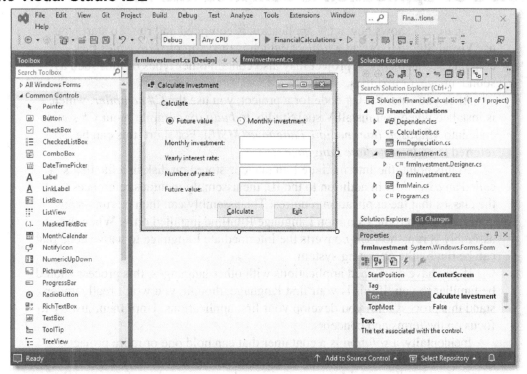

Description

- Visual Studio includes drag-and-drop designers that can be used to develop Windows Forms apps and Web Forms apps.

- Visual Studio includes a code editor that can be used to work with many languages, including the .NET languages presented in figure 1-2.

Figure 1-4   The Visual Studio IDE

How a C# application is compiled and run

Figure 1-5 shows how a C# application is compiled and run. To start, you use Visual Studio to create a *project*, which is made up of *source files* that contain C# statements. A project may also contain other types of files such as sound, image, or text files.

After you enter the C# code for a project, you use the *C# compiler*, which is installed when you install Visual Studio, to *build* (or compile) your C# source code into *Microsoft Intermediate Language* (*MSIL*). For short, this can be referred to as *Intermediate Language* (*IL*).

At this point, the Intermediate Language is stored on disk in a file that's called an *assembly*. In addition to the IL, the assembly includes references to the classes that the application requires. The assembly can then be run on any computer that has the Common Language Runtime installed on it. When the assembly is run, the CLR converts the Intermediate Language to native code that can be run by the operating system.

If you have developed applications with other languages, this process should be familiar to you. If this is your first language, though, you won't really understand this process until you develop your first applications. Until then, just try to focus on the terms and concepts.

Incidentally, a *solution* is a container that can hold one or more projects. Although a solution can contain more than one project, the solution for a simple application usually contains just one project. In that case, the solution and the project are essentially the same thing.

How a C# application is compiled and run

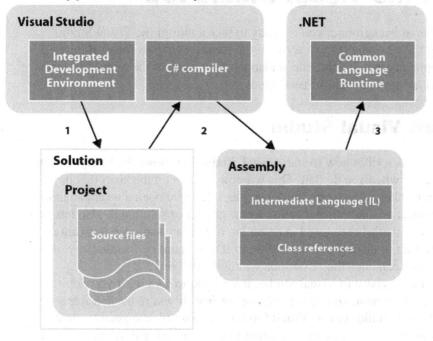

Operation

1. The programmer uses Visual Studio to create a *project*, which includes C# *source files*. In some cases, a project will also contain other types of files such as images, sound, or text files.

2. The C# *compiler* compiles (translates) the C# source code for a project into *Microsoft Intermediate Language* (*MSIL*), or just *Intermediate Language* (*IL*). This language is stored on disk in an *assembly* that also contains references to the required classes. An assembly is an executable file that has an .exe or .dll extension.

3. The assembly is run by .NET's Common Language Runtime. The CLR manages all aspects of how the assembly is run, including converting the Intermediate Language to native code that can be run by the operating system, managing memory for the assembly, and enforcing security.

About projects and solutions

- A *solution* is a container that can hold one or more projects.

Figure 1-5   How a C# application is compiled and run

A tour of the Visual Studio IDE

With that as background, you're ready to take a tour of the Visual Studio IDE. Along the way, you'll learn some of the basic techniques for working in this development environment. You'll also see how some of the terms that you just learned are applied within Visual Studio.

How to start Visual Studio

Figure 1-6 describes how to start Visual Studio and shows the Start window that's displayed when you do that. This window focuses on the tasks that developers are most likely to perform. For example, it lets you open a recent solution, open any project or solution, and create a new project or solution. It also lets you work with code that's been stored in an online repository and open individual files. If you want to display the Visual Studio IDE without performing any of these tasks, you can click the "Continue without code" link.

The first time you start Visual Studio, it asks you to sign in. If you don't already have an account, you can create one for free. If you're using a free edition of Visual Studio such as Visual Studio Community, you need to create an account or sign in to an existing account to continue using it. Also, if you run Visual Studio on multiple devices, signing in allows you to synchronize your settings across those devices.

After you sign in, Visual Studio asks you to select the default development settings. Then, you can choose the Visual C# option to make your menus look like the ones in this book. If you want, you can also select the color theme that you'd like to use. Visual Studio defaults to the Blue color theme, and that's the one shown by the screen captures in this book.

The screen captures in this book are based on Visual Studio Community 2022. If you're using another edition, you may notice some minor differences between the screens displayed by your edition and the screen captures in this book. However, the features described in this book should still work similarly on your edition of Visual Studio.

The Start window that's displayed when you start Visual Studio

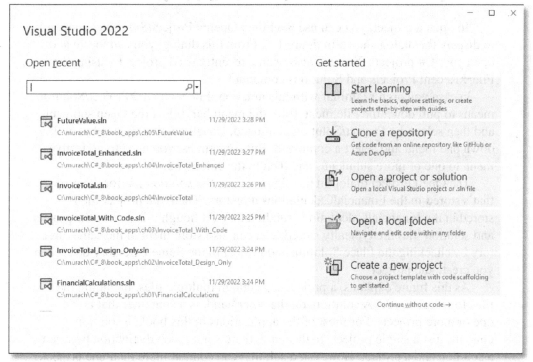

Description

- To start Visual Studio, locate and select Visual Studio from the Start menu or the Apps list.

- To make it easier to start Visual Studio, you can create a shortcut for Visual Studio and put it on the desktop or pin it to the Start menu.

- When Visual Studio starts, it displays a Start window. You can use this window to open a recent solution, open any project or solution, create a new project, and so on.

- To display the Visual Studio IDE without performing one of the available tasks, click the "Continue without code" link.

Differences between Visual Studio Community and other editions

- The screen captures in this book use Visual Studio 2022 Community. If you're using another edition of Visual Studio, you may notice some minor differences on your system, but Visual Studio should still work similarly.

Figure 1-6   How to start Visual Studio

How to open or close an existing project

To open a project, you can use the File→Open→Project/Solution command to display the dialog shown in figure 1-7. From this dialog, you can locate and open your C# projects. You can also open a recently used project by using the File→Recent Projects and Solutions command.

In case you aren't familiar with this notation, File→Open→Project/Solution means to pull down the File menu from the menu bar, select the Open submenu, and then select the Project/Solution command. Usually, you only need to pull down one menu and select a command. But sometimes, you need to go from a menu to one or more submenus and then to the command.

The Open Project dialog in this figure shows the *solution file* for the project that's stored in the FinancialCalculations directory. Then, the project file is stored in the FinancialCalculations subdirectory. Although this is how the project and solution files are typically stored, you can also store them in the same directory by checking the Place Solution and Project in the Same Directory box when you create the project.

As this figure explains, a project can contain multiple files, including the files for source code. A solution, on the other hand, is a container that holds one or more projects. For most of the applications in this book, a solution contains just a single project. In that case, there's not much distinction between a solution and a project. However, a solution can contain more than one project. This is often the case for large applications that are developed by teams of programmers.

With a multi-project solution, programmers can work independently on the projects that make up the solution. In fact, the projects don't even have to be written in the same language. For example, a solution can contain two projects, one written in C#, the other in Visual Basic.

At this point, you might wonder whether you should open a project or a solution. In this figure, for example, FinancialCalculations.sln is a solution and FinancialCalculations.csproj is a C# project. In most cases, it doesn't matter whether you open the solution or the project. Either way, both the solution and the project files will be opened. And when you use the File→Close Solution command, both the solution and the project files will be closed.

Curiously, some of the menus vary slightly based on the development settings that you set the first time you run Visual Studio. So, don't be surprised if you have to use the File→Open Project command to open a project on your system instead of the File→Open→Project/Solution command. In the next chapter, you'll learn how to change your development settings so your menus will match the ones described in this book.

The Open Project/Solution dialog

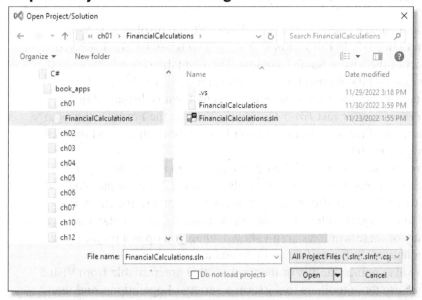

Project and solution concepts

- Every C# project has a *project file* with an extension of .csproj that keeps track of the files that make up the project and records various settings for the project. In this figure, the project file is stored in the FinancialCalculations folder just above the selected file.
- Every solution has a *solution file* with an extension of .sln that keeps track of the projects that make up the solution. In this figure, the solution file is selected.
- When you open a project file, Visual Studio opens the solution that contains the project. And when you open a solution file, Visual Studio automatically opens all the projects contained in the solution. So, either way, both the project and the solution are opened.
- Sometimes the project and solution files are stored in the same directory. Sometimes the project file is stored in a subdirectory of the directory that contains the solution file.

How to open a project

- To open an existing project, use the File→Open→Project/Solution command. Then, use the controls in the resulting dialog to locate and select the project or solution you want to open.
- After you've worked on one or more projects, their names will be listed in the File→Recent Projects and Solutions submenu. Then, you can click on a project or solution name to open it.
- You can also use the links in the Start window to open a project.

How to close a project

- Use the File→Close Solution command.

Figure 1-7   How to open or close an existing project

How to use the Form Designer

When you open an existing C# project, Visual Studio displays a screen like the one in figure 1-8. In this example, two *tabbed windows* are displayed in the main part of the Visual Studio window. The first tab is for a form named frmInvestment.cs, and the second tab is for a form named frmDepreciation. cs. Here, the tab for the first form is selected, and its form is displayed in the *Form Designer window* (or just *Form Designer*). You use the Form Designer to develop the user interface for a form, and you'll learn more about working with the Form Designer in chapter 2.

This figure also shows some of the other windows that you use as you develop Windows Forms apps. To add controls to a form, for example, you use the *Toolbox*. To set the properties of a form or control, you use the *Properties window*. And to manage the files that make up a solution, you use the *Solution Explorer*. If any of these windows aren't shown when you open a project, you can use the techniques in figure 1-11 to open and arrange them.

This figure also points out two of the toolbars that are available from Visual Studio. You can use these toolbars to perform a variety of operations, and the toolbars change depending on what you're doing. Of course, you can also perform any operation by using the menus at the top of Visual Studio. And you can perform some operations by using the context-sensitive shortcut menu that's displayed when you right-click on an item within Visual Studio.

Visual Studio with the Form Designer displayed

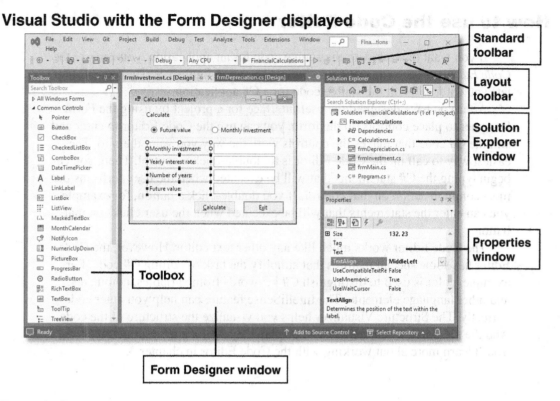

Standard toolbar

Layout toolbar

Solution Explorer window

Properties window

Toolbox

Form Designer window

Description

- The main Visual Studio workspace contains one or more tabbed windows. To design the user interface for a form, you use the *Form Designer window* (or just *Form Designer*). To develop code, you use the Code Editor window that's shown in figure 1-9.

- To open the Form Designer, you can double-click on a form in the Solution Explorer, or you can select the form in the Solution Explorer and then choose View→Designer.

- To add controls and other items to a form, you use the *Toolbox*.

- To change the way a form or control looks or operates, you use the *Properties window*. This window displays the properties of the item that's selected in the Form Designer.

- To manage the files of a project, you use the Solution Explorer window as shown in figure 1-10.

- Several toolbars are available from Visual Studio. The Standard toolbar includes standard buttons such as Open, Save, and Save All as well as other buttons that you'll learn about as you progress through this book.

- As you work with Visual Studio, you'll find that other toolbars are displayed, depending on what you're doing.

Figure 1-8   How to use the Form Designer

How to use the Code Editor

If you want to work with the source code for an application, you can use the *Code Editor window* (or just *Code Editor*) shown in figure 1-9. The Code Editor lets you enter and edit the source code for a C# application.

After you have designed the user interface for a project by using the Form Designer to place controls on the form, you can use the Code Editor to enter and edit the C# code that makes the controls work the way you want them to. The easiest way to call up the Code Editor is to double-click a control. Then, you can begin typing the C# statements that will be executed when the user performs the most common action on that control. If you double-click a button, for example, you can enter the statements that will be executed when the user clicks on that button.

The Code Editor works much like any other text editor. However, the Code Editor has some special features that simplify the task of editing C# code. For example, color is used to distinguish C# keywords from variables, comments, and other language elements. The IntelliSense feature can help you enter code correctly. The Structure Visualizer helps you visualize the structure of the code. And the file preview feature lets you display the code in a file without opening it. You'll learn more about working with the Code Editor in chapter 3.

Visual Studio with the Code Editor displayed

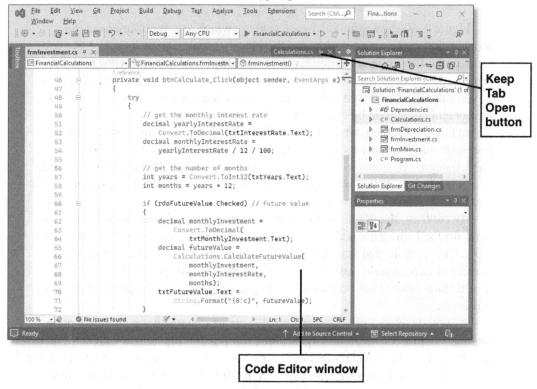

Code Editor window

Description

- The *Code Editor window* (or just *Code Editor*) is where you create and edit the C# code that your application requires. The Code Editor works much like any other text editor, so you shouldn't have much trouble learning how to use it.

- You can display the Code Editor by double-clicking the form or one of the controls in the Form Designer window. Or, you can right-click the form in the Solution Explorer and select the View Code command from the resulting menu.

- You can also preview the code in a file by selecting the file in the Solution Explorer. Then, a tab for the window appears at the right side of the Code Editor window as shown above. If you modify the file or click the Keep Tab Open button in the tab, the file is opened.

- Once you've opened the Code Editor, you can return to the Form Designer by clicking the [Design] tab for that window. You can also move among these windows by pressing Ctrl+Tab or Shift+Ctrl+Tab, or by selecting a form from the Active Files drop-down list that's available to the right of the tabs.

- The Form Designer and the Code Editor give you two different views of a form. The Form Designer gives you a visual representation of the form. The Code Editor shows you the C# code that makes the form work the way you want it to.

Figure 1-9   How to use the Code Editor

How to use the Solution Explorer

Figure 1-10 shows the *Solution Explorer*, which you use to manage the projects that make up a solution and the files that make up each project. As you can see, the files in the Solution Explorer are displayed in a tree view with the project node subordinate to the solution node. If a node has a ▷ symbol next to it, you can click the ▷ symbol to display its contents. Conversely, you can hide the contents of a node by clicking the ◢ symbol next to it.

In this figure, the form that's stored in the file named frmInvestment.cs has been expanded to show its supporting files. Here, the file named frmInvestment.Designer.cs stores most of the code that's generated by the Form Designer in a *partial class*. If you want, you can use the Code Editor to view this code, but you usually won't want to modify it.

By contrast, the file named frmInvestment.cs contains the C# code that you enter for the form. This is the code that determines how the controls on the form work. This code is also stored in a partial class, and the two partial classes are combined into a single class for the Investment form when the project is built. You'll learn more about both classes and partial classes as you progress through this book.

As you develop a project, you can also create classes that contain C# code but don't define forms. In this figure, for example, the file named Calculations.cs is a file that contains a class that isn't for a form. In this case, you can preview the class in the Code Editor by selecting it in the Solution Explorer as shown in the previous figure. Or, you can open it for editing by double-clicking it.

To identify the files that make up a project, you can look at the icon that's displayed to the left of the file name. The icon for a form file, for example, is a form, and the icon for a C# class file has a C# on it.

As you develop your applications, we recommend that you name your files in a way that identifies their contents. For example, we add a prefix of frm to the names of our form files. That way, it's easy to identify the form files when you work with them outside of the Solution Explorer.

This project also includes a group item named Dependencies. When you create a new project for a Windows Forms app for .NET, Visual Studio automatically adds several analyzers, as well as references to the two frameworks that contain the assemblies required by that application as dependencies. The analyzers inspect the code you write and notify you of any problems. And the assemblies are for *namespaces* such as System, System.Data, and System.Windows.Forms that contain the .NET classes that are available to the project such as the Form class.

This should give you some idea of how complicated the file structure for a project can be. For this relatively simple application, the developer created three form files and one class file. And Visual Studio added the namespaces and the Program.cs file to the project automatically. This Program.cs file contains the C# code that starts the application and runs the first form of the application.

The Solution Explorer

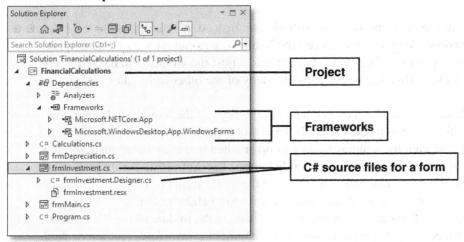

Description

- You use the *Solution Explorer* to manage and display the files and projects in a solution. The Solution Explorer lists all of the projects for the current solution, as well as all of the files that make up each project.

- The ▷ and ◢ symbols in the Solution Explorer indicate groups of files. You can click these symbols to expand and collapse the groups.

- You can use the buttons at the top of the Solution Explorer window to perform a variety of functions.

Project files

- The Solution Explorer uses different icons to distinguish between source code files that define forms and source code files that don't define forms.

- Each form is defined by two C# source files where each file contains a *partial class*. The file with the cs extension contains the code that's entered by the programmer, and the file with the Designer.cs extension contains the code that's generated when the programmer works with the Form Designer. When the project is compiled, these partial classes are combined into a single class that determines the appearance and operation of the form.

- A source code file that doesn't define a form is usually stored in a single C# source file that contains a single class.

- When you create a new app, Visual Studio creates the Program.cs file automatically. For a Windows Forms app, this file contains the C# code that starts the app and runs the first form in the app.

- When you create a new Windows Forms app for .NET, Visual Studio automatically adds two frameworks under the Dependencies group item. These frameworks contain assemblies for the *namespaces* that contain the classes available to the project.

- Visual Studio also includes several analyzers under the Dependencies group item that it uses to inspect the code you write and notify you of any problems.

Figure 1-10   How to use the Solution Explorer

How to work with Visual Studio's windows

In figure 1-11, the Toolbox isn't visible. Instead, it's hidden at the left side of the window. Then, when you need the Toolbox, you can click its tab to display it. This is just one of the ways that you can adjust the windows in the IDE so it's easier to use. This figure also presents many of the other techniques that you can use.

By default, the Toolbox is docked at the edge of the Visual Studio window and is hidden so it appears as a tab. To display a hidden window, you click its tab. If you want the window to remain open when you click on another window, you can click the window's Auto Hide button. The Auto Hide button looks like a pushpin, as illustrated by the button near the upper right corner of the Properties window. To hide the window again, click its Auto Hide button.

You can also undock a window so it floats in the middle of the IDE, outside the IDE, or even on a separate monitor. That includes windows that are docked at the edge of the IDE, like the Toolbox and the Solution Explorer, as well as the tabbed windows in the middle of the IDE. To undock one of these windows, you drag it by its title bar or tab or double-click its title bar or tab. In this figure, for example, the Solution Explorer window that was docked at the right side of the IDE is now floating in the middle of the IDE. Although we don't recommend this arrangement of windows, it should give you an idea of the many ways that you can arrange them.

You can also pin a window at the left side of the main window in the Visual Studio IDE so it's easy to access. To do that, you click the Toggle Pin Status button to the left of the Close button for the window. This is illustrated by the tab for the frmInvestment.cs file in this figure. When you pin a window, it's easy to display the window if the tabs for all the windows you have open can't be displayed at the same time.

If you experiment with these techniques for a few minutes, you'll see that they're easy to master. Then, as you get more comfortable with Visual Studio, you can adjust the windows so they work best for you. If you want, you can save a window arrangement using the Save Window Layout command in the Window menu. Then, you can use other commands in this menu to apply and manage your custom layouts and to reset the layout to its default.

Two floating windows, a hidden window, and a pinned window

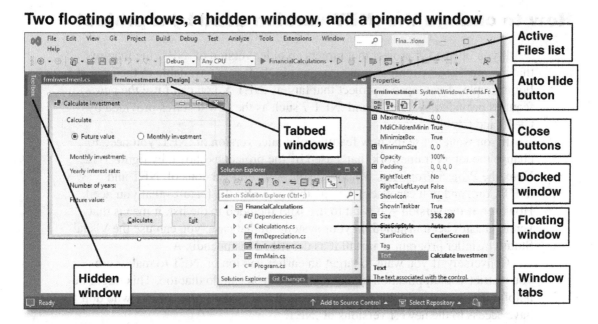

How to rearrange windows

- To close a window, click its Close button. To redisplay it, click its button in the Standard toolbar (if one is available) or select it from the View menu.

- To undock a docked window so it floats on the screen, drag it by its title bar away from the edge of the Visual Studio window or double-click its title bar.

- To dock a floating window, drag it by its title bar onto one of the positioning arrows that become available. Or, hold down the Ctrl key and then double-click its title bar to return it to its previous docked location.

- To hide a docked window, click its Auto Hide button. Then, the window is displayed as a tab at the edge of the screen, and you can display it by clicking on the tab. To change it back, display it and then click the Auto Hide button.

- To size a window, place the mouse pointer over an edge or a corner of the window and drag it.

- To display a window in a group of tabbed windows, click on its tab. To close a tabbed window, click on its Close button.

- If you dock, undock, hide, or unhide a tabbed window, all the windows in the group are docked, undocked, hidden, or unhidden.

- To pin a window at the left side of the main window, click the Toggle Pin Status button. To unpin the window, click this button again.

- You can also use the commands in the Window menu to work with windows. For example, you can use the Reset Window Layout command to return the windows to their default layout. You can also save, apply, and manage custom layouts.

Figure 1-11   How to work with Visual Studio's windows

How to change the .NET version used by a project

If you open a C# project that targets an older version of .NET, the features that are provided by more recent versions of .NET aren't available to the project. For example, if you open a project that targets .NET 5, you can't use the new features provided by .NET 6 and .NET 7 such as the new features provided by C# 10 and C# 11.

If you want to use the new features of a later version of .NET, you need to change the target framework that's used by the project as shown by figure 1-12. Here, the Project Properties window displays several versions of .NET and .NET Core, and you can select the one that provides the features that you need. However, if the version you want to use isn't included in the list, it means that version hasn't been installed on your system. In that case, you can use the Visual Studio Installer program to install it as described in appendix A.

Conversely, if you want to target an earlier version of .NET to make sure you restrict your application to older features, you can do that too. This might be helpful if you're developing an application that needs to support users who don't have access to the newest versions of .NET.

Although this figure shows a list of .NET and .NET Core versions, you should know that a list of .NET Framework versions is displayed for projects developed using the .NET Framework. Then, you can select the target framework just as you do for .NET projects. However, you can't use the target framework list to convert a project from .NET Framework to .NET or vice versa.

When you change the target framework for a project, it changes the default C# version for the project too. For example, if you select .NET 6.0, your project uses C# 10.0 by default. As a result, you can use all the features of C# 10.0 and earlier, but you can't use the features that were introduced with C# 11.0. If you want to use these features, the recommended way to do that is to select .NET 7.0 as the target framework.

If necessary, you can manually change the default C# version for a project. However, choosing a version newer than the default is not recommended since it can cause errors that are difficult to find and fix. That's why this book doesn't describe how to manually change the C# version for a project.

The Project Properties window

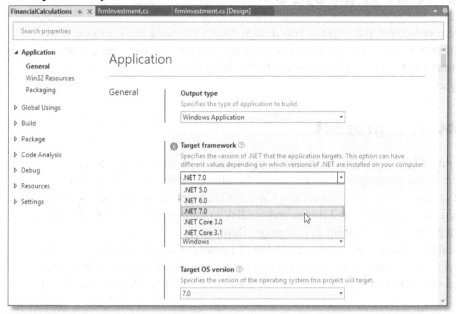

How the .NET version corresponds to the default C# version

Target framework	Default C# version
.NET 7.x	C# 11.0
.NET 6.x	C# 10.0
.NET 5.x	C# 9.0
.NET Core 3.x	C# 8.0
.NET Framework (all)	C# 7.3

Description

- To change the version of .NET that's used by a project, select the target framework you want to use from the General category of the Application group in the Project Properties window for the project.

- To display the Project Properties window, right-click on the project in the Solution Explorer and select the Properties command from the resulting menu.

- The .NET version you choose determines the features you can use in the project.

Note

- To change the target framework to a newer version of .NET, the newer version must be installed on your system. If it isn't, you can use the Visual Studio Installer program to install it as described in appendix A.

- The target framework determines the default C# version. If necessary, you can manually change the default C# version for a project. However, choosing a version newer than the default is not recommended since it can cause errors that are difficult to find and fix.

Figure 1-12   How to change the .NET version used by a project

How to test a project

When you develop a project, you design the forms using the Form Designer, and you write the C# code for the project using the Code Editor. Then, when you're ready to test the project to see whether it works, you need to build and run the project.

How to build a project

Figure 1-13 shows how to *build* a project. One way to do that is to pull down the Build menu and select the Build Solution command. If the project doesn't contain any coding errors, the C# code is compiled into the Intermediate Language for the project and it is saved on disk in an assembly. This assembly can then be run by the Common Language Runtime.

Usually, though, you don't need to build a project this way. Instead, you can simply run the project. Then, if the project hasn't been built before, or if it's been changed since the last time it was built, Visual Studio builds it before running it.

How to run a project

One easy way to *run* a project is to click the Start button that's identified in this figure. This button has a green arrowhead and the name of the project on it when the project isn't running. When it is running, though, this button is labeled Continue.

When you click the Start button, the project is built if necessary, the Intermediate Language is executed by the Common Language Runtime, and the first (or only) form of the project is displayed. This figure, for example, shows the first form that's displayed when the Financial Calculations project is run. This form contains two buttons that let you display the other forms of the project.

To test the project, you try everything that the application is intended to do. When data entries are required, you try ranges of data that test the limits of the application. When you're done running the application, you can exit it by clicking the Close button in the upper right corner of the form or on a button control that has been designed for that purpose. If the application doesn't work, of course, you need to fix it, but you'll learn more about that in chapter 3.

The form that's displayed when the Financial Calculations project is run

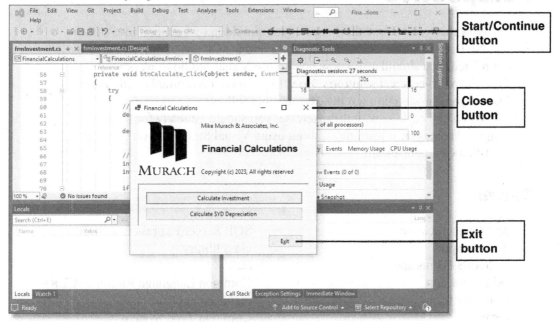

How to build a project without running it

- Use the Build→Build Solution command. Or, press F6. This *builds* the Intermediate Language for the project and saves it in an assembly.

How to run a project

- Click the Start button in the Standard toolbar. Or, press F5. This *runs* the project and displays its first form on top of the Visual Studio window.

- If the project hasn't already been built, the project is first built and then run. As a result, it isn't necessary to use the Build command before you run the program.

Two ways to exit from a project that is running

- Click the Close button in the upper right corner of the form.

- Click a button control that's designed for exiting the application. This is typically a button labeled Exit, Close, or Cancel.

Figure 1-13   How to build and run a project

Perspective

Now that you've read this chapter, you should have a general idea of how the .NET platform, the Visual Studio IDE, and the C# programming language are related. You should also know how to use Visual Studio to work with the files in projects and solutions. Now, to get more comfortable with Visual Studio, you can step through the exercise that follows.

When you're done with this exercise, you should be ready for the next chapter. There, you'll learn more about using Visual Studio as you develop your first C# application.

Terms

desktop application
desktop app
Windows Forms app
WinForms app
Windows form
form
control
WPF (Windows Presentation
    Foundation) app
XAML (Extensible Application
    Markup Language)
UWP (Universal Windows Platform)
web app
ASP.NET Web Forms app
web form
ASP.NET Core MVC app
MVC (Model-View-Controller)
ASP.NET Core Razor Pages app
Visual Studio
Integrated Development Environment
    (IDE)
.NET Framework
.NET Core
.NET

SQL Server Express LocalDB
class library
class
Common Language Runtime (CLR)
managed application
Common Type System
project
source file
C# compiler
Microsoft Intermediate Language
    (MSIL)
Intermediate Language (IL)
assembly
solution
Form Designer
Toolbox
Properties window
Code Editor
Solution Explorer
partial class
namespace
build a project
run a project

Before you do the exercises in this book

Before you do any of the exercises in this book, you need to have Visual Studio installed on your system. You also need to download the folders and files for this book from our website and install them on your computer as described in appendix A. When you're done with that, the exercises should be in the C:\C# folder.

Exercise 1-1   Tour Visual Studio

This exercise guides you through the process of opening an existing C# project, working with the windows in Visual Studio, and building and running a project. When you're done, you should have a better feel for some of the techniques that you will use as you develop C# applications.

Start Visual Studio and open an existing project

1. Start Visual Studio. If a dialog that lets you select the default environment settings and color theme is displayed, select the Visual C# development settings and the Blue color theme.

2. Review the Start window to see what it offers. When you're done, click the "Continue without code" link to display the Visual Studio IDE.

3. Use the File menu to display the Open Project dialog. Next, locate the solution file named FinancialCalculations.sln in the C:\C#\Ch01\ FinancialCalculations folder. Then, double-click the solution file to open the solution and the project it contains.

Experiment with Visual Studio

4. In the Solution Explorer, double-click the frmInvestment.cs file to display the Form Designer for the Calculate Investment form.

5. In the Solution Explorer, select the file for the Calculate Investment form (frmInvestment.cs) and press F7. This should display the C# code for this form in the Code Editor.

6. Click the tab for frmInvestment.cs [Design] to display the Form Designer again. Then, press Ctrl+Tab to move back to the Code Editor window, and do it again to move back to the Designer.

7. If the Toolbox is hidden, click its tab along the left side of the window to display it. Then, click in the Designer to see that the Toolbox is hidden again. Display the Toolbox again, locate the pushpin near its upper right corner, and click it. Now when you click in another window, the Toolbox should remain displayed.

8. Undock the Solution Explorer window by dragging its title bar to the center of the screen. Notice that the Properties window expands to fill the space that was occupied by the docked Solution Explorer window. Hold down the Ctrl key and then double-click the title bar of the Solution Explorer window to return the window to its docked position.

9. Click the ▷ symbol next to the Dependencies item in the Solution Explorer window, and then on the ▷ symbol next to the Frameworks item to see the namespaces that are included in the project. When you're done, click the ◢ symbol next to the Frameworks and Dependencies items to close them.

10. Click the ▷ symbol next to the frmInvestment.cs file to display the subordinate files. Then, click the frmInvestment.Designer.cs file to preview its code. This is the code that was generated by the Form Designer when the form was designed.

11. Click the Calculations.cs file in the Solution Explorer, and note that its code replaces the code for the frmInvestment.Designer.cs file in the preview tab. Then, click the Keep Tab Open button in the tab to open the code in the Code Editor. This is the code that performs the calculations that are required by this application. Now, close the tabbed window for this code.

Close and reopen the project

12. Select the File→Close Solution command to close the project. If a dialog is displayed that asks whether you want to save changes, click the No button.

13. If the Start window is displayed, reopen the solution by clicking on it in the Open recent list. Otherwise, reopen the solution by using the File→Recent Projects and Solutions submenu to select the appropriate project file.

Build and run the project

14. Build the project by pulling down the Build menu and selecting the Build Solution command. This compiles the project into Intermediate Language. It may also open the Output window, but you don't need to be concerned with that until the next chapter.

15. Run the project by clicking the Start button in the Standard toolbar. When the first form is displayed, click the Calculate Investment button to display the next form. Then, experiment with this form until you understand what it does. When you're through experimenting, exit from this form so you return to the first form.

16. Click the Calculate SYD Depreciation button to display another form. Then, experiment with that form to see what it does. When you exit from it, you will return to the first form.

17. Exit from the first form by clicking the Close button in the upper right corner of the form.

Close the project and exit from Visual Studio

18. Close the project.

19. If the Start window is displayed, close it by clicking the Close button in its upper right corner. Then, exit from Visual Studio by clicking the Close button in the upper right corner of the Visual Studio window.

2

How to design a Windows Forms app

In the last chapter, you learned the basic skills for working with Visual Studio, you toured a Windows Forms app, and you tested an app with three Windows forms. Now, in this chapter, you'll learn how to use Visual Studio to design the user interface for a Windows Forms app.

How to get started

This chapter starts by showing how to create and configure a new Windows Forms app. Once you do that, you can design the form by adding controls and setting properties.

How to create a new project

To create a Windows Forms app, you start by creating a new project as shown in figure 2-1. When creating a new project, Visual Studio provides several *templates* that you can use. To create a Windows Forms app using .NET, for example, you select the Windows Forms App template. Among other things, this template includes dependencies for all the features you're most likely to use as you develop a Windows app.

Note that you can select a template from the list at the right side of this dialog as shown here. You can also filter this list using the drop-down lists at the top of this dialog to make it easier to find the template you want. You can select a template from the list of recent project templates at the left side of the window. Or you can search for a template using the search text box.

This figure also shows how to change what's displayed when Visual Studio starts and the development settings that Visual uses. If you don't want the Start window to be displayed when Visual Studio starts, for example, you can change the startup option. Similarly, if you want the Visual Studio menus to appear as shown in this book, you can change the development settings option to "Visual C#".

The dialog that displays the project templates

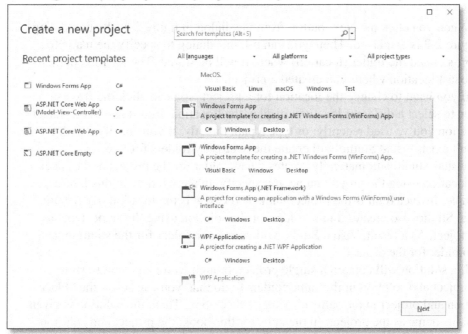

How to create a new C# project

1. Click the Create a New Project button in the Start window, or use the File→New→Project command to open the Create a New Project dialog.

2. Choose the Windows Forms App template from the list at the right side of the dialog, or choose a recently used template from the left side of the dialog.

3. Click the Next button to display the Configure Your New Project dialog shown in the next figure.

How to change the startup and development settings options

- If you don't want the Start window to be displayed when you start Visual Studio or when you close a solution, you can select the Tools→Options command, select the General category under the Environment group, and select an option from the "On startup, open" drop-down list. The other options are "Most recent solution" and "Empty environment".

- If your menus don't appear as shown in this book, you can change the development settings using the Tools→Import and Export Settings command to start the Settings Wizard. Then, choose the "Reset all settings" option, the "Yes, save my current settings" option, and the "Visual C#" option as you step through the wizard.

Description

- The project *template* that you select determines the initial files, dependencies, code, and property settings that are added to the project.

Figure 2-1   How to create a new project

How to configure a new Windows Forms app

When you click the Next button from the dialog in figure 2-1, the first dialog in figure 2-2 is displayed. Then, you can use this dialog to specify the name for the project and the folder (location) where it will be stored. The location defaults to the last location where you created a project.

If you want to change the location for a project, you can click the Browse button to select a different location; display the Location drop-down list to select a location you've used recently; or type a path directly. If you specify a path that doesn't exist, Visual Studio will create the necessary folders for you.

Visual Studio automatically creates a new folder for the project at the specified location using the project name you specify. In the window in this figure, for example, InvoiceTotal is the project name and C:\C# is the location. By default, Visual Studio also creates a new folder for the solution using the same name as the project. As a result, Visual Studio will create one folder for the solution, and a subfolder for the project.

If a solution will contain a single project, though, you may want to store the project and solution in the same folder. To do that, you can select the "Place solution and project in the same directory" check box. Then, the solution is given the same name as the project. In the apps for this book, the project and solution files are typically stored in separate folders even though most solutions contain a single project.

Incidentally, the terms *folder* and *directory* are used as synonyms throughout this book. Although Microsoft started referring to directories as folders some time ago, most of the Visual Studio documentation still uses the term *directory*. That's why this book uses whichever term seems more appropriate at the time.

When you click the Next button from this dialog, the second dialog in this figure is displayed. This dialog lets you choose the framework version you want to use for the app. In this figure, .NET 7.0 (Standard Term Support) is selected. This is the version that supports C# 11.

The dialogs for configuring a new Windows Forms app

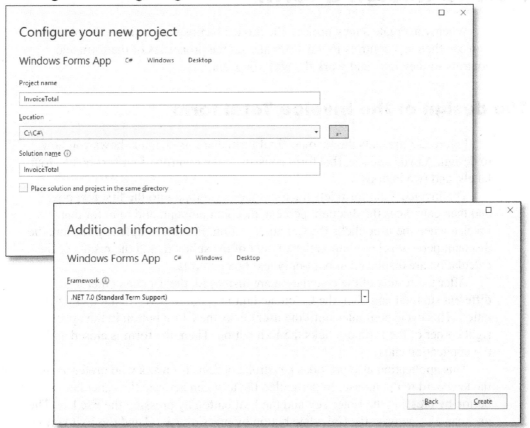

How to configure a new Windows Forms app

1. Enter a name for the project, which will enter the same name for the solution.
2. Enter the location (folder) for the project (and solution). To do that, you can click the Browse […] button.
3. Edit the solution name if necessary, then click the Next button to display the Additional Information dialog.
4. Select the framework you want to use for the app, then click the Create button to create the new project.

Description

- Visual Studio remembers the location you specify when you create a new project and uses it as the default location the next time you create a project.
- If the "Place solution and project in the same directory" box is checked, Visual Studio stores the solution and project files in the same folder. Otherwise, it creates a folder for the solution and a subfolder for the project.

Figure 2-2   How to configure a new Windows Forms app

How to design a form

When you create a new project, the project begins with a single, blank form. You can then add controls to this form and set the properties of the form and controls so they look and work the way you want.

The design of the Invoice Total form

Figure 2-3 presents the Invoice Total form that this chapter shows you how to design. As you can see, this form consists of ten controls: four text boxes, four labels, and two buttons.

The Invoice Total form lets the user enter a subtotal into the first text box, and then calculates the discount percent, discount amount, and total for that invoice when the user clicks the Calculate button. For this simple application, the discount percent is based upon the amount of the subtotal, and the results of the calculation are displayed in read-only text box controls.

After the results of the calculation are displayed, the user can enter a different subtotal and click the Calculate button again to perform another calculation. This cycle continues until the user clicks the Close button in the upper right corner of the form or clicks the Exit button. Then, the form is closed and the application ends.

This application also provides keystroke options for users who prefer using the keyboard to the mouse. In particular, the user can activate the Calculate button by pressing the Enter key and the Exit button by pressing the Esc key. The user can also activate the Calculate button by pressing Alt+C and the Exit button by pressing Alt+X.

In the topics that follow, you'll learn how to use the Form Designer to design the form shown here. As you do that, Visual Studio automatically generates the C# code that's needed to define the form and its controls. In other words, the form that you see in the Form Designer is just a visual representation of the form that the C# code is going to display later on. Then, all you have to do is write the C# code that gives the form its functionality, and you'll learn how to do that in the next chapter.

The Invoice Total form

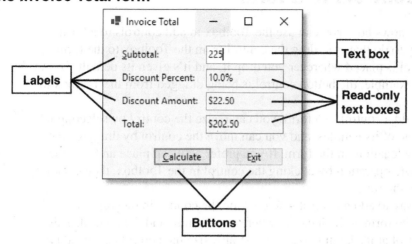

Description

- A text box is used to get the subtotal from the user. Read-only text boxes are used to display the discount percent, discount amount, and total. And label controls are used to identify the values that are in the text boxes on the form.

- After entering a subtotal, the user can click the Calculate button to calculate the discount percent, discount amount, and total. Alternatively, the user can press the Enter key to perform the calculation.

- To calculate another invoice total, the user can enter another subtotal and then click the Calculate button or press the Enter key again.

- To close the form and end the application, the user can click the Close button in the upper right corner of the form or click the Exit button. Alternatively, the user can press the Esc key to exit from the form.

- The user can press Alt+C to activate the Calculate button or Alt+X to activate the Exit button. On most systems, the letters that activate these buttons aren't underlined until the user presses the Alt key.

Three types of controls

- A *label* displays text on a form.
- A *text box* lets the user enter text on a form.
- A *button* initiates form processing when clicked.

Figure 2-3   The design of the Invoice Total form

How to add controls to a form

Figure 2-4 shows how you can use the Toolbox to add controls to a form. The easiest way to do that is to drag the control from the Toolbox to the form. Then, the control is placed wherever you drop it, and it's given its default size. In this figure, for example, the button control is being dragged from the Toolbox to the form.

Once you add a control to a form, you can resize the control by selecting it and dragging one of its handles, and you can move the control by dragging the control to a new location on the form. If you prefer, you can place and size the control in a single operation by clicking the control in the Toolbox, then clicking and dragging in the form.

A second way to add a control is to click on the control in the Toolbox and then click the form at the location where you want to add the control. This creates the control at its default size. You can also size the control as you add it by dragging on the form.

A third method for adding controls is to double-click the control you want to add in the Toolbox. This places the control in the upper left corner of the form at its default size. You can then move and resize the control.

If the AutoHide feature is activated for the Toolbox and you click on the Toolbox tab to display it, the display frequently obscures some or all of the form. This makes it difficult to add controls. As a result, it's a good idea to turn off the AutoHide feature when you're adding controls. To do that, just click the pushpin button in the upper right corner of the Toolbox.

After you have added controls to the form, you can work with several controls at once. For example, suppose you have four text box controls on your form and you want to make them all the same size with the same alignment. To do that, first select all four controls by holding down the Ctrl or Shift key as you click on them or by using the mouse pointer to drag a dotted rectangular line around the controls. Then, use the commands in the Format menu or the buttons in the Layout toolbar to move, size, and align the controls relative to the *primary control*. If you select the controls one at a time, the primary control will be the first control you select. If you select the controls by dragging around them, the primary control will be the last control in the group. To change the primary control, just click on it. (The primary control will have different color handles so you can identify it.)

Although these techniques may be hard to visualize as you read about them, you'll find that they're relatively easy to use. All you need is a little practice, which you'll get in the exercise for this chapter.

A form after some controls have been added to it

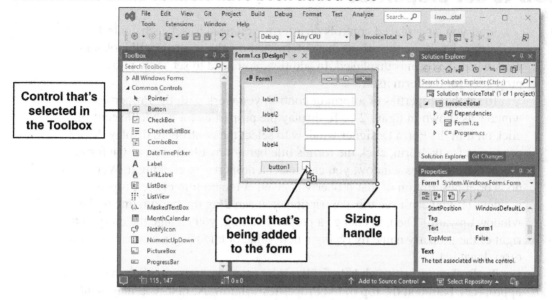

Control that's selected in the Toolbox

Control that's being added to the form

Sizing handle

Three ways to add a control to a form

- Select the control in the Toolbox. Then, click in the form where you want to place the control. Or, drag the pointer on the form to place the control and size it at the same time.

- Double-click the control in the Toolbox. Then, the control is placed in the upper left corner of the form.

- Drag the control from the Toolbox and drop it on the form. Then, the control is placed wherever you drop it.

How to select and work with controls

- To select a control on the form, click it.

- To move a control, drag it.

- To size a selected control, drag one of its handles. Note, however, that you can't size a label by dragging its handles unless you change its AutoSize property to False.

- To select more than one control, hold down the Shift or Ctrl key as you click on each control. You can also select a group of controls by clicking on a blank spot in the form and then dragging around the controls.

- To align, size, or space a group of selected controls, click on a control to make it the *primary control*. Then, use the commands in the Format menu or the buttons on the Layout toolbar to align, size, or space the controls relative to the primary control.

- You can also size all of the controls in a group by sizing the primary control in the group. And you can drag any of the selected controls to move all the controls.

- To change the size of a form, click the form and drag one of its sizing handles.

Figure 2-4   How to add controls to a form

How to set properties

After you have placed controls on a form, you need to set each control's *properties*. These are the values that determine how the controls will look and work when the form is displayed. In addition, you need to set some of the properties for the form itself.

To set the properties of a form or control, you work with the Properties window as shown in figure 2-5. To display the properties for a specific control, click on it in the Form Designer window to select the control. To display the properties for the form, click the form's title bar or any blank area of the form.

In the Properties window, you can select a property by clicking it. When you do, a brief description of that property is given at the bottom of the Properties window. (If you can't see this description, you can drag the bottom line of the window upward.) Then, to change a property setting, you change the entry to the right of the property name by typing a new value or choosing a new value from a drop-down list.

To display properties alphabetically or by category, you can click the appropriate button at the top of the Properties window. At first, you may want to display the properties by category so you have an idea of what the different properties do. Once you become more familiar with the properties, though, you may be able to find the ones you're looking for faster if you display them alphabetically.

As you work with properties, you'll find that most are set the way you want by default. In addition, some properties such as Height and Width are set interactively as you size and position the form and its controls in the Form Designer window. As a result, you usually only need to change a few properties for each object.

A form after the properties have been set

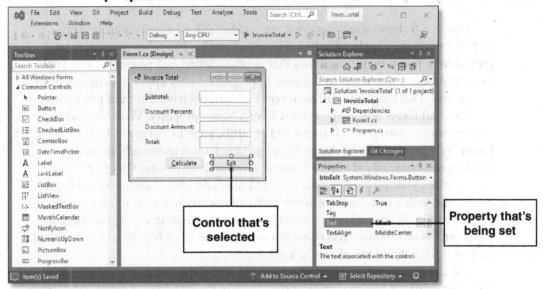

Description

- The Properties window displays the *properties* for the object that's currently selected in the Form Designer window. To display the properties for another object, click on that object or select the object from the drop-down list at the top of the Properties window.

- To change a property, enter a value into the text box or select a value from its drop-down list if it has one. If a button with an ellipsis (…) appears at the right side of a property's text box, you can click on the ellipsis to display a dialog that lets you set options for the property.

- To change the properties for two or more controls at the same time, select the controls. Then, the common properties of the controls are displayed in the Properties window.

- When you click on a property in the Properties window, a brief explanation of the property appears in a pane at the bottom of the window. For more information, press F1 to display the help information for the property.

- You can use the first two buttons at the top of the Properties window to sort the properties by category or alphabetically.

- You can use the plus (+) and minus (-) signs displayed to the left of some of the properties and categories in the Properties window to expand and collapse the list of properties.

Note

- If a description isn't displayed when you click on a property in the Properties window, right-click on the window and select Description from the shortcut menu.

Figure 2-5   How to set properties

Common properties for forms and controls

Figure 2-6 shows some common properties for forms and controls. The first two properties apply to both forms and controls. The other properties are presented in two groups: properties that apply to forms and properties that apply to controls. Note that some of the control properties only apply to certain types of controls. That's because different types of controls have different properties.

Since all forms and controls must have a Name property, Visual Studio creates generic names for all forms and controls, such as Form1 or button1. Often, though, you should change these generic names to something more meaningful, especially if you're going to refer to them in your C# code.

To make your program's code easier to read and understand, you can begin each name with a two- or three-letter prefix in lowercase letters to identify the control's type. Then, you can complete the name by describing the function of the control. For instance, you can use a name like btnExit for the Exit button and txtSubtotal for the Subtotal text box.

For Label controls, you can leave the generic names unchanged unless you plan on modifying the properties of the labels in your code. For example, if you want to use a label control to display a message to the user, you can give that label a meaningful name such as lblMessage. But there's no reason to change the names for label controls that display text that won't be changed by the program.

Forms and most controls also have a Text property that is visible when the form is displayed. A form's Text property is displayed in the form's title bar. For a control, the Text property is usually displayed somewhere within the control. The Text property of a button, for example, is displayed on the button, and the Text property of a text box is displayed in the text box.

As you work with properties, you'll find that you can set some of them by selecting a value from a drop-down list. For example, you can select a True or False value for the TabStop property of a control. For other properties, you have to enter a number or text value. And for some properties, a button with an ellipsis (...) is displayed. Then, when you click this button, a dialog appears that lets you set the property.

The Name property

- Sets the name you use to identify a form or control in your C# code.
- Can be changed to provide a more descriptive and memorable name for forms and controls that you will refer to when you write your code.
- Doesn't need to be changed for controls that you won't refer to when you write your code (such as most labels).
- Can use a three-letter prefix to indicate whether the name refers to a form (frm), button (btn), label (lbl), or text box (txt).

The Text property

- Sets the text that's displayed on a form or control. Some controls such as labels display the generic name that's generated by Visual Studio, which you'll almost always want to change.
- For a form, the Text value is displayed in the title bar. For controls, the Text value is displayed directly on the control.
- For a text box, the Text value changes when the user types text into the control, and you can write code that uses the Text property to get the text that was entered by the user.

Other properties for forms

Property	Description
AcceptButton	Identifies the button that will be activated when the user presses the Enter key.
CancelButton	Identifies the button that will be activated when the user presses the Esc key.
StartPosition	Sets the position at which the form is displayed. To center the form, set this property to CenterScreen.

Other properties for controls

Property	Description
Enabled	Determines whether the control will be enabled or disabled.
ReadOnly	Determines whether the text in some controls like text boxes can be edited.
TabIndex	Indicates the control's position in the tab order, which determines the order in which the controls will receive the focus when the user presses the Tab key.
TabStop	Determines whether the control will accept the focus when the user presses the Tab key to move from one control to another. Some controls, like labels, don't have the TabStop property because they can't receive the focus.
TextAlign	Sets the alignment for the text displayed on a control.

Figure 2-6   Common properties for forms and controls

How to add navigation features

Windows forms have features that make it easier for users to move around in the forms without using the mouse. These navigation features are described in figure 2-7.

The *tab order* is the order in which the controls on a form receive the *focus* when the user presses the Tab key. The tab order should usually be set so the focus moves left-to-right and top-to-bottom, beginning at the top left of the form and ending at the bottom right. However, in some cases you'll want to deviate from that order. For example, if you have controls arranged in columns, you may want the tab order to move down each column.

The tab order is initially set based on the order in which you add controls to the form. So, if you add the controls in the right order, you won't need to alter the tab order. But if you do need to change the tab order, you can do so by adjusting the TabIndex property settings. The TabIndex property is simply a number that represents the control's position in the tab order, beginning with zero. So, the first control in the tab order has a TabIndex of 0, the second control's TabIndex is 1, and so on.

Access keys are shortcut keys that let the user move the focus directly to a control. You set a control's access key by using the Text property. Just precede the letter in the Text property value that you want to use as the access key with an ampersand (&). Then, the user can move the focus to the control by pressing Alt plus the access key.

If you assign an access key to a control that can't receive the focus, such as a label control, pressing the access key causes the focus to move to the next control in the tab order that can receive the focus. As a result, you can use an access key with a label control to create a shortcut for a text box control, which can't have an access key.

If you assign an access key to a button control, you should know that pressing Alt plus the access key doesn't simply move the focus to the control. Instead, it activates the control just as if it was clicked. Without an access key, a user would have to tab to the button control and then press the Enter key to activate it using the keyboard. The exception is if the button is selected for the AcceptButton or CancelButton property for the form.

The AcceptButton and CancelButton properties specify the buttons that are activated when the user presses the Enter and Esc keys. That can make it easier for a user to work with a form. If, for example, the AcceptButton property of the Invoice Total form in figure 2-3 is set to the Calculate button, the user can press the Enter key after entering a subtotal instead of using the mouse to click the Calculate button or using the access key to activate it.

How to adjust the tab order

- *Tab order* refers to the sequence in which the controls receive the *focus* when the user presses the Tab key. You should adjust the tab order so the Tab key moves the focus from one control to the next in a logical sequence.

- Each control has a TabIndex property that indicates the control's position in the tab order. You can change this property to change a control's tab order position.

- If you don't want a control to receive the focus when the user presses the Tab key, change that control's TabStop property to False.

- Label controls don't have a TabStop property so they can't receive the focus.

How to set access keys

- *Access keys* are shortcut keys that the user can use in combination with the Alt key to quickly move to individual controls on the form.

- You use the Text property to set the access key for a control by placing an ampersand immediately before the letter you want to use for the access key. For example, &Invoice sets the access key to *I*, but I&nvoice sets the access key to *n*.

- Since the access keys aren't case sensitive, &N and &n set the same access key.

- When you set access keys, make sure to use a unique letter for each control. If you don't, the user may have to press the access key two or more times to select a control.

- You can't set the access key for a text box. However, if you set an access key for a label that immediately precedes the text box in the tab order, the access key will take the user to the text box.

- If you assign an access key to a button, the button is activated when you press Alt plus the access key.

How to set the Enter and Esc keys

- The AcceptButton property of the form sets the button that will be activated if the user presses the Enter key.

- The CancelButton property of the form sets the button that will be activated if the user presses the Esc key. This property should usually be set to the Exit button.

- You set the AcceptButton or CancelButton values by choosing the button from a drop-down list that shows all the buttons on the form. So be sure to create and name the buttons you want to use before you attempt to set these values.

Another way to set the tab order

- In chapter 10, you'll learn how to use Tab Order view to set the tab order of the controls on the form. If the form consists of more than a few controls, that is the best way to set that order.

Figure 2-7   How to add navigation features

The property settings for the Invoice Total form

Figure 2-8 shows the property settings for the Invoice Total form. As you can see, you don't need to change many properties to finish the design of this form. You only need to set four properties for the form, and you only use six of the properties (Name, Text, TextAlign, ReadOnly, TabStop, and TabIndex) for the controls. Depending on the order in which you create the controls, though, you may not need to change the TabIndex settings.

Notice that the three text boxes that display the form's calculations have their ReadOnly property set to True. This setting gives the text boxes a shaded appearance, as you saw in figure 2-3, and it prevents the user from entering text into these controls. In addition, the TabStop property for these text boxes has been set to False so the user can't use the Tab key to move the focus to these controls.

Finally, the settings for the TabIndex properties of the text box and the two buttons are 1, 2, and 3. Since the label controls can't receive the focus, and since the TabStop property for the three read-only text boxes has been set to False, the user can press the Tab key to move the focus from the Subtotal text box to the Calculate button to the Exit button.

In addition, the Subtotal label has a TabIndex property of 0 and a Text property that includes an access key of S. As a result, the user can press Alt+S to move the focus to the control that has the next available tab index. In this case, that control is the Subtotal text box, which has a TabIndex property of 1.

Of course, this is just one way that the TabIndex properties could be set. If, for example, the TabIndex properties for the 10 controls were set from 0 through 9, from top to bottom in this summary, the tab order would work the same.

The property settings for the form

Default name	Property	Setting
Form1	Text	Invoice Total
	AcceptButton	btnCalculate
	CancelButton	btnExit
	StartPosition	CenterScreen

The property settings for the controls

Default name	Property	Setting
label1	Text	&Subtotal:
	TextAlign	MiddleLeft
	TabIndex	0
label2	Text	Discount percent:
	TextAlign	MiddleLeft
label3	Text	Discount amount:
	TextAlign	MiddleLeft
label4	Text	Total:
	TextAlign	MiddleLeft
textBox1	Name	txtSubtotal
	TabIndex	1
textBox2	Name	txtDiscountPercent
	ReadOnly	True
	TabStop	False
textBox3	Name	txtDiscountAmount
	ReadOnly	True
	TabStop	False
textBox4	Name	txtTotal
	ReadOnly	True
	TabStop	False
button1	Name	btnCalculate
	Text	&Calculate
	TabIndex	2
button2	Name	btnExit
	Text	E&xit
	TabIndex	3

Note

- To provide an access key for the Subtotal text box, you can set the TabIndex and Text properties for the Subtotal label as shown above.

Figure 2-8   The property settings for the Invoice Total form

How to finish your design

When you're working on a project, you may want to change the names of some of the files from their defaults. Then, you'll want to save the files with their new names.

How to rename the files of a project

You may have noticed throughout this chapter that I didn't change the default name of the form (Form1.cs) that was added to the Invoice Total project when the project was created. In practice, though, you usually change the name of this form so it's more descriptive. For example, figure 2-9 shows how to use the Solution Explorer to change the name of the form file from Form1.cs to frmInvoiceTotal.cs. When you do that, Visual Studio will also change the File Name property for the form from Form1 to frmInvoiceTotal, and it will ask you if you want to modify any references to the form.

You may also want to change the name of the project or solution. For example, if you accepted the default project name when you started the project (WindowsApp1.csproj), you may want to change it to something more meaningful. Or, you may want to change the name of the solution so it's different from the project name. If so, you can use the technique presented in this figure to do that too.

How to save the files of a project

Figure 2-9 also describes how to save the files of a project. Because Visual Studio saves any changes you make to the files in a project when you build the project, you won't usually need to save them explicitly. However, it's easy to do if you need to.

When using the Save or Save All command, two factors determine which files are saved: what's selected in the Solution Explorer and the command you use to perform the save operation. If, for example, a single file is selected, you can use the Save command to save just that file, and you can use the Save All command to save the file along with the project and solution that contain the file. By contrast, if a project is selected in the Solution Explorer, the Save command causes the entire project to be saved, and the Save All command causes the entire solution to be saved.

If you haven't saved all of your recent changes when you close a project, Visual Studio will ask whether you want to save them. As a result, you don't need to worry that your changes will be lost.

The Solution Explorer as a form file is being renamed

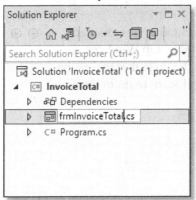

How to rename a file, project, or solution

- You can rename a file, project, or solution by right-clicking on it in the Solution Explorer window and selecting the Rename command from the shortcut menu. Or, you can select the file, project, or solution in the Solution Explorer and press F2. Then, you can enter the new name for the file, project, or solution.

- Be sure not to change or omit the file extension when you rename a file. Remember too that using a three-letter prefix to indicate the contents of the file (like *frm* for a form file) makes it easier to tell what each file represents.

- When you change the name of a form file, Visual Studio also changes the File Name property for the file. It also asks you if you want to change all references to the file, which is usually what you want.

How to save a file, project, or solution

- You can use the Save All button in the Standard toolbar or the Save All command in the File menu to save all files and projects in the solution.

- You can use the Save button in the Standard toolbar or the Save command in the File menu to save a file, project, or solution. The files that are saved depend on what's selected in the Solution Explorer window. If a single file is selected, just that file is saved. If a project is selected, the entire project and its solution are saved. And if a solution is selected, the entire solution and all its projects are saved.

- If you try to close a solution that contains modified files, a dialog is displayed that asks you if you want to save those files.

Figure 2-9   How to name and save the files of a project

Perspective

If you can design the Invoice Total form that's presented in this chapter, you've taken a critical first step toward learning how to develop Windows Forms apps with Visual Studio. The next step is to add the code that makes the form work the way you want it to, and that's what you'll learn to do in the next chapter.

Terms

template
label
text box
button
primary control
property
tab order
focus
access key

Exercise 2-1   Design the Invoice Total form

This exercise will guide you through the process of starting a new project and developing the user interface for the Invoice Total form shown in this chapter.

Set the default path and start a new project

1. Start Visual Studio. If the Start window is displayed, click the "Continue without code" link to display the IDE.

2. If you need to change the development settings so your menus are the same as the ones in this book, use the procedure described in figure 2-1 to select the default Visual C# settings.

3. If you want to stop the Start window from being displayed each time you start Visual Studio, use the procedure described in figure 2-1 to change the startup option to "Most recent solution" or "Empty environment".

4. Start a new project as shown in figure 2-2. The project should be named InvoiceTotal, it should be stored in the C:\C#\Ch02 folder, and the solution should be stored in its own folder.

Add controls to the new form and set the properties

5. Use the techniques in figure 2-4 to add controls to the form so they have approximately the same sizes and locations as in figure 2-5. But don't worry about the size of the labels, just their locations.

6. Select groups of controls and use the buttons in the Layout toolbar to size and align the controls. But here again, let the labels automatically size themselves. Then, size the form so it looks like the one in figure 2-4.

7. Use the Properties window to set the properties for the form and its controls so it looks like the form in figure 2-3. These properties are summarized in figure 2-8.

Test the user interface

8. Press F5 to build and run the project. That should display the form in the center of the screen, and it should look like the one in figure 2-3.

9. Experiment with the form to see what it can do. When you press the Tab key, notice how the focus moves from one control to another. When you click a button, notice how it indents and then pops back out just like any other Windows button control. Nothing else happens in response to these button clicks, though, because you haven't written the code for them yet.

    Notice that the Calculate button has a dark outline around it to indicate that its function will be executed if you press the Enter key. (If it doesn't have a dark outline, you haven't set the AcceptButton property of the form to the button.)

    When you press the Alt key, notice that an underline appears under the s in Subtotal, the first c in Calculate, and the x in Exit to indicate that you can use an access key to work with these controls. (If the underlines don't show, you haven't entered the Text properties correctly.)

10. If you notice that some of the properties are set incorrectly, click the Close button in the upper right corner of the form to close the form. Then, make the necessary changes and run the project again. When you're satisfied that the form is working right, close the form to return to the Form Designer.

Experiment with the properties for the form and its controls

11. In the Form Designer, click on the form so it is selected. Then, if necessary, adjust the Properties window so you can see the description for each property. To do that, drag the bottom boundary of the window up.

12. Click on the Categorized button at the top of the Properties window to display the properties by category. Then, review the properties in the Appearance, Behavior, Layout, and Window Style categories. Although you won't understand all of the descriptions, you should understand some of them.

13. In the Window Style category, change the settings for the MaximizeBox and MinimizeBox to false to see how that changes the form. Then, to undo those changes, click twice on the Undo button in the Standard toolbar or press Ctrl+Z twice.

14. Click on the first text box and review the Appearance, Behavior, and Layout properties for that control. Then, repeat this process for one of the labels and one of the buttons. Here again, you won't understand all of the descriptions, but you should understand some of them.

15. Select all four of the labels, click on the plus sign before the Font property in the Appearance group, and change the Bold setting to True to see how that changes the form. Then, undo that change.

Change the name of the form files

16. Use one of the techniques presented in figure 2-9 to change the name of the form file from Form1.cs to frmInvoiceTotal.cs. When you do that, a dialog is displayed that asks whether you want to change all the references to the form name too. Click on Yes to close that dialog, and Visual Studio changes all references to Form1 in the C# code to frmInvoiceTotal.

17. Note in the Solution Explorer that this also changes the name of the two subordinate files to frmInvoiceTotal.Designer.cs and frmInvoiceTotal.resx.

Close the project and exit from Visual Studio

18. Use the File→Close Solution command to close the project. If you've made any changes to the project since the last time you tested it, a dialog is displayed that asks whether you want to save the changes that you made. If you want to save those changes, click Yes.

19. Use the File→Exit command to exit from Visual Studio.

3

How to code and test a Windows Forms app

In the last chapter, you learned how to design a form for a Windows Forms app. In this chapter, you'll learn how to code and test a Windows Forms app. When you're done, you'll be able to develop simple apps of your own.

An introduction to coding

Before you learn the mechanics of adding code to a form, it's important to understand some of the concepts behind object-oriented programming.

Introduction to object-oriented programming

Whether you know it or not, you are using *object-oriented programming* as you design a Windows form with Visual Studio's Form Designer. That's because each control on a form is an object, and the form itself is an object. These objects are derived from classes that are part of the .NET class libraries.

When you start a new project from the Windows Forms App template, you are creating a new *class* that inherits the characteristics of the Form class that's part of the Windows.Forms class library. Later, when you run the form, you are creating an *instance* of your form class, and this instance is known as an *object*.

Similarly, when you add a control to a form, you are adding a control object to the form. Each control is an instance of a specific class. For example, a text box control is an object that is an instance of the TextBox class. Similarly, a label control is an object that is an instance of the Label class. This process of creating an object from a class can be called *instantiation*.

As you progress through this book, you will learn much more about classes and objects because C# is an *object-oriented language*. In chapter 12, for example, you'll learn how to use the C# language to create your own classes. At that point, you'll start to understand what's happening as you work with classes and objects. For now, though, you just need to get comfortable with the terms and accept the fact that a lot is going on behind the scenes as you design a form and its controls.

Figure 3-1 summarizes these class and object concepts. It also introduces you to the properties, methods, and events that are defined by classes and used by objects. As you've already seen, the *properties* of an object define the object's characteristics and data. For instance, the Name property gives a name to a control, and the Text property determines the text that is displayed within the control. By contrast, the *methods* of an object determine the operations that can be performed by the object.

An object's *events* are signals sent by the object to your app that something has happened that can be responded to. For example, a Button control object generates an event called Click if the user clicks the button. Then, your app can respond by running a C# method to handle the Click event.

By the way, the properties, methods, and events of an object or class are called the *members* of the object or class. You'll learn more about properties, methods, and events in the next two figures.

A form object and its ten control objects

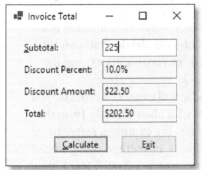

Class and object concepts

- An *object* is a self-contained unit that combines code and data. Two examples of objects you have already worked with are forms and controls.
- A *class* is the code that defines the characteristics of an object. You can think of a class as a template for an object.
- An object is an *instance* of a class, and the process of creating an object from a class is called *instantiation*.
- More than one object instance can be created from a single class. For example, a form can have several button objects, all instantiated from the same Button class. Each is a separate object, but all share the characteristics of the Button class.

Property, method, and event concepts

- *Properties* define the characteristics of an object and the data associated with an object.
- *Methods* are the operations that an object can perform.
- *Events* are signals sent by an object to the app telling it that something has happened that can be responded to.
- Properties, methods, and events can be referred to as *members* of an object.
- If you instantiate two or more instances of the same class, all of the objects have the same properties, methods, and events. However, the values assigned to the properties can vary from one instance to another.

Objects and forms

- When you use the Form Designer, Visual Studio automatically generates C# code that creates a new class based on the Form class. Then, when you run the project, a form object is instantiated from the new class.
- When you add a control to a form, Visual Studio automatically generates C# code in the class for the form that instantiates a control object from the appropriate class and sets the control's default properties. When you move and size a control, Visual Studio automatically sets the properties that specify the location and size of the control.

Figure 3-1 Introduction to object-oriented programming

How to refer to properties, methods, and events

As you enter the code for a form in the Code Editor window, you often need to refer to the properties, methods, and events of its objects. To do that, you type the name of the object, a period (also known as a *dot operator*, or *dot*), and the name of the member. This is summarized in figure 3-2.

In addition to referring to the properties, methods, and events of objects, you can also refer to some of the properties and methods of a class directly from that class. The code shown in the Code Editor in this figure, for example, refers to the ToDecimal() method of the Convert class. A property or method that you can refer to directly from a class like this is called a *static member*. You'll learn more about static members in chapter 4. For now, you just need to realize that you can refer to static properties and methods using the same techniques that you use to refer to the properties and methods of an object.

To make it easier for you to refer to the members of an object or class, Visual Studio's IntelliSense feature displays a list of the members that are available for that object or class after you type the object or class name and a period. Then, you can highlight the entry you want by clicking on it, typing one or more letters of its name, or using the arrow keys to scroll through the list. In most cases, you can then complete the entry by pressing the Tab or Enter key or entering a space. If the member name is followed by another character, such as another period, you can also complete the entry by typing that character.

To give you an idea of how properties, methods, and events are used in code, this figure shows examples of each. In the first example for properties, code is used to set the value that's displayed for a text box to 10. In the second example, code is used to set the ReadOnly property of a text box to true. Although you can also use the Properties window to set these values, that just sets the properties at the start of the app. By using code, you can change the properties as an app is running.

In the first example for methods, the Focus() method of a text box is used to move the focus to that text box. In the second example, the Close() method of a form is used to close the active form. In this example, the *this* keyword is used instead of the name of the form. Here, *this* refers to the current instance of the active form. Note that the names of the methods are followed by parentheses.

As you progress through this book, you'll learn how to use the methods for many types of objects, and you'll learn how to supply arguments within the parentheses of a method. For now, though, just try to understand that you can call a method from a class or an object and that you must code a set of parentheses after the method.

Although you'll frequently refer to properties and methods as you code an app, you'll rarely need to refer to an event. That's because Visual Studio automatically generates the code for working with events, as you'll see later in this chapter. To help you understand the code that Visual Studio generates, however, the last example in this figure shows how you refer to an event. In this case, the code refers to the Click event of a button named btnExit.

A member list that's displayed in the Code Editor window

The syntax for referring to a member of a class or object

```
ClassName.MemberName
objectName.MemberName
```

Statements that refer to properties

`txtTotal.Text = "10";`	Assigns a string holding the number 10 to the Text property of the text box named txtTotal.
`txtTotal.ReadOnly = true;`	Assigns the true value to the ReadOnly property of the text box named txtTotal so the user can't change its contents.

Statements that refer to methods

`txtMonthlyInvestment.Focus();`	Uses the Focus() method to move the focus to the text box named txtMonthlyInvestment.
`this.Close();`	Uses the Close() method to close the form that contains the statement. In this example, *this* is a keyword that is used to refer to the current instance of the class.

Code that refers to an event

`btnExit.Click`	Refers to the Click event of a button named btnExit.

How to enter member names when working in the Code Editor

- To display a list of the available members for a class or an object, type the class or object name followed by a period (called a *dot operator*, or just *dot*). Then, you can type one or more letters of the member name, and the Code Editor will select the first entry in the list that matches those letters. Or, you can scroll down the list to select the member you want. Once it's selected, press the Tab or Enter key to insert the member into your code.

- If a member list isn't displayed, select the Tools→Options command to display the Options dialog. Then, expand the Text Editor group, select the C# category, and check the Auto List Members and Parameter Information boxes.

Figure 3-2   How to refer to properties, methods, and events

How an application responds to events

Windows Forms apps are *event-driven*. That means they work by responding to the events that occur on objects. To respond to an event, you code a special type of method known as an *event handler*. When you do that, Visual Studio generates a statement that connects, or wires, the event handler to the event. This is called *event wiring*, and it's illustrated in figure 3-3.

In this figure, the user clicks the Exit button on the Invoice Total form. Then, the application uses the event wiring to determine what event handler to execute in response to the event. In this case, the btnExit.Click event is wired to the method named btnExit_Click, so this method is executed. As you can see, this event handler contains a single statement that uses the Close() method to close the form.

This figure also lists some common events for controls and forms. One control event you'll respond to frequently is the Click event. This event occurs when the user clicks an object with the mouse. Similarly, the DoubleClick event occurs when the user double-clicks an object.

Although the Click and DoubleClick events are started by user actions, that's not always the case. For instance, the Enter and Leave events typically occur when the user moves the focus to or from a control, but they can also occur when code moves the focus to or from a control. Similarly, the Load event of a form occurs when a form is loaded into memory. For the first form of an app, this typically happens when the user starts the app. And the Closed event occurs when a form is closed. For the Invoice Total form presented in this figure, this happens when the user clicks the Exit button or the Close button in the upper right corner of the form.

In addition to the events shown here, most objects have many more events that the app can respond to. For example, events occur when the user positions the mouse over an object or when the user presses or releases a key. However, it's not as common to respond to those events.

Event: The user clicks the Exit button

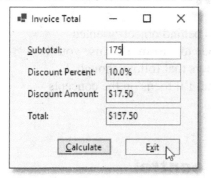

Wiring: The application determines what method to execute

```
btnExit.Click += btnExit_Click;
```

Response: The method for the Click event of the Exit button is executed

```
private void btnExit_Click(object sender, System.EventArgs e)
{
    this.Close();
}
```

Common control events

Event	Occurs when...
Click	the user clicks the control.
DoubleClick	the user double-clicks the control.
Enter	the focus is moved to the control.
Leave	the focus is moved from the control.

Common form events

Event	Occurs when...
Load	the form is loaded into memory.
Closing	the form is closing.
Closed	the form is closed.

Concepts

- Windows Forms apps work by responding to events that occur on objects.
- To indicate how an app should respond to an event, you code an *event handler*, which is a special type of method that handles the event.
- To connect the event handler to the event, Visual Studio automatically generates a statement that wires the event to the event handler. This is known as *event wiring*.
- An event can be an action that's initiated by the user like the Click event, or it can be an action initiated by program code like the Closed event.

Figure 3-3   How an application responds to events

How to add code to a form

Now that you understand some of the concepts behind object-oriented programming, you're ready to learn how to add code to a form. Because you'll learn the essentials of the C# language in the chapters that follow, though, I won't focus on the coding details right now. Instead, I'll focus on the concepts and mechanics of adding the code to a form.

How to create an event handler for the default event of a form or control

Although you can create an event handler for any event of any object, you're most likely to create event handlers for the default events of forms and controls. So that's what you'll learn to do in this chapter. Then, in chapter 6, you'll learn how to create event handlers for other events.

To create an event handler for the default event of a form or control, you double-click the object in the Form Designer. Then, Visual Studio opens the Code Editor, generates a *method declaration* for the default event of the object, and places the insertion point on a blank line between the opening and closing braces of that declaration. As a result, you can immediately start typing the C# statements that you want to include in the body of the method.

To illustrate, figure 3-4 shows the code that was generated when I double-clicked the Exit button on the Invoice Total form. In this figure, the code for the form is stored in a file named frmInvoiceTotal.cs. In addition, the name of the method is the name of the object (btnExit), an underscore, and the name of the event (Click). The statement that wires the Click event of this button to this event handler is stored in the file named frmInvoiceTotal.Designer.cs.

Before you start an event handler for a control, you should set the Name property of the control as described in chapter 2. That way, this name will be reflected in the *method name* of the event handler as shown in this figure. If you change the control name after starting an event handler for it, Visual Studio will change the name of the object in the event wiring, but it won't change the name of the object in the method name. And that can be confusing when you're first learning C#.

You should also avoid modifying the method declaration that's generated for you when you create an event handler. In chapter 6, you'll learn how to modify the method declaration. But for now, you should leave the method declaration alone and focus on adding code within the body of the method.

How to delete an event handler

If you add an event handler by mistake, you can't just delete it. If you do, you'll get an error when you try to run the project. This error will be displayed in an Error List window as shown in figure 3-7, and it will indicate that the event handler is missing.

The method that handles the Click event of the Exit button

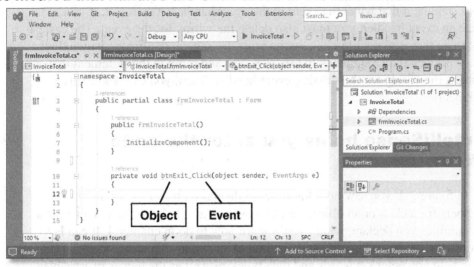

How to handle the Click event of a button

1. In the Form Designer, double-click the button. This opens the Code Editor, generates the declaration for the method that handles the event, and places the cursor within this declaration.

2. Type the C# code between the opening brace (**{**) and the closing brace (**}**) of the method declaration.

3. When you are finished writing code, you can return to the Form Designer by clicking on its tab.

How to handle the Load event for a form

*   Follow the procedure shown above, but double-click the form itself.

Description

*   The *method declaration* for the event handler that's generated when you double-click on an object in the Form Designer includes a *method name* that consists of the object name, an underscore, and the event name. The event handler is stored in the cs file for the form.

*   Most of the code that's generated when you design a form, including the statement that wires the event to the event handler, is stored in the Designer.cs file for the form. If necessary, you can open this file to view or delete the event wiring.

*   In chapter 6, you'll learn how to handle events other than the default event.

Figure 3-4   How to create an event handler for the default event of a form or control

That's because when you create an event handler, Visual Studio also generates a statement that wires the event to the event handler. As a result, if you
delete an event handler, you must also delete the wiring for the event. The easiest
way to do that is to double-click on the error message in the Error List window.
This will open the Designer.cs file for the form and jump to the statement that
contains the wiring for the missing event handler. Then, you can delete this
statement.

How IntelliSense helps you enter the code
for a form

In figure 3-2, you saw how IntelliSense displays a list of the available
members for a class or an object. IntelliSense can also help you select a type for
the variables you declare, which you'll learn how to do in chapter 4. It can help
you use the correct syntax to call a method as shown in chapters 6 and 12. And
it can help you enter keywords and data types, as well as the names of variables,
objects, and classes. Figure 3-5 illustrates how this works.

The first example in this figure shows the *completion list* that IntelliSense
displays when you start to enter a new line of code. Here, when the letter *i* is
entered, the list is positioned on the last item used that begins with that letter. In
this case, it's positioned on the if keyword. As described earlier in this chapter,
you can enter as many letters as you want, and Visual Studio will select the
appropriate item based on your entry. You can also scroll through the list to
select an item, and you can press the Tab or Enter key to insert the item into your
code.

When you select an item in a list, Visual Studio displays information about
that item in a *tool tip*. For example, the tool tip for the if keyword indicates that
there is a code snippet available for the if statement and that you can insert it by
pressing the Tab key twice. You'll learn more about using code snippets later in
this chapter.

The second example in this figure shows the completion list that's displayed
after the if keyword is inserted and a space, followed by an opening parenthesis and the initial text *su*, is typed. That makes it easy to enter the variable
named subtotal into the code, and IntelliSense adds the closing parenthesis
automatically.

If you use these IntelliSense features, you'll see that they can help you avoid
introducing errors into your code. For example, it's easy to forget the names
you've given to items such as controls and variables, so the list that's displayed
can help you locate the appropriate name.

The completion list that's displayed when you enter a letter at the beginning of a line of code

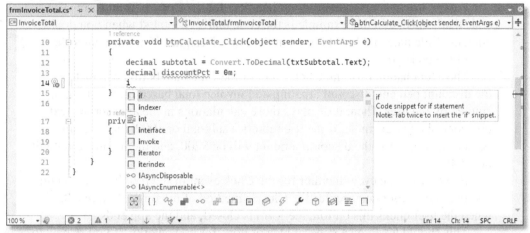

The completion list that's displayed as you enter code within a statement

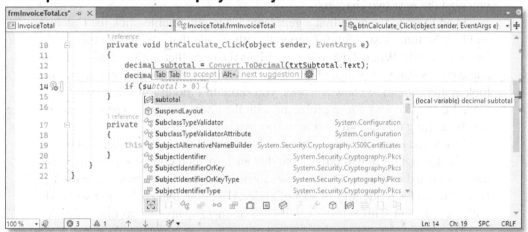

Description

- The IntelliSense that's provided for C# lists keywords, data types, variables, objects, and classes as you type so you can enter them correctly.

- When you highlight an item in a *completion list*, a *tool tip* is displayed with information about the item.

- If you need to see the code behind a completion list without closing the list, press the Ctrl key. Then, the list is hidden until you release the Ctrl key.

- If you enter an opening parenthesis or brace, the closing parenthesis or brace is added automatically.

Figure 3-5   How IntelliSense helps you enter the code for a form

The event handlers for the Invoice Total form

Figure 3-6 presents the two event handlers for the Invoice Total form. The code that's shaded in this example is the code that's generated when you double-click the Calculate and Exit buttons in the Form Designer. You must enter the rest of the code yourself.

The event handler for the Click event of the Calculate button calculates the discount percent, discount amount, and invoice total based on the subtotal entered by the user. Then, it displays those calculations in the appropriate text box controls. For example, if the user enters a subtotal of 1000, the discount percent will be 20%, the discount amount will be $200, and the invoice total will be $800.

By contrast, the event handler for the Click event of the Exit button contains just one statement that executes the Close() method of the form. As a result, when the user clicks this button, the form is closed, and the app ends.

This should give you a general idea of how this code works. If you're new to programming, however, you may not understand the code completely until after you read the next two chapters.

In addition to the code that's generated when you double-click the Calculate and Exit buttons, Visual Studio generates other code that's hidden in the Designer.cs file. When the app is run, this is the code that implements the form and controls that you designed in the Form Designer. Although you may want to look at this code to see how it works, you shouldn't modify this code with the Code Editor as it may cause problems with the Form Designer. The one exception is deleting unnecessary event wiring statements.

When you enter C# code, you must be aware of the coding rules summarized in this figure. In particular, note that each method contains a *block* of code that's enclosed in braces. As you'll see throughout this book, braces are used frequently in C# to identify blocks of code. Also, note that each *statement* ends with a semicolon. This is true even if the statement spans several lines of code.

You should also realize that C# is a case-sensitive language. As a result, you must use exact capitalization for all C# keywords, class names, object names, variable names, and so on. If you use IntelliSense to help you enter your code, this shouldn't be a problem.

The event handlers for the Invoice Total form

```
private void btnCalculate_Click(object sender, EventArgs e)
{
    decimal subtotal = Convert.ToDecimal(txtSubtotal.Text);
    decimal discountPct = 0m;
    if (subtotal >= 500)
    {
        discountPct = .2m;
    }
    else if (subtotal >= 250 && subtotal < 500)
    {
        discountPct = .15m;
    }
    else if (subtotal >= 100 && subtotal < 250)
    {
        discountPct = .1m;
    }

    decimal discountAmt = subtotal * discountPct;
    decimal invoiceTotal = subtotal - discountAmt;

    txtDiscountPct.Text = discountPct.ToString("p1");
    txtDiscountAmt.Text = discountAmt.ToString("c");
    txtTotal.Text = invoiceTotal.ToString("c");

    txtSubtotal.Focus();
}

private void btnExit_Click(object sender, EventArgs e)
{
    this.Close();
}
```

Coding rules

- Use spaces to separate the words in each statement.
- Use exact capitalization for all keywords, class names, object names, variable names, etc.
- End each *statement* with a semicolon.
- Each *block* of code must be enclosed in braces ({}). That includes the block of code that defines the body of a method.

Description

- When you double-click the Calculate and Exit buttons in the Form Designer, Visual Studio generates the shaded code shown above. Then, you can enter the rest of the code within the event handlers.
- The first event handler for the Invoice Total form is executed when the user clicks the Calculate button. This method calculates and displays the discount percent, discount amount, and total based on the subtotal entered by the user.
- The second event handler for the Invoice Total form is executed when the user clicks the Exit button. This method closes the form, which ends the app.

Figure 3-6   The event handlers for the Invoice Total form

How to detect and correct syntax errors

As you enter code, Visual Studio checks the syntax of each statement. If a *syntax error*, or *build error*, is detected, Visual Studio displays a wavy line under the code in the Code Editor. In the Code Editor in figure 3-7, for example, you can see the lines under txtDiscountPercent and txtDiscountAmount.

If you place the mouse pointer over the code in error, a brief description of the error is displayed. In this case, the error message indicates that the name does not exist. That's because the names entered in the Code Editor don't match the names used by the Form Designer. If the names are correct in the Form Designer, you can easily correct these errors by editing the names in the Code Editor. In this figure, for example, the names of the text boxes should be txtDiscountPct and txtDiscountAmt.

If the Error List window is open as shown in this figure, any errors that Visual Studio detects will also be displayed in that window. If the Error List window isn't open, you can display it using the View→Error List command. Then, you can jump to the error in the Code Editor by double-clicking on it in the Error List window.

When you're first getting started with C#, you will inevitably encounter a lot of errors. As a result, you may want to keep the Error List window open all the time. This makes it easy to see errors as soon as they occur. Then, once you get the hang of working with C#, you can conserve screen space by using the Auto Hide button so this window is only displayed when you click the Error List tab at the lower edge of the screen.

If you need additional help determining the cause of a syntax error, you can use the *live code analysis* feature. To use this feature, you can click the light bulb or link that appears when you place the mouse pointer over the error to display a list of potential fixes. Then, you can highlight a fix to preview the changes that will be made, and you can press the Enter key to apply the fix. Alternatively, you can click on a fix to apply it.

By the way, Visual Studio can't detect all syntax errors as you enter code. Instead, some syntax errors aren't detected until the project is built. You'll learn more about building projects later in this chapter.

The Code Editor and Error List windows with syntax errors displayed

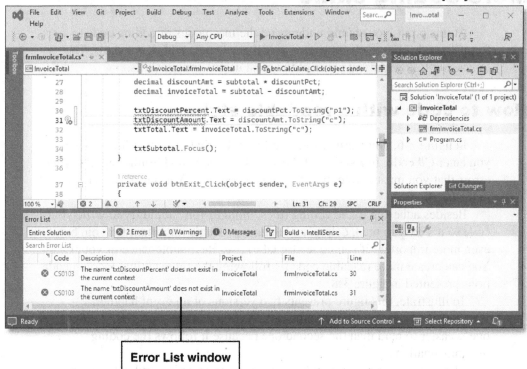

Error List window

Description

- Visual Studio checks the syntax of your C# code as you enter it. If a *syntax error* (or *build error*) is detected, it's highlighted with a wavy underline in the Code Editor, and you can place the mouse pointer over it to display a description of the error.
- If the Error List window is open, all of the build errors are listed in that window. Then, you can double-click on any error in the list to take you to its location in the Code Editor. When you correct the error, it's removed from the error list.
- If the Error List window isn't open, you can display it by selecting the Error List command from the View menu. Then, if you want to hide this window, you can click its Auto Hide button.
- To display a list of potential fixes for an error, you can click the Show Potential Fixes link that's displayed below the description of the error when you point to the error. You can also display this list by clicking the light bulb that appears below the error when you point to it or in the margin to the left of the error when you click in it. This is part of a feature called *live code analysis*.
- You can highlight a potential fix in the list to preview the changes, and you can apply a fix by clicking on it or highlighting it and pressing Enter.
- Visual Studio doesn't detect some syntax errors until the project is built. As a result, you may encounter more syntax errors when you build the project.

Figure 3-7   How to detect and correct syntax errors

More coding skills

At this point, you should understand the mechanics of adding code to a form. To code effectively, however, you'll need some additional skills. The topics that follow present some of the most useful coding skills.

How to code with a readable style

In figure 3-6, you learned some coding rules that you must follow when you enter C# code. If you don't follow these rules, Visual Studio reports syntax errors that you must correct before you can continue. You saw how that worked in the last figure.

Besides adhering to the coding rules, though, you should try to write your code so it's easy to read, debug, and maintain. That's important for you, but it's even more important if someone else takes over the maintenance of your code. You can create more readable code by following the three coding recommendations presented in figure 3-8.

To illustrate, this figure presents two versions of an event handler. Both versions accomplish the same task. As you can see, however, the first one is easier to read than the second one because it follows the coding recommendations.

The first coding recommendation is to use indentation and extra spaces to align related elements in your code. This is possible because you can use one or more spaces, tabs, or returns to separate the elements in a C# statement. In this example, all the statements within the event handler are indented. In addition, the if-else statement is indented and aligned so you can easily identify the parts of this statement.

The second recommendation is to separate the words, values, and operators in each statement with spaces. In the less readable code example, you can see that each line of code except for the method declaration includes at least one operator. Because the operators aren't separated from the word or value on each side of the operator, the code is difficult to read. By contrast, the readable code includes a space on both sides of each operator.

The third recommendation is to use blank lines before and after groups of related statements to set them off from the rest of the code. This too is illustrated by the first method in this figure. Here, the code is separated into five groups of statements. In a short method like this one, this isn't too important, but it can make a long method easier to follow.

Throughout this book, you'll see code that illustrates the use of these recommendations. You will also learn other coding recommendations that will help you write code that is easy to read, debug, and maintain.

As you enter code, the Code Editor will automatically assist you in formatting your code. When you press the Enter key at the end of a statement, for example, the Editor will indent the next statement to the same level. Although you can change how this works, you probably won't want to do that.

A method written in a readable style

```
private void btnCalculate_Click(object sender, EventArgs e)
{
    decimal subtotal = Convert.ToDecimal(txtSubtotal.Text);

    decimal discountPct = 0m;
    if (subtotal >= 500)
    {
        discountPct = .2m;
    }
    else if (subtotal >= 250 && subtotal < 500)
    {
        discountPct = .15m;
    }
    else if (subtotal >= 100 && subtotal < 250)
    {
        discountPct = .1m;
    }

    decimal discountAmt = subtotal * discountPct;
    decimal invoiceTotal = subtotal - discountAmt;

    txtDiscountPct.Text = discountPct.ToString("p1");
    txtDiscountAmt.Text = discountAmt.ToString("c");
    txtTotal.Text = invoiceTotal.ToString("c");

    txtSubtotal.Focus();
}
```

A method written in a less readable style

```
private void btnCalculate_Click(object sender, EventArgs e){
decimal subtotal=Convert.ToDecimal(txtSubtotal.Text);
decimal discountPct=0m;
if (subtotal>=500) discountPct=.2m;
else if (subtotal>=250&&subtotal<500) discountPct=.15m;
else if (subtotal>=100&&subtotal<250) discountPct=.1m;
decimal discountAmt=subtotal*discountPct;
decimal invoiceTotal=subtotal-discountAmt;
txtDiscountPct.Text=discountPct.ToString("p1");
txtDiscountAmt.Text=discountAmt.ToString("c");
txtTotal.Text=invoiceTotal.ToString("c");txtSubtotal.Focus();}
```

Coding recommendations

- Use indentation and extra spaces to align statements and blocks of code so they reflect the structure of the app.
- Use spaces to separate the words, operators, and values in each statement.
- Use blank lines before and after groups of related statements.

Note

- As you enter code in the Code Editor, Visual Studio automatically adjusts its formatting by default.

Figure 3-8   How to code with a readable style

How to code comments

Comments are used to document what the app does and what specific blocks and lines of code do. Since the C# compiler ignores comments, you can include them anywhere in an app without affecting your code. Figure 3-9 shows how to code two types of comments.

First, this figure shows a *delimited comment* at the start of a method. This type of comment is typically used to document information that applies to an entire method or to any other large block of code. You can include any helpful information in a delimited comment such as a general description of the block, the author's name, the completion date, the files used by the block, and so on.

To document the purpose of a single line of code or a block or code, you can use *single-line comments*. Once the compiler reads the slashes (//) that start this type of comment, it ignores all characters until the end of the current line. In this figure, single-line comments have been used to describe each group of statements. In addition, single-line comments have been used at the end of some lines of code to clarify the code.

Although many programmers sprinkle their code with comments, that shouldn't be necessary if you write your code so it's easy to read and understand. Instead, you should use comments only to clarify code that's difficult to understand. The trick, of course, is to provide comments for the code that needs explanation without cluttering the code with unnecessary comments. For example, an experienced C# programmer wouldn't need any of the comments shown in this figure.

One problem with comments is that they may not accurately represent what the code does. This often happens when a programmer changes the code, but doesn't change the comments that go along with it. Then, it's even harder to understand the code, because the comments are misleading. So, if you change code that has comments, be sure to change the comments too.

Incidentally, all comments are displayed in the Code Editor in green by default, which is different from the color of the words in the C# statements. That makes it easy to identify the comments.

A method with comments

```csharp
private void btnCalculate_Click(object sender, EventArgs e)
{
    /**************************************
     * this method calculates the total
     * for an invoice depending on a
     * discount that's based on the subtotal
     **************************************/

    // get the subtotal amount from the Subtotal text box
    decimal subtotal = Convert.ToDecimal(txtSubtotal.Text);

    // set the discountPct variable based
    // on the value of the subtotal variable
    decimal discountPct = 0m;              // the m indicates a decimal value
    if (subtotal >= 500)
    {
        discountPct = .2m;
    }
    else if (subtotal >= 250 && subtotal < 500)
    {
        discountPct = .15m;
    }
    else if (subtotal >= 100 && subtotal < 250)
    {
        discountPct = .1m;
    }

    // calculate and assign the values for the
    // discountAmt and invoiceTotal variables
    decimal discountAmt = subtotal * discountPct;
    decimal invoiceTotal = subtotal - discountAmt;

    // format the values and display them in their text boxes
    txtDiscountPct.Text =                  // percent format
        discountPct.ToString("p1");        // with 1 decimal place
    txtDiscountAmt.Text =
        discountAmt.ToString("c");         // currency format
    txtTotal.Text =
        invoiceTotal.ToString("c");

    // move the focus to the Subtotal text box
    txtSubtotal.Focus();
}
```

Description

- *Comments* are used to help document what an app does and what the code within it does.

- To code a *single-line comment*, type // before the comment. You can use this technique to add a comment on its own line or to add a comment at the end of a line.

- To code a *delimited comment*, type /* at the start of the comment and */ at the end. You can also code asterisks to identify the lines in the comment, but that isn't necessary.

Figure 3-9   How to code comments

How to work with the Text Editor toolbar

Figure 3-10 shows how you can use the Text Editor toolbar to work with code. If you experiment with this toolbar, you'll find that its buttons provide some useful functions for working with comments and for moving from one place to another.

In particular, you can use the Text Editor toolbar to *comment out* several lines of code during testing by selecting the lines of code and then clicking on the Comment Out button. Then, you can test the app without those lines of code. If necessary, you can use the Uncomment button to restore those lines of code.

You can also use the Text Editor toolbar to work with *bookmarks*. After you use the Toggle Bookmark button to mark lines of code, you can easily move between the marked lines of code by using the Next and Previous buttons. Although you usually don't need bookmarks when you're working with simple apps like the one shown here, bookmarks can be helpful when you're working with apps that contain more than a few pages of code.

How to collapse or expand blocks of code

As you write the code for an app, you may want to *collapse* or *expand* some of the regions, comments, and methods to make it easier to scroll through the code and locate specific sections of code. To do that, you can use the techniques described in figure 3-10. In this figure, for example, the frmInvoiceTotal method has been collapsed so all you can see is its method declaration.

The Code Editor and the Text Editor toolbar

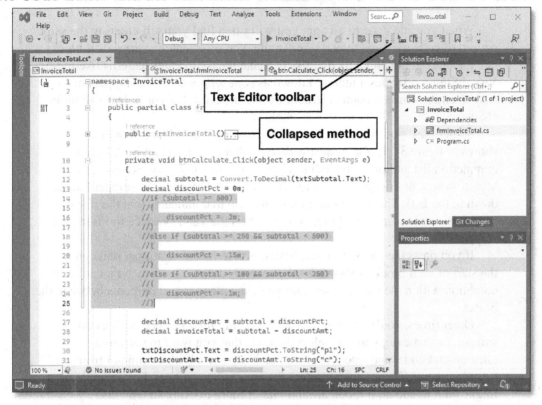

How to use the buttons of the Text Editor toolbar

- To display or hide the Text Editor toolbar, right-click in the toolbar area and choose Text Editor from the shortcut menu.

- To comment or uncomment several lines of code, select the lines and click the Comment Out or Uncomment button. During testing, you can *comment out* lines of code so they won't be executed. That way, you can test new statements without deleting the old statements.

- To move quickly between lines of code, you can use the last four buttons on the Text Editor toolbar to set and move between *bookmarks*.

How to collapse or expand regions of code

- If a region of code appears in the Code Editor with a minus sign (-) next to it, you can click the minus sign to *collapse* the region so just the first line is displayed.

- If a region of code appears in the Code Editor with a plus sign (+) next to it, you can click the plus sign to *expand* the region so all its code is displayed.

Figure 3-10   How to use the Text Editor toolbar and collapse or expand code

How to use code snippets

When you add code to an app, you will often find yourself entering the same pattern of code over and over. For example, you often enter a series of if blocks like the ones in the previous figures. To make it easy to enter patterns like these, Visual Studio provides a feature known as *code snippets*. Code snippets make it easy to enter common control structures like the ones that you'll learn about in chapter 5.

Sometimes, you'll want to insert a code snippet on a blank line of text as shown in figure 3-11. The easiest way to do that is to select an item from a completion list and press the Tab key twice. In this figure, for example, the first screen shows the completion list for the if keyword (not the #if snippet farther down in the list). This screen includes a tool tip that indicates that the if statement has a code snippet and that you can press the Tab key twice to insert that snippet.

If you press the Tab key twice, Visual Studio inserts a snippet that contains the start of an if block as shown by the second screen. That way, you can enter a condition within the parentheses, and you can enter some statements between the braces.

Other times, you'll want to surround existing lines of code with a code snippet. In that case, you can select the code that you want to surround, right-click on that code, and select the Snippet→Surround With command from the resulting menu. Then, you can select the appropriate snippet. For example, you might want to add an if block around one or more existing statements.

If you find that you like using code snippets, you should be aware that it's possible to add or remove snippets from the default list. To do that, you can choose the Code Snippets Manager command from the Tools menu. Then, you can use the resulting dialog to remove code snippets that you don't use or to add new code snippets. Be aware, however, that writing a new code snippet requires creating an XML file that defines the code snippet. To learn how to do that, you can consult the documentation for Visual Studio.

Incidentally, if you're new to programming and don't understand the if statements in this chapter, don't worry about that. Instead, just focus on the mechanics of using code snippets. In chapter 5, you'll learn everything you need to know about coding if statements.

The completion list for the if keyword

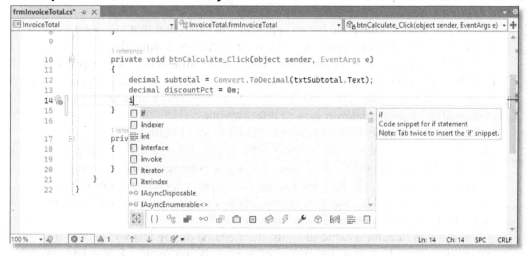

The if snippet after it has been inserted

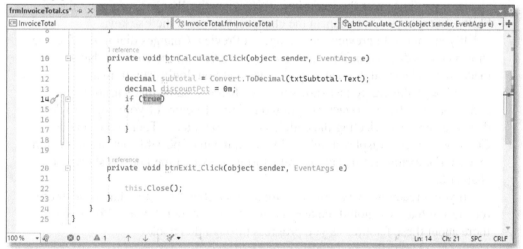

Description

- To insert a code snippet, select an item from a completion list that has a code snippet and then press the Tab key twice.

- To surround existing code with a code snippet, select the code, right-click on it, and select the Snippet→Surround With command from the resulting menu. Then, select the appropriate snippet.

- You can use the Tools→Code Snippets Manager command to display a dialog that you can use to edit the list of available code snippets and to add custom code snippets.

Figure 3-11   How to use code snippets

How to refactor code

As you work on the code for an app, you will often find that you want to revise your code. For example, you may want to change a name that you've used to identify a variable in your code to make the name more meaningful and readable. However, if you change the name in one place, you need to change it throughout your code. This is known as *refactoring*, and Visual Studio's live code analysis feature makes it easy to refactor your code.

Figure 3-12 shows how you can use Visual Studio to quickly and easily change the names that you use within your code. In this figure, for example, the first screen shows the Code Editor after one occurrence of the discountPct variable was selected, the Rename dialog was displayed, and the name of the variable was changed to discountPercent. Then, all occurrences of that variable were changed. This is referred to as *inline renaming*.

When you refactor a name like this, the Rename dialog lets you choose if you want to include names that appear in comments and strings. It also lets you choose if you want to preview the changes before they're applied. To apply the changes, you just press the Enter key. To preview the changes, you press the Shift + Enter keys. Or, to cancel the changes, you press the Esc key.

If you choose to preview the changes, a Preview Changes dialog like the one shown here is displayed. This dialog lets you review all the changes that will be made. It also lets you deselect any changes that you don't want to make.

Although this figure just shows how to change a name that's used by the code, you can also use refactoring to modify the structure of your code. To do that, you begin by selecting the code you want to refactor. Then, you can click Ctrl + period (.) to display a light bulb with a menu of possible actions in the left margin. For example, you can use refactoring to extract methods as shown in chapter 6.

If you already have experience with another object-oriented language, these refactoring features should make sense to you. If not, don't worry. You'll learn more about these features as you progress through this book.

How to get help information

As you develop apps in C#, it's likely that you'll need some additional information about Visual Studio, the C# language, or the classes that are available from .NET. The easiest way to get that information is to search the internet. When you do, your searches will often lead to Microsoft's official online documentation, a great source of information about C# and .NET programming.

Because you use your web browser to access this help information, you can work with it just as you would any other web page. For example, to jump to a topic, you can click on the appropriate link. Or, to move back through previously displayed topics, you can use your browser's Back button. As a result, with a little practice, you shouldn't have much trouble getting help information.

The options that are displayed when you rename a variable

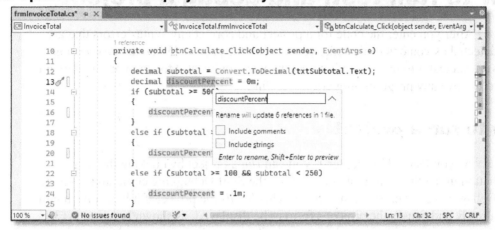

The Preview Changes - Rename dialog

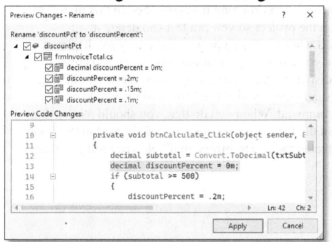

Description

- The process of revising and restructuring existing code is known as *refactoring*. Refactoring is part of the live code analysis feature.

- To change a name that's used in your code, you can highlight the name, right-click on it, and select Rename from the shortcut menu that's displayed. Then, enter the new name and press the Enter key in the dialog that's displayed. You can also press Shift + Enter to preview the changes before they're made.

- You can also use refactoring to modify the structure of your code by introducing constants or variables, extracting methods, and so on. To do that, you begin by selecting the code you want to refactor. Then, you press Ctrl + period (.) to display a menu of actions and select the appropriate refactoring action.

- Some refactoring commands display a dialog that lets you preview the changes before you make them. Then, you can deselect any changes that you don't want to make.

Figure 3-12   How to refactor code

How to run, test, and debug a project

After you enter the code for a project and correct any syntax errors that are detected as you enter this code, you can run the project. When the project runs, you can test it to make sure it works the way you want it to, and you can debug it to remove any programming errors you find.

How to run a project

As you learned in chapter 1, you can *run* a project by clicking the Start button in the Standard toolbar, selecting the Start Debugging command from the Debug menu, or pressing the F5 key. This *builds* the project if it hasn't been built already and causes the project's form to be displayed, as shown in figure 3-13. When you close this form, the app ends. Then, you're returned to Visual Studio where you can continue working on your app.

You can also build a project without running it as described in this figure. In most cases, though, you'll run the project so you can test and debug it.

If build errors are detected when you run a project, the errors are displayed in the Error List window, and you can use this window to identify and correct the errors. If it isn't already displayed, you can display this window by clicking on the Error List tab that's usually displayed at the bottom of the window or by using the View→Error List command. When you do that, you should realize that the errors will still be listed in the Error List window and highlighted in the Code Editor even after you've corrected them. The errors aren't cleared until you build the project again.

The form that's displayed when you run the Invoice Total project

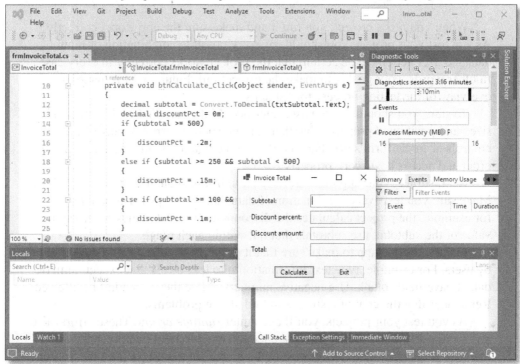

Description

- To *run* a project, click the Start button in the Standard toolbar (the one with the green arrowhead and project name on it), select the Debug→Start Debugging menu command, or press the F5 key. This causes Visual Studio to *build* the project and create an assembly. Then, if there are no build errors, the assembly is run so the project's form is displayed as shown above.

- When a project is run with debugging, the Diagnostic Tools window is displayed by default. This window shows information related to events, process memory usage, and CPU usage. This information is most helpful for checking the performance of an app as well as inefficient memory and memory leaks.

- If syntax errors are detected when a project is built, they're listed in the Error List window and the project does not run.

- To locate the statement that contains the error, you can double-click on the error description in the Error List window. After you've corrected all the errors, run the project again to rebuild it and clear the errors.

- You can build a project without running it by selecting the Build→Build Solution command.

- When you build a project for the first time, all of the components of the project are built. After that, only the components that have changed are rebuilt. To rebuild all components whether or not they've changed, use the Build→Rebuild Solution command.

Figure 3-13   How to run a project

How to test a project

When you *test* a project, you run it and make sure the app works correctly. As you test your project, you should try every possible combination of input data and user actions to be certain that the project works correctly in every case. In other words, your goal is to make the project fail. Figure 3-14 provides an overview of the testing process for C# apps.

To start, you should test the user interface. Make sure that each control is sized and positioned properly, that there are no spelling errors in any of the controls or in the form's title bar, and that the navigation features such as the tab order and access keys work properly.

Next, subject your app to a carefully thought-out sequence of valid test data. Make sure you test every combination of data that the project will handle. If, for example, the project calculates the discount at different values based on the value of the subtotal, use subtotals that fall within each range.

Finally, test the app to make sure that it properly handles invalid data entered by users. For example, type text information into text boxes that expect numeric data. Leave fields blank. Use negative numbers where they shouldn't be allowed. Remember that the goal of testing is to find all the problems.

As you test your projects, you'll encounter *runtime errors*. These errors, also known as *exceptions*, occur when C# encounters a problem that prevents a statement from being executed. If, for example, a user enters "$100" into the Subtotal text box on the Invoice Total form, a runtime error will occur when the app tries to assign that value to a decimal variable.

When a runtime error occurs, Visual Studio breaks into the debugger and displays an Exception Helper window like the one in this figure. Then, you can use the debugging tools that you'll be introduced to in the next figure to debug the error.

Runtime errors, though, should only occur when you're testing an app. Before an app is put into production, it should be coded and tested so all runtime errors are caught by the app and appropriate messages are displayed to the user. You'll learn how to do that in chapter 7 of this book.

The Exception Helper that's displayed when a runtime error occurs

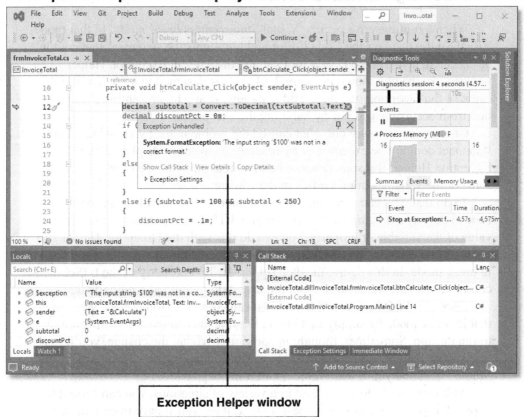

Exception Helper window

How to test a project

1. Test the user interface. Visually check all the controls to make sure they are displayed properly with the correct text. Use the Tab key to make sure the tab order is set correctly, verify that the access keys work right, and make sure that the Enter and Esc keys work properly.

2. Test valid input data. For example, enter data that you would expect a user to enter.

3. Test invalid data or unexpected user actions. For example, leave required fields blank, enter text data into numeric input fields, and use negative numbers where they are not appropriate. Try everything you can think of to make the app fail.

Description

*   To *test* a project, you run the project to make sure it works properly no matter what combinations of valid or invalid data you enter or what sequence of controls you use.

*   If a statement in your app can't be executed, a *runtime error*, or *exception*, occurs. Then, if the exception isn't handled by your app, the statement that caused the exception is highlighted and an Exception Helper window like the one above is displayed. At that point, you need to debug the app.

Figure 3-14   How to test a project

How to debug runtime errors

When a runtime error occurs, Visual Studio enters *break mode*. In that mode, Visual Studio displays the Code Editor and highlights the statement that couldn't be executed, displays the Debug toolbar, and displays an Exception Helper window like the one shown in figure 3-14. This is designed to help you find the cause of the exception (the *bug*), and to *debug* the app by preventing the exception from occurring again or by handling the exception.

Often, you can figure out what caused the problem just by knowing what statement couldn't be executed or by reading the message displayed by the Exception Helper. But sometimes, it helps to find out what the current values in some of the variables or properties in the app are.

To do that, you can place the mouse pointer over a variable or property in the code to display a *data tip* as shown in figure 3-15. This tip displays the current value of the variable or property. You can do this with the Exception Helper still open, or you can click on its Close button to close it. Either way, the app is still in break mode. In this figure, the data tip for the Text property of the txtSubtotal control is "$100", which shows that the user didn't enter valid numeric data.

Once you find the cause of a bug, you can correct it. Sometimes, you can do that in break mode by simply making and saving the change and then continuing to run the app. Sometimes, though, in addition to saving the change, you'll have to click the Hot Reload button to apply it. Hot Reload is a new feature of Visual Studio 2022, and you'll learn more about it in chapter 11.

Although Hot Reload is useful in a variety of situations, you can't use it to apply all types of changes. If it doesn't work, then, you'll have to end the app before fixing the code. To do that, you can click the Stop Debugging button in the Debug toolbar. Then, you can correct the code and test the app again.

For now, don't worry if you don't know how to correct the problem in this example. Instead, you can assume that the user will enter valid data. In chapter 7, though, you'll learn how to catch exceptions and validate all user entries for an app because that's what a professional app must do. And in chapter 11, you'll learn a lot more about debugging.

How a project looks in break mode

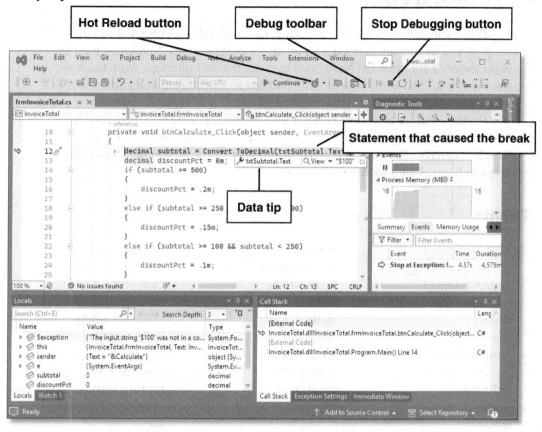

Description

- When an app encounters a runtime error, you need to fix the error. This is commonly referred to as *debugging*, and the error is commonly referred to as a *bug*.

- When an app encounters a runtime error, it enters *break mode*. In break mode, the Debug toolbar is displayed along with the Exception Helper window.

- The Exception Helper window suggests what the error might be.

- If you close the Exception Helper window, the app remains in break mode.

- To display a *data tip* for a property or variable, move the mouse pointer over it in the C# code.

- To exit break mode and end the app, click the Stop Debugging button in the Debug toolbar or press Shift+F5.

- You'll learn more about debugging in chapter 11.

Figure 3-15   How to debug runtime errors

Perspective

If you can code and test the Invoice Total project that's presented in this chapter, you've already learned a lot about C# programming. You know how to enter the code for the event handlers that make the user interface work the way you want it to. You know how to build and test a project. And you know some simple debugging techniques.

On the other hand, you've still got a lot to learn. For starters, you need to learn the C# language. So, in the next six chapters, you'll learn the essentials of the C# language. Then, in chapter 11, you'll learn some debugging techniques that can be used with more advanced code.

Terms

object-oriented programming	event-driven app	collapse
object-oriented language	event handler	expand
	event wiring	code snippet
object	method declaration	refactoring
class	method name	inline renaming
instance	statement	build a project
instantiation	block of code	run a project
property	syntax error	test a project
method	build error	runtime error
event	live code analysis	exception
member	comment	bug
dot operator	single-line comment	debug
dot	delimited comment	break mode
static member	comment out a line	data tip
	bookmark	

Exercise 3-1   Code and test the Invoice Total form

In this exercise, you'll add code to the Invoice Total form that you designed in exercise 2-1. Then, you'll build and test the project to be sure it works correctly. You'll also experiment with debugging and review some help information.

Copy and open the Invoice Total app

1. Use Windows Explorer to copy the Invoice Total project that you created for chapter 2 from the C:\C#\Ch02 directory to the C:\C#\Ch03 directory.

2. Open the Invoice Total solution (InvoiceTotal.sln) that's now in the C:\C#\ch03\InvoiceTotal directory.

Add code to the form and correct syntax errors

3. Display the Invoice Total form in the Form Designer, and double-click on the Calculate button to open the Code Editor and generate the method declaration for the Click event of this object. Then, enter the code for this method as

shown in figure 3-6. As you enter the code, be sure to take advantage of all the Visual Studio features for coding including snippets.

4. Return to the Form Designer, and double-click the Exit button to generate the method declaration for the Click event of this object. Enter the statement shown in figure 3-6 for this event handler.

5. Open the Error List window as described in figure 3-7. If any syntax errors are listed in this window, double-click on each error to move to the error in the Code Editor. Then, correct the error.

Test the project

6. Press F5 to build and run the project. If you corrected all the syntax errors in step 5, the build should succeed and the Invoice Total form should appear. If not, you'll need to correct the errors and press F5 again.

7. Enter a valid numeric value in the first text box and click the Calculate button or press the Enter key to activate this button. If the calculation works, click the Exit button or press the Esc key to close the form and return to Visual Studio. If either of these methods doesn't work right, of course, you need to debug the problems and test the project again.

Enter invalid data and display data tips in break mode

8. Run the project again. This time, enter "xx" for the subtotal. Then, click the Calculate button. This will cause Visual Studio to enter break mode and display the Exception Helper as shown in figure 3-14.

9. Note the highlighted statement and read the message that's displayed in the Exception Helper. Then, move the mouse pointer over the variable and the property in this statement to display their data tips. This shows that the code for this form needs to be enhanced so it checks for invalid data. You'll learn how to do that in chapter 7. For now, though, click the Stop Debugging button in the Debug toolbar to end the app.

Create a syntax error and see how it affects the IDE

10. When you return to the Code Editor, hide the Error List window by clicking on its Auto Hide button. Next, change the name of the Subtotal text box from txtSubtotal to txtSubTotal. This creates an error since the capitalization doesn't match the capitalization used by the Name property of the text box.

11. Try to run the project, and click No when Visual Studio tells you the build had errors and asks whether you want to continue with the last successful build. Then, double-click on the error in the Error List window, correct the error, and run the project again to make sure the problem is fixed.

Use refactoring

12. Highlight the name of the subtotal variable, then right-click on the name and select the Rename command from the shortcut menu that's displayed. When the Rename dialog appears, enter the name invoiceSubtotal and notice that all occurrences of the variable are changed.

13. Press the Enter key to apply the changes, and then run the project to make sure it still works correctly.

Generate and delete an event handler

14. Display the Form Designer for the Invoice Total form and double-click a blank area on the form. This should generate an event handler for the Load event of the form.

15. Delete the event handler for the Load event of the form. Then, run the project and click No when Visual Studio tells you the build had errors.

16. Double-click on the error in the Error List window that tells you the form does not contain a definition for the Load event handler. This opens the Designer.cs file for the form and jumps to the statement that wires the event handler. Delete this statement to correct the error.

17. If you're curious, review the generated code that's stored in the Designer.cs file for this simple form. Then, click the minus sign to the left of the region named "Windows Form Designer generated code" to collapse this region.

18. Run the project to make sure it's working correctly. When you return to the Code Editor, close the Designer.cs file for the form.

Exit from Visual Studio

19. Click the Close button for the Visual Studio window to close the solution and exit from Visual Studio. If you did everything and got your project to work right, you've come a long way!

Section 2

The C# language essentials

In section 1, you were introduced to C# programming. In particular, you learned how to use Visual Studio to design a Windows form, to enter the code for that form, and to test that code. However, you didn't learn the details for coding C# statements.

Now, in this section, you'll learn the C# language essentials. In chapter 4, for example, you'll learn how to perform arithmetic operations. In chapter 5, you'll learn how to code selection and iteration statements. In chapter 6, you'll learn how to code methods and event handlers. In chapter 7, you'll learn how to check the user's entries to make sure they're valid. In chapter 8, you'll learn how to use arrays and collections. And in chapter 9, you'll learn how to work with dates and strings. This gets you off to a great start.

After that, chapter 10 presents more skills for developing Windows Forms apps. These expand upon the skills you learned in chapter 2 and require many of the language skills that you will learn in chapters 4 through 9. To conclude your mastery of these essentials, chapter 11 presents more of the Visual Studio features for debugging that you were introduced to in chapter 3.

4

How to work with numeric and string data

To start your mastery of the C# language, this chapter shows you how to work with the various types of data that C# offers. In particular, you'll learn how to perform arithmetic operations on numeric data, how to work with string data, and how to convert one type of data to another.

How to work with the built-in value types

To start, this chapter shows you how to work with the *built-in data types* that .NET provides. As you will see, these consist of value types and reference types.

The built-in value types

Figure 4-1 summarizes the *value types* that .NET provides. To refer to each of these data types, C# provides a keyword. You can use the first eleven data types to store numbers, and you can use the last two data types to store characters and true or false values.

The first eight data types are used to store *integers*, which are numbers that don't contain decimal places (whole numbers). When you use one of the integer types, you should select an appropriate size. Most of the time, you can use the *int* type. However, you may need to use the *long* type if the value is too large for the int type. On the other hand, if you're working with smaller numbers and you need to save system resources, you can use the *short* or *byte* type. If you're working with positive numbers, you can also use the unsigned versions of these types.

You can use the next three data types to store numbers that contain decimal places. Since the *decimal* type is more accurate than the *double* and *float* types, it's commonly used for monetary values. If you need to save system resources, however, the double and float types are adequate for most situations.

You can use the *char* type to store a single character. Since C# supports the two-byte *Unicode character set*, it can store practically any character from any language around the world. As a result, you can use C# to create programs that read and print Greek or Chinese characters. In practice, though, you'll usually work with the characters that are stored in the older one-byte *ASCII character set*. These characters are the first 256 characters of the Unicode character set.

Last, you can use the *bool* type to store a true value or false value. This type of value is known as a *Boolean value*.

The built-in value types

C# keyword	Bytes	.NET type	Description
byte	1	Byte	A positive integer value from 0 to 255
sbyte	1	SByte	A signed integer value from -128 to 127
short	2	Int16	An integer from −32,768 to +32,767
ushort	2	UInt16	An unsigned integer from 0 to 65,535
int	4	Int32	An integer from −2,147,483,648 to +2,147,483,647
uint	4	UInt32	An unsigned integer from 0 to 4,294,967,295
long	8	Int64	An integer from −9,223,372,036,854,775,808 to +9,223,372,036,854,775,807
ulong	8	UInt64	An unsigned integer from 0 to +18,446,744,073,709,551,615
float	4	Single	A non-integer number with approximately 7 significant digits
double	8	Double	A non-integer number with approximately 14 significant digits
decimal	16	Decimal	A non-integer number with up to 28 significant digits (integer and fraction) that can represent values up to 7.9228 x 1028
char	2	Char	A single Unicode character
bool	1	Boolean	A true or false value

Description

- The *built-in data types* are actually aliases for the data types defined by the Common Type System of .NET.
- All of the data types shown in this figure are *value types*, which means that they store their own data. By contrast, *reference types* store a reference to the area of memory where the data is stored. See figure 4-13 for more information on value types and reference types.
- A *bit* is a binary digit that can have a value of one or zero. A *byte* is a group of eight bits. As a result, the number of bits for each data type is the number of bytes multiplied by 8.
- *Integers* are whole numbers, and the first eight data types above provide for signed and unsigned integers of various sizes.
- Since the decimal type is the most accurate non-integer data type, it's typically used to store monetary values.
- The *Unicode character set* provides for over 65,000 characters, with two bytes used for each character. Each character maps to an integer value.
- The older *ASCII character set* that's used by most operating systems provides for 256 characters with one byte used for each character. In the Unicode character set, the first 256 characters correspond to the 256 ASCII characters.
- A *bool* data type stores a *Boolean value* that's either true or false.

Figure 4-1   The built-in value types

How to declare and initialize variables

A *variable* stores a value that can change as the program executes. Before you can use a variable, you must declare its data type and name and then initialize it by assigning a value to it. Figure 4-2 shows two ways you can do that.

First, you can use separate statements to *declare* and *initialize* a variable as shown in the first example in this figure. Second, you can use a single statement that declares the variable and assigns a value to it. This figure presents several examples that use this technique. Notice that the last example declares and initializes two variables with the same data type.

Although you can declare a variable without assigning a value to it, you must assign a value to the variable before you can use it in your code. Otherwise, you'll get a build error when you try to run the project. As a result, it's a good coding practice to declare and initialize a variable in one statement or to assign a value to a variable immediately after you declare it.

You can also let the type of some variables be inferred from the values that are assigned to them. To do that, you code the *var* keyword instead of a type. This is useful when you're working with tuples, as you'll see in chapter 6, and with LINQ, as you'll see in chapter 18.

You should also notice in the examples in this figure that the first word of each variable name starts with a lowercase letter, and the remaining words start with an uppercase letter. This is known as *camel notation*, and it's a common coding convention in C#.

When you work with variables, you can assign a *literal value*, or *literal*, to the variable. For example, you can assign a literal value of 1 to an int variable. When you code a number that has a decimal point, such as 8.125, the C# compiler assumes that you want that literal value to be a double value. As a result, if you want it to be interpreted as a decimal value, you need to code the letter *m* or *M* after the value (think *m* for *money*). Similarly, for a float type, you code the letter *f* or *F* after the value. If you omit the letter, you'll get a build error when you try to run the project.

With C# 7.0 and later, you can also use underscores in a numeric literal to separate the digits in the literal. This is particularly useful for coding literals with a large number of digits, since you can't use commas in numeric literals. These underscores are referred to as *digit separators*, and you'll want to use them whenever that improves the readability of your code.

You can use *scientific notation* to express the value of extremely large or small non-integer numbers. To use this notation, you code the letter *e* or *E* followed by a power of 10. For instance, 3.65e+9 is equal to 3.65 times 10^9 (or 3,650,000,000), and 3.65e-9 is equal to 3.65 times 10^{-9} (or .00000000365). If you have a scientific or mathematical background, you're already familiar with this notation. Otherwise, you probably won't ever use this notation.

You can also assign a literal value to a variable with the char data type. To do that, you enclose the value in single quotes. To assign a literal value to a variable with the bool type, you can use the *true* and *false* keywords.

How to declare and initialize a variable in two statements

Syntax
```
type variableName;
variableName = value;
```

Example
```
int counter;            // declaration statement
counter = 1;            // assignment statement
```

How to declare and initialize a variable in one statement

Syntax
```
type variableName = value;
```

Examples
```
int counter = 1;
long numberOfBytes = 2000000;
float interestRate = 8.125f;   // f or F indicates a float value
double price = 14.95;
decimal total = 24218.1928m;   // m or M indicates a decimal value
int population1 = 1734323;
int population2 = 1_734_323    // improve readability - C# 7.0 and later
double starCount = 3.65e+9;    // scientific notation
char letter = 'A';             // enclose a character value in single quotes
bool valid = false;
int x = 0, y = 0;              // initialize 2 variables with 1 statement
```

Description

- A *variable* stores a value that can change as a program executes. In other words, the value of a variable can vary as an app executes.

- Before you can use a variable, you must declare its type and assign an initial value to it.

- Common initial values are 0 for variables that store integer values, 0.0 for variables that store decimal values, and false for variables that store Boolean values.

- To declare or initialize more than one variable for a single data type in a single statement, use commas to separate the variable names or assignments.

- To identify *literal values* as float values, you must type the letter *f* or *F* after the number. To identify decimal values, you must type the letter *m* or *M* after the number.

- The keywords for data types must be coded with all lowercase letters.

Naming conventions

- Start the names of variables with a lowercase letter, and capitalize the first letter of each word after the first word. This is known as *camel notation*.

- Try to use meaningful names that are easy to remember as you code.

Figure 4-2   How to declare and initialize variables

How to declare and initialize constants

Unlike a variable, a *constant* stores a value that can't be changed as the program executes. Many of the skills for declaring and initializing variables also apply to declaring and initializing constants. However, you always use a single statement to declare and initialize a constant, and that statement must begin with the *const* keyword. In addition, it's a common coding convention to capitalize the first letter in each word of a constant, including the first word, as shown in figure 4-3. This is known as *Pascal notation*.

How to declare and initialize a constant

Syntax

```
const type ConstantName = value;
```

Examples

```
const int DaysInNovember = 30;
const decimal SalesTax = .075m;
```

Description

- A *constant* stores a value that can't be changed. In other words, the value of a constant remains constant as an app executes.

- To declare a constant, you begin the declaration statement with the const keyword. After that, the skills for initializing variables also apply to constants, except that you must always declare and initialize a constant using a single statement.

Naming conventions

- Capitalize the first letter of each word of a constant name. This is known as *Pascal notation*.

- Try to use meaningful names that are easy to remember.

Figure 4-3   How to declare and initialize constants

How to code arithmetic expressions

Figure 4-4 shows how to code *arithmetic expressions*. To create an arithmetic expression, you use the *arithmetic operators* to indicate what operations are to be performed on the *operands* in the expression. An operand can be a literal or a variable.

The first five operators listed in this figure work on two operands. As a result, they're referred to as *binary operators*. For example, when you use the subtraction operator (-), you subtract one operand from the other. By contrast, the last four operators work on one operand. As a result, they're referred to as *unary operators*. For example, you can code the negative sign operator (-) in front of an operand to reverse the value of the operand. You can also code a positive sign operator (+) in front of an operand to return the value of the operand. Since that doesn't change the value of the operand, however, the positive sign is rarely used as a unary operator.

While the addition (+), subtraction (-), and multiplication (*) operators are self-explanatory, the division (/) and modulus (%) operators require some additional explanation. If you're working with integer data types, the division operator returns an integer value that represents the number of times the right operand goes into the left operand. Then, the modulus operator returns an integer value that represents the remainder (which is the amount that's left over after dividing the left operand by the right operand).

If you're working with non-integer data types, the division operator returns a value that uses decimal places to indicate the result of the division, which is usually what you want. The modulus operator also uses decimal places to indicate the amount that's left over after dividing the left operand by the right operand and returning an integer. The modulus operator is rarely used with non-integer data types.

When you code an increment (++) or decrement (--) operator, you can *prefix* the operand by coding the operator before the operand. This is illustrated by the last two examples in the first two groups. Then, the operand is incremented or decremented before the result is assigned.

You should realize, though, that you can also *postfix* the operand by coding the operator after the operand. Then, the result is assigned before the operand is incremented or decremented. When an entire statement does nothing more than increment a variable, as in

```
counter++;
```

both the prefix and postfix forms yield the same result.

Arithmetic operators

Operator	Name	Description
+	Addition	Adds two operands.
-	Subtraction	Subtracts the right operand from the left operand.
*	Multiplication	Multiplies the right operand and the left operand.
/	Division	Divides the right operand into the left operand. If both operands are integers, then the result is an integer.
%	Modulus	Returns the value that is left over after dividing the right operand into the left operand. The division that's used by this operator always results in an integer.
+	Positive sign	Returns the value of the operand.
-	Negative sign	Changes a positive value to negative, and vice versa.
++	Increment	Adds 1 to the operand (x = x + 1).
--	Decrement	Subtracts 1 from the operand (x = x - 1).

Examples of arithmetic expressions

```
// integer arithmetic
int x = 14;
int y = 8;
int result1 = x + y;         // result1 = 22
int result2 = x - y;         // result2 = 6
int result3 = x * y;         // result3 = 112
int result4 = x / y;         // result4 = 1
int result5 = x % y;         // result5 = 6
int result6 = -y + x;        // result6 = 6
int result7 = --y;           // result7 = 7, y = 7
int result8 = ++x;           // result8 = 15, x = 15

// decimal arithmetic
decimal a = 8.5m;
decimal b = 3.4m;
decimal result11 = a + b;    // result11 = 11.9
decimal result12 = a - b;    // result12 = 5.1
decimal result13 = a / b;    // result13 = 2.5
decimal result14 = a * b;    // result14 = 28.90
decimal result15 = a % b;    // result15 = 1.7
decimal result16 = -a;       // result16 = -8.5
decimal result17 = --a;      // result17 = 7.5, a = 7.5
decimal result18 = ++b;      // result18 = 4.4, b = 4.4
```

Description

- An *arithmetic expression* consists of one or more *operands* and *arithmetic operators*.

- The first five operators above are called *binary operators* because they operate on two operands. The next four are called *unary operators* because they operate on just one operand.

Figure 4-4   How to code arithmetic expressions

How to code assignment statements

Figure 4-5 shows how you can code an *assignment statement* to assign a new value to a variable. In a simple assignment statement, you code the variable name, an equal sign, known as the *assignment operator*, and an expression. This is illustrated by the first group of assignment statements in this figure. Notice that the expression can be a literal value, the name of another variable, or any other type of expression, such as an arithmetic expression. After the expression is evaluated, the result is assigned to the variable.

When you code assignment statements, you sometimes need to code the same variable on both sides of the equal sign as shown in the second group of statements. That way, you use the current value of the variable in an expression and then update the variable by assigning the result of the expression to it. For example, you can easily add 100 to the value of a variable and store the new value in the same variable.

Since it's common to use a variable on both sides of an assignment statement, C# provides the five *shortcut assignment operators* shown in this figure. These operators are illustrated in the third group of statements. Notice that these statements perform the same functions as the second group of statements. However, the statements that use the shortcut operators are more compact.

If you need to increment or decrement a variable by a value of 1, you can use the increment or decrement operator instead of an assignment statement. For example:

```
month = month + 1;
```

is equivalent to

```
month += 1;
```

which is equivalent to

```
month++;
```

The technique you use is mostly a matter of preference. Of course, the last technique requires the least amount of typing and is most commonly used.

Operators for assigning values to variables

Operator	Name	Description
=	Assignment	Assigns a new value to the variable.
+=	Addition	Adds the right operand to the value stored in the variable and assigns the result to the variable.
-=	Subtraction	Subtracts the right operand from the value stored in the variable and assigns the result to the variable.
*=	Multiplication	Multiplies the variable by the right operand and assigns the result to the variable.
/=	Division	Divides the variable by the right operand and assigns the result to the variable. If the variable and the operand are both integers, then the result is an integer.
%=	Modulus	Divides the variable by the right operand and assigns the remainder to the variable.

The syntax for a simple assignment statement

```
variableName = expression;
```

Typical assignment statements

```
counter = 7;
newCounter = counter;
discountAmount = subtotal * .2m;
total = subtotal - discountAmount;
```

Statements that use the same variable on both sides of the equal sign

```
total = total + 100m;
total = total - 100m;
price = price * .8m;
```

Statements that use the shortcut assignment operators

```
total += 100m;
total -= 100m;
price *= .8m;
```

Description

- A simple *assignment statement* consists of a variable, an equal sign, and an expression. When the assignment statement is executed, the expression is evaluated and the result is stored in the variable.

- Besides the equal sign, known as the *assignment operator*, C# provides the five other *shortcut assignment operators* shown above. These operators provide a shortcut way to code common assignment operations.

Figure 4-5   How to code assignment statements

How to work with the order of precedence

Figure 4-6 gives more information for coding arithmetic expressions. Specifically, it gives the *order of precedence* of the arithmetic operations. This means that all the prefixed increment and decrement operations in an expression are done first, followed by all the positive and negative operations, and so on. If there are two or more operations at each order of precedence, the operations are done from left to right.

Because this sequence of operations doesn't always work the way you want it to, you may need to override the sequence by using parentheses. Then, the expressions in the innermost sets of parentheses are done first, followed by the expressions in the next sets of parentheses, and so on. Within each set of parentheses, though, the operations are done from left to right in the order of precedence.

The need for parentheses is illustrated by the two examples in this figure. Because parentheses aren't used in the first example, the multiplication operation is done before the subtraction operation, which gives an incorrect result. By contrast, because the subtraction operation is enclosed in parentheses in the second example, this operation is performed before the multiplication operation, which gives a correct result.

In practice, you should use parentheses to dictate the sequence of operations whenever there's any doubt about it. That way, you don't have to worry about the order of precedence.

This figure also summarizes the information on prefixed and postfixed increment and decrement operations mentioned earlier, and the last set of examples shows the differences in these operations. Because this can get confusing, it's best to limit these operators to simple expressions and to use the prefix form whenever there's any doubt about how an expression will be evaluated.

The order of precedence for arithmetic operations

1. Increment and decrement
2. Positive and negative
3. Multiplication, division, and modulus
4. Addition and subtraction

A calculation that uses the default order of precedence

```
decimal discountPercent = .2m;        // 20% discount
decimal price = 100m;                 // $100 price
price = price * 1 - discountPercent;  // price = $99.8
```

A calculation that uses parentheses to specify the order of precedence

```
decimal discountPercent = .2m;          // 20% discount
decimal price = 100m;                    // $100 price
price = price * (1 - discountPercent);  // price = $80
```

The use of prefixed and postfixed increment and decrement operators

```
int a = 5;
int b = 5;
int y = ++a;      // a = 6, y = 6
int z = b++;      // b = 6, z = 5
```

Description

- Unless parentheses are used, the operations in an expression take place from left to right in the *order of precedence*.

- To specify the sequence of operations, you can use parentheses. Then, the operations in the innermost sets of parentheses are done first, followed by the operations in the next sets, and so on.

- When you use an increment or decrement operator as a *prefix* to a variable, the variable is incremented or decremented and then the result is assigned. But when you use an increment or decrement operator as a *postfix* to a variable, the result is assigned and then the variable is incremented or decremented.

Figure 4-6   How to work with the order of precedence

How to use casting

As you develop C# programs, you'll frequently need to convert data from one data type to another. To do that, you can sometimes use a technique called *casting*. Figure 4-7 illustrates how casting works.

As you can see, C# provides for two types of casting. *Implicit casts* are performed automatically and can be used to convert data with a less precise type to a more precise type. This is called a *widening conversion* because the resulting value is always wider than the original value. The first statement in this figure, for example, causes an int value to be converted to a double value. Similarly, the second statement causes a char value to be converted to an int value.

C# will also perform an implicit cast on the values in an arithmetic expression if some of the values have more precise data types than other values. This is illustrated by the next three statements in this figure. Here, the variables a, b, and c are used in an arithmetic expression. Notice that a is declared with the double data type, while b and c are declared with the int data type. Because of that, both b and c will be converted to double values when this expression is evaluated.

A *narrowing conversion* is one that casts data from a more precise data type to a less precise data type. With this type of conversion, the less precise data type may not be wide enough to hold the original value. Because C# uses *strict type semantics*, you must use an *explicit cast* to perform narrowing conversions.

To perform an explicit cast, you code the data type in parentheses before the variable that you want to convert. When you do this, you should realize that you may lose some information. This is illustrated by the first example in this figure that performs an explicit cast. Here, a double value of 93.75 is cast to an int value of 93. An explicit cast is required in this example because C# won't automatically cast a double value to an integer value since an integer value is less precise. Notice here that the double value is truncated rather than rounded.

When you use explicit casting in an arithmetic expression, the casting is done before the arithmetic operations. This is illustrated by the last two examples of explicit casts. In the last example, two integer types are cast to decimal types before the division is done so the result will have decimal places if they are needed. Without explicit casting, the expression would return an integer value that would then be cast to a decimal.

When you code an explicit cast, an exception may occur at runtime if the new data type isn't wide enough to hold the result of the expression. As a result, you should use an explicit cast only when you're sure that the new data type can hold the value.

Although you typically cast between numeric data types, you should know that you can also cast between the int and char types. That's because every char type corresponds to an int value that identifies it in the Unicode character set.

How implicit casting works

Casting from less precise to more precise data types

byte→short→int→long→decimal

int→double

short→float→double

char→int

Examples

```
double grade = 93;                // convert int to double

int letter = 'A';                 // convert char to int

double a = 95.0;
int b = 86, c = 91;
double average = (a+b+c)/3;        // convert b and c to double values
                                   // (average = 90.666666...)
```

How to code an explicit cast

The syntax for coding an explicit cast

```
(type) expression
```

Examples

```
int grade = (int)93.75;           // convert double to int (grade = 93)

char letter = (char)65;           // convert int to char (letter = 'A')

double a = 95.0;
int b = 86, c = 91;
int average = ((int)a+b+c)/3;      // convert a to int value (average = 90)

decimal result = (decimal)b/(decimal)c; // result has decimal places
```

Description

- If you code an assignment statement that assigns a value with a less precise data type to a variable with a more precise data type, C# automatically converts the less precise data type to the more precise data type. This can be referred to as an *implicit cast* or a *widening conversion*.

- No implicit casts can be done between floating-point types and the decimal type.

- When you code an arithmetic expression, C# implicitly casts operands with less precise data types to the most precise data type used in the expression.

- To code an assignment statement that assigns a value with a more precise data type to a variable with a less precise data type, you must code the less precise data type in parentheses preceding the value to be assigned. This can be referred to as an *explicit cast* or a *narrowing conversion*.

- You can also use an explicit cast in an arithmetic expression. Then, the casting is done before the arithmetic operations.

Figure 4-7   How to use casting

How to use the Math class

Figure 4-8 presents five methods of the Math class that you can use to work with numeric data. Although this class provides a variety of methods for performing mathematical operations, these are the ones you're most likely to use. In the syntax summaries, the bar (|) means that you select one of the options separated by the bar, square brackets indicate that a clause is optional, braces indicate a choice between two or more elements, and bold type indicates language elements that must be entered exactly as shown.

The five methods shown in this figure are *static methods*. This means that you call these methods directly from the Math class by coding the name of the class, a dot, the name of the method, and one or more *arguments* enclosed in parentheses and separated by commas. For example, the Round() method requires at least one argument that represents the value to be rounded, plus optional second and third arguments. The Sqrt() method requires just one argument. And the Pow(), Min(), and Max() methods require two arguments.

You use the Round() method to round a decimal, double, or float value to a specified number of decimal digits, called the *precision*. For instance, the first statement in this figure rounds the value in the shipWeightDouble variable to a whole number, because that's the default. By contrast, the second statement specifies two decimal places.

If you use the Round() method of the Math class, you should know that by default, it uses a special type of rounding called *banker's rounding*. With this type of rounding, if you round a number that ends in 5, it's always rounded to the even number. This is illustrated by the first and second statements in the second set of examples in this figure. Here, you can see that both the numbers 23.75 and 23.85 are rounded to 23.8. That can help eliminate the errors that can occur from always rounding a decimal value up to the nearest number, which is how standard rounding techniques work.

If you prefer to use standard rounding techniques, you can do that by including the mode argument as shown in the fifth statement in this set of examples. If you compare the result of this statement with the result of the fourth statement, you'll see how the mode argument works.

You use the Pow() method to raise a number to the specified power. The third statement in this figure, for example, raises the variable named radius to the second power. In other words, it calculates the square of this variable, which is used to calculate the area of a circle. Note that PI is a field of the Math class that represents the mathematical constant ϖ (3.14159265...). C# doesn't provide an arithmetic operator for raising a number to a power like some other languages do. Because of that, you'll want to use the Pow() method any time you need to perform this operation.

This figure also presents three other static methods of the Math class: Sqrt(), Min(), and Max(). The Sqrt() method calculates the square root of a number. The Min() and Max() methods return the minimum or maximum of two numeric values that you specify. These three methods can be used with any of the numeric data types. However, when you use the Min() or Max() method, the two values you specify must be of the same type.

Five static methods of the Math class

The syntax of the Round() method
```
Math.Round(decimalNumber[, precision[, mode]])
```

The syntax of the Pow() method
```
Math.Pow(number, power)
```

The syntax of the Sqrt() method
```
Math.Sqrt(number)
```

The syntax of the Min() and Max() methods
```
Math.{Min|Max}(number1, number2)
```

Statements that use static methods of the Math class
```
int shipWeight = Math.Round(shipWeightDouble);   // round to a whole number
double orderTotal = Math.Round(orderTotal, 2);   // round to 2 decimal places
double area = Math.Pow(radius, 2) * Math.PI;     // area of circle
double sqrtX = Math.Sqrt(x);
double maxSales = Math.Max(lastYearSales, thisYearSales);
int minQty = Math.Min(lastYearQty, thisYearQty);
```

Results from static methods of the Math class

Statement	Result	Statement	Result
Math.Round(23.75, 1)	23.8	Math.Pow(5, 2)	25
Math.Round(23.85, 1)	23.8	Math.Sqrt(20.25)	4.5
Math.Round(23.744, 2)	23.74	Math.Max(23.75, 20.25)	23.75
Math.Round(23.745, 2)	23.74	Math.Min(23.75, 20.25)	20.25
Math.Round(23.745, 2, MidpointRounding.AwayFromZero)			23.75

Description

- To use one of the *static methods* of the Math class, code the class name, a dot, the method name, and one or more *arguments* in parentheses. The arguments provide the values that are used by the method.

- The Round() method rounds a decimal argument to the specified *precision*, which is the number of significant decimal digits. If the precision is omitted, the number is rounded to the nearest whole number.

- By default, if you round a decimal value that ends in 5, the number is rounded to the nearest even decimal value. This is referred to as *banker's rounding*. You can also code the mode argument with a value of MidpointRounding.AwayFromZero to round positive values up and negative values down.

- The Pow() method raises the first argument to the power of the second argument. Both arguments must have the double data type.

- The Sqrt() method returns the square root of the specified argument, which can have any numeric data type.

- The Min() and Max() methods return the minimum and maximum of two numeric arguments. The two arguments must have the same data type.

Figure 4-8   How to use the Math class

How to generate random numbers

When learning how to program, it's often helpful to be able to generate random numbers. They're useful if you want to develop games that involve dice, cards, or other elements of random chance. They're also useful for simulations such as testing a method with a range of random numbers.

To generate random numbers with C#, you can use the methods of the Random class shown in figure 4-9. Unlike the static methods of the Math class that you saw in the previous figure, the methods of the Random class are *instance methods*. That means you call them from an object that's created, or *instantiated*, from the Random class. To create an instance of the Random class, you use the *new* keyword as shown by the statement in the first example in this figure. Here, the Random object is created and assigned to a variable named number.

After you create a Random object, you can use the methods shown here to generate random numbers. This is illustrated by the statements in the second example. The first statement uses a Next() method without any arguments. Because of that, it gets an integer that's greater than or equal to zero and less than the maximum value of an integer (Int32.MaxValue).

The second statement is similar, but it includes an argument that specifies the maximum value of the random number. Note that the maximum value isn't included in the range of values that can be returned by the method. In this case, then, the random number can have a value from 0 to 100.

The third statement includes both a minimum and a maximum value. Unlike a maximum value, a minimum value is included in the range. Because of that, this statement will return a value from 1 to 100.

If you want to get a random number that is a double instead of an int, you can use the NextDouble() method. Unlike the Next() method, the NextDouble() method always returns a value that's greater than or equal to 0.0 and less than 1.0. If you need to, though, you can multiply the random number by another number to get a number within a specified range. If you multiply the number by 100, for example, it will be greater than or equal to 0.0 and less than 100.0.

The third example in this figure presents code that uses the Random class to simulate the roll of two dice. To start, this code creates an instance of the Random class. Then, it calls the Next() method with a minimum value of 1 and a maximum value of 7. That will return a random number from 1 to 6, and that number is assigned to an int variable named die1. Then, the Next() method is called again and the result is assigned to an int variable named die2.

When you use the Random class, you should know that its methods generate *pseudorandom numbers*. That's because the generated numbers are based on a mathematical algorithm that depends on a starting value, called a *seed value*. When you create an instance of the Random class, this seed value is determined by the system clock by default. In most cases, that's what you want. If you need to generate two series of random numbers, though, you may want to specify a specific seed value to be sure that the two series contain different numbers. Or, you can specify a seed value to be sure that a series always contains the same numbers. For more information on specifying a seed value, see the online documentation for the Random class.

Instance methods of the Random class

Method	Description
`Next()`	Returns a random int value that is greater than or equal to 0 and less than the maximum value for the int type.
`Next(maxValue)`	Returns a random int value that is greater than or equal to 0 and less than the specified maximum value.
`Next(minValue, maxValue)`	Returns a random int value that is greater than or equal to the specified minimum value and less than the specified maximum value.
`NextDouble()`	Returns a double value that is greater than or equal to 0.0 and less than 1.0.

A statement that creates an instance of the Random class

```
Random number = new Random();
```

Statements that use the methods of the Random class

```
number.Next();            // an int >= 0 and < Int32.MaxValue
number.Next(101);         // an int >= 0 and < 101
number.Next(1,101);       // an int >= 1 and < 101
number.NextDouble();      // a double >= 0.0 and < 1.0
```

Code that simulates the roll of two dice

```
Random number = new Random();
int die1 = number.Next(1, 7);    // die1 is >= 1 and < 7
int die2 = number.Next(1, 7);    // die2 is >= 1 and < 7
```

Description

- The Random class provides methods that you can use to generate a series of *pseudorandom numbers*, which is a series of numbers that appears to be random but is actually based on a mathematical algorithm.

- To generate random numbers, you create an object that's an instance of the Random class by using the *new* keyword as shown above.

- When you create an instance of the Random class, you can provide a starting value to the algorithm, called a *seed value*. The default seed value is based on the system clock. For information on using other seed values, see the online documentation for the Random class.

- The methods of the Random class are called *instance methods* because you call them from an instance of the class.

- When you use the forms of the Next() method that accept a maximum value, that value is exclusive of the values that can be generated.

Figure 4-9   How to generate random numbers

How to work with strings

In the topics that follow, you'll learn some basic skills for working with
the string data type. These skills should be all you need for many of your
apps. Then, in chapter 9, you'll learn the skills you need for advanced string
operations.

How to declare and initialize a string

A *string* can consist of any letters, numbers, and characters. Figure 4-10
summarizes the techniques that you can use to work with string variables. To
start, you use the *string* keyword to declare a string. Then, you can assign a
string literal to a string by enclosing the characters within double quotes.

To assign an *empty string* to a variable, you can code a set of double quotes
with nothing between them. You do that when you want the string to have a
value, but you don't want it to contain any characters. Another option is to assign
the String.Empty field to the variable like this:

```
string message2 = String.Empty;
```

This makes it clear that the code is assigning an empty string. In this book,
though, we use double quotes with nothing between them because it's shorter
and easier to type.

A third alternative is to assign a *null value* to a string by using the *null*
keyword, which usually indicates that the value of the string is unknown. In
this example, the null keyword is followed by the *null-forgiving operator* (!).
This operator tells Visual Studio to suppress the null-reference warning that's
issued if a null value is assigned to a string that can't contain a null value. It's
necessary because with .NET 6 and later, all reference types including strings are
non-nullable by default.

How to join and append strings

Figure 4-10 also shows how to join, or *concatenate*, two or more strings into
one string. To do that, you use the + operator as shown in the second example in
this figure. Here, two string variables are concatenated with a string literal that
consists of one space. The result is then stored in another string variable.

You can also join a string with a value data type. This is illustrated in the
third example. Here, a variable that's defined with the decimal data type is
appended to a string. When you use this technique, C# automatically converts
the value to a string.

You can also use the + and += operators to *append* a string to the value of a
string variable. This is illustrated in the last two examples in this figure. Notice
that when you use the + operator, you include the string variable in the expression that you're assigning to this variable. By contrast, when you use the +=
operator, you can omit the string variable from the expression. Because of that,
it's common to use this operator to simplify your code.

How to declare and initialize a string

```
string message1 = "Invalid data entry.";
string message2 = "";
string message3 = null!;
```

How to join strings

```
string firstName = "Bob";               // firstName is "Bob"
string lastName = "Smith";               // lastName is "Smith"
string name = firstName + " " + lastName; // name is "Bob Smith"
```

How to join a string and a number

```
decimal price = 14.95m;
string priceString = "Price: $" + price;   // priceString is "Price: $14.95"
```

How to append one string to another string

```
string firstName = "Bob";               // firstName is "Bob"
string lastName = "Smith";               // lastName is "Smith"
string name = firstName + " ";           // name is "Bob "
name = name + lastName;                   // name is "Bob Smith"
```

How to append one string to another with the += operator

```
string firstName = "Bob";               // firstName is "Bob"
string lastName = "Smith";               // lastName is "Smith"
string name = firstName + " ";           // name is "Bob "
name += lastName;                         // name is "Bob Smith"
```

Description

- A *string* can consist of any characters in the character set including letters, numbers, and special characters like $, *, &, and #.

- To specify the value of a string, you can enclose text in double quotes. This is known as a *string literal*.

- To assign an *empty string* to a string, you can code a set of double quotes with nothing between them. This usually indicates that the value of the string is known, but the string doesn't contain any characters.

- To assign a *null value* to a string, you can use the *null* keyword. This means that the value of the string is unknown.

- Because a string is a reference type and because reference types can't contain null by default with .NET 6 and later, a warning will occur if you try to assign null to a string. To suppress this warning, you can code the *null-forgiving operator* (!) as shown above.

- To join, or *concatenate*, a string with another string or a value data type, use a plus sign. If you concatenate a value data type to a string, C# will automatically convert the value to a string so it can be used as part of the string.

- When you *append* one string to another, you add one string to the end of another. To do that, you can use assignment statements.

- The += operator is a shortcut for appending a string expression to a string variable.

Figure 4-10   Basic skills for working with strings

How to include special characters in strings

Figure 4-11 shows two techniques that you can use to include certain types of special characters within a string. That includes backslashes and quotation marks, as well as control characters such as new lines, tabs, and returns.

One technique you can use to include these characters in a string is to use the *escape sequences* shown in this figure. Although these escape sequences are the ones you'll use most often, C# provides other escape sequences for hexadecimal and Unicode characters.

If you're assigning a string literal to a string, you may prefer to use a *verbatim string literal* instead of escape sequences. To use a verbatim string literal, you code an @ sign before the opening quote for the string. Then, you can enter special characters without escape sequences between the opening and closing quotes. In most cases, you'll use verbatim string literals for simple strings like the ones shown in this figure that contain backslashes and quotes.

Although verbatim string literals work well for literals that include backslashes and single quotes, a complication occurs when you need to include a double quote in the literal. That's because double quotes are used to indicate the beginning and end of the literal. To include a double quote in a verbatim string literal, then, you must enter two double quotes.

At this point, you may be wondering when you should use escape sequences to include special characters in a string and when you should use verbatim string literals. The answer is that each technique is appropriate for certain types of coding situations. For example, verbatim string literals work well for coding file locations. On the other hand, it's often easier to use escape sequences to include new line characters and tabs in a string. Because of that, you'll want to become familiar with both techniques. Then, you can decide which technique works best for a given situation.

Common escape sequences

Key	Description
\n	New line
\t	Tab
\r	Return
\\	Backslash
\"	Quotation

Examples that use escape sequences

Code	Result
| ```
string code = "JSPS";
decimal price = 49.50m;
string result =
    "Code: " + code + "\n" +
    "Price: $" + price + "\n";
``` | ```
Code: JSPS
Price: $49.50
``` |
| ```
string names =
    "Joe\tSmith\rKate\tLewis\r";
``` | ```
Joe    Smith
Kate   Lewis
``` |
| ```
string path = "c:\\c#\\files";
``` | `c:\c#\files` |
| ```
string message =
    "Type \"x\" to exit";
``` | `Type "x" to exit` |

Examples that use verbatim string literals

Code	Result
| ```
string path = @"c:\c#\files";
``` | `c:\c#\files` |
| ```
string message =
    @"Type ""x"" to exit";
``` | `Type "x" to exit` |

Description

- Within a string, you can use *escape sequences* to include certain types of special characters.

- To code a *verbatim string literal*, you can code an @ sign, followed by an opening double quote, the string, and a closing double quote. Within the string, you can enter backslashes, tabs, new line characters, and other special characters without using escape sequences. However, to enter a double quote within a verbatim string literal, you must enter two double quotes.

Figure 4-11   How to include special characters in strings

How to code raw string literals

In addition to regular string literals and verbatim string literals, C# 11 provides support for *raw string literals*. Raw string literals are typically used for multi-line strings of formatted text. They can include standard text characters, whitespace, and special characters. Figure 4-12 shows how raw string literals work.

To code a raw string literal, you enclose it in three or more sets of quotes as shown in the first example in this figure. That way, if the string includes quotes, it isn't necessary to code double quotes like you do for a verbatim string literal. If the string includes text that's enclosed in more than one set of quotes, though, you must enclose the raw string literal in additional sets of quotes.

The raw string literal shown here includes text that's enclosed in quotes as well as a new line character at the end of each line and whitespace before two of the lines that indent the lines. The Text Visualizer dialog in this figure shows how this raw string literal is displayed. You'll learn more about the Text Visualizer dialog in chapter 11. For now, just notice that the formatting of the text in this dialog is identical to the formatting of the code shown in the example. It would be much more difficult to code a regular string literal with escape sequences or a verbatim string literal that produces this text.

A raw string literal with whitespace, new lines, and quotes

```
string rawMessage = """
    Once upon a midnight dreary, while I pondered, weak and weary,
    Over many a quaint and curious volume of forgotten lore--
        While I nodded, nearly napping, suddenly there came a tapping,
    As of some one gently rapping, rapping at my chamber door.
    "'Tis some visitor," I muttered, "tapping at my chamber door--
              Only this and nothing more."

    --Edgar Alan Poe
""";
```

The result in the Text Visualizer

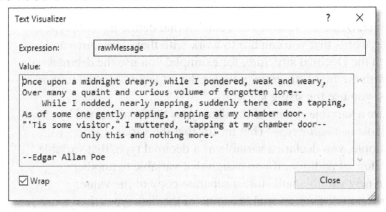

Description

- A *raw string literal* can contain standard text characters, whitespace, and special characters such as new lines and quotation marks. They are typically used for lengthy strings of formatted text.

- Like verbatim string literals, raw string literals don't require escape sequences.

- To code a raw string literal, you code three or more double quotes at the beginning and end of the string. Then, you can include quoted text within the literal.

- If you need to include text that's enclosed in more than one set of quotes, you must increase the number of quotes used to enclose the literal. The number of quotes at the start and end of the literal must be the same.

- The content of a raw string literal is typically coded on separate lines from the opening quotes and closing quotes as shown above. In that case, the new lines after the opening quote and before the closing quotes are not included in the literal. In addition, any whitespace before the closing quotes is not included in the literal.

Figure 4-12   How to code raw string literals

How to convert data types

In chapter 3, you were introduced to the use of classes, which provide properties and methods for the objects that are instantiated from the classes. Now, you'll be introduced to *structures*, which are similar to classes. Then, you'll learn how to use these structures and classes to convert data from one type to another.

The .NET structures and classes that define data types

Figure 4-13 summarizes the structures and classes that define the data types, along with the C# keywords that you can use to work with these structures and classes. To work with the Decimal structure, for example, you use the decimal keyword. To work with the Int32 structure, you use the int keyword. And to work with the String class, you use the string keyword.

When you declare a variable as one of the data types that's supported by a structure, that variable is a *value type*. That means that the variable stores its own data. If, for example, you declare a variable as a decimal type, that variable stores the decimal value. In addition, if you assign that variable to another decimal variable, the new variable will store a separate copy of the value.

By contrast, when you declare a variable as one of the data types that's supported by a class, an object is created from the class. Then, the variable stores a reference to the object, not the object itself. Because of that, object data types are called *reference types*.

In this figure, the two reference types defined by .NET are string and object. So, when you declare a variable as a string, that variable holds a reference to a String object that contains the data for the string. As a result, it's possible for two or more variables to refer to the same String object.

In addition to the String class, .NET also provides a generic Object class. You can use a variable created from this class to hold a reference to any type of object. You'll learn more about working with the Object class in chapter 14.

Common .NET structures that define value types

Structure	C# keyword	What the value type holds
Byte	**byte**	An 8-bit unsigned integer
Int16	**short**	A 16-bit signed integer
Int32	**int**	A 32-bit signed integer
Int64	**long**	A 64-bit signed integer
Single	**float**	A single-precision floating-point number
Double	**double**	A double-precision floating-point number
Decimal	**decimal**	A 96-bit decimal value
Boolean	**bool**	A true or false value
Char	**char**	A single character

Common .NET classes that define reference types

Class	C# keyword	What the reference type holds
String	**string**	A reference to a String object
Object	**object**	A reference to any type of object

Description

- Each built-in data type is supported by a structure or a class within the .NET Framework. When you use a C# keyword to refer to a data type, you're actually using an alias for the associated structure or class.
- A *structure* defines a *value type*, which stores its own data.
- A class defines a *reference type*. A reference type doesn't store the data itself. Instead, it stores a reference to the area of memory where the data is stored.
- All of the structures and classes shown in this figure are in the System namespace of .NET.

Note

- .NET also provides structures for the other built-in data types that were listed in figure 4-1.

Figure 4-13   The .NET structures and classes that define data types

How to use methods to convert data types

Figure 4-14 presents two ways you can use methods to convert data from one type to another. First, you can use the ToString(), Parse(), and TryParse() methods, which are available from any of the data structures defined by .NET. Second, you can use the static methods of the Convert class to convert a value to any of the data structures defined by .NET.

The ToString() method lets you convert any value to a string. In the first group of statements in this figure, for example, the ToString() method is used to convert a decimal value to a string value. Notice in this example that no arguments are provided on the ToString() method. In the next figure, you'll learn how to code an argument that formats the resulting string.

Before going on, you should realize that C# calls the ToString() method implicitly in certain situations. You learned about one of those situations earlier in this chapter, and that example is repeated here. In this case, a double value is automatically converted to a string when it's joined with another string.

The Parse() method is a static method that performs the reverse operation of the ToString() method. In other words, it converts a string value to another data type. In the third statement in the first group of statements, for example, the Parse() method of the Decimal structure is used to convert the value of a string variable to a decimal value. However, this method only recognizes standard numeric characters when coded as shown here. As a result, an exception will occur if you try to convert a string that includes non-numeric characters like a dollar sign or parentheses.

One way to avoid this is to code another argument on the Parse() method that indicates the characters that are allowed. You'll learn more about that in chapter 9. Another way is to use the TryParse() method instead of the Parse() method. This method also converts a string value to another data type as illustrated by the last statement in the first group of statements. Notice here that you don't assign the result of the TryParse() method to a variable like you do when you use Parse(). Instead, you name the variable on the second argument of the method, and you precede the name of the variable with the *out* keyword. You'll learn more about this keyword in chapter 6. For now, just realize that if the conversion can't be performed, the TryParse() method stores a value of zero in the variable and returns a false value instead of throwing an exception. Then, you can test the return value to determine if the conversion was successful. You'll see an example of that in chapter 7.

The Convert class provides static methods that you can use to convert a value with any data type to any other data type. This is illustrated by the last group of statements in this figure. Here, the first statement uses the ToDecimal() method to convert a string that's entered in a text box to a decimal value. The second statement uses the ToInt32() method to convert a string that's entered in a text box to an integer value. The third statement uses the ToString() method to convert a decimal value to a string value. And the fourth statement uses the ToInt32() method to convert a decimal value to an integer value.

When you use the Convert class, you should realize that the results of the conversion will vary depending on the type of conversion that you perform. If,

Common methods for data conversion

Method	Description
`ToString([format])`	A method that converts the value to its equivalent string representation using the specified format. If the format is omitted, the value isn't formatted.
`Parse(string)`	A static method that converts the specified string to an equivalent data value. If the string can't be converted, an exception occurs.
`TryParse(string, result)`	A static method that converts the specified string to an equivalent data value and stores it in the result variable. Returns a true value if the string is converted. Otherwise, returns a false value.

Some of the static methods of the Convert class

Method	Description
`ToDecimal(value)`	Converts the value to the decimal data type.
`ToDouble(value)`	Converts the value to the double data type.
`ToInt32(value)`	Converts the value to the int data type.
`ToChar(value)`	Converts the value to the char data type.
`ToBool(value)`	Converts the value to the bool data type.
`ToString(value)`	Converts the value to a string object.

Conversion statements that use the ToString(), Parse(), and TryParse() methods

```
decimal sales = 2574.98m;
string salesString = sales.ToString();        // decimal to string
sales = Decimal.Parse(salesString);           // string to decimal
Decimal.TryParse(salesString, out sales);     // string to decimal
```

An implicit call of the ToString() method

```
double price = 49.50;
string priceString = "Price: $" + price;      // automatic ToString() call
```

A TryParse() method that handles invalid data

```
string salesString = "$2574.98";
decimal sales = 0m;
Decimal.TryParse(salesString, out sales);     // sales is 0
```

Conversion statements that use the Convert class

```
decimal subtotal = Convert.ToDecimal(txtSubtotal.Text); // string to decimal
int years = Convert.ToInt32(txtYears.Text);             // string to int
txtSubtotal.Text = Convert.ToString(subtotal);          // decimal to string
int subtotalInt = Convert.ToInt32(subtotal);            // decimal to int
```

Description

- The ToString(), Parse(), and TryParse() methods are included in all of the data structures.

- In some situations where a string is expected, the compiler will automatically call the ToString() method.

- The Convert class contains static methods for converting all of the built-in types. To see all of the methods of this class, you can look up the Convert class in online help.

Figure 4-14   How to use methods to convert data types

for example, you convert a decimal to an integer as illustrated in the last statement in figure 4-14, the conversion will round the decimal digits using banker's rounding. In other cases, C# won't be able to perform the conversion, and an exception will occur.

How to use methods to convert numbers to formatted strings

Figure 4-15 shows how to use methods to convert numbers to formatted strings. The table at the start of this figure summarizes the standard codes that you can use to format a number when you use its ToString() method. To use these codes, you code them as arguments, as illustrated in the first group of statements in this figure. Notice that the formatting code must be enclosed in double quotes.

You can also include an integer after any of the numeric formatting codes. In most cases, this integer indicates the number of decimal places in the resulting string. For example, if you specify the code "c0" for the value 19.95, that number will be converted to $20. Note that if you don't specify the number of decimal places, two decimal places are assumed.

If you specify a number on the D or d formatting code, it indicates the minimum number of digits in the result. Since these formatting codes are used with integers, that means that the value is padded on the left with zeros if the number you specify is greater than the number of digits in the integer. If, for example, you specify the code "d3" for the number 28, it will be converted to 028.

Another way to format numbers is to use the Format() method of the String class. Since this is a static method, you access it directly from the String class rather than from an instance of this class. You must also provide two arguments.

The first argument is a string literal that contains the format specification for the value to be formatted, and the second argument is the value to be formatted. The syntax for the format specification is shown in this figure. Here, the index indicates the value to be formatted, and the format code specifies how the value is to be formatted. Although you can format multiple values using the Format() method, you'll typically use it to format a single value. In that case, the index value will be 0. In chapter 9, you'll learn how to use this method to format two or more values.

The second group of statements in this figure shows how to use the Format() method. As you can see, these statements perform the same functions as the statements that use the ToString() method. In this case, though, these statements use literal values so you can see what the values look like before they're formatted. Notice in these statements that the format specification is enclosed in braces. In addition, the entire argument is enclosed in double quotes.

Standard numeric formatting codes

Code	Format	Description
c or c	Currency	Formats the number as currency with the specified number of decimal places.
P or p	Percent	Formats the number as a percent with the specified number of decimal places.
N or n	Number	Formats the number with thousands separators and the specified number of decimal places.
F or f	Float	Formats the number as a decimal with the specified number of decimal places.
D or d	Digits	Formats an integer with the specified number of digits.
E or e	Exponential	Formats the number in scientific (exponential) notation with the specified number of decimal places.
G or g	General	Formats the number as a decimal or in scientific notation depending on which is more compact.

How to use the ToString() method to format a number

Statement	Example
`string monthlyAmount = amount.ToString("c");`	$1,547.20
`string interestRate = interest.ToString("p1");`	2.3%
`string quantityString = quantity.ToString("n0");`	15,000
`string paymentString = payment.ToString("f3");`	432.818

How to use the Format() method of the String class to format a number

Statement	Result
`string monthlyAmount = String.Format("{0:c}", 1547.2m);`	$1,547.20
`string interestRate = String.Format("{0:p1}", .023m);`	2.3%
`string quantityString = String.Format("{0:n0}", 15000);`	15,000
`string paymentString = String.Format("{0:f3}", 432.8175);`	432.818

The syntax of the format specification used by the Format() method

```
{index:formatCode}
```

Description

- You can include a number after some of the numeric formatting codes to specify the number of decimal places in the result. If the numeric value contains more decimal places than are specified, the result will be rounded using standard rounding. If you don't specify the number of decimal places, the default is 2.

- You can include a number after the D or d formatting code to specify the minimum number of digits in the result. If the integer has fewer digits than are specified, zeros are added to the beginning of the integer.

- You can use the Format() method of the String class to format two or more values. For more information, see chapter 9.

Figure 4-15   How to use methods to convert numbers to formatted strings

Four other skills for working with data

To complete the subject of working with data, the next four figures present four more useful skills: how to work with scope, how to work with enumerations, how to allow value types to store null values, and how to allow reference types to store null values.

How to work with scope

When you work with C#, the *scope* of a variable is determined by where you declare it, and the scope determines what code can access the variable. If, for example, you declare a variable within an event handler, the variable has *method scope* because an event handler is a method. In that case, the variable can only be referred to by statements within that method.

Often, though, you want all the methods of a form to have access to a variable. Then, you must declare the variable within the class for the form, but outside all the methods. In that case, the variable has *class scope* and can be called a *class variable*.

This is illustrated and summarized in figure 4-16. Here, you can see that two variables are declared after the last of the generated code for the form class, but before the first event handler for the form. As a result, these variables have class scope. By contrast, the four variables that are declared at the start of the first event handler have method scope. Note that the variables with class scope are used by both event handlers in this example, which is one reason for using class scope.

The other reason for using variables with class scope is to retain data after a method finishes executing. This has to do with the *lifetime* of a variable. In particular, a method variable is available only while the method is executing. When the method finishes, the variable is no longer available and the data is lost. Then, when the method is executed the next time, the method variables are declared and initialized again.

By contrast, a class variable lasts until the instance of the class is terminated. For a form, that happens when you exit the form and the form is closed. As a result, class variables can be used for accumulating values like invoice totals. You'll see this illustrated by the last app in this chapter.

Code that declares and uses variables with class scope

```
public frmInvoiceTotal()
{
    InitializeComponent();
}
```
— Last generated method

```
decimal numberOfInvoices = 0m;
decimal totalOfInvoices = 0m;
```
— Class scope

```
private void btnCalculate_Click(object sender, EventArgs e)
{
    decimal subtotal = Convert.ToDecimal(txtEnterSubtotal.Text);
    decimal discountPercent = .25m;
    decimal discountAmount = subtotal * discountPercent;
    decimal invoiceTotal = subtotal - discountAmount;
```
— Method scope

```
    numberOfInvoices++;
    totalOfInvoices += invoiceTotal;
```
— Class scope

```
    // the rest of the code for the method
}

private void btnClearTotals_Click(object sender, EventArgs e)
{
    numberOfInvoices = 0m;
    totalOfInvoices = 0m;
}
```
— Class scope

Description

- The *scope* of a variable determines what code has access to it. If you try to refer to a variable outside of its scope, it will cause a build error.

- The scope of a variable is determined by where you declare it. If you declare a variable within a method, it has *method scope*. If you declare a variable within a class but not within a method, it has *class scope*.

- A variable with method scope can only be referred to by statements within that method. A variable with class scope can be referred to by all of the methods in the class.

- The *lifetime* of a variable is the period of time that it's available for use. A variable with method scope is only available while the method is executing. A variable with class scope is available while the class is instantiated.

- You can declare *class variables* right after the code that is generated for a form.

Figure 4-16   How to work with scope

How to declare and use enumerations

An *enumeration* is a set of related constants that defines a value type where each constant is known as a *member* of the enumeration. The enumerations provided by.NET are generally used to set object properties and to specify the values that are passed to methods. For example, the FormBorderStyle enumeration includes a group of constants that you can use to specify the settings for the FormBorderStyle property of a form.

The table in figure 4-17 summarizes three of the constants within the FormBorderStyle enumeration, and the first example shows how you can use code to set this form property. Normally, though, you'll use the Properties window to choose the constant from the enumeration for this form property.

When writing code, you often need to select one option from a group of related options. For example, you may need to let a user choose the payment terms for an invoice. In that case, it often makes sense to define an enumeration that contains each option.

To define an enumeration, you can use the syntax shown in this figure. After you provide a name for an enumeration, you code the constant names within braces. In the first example, the enumeration is named Terms, and the constants are named Net30Days, Net60Days, and Net90Days. In this case, because values aren't provided for these constants, the default values of 0, 1, and 2 are assigned to the constants.

If you want to assign other values to the constants, you can provide a value for each constant as shown in the second example. Here, the values 30, 60, and 90 are assigned to the constants for the TermValues enumeration. In this case, these values are stored as short data types because a colon and the data type are coded after the enumeration name. If the data type is omitted, the constant values are stored as integers.

To refer to a constant value in an enumeration, you code the name of the enumeration followed by a dot and the name of the constant. This is illustrated by the first three statements in the third group of examples. Here, the first statement returns a value of the Terms type, the second statement returns the int type that corresponds to a member of the Terms enumeration, and the third statement returns the int type that corresponds to a member of the TermValues enumeration. If you want to refer to the name of a constant instead of its value, you can use the ToString() method as in the last example in this group.

For now, when you code an enumeration, you can code it with class scope. In other words, you can code the enumeration after the generated code for a class as shown in the previous figure. That way, it will be available to all the methods in the class. Later, when you learn how to add classes to a project, you can store an enumeration in its own file so it's easily accessible from all classes in the project.

Some of the constants in the FormBorderStyle enumeration

Constant	Description
`FormBorderStyle.FixedDialog`	A fixed, thick border sometimes used for dialogs
`FormBorderStyle.FixedSingle`	A single-line border that isn't resizable
`FormBorderStyle.Sizable`	A resizable border

A statement that uses the FormBorderStyle enumeration

```
this.FormBorderStyle = FormBorderStyle.FixedSingle;
```

The syntax for declaring an enumeration

```
enum EnumerationName [: type]
{
    ConstantName1 [= value][,
    ConstantName2 [= value]]...
}
```

An enumeration that sets the constant values to 0, 1, and 2

```
enum Terms
{
    Net30Days,
    Net60Days,
    Net90Days
}
```

An enumeration that sets the constant values to 30, 60, and 90

```
enum TermValues : short
{
    Net30Days = 30,
    Net60Days = 60,
    Net90Days = 90
}
```

Statements that use the constants in these enumerations

```
Terms t = Terms.Net30Days;
int i = (int) Terms.Net30Days;           // i is 0
int i = (int) TermValues.Net60Days;      // i is 60
string s = Terms.Net30Days.ToString();   // s is "Net30Days"
```

Description

- An *enumeration* defines a set of related constants. Each constant is known as a *member* of the enumeration.

- By default, an enumeration uses the int type and sets the first constant to 0, the second to 1, and so on.

- To use one of the other integer data types, you can code a colon after the enumeration name followed by the data type.

- To specify other values for the constants, you can code an equal sign after the constant name followed by the integer value.

Figure 4-17   How to declare and use enumerations

How to work with nullable value types and the null-coalescing operators

By default, value types (such as the int, decimal, and bool types) can't store null values. Most of the time, you won't need to use a value type to store null values. However, a feature of C# known as *nullable types* allows you to store a null value in a value type, and figure 4-18 shows how this feature works.

To declare a *nullable value type*, you type a question mark (?) immediately after the type in the declaration of a value type. Except for the question mark, this works just as it does for any other value type variable. In this figure, for example, the first statement declares an int variable as a nullable type. Then, the second statement uses the null keyword to assign a null value to this type.

Typically, you use a null value to indicate that the value of the variable is unknown. For example, if a user didn't enter a quantity, you might want to assign a null value to the quantity variable to indicate that the user didn't enter a value. When working with value types, however, it's more common to assign a default value such as zero to indicate that the user didn't enter a value. As a result, unless you're working with a database that returns null values, you probably won't need to use nullable value types.

In addition to the built-in value types, this figure shows that you can declare the Terms enumeration shown in figure 4-17 as a nullable type. That makes sense because enumerations define value types.

Once you declare a value type as nullable, you can use the HasValue property to check if the type stores a value or if it contains a null value. Then, if it stores a value, you can use the Value property to get that value as shown in the second example. You can also execute different statements if the type is null.

Another way to test the value of a nullable type is to use the *null-coalescing operator*. This operator returns the value of the left operand—in this case, the nullable type—if it isn't null. Otherwise, it returns the value of the right operand. This operator makes it easy to assign a default value to a variable if a nullable type contains null. In the statement in this figure, for example, a value of -1 will be assigned to the variable named qty if the nullable type named quantity is null.

Sometimes, you only want to assign a value to a variable if that variable is null. To do that, you can use the *null-coalescing assignment operator*. In this figure, for example, a value of 0.0 will be assigned only if salesTotal is null.

You can also use nullable values types in arithmetic expressions. In that case, if the value of the nullable type is null, the result of the arithmetic expression is always null. This is illustrated in the last example in this figure.

How to declare a value type that can contain null values

```
int? quantity;
quantity = null;
quantity = 0;
quantity = 20;

decimal? salesTotal = null;

Terms? paymentTerm = null;
```

Two properties and one method for working with nullable value types

Property	Description
HasValue	Returns a true value if the nullable type contains a value. Returns a false value if the nullable type is null.
Value	Returns the value of the nullable type.

How to use the properties of a nullable value type

```
if (quantity.HasValue) {
    int qty = quantity.Value;
}
```

How to use the null-coalescing operator to assign a default value

```
int qty = quantity ?? -1;
```

How to use the null-coalescing assignment operator

```
salesTotal ??= 0.0m;
```

How to use nullable value types in arithmetic expressions

```
decimal? sales1 = 3267.58m;
decimal? sales2 = null;
decimal? salesTotal = sales1 + sales2;  // result = null
```

Description

- A *nullable value type* is a value type that can store a null value. Null values are typically used to indicate that the value of the variable is unknown.
- To declare a value type as nullable, code a question mark (?) immediately after the keyword for the type.
- The *null-coalescing operator* (??) returns the value of the left operand if it isn't null or the right operand if it is.
- The *null-coalescing assignment operator* (??=) assigns the value of the right operand only if the left operand is null.
- If you use a variable with a nullable type in an arithmetic expression and the value of the variable is null, the result of the arithmetic expression is always null.

Figure 4-18   How to work with nullable value types and the null-coalescing operators

How to work with nullable reference types

With .NET 6.0 and later, *nullable reference types* are enabled by default. In many respects, nullable reference types work like nullable value types as shown in figure 4-18. However, there are some differences in the way you work with nullable reference types, as shown in figure 4-19

To start, this figure shows how to enable nullable reference types if you're using a version of .NET prior to .NET 6. In most cases, you'll want to enable it for an entire project. To do that, you can use the procedure shown at the top of this figure.

You can also enable nullable reference types for an individual file. To do that, you add a #nullable *preprocessor directive* at the beginning of the file like the one shown in the first example. A preprocessor directive provides conditional information to the compiler that determines how a file is compiled.

Although the default for reference types is for them to be non-nullable, you'll still want to use reference types that can contain null values in some cases. To declare a reference type that can contain a null value, you code a question mark (?) after the type as shown by the first statement in the second example. This works the same as it does for nullable value types.

When you enable nullable reference types, the compiler will display warnings when you use nullable and non-nullable variables incorrectly. If, for example, you try to get the length of a nullable variable as shown in the second statement and the compiler can't determine that you've assigned a non-null value to that variable, it will display a warning that the variable may be null. This figure lists other common situations when warnings are displayed. These warnings are intended to help you identify problem areas in your code so you can fix them. For example, before you get the length of a variable that may contain a null value, you should check to be sure it isn't null as shown in the third statement. This is true regardless of whether nullable reference types are enabled.

In some cases, the compiler won't be able to tell whether a nullable variable might contain a null value, and it will display a warning. If you're sure that the variable won't contain a null value, though, you can suppress the warning. To do that, you code a null-forgiving operator (!) after the name of the variable as shown in the fourth statement.

Because nullable reference types are enabled by default with .NET 6 and later, all the applications in this book use them. As you progress through this book, then, you'll see more examples of how to work with nullable reference types. Of course, you can also disable nullable reference types if you don't want to use them. You do that using techniques like those shown at the top of this figure, except you select Disable from the Nullable drop-down list or you set the #nullable preprocessor directive to disable. Because nullable reference types can help you find potential null reference errors, however, you should use them whenever possible.

How to enable nullable reference types (prior to .NET 6)

At the project level

1. In the Solution Explorer, right-click on the project name and select Properties.
2. Select the Build category.
3. From the Nullable drop-down list, select Enable.

At the file level

```
#nullable enable
using System.Windows.Forms;
...
```

How to work with nullable reference types

```
string? message = null;              // declare a nullable reference type

int length = message.Length;         // message may produce null warning

int length = 0;
if (message != null)                 // check that the message isn't null
    length = message.Length;

int length = message!.Length;        // stop compiler from displaying warning
```

Common situations when warnings are displayed

- When you assign or pass a null value to a non-nullable reference type.
- When you assign or pass a nullable reference type to a non-nullable one.
- When you refer to a nullable reference type that may be null.
- When a non-nullable field of a new object isn't initialized to a non-null value.

Description

- Prior to .NET 6, reference types could contain null values by default. If that wasn't what you wanted, you could enable *nullable reference types* at the project or file level as shown above.
- With .NET 6 and later, all project templates enable nullable reference types by default.
- To declare a reference type as nullable, you code a question mark (?) immediately after the keyword for the type just like you do for value types.
- When you use nullable reference types, the compiler tries to determine when nullable and non-nullable variables are used incorrectly and then displays a warning.
- If a warning is displayed indicating that a non-nullable variable may contain a null value and you're sure it won't, you can code the null-forgiving operator (!) after the variable name or null keyword to keep the warning from being displayed.
- Before referring to a nullable reference type, you should check that it doesn't contain a null value.
- You can use the null-coalescing and null-coalescing assignment operators shown in figure 4-18 with nullable reference types just as you can with nullable value types.

Figure 4-19   How to work with nullable reference types

Two versions of the Invoice Total app

To give you a better idea of how you can use data, arithmetic expressions, data conversion, and scope, this chapter concludes by presenting two illustrative apps.

The basic Invoice Total app

Figure 4-20 presents a simple version of the Invoice Total app that's similar to the one presented in chapter 3. Now that you have learned how to work with data, you should be able to understand all the code in this app.

To start, this figure shows the user interface for this app, which is the same as it was in the last chapter. Then, this figure lists the six controls that the code refers to so you can see how the code relates to those controls.

This figure also presents the code for the two event handlers of the Invoice Total app. If you study the code for the Click event of the Calculate button, you'll see that it begins by converting the string value that's entered by the user to a decimal value. Then, it sets the discount percent to .25, or 25%. This percent is then used to calculate the discount for the invoice, and the discount is subtracted from the subtotal to get the invoice total. Finally, the calculated values are formatted and displayed on the form.

If rounding is necessary when the values are displayed, the formatting statements in this app will do the rounding. Note, however, that the values stored in discountAmt and invoiceTotal aren't rounded. To round these values, you would need to use the Round() method of the Math class. You often need to do that when you work with values that are going to be stored in a file or database.

You should also realize that this app will work only if the user enters a numeric value into the Subtotal text box. If the user enters any non-numeric characters, an exception will occur when the app tries to convert that value to a decimal value. One way to prevent this type of error is to use the TryParse() method you learned about earlier in this chapter. Then, you can use the techniques presented in the next chapter to test if the value the user entered is valid, and you can use the technique presented in chapter 7 to display an error message to the user if the entry is invalid. Chapter 7 also presents some additional techniques you can use to prevent exceptions.

The Invoice Total form

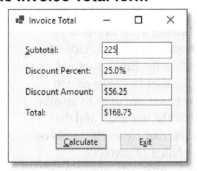

The controls that are referred to in the code

Object type	Name	Description
TextBox	txtSubtotal	A text box that accepts a subtotal amount
TextBox	txtDiscountPct	A read-only text box that displays the discount percent
TextBox	txtDiscountAmt	A read-only text box that displays the discount amount
TextBox	txtTotal	A read-only text box that displays the invoice total
Button	btnCalculate	Calculates the discount amount and invoice total when clicked
Button	btnExit	Closes the form when clicked

The event handlers for the Invoice Total form

```
private void btnCalculate_Click(object sender, EventArgs e)
{
    decimal subtotal = Convert.ToDecimal(txtSubtotal.Text);
    decimal discountPct = .25m;
    decimal discountAmt = subtotal * discountPct;
    decimal invoiceTotal = subtotal - discountAmt;

    txtDiscountPct.Text = discountPct.ToString("p1");
    txtDiscountAmt.Text = discountAmt.ToString("c");
    txtTotal.Text = invoiceTotal.ToString("c");

    txtSubtotal.Focus();
}

private void btnExit_Click(object sender, EventArgs e)
{
    this.Close();
}
```

Figure 4-20   The basic Invoice Total app

The enhanced Invoice Total app

Figure 4-21 presents an enhanced version of the Invoice Total app that illustrates some of the other skills presented in this chapter. On the left side of the form, a new label and text box have been added below the Enter Subtotal text box. These controls display the last subtotal that the user has entered. On the right side of the form, three pairs of labels and text boxes are used to display the number of invoices that have been entered, a total of the invoices, and the average of the invoices. The form also has a Clear button that clears the totals on the right side of the form so the user can enter another batch of invoices.

The controls that have been added to this form are named with our standard naming conventions, which are based on the names that are used to identify text boxes and labels. In this case, txtEnterSubtotal is used for the text box that lets the user enter a subtotal, txtSubtotal is used for the text box that displays the last subtotal that the user has entered, txtNumberOfInvoices is used for the text box that displays the number of invoices, txtTotalOfInvoices is used for the text box that displays the total of the invoices, txtAvgOfInvoices is used for the text box that displays the average of the invoices, and btnClearTotals is used for the Clear button.

In the code for this form, the enhancements are shaded so they're easy to review. This code starts with the declarations of the three class variables: numberOfInvoices, totalOfInvoices, and avgOfInvoices. These are the variables whose values need to be retained from one execution of an event handler to another. They are initialized with zero values.

In the event handler for the Click event of the Calculate button, the second and third shaded lines add rounding to the calculations for the discount amount and invoice total. That's necessary so only the exact amount of the invoice is added to the total for the invoices. Otherwise, the total for the invoices may become incorrect. Then, the next shaded statement displays the subtotal entered by the user in the Subtotal text box. That way, all the data for the last invoice is shown in the text boxes on the left side of the form while the user enters the subtotal for the next invoice.

The next set of shaded statements shows how the class variables are used after each subtotal entry has been processed. The first three statements add 1 to the number of invoices, add the invoice total to the total of invoices, and calculate the average of the invoices. Then, the next three statements assign the new values of the class variables to the text boxes that will display them. The last shaded statement in this event handler assigns an empty string to the Enter subtotal text box so the user can enter the subtotal for the next invoice.

In the event handler for the Click event of the Clear button, the first three statements reset the class variables to zeros so the user can enter the subtotals for another batch of invoices. Then, the next three statements set the text boxes that display these variables to empty strings. The last statement moves the focus to the Enter Subtotal text box so the user can start the first entry of another batch of invoices.

The enhanced Invoice Total form

The code for the class variables and two event handlers

```
int numberOfInvoices = 0;
decimal totalOfInvoices = 0m;
decimal avgOfInvoices = 0m;

private void btnCalculate_Click(object sender, EventArgs e)
{
    decimal subtotal = Convert.ToDecimal(txtEnterSubtotal.Text);
    decimal discountPct = .25m;
    decimal discountAmt = Math.Round(subtotal * discountPct, 2);
    decimal invoiceTotal = Math.Round(subtotal - discountAmt, 2);

    txtSubtotal.Text = subtotal.ToString("c");
    txtDiscountPct.Text = discountPct.ToString("p1");
    txtDiscountAmt.Text = discountAmt.ToString("c");
    txtTotal.Text = invoiceTotal.ToString("c");

    numberOfInvoices++;
    totalOfInvoices += invoiceTotal;
    avgOfInvoices = totalOfInvoices / numberOfInvoices;

    txtNumberOfInvoices.Text = numberOfInvoices.ToString();
    txtTotalOfInvoices.Text = totalOfInvoices.ToString("c");
    txtAvgOfInvoices.Text = avgOfInvoices.ToString("c");

    txtEnterSubtotal.Text = "";
    txtEnterSubtotal.Focus();
}

private void btnClearTotals_Click(object sender, System.EventArgs e)
{
    numberOfInvoices = 0;
    totalOfInvoices = 0m;
    avgOfInvoices = 0m;

    txtNumberOfInvoices.Text = "";
    txtTotalOfInvoices.Text = "";
    txtAvgOfInvoices.Text = "";

    txtEnterSubtotal.Focus();
}
```

Figure 4-21   The enhanced Invoice Total app

Perspective

If you understand the code in the enhanced Invoice Total app, you've come a long way. If not, you should get a better understanding for how this app works when you do the exercises for this chapter. Once you understand it, you'll be ready to learn how to code selection and iteration statements so you can add logical operations to your apps.

Terms

built-in data type	precision
bit	banker's rounding
byte	instance method
integer	instantiation
Unicode character set	pseudorandom number
ASCII character set	seed value
Boolean value	string
variable	string literal
constant	null value
declare a variable or constant	empty string
initialize a variable or constant	concatenate strings
camel notation	append a string
digit separator	escape sequence
Pascal notation	verbatim string literal
literal	raw string literal
scientific notation	structure
arithmetic expression	value type
arithmetic operator	reference type
operand	scope
binary operator	class scope
unary operator	class variable
prefix an operand	method scope
postfix an operand	lifetime
assignment statement	enumeration
assignment operator	member
shortcut assignment operators	nullable type
order of precedence	nullable value type
casting	null-coalescing operator
implicit cast	null-coalescing assignment operator
widening conversion	nullable reference type
explicit cast	
narrowing conversion	
strict type semantics	
static method	
argument	

Exercise 4-1   Modify the Invoice Total app

In this exercise, you'll modify the Invoice Total app that's presented in this chapter.

Open the Invoice Total app

1. Open the app that's in the C:\C#\Ch04\InvoiceTotal directory. This is the app that's presented in figure 4-20.

Test the code for the Invoice Total app

2. Build and run the app, and enter a valid subtotal to verify that the correct discount is being taken. Then, enter a valid subtotal like 225.50 that will yield a discount amount that has more than two decimal places, and make sure that only two decimal places are displayed for the discount amount and total.

3. Enter "$1000" for the subtotal and click the Calculate button. This time, an exception should occur, Visual Studio should enter break mode, and the Exception Helper should display a message that indicates that the input string was not in a correct format.

4. Note the highlighted statement. This shows that the assignment statement can't convert the string that was entered to the decimal data type. Next, move the mouse pointer over txtSubtotal.Text so you can see the data tip that shows that the current value is $1000. Then, click the Stop Debugging button in the Debug toolbar to end the app.

Experiment with the code

5. Modify the first statement in the btnCalculate_Click() method so it uses the Parse() method of the Decimal class instead of the ToDecimal() method of the Convert class. Then, test the app to verify that it still works the same.

6. Round the values that are stored in the discountAmt and invoiceTotal variables to two decimal places, and delete the formatting codes for the statements that convert these variables to strings. Then, test the app to make sure that only two decimal places are displayed for the discount amount and total. Note that dollar signs are no longer included for the discount amount and invoice total since the formatting codes for those values were deleted.

7. Add the formatting codes back so the dollar signs are displayed once again.

Save and close the project

8. Save the solution and close it.

Exercise 4-2   Enhance the Invoice Total app

This exercise will guide you through the process of enhancing the Invoice Total app of exercise 4-1 so it works like the app in figure 4-21. This will give you more practice in developing forms and working with data.

Open the Invoice Total app and enhance the form

1. Open the app in the C:\C#\Ch04\InvoiceTotalEnhanced directory.

2. Use the techniques that you learned in chapter 2 to enlarge the form and to add the new controls that are shown in figure 4-21 to the form.

3. Set the properties for each of the controls. You should be able to do this without any guidance, but try to name each control that's going to be referred to by code with the proper prefix followed by the name that identifies it in the form (like txtNumberOfInvoices).

Add the code for the enhancements

4. Switch to the Code Editor and enter the three class variables shown in figure 4-21. These are the variables that will accumulate the data for all the invoices.

5. Enhance the code for the Click event of the Calculate button so it calculates and displays the new data. Try to do this without referring to figure 4-21.

6. Use the techniques you learned in chapter 3 to start the event handler for the Click event of the Clear button. Then, add the code for this event. Here again, try to do this without referring to the code in figure 4-21.

7. Test the app and fix any errors until the app works properly. Be sure that it restarts properly when you click the Clear button and enter another batch of invoices.

Add more controls and code

8. Add two more labels and two more text boxes below the two columns of text boxes and labels on the right side of the form. The two labels should say "Largest invoice" and "Smallest invoice". The text boxes to the right of the labels should display the values for the largest invoice total and the smallest invoice total.

9. Add the code that makes this work. If you're new to programming, this may challenge you. (Hint: To find the smallest invoice total, use the Math.Min() method to compare each invoice total to a variable that contains the smallest invoice total to that point. Then, replace the variable value with the smaller of the two invoice totals. To make this work for the first invoice, you can initialize this variable to a large number like the MaxValue member of the Decimal class.)

10. Test the app and fix any errors until the app works properly. Then, close the project.

5

How to code control structures

In the last chapter, you learned how to write code that works with the most common data types. Now, you'll learn how to code the three types of control structures that are common to all modern programming languages: the selection, case, and iteration structures. When you finish this chapter, you'll be able to write apps that perform a wide range of logical operations.

How to code Boolean expressions

When you code an expression that evaluates to a true or false value, that expression can be called a *Boolean expression*. Because you use Boolean expressions within the control structures you code, you need to learn how to code Boolean expressions before you learn how to code control structures.

How to use the relational operators

Figure 5-1 shows how to use six *relational operators* to code a Boolean expression. These operators let you compare two operands, as illustrated by the examples in this figure. An operand can be any expression, including a variable, a literal, an arithmetic expression, or a keyword such as null, true, or false.

The first six expressions in this figure use the equality operator (==) to test if the two operands are equal. To use this operator, you must code two equals signs instead of one. That's because a single equals sign is used for assignment statements. As a result, if you try to code a Boolean expression with a single equals sign, your code won't compile.

The next expression uses the inequality operator (!=) to test if a variable is not equal to a string literal. The two expressions after that use the greater than operator (>) to test if a variable is greater than a numeric literal and the less than operator (<) to test if one variable is less than another. The last two expressions are similar, except they use the greater than or equal operator (>=) and less than or equal operator (<=) to compare operands.

If you want to include a Boolean variable in an expression, you often don't need to include the == or != operator. That's because a Boolean variable evaluates to a Boolean value by definition. So if isValid is a Boolean variable,

```
isValid
```

works the same as

```
isValid == true
```

When comparing numeric values, you usually compare values with the same data type. However, if you compare different types of numeric values, C# automatically casts the value with the less precise type to the more precise type. For example, if you compare an int value to a decimal value, the int value is cast to a decimal value before the comparison is performed.

If you're coming from another programming language such as Java, you may be surprised to find that you can also use some of these operators on strings, which are actually String objects. This is possible because C# allows classes and structures to define operators. In this case, since the String class defines the == and != operators, you can use these operators on strings.

Relational operators

Operator	Name	Description
==	Equality	Returns a true value if the left and right operands are equal.
!=	Inequality	Returns a true value if the left and right operands are not equal.
>	Greater than	Returns a true value if the left operand is greater than the right operand.
<	Less than	Returns a true value if the left operand is less than the right operand.
>=	Greater than or equal	Returns a true value if the left operand is greater than or equal to the right operand.
<=	Less than or equal	Returns a true value if the left operand is less than or equal to the right operand.

Examples

```
firstName == "Frank"        // equal to a string literal
txtYears.Text == ""         // equal to an empty string
message == null             // equal to a null value
discountPercent == 2.3      // equal to a numeric literal
isValid == false            // equal to the false value
code == productCode         // equal to another variable

lastName != "Jones"         // not equal to a string literal

years > 0                   // greater than a numeric literal
i < months                  // less than a variable

subtotal >= 500             // greater than or equal to a literal value
quantity <= reorderPoint    // less than or equal to a variable
```

Description

- You can use the *relational operators* to create a *Boolean expression* that compares two operands and returns a Boolean value.
- To compare two operands for equality, make sure you use two equals signs. If you use a single equals sign, the compiler will interpret it as an assignment statement, and your code won't compile.
- When comparing strings, you can only use the equality and inequality operators.
- If you compare two numeric operands with different data types, C# will cast the less precise operand to the type of the more precise operand.

Figure 5-1   How to use the relational operators

How to use the logical operators

Figure 5-2 shows how to use the *logical operators* to code a compound Boolean expression that consists of two or more Boolean expressions. For example, the first compound expression in this figure uses the **&&** operator. As a result, it evaluates to true if both the expression before the **&&** operator *and* the expression after the **&&** operator evaluate to true. Conversely, the second compound expression uses the || operator. As a result, it evaluates to true if either the expression before the || operator *or* the expression after the || operator evaluates to true.

When you use the **&&** and || operators, the second expression is only evaluated if necessary. Because of that, these operators are sometimes referred to as the *short-circuit operators*. To illustrate, suppose that the value of subtotal in the first example is less than 250. Then, the first expression evaluates to false. That means that the entire expression evaluates to false regardless of the value of the second expression. As a result, the second expression isn't evaluated. Since this is more efficient than always evaluating both expressions, you'll want to use these short-cut operators most of the time.

However, there may be times when you want to evaluate the second expression regardless of the value that's returned by the first expression. For example, the second expression may increment a variable, as illustrated by the third and fourth examples in this figure. In these cases, you can use the **&** and | operators to make sure that the second expression is evaluated.

You can also use two or more logical operators in the same expression, as illustrated by the fifth and sixth examples. When you do, you should know that And operations are performed before Or operations. In addition, both arithmetic and relational operations are performed before logical operations. If you need to change this sequence or if there's any doubt about how an expression will be evaluated, you can use parentheses to control or clarify the sequence.

If necessary, you can use the Not operator (**!**) to reverse the value of an expression as illustrated by the last example in this figure. Because this can create code that's difficult to read, however, you should avoid using this operator whenever possible. For example, instead of coding

```
!(subtotal < 100)
```

you can code

```
subtotal >= 100
```

Although both expressions return the same result, the second expression is easier to read.

Logical operators

Operator	Name	Description
&&	Conditional-And	Returns a true value if both expressions are true. This operator only evaluates the second expression if necessary.
||	Conditional-Or	Returns a true value if either expression is true. This operator only evaluates the second expression if necessary.
&	And	Returns a true value if both expressions are true. This operator always evaluates both expressions.
|	Or	Returns a true value if either expression is true. This operator always evaluates both expressions.
!	Not	Reverses the value of the expression.

Examples

```
subtotal >= 250 && subtotal < 500
timeInService <= 4 || timeInService >= 12

isValid == true & counter++ < years
isValid == true | counter++ < years

date > startDate && date < expirationDate || isValid == true
((thisYTD > lastYTD) || empType=="Part time") && startYear < currentYear

!(counter++ >= years)
```

Description

- You can use the *logical operators* to create a Boolean expression that combines two or more Boolean expressions.

- Since the && and || operators only evaluate the second expression if necessary, they're sometimes referred to as *short-circuit operators*. These operators are slightly more efficient than the & and | operators.

- By default, Not operations are performed first, followed by And operations, and then Or operations. These operations are performed after arithmetic operations and relational operations.

- You can use parentheses to change the sequence in which the operations will be performed or to clarify the sequence of operations.

Figure 5-2   How to use the logical operators

How to code conditional statements and expressions

Now that you know how to code Boolean expressions, you're ready to learn how to code conditional statements and expressions. That includes the if-else and switch statements, the switch expression, and expressions that use pattern matching and the conditional operator.

How to code if-else statements

Figure 5-3 shows how to use the *if-else statement* (or just *if statement*) to control the logic of your programs. This type of statement is the primary logical statement of all programming languages. It is the C# implementation of a control structure known as the *selection structure* because it lets you select different actions based on the results of Boolean expressions.

In the syntax summary in this figure, the brackets [ ] indicate that a clause is optional, and the ellipsis (...) indicates that the preceding element can be repeated as many times as needed. In other words, this syntax shows that you can code an *if* clause with or without *else if* clauses or an *else* clause. It also shows that you can code as many else if clauses as you need.

When an if statement is executed, C# begins by evaluating the Boolean expression in the if clause. If it's true, the statements within this clause are executed and the rest of the clauses in the if-else statement are skipped. If it's false, C# evaluates the first else if clause (if there is one). If its Boolean expression is true, the statements within this else if clause are executed and the rest of the if-else statement is skipped. Otherwise, C# evaluates the next else if clause. This continues with any remaining else if clauses. Finally, if none of the clauses contains a Boolean expression that evaluates to true, C# executes the statements in the else clause. If the statement doesn't include an else clause, C# doesn't execute any statements.

When coding if-else statements, it's often a good coding practice to code a set of braces for each clause. However, if a clause only contains a single statement, you can omit the braces. Although omitting the braces saves you some typing and takes up less vertical space, coding the braces makes it easier to identify the statements for each clause, and it makes it easier for you to add more statements later.

If you're working on an existing project that doesn't include the braces, you can add them using refactoring. To do that, place the cursor in an if, else if, or else clause, press Ctrl + period (.), and select Add Braces from the Quick Actions menu that's displayed. Then, click the Document, Project, or Solution link in the popup window to identify where you want the changes made.

In C#, whenever you use braces, you define a block of code. If you declare a variable within a block, that variable is available only to the other statements in the block. This can be referred to as *block scope*. As a result, if you need to access a variable outside of an if statement, you should declare it before the if statement.

The syntax of the if-else statement

```
if (booleanExpression) { statements }
[else if (booleanExpression) { statements }] ...
[else { statements }]
```

If statements without else if or else clauses

With a single statement

```
if (subtotal >= 100)
    discountPercent = .2m;
```

With a block of statements

```
if (subtotal >= 100)
{
    discountPercent = .2m;
    status = "Bulk rate";
}
```

An if statement with an else clause

```
if (subtotal >= 100)
    discountPercent = .2m;
else
    discountPercent = .1m;
```

An if statement with else if and else clauses

```
if (subtotal >= 100 && subtotal < 200)
    discountPercent = .2m;
else if (subtotal >= 200 && subtotal < 300)
    discountPercent = .3m;
else if (subtotal >= 300)
    discountPercent = .4m;
else
    discountPercent = .1m;
```

Nested if statements

```
if (customerType == "R")
{
    if (subtotal >= 100)                        // begin nested if
        discountPercent = .2m;
    else
        discountPercent = .1m;                  // end nested if
}
else    // customerType isn't "R"
    discountPercent = .4m;
```

Description

- An *if-else statement*, or just *if statement*, always contains an *if* clause. In addition, it can contain one or more *else if* clauses and a final *else* clause.

- If a clause requires just one statement, you don't have to enclose the statement in braces. You can just end the clause with a semicolon.

- If a clause requires more than one statement, you must enclose the block of statements in braces.

Figure 5-3   How to code if-else statements

When coding if statements, it's a common practice to code one if statement within another if statement. This is known as *nested if statements*. When you code nested if statements, it's a good practice to indent the nested statements and their clauses. This clearly identifies where the nested statement begins and ends. In the last example in figure 5-3, you can see that C# will execute the nested if statement only if the customer type is R. Otherwise, it executes the statement in the outer else clause.

How to code switch statements

Figure 5-4 shows how to use the *switch statement*. This is the C# implementation of a control structure known as the *case structure*, which lets you code different actions for different cases. The switch statement can sometimes be used in place of an if statement with else if clauses.

To code a switch statement, you start by coding the switch keyword followed by a *match expression*. This expression must evaluate to one of the data types listed in this figure. After the match expression, you can code one or more *case labels* that represent the possible values of the match expression. Then, when the match expression matches the value specified by a case label, the statements that follow the label are executed. A switch statement can also contain a *default label* that identifies the statements that are executed if none of the values specified by the case labels match the match expression. All of these case labels are coded within the switch statement braces.

When you code a case label or a default label, you must be sure to code a colon after it. Then, if the label contains one or more statements, you must code a *break statement* to exit the switch statement. Later in this chapter, you'll see that you can also use break statements to exit loops.

A break statement is required for each label within a switch statement because C# doesn't allow execution to *fall through* to the next label. This is known as the *no fall through rule*. The only exception to this rule is a case label that doesn't contain any statements. In that case, the statements within the following label are executed.

The first example in this figure shows how to code a switch statement that sets the discount percent based on the values in a string variable named customerType. If the customer type is R, the discount percent is sent to .1. If the customer type is C, the discount percent is set to .2. Otherwise, the discount percent is set to the default value of 0.

Please note in this example that even though the default label is the last label, it still ends with a break statement. You should also realize that you can code the case and default labels in any sequence. However, it's a common practice to code the default label last.

The second example is similar but it doesn't include a default label. Because of that, no code will be executed if none of the values in the case labels match the match expression. That means that the discountPercent variable must be initialized before the switch statement is executed. Otherwise, a compiler error will occur.

The syntax of the switch statement

```
switch (matchExpression)
{
    case constantExpression:
        statements
        break;
    [case constantExpression:
        statements
        break;] ...
    [default:
        statements
        break;]
}
```

A switch statement with a default label

```
switch (customerType)
{
    case "R":
        discountPercent = .1m;
        break;
    case "C":
        discountPercent = .2m;
        break;
    default:
        discountPercent = .0m;
        break;
}
```

A switch statement that falls through the first case label

```
switch (customerType)
{
    case "R":
    case "C":
        discountPercent = .2m;
        break;
    case "T":
        discountPercent = .4m;
        break;
}
```

Description

- A *switch statement* begins by evaluating its *match expression*. This expression must evaluate to a string, char, bool, enum, or any integer type.

- After evaluating the match expression, the switch statement transfers control to the appropriate *case label*. If control isn't transferred to one of the case labels, the optional *default label* is executed.

- The *break statement* exits the switch statement. If a label contains one or more statements, the label must end with a break statement.

- If a label doesn't contain any statements, code execution will *fall through* to the next label. That means that the statements contained by the next label will be executed.

Figure 5-4   How to code switch statements

The other difference is that the first case label doesn't include any statements. Because of that, if the customer type is R, execution falls through to the next case label. That means that the discount percent will be set to .2 if the customer type is either R or C.

When you use a switch statement, you can code if statements within the cases of the statement. You can also code switch statements within the cases of another switch statement. That can make switch statements more useful.

How to code switch expressions

With C# 8.0 and later, you can use *switch expressions* in addition to switch statements. Switch expressions work like switch statements, but their syntax is more concise. Figure 5-5 shows how to code switch expressions.

The syntax at the top of this figure shows that, unlike a switch statement, you code the match expression before the switch keyword for a switch expression. This was done intentionally to make it easy to distinguish between switch statements and switch expressions.

Within the braces that follow the switch keyword, you code one or more constant expressions that represent the possible values of the match expression. Although you don't code these expressions on case labels, they are still often referred to as cases since a switch expression provides another way of implementing the case structure. After each constant expression, you code a *lambda operator* (=>, read as "goes to"), followed by the expression to be returned. This is different from a switch statement, where each case label can contain multiple executable statements.

A switch expression can also include a default expression that's returned if none of the constant expressions match the match expression. To identify this expression, you use a *discard* (_). This is equivalent to the default label that you can use with switch statements. Unlike switch statements, however, switch expressions must handle all possible values of the match expression. Because of that, switch expressions frequently include a discard for one of the constant expressions.

Notice that the cases within a switch expression are separated by commas. In addition, a switch expression must end with a semicolon (;). That's because a switch expression is treated as a single statement.

The first example in this figure illustrates how a simple switch expression works. Here, the switch expression is used to assign a value to the discountPercent variable based on the value of the customerType variable. If the customer type is R, for example, the discount percent is set to .1. If the customer type is C, the discount percent is set to .2. And if the customer type is something other than R or C, the discount percent is set to 0. This accomplishes the same thing as the first switch statement in figure 5-4. If you compare this switch expression and switch statement, though, you'll see that the switch expression requires less code.

The second example is similar to the first, except it returns the same value for customer types R and C. To do that, it repeats the value for each type. That's because the cases of a switch expression can't fall through to the next case like

The syntax of the switch expression

```
matchExpression switch
{
    constantExpression => expression
    [, constantExpression => expression]...
    [, _ => expression]
};
```

A switch expression that uses a discard

```
discountPercent = customerType switch
{
    "R" => .1m,
    "C" => .2m,
    _   => .0m
};
```

A switch expression with two cases that return the same result

```
discountPercent = customerType switch
{
    "R" => .2m,
    "C" => .2m,
    "T" => .4m,
    _   => .0m
};
```

A switch expression with expressions that perform a calculation

```
discountAmount = customerType switch
{
    "R" => subtotal * .2m,
    "C" => subtotal * .2m,
    "T" => subtotal * .4m,
    _   => .0m
};
```

Description

- A *switch expression* begins by evaluating its match expression.

- After evaluating the match expression, the switch expression evaluates the expression that's associated with the matching constant expression. Here, a *lambda operator* (=>) is used to identify the expression for each constant.

- You can use a *discard* (_) for one of the constant expressions. Then, if the match expression doesn't match any of the constant expressions, the expression for the discard is evaluated.

- Switch expressions must handle all possible values of the match expression. Because of that, they frequently include a discard.

- Switch expressions became available with C# 8.0, and discards became available with C# 7.0.

Figure 5-5   How to code switch expressions

they can in a switch statement. Another way to do this is to use the logical or operator, as you'll see in the next figure.

The third example shows that the expression for each case can be more than just a constant value. Here, the switch expression returns the discount amount for each customer type. To do that, the first three expressions multiply the subtotal by a discount percent. This should help you begin to see the types of expressions that you can code for the cases of a switch expression.

Now that you've seen how switch expressions work, you may be wondering when you would use them. In most cases, you'll use them when you simply need to assign a value to a variable as shown in these examples.

How to use pattern matching

In the last two figures, you saw examples of switch statements and switch expressions that check a match expression against a constant value. Although you may not be aware of it, these examples use a feature of C# called *pattern matching*. Specifically, these examples use a *constant pattern* to test if an expression is equal to a constant value. Some of these examples also use a *discard pattern* that identifies the statements that are executed if none of the specified constants match the expression. Figure 5-6 shows how to use other types of patterns.

The first example in this figure shows how to use *relational patterns*. Relational patterns can use any of the relational operators you learned about in figure 5-1. In this example, the less than and less than or equal operators are used to calculate the discount amount based on the value of the subtotal variable.

The second example is similar, but it uses *logical patterns* along with the relational patterns to calculate the discount amount. A logical pattern can use the and, or, and not keywords to combine two relational operations. For instance, the first case in this example checks if the subtotal is greater than or equal to 100 *and* the subtotal is less than or equal to 200.

You can also use pattern matching within an *is expression* in the Boolean expression of an if statement. The third example, for instance, uses a constant pattern within an is expression to compare the value of the nullable message variable to null. It also uses the not keyword to create a logical pattern. The result is that the Boolean expression returns a true value if the message variable is not null.

The last example shows how to use a *declaration pattern* in the is expression of an if statement. Here, a string literal is assigned to a variable named message of the Object type. Then, the if statement tests if the message variable is a string type. If so, the variable is assigned to a string variable named stringMessage, and that variable can be used within the if block. If you don't need to use the string within the if block, though, you don't need to include a new variable name in the is expression. In that case, since the is expression simply checks the type of the variable, it uses a *type pattern* rather than a declaration pattern.

A switch expression with relational patterns

```
discountAmount = subtotal switch
{
    < 100 => 0m,
    <= 200.0m => subtotal * .2m,
    <= 500.0m => subtotal * .3m,
    _ => subtotal * .4m
};
```

A switch expression with logical patterns

```
discountAmount = subtotal switch
{
    >= 100.0m and <= 200.0m => subtotal * .2m,
    > 200.0m and <= 500.0m => subtotal * .3m,
    > 500.0m => subtotal * .4m,
    _ => .0m
};
```

An if statement with constant and logical patterns

```
string? message = null;
if (message is not null) {
    // code that uses the message variable
}
```

An if statement with a declaration pattern

```
Object message = "This is a string literal.";
if (message is string stringMessage) {
    // code that uses the stringMessage variable
}
```

Description

- C# 7.0 introduced *pattern matching*, which lets you test the match expression of a switch statement or switch expression for various characteristics. You can also use an *is expression* with an if statement to test the type of an expression or to check for a null value.

- A *constant pattern* lets you test if an expression is equal to a constant value.

- A *discard pattern* matches any expression that isn't matched by a previous case.

- A *relational pattern* lets you compare a match expression with a constant value using the relational operators.

- A *logical pattern* lets you combine two or more relational patterns using the and, or, and not keywords.

- You can use a *declaration pattern* within an is expression of an if statement to check the type of a variable and to assign the variable to a new variable of that type. If you don't need to assign the variable to a new variable, you can use a *type pattern* instead, which simply checks the type of the variable.

- C# 7.0 and later support constant, discard, and declaration patterns. C# 9.0 and later support relational, logical, and type patterns.

Figure 5-6   How to use pattern matching

How to use the conditional operator

So far in this book, you've seen unary operators that take a single operand and binary operators that take two operands. Now, figure 5-7 shows how to use the *conditional operator*. This operator is known as a *ternary operator* because it takes three operands. The first operand is a Boolean expression, the second operand is an expression that's evaluated and returned if the Boolean expression is true, and the third operand is an expression that's evaluated and returned if the Boolean expression is false.

The conditional operator requires two symbols to separate its three operands. This is illustrated by the syntax for a *conditional expression*, which is an expression that uses the conditional operator. As you can see, the question mark (?) is used to separate the Boolean expression and the true expression, and the colon (:) is used to separate the true and the false expressions.

The first example shows a conditional expression. Here the Boolean expression checks if the variable named subtotal is greater than or equal to 100. If it is, it returns .1. Otherwise, it returns .05.

The second example shows how you would use a conditional expression in an assignment statement. Here, the statement begins by declaring a decimal variable named discountPercent. Then, it assigns the result of the conditional expression in the first example to that variable. As a result, if the subtotal is greater than or equal to 100, the discountPercent variable is .1. Otherwise, it's .05.

The third example works the same as the second example. However, it uses parentheses to clearly identify the Boolean expression. These parentheses are optional, but some programmers prefer using them because they make it easier to read the statement.

The fourth example shows the third example after it has been rewritten to use an if statement instead of the conditional operator. This shows that a statement that uses the conditional operator can always be rewritten to use an if statement. Some programmers prefer this approach, since they consider if statements easier to read. Other programmers like to use the conditional operator because it takes fewer lines of code. As a result, even if you don't use the conditional operator in your code, you still need to understand how it works so you can understand code that has been written by other programmers.

The syntax for a conditional expression

```
booleanExpression ? trueExpression : falseExpression
```

A conditional expression

```
subtotal >= 100 ? .1m : .05m      // returns .1 or .05 depending on subtotal
```

How to use a conditional operator to set the value of a variable

```
decimal discountPercent = subtotal >= 100 ? .1m : .05m;
```

A statement that uses parentheses to identify the Boolean expression

```
decimal discountPercent = (subtotal >= 100) ? .1m : .05m;
```

An if statement that performs the same task

```
decimal discountPercent;
if (subtotal >= 100)
    discountPercent = .1m;
else
    discountPercent = .05m;
```

Description

- The *conditional operator* consists of three expressions that are separated by the question mark (?) and colon (:) symbols. The first expression is a Boolean expression, the second expression is evaluated and returned if the Boolean expression is true, and the third expression is evaluated and returned if the Boolean expression is false.

- The conditional operator provides a way to code simple if-else statements on a single line.

- An operator that works on three operands is known as a *ternary operator*. The conditional operator is an example of a ternary operator.

- With C# 7.2 and later, a conditional expression can return a reference to the result of the true or false expression. For more information, see the ?: operator in the C# Reference manual.

Figure 5-7   How to use the conditional operator

An enhanced version
of the Invoice Total app

To give you a better idea of how if-else statements can be used, figure 5-8 presents an enhanced version of the Invoice Total app that was presented in chapter 3. This time, the form for the app provides for two user entries: customer type and subtotal.

If you look at the event handler in this figure, you can see that the discount percent is determined by nested if statements. If, for example, the customer type is R and the subtotal is greater than or equal to 250, the discount percent is .25. Or, if the customer type is C and the subtotal is less than 250, the discount percent is .2.

When you code if statements like this, it's a good practice to code the conditions in a logical order. For instance, the expressions in the nested if statement for customer type R range from a subtotal that's less than 100, to a subtotal that's greater than or equal to 100 and less than 250, to a subtotal that's greater than or equal to 250. That covers all the possible subtotals from the smallest to the largest. Although you could code these conditions in other sequences, that would make it harder to tell whether all possibilities have been covered.

For efficiency, it's also good to code the conditions from the one that occurs the most to the one that occurs the least. If, for example, most customers are type R, that condition should be treated first so it will be processed first. In some cases, though, the most efficient sequence isn't logical so you have to decide whether it's worth sacrificing the readability of the code for efficiency. Typically, the performance gain isn't significant, so you may as well code the statements in the most logical sequence.

If you prefer, you can use a switch statement that contains if statements to get the same result as the nested if statements in this figure. Or, you can use a switch statement that contains other switch statements. That might make the code even easier to read. On the other hand, if you use indentation properly, an extensive series of nested if statements should be easy to read and understand.

When you enter if and switch statements into the Code Editor, remember that you can use code snippets to enter the basic if, else, and switch structures that you need, including the braces for the coding blocks. To refresh your memory about how to use code snippets, you can refer back to figure 3-11.

The enhanced Invoice Total form

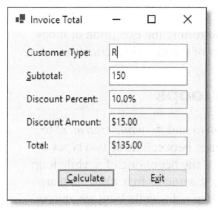

The event handler for the Click event of the Calculate button

```
private void btnCalculate_Click(object sender, EventArgs e)
{
    string customerType = txtCustomerType.Text;
    decimal subtotal = Convert.ToDecimal(txtSubtotal.Text);
    decimal discountPct = .0m;

    if (customerType == "R")
    {
        if (subtotal < 100)
            discountPct = .0m;
        else if (subtotal >= 100 && subtotal < 250)
            discountPct = .1m;
        else if (subtotal >= 250)
            discountPct =.25m;
    }
    else if (customerType == "C")
    {
        if (subtotal < 250)
            discountPct = .2m;
        else
            discountPct = .3m;
    }
    else
    {
        discountPct = .4m;
    }

    decimal discountAmt = subtotal * discountPct;
    decimal invoiceTotal = subtotal - discountAmt;

    txtDiscountPct.Text = discountPct.ToString("p1");
    txtDiscountAmt.Text = discountAmt.ToString("c");
    txtTotal.Text = invoiceTotal.ToString("c");

    txtCustomerType.Focus();
}
```

Figure 5-8   An enhanced version of the Invoice Total app

How to code loops

C# provides three different statements for controlling the execution of loops. These statements provide the C# implementations of the *iteration structure*.

How to code while and do-while loops

Figure 5-9 shows how to use the *while statement* and *do-while statement* to code *while loops* and *do-while loops*. The difference between these two types of loops is that the Boolean expression is evaluated at the beginning of a while loop and at the end of a do-while loop. As a result, the statements in a while loop are executed zero or more times, while the statements in a do-while loop are always executed at least once.

When coding while loops, it's common to use a counter variable to execute the statements in a loop a certain number of times. This is illustrated in the first example in this figure. Here, the counter variable is an int type named i, and this counter is initialized to 1. Notice that the last statement in the loop increments the counter with each iteration of the loop. As a result, the first statement in this loop will be executed as long as the counter variable is less than 5. Incidentally, it is a common coding practice to name counter variables with single letters like *i, j*, and *k*.

Most of the time, you can use either of these two types of loops to accomplish the same task. For instance, the second example in this figure uses a while loop to calculate the future value of a series of monthly payments at a specified interest rate, and the third example uses a do-while loop to perform the same calculation.

When you code loops, it's important to remember that any variables that you declare within the loop have block scope, so they can't be used outside of the loop. That's why all the variables used in the loops shown here have been declared outside of the loops. That way, you can use these variables after the loops have finished executing.

When you code loops, it's possible to code an *infinite loop*, which is a loop that never ends. That can happen, for example, if you forget to code a statement that increments the counter variable so the condition in the while or do-while loop never becomes false. Then, you can switch to Visual Studio and click the Break All button in the Debug toolbar to enter break mode and debug the program as shown later in this chapter. Or, you can click the Stop Debugging button to end the app.

The syntax of the while statement

```
while (booleanExpression)
{
    statements
}
```

A while loop that adds the numbers 1 through 4

```
int i = 1, sum = 0;
while (i < 5)
{
    sum += i;
    i++;
}
```

A while loop that calculates a future value

```
int i = 1;
while (i <= months)
{
    futureValue = (futureValue + monthlyPayment) *
        (1 + monthlyInterestRate);
    i++;
}
```

The syntax of the do-while statement

```
do
{
    statements
}
while (booleanExpression);
```

A do-while loop that calculates a future value

```
int i = 1;
do
{
    futureValue = (futureValue + monthlyPayment) *
        (1 + monthlyInterestRate);
    i++;
}
while (i <= months);
```

Description

- When you use a *while statement*, the condition is tested before the *while loop* is executed. When you use a *do-while statement*, the condition is tested after the *do-while loop* is executed.

- A while or do-while loop executes the block of statements within its braces as long as its Boolean expression is true.

- If a loop requires more than one statement, you must enclose the statements in braces. Then, any variables or constants that are declared in the block have block scope. If a loop requires just one statement, you don't have to enclose the statement in braces.

- If the conditional expression never becomes false, the loop never ends. Then, the program goes into an *infinite loop* that you can cancel by using the Break All or Stop Debugging commands from the Debug toolbar.

Figure 5-9   How to code while and do-while loops

How to code for loops

Figure 5-10 shows how to use a *for statement* to code a *for loop*. This type of loop is useful when you need to increment or decrement a counter variable that determines how many times the loop is going to be executed.

To code a for loop, you start by coding the *for* keyword followed by three expressions enclosed in parentheses and separated by semicolons. The first expression is an initialization expression that typically declares a counter variable and assigns a starting value to it. The second expression is a Boolean expression that specifies the condition under which the loop executes. And the third expression is an increment expression that determines how the counter variable is incremented or decremented each time the loop is executed.

The first example in this figure illustrates how to use these expressions. Here, the initialization expression declares a counter variable named i with the int type and assigns an initial value of 0 to it. Next, the Boolean expression specifies that the loop will be repeated as long as the counter is less than 5. Then, the increment expression adds 1 to the counter at the end of each repetition of the loop. When this loop is executed, the numbers 0 through 4 will be stored as a string variable like this:

```
0 1 2 3 4
```

This figure shows how to code this loop using a single statement or a block of statements. If you code more than one statement within the loop, you must enclose the statements in braces. But if you code only a single statement, the braces are optional.

The next example calculates the sum of the numbers 8, 6, 4, and 2. In this example, the sum variable is declared before the loop so it will be available outside the block of statements that are executed by the loop. Then, the initialization expression initializes the counter variable to 8, the Boolean expression specifies that the loop will execute as long as the counter is greater than zero, and the increment expression uses an assignment operator to subtract 2 from the counter variable with each repetition of the loop. Within the loop, the value of the counter variable is added to the value that's already stored in the sum variable. As a result, the final value for the sum variable is 20.

The last example shows how to code a for loop that calculates the future value of a series of monthly payments. Here, the loop executes one time for each month. If you compare this example with the last example in figure 5-9, you can see how a for loop improves upon a while loop when a counter variable is required.

Although it isn't shown in this figure, it's possible to declare a counter variable before the for loop. Then, this variable can be accessed outside the loop. However, if you need to access a counter variable outside of a loop, it's usually easier to use a while or do-while loop as described in figure 5-9.

You can also declare a counter variable within a for loop without specifying a type. To do that, you code the var keyword in place of the type. Then, the type is inferred from the value that's assigned to the variable. In most cases, though, you'll specify a type instead of using the var keyword.

The syntax of the for statement

```
for (initializationExpression; booleanExpression; incrementExpression)
{
    statements
}
```

A for loop that stores the numbers 0 through 4 in a string

With a single statement

```
string numbers = "";
for (int i = 0; i < 5; i++)
    numbers += i + " ";
```

With a block of statements

```
string numbers = "";
for (int i = 0; i < 5; i++)
{
    numbers += i;
    numbers += " ";
}
```

A for loop that adds the numbers 8, 6, 4, and 2

```
int sum = 0;
for (int j = 8; j > 0; j-=2)
{
    sum += j;
}
```

A for loop that calculates a future value

```
for (int i = 1; i <= months; i++)
{
    futureValue = (futureValue + monthlyPayment) *
        (1 + monthlyInterestRate);
}
```

Description

- The *for statement* is useful when you need to increment or decrement a counter that determines how many times the *for loop* is executed.

- Within the parentheses of a for loop, you code an initialization expression that declares a counter variable and assigns a starting value to it, a Boolean expression that specifies the condition under which the loop executes, and an increment expression that indicates how the counter variable should be incremented or decremented each time the loop is executed.

Figure 5-10   How to code for loops

Loops that use break and continue statements

In most cases, the statements within a loop are executed in the order that they're coded, and the loop ends when the Boolean expression for the loop evaluates to false. However, for some loops, you may need to use *jump statements* to control the order in which the statements are executed. Figure 5-11 presents two of those statements. You use the *break statement* to jump to the end of a loop, and you use the *continue statement* to jump to the start of a loop.

The first example in this figure shows how the break statement works. Here, a while loop calculates a future value as described in figure 5-9. If the future value becomes greater than 100,000, however, this loop assigns a string literal to the message variable, and it executes a break statement to end the loop.

The second example shows how to use the continue statement to jump to the beginning of a loop. When control is transferred to the beginning of the loop, the expressions that control the loop's operation are executed again. As a result, this will cause the counter variable to be incremented, and it will cause the Boolean expression to be evaluated.

In addition to the break and continue statements, C# provides other jump statements you can code within loops. You'll learn about most of these statements as you progress through this book. One statement you won't learn about, however, is the *goto statement*. That's because goto statements often result in code that's difficult to read and maintain. As a result, it's generally considered a good coding practice to avoid using them.

A loop with a break statement

```
string message = "";
int i = 1;
while (i <= months)
{
    futureValue = (futureValue + monthlyPayment) *
        (1 + monthlyInterestRate);
    if (futureValue > 100000)
    {
        message = "Future value is too large.";
        break;
    }
    i++;
}
```

A loop with a continue statement

```
string numbers = "";
for (int i = 1; i < 6; i++)
{
    numbers += i;
    numbers += "\n";
    if (i < 4)
        continue;
    numbers += "Big\n";
}
```

The result of the previous loop

```
1
2
3
4
Big
5
Big
```

Description

- You use a *break statement* to jump out of a loop.
- You use a *continue statement* to jump to the start of a loop.

Figure 5-11   Loops that use break and continue statements

Debugging techniques for programs with loops

When you code programs that use loops, debugging often becomes more difficult because it's sometimes hard to tell how the loop is operating. As a result, you may want to use the debugging techniques that are summarized in figure 5-12. These techniques let you stop the execution of a program and enter break mode when a loop starts. Then, you can observe the operation of the loop one statement at a time.

To stop the execution of a program and enter break mode, you set a *breakpoint*. To do that, you can click in the *margin indicator bar* at the left side of the Code Editor window. The breakpoint is then marked by a red dot. Later, when the app is run, execution will stop just prior to the statement at the breakpoint.

Once in break mode, a yellow arrow marks the next statement that will be executed, which is called the *execution point*. At this point, you can use the debugging windows to display the current values of the variables used by the loop and to watch how these variables change each time through the loop. For example, you can use the Locals window to display the current values of the variables within the scope of the current method.

While in break mode, you can also *step through* the statements in the loop one statement at a time. To do that, you repeatedly press the F11 key or click the Step Into button on the Debug toolbar. This lets you observe exactly how and when the variable values change as the loop executes. Once you understand how the loop works, you can remove the breakpoint and press the F5 key to continue normal execution.

Of course, these techniques are also useful for debugging problems that don't involve loops. If, for example, you can't figure out what's wrong with a complex set of nested if statements, you can set a breakpoint at the start of the statement. Then, when the program enters break mode, you can step through the clauses in the statement to see exactly how the expressions are being evaluated.

A for loop with a breakpoint and an execution point

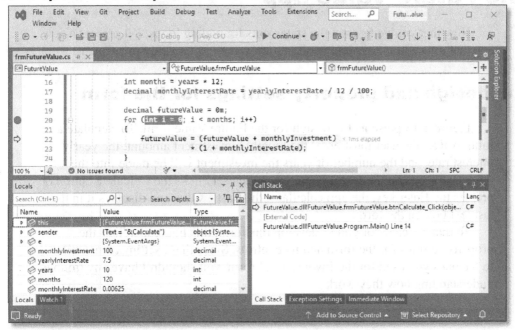

How to set and clear breakpoints

- To set a breakpoint, click in the *margin indicator bar* to the left of a statement. Or, press the F9 key to set a breakpoint at the cursor insertion point. Then, a red dot will mark the breakpoint.

- To remove a breakpoint, use any of the techniques for setting a breakpoint. To remove all breakpoints at once, use the Delete All Breakpoints command in the Debug menu.

How to work in break mode

- In break mode, a yellow arrow marks the current *execution point*, which points to the next statement that will be executed.

- To *step through* your code one statement at a time, press the F11 key or click the Step Into button on the Debug toolbar.

- To continue normal processing until the next breakpoint is reached, press the F5 key.

Description

- When you set a *breakpoint* at a specific statement, the program stops before executing that statement and enters break mode. Then, you can step through the execution of the program one statement at a time.

- In break mode, the Locals window displays the current values of the variables in the scope of the current method. If this window isn't displayed, you can display it by selecting the Locals item from the Windows submenu of the Debug menu.

Figure 5-12   Debugging techniques for programs with loops

The Future Value app

Now that you've learned the statements for coding loops, I'll present a new app that uses a loop to calculate the future value of a monthly investment.

The design and property settings for the form

Figure 5-13 presents the design for the Future Value form. To calculate a future value, the user must enter the monthly investment amount, the yearly interest rate, and the number of years the investment will be made into the three text boxes on the form. Then, when the user clicks the Calculate button or presses the Enter key, the app calculates the future value and displays it in the last text box on the form.

To make it easy for you to develop this form, this figure also lists the property settings for the form and its controls. Since these settings are similar to the ones you used for the Invoice Total form, you shouldn't have any trouble understanding how they work.

The Future Value form

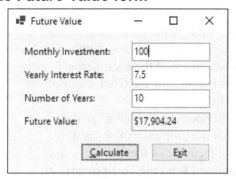

The property settings for the form

Default name	Property	Setting
Form1	Text	Future Value
	AcceptButton	btnCalculate
	CancelButton	btnExit
	StartPosition	CenterScreen

The property settings for the controls

Default name	Property	Setting
label1	Text	Monthly Investment:
label2	Text	Yearly Interest Rate:
label3	Text	Number of Years:
label4	Text	Future Value:
textBox1	Name	txtMonthlyInvestment
textBox2	Name	txtInterestRate
textBox3	Name	txtYears
textBox4	Name	txtFutureValue
	ReadOnly	True
	TabStop	False
button1	Name	btnCalculate
	Text	&Calculate
button2	Name	btnExit
	Text	E&xit

Additional property settings

- The TextAlign property of each of the labels is set to MiddleLeft.
- The TabIndex properties of the controls are set so the focus moves from top to bottom and left to right.

Figure 5-13   The form design and property settings for the Future Value app

The code for the form

Figure 5-14 presents the code for the Future Value form. Like the code for the Invoice Total form, this code consists of two event handlers: one for the Click event of the Calculate button and one for the Click event of the Exit button. Here, most of the processing occurs in the event handler for the Click event of the Calculate button.

The first three statements in this event handler declare and initialize the variables that will be used to store the values that the user enters into the three text boxes. Here, the ToDecimal() and ToInt32() methods of the Convert class are used to convert the string values that are returned from the Text property of the text boxes to the appropriate numeric data types.

The next two statements perform calculations that convert the yearly values entered by the user to monthly values. That way, all the variables used in the future value calculation will be in terms of months. The first statement converts the number of years to months by multiplying the years by 12. The second statement divides the yearly interest rate by 12 to get a monthly interest rate, and then divides that result by 100 to convert the number to a percentage.

The next group of statements uses a for loop to calculate a new future value for each month of the investment. Here, the variable that stores the future value is declared before the loop so it can be used after the loop finishes its processing. Then, within the loop, the single assignment statement that calculates the future value is executed once for each month. Since this loop contains a single statement, it doesn't require braces. However, to clearly identify the start and end of the loop, these braces are included anyway.

Within the loop, the arithmetic expression adds the monthly investment amount to the future value, which has an initial value of zero. Then, the expression multiplies that sum by 1 plus the monthly interest rate. If, for example, the monthly investment amount is $100 and the monthly interest rate is 1% (or .01), the future value is $101 after the expression is executed the first time through the loop:

```
(0 + 100) * (1 +.01) = 100 * 1.01 = 101
```

And the future value is $203.01 after the expression is executed the second time:

```
(101 + 100) * (1 + .01) = 201 * 1.01 = 203.01
```

Continue this process for as many months as the user indicates, and the future value will contain the correct result for a series of equal monthly investments.

After the loop ends, the next statement formats the future value and displays it on the form. To do that, the ToString() method converts a decimal value to a string that uses the currency format. Then, this string value is assigned to the Text property of the Future Value text box. Finally, the last statement moves the focus to the Monthly Investment text box to prepare for the next calculation.

To keep this program simple, it doesn't validate the data that's entered by the user. As a result, an exception will occur if the user enters nonnumeric data in one of the text boxes. In chapter 7, you'll learn how to add data validation to this program to prevent exceptions like this.

The code for the event handlers in the Future Value app

```
private void btnCalculate_Click(object sender, EventArgs e)
{
    decimal monthlyInvestment =
        Convert.ToDecimal(txtMonthlyInvestment.Text);
    decimal yearlyInterestRate = Convert.ToDecimal(txtInterestRate.Text);
    int years = Convert.ToInt32(txtYears.Text);

    int months = years * 12;
    decimal monthlyInterestRate = yearlyInterestRate / 12 / 100;

    decimal futureValue = 0m;
    for (int i = 0; i < months; i++)
    {
        futureValue = (futureValue + monthlyInvestment)
                    * (1 + monthlyInterestRate);
    }

    txtFutureValue.Text = futureValue.ToString("c");
    txtMonthlyInvestment.Focus();
}

private void btnExit_Click(object sender, EventArgs e)
{
    this.Close();
}
```

Description

- This app uses a for loop to calculate the future value of a monthly investment amount. For this calculation to work correctly, all of the variables that it uses must be converted to the same time period. In this case, that time period is months.

- Each time through the for loop, the assignment statement adds the monthly investment amount to the future value, which starts at zero. Then, this sum is multiplied by 1 plus the monthly interest rate. The result is stored in the futureValue variable so it can be used the next time through the loop.

- Since this app doesn't provide data validation, the user will be able to enter invalid data, which will cause an exception to occur.

Figure 5-14   The code for the Future Value app

Perspective

Now that you've finished this chapter, you should know how to code if statements, switch statements, switch expressions, conditional expressions, while statements, do-while statements, and for statements. These are the C# statements and expressions that implement the selection, case, and iteration structures, and they provide the logic of an app. Once you master them, you'll be able to develop significant C# apps.

Terms

Boolean expression	discard pattern
relational operator	relational pattern
logical operator	logical pattern
short-circuit operator	declaration pattern
if-else statement	type pattern
if statement	conditional operator
selection structure	ternary operator
block scope	conditional expression
nested if statement	iteration structure
switch statement	while statement
case structure	while loop
match expression	do-while statement
case label	do-while loop
default label	infinite loop
break statement	for statement
fall through	for loop
no fall through rule	jump statement
switch expression	continue statement
lambda operator	breakpoint
discard	margin indicator bar
pattern matching	execution point
is expression	step through code
constant pattern	

Exercise 5-1   Enhance the Invoice Total app

In this exercise, you'll use if-else and switch statements to determine the discount percent for the Invoice Total app that's in figure 5-8.

Open the app and change the if-else statement

1. Open the app that's in the C:\C#\Ch05\InvoiceTotal directory.

2. Change the if-else statement so customers of type R with a subtotal that is greater than or equal to $250 but less than $500 get a 25% discount and those with a subtotal of $500 or more get a 30% discount. Next, change the if-else

statement so customers of type C always get a 20% discount. Then, test the app to make sure this works.

3. Add another customer type to the if-else statement so customers of type T get a 40% discount for subtotals of less than $500, and a 50% discount for subtotals of $500 or more. Also, make sure that customer types that aren't R, C, or T get a 10% discount. Then, test the app.

4. Test the app again, but use lowercase letters for the customer types. Note that these letters aren't evaluated as capital letters. Now, close the app and modify the code so the users can enter either capital or lowercase letters for the customer types. Then, test the app to make sure it works correctly.

Use a switch statement with if-else statements to get the same results

5. Enter the start of a switch statement right after the if-else statement. Next, enhance this code so the switch statement provides the structure for handling the three cases for customer types: R, C, and T (but not r, c, and t). Then, within each of these cases, you can copy the related code from the if-else statement above to provide for the discounts that are based on subtotal variations. In other words, the if-else statements will be nested within the switch cases.

6. Comment out the entire if-else statement above the switch statement. Then, test to make sure the switch statement works correctly. Is this code easier to read and understand?

Use a switch expression

7. Comment out the entire switch statement. Then, enter a switch expression that sets the discount percent to 30% for the R customer type, 20% for C, and 50% for T with a default discount percent of 10%.

8. Test to make sure the switch expression works correctly. Is this code shorter and easier to read than a comparable switch statement?

9. Close the project.

Exercise 5-2   Develop the Future Value app

In this exercise, you'll develop and test the Future Value app that was presented in this chapter. You'll also step through its loop.

Develop the form, write the code, and test the app

1. Select the File→New→Project command to display the Create a New Project dialog. Then, select the Windows Forms App template, and click the Next button. In the Configure Your New Project dialog, enter "FutureValue" for the name of the project, enter "C:\C#\Ch05" for the location, and click the Next button. Be sure that .NET 7.0 is selected in the Additional Information dialog, and then click the Create button.

2. Add the controls to the form and set the properties of the form and its controls as shown in figure 5-13. Then, generate the event handlers for the Click event of the two buttons, and add the code for these handlers. If necessary, you can refer to the code in figure 5-14, but try to write the code without doing that.

3. Test the app by entering valid data in each of the three text boxes. To start, enter simple values like 100 for the monthly investment, 12 for the yearly interest rate (which is 1% per month), and 1 for the number of years. (The result should be $1,280.93).

4. After you're sure that the app works for valid data, test it with nonnumeric entries and with large values like 100 for the interest rate and 1000 for the number of years. In either case, the app will end with a runtime error, which you'll learn how to prevent in chapter 7. Then, stop the debugging.

Set breakpoints and step through the loop

5. In the Code Editor, set a breakpoint at the for statement by clicking in the margin indicator bar to the left of the statement as shown in figure 5-12. A red dot will indicate that you have set the breakpoint.

6. Run the app, and enter 100 as the monthly investment, 12 as the yearly interest rate, and 1 as the number of years. Then, click the Calculate button. This will cause the program to enter break mode. If the Locals window isn't displayed, use the Debug menu to display it.

7. Press F11 repeatedly to step through the loop. As you do this, the Locals window will display the values for i, futureValue, monthlyInvestment, and monthlyInterestRate. That way, you'll be able to see exactly how these values change as the loop is executed.

8. Press F11 to continue stepping through the app or press F5 to run the app until another breakpoint is reached.

9. Remove the old breakpoint and set a new breakpoint on the statement within the for loop. Then, run the app and note that the new breakpoint causes the app to enter break mode for each iteration of the loop. As a result, you can press F5 to move from one iteration to the next.

10. When you're through experimenting, remove the breakpoint and close the project.

6

How to code methods and event handlers

So far, you've been writing methods called event handlers for the Click events of button controls. Now, in this chapter, you'll learn how to code methods that can be called from other methods. That will help you logically divide the code for an app into manageable parts. You'll also learn how to code event handlers for events other than the Click event.

How to code and call methods

In chapter 3, you learned how to code methods that are executed automatically when a Click event occurs. Now, you'll learn how to code methods that you call explicitly from other methods in the app. That can lead to code that's easier to read and maintain.

How to code methods

Figure 6-1 shows how to code a *method*. To start, you code an *access modifier* that indicates whether the method can be called from other classes. If the method only needs to be accessed from within the class where it's coded, you can use the *private* access modifier. If the method needs to be called from another class, you can use the *public* access modifier.

After the access modifier, you code the return type for the method, which identifies the type of data that the method returns. To specify a return type, you can use the keyword for any of the built-in data types. You can also specify the name of any enumeration or the name of any of the types you'll learn about in chapter 12, including a class. Then, within the method, you must code a *return statement* that identifies the value to be returned. This value must correspond to the data type that's specified as the return type.

If the method doesn't return any data, you code the *void* keyword as the return type. Then, you don't code a return statement.

After the return type, you code the name of the method. In most cases, you'll give the method a name that indicates the action it performs. A common coding convention is to start each method name with a verb. This convention is used in the names for the methods in this figure: DisableButtons(), GetDiscountPercent(), and CalculateFutureValue().

After the method name, you code a set of parentheses. Within the parentheses, you declare the *parameters* that are required by the method. This is known as the *parameter list*. Later, when you call the method, you pass arguments that correspond to these parameters. You'll learn more about that in the next figure.

If a method doesn't require any parameters, you code an empty set of parentheses as shown in the first example in this figure. Here, a method named DisableButtons() simply assigns a false value to the Enabled properties of two buttons. However, if a method does require parameters, you code them within the parentheses as shown in the second and third examples. Here, the second method calculates and returns a decimal discount percent based on a subtotal, and the third method calculates and returns a decimal future value based on a monthly investment, a monthly interest rate, and a number of months.

When you code the name and parameter list of a method, you form the *signature* of the method. Later in this book, you'll learn how to code two or more methods with the same name but with different parameters. This is known as *overloading* a method.

Incidentally, Visual Studio doesn't provide an easy way to start the code for a new method. So, you just start the method by typing the code into the class and using the IntelliSense feature whenever it's available.

The basic syntax for coding a method

```
{public|private} returnType MethodName([parameterList])
{
    statements
}
```

A method with no parameters and no return type

```
private void DisableButtons()
{
    btnCalculate.Enabled = false;
    btnExit.Enabled = false;
}
```

A method with one parameter that returns a decimal value

```
private decimal GetDiscountPercent(decimal subtotal)
{
    decimal discountPercent = 0m;
    if (subtotal >= 500)
        discountPercent = .2m;
    else
        discountPercent = .1m;
    return discountPercent;
}
```

A method with three parameters that returns a decimal value

```
private decimal CalculateFutureValue(decimal monthlyInvestment,
    decimal monthlyInterestRate, int months)
{
    decimal futureValue = 0m;
    for (int i = 0; i < months; i++)
    {
        futureValue = (futureValue + monthlyInvestment)
                    * (1 + monthlyInterestRate);
    }
    return futureValue;
}
```

Description

- To allow other classes to access a *method*, use the *public* access modifier. To prevent other classes from accessing a method, use the *private* modifier.

- To code a method that doesn't return data, use the *void* keyword for the return type. To code a method that returns data, code a return type in the method declaration and code a *return statement* in the body of the method. The return statement ends the execution of the current method and returns the specified value to the calling method.

- Within the parentheses of a method, you can code an optional *parameter list* that contains one or more *parameters*, with the parameters separated by commas. When you code a parameter, you must code a data type and you must provide a name for the parameter.

- The name of a method plus its parameter list form the *signature* of the method, which must be unique.

Figure 6-1   How to code methods

How to call methods

Figure 6-2 shows how to *call* a method that's coded within a form class. By now, you should be familiar with the basic syntax for calling a method, so most of this figure should be review. To start, you can type the optional *this* keyword to specify that the method that's being called is in the current class, followed by the dot operator and the method name. Otherwise, you just code the method name and the current class is assumed. Because the this keyword is unnecessary and clutters the code, it isn't used in most of the examples in this book.

If the method requires *arguments*, you code the *argument list* within parentheses right after the method name. Otherwise, you code an empty set of parentheses. Before going on, you should realize that the terms *parameter* and *argument* are often used interchangeably. In this book, however, we'll use the term *parameter* to refer to the variables of a method declaration, and we'll use the term *argument* to refer to the values that are passed to a method.

When you call a method, you typically code the arguments in the same sequence that's used by the parameter list in the method. This is called *passing arguments by position*. You can also pass arguments by name, as you'll see shortly.

When you pass arguments, the data types of those arguments must be compatible with the data types of the corresponding parameters in the method. In fact, it's a good coding practice to pass arguments that have the *same* data types as the parameters in the method. Note, however, that the argument names don't have to be the same as the parameter names. But this is a common practice that makes code easier to read and write.

The three examples in this figure show how you would call the three methods you saw in figure 6-1. The first example calls the DisableButtons() method, which has no parameters. Because of that, the statement call doesn't include any arguments. In addition, the method doesn't return any data, so the statement simply calls the method.

The second example calls the GetDiscountPercent() method. Since this method is defined with one parameter, the statement that calls it passes one argument. In this case, the argument is a variable named subtotal. However, you could also code the argument as a literal value, such as 49.50m. In addition, because this method returns a value, the method call is coded as part of an assignment statement. When this statement is executed, the return value from the method, which is declared with the decimal type, is assigned to the discountPercent variable, which is also declared as a decimal.

The third example shows how to call a method that requires three arguments. In this case, all three arguments have the same data types as the corresponding parameters in the method. In addition, the arguments are listed in the same order as the corresponding parameters.

When you call a method that returns a value, you can assign that value to a variable as shown in the second and third examples in this figure. However, you can also code a method call within an expression. For example, you could use the GetDiscountPercent() method in an expression like this:

```
total = subtotal * (1 - GetDiscountPercent(subtotal));
```

In this case, the decimal value that's returned by the method will be used to perform a calculation.

The syntax for calling a method

```
[this.]MethodName([argumentList])
```

A statement that calls a method that has no parameters

```
this.DisableButtons();
```

A statement that passes one argument

```
decimal discountPercent = this.GetDiscountPercent(subtotal);
```

A statement that passes three arguments

```
decimal futureValue = CalculateFutureValue(
    monthlyInvestment, monthlyInterestRate, months);
```

The IntelliSense feature for calling a method

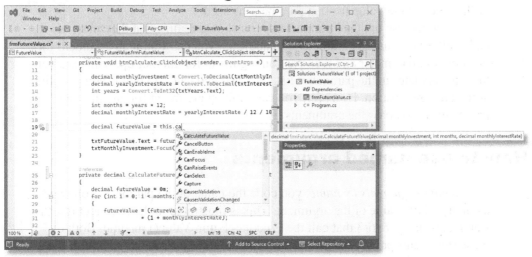

Description

- When you *call* a method, you code an *argument list* with the *arguments* that are passed to the method. You can pass arguments by position or by name. See figure 6-3 for more information on passing arguments by name.

- When you *pass arguments by position*, the arguments must be in the same order as the parameters in the parameter list defined by the method.

- The arguments you pass to a method must have data types that are compatible with their corresponding parameters. However, the names of the arguments don't need to match the names of the parameters.

- When you call a method, Visual Studio's IntelliSense feature helps you enter the name of the method and the arguments of the method.

Figure 6-2   How to call methods

How to use optional parameters

When you code a method, you may occasionally want to provide default values for one or more parameters in case the user doesn't provide values for them. To do that, you can use a feature of C# called *optional parameters*. Figure 6-3 illustrates how optional parameters work.

To declare an optional parameter, you assign a default value to the parameter. Then, if a value isn't passed to this parameter, the default value is used. In the CalculateFutureValue() method in this figure, for example, the monthly investment parameter is required, but the interest rate and months parameters are optional.

The first statement that calls this method passes arguments for all three parameters. This works just like it would if all the parameters were required. The second statement, however, omits the argument for the third parameter. Because of that, the default value for that parameter is used.

When you use optional parameters, you should realize that they must be coded after all required parameters. In addition, you can't omit an argument for one optional parameter and then pass an argument for another optional parameter that appears later in the parameter list. At least, you can't do that if you pass the arguments by position. However, you can omit an argument for any optional parameter if you pass the arguments by name.

How to use named arguments

To *pass arguments by name*, you code the name of the parameter followed by a colon and the name of the argument. This is illustrated in the third and fourth statements in figure 6-3 that call the CalculateFutureValue() method. Both of these statements pass arguments to the first and third parameters, but omit the argument for the second parameter. The only difference between the two is that the arguments are coded in a different sequence. This is another advantage of passing arguments by name.

You can also pass some arguments by position and some by name as illustrated in the last statement. Here, the first argument passes a value to the first parameter by position, and the second argument passes a value to the third parameter by name. Note that with C# 7.1 and earlier, you can't code positional arguments after named arguments. With C# 7.2 and later, though, you can do that as long as the arguments are in the correct position. For example, you can use this statement to call the CalculateFutureValue() method in C# 7.2 but not C# 7.1:

```
decimal futureValue =
    CalculateFutureValue(monthlyInvestment,
                         monthlyInterestRate:monthlyInterestRate,
                         months);
```

The syntax for an optional parameter

```
type parameterName = defaultvalue
```

The CalculateFutureValue() method with two optional parameters

```csharp
private decimal CalculateFutureValue(decimal monthlyInvestment,
        decimal monthlyInterestRate = 0.05m, int months = 12)
{
    decimal futureValue = 0m;
    for (int i = 0; i < months; i++)
    {
        futureValue = (futureValue + monthlyInvestment) *
                        (1 + monthlyInterestRate);
    }
    return futureValue;
}
```

A statement that passes arguments for all three parameters to the function

```csharp
decimal futureValue = CalculateFutureValue(
    monthlyInvestment, monthlyInterestRate, months);
```

A statement that omits the argument for the third parameter

```csharp
decimal futureValue = CalculateFutureValue(
    monthlyInvestment, monthlyInterestRate);
```

Two statements that pass the arguments for two parameters by name

```csharp
decimal futureValue = CalculateFutureValue(
    monthlyInvestment:monthlyInvestment, months:months);
```

```csharp
decimal futureValue = CalculateFutureValue(
    months:months, monthlyInvestment:monthlyInvestment);
```

A statement that passes one argument by position and one by name

```csharp
decimal futureValue = CalculateFutureValue(
    monthlyInvestment, months:months);
```

Description

- The parameter list for a method can include one or more *optional parameters*. Then, you don't have to supply a value for those parameters when you call the method.

- An optional parameter must be assigned a constant value as its default. Then, if a value isn't supplied for that parameter, the default value is used.

- If you define a parameter as optional, every parameter after that parameter in the parameter list must be defined as optional.

- If you pass a value to an optional parameter by position, you must pass a value to every other parameter before that parameter.

- When you use optional parameters, you may also want to *pass arguments by name*. To do that, you code the parameter name followed by a colon followed by the argument name.

- When you pass arguments by name, you can code the arguments in any sequence, and you can omit any of the optional parameters.

- You can also combine the two techniques for passing arguments and pass some by position and others by name.

Figure 6-3   How to use optional parameters and named arguments

How to code expression-bodied methods

In the last chapter, you saw that you can use the lambda operator (=>) to return an expression for the cases in a switch expression. Now, figure 6-4 shows how to use the lambda operator to code *expression-bodied methods*.

An expression-bodied method can return the value of an expression or execute a single statement. For instance, the first example in this figure shows a method named DisplayErrorMessage() that contains a single statement that displays a message box with the message and caption that are passed to it.

The statement that follows shows how to code this method using an expression-bodied method. To do that, you code the method signature just like you do for any other method, followed by the lambda operator and the statement to be executed. This provides a minor simplification by eliminating the need for the braces.

The second example shows a method that returns a discount percent based on the customer type that's passed to it. This method uses a switch expression like the ones you learned about in chapter 5 to get the discount percent. This switch expression is coded on a return statement so the result of the expression is returned to the calling code.

To code this method as an expression-bodied method, you add the lambda operator, omit the braces for the method, and omit the return statement as shown here. Once again, this provides a minor simplification to the code. As you continue with this book, though, you'll see that the lambda operator can be used in a number of different situations. So, it's best to become familiar with it right away by using it whenever that makes sense.

A method that executes a single statement

```
private void DisplayErrorMessage(string message, string caption)
{
    MessageBox.Show(message, caption);
}
```

The same method with an expression body

```
private void DisplayErrorMessage(string message, string caption) =>
    MessageBox.Show(message, caption);
```

A method that returns the value of an expression

```
private decimal GetDiscountPercent(string customerType)
{
    return customerType switch
    {
        "R" => .1m,
        "C" => .2m,
        "T" => .4m,
        _ => .0m
    };
}
```

The same method with an expression body

```
private decimal GetDiscountPercent(string customerType) =>
    customerType switch
    {
        "R" => .1m,
        "C" => .2m,
        "T" => .4m,
        _ => .0m
    };
```

Description

- You can code a method that executes a single statement or returns an expression as an *expression-bodied method*.

- To code an expression-bodied method, you code the method signature, followed by the lambda operator (=>) and an expression or executable statement.

- Although you can code expression-bodied methods within a form class, you're more likely to code them within user-defined classes. You can learn more about that in chapter 12.

Figure 6-4   How to code expression-bodied methods

How to use refactoring to create a new method and its calling statement

In chapter 3, you were introduced to *refactoring*, which refers to the process of revising and restructuring existing code. This can be especially helpful when you want to create a new method from some code that's in an event handler. This process is illustrated in figure 6-5. To refactor the code, you can select the code you want to create a method from, press Ctrl + period (.), and choose Extract Method from the Quick Actions menu that appears below the light bulb in the left margin. You can also display this menu by right-clicking on the selected code and choosing Quick Actions and Refactoring from the shortcut menu that's displayed. Then, you can enter a name for the new method in the Rename dialog that's displayed and press the Enter key.

In this figure, you can see that refactoring creates both a calling statement and a new method named CalculateFutureValue(). The only significant difference between this method and the CalculateFutureValue() method in figure 6-1 is that the refactored method includes the *static* keyword, which means it's a static method. Because of that, the calling statement can't use the this keyword. That's because the this keyword refers to the object that's created from the class for the form, but a static method is a member of the class. For more information about working with static methods, please see chapter 12.

Incidentally, the static keyword isn't necessary for the CalculateFutureValue() method. As a result, if you want, you can delete this keyword from the method. Then, you can use the this keyword to call this method, although that's not necessary. However, all the code that's generated when you use refactoring to create a new method works without any changes, so there's usually no need to edit it.

That's powerful stuff! With just a few mouse clicks and keystrokes, you can extract methods from event handlers. This in turn can make your code more manageable by keeping the event handlers shorter and easier to read.

The btnCalculate_Click() method with selected statements

```
private void btnCalculate_Click(object sender, EventArgs e)
{
    decimal monthlyInvestment =
        Convert.ToDecimal(txtMonthlyInvestment.Text);
    decimal yearlyInterestRate = Convert.ToDecimal(txtInterestRate.Text);
    int years = Convert.ToInt32(txtYears.Text);

    int months = years * 12;
    decimal monthlyInterestRate = yearlyInterestRate / 12 / 100;

    decimal futureValue = 0m;
    for (int i = 0; i < months; i++)
    {
        futureValue = (futureValue + monthlyInvestment)
                    * (1 + monthlyInterestRate);
    }

    txtFutureValue.Text = futureValue.ToString("c");
    txtMonthlyInvestment.Focus();
}
```

The method call that replaces the selected code

```
decimal futureValue = CalculateFutureValue(monthlyInvestment, months,
    monthlyInterestRate);
```

The method that's added to the class

```
private static decimal CalculateFutureValue(decimal monthlyInvestment,
    int months, decimal monthlyInterestRate)
{
    decimal futureValue = 0m;
    for (int i = 0; i < months; i++)
    {
        futureValue = (futureValue + monthlyInvestment)
                    * (1 + monthlyInterestRate);
    }
    return futureValue;
}
```

How to use refactoring to create a new method from existing code

1. Select the code you want to create a new method from, press Ctrl + period (.), and select Extract Method from the Quick Actions menu that's displayed. This adds a method named NewMethod() to the class, replaces the selected code with a statement that calls the method, and displays the Rename dialog for the method name.

2. Enter the name that you want to use for the new method and press the Enter key.

Description

- If you want to extract a method from existing code, refactoring makes that easy.
- Note in the code above that the refactored code doesn't use the this keyword in the method call and does include the static keyword in the method declaration. You'll learn more about the static keyword in chapter 12.

Figure 6-5   How to use refactoring to create a new method and its method call

When and how to pass arguments by reference and by value

By default, the arguments that are passed to a method are passed *by value*. That means that the value of each passed variable is assigned to the corresponding parameter in the method. Because of that, the method can change the value of the parameter without affecting the value of the variable in the calling method.

In some cases, though, you'll want to be able to change the value of the variable in the calling method from the called method. To do that, you can pass the argument *by reference* using the *ref* keyword as shown in part 1 of figure 6-6. In the example in this figure, the ref keyword is coded before the argument and before the parameter declaration. Then, when you call the method, a reference to the variable that you specify for the corresponding argument is passed to the method. As a result, if the method changes the value of the parameter, it also changes the value of the variable in the calling method.

In this figure, the first three arguments are passed by value, but the fourth is passed by reference. Then, when the method changes the fourth parameter, the variable in the calling method is also changed. As a result, there's no need for the method to return the value of the futureValue variable.

The basic syntax of the parameters in a parameter list

```
[{ref|out|in}] type variableName
```

A CalculateFutureValue() method that uses the ref keyword

```
private void CalculateFutureValue(decimal monthlyInvestment,
    decimal monthlyInterestRate, int months, ref decimal futureValue)
{
    for (int i = 0; i < months; i++)
    {
        futureValue = (futureValue + monthlyInvestment)
                    * (1 + monthlyInterestRate);
    }
}
```

Three statements that work with the CalculateFutureValue() method

```
decimal futureValue = 0m;
CalculateFutureValue(monthlyInvestment,
    monthlyInterestRate, months, ref futureValue);
txtFutureValue.Text = futureValue.ToString("c");
```

Description

- When you call a method, each argument can be passed to the method *by value* or *by reference*.

- If you pass an argument by value, the value of the variable in the calling method can't be changed by the called method. That's because the value of the variable is passed, not the variable itself.

- If you pass an argument by reference and the called method changes the value of the corresponding parameter, the value of the variable in the calling method is changed. That's because the passed argument provides a reference that points to the variable in the calling method.

- By default, arguments are passed by value. To pass an argument by reference, you use the *ref*, *out*, or *in* keyword.

- When you pass an argument by reference and update the argument in the called method, you don't have to use the return statement to return the value of the argument.

Figure 6-6   When and how to pass arguments by reference and by value (part 1 of 2)

You can also pass arguments by reference using the *out* keyword. This keyword works similarly to the ref keyword. The only difference is that a variable that's passed as an argument using the out keyword doesn't have to be initialized before it's passed. This is illustrated by the first example in part 2 of figure 6-6. Here, no value is assigned to the futureValue variable before it's passed to the CalculateFutureValue() method. However, the CalculateFutureValue() method must assign a value to this variable before it ends.

With C# 7.0 and later, you can also declare an out variable in the argument list for calling a method. To do that, you code the type of the variable after the out keyword. This is also illustrated by the first example.

You can also use a *discard* (_) for the name of an out variable if you don't need to work with that variable in the calling code. In chapter 4, for example, you learned that you can use the TryParse() method to convert a string to another data type. This method returns a true or false value that indicates whether the string could be converted. It also uses an out parameter to return the converted value. But, suppose you just wanted to test if a string could be converted and you didn't need the converted value? Then, you could call the TryParse() method with a discard like this:

```
if (Decimal.TryParse(salesString, out _) {...}
```

You'll see an example like this in the next chapter when you see the code for validating user entries.

The second example shows how to use the *in* keyword to pass arguments by reference. When you code the in keyword on a parameter declaration, the value that's passed is read-only. Because of that, the value of the parameter can't be changed by the method. Note that when you use the in keyword, you don't typically have to code it on the argument that's passed to the parameter. However, you can do that if you want to make it clear that the parameter uses the in keyword.

In general, it's better to pass arguments by value instead of by reference. That way, the data in the calling method can't be changed by the called method. In addition, it's a good coding practice to always initialize variables, in which case you can use the ref keyword instead of the out keyword. The exception is if you want to use a .NET method like the TryParse() method that you learned about in chapter 4. Because the second parameter that's defined by this method uses the out keyword, you have to use that keyword when you call the method as shown in figure 4-14.

Although it's not shown here, you can also use the ref or out keyword to return two or more values from a method. However, a better way to do that is to return one tuple or object that contains those values. You'll learn how to create and work with tuples next, and you'll learn how to create and work with objects in section 3.

For now, though, you should know about an additional complication that arises when you pass a reference type (an object) rather than a value type as an argument. If you pass a reference type by value, you still can't change its value (the reference), but you can change the values of members of the object it refers to. By contrast, if you pass a reference type by reference, you can change both its value and the values of its members. This will make more sense after you learn about creating and using your own classes in chapter 12.

A CalculateFutureValue() method that uses the out keyword

```
private void CalculateFutureValue(decimal monthlyInvestment,
    decimal monthlyInterestRate, int months, out decimal futureValue)
{
    for (int i = 0; i < months; i++)
    {
        futureValue = (futureValue + monthlyInvestment)
                    * (1 + monthlyInterestRate);
    }
}
```

Two statements that work with a CalculateFutureValue() method

```
decimal futureValue;
CalculateFutureValue(monthlyInvestment,
    monthlyInterestRate, months, out futureValue);
```

Another way to work with this method (C# 7.0 and later)

```
CalculateFutureValue(monthlyInvestment,
    monthlyInterestRate, months, out decimal futureValue);
```

A CalculateFutureValue() method that uses the in keyword (C# 7.2 and later)

```
private void CalculateFutureValue(in decimal monthlyInvestment,
    in decimal monthlyInterestRate, in int months, out decimal futureValue)
{
    for (int i = 0; i < months; i++)
    {
        futureValue = (futureValue + monthlyInvestment)
                    * (1 + monthlyInterestRate);
    }
}
```

A statement that calls the CalculateFutureValue() method

```
CalculateFutureValue(monthlyInvestment,
    monthlyInterestRate, months, out decimal futureValue);
```

Description

- When you use the out keyword to pass an argument by reference, you don't have to initialize the variable for the argument. Because of that, you have to assign a value to it within the method.

- With C# 7.0 and later, you don't have to declare an out variable before you call the method that uses it. Instead, you can declare it in the argument list by including a type on the argument.

- If you don't need to use the value of an out variable from the calling code, you can use a *discard* (_) as the name of the variable in the method call. Then, the value of the variable is discarded when it's returned by the method.

- When you use the in keyword to pass an argument by reference, you must initialize the variable for the argument, and you can't change the value of the parameter in the method.

Figure 6-6   When and how to pass arguments by reference and by value (part 2 of 2)

How to work with tuples

C# 7.0 introduced a new feature called *tuples* that lets you define simple data structures. Tuples are similar to enumerations, except the *members* of a tuple are public variables instead of constants. In the topics that follow, you'll learn the basic skills for creating tuples and referring to their members. You'll also learn how to use a tuple as the return type for a method.

How to create tuples and refer to their members

Figure 6-7 shows different ways that you can create tuples. The first example shows how to create an *unnamed tuple*. To do that, you code the var keyword as the tuple type, followed by the name of the variable that will store the tuple. Then, you assign values for the members of the tuple by coding the values in parentheses and separating them with commas.

When you use this technique, the types of the members are inferred from the values that are assigned to them. In this example, that means that the first member is given a type of string and the second member is given a type of int. In addition, the members of an unnamed tuple are given default names of Item1, Item2, and so on. Then, you can refer to a member of the tuple using its default name. To do that, you code the name of the tuple variable, followed by a dot operator and the name of the member.

In most cases, you'll want to create a *named tuple* by assigning your own names to the members of the tuple. The second example shows two ways to do that. First, you can specify a member name by coding the name and a colon before the member value. When you use this technique, the types of the members are inferred from the values that are assigned to them, just as they are when you create an unnamed tuple.

Second, you can declare the data types for the members explicitly. To do that, you code the type and name for each member before the name of the tuple variable, you separate the members with commas, and you enclose them with parentheses.

To refer to a member of a named tuple, you code the name of the tuple variable followed by the dot operator just like you do for an unnamed tuple. Instead of coding the default names, though, you can code the names you specified. These names act as synonyms for the default names and make it easier to refer to the members.

Notice in both examples that the names of the tuple members use Pascal notation (each word starts with an uppercase character). This is a common coding practice, since the members are public variables.

The third example in this figure shows another way to create a tuple that was introduced with C# 7.1. Here, the member values are specified using variable names instead of literals. When you use this technique, the members are given the same names as the variables. Because of that, the member names use Camel notation (first word starts with a lowercase character, all words after that start with an uppercase character). Then, you can refer to the members using those names.

How to create and work with an unnamed tuple

How to create a tuple with two members
```
var person = ("Anne Boehm", 62);
```

How to refer to the members of the tuple
```
person.Item1
person.Item2
```

How to create and work with a named tuple

How to create a tuple with two members
```
var person = (Name: "Anne Boehm", Age: 62);
```

How to create the tuple and declare its member types
```
(string Name, int Age) person = ("Anne Boehm", 62);
```

How to refer to the members of the tuple
```
person.Name
person.Age
```

How to create a tuple using variable names (C# 7.1 and later)

How to create a tuple with two members
```
string name = "Anne Boehm";
int age = 62;
var person = (name, age);
```

How to refer to the members of the tuple
```
person.name
person.age
```

Description

- *Tuples* are a feature introduced with C# 7.0 that lets you define simple data structures that contain two or more data items called *members*.

- Tuples can be used in place of classes and other types that you'll learn about in chapter 12 when you just need to work with a group of public variables.

- When you create a tuple, you must assign a value to each member. You can do that using any of the techniques shown above.

- An *unnamed tuple* is a tuple whose members don't have names. You can refer to the members of an unnamed tuple using the default names Item1, Item2, and so on.

- A *named tuple* is assigned synonyms that can be used in place of the default names.

- To refer to a member of a tuple, you code the name of the tuple, followed by the dot operator and the name of the member.

Figure 6-7   How to create tuples and refer to their members

How to use a tuple as the return type for a method

Earlier in this chapter, you learned how to use out parameters to return values from a method to the calling code. When you use out parameters, you can return one or more values. However, this isn't the recommended way to return multiple values from a method. A better way is to use tuples as shown in figure 6-8.

This figure starts by showing a version of the CalculateFutureValue() method that returns a tuple. Here, the return type is coded as a tuple that contains two members. The first member is a decimal named FutureValue that will store the future value that's calculated by the method, and the second member is a decimal that will store the total amount of interest that's included in the future value.

To return a tuple from a method, you code a return statement as shown here. This return statement includes the names of the variables that contain the values you want to return. These variables must be enclosed in parentheses and separated by commas, and they must be coded in the same sequence as the members of the tuple for the return type. Their data types must also correspond to member types of the tuple.

Next, this figure shows two ways that you can call the CalculateFutureValue() method. First, you can declare the data types and names for the members of the tuple and then assign the result of the method to the tuple. When you do that, the values in the tuple that's returned by the method are assigned to the corresponding members of the tuple in the calling code. This is referred to as *deconstructing the tuple*. Note that when you use this technique, you don't have to name the tuple in the calling code. If you don't, you can refer to its members directly by name.

Second, you can use the var keyword to create a tuple variable in the calling code. Then, the data types of the tuple members are inferred from the tuple that's returned by the method. In that case, you must refer to the members of the tuple using the name of the tuple variable.

Although it's not shown here, you should know that you can use a discard if you don't need one or more of the values that are returned by a tuple. For example, suppose you need just the future value that's returned by the method in this figure and not the total interest. In that case, you could call the method like this:

```
(decimal FutureValue, _) = CalculateFutureValue(
    monthlyInvestment, monthlyInterestRate, months);
```

Then, the second value that's returned by the tuple is discarded instead of being stored in a variable.

Although tuples provide an easy and efficient way to return multiple values from a method, you should know that you can accomplish the same thing using a class or one of the other types you'll learn about in chapter 12. For now, you should realize that those types can contain members like properties and methods that you can't include in tuples. If you need to return a type from a method that contains these members, then, you'll need to use one of the types presented in chapter 12.

A CalculateFutureValue() method that returns a tuple

```
private (decimal FutureValue, decimal TotalInterest)
    CalculateFutureValue(decimal monthlyInvestment,
    decimal monthlyInterestRate, int months)
{
    decimal futureValue = 0m;
    decimal totalInterest = 0m;
    decimal monthlyInterest = 0m;
    for (int i = 0; i < months; i++)
    {
        monthlyInterest = (futureValue + monthlyInvestment)
                        * monthlyInterestRate;
        totalInterest += monthlyInterest;
        futureValue += monthlyInvestment + monthlyInterest;
    }
    return (futureValue, totalInterest);
}
```

A statement that calls the method and deconstructs the tuple

```
(decimal FutureValue, decimal TotalInterest) = CalculateFutureValue(
    monthlyInvestment, monthlyInterestRate, months);
```

Two statements that refer to the members of the tuple
```
txtFutureValue.Text = FutureValue.ToString("c");
txtTotalInterest.Text = TotalInterest.ToString("c");
```

A statement that calls the method and assigns the tuple to a variable

```
var calculations = CalculateFutureValue(
    monthlyInvestment, monthlyInterestRate, months);
```

Two statements that refer to the members of the tuple
```
txtFutureValue.Text = calculations.FutureValue.ToString("c");
txtTotalInterest.Text = calculations.TotalInterest.ToString("c");
```

Description

- To define a tuple as the return type for a method, you define its members by enclosing them in parentheses and separating them with commas.

- To return a tuple from a method, you code the variables that store the values of the members on the return statement. To do that, you enclose the variables in parentheses and separate them with commas.

- To call a method that returns a tuple, you can declare each member of the tuple and then assign the result of the method to the tuple. This is referred to as *deconstructing the tuple* because the value of each member that's returned is assigned to a separate variable.

- You can also assign a tuple that's returned by a method to a single variable. Then, the members of the tuple have the same names as the members of the return type, and you can refer to those members through the tuple variable.

Figure 6-8   How to use a tuple as the return type for a method

How to work with events and delegates

In chapter 3, you learned how to generate the event handler for the default event of a control by double-clicking on the control in the Form Designer. Now, you'll learn how to create an event handler for any form or control event. In addition, you'll learn more about how event wiring works, and you'll learn how to handle two or more events with the same event handler.

How to generate an event handler for any event

Figure 6-9 shows how to generate an event handler for any event of a form or control. To do that, you select the form or control in the Form Designer and then click the Events button in the Properties window. When you do, a list of events for that form or control is displayed. In this figure, for example, you can see a list of the events for the first text box on the Future Value form. Below the list of events, you can see a short description of the highlighted event.

To generate a handler for any of these events, you can double-click on the event in this list. Then, Visual Studio will generate the method declaration for the event handler along with a statement that *wires* the event to the event handler (as you'll see in the next figure). When you use this technique, Visual Studio will give the event handler a name that combines the name of the control and the name of the event. For example, if you double-click the Validating event for the Monthly Investment text box, Visual Studio will generate an event handler with this name:

```
txtMonthlyInvestment_Validating
```

If you want to generate an event handler with a name other than the default, you can do that by entering the name next to the event in the Properties window. Then, when you press the Enter key, Visual Studio will create an event handler with that name. In most cases, you'll use this technique only when you generate an event handler that will be used to handle more than one event. You'll learn more about that in figure 6-11.

If you look through the list of events for a form or a control, you'll see that there are many events for each one. For instance, there are more than 60 events for a text box and more than 80 events for a form. In practice, though, you'll use just a few events for each form or control. As you go through this book, you'll be introduced to the ones that are commonly used.

The Events list for a text box control

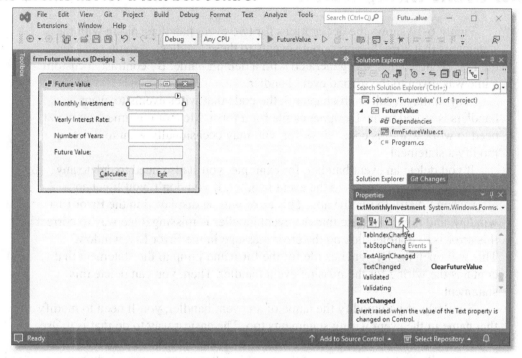

Description

- To generate the event handler for the default event of a form or control, you can double-click the form or control in the Form Designer.

- To view a list of all events for a form or control, you can select the form or control and click the Events button in the Properties window to display the Events list. Then, you can double-click on any event to generate an event handler for that event.

- By default, an event handler is given a name that consists of the form or control name, an underscore, and the event name. To generate an event handler with a custom name, you can type the name of the event handler to the right of the event in the Events list and then press Enter to generate the event handler.

- When you generate an event handler for a control, Visual Studio generates the method declaration for the event handler and it connects, or *wires*, the event to the event handler as shown in the next figure.

Figure 6-9   How to generate an event handler for any event

How event wiring works

Figure 6-10 shows the declarations for two event handlers, along with the statements that wire the appropriate events to these handlers. As you can see, the first event handler was generated with a default name. By contrast, a custom name was given to the second event handler.

As you may recall from chapter 3, the code that wires events to event handlers is stored in the Designer.cs file for a form. Most of the time, you won't need to work with this code. However, you may occasionally want to delete or modify a statement.

If you delete an event handler, for example, you'll also need to delete any statements that wire events to the event handler. If you don't, you'll get an error when you try to run the app. This error will be displayed in the Error List window, and it will indicate that the event handler is missing. One way to correct this error is to double-click on the error message in the Error List window. This will open the Designer.cs file for the form and jump to the statement that contains the wiring for the missing event handler. Then, you can delete this statement.

Similarly, if you modify the name of an event handler, you'll need to modify that name in the event wiring statements too. The easiest way to do that is to use refactoring as described in chapter 3 when you rename the event handler. This automatically updates the name of the event handler in the corresponding event wiring statements. However, if you forget to use refactoring when you rename the event handler, you can use the technique presented in this figure to wire the corresponding events to the newly renamed event handler.

To wire an event to an event handler, Visual Studio uses a *delegate*, which is an object that represents a method. By default, C# uses the EventHandler delegate that's provided by .NET. This delegate defines the return type and parameter list for a method that can handle an event.

With Visual Studio versions 17.5 and later, an EventHandler delegate is created implicitly. Then, the code uses the += operator to wire the event to the event handler. You can see how this works in the first two examples in this figure.

Prior to version 17.5, the code used the *new* keyword to explicitly create an EventHandler delegate. In this case, the name of the method that will handle the event is passed to the delegate. Then, the += operator is used to wire the event to the method specified by the delegate. You can see how this works in the third example. Because the applications for this book were created with versions of Visual Studio prior to 17.5, the event wiring looks as shown in this example.

For C# to recognize a method as an event handler, the method must include the two parameters defined by the EventHandler delegate as shown in the examples. The first parameter is an object named sender. When an event handler is executed, this parameter receives the object that the event occurred on. The second parameter identifies an EventArgs object named e that contains information about the event. The exact content of this object depends on the event that occurred.

The default event handler for a text box

The method declaration for the event handler

```
private void txtMonthlyInvestment_TextChanged(object sender, EventArgs e)
{

}
```

The generated statement that wires the event to the event handler

```
txtMonthlyInvestment.TextChanged += txtMonthlyInvestment_TextChanged;
```

A custom event handler for a text box

The method declaration for the event handler

```
private void ClearFutureValue(object sender, EventArgs e)
{

}
```

The generated statement that wires the event to the event handler

```
txtMonthlyInvestment.TextChanged += ClearFutureValue;
```

A statement that explicitly creates the delegate object

```
this.txtMonthlyInvestment.TextChanged +=
    new System.EventHandler(this.ClearFutureValue);
```

Description

- When you use the Form Designer to generate an event handler, a statement is also generated in the Designer.cs file for the form to wire the event to the method that handles the event.

- To wire an event to a method, C# uses the EventHandler *delegate*, which is an object that represents a method.

- The EventHandler delegate specifies the return type and the parameters that are required for a method that can handle an event. These objects are passed to the event handler when the event occurs. The first parameter (sender) identifies the object that the event occurred on, and the second parameter identifies an EventArgs object that contains additional information about the event.

- After C# creates the EventHandler delegate, the **+=** operator is used to wire the specified event handler to the event.

- Prior to version 17.5 of Visual Studio, the statement used to wire an event to an event handler explicitly created the EventHandler delegate using the *new* keyword as shown in the third example above. With versions 17.5 and later, however, the delegate is created implicitly as shown in the first and second examples.

Figure 6-10   How event wiring works

How to handle multiple events with one event handler

In some cases, you'll want to use the same event handler to handle two or more events. For example, it's common to use one event handler for the TextChanged event of multiple text boxes on a form. To do that, you can use the procedure shown in figure 6-11.

To start, you must generate the event handler as described in figure 6-9. Typically, you will want to give this event handler a name that's not specific to any one control. Suppose, for example, that any time the user changes the value in one of the first three text boxes on the Future Value form, you want to clear the future value that's currently displayed. Then, when you create the event handler for the first text box, you might give this event handler the name ClearFutureValue().

Once you've created this event handler, it will appear in the drop-down list of the event handlers that are available. In this figure, for example, you can see that the ClearFutureValue() event handler is included in the drop-down list for the TextChanged event of the Yearly Interest Rate text box. Then, you can select this event handler to generate a statement that wires the event to the event handler.

How to select an existing event handler for an event

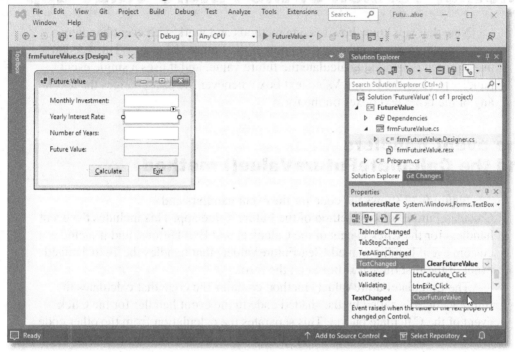

How to wire an event to an existing event handler

1. Select the control in the Form Designer.
2. If necessary, click the Events button in the Properties window to display a list of the events for the control.
3. Click to the right of the event you want to handle and display the drop-down list.
4. Select the event handler you want to use for that event.

Description

- The drop-down list that's available for each event includes all the existing event handlers for the current form.
- When you select an event handler from the drop-down list, Visual Studio generates a statement that wires the event to the event handler.

Figure 6-11   How to handle multiple events with one event handler

Another version of the Future Value app

Now that you know how to code methods and work with event handlers, you're ready to see an enhanced version of the Future Value app. This version uses a private method to calculate the future value, and it uses a single event handler to clear the Future Value text box whenever the user changes the text in any of the other text boxes on the form.

The event handlers and the CalculateFutureValue() method

Figure 6-12 shows the code for the event handlers and CalculateFutureValue() method of the Future Value app. This includes the event handlers for the Click events of the Calculate and Exit buttons, and it includes a custom event handler named ClearFutureValue() that handles the TextChanged event of the first three text boxes on the form.

The CalculateFutureValue() method contains the code that calculates the future value. It's called by the shaded code in the event handler for the Click event of the Calculate button. This separates the calculation from the other code for the event. In a lengthy event handler, using methods like this can make it easier to code, test, and debug an app. You'll see more of this in the next chapter.

The ClearFutureValue() event handler contains a single statement that sets the Text property of the Future Value text box to an empty string. In other words, it clears the future value that's displayed on the form. Since this event handler is wired to the TextChanged event of the first three text boxes on this form, this code clears the Future Value text box every time the user changes a value in any of the other text boxes. Then, the future value isn't displayed until the user clicks the Calculate button again. As a result, this code prevents the Future Value text box from displaying a value that isn't accurate for the values that are displayed in the other text boxes.

The code for the methods of the Future Value app

```
private void btnCalculate_Click(object sender, EventArgs e)
{
    decimal monthlyInvestment = Convert.ToDecimal(txtMonthlyInvestment.Text);
    decimal yearlyInterestRate = Convert.ToDecimal(txtInterestRate.Text);
    int years = Convert.ToInt32(txtYears.Text);

    int months = years * 12;
    decimal monthlyInterestRate = yearlyInterestRate / 12 / 100;

    decimal futureValue = CalculateFutureValue(
        monthlyInvestment, monthlyInterestRate, months);
    txtFutureValue.Text = futureValue.ToString("c");
    txtMonthlyInvestment.Focus();
}

private decimal CalculateFutureValue(decimal monthlyInvestment,
    decimal monthlyInterestRate, int months)
{
    decimal futureValue = 0m;
    for (int i = 0; i < months; i++)
    {
        futureValue = (futureValue + monthlyInvestment)
                    * (1 + monthlyInterestRate);
    }
    return futureValue;
}

private void btnExit_Click(object sender, EventArgs e)
{
    this.Close();
}

private void ClearFutureValue(object sender, EventArgs e)
{
    txtFutureValue.Text = "";
}
```

Description

- The CalculateFutureValue() method separates the calculation from the rest of the code for the event handler for the Click event of the Calculate button.

- The TextChanged event of the Monthly Investment, Yearly Interest Rate, and Number of Years text boxes is wired to the ClearFutureValue() event handler. As a result, the Future Value text box will be cleared every time the user changes the value in one of those text boxes.

Figure 6-12   The event handlers and the other method of the Future Value app

Some of the generated code

Figure 6-13 shows a partial listing of the generated code for the Future Value app. This code is stored in the Designer.cs file for the form within the Windows Form Designer generated code region. In this figure, you can see the code that's generated for three controls: one button and two text boxes.

To start, the InitializeComponent() method creates objects from the appropriate control classes and assigns those objects to the appropriate variables, which have already been declared. Next, the InitializeComponent() method includes a group of statements for each control. Most of these statements set the starting properties for these controls.

However, the last statement in each group wires an event to an event handler. Here, the Click event of the Calculate button is wired to an event handler named btnCalculate_Click(), and the TextChanged events of the two text boxes are wired to an event handler named ClearFutureValue(). (Although it isn't shown in this listing, the TextChanged event of the third text box on this form is also wired to the ClearFutureValue() event handler.)

As the warning at the top of this listing suggests, you should avoid modifying this code with a code editor. However, you should also be aware that this generated code exists and that it is essential to the proper operation of your app. In addition, there are times when using the Code Editor to directly modify this code may be easier than using the Form Designer to indirectly modify this code. If, for example, you start an event handler and decide to delete it, you may want to use the Code Editor to delete the wiring statement. Fortunately, this doesn't cause any problems for the Form Designer.

Some of the generated code in the Designer.cs file for the form

```
#region Windows Form Designer generated code

/// <summary>
/// Required method for Designer support - do not modify
/// the contents of this method with the code editor.
/// </summary>
private void InitializeComponent()
{
    btnCalculate = new Button();
    txtInterestRate = new TextBox();
    txtMonthlyInvestment = new TextBox();
    ...
    //
    // btnCalculate
    //
    btnCalculate.Location = new Point(93, 137);
    btnCalculate.Name = "btnCalculate";
    btnCalculate.Size = new Size(75, 23);
    btnCalculate.TabIndex = 8;
    btnCalculate.Text = "&Calculate";
    btnCalculate.UseVisualStyleBackColor = true;
    btnCalculate.Click += btnCalculate_Click;
    //
    // txtInterestRate
    //
    txtInterestRate.Location = new Point(158, 41);
    txtInterestRate.Name = "txtInterestRate";
    txtInterestRate.Size = new Size(100, 23);
    txtInterestRate.TabIndex = 3;
    txtInterestRate.TextChanged += ClearFutureValue;
    //
    // txtMonthlyInvestment
    //
    txtMonthlyInvestment.Location = new Point(158, 12);
    txtMonthlyInvestment.Name = "txtMonthlyInvestment";
    txtMonthlyInvestment.Size = new Size(100, 23);
    txtMonthlyInvestment.TabIndex = 1;
    txtMonthlyInvestment.TextChanged += ClearFutureValue;
    ...
}

#endregion

private Button btnCalculate;
private TextBox txtInterestRate;
private TextBox txtMonthlyInvestment;
...
```

Description

- The InitializeComponent() method creates an instance of each control on the form, assigns each control to a variable, sets the properties of each control, and wires control events to the appropriate event handlers.

Figure 6-13   Some of the generated code for the Future Value app

Perspective

Now that you have finished this chapter, you should be able to code and call methods. You should also be able to code event handlers for any event of a form or control. With those skills, you are well on your way toward developing programs at a professional level.

Terms

method	pass arguments by name
access modifier	expression-bodied method
return statement	pass arguments by value
parameter	pass arguments by reference
parameter list	discard
signature of a method	tuple
overload a method	member
call a method	unnamed tuple
argument	named tuple
argument list	deconstructing a tuple
pass arguments by position	event wiring
optional parameter	delegate

Exercise 6-1   Enhance the Future Value app

In this exercise, you'll enhance the Future Value app that you created in chapter 5 so it works like the one in figure 6-12.

Use refactoring to create the CalculateFutureValue() method

1. Open the app that's in the C:\C#\Ch06\FutureValue directory.

2. Use refactoring as shown in figure 6-5 to refactor the calculation in the event handler and create a new method named CalculateFutureValue().

3. Test the app to make sure the new method works correctly.

Add the CalculateFutureValue() method without using refactoring

4. Press Ctrl+Z twice to return the code to the way it was before you refactored it.

5. Add a method named CalculateFutureValue() that works like the one in figure 6-12. To do that, type the start of the new method including its opening brace, and its closing brace will be added automatically. Then, move the related code from the btnCalculate_Click() method to the block within the new method and modify it where necessary.

6. Modify the code in the btnCalculate_Click() method so it calls the CalculateFutureValue() method. As you enter the call to the method, note how the IntelliSense feature helps you enter the arguments.

7. Test the app to make sure this new method works correctly.

Add an event handler for the TextChanged events

8. In the Form Designer, select the first text box. Then, click the Events button in the Properties window to display the Events list for that text box. Review the events that are available.

9. Enter "ClearFutureValue" to the right of the TextChanged event and press Enter. When you do, the Code Editor will open and an event handler named ClearFutureValue will be created. Enter a statement that clears the Future Value text box as shown in figure 6-12.

10. Open the frmFutureValue.Designer.cs file for the form, expand the Windows Form Designer generated code region if necessary, and locate the statements that set the properties of the Monthly Investment text box. At the end of those statements, you'll find a statement that wires the TextChanged event of this control to the ClearFutureValue event handler.

11. Return to the Form Designer and select the Yearly Interest Rate text box. Drop down the list for the TextChanged event of this control, and notice that the ClearFutureValue() event handler is included in this list. Select this event handler to wire the event to it. Repeat this process for the Number of Years text box.

12. Run the app and perform a calculation. Then, change the value that's displayed in one of the text boxes. When you do, the value that's displayed for the Future Value text box should be cleared.

13. When you're sure the enhancements are working correctly, close the app.

Exercise 6-2   Experiment with events

This exercise will give you a chance to experiment with events and the event wiring for the Future Value app.

Generate and delete an event handler

1. Open the Future Value app that you enhanced in exercise 6-1.

2. In the Form Designer, double-click on the form to generate the handler for the default event of a form, which is the Load event. Then, delete this event handler in the Code Editor, and try to build and run the app. This should lead to one build error.

3. Double-click on the error message, which will lead you to the event wiring for the event handler. Then, delete that wiring, and try to build and run the app again. This time, it should work.

Use a form event and two more control events

4. In the Form Designer, select the form, click the Events button in the Properties window, and double-click on the DoubleClick event to generate its event handler. Next, write the code for this handler so it sets the Text property for all four text boxes to an empty string. Then, test the app to make sure this works. (Be sure to double-click on the form, not on a control or the form's title bar.)

5. In the Form Designer, select the Monthly Investment text box. Next, select the MouseHover event, read its description, drop down its list, and select the ClearFutureValue() event handler so it will be executed whenever the user lets the mouse hover over this text box. Then, test the app to make sure this works.

6. In the Form Designer, select the Yearly Interest Rate text box, and double-click on the DoubleClick event to generate its event handler. Next, write the code for this handler so it sets the value in the Yearly Interest Rate text box to 12. Then, test this enhancement.

7. Use your own imagination to work with other events. When you're through experimenting with events, close the app.

Exercise 6-3   Enhance the Invoice Total app

In this exercise, you'll enhance the Invoice Total app from chapter 5 so it uses a method with a tuple.

Add a GetInvoiceAmounts() method

1. Open the app that's in the C:\C#\Ch06\InvoiceTotal directory.

2. Add a method named GetInvoiceAmounts() that accepts the customer type and subtotal and returns the discount percent. You can do that manually or using refactoring.

3. Test the app to make sure the new method works correctly.

Add a tuple

4. Modify the declaration for the GetInvoiceAmounts() method so it returns a tuple that includes the discount percent, discount amount, and invoice total. Then, modify the code for this method so it works with the tuple.

5. Modify the calling code so it deconstructs the tuple that's returned by the GetInvoiceAmounts() method. When you do that, you can delete the statements that declare and calculate the discount amount and invoice total.

6. Test the app to make sure the changes work.

7

How to handle exceptions and validate data

In the last two chapters, you learned how to code a Future Value app that calculates the future value of a series of monthly payments. However, if the user enters data that can't be handled by this app, an exception will occur and the app will crash. In this chapter, you'll learn how to prevent that from happening by handling any exceptions that occur and by validating data to prevent exceptions.

An introduction to exceptions

Before you learn how to handle exceptions, it's helpful to know more about how exceptions work. In addition, it's helpful to know how to display a dialog that contains a message about an exception that has occurred. So that's what you'll learn in the two topics that follow.

It's inevitable that your apps will encounter exceptions. For example, a user may enter data that's not appropriate for the app. Then, if the app doesn't check to be sure that the data is valid, the .NET runtime environment will *throw* an *exception* when it tries to work with that data. An exception is an object that's created from the Exception class or one of its subclasses like the ones shown in figure 7-1. Exception objects represent errors that have occurred, and they contain information about those errors.

How exceptions work

A well-coded app will *catch* specific exceptions that might be thrown and handle them. This is known as *exception handling*. Exception handling can be as simple as notifying users that they must enter valid data. However, for more serious exceptions, exception handling may involve notifying users that the app is being shut down, saving as much data as possible, cleaning up resources, and exiting the app as smoothly as possible.

When you're testing an app, it's common to encounter exceptions that haven't been handled. In that case, Visual Studio will enter break mode and display an Exception Helper dialog like the one shown in this figure. This dialog includes the name of the class for the exception and a brief message that describes the cause of the exception.

All exceptions are *subclasses* of the Exception class. For example, the FormatException class is a subclass of the Exception class that represents a specific type of exception that occurs when a value of one data type can't be converted to another data type. This exception can be thrown by the To() methods of the Convert class or the Parse() method of any class.

The ArithmeticException class is also a subclass of the Exception class. It represents an exception that occurs during an arithmetic, casting, or conversion operation. This class contains other subclasses, including the OverflowException and DivideByZeroException classes shown here. An overflow exception occurs when the result of an arithmetic, casting, or conversion operation is too large for the receiving variable. A divide-by-zero exception occurs if an app attempts to divide a number by zero.

For now, that's all you need to know about the Exception hierarchy. As you progress through this book, though, you'll learn about other types of exceptions. In section 5, for example, you'll learn how to work with the exceptions that can occur when you're working with databases. You'll also learn more about subclasses and how they work in chapter 14.

The dialog for an unhandled exception

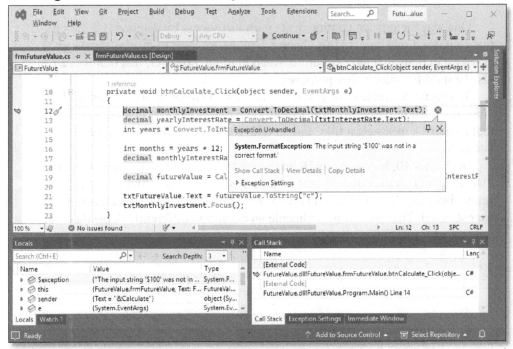

The Exception hierarchy for five common exceptions

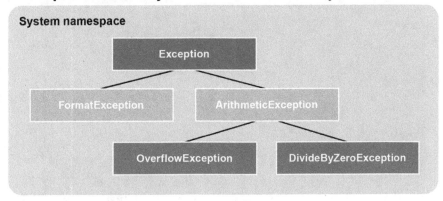

Methods that might throw exceptions

Class	Method	Exception
Convert	ToDecimal(string)	FormatException OverflowException
Convert	ToInt32(string)	FormatException OverflowException
Decimal	Parse(string)	FormatException OverflowException
DateTime	Parse(string)	FormatException

Figure 7-1   How exceptions work

How to display a dialog

One way an app can communicate with its users is by displaying a dialog that contains a message. In this chapter, dialogs are used to display messages about exceptions that have occurred. Keep in mind, however, that dialogs can also be used for many other purposes.

To display a simple dialog, you use the Show() method of the MessageBox class as shown in figure 7-2. The syntax shown here lets you display a dialog that contains a message, a title, and an OK button. For now, this simple dialog is adequate.

In chapter 10, however, you'll learn how to use the MessageBox class to display more complex dialogs that include Yes, No, Cancel, Abort, Retry, and Ignore buttons, and you'll learn how to write code that checks which button the user selected. That way, you can handle an exception differently depending on how the user responds to the dialog.

The syntax to display a dialog with an OK button

```
MessageBox.Show(text[, caption]);
```

A dialog with an OK button

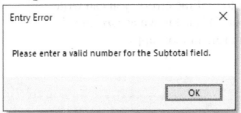

The statement that displays this dialog

```
MessageBox.Show(
    "Please enter a valid number for the Subtotal field.",
    "Entry Error");
```

Description

- You can use the static Show() method of the MessageBox class to display a dialog. Dialogs can be used to display information about an exception to the user.
- If you omit the caption argument, the dialog will be displayed without a caption in its title bar.

Note

- In chapter 10, you'll learn how to use the MessageBox class to display more complex dialogs that contain other buttons and accept a response from the user.

Figure 7-2   How to display a dialog

How to use structured exception handling

To prevent your apps from crashing due to runtime errors, you can write code that handles exceptions when they occur. This is known as *structured exception handling*, and it plays an important role in most apps.

How to catch an exception

Figure 7-3 shows how to use *try-catch statements* to catch and handle exceptions. First, you code a *try block* around the statement or statements that may throw an exception. Then, immediately after the try block, you code a *catch block* that contains the statements that will be executed if an exception is thrown by a statement in the try block. This is known as an *exception handler*.

The try-catch statement in this figure shows how you might catch any exceptions thrown by four of the statements in the Invoice Total app. For example, if the user enters a non-numeric value into the Subtotal text box, the ToDecimal() method of the Convert class will throw an exception. Then, the app will jump into the catch block, skipping all the remaining statements in the try block. In this case, the catch block simply displays a dialog that notifies the user of the problem. Then, the user can click the OK button and enter a valid number.

The syntax for a simple try-catch statement

```
try { statements }
catch { statements }
```

A try-catch statement

```
try
{
    decimal subtotal = Convert.ToDecimal(txtSubtotal.Text);
    decimal discountPercent = .2m;
    decimal discountAmount = subtotal * discountPercent;
    decimal invoiceTotal = subtotal - discountAmount;
}
catch
{
    MessageBox.Show(
        "Please enter a valid number for the Subtotal field.",
        "Entry Error");
}
```

The dialog that's displayed if an exception occurs

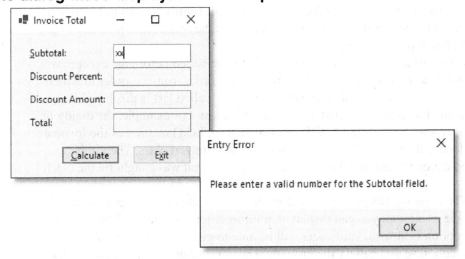

Description

- You can use a *try-catch statement* to code an *exception handler* that catches and handles any exceptions that are thrown.

- You can code a *try block* around any statements that may throw an exception. Then, you can code a *catch block* that contains the statements to be executed when an exception is thrown in the try block.

Figure 7-3   How to catch an exception

How to use the properties and methods of an exception

Since an exception is an object, it has properties and methods. If you want to use the properties or methods of an exception in the catch block that catches the exception, you must supply a name for the exception as shown in figure 7-4. To do that, you code a set of parentheses after the catch keyword. Within those parentheses, you code the name of the exception class, followed by a name for the exception.

If you're coding the try-catch statement within an event handler, you can't use e as the name of the exception. That's because, by default, the event handler already uses this name for its EventArgs parameter. As a result, you must specify another name such as x or ex. Or, you must change the name of the EventArgs parameter from e to another name.

Once you specify a name for an exception, you can use the Message property to get a brief description of the error. You can also use the GetType() method to get the type of class that was used to create the exception object. Then, to get the name of that type, you can use the ToString() method as shown in the example in this figure. Finally, you can use the StackTrace property to get a string that represents the *stack trace*.

A stack trace is a list of the methods that were called before the exception occurred. These methods are listed in the reverse order from the order in which they were called. As a result, the method that was called last is displayed first, and the method that was called first is displayed last. For example, the dialog in this figure shows that line 14 of the btnCalculate_Click() method of the Invoice Total form called the ToDecimal() method of the Convert class. Then, this method called the method that threw the exception that was caught by the catch block.

When you use the properties and methods of an exception to get information about the exception, you can display that information in a dialog. That way, if an exception is thrown, your users will be able to give you information about the exception so you can fix the problem. Or, if a serious exception occurs that prevents the app from continuing, you can write information about the exception to a log file so you can monitor and review these exceptions. You'll learn how to write data to files in chapter 17.

The syntax for a try-catch statement that accesses the exception

```
try { statements }
catch(ExceptionClass exceptionName) { statements }
```

Two common properties for all exceptions

Property	Description
Message	Gets a message that briefly describes the current exception.
StackTrace	Gets a string that lists the methods that were called before the exception occurred.

A common method for all exceptions

Method	Description
GetType()	Gets the type of the current exception.

A try-catch statement that accesses the exception

```
try
{
    decimal subtotal = Convert.ToDecimal(txtSubtotal.Text);
}
catch(Exception ex)
{
    MessageBox.Show(ex.Message + "\n\n" + ex.GetType().ToString() + "\n" +
                    ex.StackTrace, "Exception");
}
```

The dialog that's displayed if an exception occurs

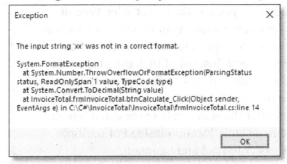

```
Exception                                              ×

The input string 'xx' was not in a correct format.

System.FormatException
   at System.Number.ThrowOverflowOrFormatException(ParsingStatus
status, ReadOnlySpan`1 value, TypeCode type)
   at System.Convert.ToDecimal(String value)
   at InvoiceTotal.frmInvoiceTotal.btnCalculate_Click(Object sender,
EventArgs e) in C:\C#\InvoiceTotal\InvoiceTotal\frmInvoiceTotal.cs:line 14

                                              [  OK  ]
```

Description

- If you want to use the properties or methods of the exception in the catch block, you must supply a name for the exception.

- The *stack trace* is a list of the methods that were called before the exception occurred. The list appears in reverse order, from the last method called to the first method called.

Note

- If you're coding the try-catch statement within an event handler, you can't use e for the name of the exception because it's used as the name of a parameter for the handler.

Figure 7-4   How to use the properties and methods of an exception

How to catch specific types of exceptions

In some cases, the statements in the try block of a try-catch statement can throw more than one type of exception. Then, you may want to handle each exception differently. To do that, you can code catch blocks like the ones shown in figure 7-5. Here, the first catch block catches a FormatException, the second catch block catches an OverflowException, and the third catch block catches any other exceptions.

When you catch specific exceptions, you should realize that you must code the catch blocks for the most specific exceptions in a class hierarchy first, and you must code the catch blocks for the least specific exceptions last. In this figure, for example, the FormatException type and the OverflowException type are both more specific than the Exception type. As a result, their catch blocks must be coded before the catch block for the Exception type. If they were coded after the Exception type, you would get a build error when you tried to compile the project. That's because the catch blocks are evaluated in sequence, which means that the catch block for the Exception type would catch any exception that occurred. In other words, the other catch blocks would never be executed.

Although you have to code the catch blocks for the FormatException and OverflowException types before the catch block for the Exception type, you don't have to code the catch block for the FormatException type before the OverflowException type. That's because the OverflowException class is a subclass of the ArithmeticException class, not the FormatException class. In other words, the least specific exception to most specific exception rule applies only within subclasses that are based on the same class.

When you code try-catch statements, you may find that you have some code that should run regardless of whether an exception is thrown or what type of exception is thrown. For example, if your app is using system resources such as database connections, it's common to perform some cleanup code that releases those resources when they're no longer needed. Instead of including this code in the try block and each catch block, you can code it in a *finally block*. Then, this code is executed after all the statements in the try block are executed. Or, if an exception is thrown, it's executed after the statements in the catch block. This allows you to store cleanup code in a single location instead of multiple locations, which results in code that's easier to read and maintain.

The syntax for a try-catch statement that catches specific types of exceptions

```
try { statements }
[catch(MostSpecificException [exceptionName]) { statements }]...
[catch(NextMostSpecificException [exceptionName]) { statements }]...
[catch([LeastSpecificException [exceptionName]]) { statements }]
[finally { statements }]
```

A try-catch statement that catches two specific exceptions

```
try
{
    decimal monthlyInvestment =
        Convert.ToDecimal(txtMonthlyInvestment.Text);
    decimal yearlyInterestRate =
        Convert.ToDecimal(txtInterestRate.Text);
    int years = Convert.ToInt32(txtYears.Text);
}
catch(FormatException)    // a specific exception
{
    MessageBox.Show(
        "A format exception has occurred. Please check all entries.",
        "Entry Error");
}
catch(OverflowException) // another specific exception
{
    MessageBox.Show(
        "An overflow exception has occurred. Please enter smaller values.",
        "Entry Error");
}
catch(Exception ex)        // all other exceptions
{
    MessageBox.Show(ex.Message, ex.GetType().ToString());
}
finally        // this code runs whether or not an exception occurs
{
    PerformCleanup();
}
```

Description

- You can code one catch block for each type of exception that may occur in the try block. If you code more than one catch block, you must code the catch blocks for the most specific types of exceptions first.

- Since all exceptions are subclasses of the Exception class, a catch block for the Exception class will catch all types of exceptions.

- You can code a *finally block* after all the catch blocks. The code in this block is executed whether or not an exception occurs. It's often used to free any system resources.

Figure 7-5   How to catch specific types of exceptions

How to throw an exception

Now that you've learned how to catch exceptions, you're ready to learn how to throw exceptions from the methods that you code. To do that, you can use the *throw statement* as shown in figure 7-6. As you can see, you can use this statement either to throw a new exception or to throw an existing exception.

To throw a new exception, you code the throw keyword followed by the *new* keyword and the name of the exception class you want to create the exception from. (As you'll see later in this book, the new keyword is the keyword that's used to create an object from a class.) When you do that, you can also supply a string argument that provides a brief description of the exception. This argument is assigned to the Message property of the exception. Then, when you handle the exception, you can use the Message property to get this string.

This use of the throw statement is illustrated in the first example in this figure. Here, before performing its calculation, the CalculateFutureValue() method checks if the values used in the calculation are less than or equal to zero. If so, an exception that's created from the Exception class is thrown. Both throw statements shown here include a string that briefly describes the cause of the exception.

In general, you should throw an exception only when a truly exceptional condition occurs. In the first example, the CalculateFutureValue() method can't perform the calculation when it receives a negative number. As a result, this is an exceptional condition, and it makes sense to throw an exception. Another way to handle this situation would be to return a negative decimal value (such as -1.0m) to indicate that the calculation can't be performed. However, throwing an exception allows you to provide a description of the exceptional condition, which is often helpful to other programmers who might want to use this method.

You can also use the throw statement to test an exception handling routine as shown in the second example. Here, the throw statement is coded within the try block of a try-catch statement. Then, when this statement is executed, the code within the catch block is executed so you can be sure it works properly.

The third example in this figure shows how to throw an existing exception. This technique is useful if you need to catch an exception, perform some processing that partially handles the exception, and then throw the exception again so another exception handler can finish handling the exception. In this case, the ToDecimal() method is used within a try block to convert the value the user enters into a text box to a decimal. If the user enters a value that's not a valid decimal, a FormatException is thrown. Then, the catch block catches this exception, moves the focus to the text box, and rethrows the exception. That way, the calling method can also catch the exception and perform some additional processing.

With C# 7.0 and later, you can also throw an exception using a *throw expression*. Throw expressions are written just like throw statements, but they can be used in some contexts where throw statements can't be used. For example, they can be used in a null-coalescing expression as shown in the last example in this figure. They can also be used in conditional expressions like the ones you

The syntax for throwing a new exception

```
throw new ExceptionClass([message]);
```

The syntax for throwing an existing exception

```
throw exceptionName;
```

A method that throws an exception when an exceptional condition occurs

```
private decimal CalculateFutureValue(decimal monthlyInvestment,
        decimal monthlyInterestRate, int months) {
    if (monthlyInvestment <= 0)
        throw new Exception("Monthly Investment must be greater than 0.");
    if (monthlyInterestRate <= 0)
        throw new Exception("Interest Rate must be greater than 0.");
    ...
}
```

Code that throws an exception for testing purposes

```
try {
    decimal subtotal = Convert.ToDecimal(txtSubtotal.Text);
    throw new Exception("An unknown exception occurred.");
}
catch (Exception ex) {
    MessageBox.Show(ex.Message + "\n\n"
        + ex.GetType().ToString() + "\n"
        + ex.StackTrace, "Exception");
}
```

Code that rethrows an exception

```
try {
    Convert.ToDecimal(txtSubtotal.Text);
}
catch (FormatException fe) {
    txtSubtotal.Focus();
    throw fe;
}
```

Code that uses a throw expression to throw an exception (C# 7.0 or later)

```
string? productCode = null;
string code = productCode ?? throw new Exception("Code cannot be null.");
```

When to throw an exception

- When a method encounters a situation where it isn't able to complete its task.

- When you want to generate an exception to test an exception handler.

- When you want to catch the exception, perform some processing, and then throw the exception again.

Description

- You can use a *throw statement* or a *throw expression* to throw a new or existing exception. When you create a new exception, you can specify a string that's assigned to the Message property.

- Throw expressions became available with C# 7.0 and can be used in some contexts where throw statements can't, such as in conditional and null-coalescing expressions.

Figure 7-6   How to throw an exception

learned about in chapter 5, expression-bodied methods like the ones you learned about in chapter 6, and in other lambda expressions like the ones you'll learn about later in this book.

The Future Value app with exception handling

Figure 7-7 presents an improved version of the Future Value app you saw in the last chapter. This version uses structured exception handling to catch any exceptions that might be thrown when the user clicks the Calculate button on the form.

To catch exceptions, all of the statements in the btnCalculate_Click() method are coded within a try block. Then, the first catch block handles any format exceptions that are thrown if the user enters data with an invalid numeric format in one of the text boxes. Next, the second catch block handles any overflow exceptions that are thrown if the user enters numbers that are too large. If either of these exceptions is thrown, the code in the catch block displays a dialog that describes the exception and indicates a corrective action that the user can take.

While the first two catch blocks catch specific exceptions, the third catch block catches all other exceptions. Since the cause of these exceptions isn't known, the app uses the properties and methods of the exception to display some information about the exception in a dialog. In this case, the name of the exception class is displayed in the title bar of the dialog, and a brief description of the exception is displayed in the body of the dialog. That way, the user will be able to provide some information about the exception to the person who is going to fix the bug.

Note that the third catch block can't use e as the name of the exception because e is used for the EventArgs parameter. Instead, this catch block uses ex as the name of the Exception object.

Note also that if an exception occurs in the CalculateFutureValue() method, the exception isn't caught by that method. As a result, the exception is passed back to the calling method, in this case, btnCalculate_Click(). Then, the appropriate catch block in that method handles the exception.

The code for the Future Value app with exception handling

```csharp
private void btnCalculate_Click(object sender, EventArgs e)
{
    try
    {
        decimal monthlyInvestment =
            Convert.ToDecimal(txtMonthlyInvestment.Text);
        decimal yearlyInterestRate =
            Convert.ToDecimal(txtInterestRate.Text);
        int years = Convert.ToInt32(txtYears.Text);

        decimal monthlyInterestRate = yearlyInterestRate / 12 / 100;
        int months = years * 12;

        decimal futureValue = CalculateFutureValue(
            monthlyInvestment, monthlyInterestRate, months);
        txtFutureValue.Text = futureValue.ToString("c");
        txtMonthlyInvestment.Focus();
    }
    catch(FormatException)
    {
        MessageBox.Show(
            "Invalid numeric format. Please check all entries.",
            "Entry Error");
    }
    catch(OverflowException)
    {
        MessageBox.Show(
            "Overflow error. Please enter smaller values.",
            "Entry Error");
    }
    catch(Exception ex)
    {
        MessageBox.Show(
            ex.Message,
            ex.GetType().ToString());
    }
}

private decimal CalculateFutureValue(decimal monthlyInvestment,
    decimal monthlyInterestRate, int months)
{
    decimal futureValue = 0m;
    for (int i = 0; i < months; i++)
    {
        futureValue = (futureValue + monthlyInvestment)
                    * (1 + monthlyInterestRate);
    }

    return futureValue;
}
```

Figure 7-7   The Future Value app with exception handling

How to validate data

When a user enters data, that data usually needs to be checked to make sure that it's valid. This is known as *data validation*. When an entry is invalid, the app needs to display an error message and give the user another chance to enter valid data. This needs to be repeated until all the entries on the form are valid.

How to validate a single entry

When a user enters text into a text box, you may want to perform several types of data validation. In particular, it's common to perform the three types of data validation shown in figure 7-8.

First, if the app requires that the user enters a value into a text box, you can check the Text property of the text box to make sure the user has entered one or more characters. Second, if the app requires that the user enters a number in the text box, you can use the TryParse() method of the appropriate class within an if statement to check that the Text property of the text box can be converted to the appropriate numeric data type. Notice here that a discard is used for the out argument, since its value isn't needed by this code. Third, if the app requires that the user enters a number within a specified range, you can use if-else statements to check that the number falls within that range. This is known as *range checking*.

In the examples shown here, all three types of validation are performed on the Monthly Investment text box. Because this text box requires a numeric entry, however, you should know that you could accomplish the same validation without testing if the Text property of the control is equal to an empty string. That's because, when you test for a valid decimal format, it will detect if no value was entered. Because of that, you'll typically test the Text property only if a string entry is required.

Although this figure only shows how to check data that the user has entered into a text box, the same principles apply to other types of controls. In chapter 10, you'll learn more about validating entries made in other types of controls. In addition, although this figure only shows how to check the range of a number, you can also check strings and dates to make sure that they fall within certain ranges. You'll learn more about working with dates and strings in chapter 9.

Often, the code that performs the data validation prevents exceptions from being thrown. For example, if the user doesn't enter a value in the Monthly Investment text box, the code in this figure displays a dialog and moves the focus to the Monthly Investment text box. If you didn't include this code, an exception would occur when the app tried to convert the empty string to a numeric data type.

Code that checks that an entry has been made

```
if (txtMonthlyInvestment.Text == "")
{
    MessageBox.Show(
        "Monthly Investment is a required field.", "Entry Error");
    txtMonthlyInvestment.Focus();
}
```

Code that checks an entry for a valid decimal value

```
if (!(Decimal.TryParse(txtMonthlyInvestment.Text, out _)))
{
    MessageBox.Show(
        "Monthly Investment must be a valid decimal value.", "Entry Error");
    txtMonthlyInvestment.Focus();
}
```

Code that checks an entry for a valid range

```
decimal monthlyInvestment = Convert.ToDecimal(txtMonthlyInvestment.Text);
if (monthlyInvestment <= 0)
{
    MessageBox.Show(
        "Monthly Investment must be greater than 0.", "Entry Error");
    txtMonthlyInvestment.Focus();
}
else if (monthlyInvestment >= 1000)
{
    MessageBox.Show(
        "Monthly Investment must be less than 1,000.", "Entry Error");
    txtMonthlyInvestment.Focus();
}
```

Description

- When a user enters data, that data usually needs to be checked to make sure that it is valid. This is known as *data validation*.

- When an entry is invalid, the program needs to display an error message and give the user another chance to enter valid data.

- Three common types of validity checking are (1) to make sure that a required entry has been made, (2) to make sure that an entry has a valid numeric format, and (3) to make sure that an entry is within a valid range (known as *range checking*).

- To test whether a value has been entered into a text box, you can check whether the Text property of the box is equal to an empty string.

- To test whether a text box contains valid numeric data, you can code an if statement with a condition that tests if a TryParse() method that converts the data is successful.

- To test whether a value is within an acceptable range, you can use if-else statements.

Figure 7-8   How to validate a single entry

How to code generic methods for data validation

Since it's common to check entries for valid data, it often makes sense to create generic methods like the ones shown in figure 7-9 for data validation. These methods perform the same types of validation described in the previous figure, but they work for any entry instead of a specific text box. That includes entries on non-Windows forms, since these methods don't require the Windows. Forms namespace. In this chapter, of course, these methods are coded within a Windows form, so they could use this namespace. In a real-world app, though, methods like these would be coded in a separate class and stored in a class library. You'll learn how to code classes like this in chapter 12, and you'll learn how to create and use class libraries in chapter 16.

In this figure, the IsPresent() method checks that the user has entered a value. To do that, it accepts two parameters that contain the value to be validated and a name that describes the value. This method starts by setting a variable named msg to an empty string. Then, if the user hasn't entered any characters into the text box, it adds a message to the msg variable that includes the name parameter. Finally, it returns the value of the msg variable.

The IsDecimal() method accepts the same parameters as the IsPresent() method, but it uses an if statement that calls the TryParse() method of the Decimal class to check if the value entered by the user is a decimal value. If it isn't, the TryParse() method will return a false value and a message will be added to the msg variable. Then, the method returns the value of this variable.

Once you understand how the IsDecimal() method works, you can code methods for other numeric types. For example, you can code an IsInt32() method that uses the Int32.TryParse() method to check if the user has entered a valid int value.

The IsWithinRange() method accepts two additional parameters that contain the minimum and maximum values that can be entered into the text box. Before it checks the range, it calls the TryParse() method of the Decimal class to be sure the value is numeric. You'll see why that's necessary when you see the code that calls these methods in the next figure. If the value is numeric, the IsWithinRange() method uses an if statement to check if the decimal value is within the range specified by the min and max parameters. If not, this method adds a message to the msg variable and returns the value of this variable.

Since the IsWithinRange() method uses the decimal type, which is the widest (most accurate) numeric data type, this method works with all numeric types. That's because all numeric types can be automatically cast to the decimal type. If, for example, you pass arguments of the int type to the min and max parameters, they will be cast to the decimal type.

A method that checks for a required field

```
private string IsPresent(string value, string name)
{
    string msg = "";
    if (value == "")
    {
        msg = name + " is a required field.\n";
    }
    return msg;
}
```

A method that checks for a valid numeric format

```
private string IsDecimal(string value, string name)
{
    string msg = "";
    if (!Decimal.TryParse(value, out _))
    {
        msg = name + " must be a valid decimal value.\n";
    }
    return msg;
}
```

A method that checks for a valid numeric range

```
private string IsWithinRange(string value, string name, decimal min,
    decimal max)
{
    string msg = "";
    if (Decimal.TryParse(value, out decimal number))
    {
        if (number < min || number > max)
        {
            msg = name + " must be between " + min + " and " + max + ".\n";
        }
    }
    return msg;
}
```

Description

- Since it's common to need to check text boxes for valid data, it often makes sense to create generic methods like these for data validation.

- These methods can be used to validate entries on Windows and non-Windows forms, since they don't require the Windows.Forms namespace. Then, you can code them in a separate class as shown in chapter 12, and you can store the class in a class library as shown in chapter 16.

Figure 7-9   How to code generic methods for data validation

How to validate multiple entries

Figure 7-10 shows how to code a method named IsValidData() that validates multiple entries on a form. The method shown here validates the Monthly Investment and Interest Rate text boxes on the Future Value form using the IsDecimal() and IsWithinRange() methods you saw in figure 7-9. In addition, it uses the IsWithinRange() method and a method named IsInt32() to validate the Years text box. The IsInt32() method works similarly to the IsDecimal() method, but it checks for an integer value using the TryParse() method of the Int32 class. Because this method checks every entry on the form for validity, all the validation code is in one location, which makes the code easy to read and maintain.

This code starts by declaring two variables named success and errorMessage. The success variable is a Boolean that will be used to determine if the validation is successful. The errorMessage variable is a string that will store any error messages to be displayed.

Next, this method calls the IsDecimal() method and passes the Text property of the Monthly Investment text box and a string that describes the text box as arguments. This string is included in any error messages that the method creates.

If the Text property doesn't contain a decimal value, the error message that's returned by the IsDecimal() method is appended to the errorMessage variable. Then, the IsValidData() method calls the IsWithinRange() method to make sure that the value is greater than or equal to 1 and less than or equal to 1000. Remember that the IsWithinRange() method starts by checking if the value is a valid decimal, and it doesn't check the range if it isn't. Although that means that the value is checked twice to be sure it's a decimal, this prevents an exception from being thrown when the range is checked.

The IsValidData() method uses similar code to validate the Interest Rate and Years text boxes. Then, it checks the errorMessage variable to see if any of the validation methods returned an error. If they did, the success variable is set to false and a dialog like the one at the top of this figure is displayed. This method ends by passing the success variable to the calling method.

A dialog that displays three error messages

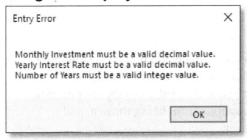

Entry Error   ×

Monthly Investment must be a valid decimal value.
Yearly Interest Rate must be a valid decimal value.
Number of Years must be a valid integer value.

OK

Code that validates multiple entries

```
private bool IsValidData()
{
    bool success = true;
    string errorMessage = "";

    // Validate the Monthly Investment text box
    errorMessage += IsDecimal(txtMonthlyInvestment.Text,
                            "Monthly Investment");
    errorMessage += IsWithinRange(txtMonthlyInvestment.Text,
                                "Monthly Investment", 1, 1000);

    // Validate the Yearly Interest Rate text box
    errorMessage += IsDecimal(txtInterestRate.Text,
                            "Yearly Interest Rate");
    errorMessage += IsWithinRange(txtInterestRate.Text,
                                "Yearly Interest Rate", 1, 20);

    // Validate the Number of Years text box
    errorMessage += IsInt32(txtYears.Text, "Number of Years");
    errorMessage += IsWithinRange(txtYears.Text, "Number of Years", 1, 40);

    if (errorMessage != "")
    {
        success = false;
        MessageBox.Show(errorMessage, "Entry Error");
    }
    return success;
}
```

Description

- You can use the validation methods shown in the previous figures to validate multiple entries. Then, if any of the entries are invalid, you can display a dialog that describes the errors.

Figure 7-10   How to validate multiple entries

The Future Value app
with data validation

In figure 7-7, you saw a version of the Future Value app that used structured exception handling to catch all exceptions that might be thrown. Now, you'll see an improved version of this app that includes code that validates the user entries. This code prevents format and overflow exceptions from being thrown, and it provides more descriptive messages to the user.

The dialogs

Figure 7-11 shows the Future Value app after the user has entered invalid data in all three fields. Then, it shows the dialog that's displayed to identify those errors. Here, you can see that the monthly investment is outside the valid range, the yearly interest rate is invalid because it includes a percent sign, and the number of years is invalid because the user didn't enter a value.

The last dialog is displayed if an exception that hasn't been anticipated is thrown. To test this dialog, you can code a throw statement within the code for the Future Value app as shown in figure 7-6.

The code

Figure 7-12 shows the code for this version of the Future Value app. To start, the btnCalculate_Click() method contains an exception handler that catches and handles any unanticipated exceptions. Within the try block, an if statement checks whether the IsValidData() method returns a true value. If it does, the future value is calculated and displayed. Otherwise, none of the statements within the if block are executed. However, the IsValidData() method will display a dialog with appropriate messages. Because this method is identical to the one you saw in the previous figure, you shouldn't have any trouble understanding how it works.

Each method in this app performs a specific task. For example, the btnCalculate_Click() method contains the code that gets the values from the form and displays values on the form. The IsValidData(), IsDecimal(), IsInt32(), and IsWithinRange() methods contain the code that validates the data that's entered by the user. And the CalculateFutureValue() method contains the code that performs the calculation. This is a good design because it leads to code that's reusable and easy to maintain.

However, this code could be more efficient. For example, if the user enters a valid decimal value in the Monthly Investment text box, the value is converted to a decimal three times: once by the IsDecimal() method, once by the IsWithinRange() method, and once by the btnCalculate_Click() method. For most apps, however, the benefits that result from being able to reuse and easily maintain this code far outweigh any performance issues.

The Future Value form with three invalid fields

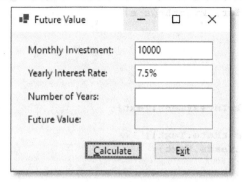

The dialog that displays the errors

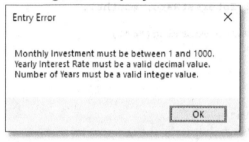

The dialog for an unanticipated exception

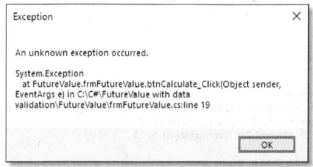

Description

- The first dialog is displayed if the user enters invalid data, such as invalid decimal or integer values or values outside the range specified by the app.
- The second dialog is displayed if an unanticipated exception occurs.

Figure 7-11   The dialogs of the Future Value app

The code for the Future Value app   Page 1

```csharp
private void btnCalculate_Click(object sender, EventArgs e)
{
    try
    {
        if (IsValidData())
        {
            decimal monthlyInvestment =
                Convert.ToDecimal(txtMonthlyInvestment.Text);
            decimal yearlyInterestRate =
                Convert.ToDecimal(txtInterestRate.Text);
            int years = Convert.ToInt32(txtYears.Text);

            int months = years * 12;
            decimal monthlyInterestRate = yearlyInterestRate / 12 / 100;
            decimal futureValue = CalculateFutureValue(
                monthlyInvestment, monthlyInterestRate, months);

            txtFutureValue.Text = futureValue.ToString("c");
            txtMonthlyInvestment.Focus();
        }
    }
    catch(Exception ex)
    {
        MessageBox.Show(ex.Message + "\n\n" +
            ex.GetType().ToString() + "\n" +
            ex.StackTrace, "Exception");
    }
}

private bool IsValidData()
{
    bool success = true;
    string errorMessage = "";

    // Validate the Monthly Investment text box
    errorMessage += IsDecimal(txtMonthlyInvestment.Text, "Monthly Investment");
    errorMessage += IsWithinRange(txtMonthlyInvestment.Text,
                            "Monthly Investment", 1, 1000);

    // Validate the Yearly Interest Rate text box
    errorMessage += IsDecimal(txtInterestRate.Text,
                            "Yearly Interest Rate");
    errorMessage += IsWithinRange(txtInterestRate.Text,
                            "Yearly Interest Rate", 1, 20);

    // Validate the Number of Years text box
    errorMessage += IsInt32(txtYears.Text, "Number of Years");
    errorMessage += IsWithinRange(txtYears.Text, "Number of Years", 1, 40);

    if (errorMessage != "")
    {
        success = false;
        MessageBox.Show(errorMessage, "Entry Error");
    }
    return success;
}
```

Figure 7-12   The code for the Future Value app (part 1 of 2)

The code for the Future Value app   **Page 2**

```
private string IsDecimal(string value, string name)
{
    string msg = "";
    if (!Decimal.TryParse(value, out _))
    {
        msg = name + " must be a valid decimal value.\n";
    }
    return msg;
}

private string IsInt32(string value, string name)
{
    string msg = "";
    if (!Int32.TryParse(value, out _))
    {
        msg = name + " must be a valid integer value.\n";
    }
    return msg;
}

private string IsWithinRange(string value, string name, decimal min,
    decimal max)
{
    string msg = "";
    if (Decimal.TryParse(value, out decimal number))
    {
        if (number < min || number > max)
        {
            msg = name + " must be between " + min + " and " + max + ".\n";
        }
    }
    return msg;
}

private decimal CalculateFutureValue(decimal monthlyInvestment,
    decimal monthlyInterestRate, int months)
{
    decimal futureValue = 0m;
    for (int i = 0; i < months; i++)
    {
        futureValue = (futureValue + monthlyInvestment)
                    * (1 + monthlyInterestRate);
    }
    return futureValue;
}
```

Figure 7-12   The code for the Future Value app (part 2 of 2)

Perspective

In this chapter, you learned how to handle exceptions and validate data so you can code apps that are "bulletproof." This means that your apps won't throw unhandled exceptions no matter what data the user enters or how the user works with the user interface. This is an essential feature of any professional app.

But there's still a lot more for you to learn about the C# language. So, in chapter 8, you'll learn how to work with arrays and collections. In chapter 9, you'll learn how to work with dates, and you'll learn more about working with strings. And in chapter 10, you'll learn how to develop forms that use other types of controls. When you finish these chapters, you'll be able to develop apps of considerable complexity.

Terms

exception	try block
throw an exception	catch block
catch an exception	stack trace
exception handling	finally block
subclass	throw statement
structured exception handling	data validation
try-catch statement	range checking
exception handler	

Exercise 7-1   Enhance the Invoice Total app

This exercise guides you through the process of enhancing the Invoice Total app so it catches any runtime errors and validates the Subtotal entry.

1. Open the app that's in the C:\C#\Ch07\InvoiceTotal directory. This is the version that you worked on in chapter 4.

2. Add a try-catch statement to the btnCalculate_Click() method so it catches any exception that the ToDecimal() method of the Convert class might throw. The catch block should display a dialog like the one in figure 7-2. Then, test the app to make sure this works correctly.

3. Add code to the try block that checks that the user enters a value in the Subtotal text box. If a value isn't entered, display a dialog with a message indicating that Subtotal is a required field. Then, test this enhancement.

4. Add code to the try block that range checks the user entry so it's greater than zero and less than 10,000. If it isn't, display a dialog that specifies the acceptable range. Then, test this enhancement. When you're satisfied that the app works correctly, close it.

Exercise 7-2   Enhance the Future Value app

This exercise guides you through the process of enhancing the Future Value app that you worked on in chapter 6.

1. Open the app that's in the C:\C#\Ch07\FutureValue directory.

2. Add a try-catch statement to the btnCalculate_Click() method that catches and handles any FormatException or OverflowException that might occur. These catch blocks should display dialogs with appropriate messages. Then, test these enhancements.

3. Add another catch block to the try-catch statement that will catch any other exception that might occur. This catch block should display a dialog that displays the message contained in the exception object, along with the exception type and the stack trace.

4. Add a throw statement before the return statement in the CalculateFuture-Value() method that throws a new exception of the Exception class regardless of the result of the calculation. This statement will be used to test the enhancements of step 3, and it should specify a generic message that indicates an unknown error. Then, test the app by entering valid values in the three text boxes and clicking the Calculate button. If the exception is thrown and the last catch block works correctly, end the app and comment out the throw statement.

5. Code three generic validation methods named IsDecimal(), IsInt32(), and IsWithinRange() that test whether a text box contains a valid decimal value, a valid int value, and a value within a given range. If the validation is unsuccessful, each method should return an error message that includes the name of the text box that's being validated. If you need help in coding these methods, you can refer to figure 7-9.

6. Code an IsValidData() method that calls the three generic methods you created in step 5 to validate the data the user enters into the three text boxes. Each text box should be tested for two types of invalid data: (1) invalid format and (2) invalid range. If any errors occur, a dialog should be displayed with those errors. Also, be sure this method returns a Boolean value indicating if the validation was successful.

7. Modify the code in the event handler for the Calculate button so it uses the IsValidData() method to validate the data before it processes it. Then, test the app to be sure it works correctly. If it does, end the app and comment out the FormatException and OverflowException catch blocks since these exceptions are now prevented by the data validation.

8. Do a final test of the app, and then close it.

8

How to use arrays and collections

Arrays and collections are objects that act as containers. As you develop C# apps, you'll find many uses for arrays and collections. For example, you can use a sales array or a sales collection to hold the sales amounts for each of the 12 months of the year. Then, you can use that array or collection to perform calculations on those amounts. In this chapter, you'll learn the basic concepts and techniques for working with arrays and collections.

How to work with one-dimensional arrays

You can use an *array* to store a set of related data. Since a one-dimensional array is the simplest type of array, you'll start by learning how to create and use one-dimensional arrays.

How to create an array

To create a *one-dimensional array*, you use the syntax shown in figure 8-1. As you can see, you can create an array using either one or two statements. This is similar to the techniques you use to declare variables, except that you code square brackets after the data type to indicate that the variable refers to an array. Within the second set of brackets, you code a number that indicates the *length*, or *size*, of the array. This specifies the number of elements that the array can hold.

Notice that you also use the new keyword to create an array. That's because, as you'll learn later in this chapter, arrays are created from the Array class that's provided by .NET. So, when you create an array, you're creating an instance of this class.

When you create an array, each *element* in the array is initialized to a default value. This value depends on the data type of the array as indicated by the table in this figure. Specifically, numeric types are set to zero, char types are set to the null character, Boolean types are set to false, DateTime types are set to 12:00:00 AM on January 1, 0001, and reference types are set to null. In the next figure, you'll learn how to assign new values to the elements of an array.

In most cases, all the elements in an array will contain the same type of data, and you'll declare the array with that data type. However, if you don't know what type of data an array will contain, you can declare it with the object data type. Then, each element can contain data of any type.

The syntax for creating a one-dimensional array

With two statements
```
type[] arrayName;                      // declaration statement
arrayName = new type[arrayLength];     // assignment statement
```

With one statement
```
type[] arrayName = new type[arrayLength];
```

Examples that create an array of decimal types

With two statements
```
decimal[] totals;
totals = new decimal[4];
```

With one statement
```
decimal[] totals = new decimal[4];
```

Other examples

An array of strings
```
string[] description = new string[3];
```

Two arrays in one statement
```
const int MaxCount = 100;
decimal[] prices = new decimal[MaxCount],
          discountPercentages = new decimal[MaxCount];
```

Default values for array elements

Data type	Default value
numeric	**0** (zero)
char	**'\0'** (the null character)
Boolean	**false**
DateTime	**01/01/0001 00:00:00**
reference types	**null**

Description

- An *array* can store one or more *elements*. The *length*, or *size*, of an array is the number of elements in the array.

- When you create an array, each element of the array is set to a default value. If the array contains value types, each element is set to the value shown above. If the array contains reference types, each element is set to null.

Figure 8-1   How to create an array

How to assign values to the elements of an array

Figure 8-2 shows how to assign values to the elements of an array. As the syntax at the top of this figure indicates, you refer to an element in an array by coding the array name followed by its *index* in brackets. The index that you specify must be from 0, which refers to the first element in the array, to the *upper bound* of the array, which is one less than the length of the array.

To understand how this works, take a look at the first example in this figure. This example declares an array of decimals that contains four elements. Then, it uses indexes 0 through 3 to assign values to those four elements. Here, the length of the array is 4, and the upper bound of the array is 3. Note that if you use an index that's greater than the upper bound, an IndexOutOfRangeException will be thrown.

The syntax and examples at the bottom of this figure show how to declare an array and assign values to its elements in a single statement. Here, you start the array declaration as before, but you code a list of values in braces after the declaration. Notice that when you use this technique, you can omit the new keyword and the type and length specification. Then, C# automatically sets the length of the array to the number of elements within the braces. If you include the data type and length specification, however, they must match the list of values you provide.

The next three statements show how this works. The first statement creates the same array as the first example in this figure. Notice that this statement specifies the data type and length of the array. The second statement creates the same array, but the data type and length are omitted. Finally, the third statement creates the same array of strings that was created by the second example in this figure. Like the second statement, the data type and length are omitted from this statement.

You may remember from chapter 4 that you can use the var keyword to declare a variable that infers its type from the value that's assigned to it. You can also use the var keyword with an array, as illustrated in the last statement in this figure. This statement creates an array that contains four int values.

Although we recommend that you specify the type of an array whenever possible, you should notice three differences in how this statement is coded in case you ever want to use this technique. First, you don't code square brackets following the var keyword like you do when you specify a type. Second, you must include the new keyword followed by square brackets on the assignment statement. And third, you must not specify the length of the array within the square brackets.

The syntax for referring to an element of an array

```
arrayName[index]
```

Examples that assign values by accessing each element

Code that assigns values to an array of decimal types

```
decimal[] totals = new decimal[4];
totals[0] = 14.95m;
totals[1] = 12.95m;
totals[2] = 11.95m;
totals[3] = 9.95m;
//totals[4] = 8.95m;    // this would throw an IndexOutOfRangeException
```

Code that assigns objects to an array of strings

```
string[] names = new string[3];
names[0] = "Ted Lewis";
names[1] = "Sue Jones";
names[2] = "Ray Thomas";
```

The syntax for creating an array and assigning values in one statement

```
type[] arrayName = [new type[length]] {value1[, value2][, value3]...};
```

Examples that create an array and assign values in one statement

```
decimal[] totals = new decimal[4] {14.95m, 12.95m, 11.95m, 9.95m};
decimal[] totals = {14.95m, 12.95m, 11.95m, 9.95m};
string[] names = {"Ted Lewis", "Sue Jones", "Ray Thomas"};
```

A statement that creates an array whose type is inferred from its values

```
var grades = new[] {95, 89, 91, 98};
```

Description

- To refer to the elements in an array, you use an *index* where 0 is the first element, 1 is the second element, 2 is the third element, and so on. The index of the last element in an array is known as the *upper bound*.

- If you list the values to be assigned to an array without using the new keyword to create the array, an array is created with a length equal to the number of values in the list. If you use the new keyword with a list of values, the length you specify for the array must match the number of values in the list, and the values must match the type you specify.

- You can also create an array without specifying a data type. To do that, you use the var keyword. Then, the data type is inferred from the values that are assigned to the array. When you use this technique, you must not code square brackets following the var keyword, you must code the new keyword followed by square brackets, and you must not specify a length.

- If you specify an index that's less than zero or greater than the upper bound of an array, an IndexOutOfRangeException will be thrown when the statement is executed.

Figure 8-2   How to assign values to the elements of an array

How to work with arrays

Now that you understand how to declare an array and assign values to its elements, you're ready to learn how to work with the values in an array. Figure 8-3 presents some of the basic techniques for doing that.

This figure starts by presenting the Length property of an array, which gets the number of elements in the array. You'll use this property frequently as you work with arrays.

The first example in this figure shows how to get the values from an array and calculate the average value of the elements. Here, the first statement declares a totals array that contains four decimal values. Then, the second statement sets the sum variable equal to the sum of the four elements in the array. Finally, the third statement computes the average value of these elements by dividing the sum by the Length property of the array, which contains a value of four.

The second example uses a for loop to put the numbers 0 through 9 into an array. Here, the first statement declares an array named numbers that contains 10 int values. Then, the for loop assigns the value of the loop's counter to each of the elements in the array.

The third example uses a for loop to display the elements of the numbers array in a dialog. Here, the first statement declares a string variable. Then, the for loop accesses each element of the numbers array and appends the number and a space to the string variable. When the for loop finishes, the next statement displays the string that contains the numbers in a dialog.

The fourth example shows how to use a loop to calculate the average value of the elements in the totals array. Here, the first statement declares the sum variable. Then, the for loop gets the value of each element of the array and adds that value to the current value of the sum variable. After the loop, the next statement uses the sum variable and the Length property of the array to calculate the average. If you compare this code to the code in the first example, you'll see that they both accomplish the same task. However, the code in this example will work equally well whether the totals array contains 4 or 400 values. As a result, it usually makes sense to use loops when working with arrays.

The last example shows how to display the elements of the totals array, along with the sum and average for the array, in a dialog. Like the third example, this one uses a for loop to format the values in the array as a string. Then, it displays the string and the sum and average values in a dialog.

The syntax for using the Length property of an array

```
arrayName.Length
```

Code that computes the average of an array of totals

```
decimal[] totals = {14.95m, 12.95m, 11.95m, 9.95m};
decimal sum = totals[0] + totals[1] + totals[2] + totals[3];
decimal average = sum/totals.Length;
```

Code that puts the numbers 0 through 9 into an array

```
int[] numbers = new int[10];
for (int i = 0; i < numbers.Length; i++)
    numbers[i] = i;
```

Code that displays the numbers array in a dialog

```
string numbersString = "";
for (int i = 0; i < numbers.Length; i++)
    numbersString += numbers[i] + " ";
MessageBox.Show(numbersString, "Numbers Test");
```

Code that uses a for loop to compute the average of the totals array

```
decimal sum = 0.0m;
for (int i = 0; i < totals.Length; i++)
    sum += totals[i];
decimal average = sum/totals.Length;
```

Code that displays the totals array in a dialog

```
string totalsString = "";
for (int i = 0; i < totals.Length; i++)
    totalsString += totals[i] + "\n";
MessageBox.Show("The totals are:\n" +
    totalsString + "\n" +
    "Sum: " + sum + "\n" +
    "Average: " + average, "Totals Test");
```

Figure 8-3   How to work with arrays

How to use foreach loops to work with arrays

Although you can use for loops to work with the elements of an array, it's often easier to use a *foreach statement* to code a *foreach loop*. Figure 8-4 shows how to do that.

To code a foreach loop, you begin by coding the foreach keyword followed by a set of parentheses. Within the parentheses, you code the data type of the elements in the array, the name you want to use to access the elements, the in keyword, and the name of the array. You can also code the var keyword in place of the data type, in which case the type is inferred from the type of the array.

Next, you can code one or more statements that use the element name to work with an element. If the foreach loop contains two or more statements, you must code braces around them. Otherwise, you can omit the braces.

When a foreach loop is executed, its statements are executed once for each element in the array. For instance, the first example in this figure shows how you can use a foreach loop to display the elements in the numbers array that you saw in the previous figure. Similarly, the second example computes the average of the totals array, and the third example displays the elements in the totals array.

If you compare these examples to the for loop examples in the previous figure, you'll see that foreach loops are less complicated. In particular, when you use a foreach loop, you don't need to use a counter variable, and you don't need to use an index to get an element from the array. As a result, it's often easier to use a foreach loop than a for loop.

You should realize, however, that there are still times when you'll need to use a for loop to work with an array. For example, if you only want to access some of the elements in an array, you'll need to use a for loop. You'll also need to use a for loop if you want to use a counter variable to assign values to the elements of the array as shown in the second example in figure 8-3.

The syntax of a foreach loop

```
foreach (type elementName in arrayName)
{
    statements
}
```

Code that displays the numbers array in a dialog

```
string numbersString = "";
foreach (int number in numbers)
{
    numbersString += number + " ";
}
MessageBox.Show(numbersString, "Numbers Test");
```

Code that computes the average of the totals array

```
decimal sum = 0.0m;
foreach (decimal total in totals)
    sum += total;
decimal average = sum/totals.Length;
```

Code that displays the totals array in a dialog

```
string totalsString = "";
foreach (decimal total in totals)
    totalsString += total + "\n";
MessageBox.Show("The totals are:\n" +
    totalsString + "\n" +
    "Sum: " + sum + "\n" +
    "Average: " + average,
    "Totals Test");
```

Description

- You can use a *foreach loop* to access each element of an array. You can also use foreach loops to work with collections like the ones you'll learn about later in this chapter.

Figure 8-4   How to use foreach loops to work with arrays

How to work with rectangular arrays

So far, this chapter has shown how to work with an array that uses one index to store elements in a one-dimensional array. Now, you'll learn how to work with rectangular arrays that use two indexes. You can think of a *rectangular array* as a table that has rows and columns. Since rectangular arrays store data in two dimensions, they're also known as *two-dimensional arrays*.

Although it's possible to create arrays that contain more than two dimensions, that's rarely necessary. However, if you do need to use an array that has three or more dimensions, you can extend the two-dimensional techniques that you'll learn next.

How to create a rectangular array

Figure 8-5 shows how to create a rectangular array. To do that, you code a comma within the set of brackets that follows the data type declaration. This indicates that the array will have two dimensions. Then, when you use the new keyword to create the array, you specify the number of rows in the array, followed by a comma, followed by the number of columns in the array.

The first example in this figure creates a rectangular array of integers. In this case, the array has three rows and two columns. After this statement executes, each element in the array will be assigned the default value of 0 as described in figure 8-1.

How to assign values to a rectangular array

After you create an array, you can assign values to it. To do that, you refer to each element of the array using its row and column index. This is illustrated by the table of index values shown in figure 8-5. Because this array consists of four rows and four columns, the index values range from 0,0 to 3,3.

To assign values to the elements of a rectangular array, you can code one statement for each element as shown in the second example. These statements assign values to the elements of the numbers array that was created by the first statement in this figure.

You can also assign values to a rectangular array when you declare it, as illustrated by the third, fourth, and fifth examples. Here, the third example creates the numbers array and assigns values to it by coding three sets of braces within an outer set of braces. The three inner braces represent the three rows in the array, and the values in these braces are assigned to the two columns in each row. The fourth example works the same except that it uses string objects instead of int values. The fifth example also creates a string array, but it infers the data type from the specified values. Because of that, it uses the new keyword.

How to create a rectangular array

The syntax for creating a rectangular array

```
type[,] arrayName = new type[rowCount,columnCount];
```

A statement that creates a 3x2 array

```
int[,] numbers = new int[3,2];
```

How to assign values to a rectangular array

The syntax for referring to an element of a rectangular array

```
arrayName[rowIndex, columnIndex]
```

The index values for the elements of a 4x4 rectangular array

```
0,0    0,1    0,2    0,3
1,0    1,1    1,2    1,3
2,0    2,1    2,2    2,3
3,0    3,1    3,2    3,3
```

Code that assigns values to the numbers array

```
numbers[0,0] = 1;
numbers[0,1] = 2;
numbers[1,0] = 3;
numbers[1,1] = 4;
numbers[2,0] = 5;
numbers[2,1] = 6;
```

Code that creates a 3x2 array and assigns values with one statement

```
int[,] numbers = { {1,2}, {3,4}, {5,6} };
```

Code that creates and assigns values to a 3x2 array of strings

```
string[,] products =
    {{"C#", "Murach's C#"},
     {"JAVA", "Murach's Java Programming"},
     {"ASPMVC", "Murach's ASP.NET MVC"}};
```

Another way to create the array of strings

```
var products = new[,]
    {{"C#", "Murach's C#"},
     {"JAVA", "Murach's Java Programming"},
     {"ASPMVC", "Murach's ASP.NET MVC"}};
```

Description

- A *rectangular array* uses two indexes to store data. You can think of this type of array as a table that has rows and columns. Rectangular arrays are sometimes referred to as *two-dimensional arrays*.

- Although it's rarely necessary, you can extend this two-dimensional syntax to work with arrays that have more than two dimensions.

Figure 8-5   How to create a rectangular array and assign values to its elements

How to work with rectangular arrays

Figure 8-6 presents some examples that show how to work with rectangular arrays. The first example shows how to use the GetLength() method to get the number of elements in a dimension of an array. Here, the first statement gets the number of rows in the numbers array by calling the GetLength() method and specifying 0 to get the length of the first dimension. Then, the second statement gets the number of columns in the array by calling the GetLength() method and specifying 1 to get the length of the second dimension. Finally, the third statement uses indexes to get the values from both elements in the first row of the array and add them together.

The second example shows how to use nested for loops to display the elements of a rectangular array in a dialog. In this case, the elements of the numbers array you saw in figure 8-5 are displayed. As you can see, the outer for loop uses a counter variable to cycle through the rows in the array. To determine the number of rows in the array, this loop uses the GetLength() method. Then, the inner for loop uses another counter variable to cycle through each column of each row in the array. Just like the outer for loop, the inner for loop uses the GetLength() method to determine the number of columns in the array.

To display the value of each element, the statement within the inner for loop uses both counter variables to get the value of the element and append it to a string. Each element is also separated from the next element by a space. Then, after each row is processed by the inner loop, a new line character is appended to the string so the elements in each row will appear on a separate line. When the outer loop ends, the string is displayed in a dialog as shown in this figure.

The third example is similar, except it displays the array of products you saw in figure 8-5. If you compare this code with the code in the second example, you'll see the only difference is that the elements in the two columns are separated by tab characters so they're aligned as shown here.

***

Now that you've learned how to work with one- and two-dimensional arrays, you should be aware of another type of array called a *jagged array*. Jagged arrays let you store data in a table that can have rows of unequal lengths. Each row in a jagged array is stored as a separate array. Because of that, a jagged array is also known as an *array of arrays*. Because jagged arrays are used infrequently, they aren't covered in this book. For more information, refer to the online documentation.

The syntax for using the GetLength() method of a rectangular array

```
arrayName.GetLength(dimensionIndex)
```

Code that works with the numbers array

```
int numberOfRows = numbers.GetLength(0);
int numberOfColumns = numbers.GetLength(1);
int sumOfFirstRow = numbers[0,0] + numbers[0,1];
```

Code that displays the numbers array in a dialog

```
string numbersString = "";
for (int i = 0; i < numbers.GetLength(0); i++)
{
    for (int j = 0; j < numbers.GetLength(1); j++)
        numbersString += numbers[i,j] + " ";

    numbersString += "\n";
}
MessageBox.Show(numbersString, "Numbers Test");
```

```
Numbers Test   X

1 2
3 4
5 6

       OK
```

Code that displays the products array in a dialog

```
string productsString = "";
for (int i = 0; i < products.GetLength(0); i++)
{
    for (int j = 0; j < products.GetLength(1); j++)
        productsString += products[i,j] + "\t\t";

    productsString += "\n";
}
MessageBox.Show(productsString, "Products Test");
```

```
Products Test                                          X

C#            Murach's C#
JAVA          Murach's Java Programming
ASPMVC        Murach's ASP.NET MVC

                                         OK
```

Description

- You use the GetLength() method to get the number of rows or columns in a rectangular array. To get the number of rows, specify 0 for the dimensionIndex argument. To get the number of columns, specify 1 for this argument.
- You use nested for loops to iterate through the rows and columns of a rectangular array.

Figure 8-6   How to work with rectangular arrays

More skills for working with arrays

Now that you know how to work with one-dimensional and rectangular arrays, you're ready to learn some additional skills for working with arrays.

How to use the Array class

Because an array is an instance of the Array class, you can use the properties and methods of this class to work with your arrays. Figure 8-7 presents the properties and methods you're most likely to use.

You've already seen how to use the Length property and the GetLength() method. Another property you may want to use is the GetUpperBound() method, which returns the index of the last element in a given dimension of an array. The first example in this figure illustrates the difference between the GetLength() and GetUpperBound() methods. Here, you can see that the GetLength() method returns a value of 4 for a one-dimensional array that contains four elements. By contrast, the GetUpperBound() method returns a value of 3 because the four elements are referred to with the index values of 0 through 3.

Although values have been assigned to the elements of the array that's used in this example, you should realize that the GetLength() and GetUpperBound() methods return the same values whether or not values have been assigned to the array. In other words, these methods depend only on the number of elements that were declared for the array. That's true of the Length property as well.

The Sort() method of the Array class lets you sort the elements in a one-dimensional array. This is illustrated by the second example in this figure. Here, the first statement declares an array that consists of three last names. Then, the Sort() method is used to sort the names in that array. Notice that because this method is a static method, it's called from the Array class, not from the array itself. After the array is sorted, a string is created that contains the values of the elements in ascending order. Then, the string is displayed in a dialog.

The third example shows how you can use the BinarySearch() method to locate a value in a one-dimensional array. This code uses the BinarySearch() method to get the index of the specified employee in an employees array. Then, this index is used to get the corresponding sales amount from a salesAmounts array.

For the BinarySearch() method to work properly, the array must be sorted in ascending sequence. If it's not, this method usually won't be able to find the specified value, even if it exists in the array. When the BinarySearch() method can't find the specified value, it returns a negative value. Then, if you try to use this value to access an element of an array, an IndexOutOfRangeException will be thrown.

Common properties and methods of the Array class

Property	Description
`Length`	Gets the number of elements in all of the dimensions of an array.

Instance method	Description
`GetLength(dimension)`	Gets the number of elements in the specified dimension of an array.
`GetUpperBound(dimension)`	Gets the index of the last element in the specified dimension of an array.

Static method	Description
`Copy(array1, array2, length)`	Copies some or all of the values in one array to another array. For more information, see figure 8-8.
`BinarySearch(array, value)`	Searches a one-dimensional array that's in ascending order for an element with a specified value and returns the index for that element.
`Sort(array)`	Sorts the elements in a one-dimensional array into ascending order.

Code that uses the GetLength() and GetUpperBound() methods

```
int[] numbers = new int[4] {1, 2, 3, 4};
int length = numbers.GetLength(0);               // length = 4
int upperBound = numbers.GetUpperBound(0);       // upperBound = 3
```

Code that uses the Sort() method

```
string[] lastNames = {"Boehm", "Taylor", "Murach"};
Array.Sort(lastNames);
string message = "";
foreach (string lastName in lastNames)
    message += lastName + "\n";
MessageBox.Show(message, "Sorted Last Names");
```

Code that uses the BinarySearch() method

```
string[] employees = {"AdamsA", "FinkleP", "LewisJ", "PotterE"};
decimal[] salesAmounts = {3275.68m, 4298.55m, 5289.57m, 1933.98m};
int index = Array.BinarySearch(employees, "FinkleP");
decimal salesAmount = salesAmounts[index];        // salesAmount = 4298.55
```

Note

- The BinarySearch() method only works on arrays whose elements are in ascending order. If the array isn't in ascending order, you must use the Sort() method to sort the array before using the BinarySearch() method.

Figure 8-7   How to use the Array class

How to refer to and copy arrays

Because arrays are created from a class, they are reference types. That means that an array variable contains a reference to an array object and not the actual values in the array. Because of that, you can use two or more variables to refer to the same array. This is illustrated in the first example in figure 8-8.

The first statement in this example declares an array variable named inches1, creates an array with three elements, and assigns values to those elements. Then, the second statement declares another array variable named inches2 and assigns the value of the inches1 variable to it. Because the inches1 variable contains a reference to the array, that means that the inches2 variable now contains a reference to the same array. As a result, if you use the inches2 variable to change any of the elements in the array as shown in the third statement, those changes will be reflected if you use the inches1 variable to refer to the array.

Once you declare the length of an array, it can't grow or shrink. In other words, arrays are *immutable*. However, you can use an existing array variable to refer to another array with a larger or smaller number of elements. To do that, you simply create the new array and assign it to the existing variable as shown in the second example in this figure. Here, an array that contains 20 elements is assigned to the inches1 variable, which originally contained only three elements. Note that when this statement is executed, the original array is discarded unless another array variable refers to it. In this case, the inches2 variable refers to the original array, so the array is maintained.

If you want to create a copy of an array, you can use the Copy() method of the Array class as shown in this figure. Then, each array variable will point to its own copy of the elements of the array, and any changes that are made to one array won't affect the other array.

You can use two techniques to copy the elements of an array. First, you can copy one or more elements of the array starting with the first element by specifying the source array, the target array, and the number of elements to be copied. This is illustrated by the third example in this figure. Here, all the elements of an array named inches are copied to an array named centimeters. Notice that the Length property of the inches array is used to specify the number of elements to be copied.

You can also copy one or more elements of an array starting with an element other than the first. To do that, you specify the index of the first element you want to copy. In addition, you specify the index of the element in the target array where you want to store the first element from the source array.

This is illustrated by the last example in this figure. Here, the first statement creates an array that contains three string values, and the second statement creates an array that can hold two string values. Then, the third statement copies the second and third strings from the first array into the second array. To do that, the first two arguments specify the source array and a starting index of 1 (the second element). Then, the next two arguments specify the target array and a starting index of 0 (the first element). Finally, the last argument specifies that two elements should be copied.

Code that creates a reference to another array

```
double[] inches1 = new double[3] {1,2,3};
double[] inches2 = inches1;
inches2[2] = 4;     // changes the third element
```

Code that reuses an array variable

```
inches1 = new double[20];   // make a new array with 20 elements
```

How to copy elements of one array to another array

The syntax for copying elements of an array

```
Array.Copy(fromArray, toArray, length);
```

Another way to copy elements from one array to another

```
Array.Copy(fromArray, fromIndex, toArray, toIndex, length);
```

Code that copies all the elements of an array

```
double[] inches = new double[3] {1,2,3};
double[] centimeters = new double[3];
Array.Copy(inches, centimeters, inches.Length);
for (int i = 0; i < centimeters.Length; i++)
    centimeters[i] *= 2.54;     // set the new values for this array
```

Code that copies some of the elements of an array

```
string[] names = {"Murach", "Boehm", "Delamater"};
string[] lastTwoNames = new string[2];
Array.Copy(names, 1, lastTwoNames, 0, 2);
```

Description

- An array is a reference type, which means that an array variable contains a reference to an array object. To create another reference to an existing array, you assign the array to another array variable. Then, both array variables point to the same array in memory.

- To reuse an array variable so it refers to an array with a larger or smaller number of elements, you create a new array and assign it to that variable. When you do, the original array is discarded unless another array variable refers to it.

- To copy the elements of one array to another array, you use the Copy() method of the Array class.

- To copy a specified number of elements from an array beginning with the first element, you can use the first syntax shown above. Then, you use the length argument to specify the number of elements to copy.

- To specify the first element in an array that you want to copy, you use the second syntax shown above. Then, the fromIndex argument specifies the index of the first element that's copied, the toIndex argument specifies the index where the first element is copied to, and the length argument specifies the number of elements that are copied.

- When you copy an array, the target array must have a type that's compatible with the source array and it must be large enough to receive all of the elements that are copied to it.

Figure 8-8   How to refer to and copy arrays

How to code methods that work with arrays

Figure 8-9 presents the techniques you can use to code methods that return and accept arrays. To return an array from a method, you follow the return type for the method with brackets as shown in the first example. Then, you define an array within the code for the method and use the return statement to return that array.

To call a method that returns an array, you use the same techniques that you use for calling any other method. In this figure, the statement that calls the GetRateArray() method declares an array variable and assigns the return value of the method to this variable. In this case, the method requires an argument that supplies the number of elements that the array should contain.

The second example shows how to code a method that accepts an array as an argument. To do that, you follow the data type of the parameter that accepts the argument with brackets to indicate that it's an array. Then, within the method, you can use all the techniques that you've learned for working with arrays to work with this parameter. In this case, a method named ToCentimeters() is used to convert the inch measurements in an array to centimeters.

To call a method that's defined with an array parameter, you just pass an array argument as shown here. Note, however, that unlike other arguments, arrays are automatically passed by reference. As a result, any changes that you make to the values stored in the array parameter will be reflected in any array variables in the calling method that refer to the array. In this figure, for example, the values in the measurements array are updated after the ToCentimeters() method is called.

The third example shows how to use the params keyword with an array parameter. When you use this keyword, the statement that calls the method can pass an array to the method, or it can pass a list of values. This is illustrated in the third example in this figure. Here, the statement that calls the method passes three values, which are then stored in the array parameter. Then, after these values are converted to centimeters, the array is passed back to the calling method.

Because the ToCentimeters() method that uses the params keyword can accept either an array or a list of values, it's more flexible than the first ToCentimeters() method. However, you should be aware of some restrictions when you use the params keyword. First, you can only use this keyword on one parameter within a method. Second, if a method is defined with two or more parameters, this keyword must be coded on the last parameter.

How to return an array from a method

The code for a method that returns an array

```
private decimal[] GetRateArray(int elementCount)
{
    decimal[] rates = new decimal[elementCount];
    for (int i = 0; i < rates.Length; i++)
        rates[i] = (decimal) (i + 1) / 100;
    return rates;
}
```

A statement that calls the method

```
decimal[] rates = this.GetRateArray(4);
```

How to code a method that accepts an array argument

A method that converts inches to centimeters

```
private void ToCentimeters(double[] measurements)
{
    for (int i = 0; i < measurements.Length; i++)
        measurements[i] *= 2.54;
}
```

Statements that declare the array and call the method

```
double[] measurements = {1,2,3};
ToCentimeters(measurements);
```

How to code a method that uses the params keyword

A method that converts inches to centimeters

```
private double[] ToCentimeters(params double[] measurements)
{
    for (int i = 0; i < measurements.Length; i++)
        measurements[i] *= 2.54;
    return measurements;
}
```

A statement that calls the method

```
double[] measurements = ToCentimeters(1,2,3);
```

Description

- To return an array from a method, you code a set of brackets after the return type declaration to indicate that the return type is an array.

- To accept an array as a parameter of a method, you code a set of brackets after the parameter type to indicate that the parameter is an array. By default, arrays are passed by reference.

- If you want to pass two or more arguments that haven't been grouped in an array to a method and have the method store the values in an array, you can include the *params* keyword on the parameter declaration. You code this keyword before the array type and name, you can code it on a single parameter, and you must code it on the last parameter.

Figure 8-9   How to code methods that work with arrays

How to use the null-conditional operator

When you work with objects like the arrays you've seen in this chapter as well as the elements of arrays, you may need to test for null values. The easiest way to do that is to use the *null-conditional operator* as shown in figure 8-10.

Here, the statement in the first example creates an array named initials and assigns a null value to it. Then, the statement in the second example attempts to access the first element in the array and convert it to uppercase. Because the array has a null value, though, this statement will throw a NullReferenceException.

The same is true if the array doesn't contain a null value, but the elements do. For example, suppose that the array is created with three elements like this:

```
string[] initials = new string[3];
```

Then, because the elements are reference types, they're assigned null values by default. So, if a statement tries to access any of the elements of the array, it will throw a NullReferenceException.

One way to prevent a NullReferenceException is to use nested if statements like the ones in the third example in this figure. Here, the outer if statement checks that the array itself doesn't contain a null value. Then, the inner if statement checks that the first element of the array doesn't contain a null value. If both of these conditions are true, the first element of the array can be accessed without a NullReferenceException being thrown.

The fourth example shows how to use null-conditional operators to check for null values in arrays and array elements. This operator consists of a single question mark (?) that you code after the object or element you want to check. Here, the first null-conditional operator checks if the initials array contains a null value. If it does, a null value is assigned to the firstInitial variable and no further processing takes place.

If the array doesn't contain a null value, processing continues. Then, the second null-conditional operator checks if the first element of the array contains a null value. If it does, a null value is assigned to the firstInitial variable and no further processing takes place. If the element doesn't contain a null value, though, it's converted to uppercase and assigned to the firstInitial variable. As you can see, this is much more succinct than using nested if statements.

Note that because the null-conditional operator can return a null value, the variable that receives the return value must be able to store a null value. That's why the firstInitial variable in this example is declared with a nullable type.

Although this figure shows only how to use the null-conditional operator with arrays, you should know that you can use it with any object. For example, you can use it with the collections that you'll learn about next. You can also use it with the custom objects that you'll learn to create in section 3.

A statement that creates a null array

```
string[] initials = null;
```

A statement that will throw a NullReferenceException

```
string firstInitial = initials[0].ToUpper();
```

Code that uses if statements to prevent a NullReferenceException

```
if (initials != null)
{
    if (initials[0] != null)
    {
        string firstInitial = initials[0].ToUpper();
    }
}
```

A statement that uses null-conditional operators to prevent a NullReferenceException

```
string? firstInitial = initials?[0]?.ToUpper();
```

Description

- If you try to access a member or element of an object that contains a null value, a NullReferenceException will occur. That's the case with the second example above, since the array it accesses contains a null value.

- One way to prevent a NullReferenceException is to use an if statement to check for a null value before accessing a member or element of the object.

- An easier way to prevent a NullReferenceException is to use the *null-conditional operator* (?). This operator checks the object or element that precedes it for a null value. If it finds a null value, no further operations take place and a null value is returned.

- Because the null-conditional operator can cause a null value to be returned, the variable that the return value is assigned to must be defined as a nullable type.

- You can use the null-conditional operator with any object and any element. That includes collection objects and elements like the ones you'll learn about later in this chapter, as well as custom objects and elements like the ones you'll learn about in section 3.

Figure 8-10   How to use the null-conditional operator

More ways to refer to array elements

Figure 8-11 presents some additional skills for referring to the elements of an array that were introduced with C# 8.0. To start, you can refer to an element by its index from the end of the array by coding the ^ operator before the index. To illustrate how this works, the first example presents an array of eight decimals that's used by the other examples in this figure. Then, the second example shows how to retrieve the second element from the end of the array. Note that when you refer to an element from the end of an array, the index of the last element is 1, not 0 as you might expect.

You can also refer to a *range of elements*. To do that, you use the range operator (..) as illustrated by the statements in the third example. Here, the first statement refers to the elements in the range that starts with index 0 and ends with index 2. Note that the starting index is inclusive, so the element with that index is included in the range, but the ending index is exclusive, so the element with that index isn't included in the range. Also note that the elements retrieved by this statement are stored in a variable that's declared with the var keyword. That way, the range can be stored in a variable with the appropriate type, whether that's an array or an individual variable.

When you refer to a range of elements, you can omit the starting index, the ending index, or both the starting and ending indexes. For instance, the second statement in this example doesn't include a starting index, so it defaults to 0. Because of that, it gets the same range as the first statement.

The third statement doesn't include an ending index, so it defaults to ^0. This refers to the element after the last element in the array. So, the range in this example includes the element with index 6 through the last element in the array, which has index 7.

The fourth statement doesn't include a starting or ending index. Because of that, the range includes all the elements in the array. In most cases, you won't use this technique unless you need to create a copy of the array. Instead, you can just refer to the original array.

The last statement in this example shows how to code a range that includes an index from the end of the array. Here, the starting index is 3 and the ending index is ^2. This is the same as coding 3..6, which is much easier to understand. Because of that, you won't typically use indexes from the end of an array in a range unless it's the index that refers to the element after the last element in the array (^0).

You can use a range to copy selected elements from one range to another instead of using the Array class. If you just need to process the elements without storing them in a separate array, though, you can use a foreach loop as shown in the fourth example. Here, instead of just naming the array as you saw earlier in this chapter, you include the range of elements you want to process.

The last example shows that you can store an index in a variable with the Index type, and you can store a range in a variable with the Range type. Then, you can use those variables to refer to the index and range.

The array that's used in the examples

```
decimal[] sales = { 22125.67m, 25362.35m, 21478.93m, 27495.72m,
                    26405.61m, 19476.29m, 31837.56m, 28649.01m };
```

How to refer to an element from the end of an array

```
decimal previousMonthSales = sales[^2];                    // 31837.56
```

How to refer to a range of elements

By including starting and ending indexes

```
var firstQtrSales = sales[0..3];                // indexes 0 through 2
```

By including just an ending index

```
var firstQtrSales = sales[..3];                 // indexes 0 through 2
```

By including just a starting index

```
var secondHalfSales = sales[6..];               // indexes 6 through 7
```

By including no starting or ending index

```
var YTDSales = sales[..];                        // indexes 0 through 7
```

By including an index from the end of the array

```
var secondQtrSales = sales[3..^2];              // indexes 3 through 5
```

How to use a range in a foreach loop

```
totalSales = 0.0m;
foreach (decimal sale in sales[3..6])           // indexes 3 through 5
{
    totalSales += sale;
}
```

How to use the Index and Range types (.NET Core 3.0 and later)

```
Index previousMonthIndex = ^2;
decimal previousMonthSales = sales[previousMonthIndex];   // 31837.56

Range secondQtrRange = 3..6;
var secondQtrSales = sales[secondQtrRange];     // indexes 3 through 5
```

Description

- With C# 8.0 and later, you can refer to an element from the end of an array by coding the ^ operator before the index. The element indexes start with ^1 for the last element, ^2 for the next to last element, and so on.

- With C# 8.0 and later, you can also refer to a *range of elements* in an array. To do that, you code the first index, the range operator (..), and one past the last index.

- To refer to one element past the last element in an array, you code ^0.

- If you omit the first index in a range, it defaults to 0. If you omit the last index in a range, it defaults to ^0.

- You can also store an index in a variable with the Index type, and you can store a range in a variable with the Range type. Then, you can use these variables in place of an index or range.

Figure 8-11   More ways to refer to array elements

How to work with list patterns

In chapter 5, you learned how to use pattern matching with if statements, switch statements, and switch expressions. Now, figure 8-12 shows how to use pattern matching with the elements of an array. This type of pattern is known as a *list pattern*, and it can be used with arrays as well as with collections like the ones you'll learn about later in this chapter.

The first example in this figure presents an array named quantity that's used by all the other examples. This array contains four int values. Then, the second example presents several if statements that show some basic techniques for using list patterns with this array. As you can see, all these statements use an is expression to match the elements in the array. To do that, zero or more patterns are enclosed in square brackets and separated by commas.

Here, the list pattern in the first if condition uses constant patterns that match the values in the array, so the condition is true. In the second condition, however, the third pattern doesn't match, so the condition is false. Similarly, the third condition is false because the list pattern includes only three patterns and the array has four elements. The fourth condition shows that you can use a discard pattern within a list pattern to match an element with any value. And the fifth condition shows that you can use relational and logical patterns within a list pattern.

The if conditions in the third example show how to use *slice patterns* within list patterns. A slice pattern is represented by two periods (. .), and it can be coded in place of zero or more patterns within a list pattern. For instance, the first if condition uses a slice pattern that represents the third and fourth elements. That means that those elements will match the pattern regardless of their values. Although you could also use two discard patterns in place of this slice pattern, the slice pattern is more versatile because it can be used to represent any number of elements.

The second if condition in this example is similar to the first, but it uses a slice pattern at the beginning of the list pattern in place of the first three elements. The third if condition uses a slice pattern in the middle of the list pattern in place of the second and third elements.

The fourth example shows another type of pattern that you can code within a list pattern, called a *var pattern*. A var pattern is like a discard pattern because it matches an element with any value. Unlike a discard pattern, though, a var pattern stores the value of the element in a variable with the name you specify. Then, you can use that variable within the scope in which it's declared. In this case, you can use it within the if block.

The last example in this figure shows how to use list patterns with a switch expression. In this case, the switch expression returns an integer that represents the index of the first element with a value that's less than or equal to zero. To do that, the first pattern tests if all elements have a value greater than zero. If so, a value of -1 is returned to indicate that none of the elements have a value that's less than or equal to zero. The second pattern tests if the fourth element is less than or equal to zero and returns a value of 3 if it is. The third and fourth patterns are similar. Finally, if none of the patterns match, a value of 0 is returned.

The list used in the following examples
```
int[] quantity = { 100, 200, 300, 400 };
```

Some if conditions that use list patterns to test the values
```
if (quantity is [100, 200, 300, 400])      // true
if (quantity is [100, 200, 400, 400])      // false
if (quantity is [100, 200, 300])           // false
if (quantity is [100, 200, 300, _])        // true
if (quantity is [< 200, 200 or 300, >= 300 and < 400, > 200])    // true
```

Some if conditions that use slice patterns within list patterns
```
if (quantity is [100, 200, ..])      // true
if (quantity is [.., 400])           // true
if (quantity is [> 0, .., > 500])    // false
```

An if condition that uses a var pattern within a list pattern
```
if (quantity is [100, 200, 300, var fourth])      // true
```

A switch expression that uses list patterns
```
int index = quantity switch
{
    [> 0, > 0, > 0, > 0] => -1,
    [> 0, > 0, > 0, <= 0] => 3,
    [> 0, > 0, <= 0, ..] => 2,
    [> 0, <= 0, ..] => 1,
    _ => 0
};
```

Description
- A *list pattern* lets you match a sequence of patterns against the elements in an array. You can also use a list pattern to match the elements in a collection.
- You can use a list pattern with the is operator and, optionally, the not operator of an if statement. You can also use list patterns with the cases of switch statements and switch expressions.
- You can use a *slice pattern* within a list pattern to match zero or more elements at the beginning, at the end, or in the middle of the array. You can code only one slice pattern within a list pattern.
- You can use a discard pattern within a list pattern to match any single element. If you need to get the value of the element, you can use a *var pattern* instead of a discard pattern to assign the value to a variable.

Figure 8-12   How to work with list patterns

How to work with collections

Like an array, a *collection* can hold one or more elements. Unlike arrays, collections don't have a fixed size. Instead, the size of a collection is increased automatically when elements are added to it. In addition, most types of collections provide methods you can use to change the capacity of a collection. In other words, collections are *mutable*. As a result, collections are usually more appropriate and can usually manage system resources better than arrays when you need to work with a varying number of elements.

In the topics that follow, you'll learn how to use five types of collections: lists, sorted lists, queues, stacks, and array lists. Although .NET provides for other collections, these are the ones you'll use most often.

Commonly used collection classes

.NET provides two types of collection classes. First, it includes collection classes that can store any type of object. As a result, the collections created from these classes are sometimes referred to as *untyped collections*. In fact, you can store different types of objects in the same collection, even though that's usually not a good idea. However, if you accidentally write code that adds the wrong type of object to an untyped collection, it will result in an error that won't be discovered until you run the app.

The second type of collection classes prevents errors like this by using a feature known as *generics* to allow you to create *typed collections*. With a typed collection, you specify the data type in angle brackets (<>) after the name of the collection class. Then, you can only store objects of the specified data type in that collection, and any errors will be discovered when you attempt to compile the app.

Figure 8-13 shows four of the most commonly used typed and untyped collections. The classes for the typed collections are stored in the System.Collections.Generic namespace. The classes for the untyped collections are stored in the System.Collections namespace.

As you'll see in the next figure, typed collections have several advantages over untyped collections. As a result, you'll typically want to use typed collections for most new development. However, you may need to use untyped collections when working with legacy apps.

How arrays and collections are similar

- Both can store multiple elements, which can be value types or reference types.

How arrays and collections are different

- An array is a feature of the C# language. Collections are .NET classes.
- Collection classes provide methods to perform operations that arrays don't provide.
- Arrays are fixed in size. Collections are variable in size.

Commonly used collection classes

Typed	Untyped	Description
List<T>	ArrayList	Uses an index to access each element. Is very efficient for accessing elements sequentially. Can be inefficient when inserting elements into the middle of a list.
SortedList<K, V>	SortedList	Uses a key to access a value, which can be any type of object. Can be inefficient for accessing elements sequentially. Is very efficient for inserting elements into the middle of a list.
Queue<T>	Queue	Uses methods to add and remove elements.
Stack<T>	Stack	Uses methods to add and remove elements.

Description

- A *collection* is an object that can hold one or more *elements*.
- The collection classes in the System.Collections.Generic namespace use a feature known as *generics* to allow you to create *typed collections* that can only store the specified data type. With a typed collection, you specify the data type in angle brackets (<>) after the name of the collection class.
- The collection classes in the System.Collections namespace allow you to create *untyped collections*. With an untyped collection, you can store any type of object in the collection.

Figure 8-13   Commonly used collection classes

Typed vs. untyped collections

Figure 8-14 shows the differences between typed and untyped collections. In particular, it shows that typed collections have two advantages over untyped collections. First, they check the type of each element at compile-time and thus prevent runtime errors from occurring. Second, they reduce the amount of casting that's needed when retrieving objects.

The first example shows how to use the ArrayList class from the System. Collections namespace to create an untyped collection. To start, the statement that creates the ArrayList object doesn't specify a data type. As a result, the Add() method can be used to add elements of any type to the collection. In this figure, for example, the code adds two int types and a string type to the collection. This is possible because each element in the ArrayList object is stored as an object type.

Once the elements have been added to the untyped list, a for loop is used to calculate the sum of the elements. To accomplish this, the first statement in the loop casts each element to the int type. This is necessary because each element is an object data type. However, since a string type has been added to the collection, this will cause a runtime error when the loop reaches the string type.

The second example shows how to use the List<T> class from the System.Collections.Generic namespace to create a typed collection. To start, the statement that creates the list uses angle brackets (<>) to specify the int type. As a result, the Add() method can only be used to add int types to the collection. In this figure, for example, the code adds two int types to the collection. If you tried to add another type such as a string type to the collection, you would get a compile-time error.

Once the elements have been added to the typed list, a for loop is used to calculate the sum of the elements. To accomplish this, the first statement in the loop retrieves each element and stores it in an int variable. Since this is a typed collection, no casting is necessary.

Since typed collections have several advantages over untyped collections, Visual Studio includes a *using directive* for the System.Collections.Generic namespace in all Windows Forms apps that you create. This directive makes it possible to use any type in this namespace without having to specify the name of the namespace. In addition, starting with C# 10.0, this using directive is stored in a special file with other *global using directives* that are available to every file in your project. You'll learn more about global using directives in chapter 10. For now, just realize that you will usually work with typed collections in your apps, so you won't have to add a using directive.

In some cases, you may want to upgrade an app that uses untyped collections to one that uses typed collections. If the app was created before C# 10.0, you can start by changing the using directive for the System.Collections namespace near the beginning of the form to System.Collections.Generic. Then, you can edit the statements that work with the collection. That usually means editing the statement that creates the collection, and adding or removing any casting as necessary.

Untyped collections

The using directive

```
using System.Collections;
```

An example

```
ArrayList numbers = new ArrayList();
numbers.Add(3);
numbers.Add(7);
numbers.Add("Test");     // will compile - causes runtime error
int sum = 0;
for (int i = 0; i < numbers.Count; i++)
{
    int number = (int)numbers[i];   // cast is required
    sum += number;
}
```

Typed collections

The using directive

```
using System.Collections.Generic;
```

An example

```
List<int> numbers = new List<int>();
numbers.Add(3);
numbers.Add(7);
//numbers.Add("Test");     // won't compile - prevents runtime error
int sum = 0;
for (int i = 0; i < numbers.Count; i++)
{
    int number = numbers[i];  // no cast needed
    sum += number;
}
```

Description

- Typed collections have two advantages over untyped collections. First, they check the type of each element at compile-time and prevent runtime errors from occurring. Second, they reduce the amount of casting that's needed when retrieving objects.

- By default, Visual Studio adds a *using directive* for the System.Collections.Generic namespace to each Windows Forms app you create. Prior to C# 10.0, this using directive was added to each class, including form classes. For C# 10.0 or later, this using directive is added to a special file along with other *global using directives* that are available to the entire project. See chapter 10 for more on global using directives.

- If you want to use untyped collections, you can add a using directive at the beginning of the form class for the System.Collections namespace. Then, you need to make sure to cast the elements to the appropriate type when you retrieve them from the collection.

Figure 8-14   Typed vs. untyped collections

How to work with a list

Now that you understand the difference between typed and untyped collections, you're ready to learn how to use the List<T> class to create and work with a *list*, the most common of the typed collections. To create a list, you use the new keyword to create an object from the List<T> class as shown in part 1 of figure 8-15. When you do this, you must specify the data type for each element within angle brackets (<>) immediately after the class name. In this figure, for example, the first statement specifies the string type, and the second statement specifies the decimal type. However, you could also specify any other .NET data type (such as the DateTime type) or any custom data type (such as a Product type like the one you'll learn about in chapter 12).

When you create a list, you can specify its initial capacity by coding it within parentheses after the class name. In this figure, for example, the third statement sets the initial capacity to 3. If you omit the initial capacity as illustrated by the first two statements, though, it's set to 0.

Part 1 of this figure also lists some common members of the List<T> class. You'll see how to use some of these members in part 2 of this figure. For now, you should notice that some of these members provide functions that aren't available with arrays. For example, you can use the Insert() method to insert an element into the middle of a list, and you can use the RemoveAt() method to remove an element from a list.

You should also realize that when you use the Add() or Insert() method to add elements to a list, the capacity of the list is doubled each time its capacity is exceeded. This is illustrated by the last seven statements in part 1 of this figure. Each of these statements adds another element to the lastNames list that is created with an initial capacity of three elements by the first statement. Then, when the fourth element is added, the capacity is increased to six elements. Similarly, when you add the seventh element, the capacity is doubled again to 12.

A statement that creates a list of string elements

```
List<string> titles = new List<string>();
```

A statement that creates a list of decimal elements

```
List<decimal> prices = new List<decimal>();
```

A statement that creates a list of strings with a capacity of 3

```
List<string> lastNames = new List<string>(3);
```

Common members of the List<T> class

Indexer	Description
[index]	Gets or sets the element at the specified index. The index for the first item in a list is 0.

Property	Description
Capacity	Gets or sets the number of elements a list can hold.
Count	Gets the number of elements in a list.

Method	Description
Add(object)	Adds an element to the end of a list and returns the element's index.
Clear()	Removes all elements from a list and sets its Count property to zero.
Contains(object)	Returns a Boolean value that indicates if a list contains the specified object.
Insert(index, object)	Inserts an element into a list at the specified index.
Remove(object)	Removes the first occurrence of the specified object from a list.
RemoveAt(index)	Removes the element at the specified index of a list.
BinarySearch(object)	Searches a list for a specified object and returns the index for that object.
Sort()	Sorts the elements in a list into ascending order.

Code that causes the size of a list of names to be increased

```
List<string> lastNames = new List<string>(3);
lastNames.Add("Boehm");
lastNames.Add("Delamater");
lastNames.Add("Murach");
lastNames.Add("Taylor");                //Capacity is doubled to 6 elements
lastNames.Add("Baylon");
lastNames.Add("McCoy");
lastNames.Add("Slivkoff");              //Capacity is doubled to 12 elements
```

Description

- A *list* is a collection that automatically adjusts its capacity to accommodate new elements.
- The default capacity of a list is 0 elements, but you can specify a different capacity when you create a list. When the number of elements in a list exceeds its capacity, the capacity is automatically doubled.
- The List<T> class is in the System.Collections.Generic namespace.

Figure 8-15   How to work with a list (part 1 of 2)

Part 2 of figure 8-15 shows how to use some of the methods of the List<T> class to work with the elements in a list. Here, the first example creates a list of decimal values. Unlike the statements you saw in part 1 of this figure, this example uses a *collection initializer* to assign values to the list. When you use a collection initializer, you don't have to use the Add() method to add elements to the list. Instead, you code the elements within braces as shown here.

Note that if you're working with existing code that doesn't use collection initializers, you can use refactoring to modify the code so it does use collection initializers. To do that, place the cursor in the statement that declares the list, press Ctrl + period (.), and select Collection Initialization can be Simplified from the Quick Actions menu that's displayed. You can also refactor all the code in a document, project, or solution by clicking the appropriate link in the popup window that's displayed. This capability became available with Visual Studio 2017.

The second example shows how to use an index to refer to an element in a list. The syntax for doing that is the same as the syntax for referring to an element in an array. You just specify the index in square brackets after the name of the list and the element is returned.

The third example shows how to insert and remove elements from a list. Here, a new element with a decimal value of 2745.73 is inserted at the beginning of the list named salesTotals. As a result, the other four values in the list are pushed down one index. Then, the second element of the list is removed, and the other three values are moved back up one index. The final result is that the first element is replaced with a new element.

The fourth example uses a foreach loop to display the elements in the salesTotals list in a dialog. As you can see, this works the same as it does for an array.

The fifth example shows how to use the Contains() method to check if the salesTotals list contains an object. If it does, the Remove() method is used to remove the object from the list. In this case, the object contains a decimal value of 2745.73. However, this would work regardless of the data type the object contained.

The sixth example shows how you can sort and search the elements in a list. Here, the first statement uses the Sort() method to sort the elements in the salesTotals list. Then, the second statement uses the BinarySearch() method to search for an element that contains a decimal value of 4398.55.

You should notice in this example that, unlike the Sort() method of the Array class, the Sort() method of the List<T> class is an instance method. Because of that, you call it from the list object. That's true for the BinarySearch() method too. Otherwise, these methods work similarly.

The syntax for retrieving a value from a list

```
listName[index]
```

Code that creates a list that holds decimal values

```
List<decimal> salesTotals = new List<decimal>
    { 3275.68m, 4398.55m, 5289.75m, 1933.98m };
```

Code that retrieves the first value from the list

```
decimal sales1 = salesTotals[0];                   // sales1 = 3275.68
```

Code that inserts and removes an element from the list

```
salesTotals.Insert(0, 2745.73m);         // insert a new first element
sales1 = salesTotals[0];                  // sales1 = 2745.73
decimal sales2 = salesTotals[1];          // sales2 = 3275.68
salesTotals.RemoveAt(1);                  // remove the second element
sales2 = salesTotals[1];                  // sales2 = 4398.55
```

Code that displays the list in a dialog

```
string salesTotalsString = "";
foreach (decimal d in salesTotals)
    salesTotalsString += d.ToString() + "\n";
MessageBox.Show(salesTotalsString, "Sales Totals");
```

Code that checks for an element in the list and removes it if it exists

```
decimal x = 2745.73m;
if (salesTotals.Contains(x))
    salesTotals.Remove(x);
```

Code that sorts and searches the list

```
salesTotals.Sort();
int sales2Index = salesTotals.BinarySearch(sales2);
```

A dialog that displays the results of the sort and search operation

Figure 8-15   How to work with a list (part 2 of 2)

How to work with a sorted list

You can also implement a typed collection by using the SortedList<T> class, which defines a *sorted list*. A sorted list is useful when you need to look up values in the list based on a key value. If, for example, a sorted list consists of item numbers and unit prices, the keys are the item numbers. Then, the item number can be used to look up the unit price for any item in the list. The first table in figure 8-16 describes some common members of the SortedList<T> class.

The keys in a sorted list along with their corresponding values are typically referred to as *key/value pairs*. That's because each item is created from a KeyValuePair<K, V> structure. The second table in this figure describes the two properties of this structure: Key and Value. Here, the Value property can store value types or reference types.

Like a list, you can set the initial capacity of a sorted list by specifying the number of elements in parentheses when the list is created. Then, if the number of elements in the list exceeds the capacity as the program executes, the capacity is automatically doubled.

The examples in part 1 of this figure show three ways to create and load a sorted list. In the first example, the first statement creates the sorted list and the next four statements use the Add() method to add an element to the list. When you add an element to a sorted list, you specify the key along with the value associated with that key. In this example, the keys are the names of employees, and the values are the sales totals for those employees. Note that as elements are added, the sorted list automatically sorts itself by key values.

Instead of using the Add() method to add elements to the sorted list, the second example uses a collection initializer. Notice that because each element of a sorted list consists of two values, each element is enclosed in braces within the outer braces.

The third example also uses a collection initializer, but it's used along with an *index initializer*. When you use an index initializer, you don't code the key and value within braces. Instead, you code the key within square brackets, and you follow it with an equal sign and the value that's associated with that key. Although this may seem like a minor variation, this syntax is more in keeping with the way you refer to other indexes.

Just as you can for a list, you can refactor code that creates and loads a sorted list without using a collection initializer so it uses a collection initializer. When you do that, the code is refactored so it looks like the second example in this figure. In other words, an index initializer isn't used.

Common members of the SortedList<T> class

Indexer	Description
`[key]`	Gets or sets the value of the element with the specified key.

Property	Description
`Keys`	Gets a collection that contains the keys in the list.
`Values`	Gets a collection that contains the values in the list.
`Capacity`	Gets or sets the number of elements the list can hold.
`Count`	Gets the number of elements in the list.

Method	Description
`Add(key, value)`	Adds an element with the specified key and value to the sorted list.
`Clear()`	Removes all elements from the sorted list.
`ContainsKey(key)`	Returns a Boolean value that indicates whether or not the sorted list contains the specified key.
`ContainsValue(value)`	Returns a Boolean value that indicates whether or not the sorted list contains the specified value.
`Remove(key)`	Removes the element with the specified key from the sorted list.
`RemoveAt(index)`	Removes the element at the specified index from the sorted list.

Properties of the KeyValuePair<K, V> structure

Property	Description
`Key`	The key for the SortedList item.
`Value`	The value associated with the key.

How to create and load a sorted list

With separate statements

```
SortedList<string, decimal> salesList = new SortedList<string, decimal>(4);
salesList.Add("FinkleP", 4398.55m);
salesList.Add("AdamsA", 3275.68m);
salesList.Add("PotterE", 1933.98m);
salesList.Add("LewisJ", 5289.75m);
```

With a collection initializer

```
SortedList<string, decimal> salesList = new SortedList<string, decimal>
    { { "FinkleP", 4398.55m }, { "AdamsA", 3275.68m },
      { "PotterE", 1933.98m }, { "LewisJ", 5289.75m } };
```

With an index initializer inside a collection initializer

```
SortedList<string, decimal> salesList = new SortedList<string, decimal>
    { ["FinkleP"] = 4398.55m, ["AdamsA"] = 3275.68m,
      ["PotterE"] = 1933.98m, ["LewisJ"] = 5289.75m };
```

Description

- The items in a *sorted list* consist of *key/value pairs*, and the items are always sorted by key value.

Figure 8-16   How to work with a sorted list (part 1 of 2)

The first example in part 2 of figure 8-16 shows how to look up a value in a sorted list using an *indexer*. You'll learn more about indexers in chapter 13. For now, you just need to know that the indexer for a sorted list lets you access the value of the element with the key you specify. Here, a value of "LewisJ" is specified as the key for the element. As a result, this key returns a decimal value of 5289.75.

The second example creates a string that contains the keys and values in a sorted list. To start, it declares and initializes the string. Then, it uses a foreach loop to retrieve each KeyValuePair value in the sorted list. The code within this loop uses the Key and Value properties of the KeyValuePair structure to access each element's key and value. In this example, a tab character is placed between the key and the value and a new line character is placed after the key/value pair.

Notice here that the elements are no longer in the sequence they were added to the list as shown in part 1 of this figure. Instead, they're sorted by their key values.

Since a sorted list makes it easy to look up a key and return its corresponding value, it's the ideal collection to use when you need to do this type of lookup. It would be much more difficult to perform the same task with a regular list. However, a regular list works fine when you need to look up an element by an index.

Code that looks up a value in the sorted list based on a key

```
string employeeKey = "LewisJ";
decimal salesTotal = salesList[employeeKey];
```

Code that converts the sorted list to a tab-delimited string

```
string salesTableString = "";
foreach (KeyValuePair<string, decimal> employeeSalesEntry in salesList)
{
    salesTableString += employeeSalesEntry.Key + "\t"
                     + employeeSalesEntry.Value + "\n";
}
MessageBox.Show(salesTableString, "Employee Sales Totals");
```

Description

- You can use the key for any item to look up the value of that item.
- The items in a sorted list are created from the KeyValuePair structure. You can use the Key and Value properties of this structure to access the key and value of any item.

Figure 8-16   How to work with a sorted list (part 2 of 2)

How to work with queues and stacks

Figure 8-17 shows the properties and methods of the Queue<T> and Stack<T> classes that you can use to create typed queues and stacks. Unlike other collections, queues and stacks do not use the Add() method to add items or an index to retrieve items. Instead, queues use the Enqueue() and Dequeue() methods to add and retrieve items, and stacks use the Push() and Pop() methods. This also means that you can't use collection initializers with stacks and queues. That's because collection initializers are implemented using the Add() method.

You can think of a *queue* (pronounced cue) as a line of items waiting to be processed. When you use the Enqueue() method to add an item to the queue, the item is placed at the end of the queue. When you use the Dequeue() method to retrieve an item from the queue, the item is taken from the front of the queue. Because items are retrieved from a queue in the same order in which they were added, a queue can be referred to as a *first-in, first-out* (*FIFO*) collection.

By contrast, a *stack* is a *last-in, first-out* (*LIFO*) collection. When you use the Push() method to place an item on a stack, that item is placed on the top of the stack. If you then push another item onto the stack, the new item is placed on the top of the stack and the item that was previously on the top of the stack moves to second from the top. When you use the Pop() method to retrieve an item from the stack, the item is taken from the top of the stack and the item that was second from the top moves to the top position. If it helps you, you can think of a stack as a stack of dishes. The last dish that you put on the stack is also the first dish that you take off the stack.

The two examples in this figure illustrate the differences between queues and stacks. Each example begins by defining a new queue or stack, and then adding three names. Next, a while loop is used to build a string that contains the names in the order that they are retrieved from the queue or stack, and the resulting list is displayed in a dialog. If you compare the dialogs for these examples, you can see that the queue names are displayed in the same order that they were added to the queue. But in the stack example, the names are retrieved in the opposite order.

In both examples, the while loop repeats as long as the Count property is greater than zero. This works because the Dequeue() and Pop() methods remove the item from the queue or stack, so the Count property is automatically decreased by one each time through the loop. When all the items have been read from the queue or stack, the Count property reaches zero and the while loop terminates.

Compared to lists, queues and stacks don't provide as many properties and methods. However, if you need to implement a strictly FIFO or LIFO collection, you won't need any of those extra properties and methods. In that case, it makes sense to use a queue or stack as described in this figure.

Properties and methods of the Queue<T> class

Property	Description
Count	Gets the number of items in the queue.
Method	**Description**
Enqueue(object)	Adds the specified object to the end of the queue.
Dequeue()	Gets the object at the front of the queue and removes it from the queue.
Clear()	Removes all items from the queue.
Peek()	Retrieves the next item in the queue without deleting it.

Code that uses a queue

```
Queue<string> nameQueue = new Queue<string>();
nameQueue.Enqueue("Boehm");
nameQueue.Enqueue("Taylor");
nameQueue.Enqueue("Murach");
string nameQueueString = "";
while (nameQueue.Count > 0)
    nameQueueString += nameQueue.Dequeue() + "\n";
MessageBox.Show(nameQueueString, "Queue");
```

```
Queue                    ×

Boehm
Taylor
Murach

          [ OK ]
```

Properties and methods of the Stack<T> class

Property	Description
Count	Gets the number of items in the stack.
Method	**Description**
Push(object)	Adds the specified object to the top of the stack.
Pop()	Gets the object at the top of the stack and removes it from the stack.
Clear()	Removes all items from the stack.
Peek()	Retrieves the next item in the stack without deleting it.

Code that uses a stack

```
Stack<string> nameStack = new Stack<string>();
nameStack.Push("Boehm");
nameStack.Push("Taylor");
nameStack.Push("Murach");
string nameStackString = "";
while (nameStack.Count > 0)
    nameStackString += nameStack.Pop() + "\n";
MessageBox.Show(nameStackString, "Stack");
```

```
Stack                    ×

Murach
Taylor
Boehm

          [ OK ]
```

Description

- *Queues* and *stacks* provide distinct features that let you process them like lists.
- A queue is sometimes called a *first-in, first-out* (*FIFO*) collection because its items are retrieved in the same order in which they were added.
- A stack is sometimes called a *last-in, first-out* (*LIFO*) collection because its items are retrieved in the reverse order from the order in which they were added.

Figure 8-17   How to work with queues and stacks

How to work with an array list

Although you'll probably want to use typed lists whenever possible, figure 8-18 shows how to work with an *array list*, the most common untyped collection. This should illustrate both the similarities and differences between typed and untyped lists. For the most part, an array list works like a list. However, since an array list defines an untyped collection, there are a few differences.

First, when you create an object from the ArrayList class, you don't define the type within angle brackets (<T>). Instead, each element in an array list is stored as an object type. As a result, any value type you store in an array list must be converted to a reference type. To do that, an object is created and then the value is stored in that object. The process of putting a value in an object is known as *boxing*, and it's done automatically whenever a value type needs to be converted to a reference type. In the first example, for instance, the decimal values in the array named newSalesTotals are converted to object types before they're stored in the array list named salesTotals. The second example is similar except it uses a collection initializer to load the values into the list.

Second, when you retrieve an element from an array list, you must cast the object type to the appropriate data type. In the third example, for instance, the first element in the array list named salesTotal is cast from the object type to the decimal type. The process of getting a value out of the object is known as *unboxing*, and you must write code like this whenever you need to unbox a value.

The rest of the examples work the same as the examples for the List<T> class shown in figure 8-15. The only difference is that you must cast an object to the appropriate data type when you retrieve it from an array list. If you compare the examples in this figure to the ones for the List<T> class, you'll see that they're very similar. As a result, it's easy to convert code that uses the ArrayList class to code that uses the List<T> class and vice versa. Once you understand how to do that, you should be able to convert code from any untyped collection to any typed collection and vice versa.

The syntax for retrieving a value from an array list

```
(type) arrayName[index]
```

Code that creates an array list that holds decimal values

```
decimal[] newSalesTotals = {3275.68m, 4398.55m, 5289.75m, 1933.98m};
ArrayList salesTotals = new ArrayList();
foreach (decimal d in newSalesTotals)
    salesTotals.Add(d);
```

Another way to create the array list

```
ArrayList salesTotals = new ArrayList
    { 3275.68m, 4398.55m, 5289.75m, 1933.98m };
```

Code that retrieves the first value from the array list

```
decimal sales1 = (decimal) salesTotals[0];  // sales1 = 3275.68
```

Code that inserts and removes an element from the array list

```
salesTotals.Insert(0, 2745.73m);                 // insert a new first element
sales1 = (decimal) salesTotals[0];               // sales1 = 2745.73
decimal sales2 = (decimal) salesTotals[1];       // sales2 = 3275.68
salesTotals.RemoveAt(1);                          // remove the second element
sales2 = (decimal) salesTotals[1];               // sales2 = 4398.55
```

Code that displays the array list in a dialog

```
string salesTotalsString = "";
foreach (decimal d in salesTotals)
    salesTotalsString += d + "\n";
MessageBox.Show(salesTotalsString, "Sales Totals");
```

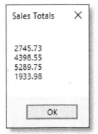

Code that checks for an element in the array list and removes it if it exists

```
decimal x = 2745.73m;
if (salesTotals.Contains(x))
    salesTotals.Remove(x);
```

Code that sorts and searches the array list

```
salesTotals.Sort();
int sales2Index = salesTotals.BinarySearch(sales2);
```

Description

- The ArrayList class is part of the System.Collections namespace.
- The ArrayList class has the same properties and methods as the List<T> class in the System.Collections.Generic namespace. As a result, it's easy to convert code that uses the ArrayList class to code that uses the List<T> class and vice versa.

Figure 8-18   How to work with an array list

Perspective

In this chapter, you've learned how to use both arrays and collections for working with groups of related data. You've also learned that .NET provides several different classes that offer useful properties and methods for working with arrays and collections. These include the Array, List<T>, SortedList<T>, Queue<T>, Stack<T>, and ArrayList classes.

As you develop your own apps, you need to decide between the use of an array or a collection. Then, if you decide to use a collection, you need to choose the most appropriate type of collection. If you make the right decisions, your code will be easier to write, debug, and maintain.

Terms

array	collection
element	mutable
length	typed collection
size	generics
one-dimensional array	untyped collection
index	using directive
upper bound	list
foreach statement	collection initializer
foreach loop	sorted list
rectangular array	key/value pair
two-dimensional array	index initializer
jagged array	queue
array of arrays	stack
immutable	first-in first-out (FIFO)
range of elements	last-in first-out (LIFO)
list pattern	array list
slice pattern	boxing
var pattern	unboxing

Exercise 8-1   Use an array and a list

This exercise will guide you through the process of adding an array and a list to the Invoice Total app that you enhanced in the last chapter.

Open the Invoice Total app

1. Open the Invoice Total app that's in the C:\C#\Ch08\InvoiceTotal directory.

Use an array to store invoice totals

2. Declare two class variables: (1) an array that can hold up to five invoice totals and (2) an index that you can use to work with that array.

3. Add code that adds the invoice total to the next element in the array each time the user clicks the Calculate button.

4. Add code that displays all the invoice totals in the array in a dialog when the user clicks the Exit button. To do that, use a foreach loop to loop through the totals and format the message for the dialog. Within this loop, you should include an if statement so you only display totals that are not equal to zero.

5. Test the program by entering subtotals for up to five invoices and then clicking the Exit button. This should display a dialog like this one:

6. Test the program by entering more than five invoices. When you do, an IndexOutOfRangeException should be thrown, and it will be caught by the catch block. Then, modify the try-catch statement so it handles this specific exception.

Sort the invoice totals

7. Add code to sort the invoice totals in the array.

8. Test the program again to be sure that the dialog displays the invoice totals in the correct sequence.

Modify the program so it uses a list

9. Without changing any of the current code, repeat steps 2 through 8 but use a list to hold the totals and add a second foreach loop to format and display the totals stored in the list in a second dialog. In other words, display two dialogs: one for the array and one for the list.

10. When you've got this working right, close the solution.

Exercise 8-2   Use a rectangular array

This exercise will guide you through the process of adding a rectangular array to the Future Value app. This array will store the values for each calculation that's performed.

Open the Future Value app

1. Open the Future Value app that's in the C:\C#\Ch08\FutureValue directory.

Use a rectangular array to store future value calculations

2. Declare class variables for a row counter and a rectangular array of strings that provides for 10 rows and 4 columns.

3. Add code that stores the values for each calculation in the next row of the array when the user clicks the Calculate button. Store the monthly investment and future value in currency format, and store the interest rate in percent format.

4. Add code to display the elements in the array in a dialog when the user clicks the Exit button. Use tab characters to format the dialog so it looks like this:

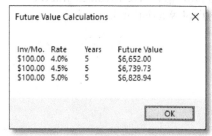

5. Test the program by making up to 10 future value calculations. When you've got this working right, close the solution.

9

How to work with dates and strings

In chapter 4, you learned some basic skills for working with strings. In this chapter, you'll learn more about working with strings, and you'll learn how to work with dates. Because you'll use dates and strings in many of the apps you develop, you'll want to be sure you know how to use the skills presented in this chapter.

How to work with dates and times

To work with dates and times in C#, you use the DateTime structure. As you'll see, this structure provides a variety of properties and methods for getting information about dates and times, formatting DateTime values, and performing operations on dates and times.

How to create a DateTime value

Figure 9-1 presents three ways that you can create a DateTime value. First, you can use the new keyword to create a DateTime value from the DateTime structure. This is different from the way you create other built-in value types. That's because C# doesn't provide a keyword for working with this structure like it does for the other value types.

When you create a DateTime value using the new keyword, you must always specify the year, month, and day. In addition, you can optionally specify the time in hours, minutes, seconds, and milliseconds. If you don't specify the time, it's set to 12:00 AM. This is illustrated by the first statement in this figure.

You can also create a DateTime value using the static Parse() or TryParse() method of the DateTime structure. When you use one of these methods, you specify the date and time as a string as illustrated by the third, fourth, and fifth statements in this figure. Here, the third statement specifies just a date. Because of that, the time portion of the DateTime value is set to 12:00 AM. The fourth statement specifies both a date and time. The fifth statement illustrates that you can create a DateTime value from a property or variable that contains a date/time string. In this case, a DateTime value is created from the Text property of a text box.

The last statement shows how you would perform the same processing as the fifth statement using the TryParse() method. Remember that when you use this method, you use the out keyword and a type, in this case, DateTime, to declare the variable where the date will be stored. Then, if the string can't be converted to a DateTime value, this method returns a false value. By contrast, if the Parse() method can't convert the string, a format exception occurs.

When you use the Parse() or TryParse() method to create a DateTime value, the date and time you specify must be in a valid format. Some of the most common formats are listed in this figure. Later in this chapter, you'll learn more about the acceptable date and time formats.

Although the statements in this figure indicate the DateTime values that are created, you should realize that these aren't the actual values that are stored in the variables. Instead, they show what happens when a DateTime value is converted to a string. The date and time are actually stored as the number of *ticks* (100 nanosecond units) that have elapsed since 12:00:00 AM, January 1, 0001. That makes it easy to perform arithmetic operations on dates and times, as you'll see later in this chapter.

The syntax for creating a DateTime value

```
DateTime variableName = new DateTime(year, month, day
    [, hour, minute, second[, millisecond]]);
```

How to create a DateTime value using the Parse() method

```
DateTime variableName = DateTime.Parse(string);
```

How to create a DateTime value using the TryParse() method

```
DateTime.TryParse(string, out DateTime variableName);
```

Statements that create DateTime values

```
DateTime startDate = new DateTime(2023, 01, 30);   // 1/30/2023 12:00 AM
DateTime startDateAndTime =
    new DateTime(2023, 1, 30, 14, 15, 0);          // 1/30/2023 2:15 PM

DateTime startDate = DateTime.Parse("01/30/23");   // 1/30/2023 12:00 AM
DateTime startDateAndTime
    = DateTime.Parse("Jan 30, 2023 2:15 PM");      // 1/30/2023 2:15 PM
DateTime invoiceDate = DateTime.Parse(txtInvoiceDate.Text);

DateTime.TryParse(txtInvoiceDate.Text, out DateTime invoiceDate);
```

Valid date formats

```
01/30/2023
1/30/23
01-01-2023
1-1-23
2023-01-01
Jan 30 2023
January 30, 2023
```

Valid time formats

```
2:15 PM
14:15
02:15:30 AM
```

Description

- You can use the DateTime structure to create and work with dates and times.
- To create a DateTime value, you can use the new keyword and then specify the date and time values you want to use to create the date.
- You can also use the static Parse() or TryParse() method of the DateTime structure to create a DateTime value from a string.
- If you omit the time specification when you create a DateTime value, the time is set to 12:00 AM. You can also omit the date specification when you create a DateTime value using the Parse() or TryParse() method. Then, the date is set to the current date.
- A date is stored as a 64-bit signed integer that represents the number of *ticks* (100 nanosecond units) that have elapsed since 12:00 AM, January 1, 0001.

Figure 9-1   How to create a DateTime value

How to get the current date and time

Figure 9-2 presents two static properties of the DateTime structure that you can use to get the current date and time. If you use the Now property, both the date and time are returned. If you use the Today property, only the date is returned, and the time is set to 12:00:00 AM. The first two statements in this figure illustrate how this works.

How to format DateTime values

To format dates and times, you can use the four methods of the DateTime structure that are shown in figure 9-2. Note, however, that these formats may vary somewhat from the formats that are used on your system. The exact formats depend on your computer's regional settings. If these methods don't provide the format you need, you can use the formatting techniques you'll learn about later in this chapter to format the date and time the way you want them.

DateTime properties for getting the current date and time

Property	Description
Now	Returns the current date and time.
Today	Returns the current date.

Statements that get the current date and time

```
DateTime currentDateTime = DateTime.Now;      // 1/30/2023 4:24:59 PM
DateTime currentDate = DateTime.Today;        // 1/30/2023 12:00:00 AM
```

DateTime methods for formatting a date or time

Method	Description
ToLongDateString()	Converts the DateTime value to a string that includes the name for the day of the week, the name for the month, the day of the month, and the year.
ToShortDateString()	Converts the DateTime value to a string that includes the numbers for the month, day, and year.
ToLongTimeString()	Converts the DateTime value to a string that includes the hours, minutes, and seconds.
ToShortTimeString()	Converts the DateTime value to a string that includes the hours and minutes.

Statements that format dates and times

```
string longDate =
    currentDateTime.ToLongDateString();       // Monday, January 30, 2023
string shortDate =
    currentDateTime.ToShortDateString();      // 1/30/2023
string longTime =
    currentDateTime.ToLongTimeString();       // 4:24:59 AM
string ShortTime =
    currentDateTime.ToShortTimeString();      // 4:24 AM
```

Description

- The Now and Today properties are static properties of the DateTime structure.
- The format that's used for a date or time depends on your computer's regional settings.

Figure 9-2   How to get the current date and format DateTime values

How to get information about dates and times

The DateTime structure provides a variety of properties and methods for getting information about dates and times. These properties and methods are listed in figure 9-3, and the statements presented here show how to work with most of them.

The first statement uses the Now property to get the current date and time. Then, the second statement uses the Month property to get the month of that date, the third statement uses the Hour property to get the hour of that time, and the fourth statement uses the DayOfYear property to get an int value from 1 to 366 that represents the day of the year.

The next two statements show how to use the two methods for getting information about a date. Since both of these methods are static, they're accessed through the DateTime structure. The first method, DaysInMonth(), returns the number of days in a given month and year. In this example, since 2023 isn't a leap year, there are 28 days in February. However, if you specified 2024, which is a leap year, there would be 29 days in February. The second method, IsLeapYear(), returns a true or false value that indicates whether the specified year is a leap year.

The last code example in this figure shows how to use the DayOfWeek property. Note that this property returns a member of the DayOfWeek enumeration. In this case, the first statement gets the day of the week for the current date. Then, an if statement checks if the current date is a Saturday or a Sunday. If it is, a string variable named message is set to "Weekend". Otherwise, it's set to "Weekday".

Properties for working with dates and times

Property	Description
Date	Returns the DateTime value with the time portion set to 12:00:00 AM.
Month	Returns an integer for the month portion of the DateTime value.
Day	Returns an integer for the day portion of the DateTime value.
Year	Returns an integer for the year portion of the DateTime value.
Hour	Returns an integer for the hour portion of the DateTime value.
Minute	Returns an integer for the minute portion of the DateTime value.
Second	Returns an integer for the second portion of the DateTime value.
TimeOfDay	Returns a TimeSpan value that represents the amount of time that has elapsed since 12:00:00 AM. For more information about the TimeSpan structure, see figure 9-4.
DayOfWeek	Returns a member of the DayOfWeek enumeration that represents the day of the week of a DateTime value.
DayOfYear	Returns an integer for the numeric day of the year.

Methods for working with dates and times

Method	Description
DaysInMonth(year, month)	Returns the number of days in a specified month and year.
IsLeapYear(year)	Returns a Boolean value that indicates whether a specified year is a leap year.

Statements that get information about a date or time

```
DateTime currentDateTime = DateTime.Now;              // 1/30/2023 10:26:35 AM
int month = currentDateTime.Month;                    // 1
int hour = currentDateTime.Hour;                      // 10
int dayOfYear = currentDateTime.DayOfYear;            // 30
int daysInMonth = DateTime.DaysInMonth(2023, 2);      // 28
bool isLeapYear = DateTime.IsLeapYear(2023);          // false
```

Code that uses the DayOfWeek property and enumeration

```
DayOfWeek dayOfWeek = currentDateTime.DayOfWeek;
string message = "";
if (dayOfWeek == DayOfWeek.Saturday || dayOfWeek == DayOfWeek.Sunday)
{
    message = "Weekend";
}
else
{
    message = "Weekday";
}
```

Figure 9-3   How to get information about dates and times

How to perform operations on dates and times

Figure 9-4 presents some of the methods of the DateTime structure that you can use to perform operations on dates and times. Most of these methods let you add a specific number of intervals, like hours, days, or months, to a DateTime value. However, you can use the Add() method to add a TimeSpan value to a date, and you can use the Subtract() method to determine the time span between two dates, which is often required in business apps.

Like DateTime values, TimeSpan values are based on a structure defined by .NET. TimeSpan values also hold a number of ticks, just like DateTime values. However, a TimeSpan value represents a time interval. By contrast, a DateTime value represents a specific point in time.

The first group of statements in this figure shows how some of the Add methods work. For example, the second statement shows how to add two months to a DateTime value, and the third statement shows how to add 60 days. Similarly, the fourth statement shows how to add 30 minutes, and the fifth statement shows how to add 12 hours.

The second group of statements shows how you can use a TimeSpan variable to determine the number of days between two DateTime values. Here, the first statement retrieves the current date, and the second statement assigns a date to another DateTime variable. Next, the third statement uses the Subtract() method to subtract the two date values and assign the result to a TimeSpan variable, which represents the number of days, minutes, hours, and seconds between the two dates. Finally, the last statement uses the Days property of the TimeSpan structure to extract the number of days from the TimeSpan value. This is one of several properties of this structure that let you extract the data from a TimeSpan value.

In addition to the properties and methods provided by the DateTime structure for working with dates, you can use some of the standard operators to work with dates. For instance, the third example in this figure shows how to use the subtraction operator to calculate the time between two dates instead of using the Subtract() method. The last example shows that you can also use DateTime values in a conditional expression. Here, the conditional expression tests if one DateTime value is greater than another.

Methods for performing operations on dates and times

Method	Description
`AddDays(days)`	Adds the specified numbers of days to a DateTime value and returns another DateTime value.
`AddMonths(months)`	Adds the specified number of months to a DateTime value and returns another DateTime value.
`AddYears(years)`	Adds the specified number of years to a DateTime value and returns another DateTime value.
`AddHours(hours)`	Adds the specified number of hours to a DateTime value and returns another DateTime value.
`AddMinutes(minutes)`	Adds the specified number of minutes to a DateTime value and returns another DateTime value.
`AddSeconds(seconds)`	Adds the specified number of seconds to a DateTime value and returns another DateTime value.
`Add(timespan)`	Adds the specified TimeSpan value to a DateTime value and returns another DateTime value.
`Subtract(datetime)`	Subtracts the specified DateTime value from a DateTime value and returns a TimeSpan value.

Statements that perform operations on dates and times

```
DateTime dateTime =
    DateTime.Parse("3/1/2023 13:28");            // 3/1/2023 1:28:00 PM
DateTime dueDate = dateTime.AddMonths(2);        // 5/1/2023 1:28:00 PM
dueDate = dateTime.AddDays(60);                  // 4/30/2023 1:28:00 PM
DateTime runTime = dateTime.AddMinutes(30);      // 3/1/2023 1:58:00 PM
runTime = dateTime.AddHours(12);                 // 3/2/2023 1:28:00 AM
```

Code that results in a TimeSpan value

```
DateTime currentDate = DateTime.Today;                      // 1/30/2023
dueDate = DateTime.Parse("2/15/2020");                      // 2/15/2023
TimeSpan timeTillDue = dueDate.Subtract(currentDate);       // 16:00:00:00
int daysTillDue = timeTillDue.Days;                         // 16
```

A statement that uses the - operator to subtract two dates

```
TimeSpan timeTillDue = dueDate - currentDate;     // 16:00:00:00
```

An if statement that uses the > operator on DateTime values

```
bool pastDue = false;
if (currentDate > dueDate)
    pastDue = true;
```

Description

- A TimeSpan value represents a period of time stored as ticks. You can use the Days, Hours, Minutes, and Seconds properties of a TimeSpan value to get portions of that value.
- In addition to the DateTime methods, you can use the +, -, ==, !=, >, >=, <, and <= operators to work with DateTime values.

Figure 9-4   How to perform operations on dates and times

How to work with strings

Many types of programs require that you work with the characters within strings. If, for example, a user enters the city, state, and zip code of an address as a single entry, your program may need to divide (or parse) that single string into city, state, and zip code variables. Or, if a user enters a telephone number that includes parentheses and hyphens, you may need to remove those characters so the number can be stored as a 10-digit integer.

When you create a string, you are actually creating a String object from the String class. Then, you can use the properties and methods of the String class to work with the String object. Another alternative, though, is to create StringBuilder objects from the StringBuilder class so you can use the properties and methods of that class to work with strings. In the topics that follow, you'll learn both ways of working with strings.

The members of the String class

Figure 9-5 summarizes some of the members of the String class that you can use as you work with String objects. When you use these members, you often need to use an index to refer to a specific character within a string. To do that, you use 0 to refer to the first character, 1 to refer to the second character, and so on. For example, when you use the Insert() method, you specify the starting index where the specified string is to be inserted. Similarly, when you use the Substring() method, you specify the starting index for the string to be returned.

You can also refer directly to a character in a string using an *indexer*. You'll learn more about indexers in chapter 13. For now, you should realize that an indexer allows you to access individual items by their index values. For a string, the items are the characters in the string. When you refer to a character in a string, you code the index value for the character within brackets. This is the same technique that you use to refer to an element of an array. In fact, it sometimes helps to think of a string as an array of characters.

One method that's particularly useful for parsing strings is Split(). This method returns an array where each element contains a substring of the original string. The argument that you specify for this method identifies the character that's used to delimit each substring. You'll see examples of this method in figure 9-7.

Unlike the other methods presented in this figure, which are instance methods of the String class, the last method, IsNullOrEmpty(), is a static method. To call this method, then, you code the name of the String class followed by the dot operator and the method name. As its name implies, you use this method when you want to check if a string variable is null or contains an empty string. You'll see an example of this method in figure 9-7 as well.

Common members of the String class

Indexer	Description
`[index]`	Gets the character at the specified position.

Property	Description
`Length`	Gets the number of characters in the string.

Method	Description
`StartsWith(string)`	Returns a Boolean value that indicates whether or not the string starts with the specified string.
`EndsWith(string)`	Returns a Boolean value that indicates whether or not the string ends with the specified string.
`IndexOf(string[, startIndex])`	Returns an integer that represents the position of the first occurrence of the specified string starting at the specified position, or starting at the beginning of the string if no position is specified. If the string isn't found, -1 is returned.
`LastIndexOf(string[, startIndex])`	Returns an integer that represents the position of the last occurrence of the specified string starting at the specified position, or starting at the end of the string if no position is specified. If the string isn't found, -1 is returned.
`Insert(startIndex, string)`	Returns a string with the specified string inserted beginning at the specified position.
`PadLeft(totalWidth)`	Returns a string that's right-aligned and padded on the left with spaces so it's the specified width.
`PadRight(totalWidth)`	Returns a string that's left-aligned and padded on the right with spaces so it's the specified width.
`Remove(startIndex, count)`	Returns a string with the specified number of characters removed starting at the specified position.
`Replace(oldString, newString)`	Returns a string with all occurrences of the old string replaced with the new string.
`Substring(startIndex[, length])`	Returns the string that starts at the specified position and has the specified length, or all of the characters to the end of the string if the length isn't specified.
`ToLower()`	Returns a string in lowercase.
`ToUpper()`	Returns a string in uppercase.
`Trim()`	Returns a string with leading and trailing spaces removed.
`Split(splitCharacters)`	Returns an array of strings where each element is a substring that's delimited by the specified character or characters.
`IsNullOrEmpty(string)`	Static method that returns a Boolean value that indicates whether or not the string is null or contains an empty string.

Description

- You can use an index to access each character in a string, where 0 is the index for the first character, 1 is the index for the second character, and so on.

Figure 9-5   The members of the String class

Code examples that work with strings

Figure 9-6 shows how to use most of the members summarized in the last figure. The first example shows how you can use an indexer to return a character from a string. Then, the second example shows how you can use an indexer and the Length property in a for loop to insert a space character between each character in the string. The third example performs the same operation as the second example, but it uses a foreach loop instead of a for loop.

The fourth example shows how you can use the StartsWith() and EndsWith() methods. Here, the first statement checks if the string named chars that was created in the first example starts with the string "abc", and the second statement checks if this string ends with "abc". As you can see, the result of the first statement is true, and the result of the second statement is false.

The fifth example shows how to use the IndexOf() and LastIndexOf() methods. Here, the first statement sets the value of the string. Then, the second and third statements use the IndexOf() method to retrieve the index of the first space in the string. The fourth statement uses the same method to return the index of a string of characters. Since the characters don't exist in the string, this method returns a value of -1. The last statement uses the LastIndexOf() method to return the index of the last space in the string.

The sixth example shows how to use the Remove(), Insert(), and Replace() methods to work with the string in the fifth example. Here, the first statement removes the first five characters of the string. In this statement, the first argument specifies the starting index, and the second argument specifies the number of characters to remove. In this case, the number of characters to remove is calculated by adding 1 to the index of the first space, which is 4. Then, the second statement uses the Insert() method to insert ", Inc." at the end of the string. Here, the first argument uses the Length property to set the starting index at the end of the string, and the second argument specifies the string to be inserted. Finally, the third statement uses the Replace() method to replace all occurrences of "and" with "And".

The seventh example shows how to use the Substring(), ToUpper(), and ToLower() methods to make sure a string is lowercase with an initial cap. Here, the second statement returns a substring that contains the first character in the string. To do that, the first argument specifies a starting index of 0 and the second argument specifies a length of 1. Then, to convert the returned substring to uppercase, this statement calls the ToUpper() method. The third statement is similar, but it uses the ToLower() method to return the remaining characters in the string and convert them to lowercase. The last statement combines the two strings into a single string.

The eighth example shows how to use the = operator to copy one string to another string. Because a string is a reference type, you might think that the second statement would copy the reference to the string object created by the first statement to the second string variable. In this case, however, a new string object is created and the value in the original string is copied to that object. Then, a reference to the new object is assigned to the new string variable.

Code that uses an indexer to access a character in a string

```
string chars = "abcdefg";
char a = chars[0];                // 'a'
char b = chars[1];                // 'b'
```

Code that uses a for loop to access each character in the string

```
string charsAndSpaces = "";
for (int i = 0; i < chars.Length; i++)
    charsAndSpaces += chars[i] + " ";
MessageBox.Show(charsAndSpaces, "String Test");
```

The message box that's displayed

Code that uses a foreach loop to access each character in the string

```
string charsAndSpaces = "";
foreach (char c in chars)
    charsAndSpaces += c + " ";
MessageBox.Show(charsAndSpaces, "String Test");
```

Code that uses the StartsWith() and EndsWith() methods

```
bool startsWithABC = chars.StartsWith("abc");   // true
bool endsWithABC = chars.EndsWith("abc");       // false
```

Code that uses the IndexOf() and LastIndexOf() methods

```
string companyName = "Mike Murach and Associates";
int index1 = companyName.IndexOf(" ");          // 4
int index2 = companyName.IndexOf(' ');          // 4
int index3 = companyName.IndexOf("Inc.");       // -1
int index4 = companyName.LastIndexOf(" ");      // 15
```

Code that uses the Remove(), Insert(), and Replace() methods

```
companyName = companyName.Remove(0, index1 + 1);
companyName = companyName.Insert(companyName.Length, ", Inc.");
companyName
    = companyName.Replace("and", "And");        // Murach And Associates, Inc.
```

Code that uses the Substring(), ToUpper(), and ToLower() methods

```
string firstName = "anne";
string firstLetter = firstName.Substring(0, 1).ToUpper();
string otherLetters = firstName.Substring(1).ToLower();
firstName = firstLetter + otherLetters;         // Anne
```

Code that copies one string to another string

```
string s1 = "abc";
string s2 = s1;     // this copies the value stored in s1 to s2
s2 = "def";         // this doesn't change the value stored in s1
```

Figure 9-6   Code examples that work with strings

More code examples that work with strings

Figure 9-7 presents some additional string-handling routines. The first four parse the data in strings. The fifth one adds characters to a string. And the sixth one replaces some of the characters in a string with other characters. If you can understand the code in these routines, you should be able to write your own routines whenever needed.

Each of the routines in this figure starts by assigning a string value to a variable, so you can visualize how the statements that follow work with that string. In practice, though, the value would be entered by a user or read from a file so you wouldn't know what it was.

The first routine shows how to parse the first name from a string that contains a full name. To start, this routine uses the Trim() method to remove any spaces from the beginning and end of the string that a user may have typed accidentally. Next, the IndexOf() method is used to get the position of the first space in the string, which should be between the first name and the middle name or last name. If this method doesn't find a space in the string, though, it returns a -1. In that case, the if-else statement that follows assigns the entire string to the first name variable. Otherwise, it uses the Substring() method to set the first name variable equal to the string that begins at the first character of the string and that has a length that's equal to the position of the first space.

The second routine in this figure shows how to parse a string that contains an address into the components of the address. In this case, a pipe character (|) separates each component of the address. In addition, the string may begin with one or more spaces followed by a pipe character, and it may end with a pipe character followed by one or more spaces.

To remove the spaces from the beginning and end of the string, this routine also uses the Trim() method. Then, it uses the StartsWith() and EndsWith() methods to determine whether the first or last character in the string is a pipe character. If it is, the Remove() method removes that character from the string.

The next three statements use the IndexOf() method to determine the index values of the first character for each substring other than the first. (The first substring will start at index 0.) To do that, it determines the index of the next pipe character and then adds 1. After that, the next four statements use these index variables as arguments of the Substring() method to return the street, city, state, and zip code substrings. To calculate the length of each substring, this code subtracts the starting index from the ending index and then subtracts 1 from that value. This results in the length of the substring without the pipe character.

The third and fourth routines use the Split() method to perform the same operations as the first and second routines. As you can see, the Split() method can simplify your code significantly, particularly if the string you're parsing consists of several elements.

The fifth and sixth routines show how to add hyphens to a phone number and change the hyphens in a date to slashes. To add hyphens, you simply use the Insert() method to insert the hyphens at the appropriate index. And to change hyphens to slashes, you use the Replace() method. The last routine also uses the IsNullOrEmpty() method to ensure that the string has a value before processing it.

Code that parses a first name from a name string

```
string fullName = " Edward C Koop    ";              // " Edward C Koop    "
fullName = fullName.Trim();                          // "Edward C Koop"
int firstSpace = fullName.IndexOf(" ");              // 6
string firstName = "";
if (firstSpace == -1)
    firstName = fullName;
else
    firstName = fullName.Substring(0, firstSpace);   // Edward
```

Code that parses a string that contains an address

```
string address = " |805 Main Street|Dallas|TX|12345| ";
address = address.Trim();
if (address.StartsWith("|"))
    address = address.Remove(0, 1);
if (address.EndsWith("|"))
    address = address.Remove(address.Length - 1, 1);
int cityIndex = address.IndexOf("|") + 1;
int stateIndex = address.IndexOf("|", cityIndex) + 1;
int zipIndex = address.IndexOf("|", stateIndex) + 1;
string street = address.Substring(0, cityIndex - 1);
string city = address.Substring(cityIndex, stateIndex - cityIndex - 1);
string state = address.Substring(stateIndex, zipIndex - stateIndex - 1);
string zipCode = address.Substring(zipIndex);
```

Code that uses the Split() method to parse the name string

```
string fullName = " Edward C Koop    ";
fullName = fullName.Trim();
string[] names = fullName.Split(' ');
string firstName = names[0];                         // Edward
```

Code that uses the Split() method to parse the address string

```
string address = " |805 Main Street|Dallas|TX|12345| ";
address = address.Trim();
if (address.StartsWith("|"))
    address = address.Remove(0, 1);
string[] columns = address.Split('|');
string street = columns[0];          // 805 Main Street
string city = columns[1];            // Dallas
string state = columns[2];           // TX
string zipCode = columns[3];         // 12345
```

Code that adds hyphens to a phone number

```
string phoneNumber = "9775551212";
phoneNumber = phoneNumber.Insert(3, "-");
phoneNumber = phoneNumber.Insert(7, "-");   // 977-555-1212
```

Code that replaces the hyphens in a date with slashes

```
string date = "12-27-2022";
if (!String.IsNullOrEmpty(date))
    date = date.Replace("-", "/");          // 12/27/2022
```

Figure 9-7   More code examples that work with strings

How to use interpolated strings for join operations

Up until now, you've used the + operator to join a string with another string or value type. Now, figure 9-8 shows how to use a feature that became available with C# 6.0 called *interpolated strings* in join operations.

To create an interpolated string, you code a $ sign followed by a string literal. Within the string literal, you code one or more *interpolated expressions* within braces. These expressions contain the values you want to add to the string literal and can be strings, value types, or expressions that result in strings or value types. Then, the value, object, or expression in each interpolated expression is evaluated, its resulting value is converted to a string, and that string is added to the string literal at the position of the interpolated expression.

The first example in this figure shows how to use an interpolated string to join two strings named firstName and lastName that are declared and initialized in the first two statements. Then, the interpolated string in the third statement consists of an interpolated expression that contains the lastName variable, followed by the characters ", ", followed by another interpolated expression that contains the firstName variable. This statement joins the two variables and the text into a single string.

The second example shows how to join a string and a number. Here, the value of the interpolated expression is of type decimal. When it's evaluated, the ToString() method of the decimal variable is implicitly called, and the resulting string is added to the string literal at the position of the interpolated expression.

The third example shows how to use an interpolated string to initialize a constant, which is a feature that became available with C# 10.0. This works just like the first two examples, except that the value in the interpolated expression is a constant. If you try to use anything other than a constant for an interpolated expression, your code won't compile.

The fourth and fifth examples in this figure present features of interpolated strings that became available with C# 11.0. The fourth example shows how to code an interpolated expression across multiple lines. This is useful when an interpolated expression contains an expression rather than a variable or constant. Here, the second interpolated expression contains a switch expression that returns a string value based on the value of a variable. And the last example shows how to code an interpolated string with a raw string literal.

You should know that you can also use interpolated strings to format the values in interpolated expressions. For instance, you could format the double variable in the second example in this figure so it displays as a currency value. You'll learn how to do that later in this chapter.

Code that joins two strings

```
string firstName = "Bob";
string lastName = "Smith";
string name = $"{lastName}, {firstName}";      // "Smith, Bob"
```

Code that joins a string and a number

```
decimal price = 14.95m;
string priceString = $"Price: {price}";        // "Price: 14.95"
```

Code that creates a constant (C# 10.0 and later)

```
const string Domain = "https://www.murach.com";
const string Url = $"{Domain}/shop-books/all";
// "http://www.murach.com/shop-books/all"
```

An interpolated expression that spans multiple lines (C# 11.0 and later)

```
string customerType = "R";
string message = $"The discount for customer type {customerType} is {
    customerType switch {
        "R" or "C" => "20 percent",
        "T" => "40 percent",
        _ => "unknown"
    }
}";
// "The discount for customer type R is 20 percent"
```

An interpolated raw string literal (C# 11.0 and later)

```
string author = "Ring Lardner";
string quote = $"""
    "Shut up", he explained.
        --{author}
    """;
```

Description

- In addition to using the + operator to join a string with another string or value type, you can use a feature that was introduced with C# 6.0 called *interpolated strings*.

- To create an interpolated string, you code a $ sign followed by a string literal that contains one or more *interpolated expressions* within braces ({}). An interpolated expression can contain a string, a value type, or an expression that results in a string or value type.

- The value in an interpolated expression is evaluated, converted to a string, and added to the string literal at its position in the string literal.

- With C# 10.0 and later, you can use an interpolated string to initialize a constant. For this to work, the values in the interpolated expressions must also be constants.

- With C# 11.0 and later, you can code an interpolated expression across multiple lines, and you can code interpolated strings with raw string literals.

Figure 9-8   How to use interpolated strings in join operations

How to use the Parse() and TryParse() methods to validate numeric entries

In chapter 4, you learned how to use the Parse() and TryParse() methods to convert a string to another data type. You also learned that when you convert a string to a numeric data type, these methods only recognize standard numeric characters. Now, you'll learn how to use the Parse() and TryParse() methods to validate a numeric user entry by specifying the exact characters you want to allow. To do that, you use the syntax of these methods shown in figure 9-9.

Here, you can see that in addition to the string that's specified for the first argument of the Parse() method, you can code one or more styles for the second argument. To do that, you use the members of the NumberStyles enumeration. This figure lists the most common members of this enumeration for working with decimal values.

The first eight members in this list provide for specific characters, like a $ sign or a decimal point. When you use one of these members, only numeric digits and the character specified by the member will be allowed. If you use the AllowCurrencySymbol member, for example, only numeric digits and a $ sign will be allowed. If the user enters any other characters, an exception will occur.

Because of that, you'll usually want to use one of the next two members since they represent a composite of some or all of the first eight members. If you use the Currency member as shown in the first example in this figure, the user will be able to enter any of the characters provided by the first eight members. And if you use the Number member, the user will be able to enter all of these characters except for a $ sign and parentheses.

Another way to provide for more than one type of character is to combine two or more members as shown in the second example in this figure. As you can see, you combine members by coding a pipe character between them. (In case you're not familiar with the pipe character, it's available from the same key as the backslash key on your keyboard.) In this case, the user will be able to enter both a $ sign and a decimal point.

Notice that this example uses the TryParse() method instead of the Parse() method. When you specify styles with this method, you also have to include a format provider as the third argument. The format provider specifies culture-specific parsing information. In most cases, you'll use the CurrentCulture property of the CultureInfo class for this argument as shown here.

The syntax of the Parse() and TryParse() methods for validating decimal values

```
Parse(string, style1[ | style2]...)
TryParse(string, style1[ | style2]..., formatProvider, result)
```

Common members of the NumberStyles enumeration for decimal values

Member	Characters allowed
AllowCurrencySymbol	Digits and a $ sign
AllowDecimalPoint	Digits and a decimal point
AllowLeadingWhiteSpace	Digits and leading whitespace
AllowTrailingWhiteSpace	Digits and trailing whitespace
AllowLeadingSign	Digits and a leading sign
AllowTrailingSign	Digits and a trailing sign
AllowParentheses	Parentheses around the digits to indicate a negative value
AllowThousands	Digits and commas used as thousands separators
Currency	Digits and all of the characters listed above
Number	Digits and all of the characters listed above except for a $ sign and parentheses
None	Digits only

A Parse() method that allows entries with any of the content above

```
decimal invoiceTotal = Decimal.Parse(txtTotal.Text, NumberStyles.Currency);
```

A TryParse() method that allows entries with a $ sign and a decimal point

```
Decimal.TryParse(txtTotal.Text,
    NumberStyles.AllowCurrencySymbol | NumberStyles.AllowDecimalPoint,
    CultureInfo.CurrentCulture, out decimal invoiceTotal);
```

Description

- By default, commas, a decimal point, and leading and trailing spaces are allowed in a decimal value when you use the Parse() or TryParse() method.

- If you want to restrict the characters that can be entered or if you want to allow additional characters, you can use the second argument of the Parse() or TryParse() method. Then, if any other characters are entered, an exception will occur.

- To indicate the characters that are allowed, you use the members of the NumberStyles enumeration. You can combine two or more members of this enumeration by coding a pipe character (|) between them as shown in the second example above.

- The Parse() and TryParse() methods remove any of the specified characters from the string that aren't allowed by the numeric data type before the value is assigned to that data type.

- When you use this syntax of the TryParse() method, you also have to include a format provider that specifies culture-specific parsing information. In most cases, you'll code this argument as shown above.

- The NumberStyles enumeration is in the System.Globalization namespace.

Figure 9-9   How to use the Parse() and TryParse() methods to validate numeric entries

How to use the StringBuilder class

When you use the String class to create a string, the string has a fixed length and value. In other words, the String class creates strings that are *immutable*. Then, when you assign a new value to a string variable, the original String object is deleted and it's replaced with a new String object that contains the new value.

Another way to work with strings, though, is to use the StringBuilder class. Then, you create StringBuilder objects that are *mutable* so you can add, delete, or replace characters in the objects. This makes it easier to write some types of string-handling routines, and these routines run more efficiently. As a result, you should use the StringBuilder class for string-handling routines that append, insert, remove, or replace characters in strings, especially if you're working with long strings that use significant system resources.

In figure 9-10, you can see some of the most useful members for working with a string that's created from the StringBuilder class. Just as you can with a String object, you can use an indexer to refer to a character in a StringBuilder object. Also like String objects, an index value for a StringBuilder object specifies the position of the character starting at 0.

You can use the Length property to get the number of characters in a string just as you can with a String object. You can also use the Insert(), Remove(), and Replace() methods with StringBuilder objects. However, instead of returning a new string, these methods change the existing string.

When you create a StringBuilder object, you can code one or two arguments that assign an initial value, an initial capacity, or both. The statements in the first example illustrate how this works. Here, the first statement doesn't include any arguments, so the StringBuilder object is created with a default capacity of 16 characters and an initial value of an empty string. The second statement creates a StringBuilder object with an initial capacity of 10. The third and fourth statements are similar, but they specify an initial value for the object.

The second example in this figure shows how you can use five methods of the StringBuilder class. Here, the first statement creates a StringBuilder object with an initial capacity of 10, and the second statement appends a 10-character phone number to the object. The third and fourth statements insert periods into the string to format the number. The fifth statement removes the area code and the period that follows it. The sixth statement replaces the remaining period with a hyphen. And the last statement converts the characters stored in the StringBuilder object to a string.

This example also shows how a StringBuilder object automatically increases its capacity when necessary. Here, the StringBuilder object has a capacity of 10 when it's created, and this capacity remains at 10 until the first period is inserted. Then, to be able to store the 11 characters, the StringBuilder object automatically doubles its capacity to 20.

The syntax for creating a StringBuilder object

```
StringBuilder variableName = new StringBuilder([value][,][capacity]);
```

Common members of the StringBuilder class

Indexer	Description
`[index]`	Gets the character at the specified position.
Property	**Description**
`Length`	Gets the number of characters in the string.
`Capacity`	Gets or sets the number of characters the string can hold.
Method	**Description**
`Append(string)`	Adds the specified string to the end of the string.
`Insert(index, string)`	Inserts the specified string at the specified index in the string.
`Remove(startIndex, count)`	Removes the specified number of characters from the string starting at the specified index.
`Replace(oldString, newString)`	Replaces all occurrences of the old string with the new string.
`ToString()`	Converts the StringBuilder object to a string.

Statements that create and initialize StringBuilder objects

```
StringBuilder address1 = new StringBuilder();          // Capacity is 16
StringBuilder address2 = new StringBuilder(10);        // Capacity is 10
StringBuilder phoneNumber1 =
    new StringBuilder("9775551212");                   // Capacity is 16
StringBuilder phoneNumber2 =
    new StringBuilder("9775551212", 10);               // Capacity is 10
```

Code that creates a phone number and inserts dashes

```
StringBuilder phoneNumber = new StringBuilder(10);   // Capacity is 10
phoneNumber.Append("9775551212");                    // Capacity is 10
phoneNumber.Insert(3, ".");                          // Capacity is 20
phoneNumber.Insert(7, ".");                          // 977.555.1212
phoneNumber.Remove(0, 4);                            // 555.1212
phoneNumber.Replace(".", "-");                       // 555-1212
lblPhoneNumber.Text = phoneNumber.ToString();        // 555-1212
```

Description

- Unlike string objects, StringBuilder objects are *mutable*, which means that they can be changed.

- The capacity of a StringBuilder object is the amount of memory that's allocated to it. That capacity is increased automatically whenever necessary. If you don't set an initial capacity when you create a StringBuilder object, the default is 16 characters.

- The StringBuilder class is a member of the System.Text namespace.

Figure 9-10   How to use the StringBuilder class

How to format numbers, dates, and times

In chapter 4, you learned how to apply standard numeric formats to numbers. Then, earlier in this chapter, you learned how to apply standard formats to dates and times. However, you can also apply custom formatting to numbers, dates, and times.

How to format numbers

Figure 9-11 shows how to use the Format() method of the String class to format numbers. Because this is a static method, you access it directly from the String class rather than from an instance of this class. The result of this method is a string that contains the formatted number.

As you can see in the syntax for this method, the first argument is a string. This string contains the format specifications for the value or values to be formatted. Following this string, you specify one or more values that you want to format. In most cases, you'll use this method to format a single value.

For each value to be formatted, you code a format specification within the string argument. This specification is divided into three parts. The first part indicates the value to be formatted. Because the values are numbered from zero, you'll usually code a zero to indicate that the first value is to be formatted. The next part indicates the width of the formatted value along with its alignment. In most cases, you'll omit this part of the specification.

The third part of the format specification contains the actual format string. This string can contain multiple formats. If only one format is specified, it's used for all numbers. If two formats are specified, the first is used for positive numbers and zero values, and the second is used for negative values. If all three formats are specified, the first is used for positive numbers, the second is used for negative numbers, and the third is used for zero values.

Each format can consist of one of the standard numeric formatting codes listed in this figure. If, for example, you want to format a number as currency, you can code a statement like the first statement in this figure. Here, the format specification, which is enclosed in braces, indicates that the first value (0) should be formatted with the currency format (c). Then, this specification is enclosed in quotes to indicate that it is a string literal. That way, it can be passed as an argument to the Format() method of the String class.

If the standard numeric formatting codes don't provide the format you want, you can create your own format using the custom codes presented in this figure. For instance, the second statement uses these codes to create a custom currency format. Here, the first format string indicates that positive numbers and the value 0 should be formatted with a decimal and thousands separators (if appropriate). In addition, the first digit to the left of the decimal point and the first two digits to the right of the decimal are always included, even if they're zero. The other digits are included only if they're non-zero.

The syntax of the Format() method of the String class

```
Format(string, value1[, value2]...)
```

The syntax of a format specification within the string argument

```
{N[, M][:formatString]}
```

Explanation

N	An integer that indicates the value to be formatted.
M	An integer that indicates the width of the formatted value. If M is negative, the value will be left-justified. If it's positive, it will be right-justified.
formatString	A string of formatting codes.

The syntax of a format string

```
positiveformat[;negativeformat[;zeroformat]]
```

Standard numeric formatting codes

C or **c**	Formats the number as currency with the specified number of decimal places.
D or **d**	Formats an integer with the specified number of digits.
E or **e**	Formats the number in scientific (exponential) notation with the specified number of decimal places.
F or **f**	Formats the number as a decimal with the specified number of decimal places.
G or **g**	Formats the number as a decimal or in scientific notation depending on which is more compact.
N or **n**	Formats the number with thousands separators and the specified number of decimal places.
P or **p**	Formats the number as a percent with the specified number of decimal places.

Custom numeric formatting codes

0	Zero placeholder	**,**	Thousands separator
#	Digit placeholder	**%**	Percentage placeholder
.	Decimal point	**;**	Section separator

Statements that format a single number

```
string balance1 = String.Format("{0:c}", 1234.56);          // $1,234.56
string balance2 =
    String.Format("{0:$#,##0.00;($#,##0.00)}", -1234.56);   // ($1,234.56)
string balance3 =
    String.Format("{0:$#,##0.00;($#,##0.00);Zero}", 0);     // Zero
string quantity = String.Format("{0:d3}", 43);              // 043
string payment =  String.Format("{0:f2}", 432.8175);        // 432.82
```

A statement that formats two numbers

```
string totalDue =
    String.Format("Invoice total: {0:c}; Amount due: {1:c}.", 354.75, 20);
// Invoice total: $354.75; Amount due: $20.00.
```

Figure 9-11   How to format numbers

The format for negative numbers is similar. However, this format includes parentheses, which means that negative numbers will be displayed with parentheses around them as shown in the result for this statement. Notice that the parentheses aren't actually formatting codes. They're simply literal values that are included in the output string. The same is true of the dollar signs.

The third statement is similar to the second one, but it includes an additional format for zero values. In this case, a zero value is displayed as the literal "Zero" as you can see in the result for this statement.

The last two statements show how to use standard formatting codes for integers and decimals. In the first statement, an integer is formatted with three digits since the number 3 is included after the formatting code. In the second statement, a decimal is formatted with two decimal places. As you can see, if the number includes more decimal places than are specified, the number is rounded.

The example at the bottom of figure 9-11 shows how you can use the Format() method to format two numbers. Here, the string argument includes text in addition to the format specification for each of the two values to be formatted. In this case, the first value is formatted according to the first format specification, and the second value according to the second format specification.

How to format dates and times

You can also use the Format() method of the String class to format dates and times. This method works the same way that it does for numeric formatting, but you use the standard and custom formatting codes for DateTime values that are presented in figure 9-12. The examples in this figure show how this works. If you understand how to use this method to format numbers, you shouldn't have any trouble using it to format dates and times.

Standard DateTime formatting codes

d	Short date	f	Long date, short time
D	Long date	F	Long date, long time
t	Short time	g	Short date, short time
T	Long time	G	Short date, long time

Custom DateTime formatting codes

d	Day of the month without leading zeros	h	Hour without leading zeros
dd	Day of the month with leading zeros	hh	Hour with leading zeros
ddd	Abbreviated day name	H	Hour on a 24-hour clock without leading zeros
dddd	Full day name	HH	Hour on a 24-hour clock with leading zeros
M	Month without leading zeros	m	Minutes without leading zeros
MM	Month with leading zeros	mm	Minutes with leading zeros
MMM	Abbreviated month name	s	Seconds without leading zeros
MMMM	Full month name	ss	Seconds with leading zeros
y	Two-digit year without leading zero	f	Fractions of seconds (one *f* for each decimal place)
yy	Two-digit year with leading zero	t	First character of AM/PM designator
yyyy	Four-digit year	tt	Full AM/PM designator
/	Date separator	:	Time separator

Statements that format dates and times

```
DateTime currentDate = DateTime.Now;                  // 1/30/2023 10:37:32 PM
String.Format("{0:d}", currentDate)                   // 1/30/2023
String.Format("{0:D}", currentDate)                   // Monday, January 30, 2023
String.Format("{0:t}", currentDate)                   // 10:37 PM
String.Format("{0:T}", currentDate)                   // 10:37:32 PM
String.Format("{0:ddd, MMM d, yyyy}",
    currentDate)                                      // Mon, Jan 30, 2023
String.Format("{0:M/d/yy}", currentDate)              // 1/30/23
String.Format("{0:HH:mm:ss}", currentDate)            // 22:37:32
```

Figure 9-12   How to format dates and times

How to use interpolated strings for formatting

In addition to using the Format() method of the String class to format numbers, dates, and times, you can use interpolated strings. Figure 9-13 shows how this works.

To start, this figure shows the syntax for an interpolated expression of an interpolated string that's used for formatting. This is similar to the syntax for a format specification that you include on the Format() method. The difference is that instead of including an integer that identifies the value to be formatted, an interpolated expression includes the value itself.

The two statements in the first example in this figure illustrate how this works. In the first statement, an interpolated string is used to format a decimal value using the currency format. In the second statement, an interpolated string is used to apply custom formatting to a decimal value. If you compare these statements to the first two statements in figure 9-11, you'll see how using interpolated strings differs from using the String.Format() method. The statement in the second example is similar, except the interpolated string formats a date.

The last example in this figure shows how you can use an interpolated string to format two values. Here, values are assigned to a decimal variable and a DateTime variable. Then, an interpolated string is used to format the two values and display them in a dialog. Notice here that you can include text within the string just like you can when you use the Format() method.

When you use interpolated strings to format numbers, dates, and times, you should realize that the compiler translates them to String.Format() methods. Because of that, the use of interpolated strings like these is slightly less efficient than using the Format() method. However, interpolated strings are typically easier to understand than Format() methods. That's particularly true if you're formatting more than one value.

The syntax of an interpolated expression of an interpolated string

```
{value[, M][:formatString]}
```

Explanation

`value`	The value to be formatted.
`M`	An integer that indicates the width of the formatted value. If M is negative, the value will be left-justified. If it's positive, it will be right-justified.
`formatString`	A string of formatting codes. See figures 9-11 and 9-12 for details.

Statements that format numbers

```
string balance1 = $"{1234.56:c}";                          // $1,234.56
string balance2 = $"{-1234.56:$#,##0.00;($#,##0.00)}";     // ($1,234.56)
```

A statement that formats a date

```
string date1 = $"{DateTime.Now:D}";     // Monday, January 30, 2023
```

Code that formats a number and a date

```
decimal balanceDue = 1234.56m;
DateTime dateDue = new DateTime(2024, 02, 07);
MessageBox.Show($"{balanceDue:c} due on {dateDue:d}.",
    "A number and a date");
```

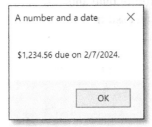

Description

- Instead of using the Format() method of the String class to format numbers, dates, and times, you can use interpolated strings with one or more interpolated expressions.

- An interpolated expression that performs formatting is similar to a format specification for the Format() method, except it includes the actual value to be formatted rather than an integer that identifies that value. That can make interpolated strings easier to understand, especially when more than one value is being formatted.

- When you use an interpolated string to format numbers, dates, and times, it's translated to a String.Format() method, which can make it less efficient.

Figure 9-13   How to use interpolated strings for formatting

Perspective

Now that you've completed this chapter, you should be able to use the DateTime structure to work with dates and times and the String and StringBuilder classes to work with strings. You should be able to use interpolated strings for join operations. And you should be able to use the Format() method of the String class and interpolated strings to provide custom formatting for numbers, dates, and times.

Terms

tick	interpolated string	immutable
indexer	interpolated expression	mutable

Exercise 9-1   Work with dates and times

In this exercise, you'll use the DateTime and TimeSpan structures.

1. Open the app that's in the C:\C#\Ch09\DateHandling directory. Within this project, you'll find a form that accepts a future date and a birth date and provides buttons for calculating days due and age.

2. Add code to calculate the due days when the user enters a future date and clicks the Calculate Due Days button. For simplicity, you can assume valid user entries. Then, display the results in a dialog like this:

3. Test your code with a variety of date formats to see what formats can be successfully parsed. When you're done, close the form.

4. Add code to calculate the age when the user enters a birth date and clicks the Calculate Age button. Then, display the results in a dialog like the one that follows. For simplicity, you can assume valid user entries.

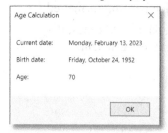

5. Test your code to make sure it works for all dates. Then, close the solution.

Exercise 9-2   Work with strings

In this exercise, you'll use methods of the String class to work with strings.

Open the app and add code to parse a name

1. Open the app that's in the C:\C#\Ch09\StringHandling directory. Within this project, you'll find a form that accepts a name and a phone number from the user and provides buttons for parsing the name and editing the phone number.

2. Add code to parse the name when the user enters a name and clicks the Parse Name button. This code should work whether the user enters a first, middle, and last name or just a first and last name. It should also convert the parsed name so the first letters are uppercase but the other letters are lowercase. The results should be displayed in a dialog like one of these:

3. Test the app to see if it works. Make sure that the names are capitalized properly no matter how they're entered.

4. Identify the variable for the middle name as one that can contain null. Be sure to check if this variable is null or empty before working with it.

5. Test the app again without entering a middle name to see if it works. When you're done, close the form.

Add code to edit a phone number

6. Add code to edit the phone number when the user enters a phone number and clicks the Edit Phone Number button. This code should remove all special characters so the number consists of 10 digits. Then, format the phone number with hyphens. These results should be displayed in a dialog like the one below. For simplicity, you can assume the user enters ten digits.

7. Test the app with a variety of entry formats to make sure it works. When you're done, close the form and then close the solution.

Exercise 9-3 Enhance the Future Value app

This exercise will guide you through the process of enhancing the Future Value app so it uses the Parse() and TryParse() methods as shown in figure 9-9.

Open the Future Value app and add the code that provides for formatted entries

1. Open the app that's in the C:\C#\Ch09\FutureValue directory.

2. Add a using directive for the System.Globalization namespace.

3. Modify the TryParse() method within the IsDecimal() method so it allows numbers and all numeric styles except for a $ sign and parentheses. If you need help, refer to figure 9-9.

4. Add another method named IsCurrency() that's like the IsDecimal() method but allows numbers and all numeric styles.

5. Modify the TryParse() method within the IsInt32() method so it allows only numbers.

6. Change the ToDecimal() method within the IsWithinRange() method to a Parse() method that allows numbers and all numeric styles.

7. Modify the IsValidData() method so it calls the IsCurrency() method instead of the IsDecimal() method for the monthly investment.

8. Modify the btnCalculate_Click() method so it uses the Parse() method to convert the values the user enters. Include a style argument that provides for the appropriate characters.

9. Modify the btnCalculate_Click() method so it catches an overflow exception and displays an appropriate error message.

10. Test the app by entering numeric values that contain characters other than numbers.

Add code to format the displayed values

11. Add statements to the btnCalculate_Click method() that format the values that are displayed in each text box like this:

12. Test the app to make sure it works correctly. Then, close it.

10

More skills for working with Windows forms and controls

In previous chapters, you learned how to work with a project that uses a single form that contains labels, text boxes, and buttons. In this chapter, you'll learn how to use some other common controls, such as combo boxes and check boxes, and you'll learn some basic skills for working with two or more forms in the same project. When you're done, you'll be able to develop a project that contains multiple forms and uses any of the controls presented in this chapter.

How to work with controls

Although you'll use label, text box, and button controls on almost every form you develop, their functionality is limited. As a result, you need to know how to use some of the other controls provided by .NET. In particular, you need to learn how to use the five controls presented in the topics that follow.

Five more types of controls

Figure 10-1 shows a form that contains two combo boxes, one list box, one group box, two radio buttons, and a check box. Although you've undoubtedly used these controls when working with Windows programs, take a moment to consider these controls from a programmer's point of view.

You can use a *combo box* to let the user select one item from a list of items. That reduces the amount of typing that's required by the user, and it reduces the chance that the user will enter invalid or inaccurate data. As you'll see in the next figure, you can also create combo boxes that let the user enter text that doesn't appear in the list.

Like a combo box, a *list box* lets the user select an item from a list of items. However, the list portion of a list box is always visible. By contrast, the list portion of a combo box is typically hidden until the user clicks the arrow at the right side of the control. The user can also select two or more items from a list box, but can only select a single item from a combo box.

Radio buttons provide a way to let the user select one item from a group of items. To create a group of radio buttons, you can place two or more radio buttons within a *group box*. Then, when the user selects one radio button, all the other radio buttons in the group are automatically deselected. Since the user can only select one radio button within each group, these buttons present mutually exclusive choices.

Check boxes provide a way to present the user with choices that are not mutually exclusive. That means that if the user checks or unchecks one check box, it doesn't affect the other check boxes on the form.

A form with five more types of controls

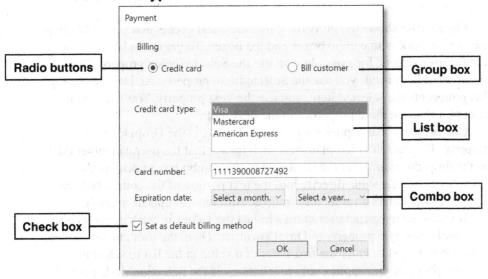

Description

- A *combo box* lets the user select one option from a drop-down list of items. A combo box can also let the user enter text into the text box portion of the combo box.

- A *list box* lets the user select one or more options from a list of items. If a list box contains more items than can be displayed at one time, a vertical scroll bar is added automatically.

- *Radio buttons* let the user select one option from a group of options.

- A *group box* can group related controls. For example, it's common to place related radio buttons within a group box. Then, the user can only select one of the radio buttons in the group.

- A *check box* lets the user select or deselect an option.

Figure 10-1   Five more types of controls

How to work with combo boxes and list boxes

Figure 10-2 shows the properties, methods, and events that you're likely to use as you work with combo boxes and list boxes. To get the index of the item that the user selects, for example, you use the SelectedIndex property. To get the selected item itself, you use the SelectedItem property. And to get a string that represents the selected item, you use the Text property. You'll see coding examples that use these properties in the next figure.

One property that applies only to a combo box is the DropDownStyle property. The default is DropDown, which means that the user can either click on the drop-down arrow at the right side of the combo box to display the drop-down list or enter a value directly into the text portion of the combo box. Note that if the user enters a value, that value doesn't have to appear in the list.

If you want to restrict user entries to just the values in the list, you can set the DropDownStyle property to DropDownList. Then, the user can only select a value from the list or enter the first letter of a value in the list to select it.

One property that applies only to a list box is the SelectionMode property. The default is One, which means that the user can only select one item from the list box. However, you can let the user select multiple items by setting this property to MultiSimple or MultiExtended. If you set it to MultiSimple, the user can only select multiple entries by clicking on them. If you set it to MultiExtended, the user can hold down the Ctrl and Shift keys to select nonadjacent and adjacent items. This works just as it does for any standard Windows app. By the way, you can also set this property to None, in which case the user can't select an entry. You might use this setting if you just want to display items.

If you allow the user to select multiple items from a list box, you can use the SelectedIndices property to return a collection of the selected indexes, and you can use the SelectedItems property to return a collection of selected items. Or, you can use the SelectedIndex and SelectedItem properties to return the first index or item in the collection of selected items.

When you work with the items in a list box or combo box, you should realize that you're actually working with the items in a collection. To refer to this collection, you use the Items property of the control. Then, you can use an *indexer* to refer to any item in the collection. You'll learn more about indexers in chapter 13. For now, you just need to know that the indexer for the collection of items in a list box or combo box is an int value starting with 0.

In addition to the indexer, you can use the properties and methods that .NET provides for working with collections. The most common properties and methods are summarized in this figure.

The most common event for working with combo boxes and list boxes is the SelectedIndexChanged event. This event occurs when the value of the SelectedIndex property changes, which happens when the user selects a different item from the list. For a combo box, you can also use the TextChanged event to detect when the user enters a value into the text portion of the control. Keep in mind, though, that this event will occur each time a single character is added, changed, or deleted.

Common members of list box and combo box controls

Property	Description
SelectedIndex	The index of the selected item. Items are numbered from 0. If no item is selected, this property has a value of -1.
SelectedItem	The selected item. This property holds a reference to an object type.
Text	The text value for the selected item.
Sorted	If set to true, the items in the list are sorted alphabetically in ascending order.
Items	The collection of items.
DropDownStyle	Determines whether the user can enter text in the text portion that's at the top of a combo box. If this property is set to DropDownList, the user must select an item from the list. If this property is set to DropDown, the user can enter data in the text box portion of the combo box. Only applies to combo boxes.
SelectionMode	Determines whether the user can select more than one item from a list box. If this property is set to One, the user can only select one item. If it's set to MultiSimple or MultiExtended, the user can select multiple items. Only applies to list boxes.

Event	Description
SelectedIndexChanged	Occurs when the user selects a different item from the list.
TextChanged	Occurs when the user enters a value into the text box portion of a combo box.

Common members of the Items collection

Indexer	Description
[index]	Gets or sets the item at the specified index in the list.

Property	Description
Count	Gets the number of items in the list.

Method	Description
Add(object)	Adds the specified item to the list.
Insert(index, object)	Inserts an item into the list at the specified index.
Remove(object)	Removes the specified item from the list.
RemoveAt(index)	Removes the item at the specified index from the list.
Clear()	Removes all items from the list.

Description

- To work with the items in a list box or combo box, you use the Items property of the control. To refer to any item in this collection, you can use an index.

Figure 10-2   Members for working with combo boxes and list boxes

After you add a combo box or list box to a form and set its properties the way you want, you can use code like that shown in figure 10-3 to work with the control. Here, the first example uses a foreach loop to load the name of each month in an array into a combo box. Each time through the loop, the Add() method is used to add a month name to the Items collection for this combo box.

The first item in the array that's loaded into the list indicates that the user should select a month from the list. This is a common technique that's used to provide instructions to the user. As you'll see later in this chapter, though, you'll need to include additional code when you use this technique to be sure that the user selects an item other than the one that provides instructions.

The second example is similar, but it uses a while loop to load eight integer values into a combo box. The first value is the current year, and the next values are the seven years that follow. Like the combo box that contains the names of the months, the first entry in this combo box provides instructions for the user.

The third example shows how you can load a list box like the one shown in figure 10-1. To make sure that no items have already been loaded into this list box, this example begins by calling the Clear() method to clear all the items. Then, it adds three items to the list box. Finally, it sets the SelectedIndex property to 0, which causes the first item in the list to be selected.

Although it's not shown here, it's common to put code that loads a combo box or list box in the event handler for the Load event of the form. That way, the control is loaded when the form is loaded. After that, the user can select an item from the combo box or list box and other methods can get information about that item.

The statements in the fourth example show four ways that you can get information from a combo box or list box. The first statement uses the SelectedIndex property to get the index of the item that's currently selected in the Years combo box. The second statement shows how to get the value that's displayed in the text box portion of this combo box. The third statement shows how to get the value of the item that's currently selected in this combo box. Notice that because the SelectedItem property returns an object type, you must cast this object to the appropriate data type to get the value of the item. Also notice that the null-coalescing operator is used to return -1 if no item is selected. You'll want to include this operator if you don't set the SelectedIndex property of the control. Finally, the fourth statement uses an index to get the second item in the Months combo box. Since the value of this item is a string type, the ToString() method is used to get the value of this item. However, you could also cast the object to a string type like this:

```
string expMonthValue = (string) cboExpirationMonth.Items[1];
```

The fifth example shows how to use the Add(), Insert(), and RemoveAt() methods to work with the items in a combo box list. This example begins with a foreach loop that adds three names to the list. Then, the Insert() method inserts a new name at the beginning of the list, and the RemoveAt() method removes the last item from the list. When you use these methods, you indicate the index where you want the item inserted or removed. Finally, the last statement shows how you can initialize a combo box so no value is selected. To do that, you set the SelectedIndex property of the control to -1.

Code that loads the Months combo box shown in figure 10-1

```
string[] months =
    {"Select a month...",
    "January", "February", "March", "April",
    "May", "June", "July", "August",
    "September", "October", "November", "December"};

foreach (string month in months)
{
    cboExpirationMonth.Items.Add(month);
}
```

Code that loads the Years combo box shown in figure 10-1

```
int year = DateTime.Today.Year;
int endYear = year + 8;
cboExpirationYear.Items.Add("Select a year...");
while (year < endYear)
{
    cboExpirationYear.Items.Add(year);
    year++;
}
```

Code that clears and loads the list box shown in figure 10-1

```
lstCreditCardType.Items.Clear();
lstCreditCardType.Items.Add("Visa");
lstCreditCardType.Items.Add("Mastercard");
lstCreditCardType.Items.Add("American Express");
lstCreditCardType.SelectedIndex = 0;                 // select the first item
```

Statements that get information from a combo box or list box

```
int expYearIndex = cboExpirationYear.SelectedIndex;
string expYearText = cboExpirationYear.Text;
int expYearValue = (int) cboExpirationYear.SelectedItem ?? -1;
string expMonthValue = cboExpirationMonth.Items[1].ToString();
```

Code that works with a combo box of names

```
string[] names = {"Judy Taylor", "Anne Boehm", "Kelly Slivkoff"};
foreach (string name in names)
{
    cboNames.Items.Add(name);
}
cboNames.Items.Insert(0, "Joel Murach");
cboNames.Items.RemoveAt(3);
cboNames.SelectedIndex = -1;                 // don't select an item
```

Notes

- You can also use the String Collection Editor to load items into a combo box or list box. To display this editor, select the control in the Form Designer and select the Edit Items command from the smart tag menu.

- In chapters 20 and 21, you'll learn techniques you can use to load combo boxes and list boxes with data that's stored in a database.

Figure 10-3   Code examples for working with combo boxes and list boxes

How to work with check boxes and radio buttons

Figure 10-4 shows you how to work with check boxes and radio buttons. The main difference between these two types of controls is that radio buttons in a group are mutually exclusive and check boxes operate independently. In other words, if the user selects one radio button in a group, all of the other buttons are automatically turned off. By contrast, when the user selects a check box, it has no effect on the other check boxes on the form, even if they appear as a group.

To group radio buttons, you typically place them in a group box control. If you place any radio buttons outside of a group, however, all the radio buttons on the form that aren't in a group box function as a group.

The property you're most likely to use when working with radio buttons and check boxes is the Checked property. This property can have a value of either true or false to indicate whether or not the control is checked.

The two statements in the first example set the Checked properties of a radio button and a check box to true. Then, the if-else statement in the second example tests the Checked property of the radio button. If the value of this property is true, a method named EnableControls() is executed. But if the value of this property is false, it indicates that another radio button is selected. In that case, a method named DisableControls() is executed.

Notice that the if-else statement in this example is coded within the event handler for the CheckedChanged event of the control. This event occurs when you select or deselect a radio button or check box, and it's the event you're most likely to use. Also note that because the Checked property contains a Boolean value, you could code the if clause without the equality operator like this:

```
if (rdoCreditCard.Checked)
```

The third example in this figure simply retrieves the Checked property of the check box and stores it in a Boolean variable. If the user has checked this box, this variable is set to true. Otherwise, it's set to false.

How to work with group boxes

Figure 10-4 also illustrates how to use a group box. For example, the group box shown at the top of this figure contains two radio buttons. That makes it clear that these controls function as a group. You specify the name of the group, which is displayed in the upper left corner of the group box, by setting the Text property of the control.

When you use a group box, you should know that all the controls it contains will move with the group box when you move it in the Form Designer. You should also know that you can't add existing controls on a form to a group box by dragging the group box over them. Instead, you have to add the group box and then drag the controls into the group box.

A group box that contains two radio buttons

Common members of radio button and check box controls

Property	Description
Checked	Gets or sets a Boolean value that indicates whether the control is checked.
Event	**Description**
CheckedChanged	Occurs when the user checks or unchecks the control.

Code that sets the value of a radio button and check box

```
rdoCreditCard.Checked = true;
chkDefault.Checked = true;
```

Code that checks the value of a radio button

```
private void rdoCreditCard_CheckedChanged(object sender, EventArgs e)
{
    if (rdoCreditCard.Checked == true)
        EnableControls();
    else
        DisableControls();
}
```

Code that gets the value of a check box

```
bool isDefaultBilling = chkDefault.Checked;
```

Description

- To determine whether a radio button or check box is checked, you test its Checked property.
- You can use a group box to group controls. Group boxes are typically used to group controls like radio buttons that function as a group.
- To add controls to a group box, drag them from the Toolbox into the group box. If you've already added the controls you want to include in the group box to the form, just drag them into the group box.
- Any radio buttons that aren't placed within a group box function as a separate group.
- If you move a group box, all of the controls it contains move with it.

Figure 10-4   How to work with radio buttons, check boxes, and group boxes

How to use Tab Order view to set the tab order

In chapter 2, you learned how to use the TabIndex property to change the *tab order* of the controls on a form. An easier way to change the tab order, though, is to use Tab Order view. This view is illustrated in figure 10-5.

When you display a form in Tab Order view, an index value is displayed at the left of each control that indicates the control's position in the tab order. Notice that the index values of the two radio button controls indicate their position in the tab order relative to the group box that contains them.

To change the tab order, you click on each control in the appropriate sequence. Then, the controls are given an index value that starts with zero and increases by one for each control you click. You can also click on the same control more than once. Then, the index value for that control is increased by one each time you click on it.

As you click on each control, the index values are displayed as shown in the second form in this figure. Here, the list box is clicked first, followed by the text box, followed by the two combo boxes, followed by the check box, followed by the two buttons and then the group box. That way, when the form is first displayed, the focus is on the list box. Then, when the user presses the Tab key, the focus moves through the controls in sequence.

Notice that when the group box control is selected, the main indexes of the radio buttons within this control change too so they're the same as the group box. However, the sub index of each radio button doesn't change. In other words, the indexes of the radio buttons relative to each other remain the same. If you want to change these indexes, though, you can do that by clicking on them just like any other control.

Also notice in the second form that the tab index isn't set for any of the labels. In most cases, it isn't necessary to change the tab order of controls that can't receive the focus. However, one case where you do want to include a label control explicitly in the tab order is if it defines an access key. In that case, you want to position the label in the tab order just before the control it identifies. Then, if the user presses the access key for that control, the focus moves to the control it identifies since it's next in the tab order.

By the way, if a form isn't displayed in Tab Order view when you select the View→Tab command as indicated in this figure, you need to change one of the Visual Studio options as described in this figure. The Optimize Rendering for Screens with Different Pixel Densities option provides for a crisp display on monitors with different display scale factors and DPIs. This is particularly useful if you work with Visual Studio on multiple monitors. In that case, you can turn this option off if you need to use Tab Order view and then turn it back on when you're done. Note that this option requires Windows 10 version 1803 and later and .NET Core 3.0 and later or .NET Framework 4.8.

A form in Tab Order view before and after the tab order is changed

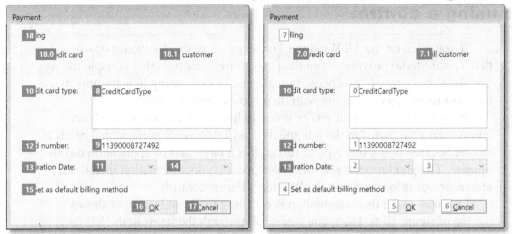

How to use Tab Order view to change the tab order

- To display a form in Tab Order view, select it and then select the View→Tab Order command. This displays the tab index for each control as in the first form above.

- If the form isn't displayed in Tab Order view, display the Options dialog (Tools→Options), select the General category in the Environment group, and uncheck the Optimize Rendering for Screens with Different Pixel Densities option.

- To change the tab indexes of the controls, click on the controls in the sequence you want to use. As you click, the new tab indexes appear as in the second form above.

- The first time you click on a control in Tab Order view, the tab index is set to the next number in sequence, starting with zero for the first control. If you click on the same control more than once, the tab index is increased by one each time you click.

- The controls in the group box are displayed with sub indexes as illustrated by the radio buttons above. Then, you can click on the group box to change its index and the main indexes of the controls it contains. To change the sub indexes of the controls in the group box, click on them individually.

Description

- The *tab order* determines the order in which controls receive the focus when the Tab key is pressed. The TabIndex property of the controls determines this order.

- By default, the value of a control's TabIndex property is determined by the sequence in which it's added to the form. The TabIndex property is set to 0 for the first control, 1 for the second control, and so on.

- A label can't receive the focus. As a result, you typically don't need to include the labels in the tab order. However, if the label defines an access key, the TabIndex property of the label should be set to one less than its related control. That way, the related control will receive the focus when the access key for the label is activated.

- When setting the tab order, you can skip controls whose TabStop, Enabled, or Visible properties have been set to false, unless those properties will change as the app runs.

Figure 10-5   How to use Tab Order view to set the tab order

How to get the information you need for using a control

If you click on the All Windows Forms group in the Toolbox, you can see that Visual Studio provides more than 50 different controls that you can use as you develop an app. In this book, though, you're only going to learn how to use the most useful controls along with their most useful members.

What that means is that you're going to have to learn how to use other controls on your own. On the job, this is a skill that every professional needs to master because doing this type of research is a large part of application development. The good news is that Microsoft's online documentation includes an abundance of information on the Windows Forms controls.

One way to get this information is by going to the web address shown at the top of figure 10-6. Then, you can scroll through the items in the left pane of the web page that's displayed to locate and display the documentation for the control you want. If you've added a control to a form, you can also display the documentation for that control by selecting it and pressing the F1 key on your keyboard. For example, this figure presents the web page that's displayed when you select a DateTimePicker control on a form and press F1.

For most controls, the documentation page for the class includes a summary of all the fields, properties, methods, and events of that class. This summary is usually near the bottom of the page. If you want to know more about a specific member, you can click on the name of the member in the summary to view the documentation for that member.

You can also display the documentation for an individual member by selecting it from the left pane. For instance, if you want to view the documentation for the BackColor property of the DateTimePicker control class, you can expand the Properties item in the left pane and then click the BackColor link.

The web address for getting help information for controls

`https://learn.microsoft.com/en-us/dotnet/api/system.windows.forms`

Some of the documentation for the DateTimePicker control class

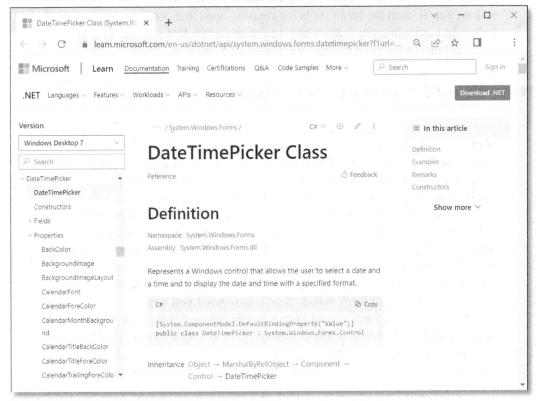

Description

- To display the information for a control class in Microsoft's online documentation, go to the web address above and scroll through the items in the left pane to find the control you want. Then, expand the item for the control and select a topic.

- If you've already added the control you want to know more about to a form, you can access the online documentation for that control by selecting it and pressing F1.

- The help information for most control classes includes a summary of all members that are available from the control. You can view more detailed information for a member by clicking on the link for that member in the summary. You can also display this information by expanding the item for the member type in the left pane and then selecting the member.

Figure 10-6   How to get the information you need for using a control

How to work with multi-form projects

In previous chapters, you learned how to create apps that consist of a single form. However, most Windows apps use two or more forms. In the topics that follow, you'll learn the basic skills for creating apps that consist of two or more forms. In particular, you'll learn how to create an app that consists of a main form and one or more forms that are displayed as dialogs.

How to add a form to a project

When you start a new project for a Windows app, it consists of a single blank form. To add another form to the project, you use the Add New Item dialog shown in figure 10-7. From this dialog, you select the Form (Windows Forms) template and then enter the name of the new form. When you click the Add button, the new form is created with the name you specify.

You can also add an existing form to a project using the Add Existing Item dialog. This can be useful if you want to use the same form in two different projects or if you want to create a form that's similar to an existing form. Note that when you add an existing form from another project, that form is copied into the new project. That way, any changes that you make to the form won't be applied to the original form, which is generally what you want.

Also note that a form you add from another project is typically in a different namespace than the forms in the current project. Because of that, you'll typically change the namespace for the form so it's the same as the namespace for the other forms. Or, you can add a using directive for the form's namespace to each form that refers to it.

The Add New Item dialog

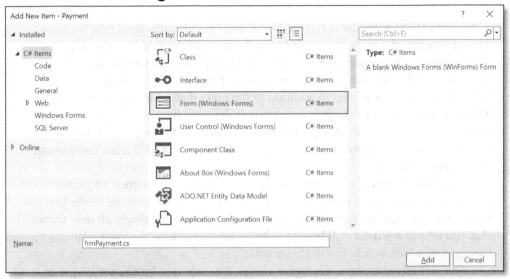

How to add a new form

- Display the Add New Item dialog by selecting the Project→Add New Item command. Or, right-click on the project in the Solution Explorer and select the Add→New Item command from the shortcut menu that's displayed.
- To add a new form, select the Form (Windows Forms) template from the Add New Item dialog, enter a name for the form, and click the Add button.

How to add an existing form

- Display the Add Existing Item dialog by selecting the Project→Add Existing Item command. Or, select the Add→Existing Item command from the shortcut menu for the project.
- To add an existing form, select the cs file for the form from the Add Existing Item dialog and then click the Add button.
- If the form is in a different namespace than the other forms in the project, you will need to either change the namespace for the form or add a using directive for the namespace to each form that refers to it.
- To change the namespace for a form, display the code for the form and then change the name on the namespace statement near the top of the code using refactoring.

Note

- When you name a form, we recommend you use the prefix *frm* so it's clear that the file contains a form.

Figure 10-7   How to add a form to a project

The code that's generated for a new form

Figure 10-8 shows the code that Visual Studio generates for a new form. This shows that the name you specify for the form in the Add New Item dialog is used within the generated code. First, it's used twice in the frmPayment.cs file. Then, it's used in the frmPayment.Designer.cs file that contains more generated code for the form. Note that in addition to the code that's shown for this file, Visual Studio generates some comments that describe the code. These comments have been omitted so the code will fit on the page. In addition, Visual Studio adds some using directives at the beginning of the form. You'll learn more about that in the next figure.

The code in both of these files is stored in a namespace named Payment, which is the same as the name of the project. You can see this name in the title bar of the Add New Item dialog in the previous figure. By default, all new forms that you add to a project will be stored in a namespace with the same name as the project, which is usually what you want.

The second example in this figure shows the code that Visual Studio generates if you double-click on a form in the Form Designer. This code consists of an event handler for the Load event of the form and a statement that wires this event handler to the Load event. The name of the form is used two more times by this generated code. First, it's used in the method declaration for the event handler. Then, it's used in the statement that wires this method to the Load event.

As you review this code, remember that, prior to Visual Studio version 17.5, the statement used to wire an event to an event handler explicitly created the EventHandler delegate. In that case, the generated event wiring code looked like this:

```
this.Load += new System.EventHandler(this.frmPayment_Load);
```

Because all the apps for this book were created with a version of Visual Studio before 17.5, this is how the event wiring code looks in these apps.

Since Visual Studio uses the name of the form when it generates code, it makes sense to specify the name you want to use in the Add New Form dialog. If you don't, however, you can modify this code by changing the name of the form as described in figure 10-10.

The generated code for a new form named frmPayment

For the frmPayment.cs file

```
namespace Payment;

public partial class frmPayment : Form
{
    public frmPayment()
    {
        InitializeComponent();
    }
}
```

For the frmPayment.Designer.cs file

```
namespace Payment;

partial class frmPayment
{
    private System.ComponentModel.IContainer components = null;

    protected override void Dispose(bool disposing)
    {
        if (disposing && (components != null))
        {
            components.Dispose();
        }
        base.Dispose(disposing);
    }

    #region Windows Form Designer generated code
}
```

The code that's generated for the Load event handler of the form

The method declaration in the frmPayment.cs file

```
private void frmPayment_Load(object sender, EventArgs e)
{

}
```

The wiring in the frmPayment.Designer.cs file

```
Load += frmPayment_Load;
```

Description

- The name you specify for the form in the Add New Item dialog is used by both files for the form class, and it appears several times in the generated code. This code is stored in a namespace that has the same name as the project.

- Visual Studio uses the name of the form when you create an event handler for one of the form's events such as the Load event.

Figure 10-8   The code that's generated for a new form

How to work with global using directives

C# 10.0 introduced *global using directives*, which are using directives that use the global keyword to make namespaces available to your entire project, rather than just a single class. For instance, the first example in figure 10-9 shows a global using directive for the System.Collections namespace. This global using directive makes it possible for you to use classes in that namespace, such as the ArrayList class, anywhere in your app without having to code a using directive or fully qualify the class name.

You can code global using directives in any class file in your app, but most developers code them in a separate class file named Usings.cs. That way, they're in a central location that's easy to find and update. Regardless of where you code them, though, you must code them before any non-global using directives.

When Visual Studio creates a new Windows Forms app, it generates global using directives by default for some common namespaces like System, System.Windows.Forms, and System.Collections.Generic. Confusingly, though, when Visual Studio creates a new form, it generates using directives for many of these same namespaces, as you can see in the second example in this figure. When you first create a form, you'll see that these using directives are dimmed, indicating that they aren't used by the form. When you're done developing a form, you may want to delete any unused using directives. An easy way to do that is to click on the lightbulb that's displayed to the left of a using directive when you click on it or hover over it, and then select Remove Unnecessary Usings.

Visual Studio stores the global using directives it generates by default in a file named *ProjectName*.GlobalUsings.g.cs in the obj/Debug/net7.0-windows directory. This directory is hidden in the Solution Explorer, and while it's possible to display it, an easier way to view the contents of this file is to use the technique described in this figure. Then you can see all the namespaces for which global using directives are provided. If you've coded any additional global using directives, those are displayed as well as you can see here.

The code for a global using directive

```
global using System.Collections;
```

The using directives Visual Studio generates by default for a new form

```
using System;
using System.Collections.Generic;
using System.ComponentModel;
using System.Data;
using System.Drawing;
using System.Linq;
using System.Text;
using System.Threading.Tasks;
using System.Windows.Forms;
```

How to remove unused using directives

- Click on or hover over one of the using directives.
- Click on the yellow light bulb that appears, then click on Remove Unnecessary Usings.

The global using directives for a Windows Forms app

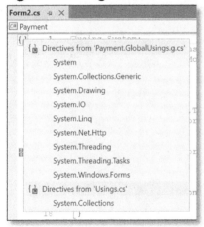

How to view the global using directives for an app

- Locate the icon in the upper left corner of a class file that looks like this: {⊡. When you hover over the icon, you'll see a tooltip that says Global 'using' directives.
- Click on the icon to view a list of the global using directives generated by Visual Studio as well as any global using directives that you've added.

Description

- With C# 10.0 and later, you can code *global using directives* that make a namespace available to an entire app. In most cases, you'll code global using directives in a class file named Usings.cs.
- Visual Studio generates global using directives for common namespaces when it creates an app. Because of that, you can often delete the using directives in a new form.

Figure 10-9   How to work with global using directives

How to rename a form

Figure 10-10 shows a procedure that you can use to rename a form. To start, you can right-click the form in the Solution Explorer and select the Rename command. Or, you can select the form in the Solution Explorer and press F2. Then, you can type the new name for the form. In the project shown in this figure, for example, the form that was originally named Form1.cs has been renamed to frmCustomer.cs. When you press the Enter key, Visual Studio displays a dialog that asks if you want to rename all references to the file. In most cases, you'll click the Yes button so the form will run correctly.

However, if you have added event handlers for form events to the form before renaming the form, the old form name will still be used by these event handlers and their wiring. Although this code should work correctly, you may want to update it so it reflects the new form name. If so, you can change the name of the form in the method declaration for the event handler using the Rename command that you learned about in chapter 3. This will also update the wiring for the event handler so it uses the same name.

A project that contains two forms

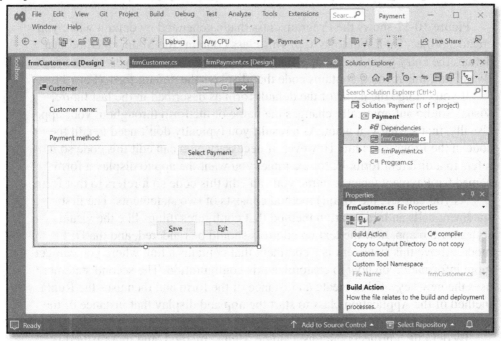

How to change the name of a form

1. Right-click the form in the Solution Explorer and select the Rename command. Or, select the form in the Solution Explorer and press F2.

2. Enter the new name for the form. When you do, Visual Studio asks if you want to rename all references to the file. In most cases, that's what you want to do.

How to change the name of any event handlers for a form's events

1. Highlight the name of the form in the method that's used by the event handler, then right-click on the name and choose Rename from the shortcut menu that's displayed.

2. Enter the new name for the form and click the Apply button in the Rename dialog.

Note

- You can also change the name that's used to identify the form in code without changing the name of the form file by using the Name property of the form. However, it's a good programming practice to use the same name for the file and the class.

Figure 10-10   How to rename a form

How to display the first form of an app

Figure 10-11 shows the Program class that's generated by default when you create a project for a Windows app. This class contains the Main() method that defines the entry point for the app, and it's executed every time you run the app. By default, this method contains code that displays the default form (Form1).

If you change the name of the default form as described in the last figure, Visual Studio automatically changes the name of the form throughout your app. Usually, that's what you want. As a result, you typically don't need to edit the code in the Program.cs file. However, if necessary, you can edit this code so it refers to a different form. If, for example, you want the app to display a form named frmPayment when it starts, you can edit this code so it refers to that form.

As you can see, the Main() method consists of two statements. The first statement calls an initialization method that configures things like the visual styles for the app, how the text on controls should be rendered, and the DPI mode. Above this statement is a comment that contains a link where you can get more information on how to customize this configuration. The second statement uses the new keyword to create an instance of the form and then uses the Run() method of the Application class to start the app and display that instance of the form.

By default, a project contains a single Main() method, and that method is stored in the Program class. However, it's possible to add additional Main() methods to your project either accidentally or on purpose. In that case, your app may use the wrong Main() method when it starts. To solve this problem, you can delete the Main() methods that you don't want to use. Or, you can display the Project Properties window by selecting the Properties command from the Project menu. Then, you can use that window to specify the class that contains the Main() method you want to use. To do that, you display the Application tab and select the class from the Startup Object combo box, which lists all the objects that contain Main() methods.

Code that defines the main entry point for an app

```
namespace Payment;

internal static class Program
{
    /// <summary>
    ///  The main entry point for the application.
    /// </summary>
    [STAThread]
    static void Main()
    {
        // To customize application configuration such as
        // set high DPI settings or default font,
        // see https://aka.ms/applicationconfiguration.
        ApplicationConfiguration.Initialize();
        Application.Run(new frmCustomer());
    }
}
```

Description

- When you create a Windows Forms app, Visual Studio automatically generates a class named Program that contains a Main() method that defines the main entry point for the app. This class is stored in the Program.cs file.

- The Main() method uses the Run() method of the Application class to display the first form for the app. If you want to change the form that's displayed when the app starts, you can change the name of the form supplied to the Run() method.

- If your project contains more than one Main() method, you can delete the Main() methods that you don't want to use. Or, you can use the Project→*ProjectName* Properties command to display the Project Properties window. Then, you can display the Application tab and select the class that contains the Main() method you want to use from the Startup Object combo box.

Figure 10-11   How to display the first form of an app

How to display a form as a dialog

When designing apps that contain two or more forms, it's common to display a form as a dialog. A form that's displayed as a dialog can also be called a *modal form*. In figure 10-12, for example, you can see a Payment form that's displayed as a dialog. This form is displayed when the user clicks the Select Payment button in the Customer form that's also shown here.

When you create a form that will be displayed as a dialog, you typically set the form properties as shown in this figure. These property settings prevent the user from closing the form other than by using the controls you provide on the form. Although setting the ControlBox property to false removes the Maximize button from a form, the user can still maximize the form by double-clicking its title bar. That's why you should also set the MaximizeBox property to false.

If you want to include a standard Close button in the title bar of a dialog, you can do that too. Just leave the ControlBox property at its default setting of true, and set the MaximizeBox and MinimizeBox properties to false. Then, the title bar will look like the one you'll see in the dialog in figure 10-14.

You can also set the FormBorderStyle property of the form to FixedDialog, which prevents the user from resizing the form by dragging its border. However, doing so can cause problems with screens that have different densities. Because of that, the FormBorderStyle property isn't presented in this figure, and the default value of Sizable is used in the examples and the app for this chapter.

To display a form as a dialog, you use the new keyword to create a new instance of the form. Then, you call the ShowDialog() method of the form object. When you use this method to display a form, the user must respond to the dialog before the code that follows the ShowDialog() method can be executed. This code typically tests the user response to determine what to do next. You'll learn more about getting the response from a dialog in the next figure.

In addition to modal forms, an app can also contain *modeless forms*. When you use modeless forms, the user can typically move back and forth between the forms as necessary. In most cases, that gives the user a wider range of possible actions, which means that the program must include code that provides for all of those actions. While this type of form is appropriate for some apps, it can make an app more difficult to develop. That's why it's common to use dialogs to control the flow of the app and to limit possible user actions.

The Payment form displayed as a dialog

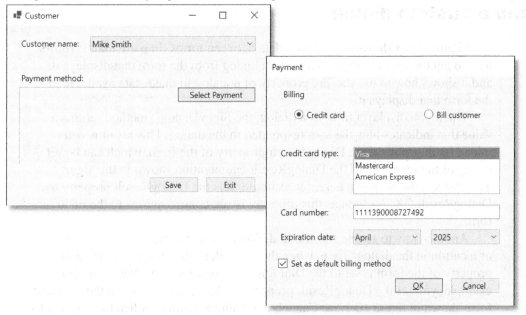

Properties for creating custom dialogs

Property	Description
`ControlBox`	Typically set to false so the control box and the Maximize, Minimize, and Close buttons don't appear in the title bar of the form.
`MaximizeBox`	Typically set to false so the user can't maximize the form by double-clicking the title bar.
`MinimizeBox`	Can be set to false to prevent the Minimize button from being displayed if the ControlBox property is set to true.

Code that creates and displays a custom dialog

```
Form paymentForm = new frmPayment();
paymentForm.ShowDialog();
// execution continues here after the user responds to the dialog
```

Description

- If you display a form as a dialog, the user must respond to the form before continuing to any other forms. A form like this is sometimes referred to as a custom dialog or a *modal form*.

- You use the ShowDialog() method of a form object to display the form as a dialog. After the user responds to the dialog, execution continues with the statement that follows the ShowDialog() method.

Figure 10-12   How to display a form as a dialog

How to pass data between a form and a custom dialog

Figure 10-13 shows how to pass data between forms. In particular, it shows how to get the user response to a custom dialog from the form that displays it, and it shows how to use the Tag property of a dialog to make data available to the form that displays it.

When you display a form as a dialog, the ShowDialog() method returns a value that indicates how the user responded to the dialog. This result is determined by the value of the DialogResult property of the form, which can be set to any of the members of the DialogResult enumeration shown in this figure. The first statement shown here, for example, sets the DialogResult property to DialogResult.OK. As soon as this property is set, control returns to the main form.

Another way to set the result of a dialog is to set the DialogResult property of a button in the dialog. Then, when the user clicks that button, the DialogResult property of the form is set to the DialogResult property of the button. If, for example, you set the DialogResult property of the Cancel button on the Payment form shown in figure 10-12 to Cancel, that value is returned when the user clicks that button and the dialog is closed. In that case, no code is required for the Click event of that button unless some additional processing is required.

You can also set the DialogResult property of a button to Cancel by setting the CancelButton property of the form. Then, the Cancel member of the DialogResult enumeration is returned when the user clicks that button. Here again, no code is required for the Click event of the button unless some additional processing is required.

After the DialogResult property is set and control returns to the form that displayed the dialog, that form can use the DialogResult enumeration to determine how the user responded. To see how this works, take a look at the third example in this figure. Here, the first statement creates an instance of the Payment form. Then, the second statement displays that form using the ShowDialog() method and stores the result of that method in a DialogResult variable named result. Next, an if statement is used to test if the result is equal to DialogResult.OK.

Another way to pass data between a dialog and another form is to use the Tag property of the dialog. The second statement in this figure, for example, sets the Tag property of a dialog to a variable named msg. Note that you must set this property before control returns to the main form.

Once control returns to the main form, you can get the data that was stored in the Tag property as shown in the last statement of the third example. Here, the Text property of a label is set to the value that was stored in the Tag property of the dialog. Notice that because the Tag property returns a nullable object type, the object must be cast to a string type before it can be assigned to the Text property. In addition, it's a good practice to check the Tag property for null before you use it. Here, the code uses the null-conditional operator (?) to do that, but you could also use an if statement.

An enumeration that works with dialogs

Enumeration	Members
DialogResult	OK, Cancel, Yes, No, Abort, Retry, Ignore, None

The Tag property of the Form class

Property	Description
Tag	Gets or sets data associated with a form or control. The Tag property holds a reference to a nullable object type, so it can hold any type of data or be null.

A statement that sets the DialogResult property of a form

```
DialogResult = DialogResult.OK;
```

A statement that sets the Tag property of a form

```
Tag = msg;
```

Code that uses the result of a dialog and the Tag property

```
Form paymentForm = new frmPayment();
DialogResult result = paymentForm.ShowDialog();
if (result == DialogResult.OK)
    lblPayment.Text = paymentForm.Tag?.ToString();
```

How to use the DialogResult enumeration

- The DialogResult enumeration provides members that represent the values that a dialog can return. The ShowDialog() method returns a member of this enumeration.
- You specify the result value of a custom dialog by setting its DialogResult property. Or, you can set the DialogResult property of a button in the dialog. Then, when the user clicks that button, the DialogResult property of the form is set accordingly.
- If you set the CancelButton property of a form to a button on that form, the DialogResult property of that button is automatically set to Cancel.
- After you set the DialogResult property of a dialog, the form is closed and control is returned to the form that displayed it. If you close a dialog without setting the DialogResult property, a value of Cancel is returned to the main form.

How to use the Tag property

- The Tag property provides a convenient way to pass data between forms in a multi-form app. A dialog can set its Tag property before it returns control to the main form. Then, the main form can get the data from this property and use it as necessary.
- Because the Tag property is an object type, you must explicitly cast it to the appropriate type to retrieve the data it contains. Or, you can use the ToString() method to convert the data to a string.
- Because the Tag property is a nullable type, you should check it for null before you use it. One way to do that is with the null-conditional operator (?) as shown above.

Figure 10-13   How to pass data between a form and a custom dialog

How to use the MessageBox class

Although you can create custom dialogs using the techniques you learned in the last two topics, it's also common to use the MessageBox class to display certain types of dialogs. In chapter 7, for example, you learned how to use the MessageBox class to display a simple dialog with an error message and an OK button. Now, you'll learn how to use the MessageBox class to display more complex dialogs, and you'll learn how to get the user's response to these dialogs.

How to display a dialog and get the user response

Figure 10-14 shows how to display a dialog and get a response from a user. To display a dialog, you use the Show() method shown at the top of this figure. As you can see, you can specify up to five arguments for this method. The first argument is the text message that you want to display. Although this is the only argument that's required, you'll typically code the second argument too, which displays a caption in the title bar of the dialog.

You can use the third argument to control the buttons that are displayed in the dialog. You can use the fourth argument to control the icon that's displayed in the dialog. And you can use the fifth argument to control the default button that's activated when the user presses the Enter key. To specify these arguments, you use the constants in the first three enumerations that are summarized in this figure.

Like the ShowDialog() method, the Show() method of the MessageBox class returns a value that indicates how the user responded to the dialog. The value that's returned is one of the members of the DialogResult enumeration. These members represent the buttons that can be displayed in a dialog, and the return value is automatically set to the appropriate member when the user clicks a button.

The first example in this figure shows how to code a Show() method that specifies all five arguments. Here, the third argument indicates that only Yes and No buttons should be included in the dialog, and the fifth argument indicates that the second button, in this case, No, should be the default button.

The second example shows how you can use the DialogResult value that's returned by the Show() method to determine which button the user clicked in the dialog. Here, an if statement tests if the DialogResult value that was returned by the Show() method is equal to DialogResult.Yes. If it is, it means that the user clicked the Yes button, and the code within the if statement is executed.

The syntax for the Show() method of the MessageBox class

```
MessageBox.Show(text[, caption[, buttons[, icon[, defaultButton]]]]);
```

The enumerations that work with the MessageBox class

Enumeration	Members
`MessageBoxButtons`	OK, OKCancel, YesNo, YesNoCancel, AbortRetryIgnore
`MessageBoxIcon`	None, Information, Error, Warning, Exclamation, Question, Asterisk, Hand, Stop
`MessageBoxDefaultButton`	Button1, Button2, Button3
`DialogResult`	OK, Cancel, Yes, No, Abort, Retry, Ignore

A statement that displays a dialog and gets the user response

```
DialogResult button =
    MessageBox.Show(
        "Are you sure you want to save this data?", "Payment",
        MessageBoxButtons.YesNo,
        MessageBoxIcon.Question,
        MessageBoxDefaultButton.Button2);
```

The dialog that's displayed

A statement that checks the user response

```
if (button == DialogResult.Yes)
{
    SaveData();
    isDataSaved = true;
}
```

Description

- You can use the Show() method of the MessageBox class to display a message to a user and accept a response from the user.

- You use the first three enumerations listed above to specify the buttons and icon that will appear in the dialog and the button that's treated as the default.

- If you omit the buttons argument, the OK button is displayed by default. If you omit the icon argument, no icon is displayed by default. If you omit the default button argument, the first button is the default.

- The Show() method returns a DialogResult value that contains one of the members of the DialogResult enumeration. You can use this value to determine which button the user clicked.

Figure 10-14   How to display a dialog and get the user response

How to use the FormClosing event

Figure 10-15 shows how you can use a dialog to cancel the FormClosing event of a form. This technique is often used when a user attempts to close a form that contains unsaved data.

To start, it's important to understand that the FormClosing event is executed when the user attempts to close the form but before the form is actually closed. This event occurs if the user clicks a button on the form that calls the Close() method of the form. It also occurs if the user clicks the Close button in the upper right corner of the form.

This figure presents an event handler for the FormClosing event of a form. This event handler receives two parameters. You can use the Cancel property of the second parameter, which is named e, to determine whether or not the form is closed. By default, this property is set to false, which means that the FormClosing event will not be canceled and the form will be closed. If you don't want to close the form, you can set this property to true to cancel the FormClosing event.

The event handler shown here starts by checking a class variable named isDataSaved to determine if the form contains unsaved data. If it doesn't, no additional processing is performed and the form is closed. If the form contains unsaved data, however, a dialog is displayed that asks the user if the data should be saved. As you can see, this dialog contains Yes, No, and Cancel buttons as well as a warning icon. Since the code for this dialog doesn't specify a default button, the first button is the default.

After the dialog is displayed, if statements are used to check the user's response and perform the appropriate action. If the user clicks the Cancel button, for example, the Cancel property of the e parameter is set to true. This cancels the FormClosing event and returns the user to the form. If the user clicks the Yes button, the code checks whether the form contains valid data. If it does, the SaveData() method is called to save the data and the form is closed. If it doesn't, the Cancel property of the parameter named e is set to true and the FormClosing event is canceled. On the other hand, if the user clicks the No button, no code is executed. As a result, the form is closed without saving the data.

The code for a dialog that cancels the Closing event

```
private void frmCustomer_FormClosing(object sender, FormClosingEventArgs e)
{
    if (isDataSaved == false)
    {
        string message =
            "This form contains unsaved data.\n\n" +
            "Do you want to save it?";

        DialogResult button =
            MessageBox.Show(message, "Customer",
            MessageBoxButtons.YesNoCancel,
            MessageBoxIcon.Warning);

        if (button == DialogResult.Yes)
        {
            if (IsValidData())
                SaveData();
            else
                e.Cancel = true;
        }
        if (button == DialogResult.Cancel)
        {
            e.Cancel = true;
        }
    }
}
```

The dialog that's displayed by the code shown above

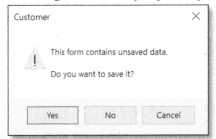

Description

- The event handler for the FormClosing event of a form receives a parameter named e that's created from the FormClosingEventArgs class. The Cancel property of this parameter lets you specify whether or not the event should be canceled. To cancel the event, set this property to true.

Figure 10-15   How to use the FormClosing event

The Payment app

This chapter closes by presenting the operation, property settings, and code for a project that contains two forms that use the controls and coding techniques that were presented in this chapter. By studying the code for this app, you will get a better idea of how you can use these controls and techniques in your own apps.

The operation

Figure 10-16 shows how the Payment app works. To start, this app displays the Customer form. On this form, the user must select a customer from the Customer Name combo box. Then, the user must click the Select Payment button to display the Payment dialog and specify payment information for the selected customer.

Within the Payment dialog, the user can select to charge the customer's credit card and then enter the required information. Or, the user can select to bill the customer directly. In either case, the user can also indicate whether the selected method should be set as the default billing method.

To complete the Payment form, the user clicks the OK button. Then, control is returned to the Customer form and the payment information is displayed on that form. To save the payment information, the user clicks the Save button.

The Customer form

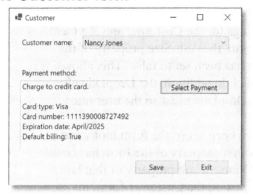

Two versions of the Payment dialog

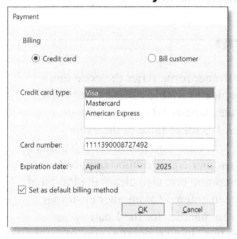

Description

- The Customer Name combo box in the Customer form lets the user select a customer.
- The Select Payment button in the Customer form displays the Payment dialog, which lets the user specify payment information for the customer.
- If the Credit Card option is selected, the user must select a credit card type, enter a card number, and select an expiration month and year.
- If the Bill Customer option is selected, the Credit Card Type, Card Number, and Expiration Date controls are disabled.
- The user can also indicate if the billing method that's selected is the default method.
- When the user clicks the OK button on the Payment form, control returns to the Customer form and the payment information is displayed in the Payment Method label.

Note

- This app doesn't actually save the data the user enters. In a production app, however, the data would be saved to a database or file.

Figure 10-16   The operation of the Payment app

The property settings

Figure 10-17 presents the property settings for the Customer and Payment forms and their controls. In the Customer form, the AutoSize property of the label that displays the payment information has been set to false. This allows you to use the Form Designer to size the label. In addition, the DropDownStyle property for the combo box has been set to DropDownList so the user must select an item from the list.

In the Payment form, the properties have been set so the form looks and acts like a dialog. In addition, the CancelButton property of the form has been set to the Cancel button, which causes the DialogResult property of that button to be set to Cancel. Finally, like the combo box on the Customer form, the DropDownStyle properties of the combo boxes on this form have been set to DropDownList so the user must select an item from the lists.

The code for the Customer form

Figure 10-18 presents the code for the Customer form. After the code that Visual Studio has generated for the form, a Boolean variable named isDataSaved is declared and set to true. This variable indicates whether the data that's currently displayed in the form has been saved. It's set to false in the event handler for the TextChanged event of the Payment label and in the event handler for the SelectedIndexChanged event of the Customer Name combo box. Notice that the event handler for the Customer Name combo box also clears the Payment label so it doesn't contain information that's been entered for another customer.

When the Customer form is loaded, the event handler for the Load event adds two names to the Customer Name combo box. In a production app, of course, the combo box would include many more names, and they would be loaded from a file or database. But for the purposes of this chapter, two names are sufficient.

When the user clicks the Select Payment button, the Click event handler for that button displays the Payment form as a dialog. Then, if the user clicks the OK button in that dialog, the payment data is displayed in the Payment Method label on the Customer form. As you can see, this data is stored in the Tag property of the Payment form.

If the user clicks the Save button, the Click event handler for that button calls the IsValidData() method shown on page 2 of this listing. This method checks that the user has selected a customer and entered a payment. If so, the event handler for the Click event of the Save button calls the SaveData() method. This method sets the SelectedIndex property of the Customer Name combo box to -1 so that no customer is selected, and it clears the Payment Method label. Then, it sets the isDataSaved variable to true and moves the focus to the combo box. In a production app, this data would be saved to a file or database.

The last method on page 2 of this listing is executed when the user tries to close the Customer form. This is the same method you saw in figure 10-15, so you shouldn't have any trouble understanding how it works.

The property settings for the Customer form

Default name	Property	Setting
Form1	Name	frmCustomer
	Text	Customer
	CancelButton	btnExit
	StartPosition	CenterScreen
comboBox1	Name	cboNames
	DropDownStyle	DropDownList
label3	Name	lblPayment
	BorderStyle	Fixed3D
	AutoSize	False
	Text	""
button1	Name	btnSave
button2	Name	btnExit
button3	Name	btnSelectPayment

The property settings for the Payment form

Default name	Property	Setting
Form2	Name	frmPayment
	Text	Payment
	AcceptButton	btnOK
	CancelButton	btnCancel
	StartPosition	CenterScreen
	ControlBox	False
	MaximizeBox	False
groupBox1	Text	Billing
radioButton1	Name	rdoCreditCard
	Checked	True
radioButton2	Name	rdoBillCustomer
listBox1	Name	lstCreditCardType
textBox1	Name	txtCardNumber
comboBox1	Name	cboExpirationMonth
	DropDownStyle	DropDownList
comboBox2	Name	cboExpirationYear
	DropDownStyle	DropDownList
checkBox1	Name	chkDefault
	Checked	True
button1	Name	btnOK
button2	Name	btnCancel
	DialogResult	Cancel

Description

- In addition to the properties shown above, you'll want to set the text and alignment properties so the forms look like the forms shown in figure 10-16.

Figure 10-17   The property settings for the Customer and Payment forms

The code for the Customer form

```csharp
public partial class frmCustomer : Form
{
    public frmCustomer()
    {
        InitializeComponent();
    }

    bool isDataSaved = true;

    private void frmCustomer_Load(object sender, EventArgs e)
    {
        cboNames.Items.Add("Mike Smith");
        cboNames.Items.Add("Nancy Jones");
    }

    private void lblPayment_TextChanged(object sender, EventArgs e)
    {
        isDataSaved = false;
    }

    private void cboNames_SelectedIndexChanged(object sender, EventArgs e)
    {
        isDataSaved = false;
        lblPayment.Text = "";
    }

    private void btnSelectPayment_Click(object sender, EventArgs e)
    {
        Form paymentForm = new frmPayment();
        DialogResult selectedButton = paymentForm.ShowDialog();

        if (selectedButton == DialogResult.OK)
        {
            lblPayment.Text = paymentForm.Tag?.ToString();
        }
    }

    private void btnSave_Click(object sender, EventArgs e)
    {
        if (IsValidData())
        {
            SaveData();
        }
    }

    private void SaveData()
    {
        cboNames.SelectedIndex = -1;
        lblPayment.Text = "";
        isDataSaved = true;
        cboNames.Focus();
    }
```

Figure 10-18   The code for the Customer form (part 1 of 2)

The code for the Customer form   Page 2

```
private bool IsValidData()
{
    bool success = true;
    string errorMessage = "";

    if (cboNames.SelectedIndex == -1)
    {
        errorMessage += "You must select a customer.\n";
    }
    if (lblPayment.Text == "")
    {
        errorMessage += "You must enter a payment.\n";
    }

    if (errorMessage != "")
    {
        success = false;
        MessageBox.Show(errorMessage, "Entry Error");
    }
    return success;
}

private void btnExit_Click(object sender, EventArgs e)
{
    Close();
}

private void frmCustomer_FormClosing(object sender,
    FormClosingEventArgs e)
{
    if (isDataSaved == false)
    {
        string message =
            "This form contains unsaved data.\n\n" +
            "Do you want to save it?";

        DialogResult button =
            MessageBox.Show(message, "Customer",
            MessageBoxButtons.YesNoCancel,
            MessageBoxIcon.Warning);

        if (button == DialogResult.Yes) {
            if (IsValidData())
                SaveData();
            else
                e.Cancel = true;
        }
        if (button == DialogResult.Cancel) {
            e.Cancel = true;
        }
    }
}
}
```

Figure 10-18   The code for the Customer form (part 2 of 2)

The code for the Payment form

Figure 10-19 presents the code for the Payment form. After the code that Visual Studio has generated for the form, the event handler for the Load event adds the appropriate items to the list box and the two combo boxes on the form. In addition, this method sets the SelectedIndex property for these controls so the first item is selected.

When the user clicks the OK button on this form, the Click event handler starts by calling the IsValidData() method shown on page 2 of this listing. If the Credit Card radio button is selected, this method checks that the user selected a credit card type and entered a credit card number. It also checks that the user selected an item other than the first one from the two combo boxes. That's necessary because the first item of these combo boxes contains user instructions ("Select a month…" and "Select a year…").

If the data is valid, the Click event handler for the OK button continues by calling the SaveData() method shown on page 3 of this listing. This method creates a string that includes the payment information. Then, it stores that string in the Tag property of the Payment form. As you've already seen, the Customer form uses this property to display the payment information. Finally, the SaveData() method sets the DialogResult property of the form to the OK member of the DialogResult enumeration. This is necessary to close the Payment form and allow the execution of the app to return to the Customer form.

When the user selects one of the radio buttons on this form, the CheckedChanged event occurs. For both radio buttons, this event is wired to the Billing_CheckChanged() event handler on page 3 of this listing. If the Credit Card radio button is selected when this event handler is executed, it calls the EnableControls() method to enable the other controls on the form so the user can enter the required information. If the Credit Card button isn't selected, however, it means that the Bill Customer button is selected. Then, this event handler calls the DisableControls() method to disable the other controls.

The code for the Payment form

```
public partial class frmPayment : Form
{
    public frmPayment()
    {
        InitializeComponent();
    }

    private void frmPayment_Load(object sender, EventArgs e)
    {
        lstCreditCardType.Items.Add("Visa");
        lstCreditCardType.Items.Add("Mastercard");
        lstCreditCardType.Items.Add("American Express");
        lstCreditCardType.SelectedIndex = 0;

        string[] months = {"Select a month...",
            "January", "February", "March", "April",
            "May", "June", "July", "August",
            "September", "October", "November", "December"};
        foreach (string month in months)
        {
            cboExpirationMonth.Items.Add(month);
        }
        cboExpirationMonth.SelectedIndex = 0;

        int year = DateTime.Today.Year;
        int endYear = year + 8;
        cboExpirationYear.Items.Add("Select a year...");
        while (year < endYear)
        {
            cboExpirationYear.Items.Add(year);
            year++;
        }
        cboExpirationYear.SelectedIndex = 0;
    }

    private void btnOK_Click(object sender, EventArgs e)
    {
        if (IsValidData())
        {
            SaveData();
        }
    }
```

Figure 10-19   The code for the Payment form (part 1 of 3)

The code for the Payment form

```
private bool IsValidData()
{
    bool success = true;

    if (rdoCreditCard.Checked)
    {
        string errorMessage = "";

        if (lstCreditCardType.SelectedIndex == -1)
        {
            errorMessage += "You must select a credit card type.\n";
        }
        if (txtCardNumber.Text == "")
        {
            errorMessage += "You must enter a credit card number.\n";
        }
        if (cboExpirationMonth.SelectedIndex == 0)
        {
            errorMessage += "You must select a month.\n";
        }
        if (cboExpirationYear.SelectedIndex == 0)
        {
            errorMessage += "You must select a year.\n";
        }

        if (errorMessage != "")
        {
            success = false;
            MessageBox.Show(errorMessage, "Entry Error");
        }
    }
    return success;
}
```

Figure 10-19   The code for the Payment form (part 2 of 3)

The code for the Payment form

```
private void SaveData()
{
    string msg = "";
    if (rdoCreditCard.Checked)
    {
        msg += "Charge to credit card." + "\n\n";
        msg += "Card type: " + lstCreditCardType.Text + "\n";
        msg += "Card number: " + txtCardNumber.Text + "\n";
        msg += "Expiration date: "
            + cboExpirationMonth.Text + "/"
            + cboExpirationYear.Text + "\n";
    }
    else
    {
        msg += "Send bill to customer." + "\n\n";
    }

    bool isDefaultBilling = chkDefault.Checked;
    msg += "Default billing: " + isDefaultBilling;

    Tag = msg;
    DialogResult = DialogResult.OK;
}

private void Billing_CheckedChanged(object sender, EventArgs e)
{
    if (rdoCreditCard.Checked)
        EnableControls();
    else
        DisableControls();
}

private void EnableControls()
{
    lstCreditCardType.Enabled = true;
    txtCardNumber.Enabled = true;
    cboExpirationMonth.Enabled = true;
    cboExpirationYear.Enabled = true;
}

private void DisableControls()
{
    lstCreditCardType.Enabled = false;
    txtCardNumber.Enabled = false;
    cboExpirationMonth.Enabled = false;
    cboExpirationYear.Enabled = false;
}
}
```

Figure 10-19   The code for the Payment form (part 3 of 3)

Perspective

In this chapter, you learned how to use five new controls for building Windows Forms apps. These controls are the ones you'll use most often. If you need to use any controls that weren't presented here, though, you should be able to figure out how to do that on your own. In most cases, it's just a matter of becoming familiar with the properties, methods, and events that are available, and you can usually do that by reviewing the documentation for the control class.

In addition, you learned how to work with a project that contains two or more forms. Specifically, you learned how to work with projects that use dialogs.

For many projects, the skills presented in this chapter are the only ones you'll need when you're working with the forms of an app. In chapter 12, though, you'll learn another technique for passing data between forms.

Terms

combo box
list box
radio button
group box
check box
tab order
global using directive
modal form
modeless form

Exercise 10-1   Create the Payment app

This exercise will guide you through the process of creating the Payment app that's described in this chapter. To make that easier for you, you'll start from an app that contains the Customer form.

Open the project and prepare the two forms

1. Open the app that's in the C:\C#\Ch10\Payment directory. This app contains a single form named Form1.

2. Rename Form1 to frmCustomer. Make sure to change both the file name and the name that's used in the code. If necessary, modify the Main() method so it displays this form when the app starts.

3. Add a second form named frmPayment to the project.

Design the Payment form

4. Add the controls to the Payment form and set the properties for this form and its controls as described in figures 10-16 and 10-17.

5. Use Tab Order view to set the tab order for the controls on the Payment form if necessary.

Add the code for the Customer form

6. Generate the event handlers for the Load event of the Customer form, for the FormClosing event of the form, and for the Click event of all three buttons. Then, add the global isDataSaved variable, and add the code for these events as shown in figure 10-18.

7. Generate event handlers for the SelectedIndexChanged event of the Customer Name combo box and the TextChanged event of the Payment Method label. Then, add the code for these event handlers so they set the isDataSaved variable to false. The event handler for the SelectedIndexChanged event should also clear the Payment Method label.

8. Add the SaveData() and IsValidData() methods.

9. Test the Customer form to make sure that it works properly. At this point, you should be able to display the Payment form, but it won't work correctly since you haven't added any code to it.

Add the code for the Payment form

10. Generate the event handlers for the Load event of the Payment form and for the Click event of the OK button. Then, add the code for these events as shown in figure 10-19.

11. Generate an event handler named Billing_CheckChanged() for the Check-Changed event of the Credit Card radio button. Then, wire this event handler to the CheckChanged event of the Bill Customer radio button and add the code for this event handler. (If you need to refresh your memory on how to wire an event to an existing event handler, see figure 6-9 in chapter 6.)

12. Add the EnableControls(), DisableControls(), IsValidData(), and SaveData() methods.

13. Test the program to be sure that it works as described in figure 10-16. When you're sure it does, close the project.

Exercise 10-2   Enhance the Future Value app

This exercise will guide you through the process of adding a combo box and a list box to the Future Value app.

Open the Future Value app and add two controls

1. Open the app that's in the C:\C#\Ch10\FutureValue directory.

2. Delete the Number of Years text box and replace it with a Number of Years combo box. Then, delete the Future Value text box and replace it with a Future Values list box.

Add the code that works with the controls

3. Generate the event handler for the Load event of the form. Then, add code that loads the numbers 1 through 20 in the Number of Years combo box, and add code that selects 3 as the default number of years.

4. Delete the code in the IsValidData() method that refers to the Number of Years text box since it isn't needed anymore.

5. Modify the event handler for the Click event of the Calculate button so it gets the number of years from the combo box and adds the future value for each year to the Future Values list box. For example, if you calculate the future value for three years, the Future Value form should return a result like this:

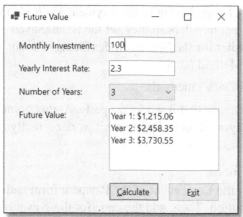

6. To get this to work correctly, you'll need to use the Clear() method of the list box to clear the list box each time the Calculate button is clicked. In addition, you can use the modulus operator (%) to add the future value after every twelve months of the calculation. For example:

```
if (month % 12 == 0) // add the future value to the list box
```

7. Test this app to make sure it works correctly.

11

How to debug an app

In chapters 3 and 5, you learned how to work in break mode when a runtime error occurs, how to use the Exception Helper to get information about the error, how to use data tips to find out what value a variable or property contains, how to use a breakpoint to enter break mode before a specific statement is executed, and how to step through the statements in an app from a breakpoint. These are the basic skills that you need for debugging simple apps.

As your apps get more complicated, though, debugging gets more complicated. In fact, if you've done much programming, you know that debugging is often the most difficult and time-consuming phase of programming. The good news is that Visual Studio offers many other tools for testing and debugging. In this chapter, you'll learn how to use the most useful ones, and you'll review the tools you've already been introduced to.

Basic debugging techniques

In the topics that follow, you'll review and expand on the basic debugging skills that you learned in previous chapters. This will help you to find and fix most types of exceptions.

How to work in break mode

By default, an app will enter *break mode* when it encounters an exception that isn't handled. You can also enter break mode by using one of the other techniques listed in figure 11-1.

When you enter break mode after an unhandled exception occurs, the statement that was executing is highlighted and the Exception Helper is displayed as shown in this figure. Then, you can use the Exception Helper to try to determine the cause of the exception. In addition, you can use data tips to display the values of variables and properties, as well as the values of array and collection elements. You can also look in the Locals window to see the values of the variables within the current scope. You'll learn more about working with data tips next, and you'll learn more about the Locals window later in this chapter.

How to work with data tips

In chapter 3, you learned the basic skills for working with *data tips*. Figure 11-1 reviews these skills and presents some additional skills for working with data tips.

First, you can display a data tip for a variable or property simply by placing the mouse pointer over it. Then, you can change the value of the variable or property by clicking on it in the data tip and entering the new value.

If a variable refers to an array or collection, you can display its elements and their values by placing the mouse pointer over the arrowhead that appears to the left of the variable name in the data tip. You can use the same technique to display the properties of an object.

You can also pin a data tip so it doesn't close when you move the mouse pointer off the variable or property. To do that, you click the pin icon that appears at the right side of the data tip.

Once you pin a data tip, three icons appear in a bar to the right of the data tip when you point to the variable or property. The top icon lets you close the data tip, the middle icon lets you unpin the data tip so it floats on top of all the open windows, and the bottom icon lets you expand or collapse an area that lets you enter a comment. Note that if a data tip is pinned, you can drag it anywhere within the Code Editor window. If a data tip is floated, however, you can drag it over any window and you will still be able to see it on top of that window.

In this figure, the data tip for the Text property of the Future Value text box has been pinned and then dragged so it's right next to the code statement that sets the value of the text box. In addition, the bottom icon has been clicked to display an area for entering a comment.

The Future Value app in break mode

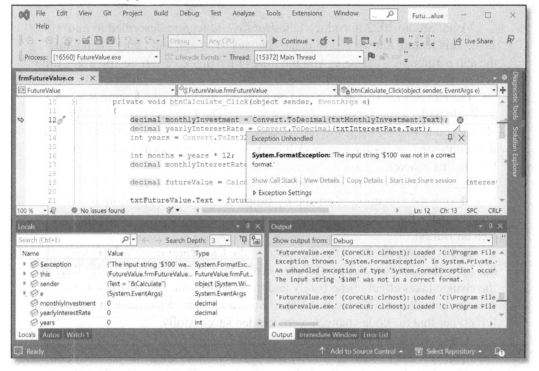

Four ways to enter break mode

- Force an unhandled exception to be thrown.
- Set a breakpoint and run the app.
- Choose the Debug→Step Into command or press F11 to begin debugging at the first line of the app.
- Choose the Debug→Break All command or press Ctrl+Alt+Break while the app is executing.

A pinned data tip for the Text property of the Future Value text box

```
txtFutureValue.Text = futureValue.ToString("c");
txtMonthlyInvestment.Focus();
```
txtFutureValue.Text View ▾ "$3,771.46"

Type a comment here

Description

- If an unhandled exception occurs, Visual Studio enters *break mode*, displays the Exception Helper, and highlights the statement that was executing when the exception occurred.
- *Data tips* allow you to see the value of a variable or property while in break mode. You can view the elements of an array or collection or the properties of an object. You can pin a data tip so it stays visible, and you can change the value of a variable or property.

Figure 11-1   How to work in break mode

How to use the Hot Reload feature

Visual Studio 2022 introduced the *Hot Reload* feature described in figure 11-2. This feature allows you to make changes to an app and apply them while the app is running. That saves you the time of having to restart an app every time you make changes.

The Hot Reload feature is based on the Edit and Continue feature that was available with earlier versions of Visual Studio. The Edit and Continue feature allows you to make changes to the C# code for an app while in break mode and then continue running the app. You'll learn more about working in break mode later in this chapter.

In contrast to the Edit and Continue feature, you can use Hot Reload at any time during the execution of an app by simply switching to Visual Studio. Then, you can make the code changes you want, save the changes, and click the Hot Reload Button.

In this figure, for example, the name of the CalculateFutureValue() method has been changed to Calculate(). After saving this change and using Hot Reload, the change takes effect immediately and the Future Value app is still able to perform calculations. Notice that Visual Studio provides a message in the bottom left corner that the code changes were applied successfully.

You should know that not all changes can be applied using Hot Reload. For example, you can't add to or modify the members of an enum. If you try to do that, Visual Studio displays the dialog in this figure. Then, you can click the Rebuild and Apply Changes button to rebuild the app so the changes are applied. You can also select the "Always rebuild when updates can't be applied" option to prevent this dialog from being displayed in the future. Or, you can click the Continue Editing button to return to the Code Editor.

The Future Value app with a change being made while it's running

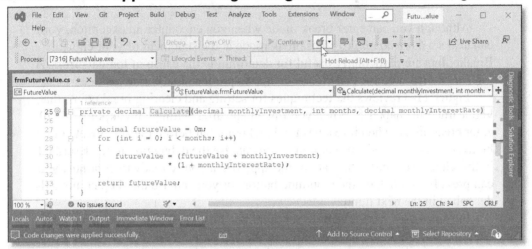

The dialog that's displayed if a change can't be made

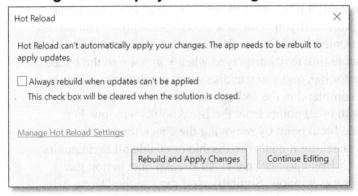

Description

- *Hot Reload* is a feature of Visual Studio 2022 that lets you apply changes to an app while it's running without restarting the app. To do that, you save the changes and then click the Hot Reload button in the Standard toolbar.

- You can use Hot Reload with most .NET 6 or later apps either with or without debugging. If you're using .NET 5 or earlier, you can only use Hot Reload with debugging.

- If Hot Reload can't apply the changes you've made while the app is running, the dialog shown above is displayed asking if you want to rebuild the app or continue editing.

- By default, you must save your changes before applying them with Hot Reload. To automatically apply your changes when you save them, display the drop-down list for the Hot Reload button, select the Settings item, and then select the "Hot Reload on File Save" option.

Figure 11-2   How to use the Hot Reload feature

How to use breakpoints

Although you can enter break mode when you encounter an exception, you can also set a *breakpoint* to enter break mode at the statement of your choice. Breakpoints are particularly useful for determining the cause of logical errors. A *logical error* is an error that causes an app to produce inaccurate results.

Figure 11-3 reviews the techniques for setting and clearing breakpoints that you learned in chapter 5. When you run an app after setting a breakpoint, it will enter break mode when it reaches the breakpoint but before the statement at the breakpoint is executed. At that point, you can use the debugging tools described in this chapter to check the state of the app. When you're ready to continue, you can press F5 or click on the Continue button, or you can use the Step commands described in the next figure.

In some cases, you'll want to set more than one breakpoint. You can do that either before you begin the execution of the app or while the app is in break mode. Then, when the app is run, it will stop at the first breakpoint. And when you continue execution, the app will run to the next breakpoint.

Once you set a breakpoint, it remains until you remove it. In fact, it remains even after you close the project. If you want to remove a breakpoint, you can use one of the techniques presented in this figure. You can also temporarily disable a breakpoint using the Disable link that's displayed when you point to the breakpoint in the margin indicator bar, and you can disable all breakpoints using the Disable All Breakpoints command in the Debug menu.

You can also work with breakpoints from the Breakpoints window. For example, you can disable a breakpoint by removing the check mark in front of it, and you can enable it by checking it again. To disable or enable all breakpoints, you can use the Disable All Breakpoints/Enable All Breakpoints button that's available from the Breakpoints window. Similarly, you can use the Delete All Breakpoints button to remove all breakpoints.

You can also use the Breakpoints window to label and filter breakpoints. You use labels to group related breakpoints. To assign a label to one or more breakpoints, select the breakpoints in the Breakpoints window. Then, right-click on the breakpoints and select Edit Labels to display the Edit Breakpoint Labels dialog. From this dialog, you can enter the label you want to use or select a label you created previously.

To filter breakpoints, select the column you want to search from the In Column drop-down list or use the default to search all columns. To search just the Labels column, for example, choose Labels from this list. Then, enter the search text in the Search box and press the Enter key. The breakpoints will be filtered so only those that contain the search text will be displayed. You can also control the columns that are displayed using the Columns drop-down menu, and you can remove the filtering using the Reset button.

If you want to set conditions for a breakpoint to be taken, you can do that too. Just point to the breakpoint in the margin indicator bar and click the Settings link that's displayed to display the Breakpoint Settings window. Then, select the Conditions option and enter one or more conditional expressions. If the expression tests if the value of a variable changes or if a variable is equal to

The Future Value app with a breakpoint

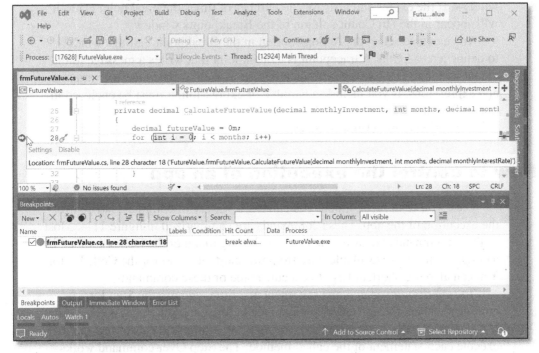

How to set and clear breakpoints

- To set a *breakpoint*, click in the margin indicator bar to the left of a statement. Or, press the F9 key to set a breakpoint at the insertion point. You can set a breakpoint before you run an app or while the app is in break mode.
- To remove a breakpoint, use any of the techniques for setting a breakpoint. To remove all breakpoints at once, use the Debug→Delete All Breakpoints command.
- To disable all breakpoints, use the Debug→Disable All Breakpoints command. To enable all breakpoints, use the Debug→Enable All Breakpoints command.

Description

- You can set a breakpoint only on a line that contains an executable statement.
- When Visual Studio encounters a breakpoint, it enters break mode before it executes the statement that contains the breakpoint.
- The current breakpoints are displayed in the Breakpoints window. To display this window, use the Debug→Windows→Breakpoints command.
- The Breakpoints window is most useful for enabling and disabling existing breakpoints, but you can also use it to add, modify, move, delete, label, or filter breakpoints.
- If you point to a breakpoint in the margin indicator bar, two links appear. The first one lets you display the Breakpoint Settings window, which you can use to set conditional breakpoints and to specify a message that's written to the Output window when a breakpoint is taken. The second one lets you disable or enable a breakpoint.

Figure 11-3   How to use breakpoints

a particular value, it will appear in the Condition column of the Breakpoints window. If the expression tests for the number of times the breakpoint is hit, it will appear in the Hit Count column of the Breakpoints window.

You can also select the Actions option in the Breakpoint Settings window to define a *tracepoint*. A tracepoint is a breakpoint that writes a message to the Ouput window. The message can include text as well as the values of variables and expressions. If you include a variable or expression, it must be enclosed in braces like this:

```
Future value: {futureValue}
```

How to control the execution of an app

Once you're in break mode, you can use a variety of commands to control the execution of the app. These commands are summarized in figure 11-4. Most of these commands are available from the Debug menu or the Debug toolbar, but a couple of them are available only from the shortcut menu for the Code Editor. You can also use shortcut keys to execute some of these commands.

To *step through* an app one statement at a time, you use the Step Into command. Then, the app enters break mode before each statement is executed. If a statement calls another method, the Step Into command causes the app to execute each statement of the called method. The Step Over command works similarly except that the statements in called methods are executed without interruption (they are "stepped over").

Although you can use either of these commands to start the execution of an app or to restart execution from break mode, you're most likely to use them from break mode. That's because if you use them to start execution of a typical form class, you first step through some of the code that's been generated for the form.

If you use the Step Into command to enter a method, you can use the Step Out command to execute the remaining statements in the method without interruption. After that, the app enters break mode before the next statement in the calling method is executed.

To skip code that you know is working properly, you can use the Run To Cursor or Set Next Statement command. You can also use the Set Next Statement command to rerun lines of code that were executed before an exception occurred. And if the next statement to be executed is no longer displayed in the Code Editor, you can use the Show Next Statement command to move to it.

If you're using Visual Studio 2017 or later, you can also use the *Run to Click feature* to control the execution of an app. To use this feature, you point to a line of code in the Code Editor and then click the green icon that appears to the left of the line. When you do, the app is executed up to that line. This eliminates the need to add a breakpoint on the line.

Although it's not shown in the last figure, you should know that when you step through code using the commands in this figure, Visual Studio displays the number of milliseconds that it took to execute the code up to that point. This is called a *PerfTip* (or performance tip). Although you won't typically need this information, it can be helpful in identifying inefficient code.

Commands in the Debug menu and toolbar

Command	Toolbar	Keyboard	Description
Start/Continue	▶ Continue ▾	F5	Start or continue execution of the app.
Break All	⏸	Ctrl+Alt+Break	Suspend execution of the app.
Stop Debugging	⏹	Shift+F5	Stop debugging and end execution of the app.
Restart	↻	Ctrl+Shift+F5	Restart the entire app.
Show Next Statement	→		Display the next statement to be executed. Also available from the shortcut menu for the Code Editor.
Step Into	⤓	F11	Execute one statement at a time.
Step Over	⇥	F10	Execute one statement at a time except for called methods.
Step Out	⇨	Shift+F11	Execute the remaining lines in the current method.

Commands in the Code Editor's shortcut menu

Command	Description
Run to Cursor	Execute the app until it reaches the statement that contains the insertion point.
Set Next Statement	Set the statement that contains the insertion point as the next statement to be executed.

Description

- If you use the Step Into or Step Over command to start the execution of an app, Visual Studio will enter break mode before it executes the first statement in the app. If you use the Run to Cursor command, Visual Studio will enter break mode when it reaches the statement that contains the insertion point.

- Once the app enters break mode, you can use the Step Into, Step Over, Step Out, and Run To Cursor commands to execute one or more statements.

- To alter the normal execution sequence of the app, you can use the Set Next Statement command. Just place the insertion point in the statement you want to execute next, issue this command, and click on the Continue button.

- With Visual Studio 2017 and later, you can use the *Run to Click* feature to run code to a line without setting a breakpoint on that line. To do that, you point to the line and then click the ▶ icon that appears to the left of the line.

- To enter break mode when you need to stop the execution of an app, you can use the Break All command.

- When you step through code or execute code to a breakpoint, the *PerfTips* feature indicates how many milliseconds it took to execute the code. This value is displayed to the right of the last statement that was executed.

Figure 11-4   How to control the execution of an app

How to use the debugging windows

Now that you know how to work with break mode, you're ready to learn how to use the primary debugging windows. These windows include the Locals window, the Autos window, the Watch windows, the Immediate window, and the Output window.

How to use the Locals window to monitor variables

If you need to see the values of several variables used in the same area of an app, you can do that using the Locals window as shown in figure 11-5. By default, this window is displayed in the group of windows in the lower left corner of Visual Studio when an app enters break mode. If it isn't, you can display it by selecting the Locals command from the Windows submenu of the Debug menu.

The Locals window displays information about the variables that are within the current scope. In this figure, for example, the Locals window shows the five variables that are within the scope of the for loop in the CalculateFutureValue() method. In addition, it shows the this keyword that includes information about the current form.

Whenever a variable contains other variables, the Locals window displays a ▷ symbol to the left of the variable. To drill down through this information, you can click this symbol to expand the entry. In this figure, for example, you can click the ▷ symbol to the left of the this keyword to view information about the current form. That includes information about all the properties for the form and all the properties for each control on the form.

By default, Visual Studio displays these properties alphabetically. Unfortunately, these groups of properties can be long, and it can take a while to find the one you're looking for. If you're using Visual Studio 2019 or later, you can pin a property to the top of its group by hovering the mouse over it and clicking the pin icon that appears to the right of its name. Later, you can unpin this property by clicking the unpin icon that's displayed to the right of its name.

Besides displaying the values of variables, you can use the Locals windows to change these values. To do that, you double-click on the value you want to change and enter a new value. Then, you can continue the execution of the app.

How to use the Autos window to monitor variables

If you want to limit the number of variables that are displayed, you can use the Autos window instead of the Locals window. This window works similarly to the Locals window, except it only displays information about the variables used in the current statement and the previous statement. As a result, it doesn't display as many variables, especially if the current block of code has a large number of variables within scope. To display this window, you can select the Autos command from the Windows submenu of the Debug menu.

The Locals window

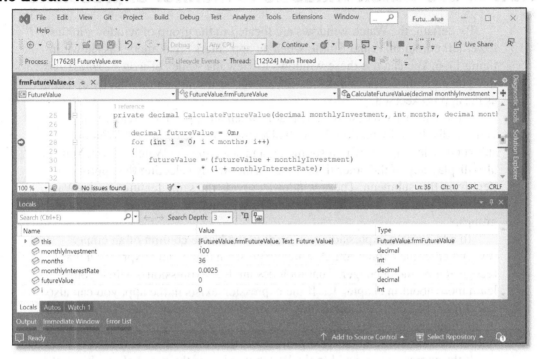

How to use the Locals window

- The Locals window displays information about the variables within the current scope.
- To display the Locals window, click on the Locals tab or use the Debug→Windows→Locals command.
- If you are debugging a form and you click on the ▷ symbol to the left of the this keyword, the properties and variables of the form are displayed. Then, if you want, you can pin a property to the top of this group by hovering the mouse over the property and clicking the pin icon that appears to the right of the property name.
- To change the value of a property or variable, double-click on the value in the Value column, then type a new value and press the Enter key.
- With Visual Studio 2019 and later, you can search for values and objects in the Locals windows, and you can specify the number of levels deep you want to search.

How to use the Autos window

- The Autos window works like the Locals window, but it only displays information about variables used by the current statement and the previous statement.
- To display the Autos window, you can use the Debug→Windows→Autos command.

Figure 11-5   How to use the Locals and Autos windows to monitor variables

How to use Watch windows to monitor expressions

By default, the Watch windows are located in the group of windows in the lower left corner of Visual Studio when an app enters break mode, as shown in figure 11-6. You can use these windows to view the values of *watch expressions* that you enter into these windows. These expressions are automatically updated as the app is executed.

If the Watch 1 window isn't available when an app enters break mode, you can display it by pulling down the Debug menu, selecting the Windows submenu, selecting the Watch submenu, and selecting the Watch 1 item. You can also display any of the other three watch windows by selecting the appropriate item from this submenu. These windows provide the same features as the Watch 1 window. You can use them if you want to separate the watch expressions into groups.

To add a watch expression, you click in the Name column of an empty row and enter the expression. A watch expression can be any expression that's recognized by the debugger. That includes lambda expressions, which you'll learn more about in chapter 13. If the expression exists in the app, you can also select it in the Code Editor and drag it to the Watch window. The Watch window in this figure shows two expressions that are recognized by the debugger: the futureValue variable and the Text property of the Future Value text box.

If the expression you add to the Watch window is the name of an object, the Watch window will display a ▷ symbol to the left of the name. Then, you can click on this symbol to display the properties of the object. A ▷ symbol is also added to an expression if it's the name of an array. Then, you can click on this symbol to display the elements in the array.

You can change the value of a watch expression by double-clicking on the value in the Value column and entering the new value. To delete a watch expression, you can use the Delete Watch command on the shortcut menu that's displayed when you right-click on an expression. To delete all watch expressions, you can use the Select All command on the shortcut menu followed by the Delete Watch command.

A Watch window

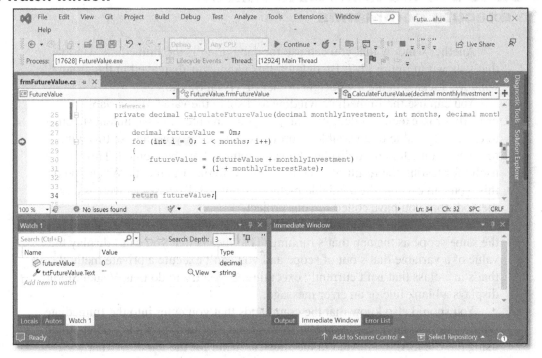

Description

- The Watch windows let you view the values of *watch expressions* while an app is in break mode. To display a Watch window, click on its Watch tab. Or, select Debug→Windows→Watch and choose Watch 1, Watch 2, Watch 3, or Watch 4.

- To add an expression to a Watch window, click on an empty row in the Name column, then type the expression. You can also highlight an expression in the Code Editor and drag it into a Watch window.

- If an expression is out of scope, it will appear dimmed in the Watch window along with a message that says the expression isn't valid in the current context.

- If you enter the name of an object or an array in the Watch window, a tree control will appear next to its name. Then, you can use this control to expand or collapse this entry.

- To change the value of a watch expression, double-click on its value in the Value column, enter the new value, and press the Enter key.

- To delete a watch expression, right-click on the expression and select the Delete Watch command from the shortcut menu. To delete all watch expressions, right-click on the Watch window, select the Select All command, and select the Delete Watch command.

- With Visual Studio 2019 and later, you can search for values and objects in the Watch windows, and you can specify the number of levels deep you want to search.

Figure 11-6   How to use Watch windows to monitor expressions

How to use the Immediate window to execute commands

Another window that you can use for debugging is the Immediate window that's shown in figure 11-7. By default, this window is displayed in the group of windows located in the lower right corner of Visual Studio.

You can use the Immediate window to display the value of a variable or property or to execute code. For example, you can enter an assignment statement to change the value of a variable or property. Similarly, you can use this window to execute a method or to display the value returned by the method. This can be useful for testing the result of a method with different arguments. When you do this, you can execute the available methods from .NET classes as well as any methods that you have coded in your project.

When you enter commands in the Immediate window, they're executed in the same scope as the app that's running. That means that you can't display the value of a variable that's out of scope and you can't execute a private method that's in a class that isn't currently executing. If you try to do that, Visual Studio displays a blank line or an error message.

You should also know that the commands that you enter into the Immediate window remain there until you exit from Visual Studio or explicitly delete them using the Clear All command in the shortcut menu for the window. That way, you can use standard Windows techniques to edit and re-use the same commands from one execution of an app to another without having to re-enter them. Unlike expressions in the Watch window, though, the command results aren't updated as the app executes.

To execute a command that you've already entered in the Immediate window, press the Up or Down arrow keys to locate the command. This displays the command at the bottom of the window. Then, if you want, you can edit the command. Or, you can press Enter to execute the command.

The Immediate window

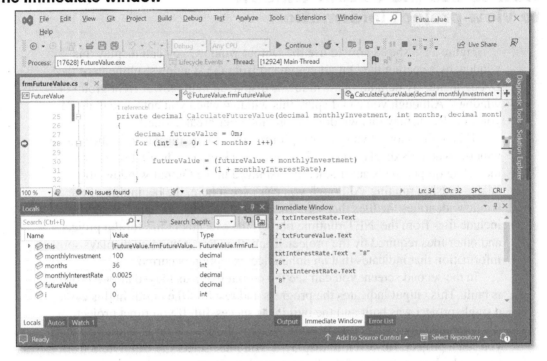

Description

- You can use the Immediate window to display and assign values from an app during execution. To display this window, click on the Immediate Window tab or use the Debug→Windows→Immediate command.

- To display a value, enter a question mark followed by the expression whose value you want to display. Then, press the Enter key.

- To assign a different value to a variable or property, enter an assignment statement. Then, press the Enter key.

- To execute a method, enter its name and any arguments it requires. Then, press the Enter key. If you want to display the result of a method, precede the method call with a question mark.

- To reissue a command, use the Up or Down arrow keys to display the command you want. Then, you can edit the command or press the Enter key to execute it.

- To remove all commands and output from the Immediate window, use the Clear All command in the shortcut menu for the window.

- You can also enter lambda expressions in the Immediate window. For more information on lambda expressions, see chapter 13.

Figure 11-7   How to use the Immediate window to execute commands

How to use the Output window
to view project information

Figure 11-8 shows how to use the Output window. You can display this window by selecting the Output command from the Windows submenu of the Debug menu. By default, this window is displayed in the lower right group of windows. Although you can display this window when you enter break mode, you can also display this window before and after break mode.

This figure shows two types of information that are displayed in the Output window when it's displayed before or after break mode. The first screen shows the debug output that's automatically displayed in the Output window after an app finishes running. Although you can't see it here, the beginning of the window identifies the files that were loaded and used by the app. These files include files from the .NET runtime library, the executable file for the project, and other files required by the project. Then, the Output window displays some information that indicates that an unhandled exception occurred.

In the second screen, you can see the output that's displayed after a project is built. This output indicates the progress and result of the build. In this case, a single project was built and the build was successful. If you run a project, it's automatically built before it's run. As a result, this output is available when you run a project. However, to display it, you must select the Build item from the combo box at the top of the Output window. On the other hand, if you build a solution by selecting one of the Build commands from the Build menu, the Output window will automatically select the Build option and show this information.

Most of the time, you won't need the information that's displayed in the Output window. If a build error occurs, for example, the error is displayed in the Error List window and you can use that window to locate and correct the error. And if an unhandled exception occurs, you can use the information in the Exception Helper window to identify the cause of the exception. Of course, once you exit break mode, the Exception Helper is no longer available. However, some information about the exception is still available in the Output window. As a result, you can use the Output window to look up this information even after you've exited break mode.

An Output window that shows debug information

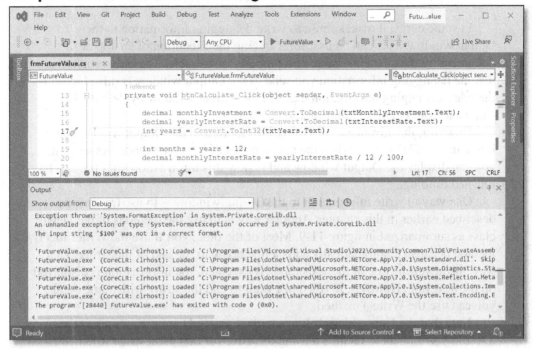

An Output window that shows build information

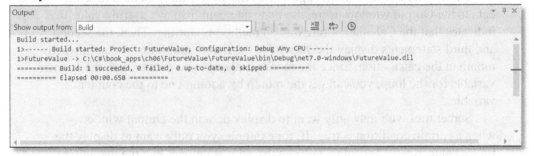

Description

- After a solution finishes running, you can use the Output window to view the debug output. This output lists the files that were loaded and used by the project, information about unhandled exceptions (if any), and a completion code.

- After you build a project or solution, you can use the Output window to view the build output. This output includes an indication of how many projects were built successfully, how many builds failed, and how many projects weren't built.

- You can use the combo box at the top of the Output window to select whether build or debug output is displayed.

- To display this window, use the Debug→Windows→Output command.

Figure 11-8   How to use the Output window to view project information

How to write data to the Output window

In some cases, it makes sense to write debugging information to the Output window. This can be useful for tracing the execution of an app or for documenting the changing value of a property or variable. The only problem is that the debugging information you send to the Output window is mixed in with the other debugging information that's in the Output window by default. This can make your debugging information hard to find.

However, the advantage of writing information to the Output window is that it remains available even when the app is no longer in break mode. As a result, you can display the Output window and review this information after the app has finished running.

One way to write information to the Output window is to use tracepoints as described earlier in this chapter. Another way is to use the methods of the Debug class as summarized in figure 11-9. Most of the time, you'll use the WriteLine() method because it automatically adds a line break to the end of the string. That way, the next time one of these methods is executed, the information is displayed on the next line. However, if you don't want to end the string with a line break, you can use the Write() method.

Note that the Debug class belongs to the System.Diagnostics namespace. As a result, you'll want to include a using directive for this namespace when you use the Debug class as shown in the first example.

The second example in this figure uses the WriteLine() method to write data to the Output window. Here, the first statement displays a string value that indicates that the CalculateFutureValue() method is starting. Then, the second and third statements display the values for the month and future value for each month in the calculation. Since the month is always one greater than the counter variable for the loop, you can get the month by adding one to the counter variable.

Sometimes, you may only want to display data in the Output window when a certain condition is true. If, for example, you only want to display the future value every 12 months, you can use an if statement like the one in the third example. Here, the modulus operator (%) is used to check if the month is a multiple of 12. If so, the WriteLine() method displays the future value in the Output window.

An Output window that displays debugging information

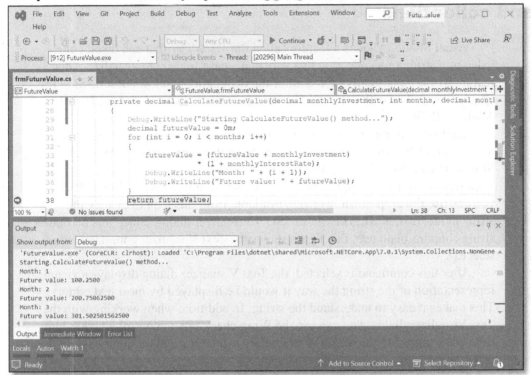

Methods of the Debug class that write data to the Output window

Method	Description
Write(string)	Displays the value of the specified string.
WriteLine(string)	Displays the value of the specified string, followed by a line break.

A using statement for the namespace that contains the Debug class

```
using System.Diagnostics;
```

Three statements that write data to the Output window

```
Debug.WriteLine("Starting CalculateFutureValue() method...");
Debug.WriteLine("Month: " + (i+1));
Debug.WriteLine("Future value: " + futureValue);
```

Code that uses an if statement to control when data is written

```
if ((i+1)%12 == 0) // every 12 months
    Debug.WriteLine("Future value: " + futureValue);
```

Description

- You can use the Write methods of the Debug class to write data to the Output window. This can be useful for tracing the execution of an app or for documenting changes in the values of variables.

Figure 11-9   How to write data to the Output window

How to use the Visualizer to view strings and collections

Visual Studio includes a feature called the *Visualizer* that can display the value of a string or a collection in a way that's easy for you to visualize. This feature works consistently across all of the debugging windows described in this chapter, as well as with data tips. For strings, it works with plain text, HTML, XML, or JSON.

The first example in figure 11-10 shows the Autos window with a variable named calculationsString that contains a string that represents a calculation. Since this variable is a string, the Visualizer icon (a magnifying glass) is displayed to the right of the value that's displayed in the Value column. Then, you can use the drop-down list that's available from this icon to display the string in the Text, XML, HTML, or JSON Visualizer dialog. Since this particular string contains plain text, this figure shows the Text Visualizer command being selected.

After this command is selected, the Text Visualizer dialog displays a visual representation of the string the way it would be displayed by most text editors. This makes it easy to understand the string. In addition, when working with the Text Visualizer dialog, you can use the Wrap check box to control whether long lines are wrapped to the next line when they extend beyond the right edge of the text box.

To help you understand how useful the Visualizer dialog can be, take a moment to consider what the string in this figure would look like without the Text Visualizer dialog. It would look something like this (without the word wrapping):

```
"Monthly Investment:\t$100.00\nYearly Interest
Rate:\t3.00\nYears:\t3\nFuture Value:\t$3,771.46\n\n"
```

You can also use the Visualizer to display the values of the items in a collection. The dialog that's displayed when you do that is called the IEnumerable Visualizer dialog. That's because every collection implements the IEnumerable or IEnumerable<T> interface. You'll learn more about interfaces in chapter 15. For now, you just need to know that these interfaces let you iterate through the items in a collection.

To illustrate how this works, the second example in this figure shows a data tip for a variable named holidays that stores a collection of tuples. Each tuple stores two string values with a day of the year and the name of the holiday on that day. Since the holidays variable stores a collection, the drop-down list for the Visualizer icon includes the IEnumerable Visualizer command. This command displays an IEnumerable Visualizer dialog like the one shown in this figure.

The IEnumerable Visualizer dialog presents the items of the collection in a tabular format. This makes it easy to see the values of the items that the collection contains. In addition, you can use the filter box in the upper left corner to filter the items that the dialog displays. And, you can use the Export drop-down list in the upper right corner to export the data to a CSV (comma-separated value) or Excel file.

The Visualizer drop-down menu for a string in the Autos window

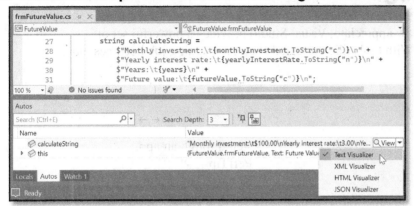

The Text Visualizer dialog

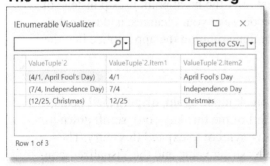

The Visualizer drop-down menu for a collection in a data tip

```
var holidays = new List<(string, string)> {
    ("4/1", "  ▷ ⊘ holidays   🔍 View ▼ Count = 3
    ("7/4      ✓  IEnumerable Visualizer
    ("12/
};
```

The IEnumerable Visualizer dialog

IEnumerable Visualizer		
🔍 ▼		Export to CSV... ▼
ValueTuple`2	ValueTuple`2.Item1	ValueTuple`2.Item2
(4/1, April Fool's Day)	4/1	April Fool's Day
(7/4, Independence Day)	7/4	Independence Day
(12/25, Christmas)	12/25	Christmas
Row 1 of 3		

Description

- You can view string and collection values in a Visualizer dialog by clicking the magnifying glass icon to the right of the value and selecting the appropriate Visualizer.

Figure 11-10   How to use the Visualizer to view strings and collections

Perspective

As you can now appreciate, Visual Studio provides a powerful set of debugging tools. With tools like these, a difficult debugging job becomes more manageable.

Terms

break mode	step through an app
data tip	PerfTip
Hot Reload	Run to Click feature
breakpoint	watch expression
logical error	Visualizer
tracepoint	

Exercise 11-1   Step through an app

If you did exercise 5-2 in chapter 5, you've already set breakpoints, used the Locals window, and stepped through an app. So in this exercise, you'll use some of the new skills that were presented in this chapter.

Use the Hot Reload feature

1. Open the app that's in the C:\C#\Ch11\FutureValue directory. Then, run the project with the default entries, and notice that the future value amount is formatted as a percent.

2. End the app and set a breakpoint on the statement in the btnCalculate_Click() method that calls the method that calculates the future value. Then, run the app with the default entries so it enters break mode.

3. In break mode, notice that the statement after the breakpoint uses p instead of c as the formatting code. Correct this code, save your changes, and press the Hot Reload button (or Alt + F10) to continue running the app. Notice that the formatting is now correct.

Use the Locals window

4. Click on the Calculate button to enter break mode again, display the Locals window, click on the ▷ symbol to the left of the this keyword, scroll down to txtMonthlyInvestment, and click on its ▷ symbol to expand this entry. Then, scroll down to the Text property to see its string value and the Visualizer icon in the Value column.

5. Click on the Visualizer icon to display the value in the Text Visualizer dialog. Then, close this dialog, and click on the ◢ symbol to the left of the this keyword to collapse this entry.

6. Press F11 to step through the statements, and notice the parameters and variables that are displayed in the Locals window at each step. Then, use the Run to Click feature to execute the code to the last statement in the

CalculateFutureValue() method (the return statement). Now, you can see the final values for the calculation.

7. Press F5 to continue execution and display the Future Value form. Click on the Calculate button to start another calculation and enter break mode again. Next, locate the months variable in the Locals window, double-click in the Value column, enter 24, and press the Enter key to change the value. Now, set a second breakpoint on the return statement in the CalculateFutureValue() method. Then, press F5 to continue execution, and notice that 24 is used as the value of the months variable in the future value calculation.

Use the Breakpoints window to disable both breakpoints

8. Display the Breakpoints window and click the Disable All Breakpoints button at the top of this window. This disables both breakpoints without removing them. Then, press F5 to continue execution. Since no breakpoints are enabled, this should display the Future Value form.

9. Click the Exit button to end the program. Then, use the Debug→Enable All Breakpoints command to enable both breakpoints, and run the app until it enters break mode at the first breakpoint.

Set a condition for a breakpoint and create a tracepoint

10. Set a breakpoint on the line that contains the closing brace for the for statement in the CalculateFutureValue() method. Then, point to the breakpoint in the margin indicator bar and click on the Settings link to display the Breakpoint Settings window.

11. Select the Conditions option in the Breakpoint Settings window. Then, choose Hit Count from the first drop-down list, choose "Is a multiple of" from the second drop-down list, and enter 12 in the text box. Then, click the Close button to close this window.

12. Press F5 to continue execution, and notice that the breakpoint is only taken each twelfth time through the loop, or at the end of each year. Continue execution until the form is displayed again, and then click on the Calculate button to start another calculation and enter break mode at the first breakpoint.

13. Display the Breakpoint Settings window for the second breakpoint again and select the Actions option. Then, enter the following in the text box that's displayed:

The future value for year {(i+1)/12} is {futureValue}

Leave the Continue Code Execution option selected so the app doesn't enter break mode when it reaches the tracepoint. Then, close the Breakpoint Settings window.

14. Continue execution until the next breakpoint is reached. Then, check the Output window to see the information that was written to it by the tracepoint. If this worked correctly, point to the tracepoint in the margin indicator bar and then click the Disable link that appears to disable it.

15. Continue execution until the form is displayed again, and then click on the Calculate button so the app enters break mode at the first breakpoint.

Use the Immediate window to work with a variable and a method

16. Display the Immediate window, and display the value of the months variable in this window. Then, display the percentage format of the monthly interest rate by calling the ToString() method from the monthlyInterestRate variable like this:

```
? monthlyInterestRate.ToString("p")
```

17. Assign a value of 12 to the months variable by entering an assignment statement in the Immediate window. Then, continue running the app so you can see that this value is used in the calculation.

Use a Watch window to monitor expressions

18. Run the app one more time with a value of 1 for the years entry. When the app enters break mode at the first breakpoint, press F11 to step into the Calculate-FutureValue() method.

19. Display a Watch window, highlight the futureValue variable, and drag it to that window. Next, drag the i variable that's used by the for loop to that window. Notice that the Name column contains an error icon and the Value column contains an error message indicating that the i variable does not exist in the current context. That's because it's only in scope within the for loop.

20. Press F11 until you reach the statement within the for loop. Then, click in the Name column of the first blank row in the Watch window and enter this expression:

```
i < months
```

21. Press F11 to step through the app and check the values in the Watch window until the value of i < months becomes false.

22. Continue execution until the form is displayed again, then exit the app.

Use the Output window

23. Use the Debug.WriteLine() method in the btnCalculate_Click() method to display the values of the monthlyInvestment, monthlyInterestRate, months, and futureValue variables. Then, run the app with the default values.

24. When the app enters break mode at the first breakpoint, use the Debug menu to disable all breakpoints.

25. Continue execution until the form is displayed again, and check the Output window to see how your debugging statements are displayed.

26. When you're through experimenting, close the project.

Section 3

Object-oriented programming

In the first two sections of this book, you learned how to use classes that are provided as part of .NET. For instance, you learned how to use the properties, methods, and events of the form and control objects that are defined by the .NET classes, and you learned how to use the List<T> class to create collection objects that can hold other objects. Although that's one aspect of object-oriented programming, it's not the whole picture.

In addition to using the .NET classes, you can create your own classes. That's what the chapters in this section teach you to do. To start, chapter 12 shows you the basics of creating classes. Then, chapter 13 expands on those basics to show you how to create classes that include advanced features such as indexers, delegates, events, and overloaded operators.

After that, chapter 14 shows you how to use inheritance, one of the most important features of object-oriented programming. Chapter 15 shows you how to use interfaces (another important feature of object-oriented programming) and generics. And Chapter 16 shows you how to organize, document, and test your classes. This includes how to work with class libraries and how to implement unit testing. When you're done, you'll not only know how to create and use your own classes, but you'll also understand how the .NET classes work.

You can read the chapters in this section any time after you complete the first 11 chapters of this book, and you should read them in sequence. However, only chapter 12 is a prerequisite for sections 4 and 5. So if you want to learn how to work with text and binary files, you can skip to chapter 17 after you read chapter 12. If you want to learn how to use LINQ to work with data, you can skip to chapter 18. And if you want to learn database programming before you learn more about object-oriented programming, you can skip to section 5. Eventually, though, you need to master the object-oriented skills that are presented in chapters 13 through 16, so be sure to return to them.

12

How to create
and use classes

This chapter presents the basics of creating and using classes in C# apps.
Here, you'll learn how to create classes that include properties, methods, and
constructors, as well as classes that contain static members. In addition, you'll
learn how to create structures, records, and record structs, which are similar to
classes.

When you complete this chapter, you'll start to see how creating your
own classes can help simplify the development of an app. As a bonus, you'll
have a better understanding of how the .NET classes work.

An introduction to classes

The topics that follow introduce you to the concepts you need before you create your own classes. First, you'll learn how classes are typically used in a business app to simplify the overall design of the app. Next, you'll learn about some of the members you can add to a class. Then, you'll see a complete example of a simple class. Finally, you'll learn how classes are instantiated to create objects.

How classes can be used to structure an app

Figure 12-1 shows how you can use classes to simplify the design of a business app using a *multi-layered architecture*. In a multi-layered app, the classes that perform different functions of the app are separated into two or more layers.

A *three-layered* application architecture like the one shown in this figure consists of a presentation layer, a middle layer, and a database layer. In practice, the middle layer is sometimes eliminated and its functions split between the database and presentation layers. On the other hand, the design of some apps further develops the middle layer into additional layers.

The classes in the *presentation layer* handle the details of the app's user interface. For a Windows Forms app, this consists of the form classes that display the user interface. One class is required for each form displayed by the app.

The classes of the *database layer* are responsible for all database access required by the app. These classes typically include methods that connect to the database and retrieve, insert, update, and delete information from the database. Then, the other layers can call these methods to access the database, leaving the details of database access to the database classes. Although we refer to this layer as the database layer, it can also contain classes that work with data that's stored in files.

The *middle layer* provides an interface between the database layer and the presentation layer. This layer often includes classes that correspond to business entities (for example, products and customers). It may also include classes that implement business rules, such as discount or credit policies. When the classes represent *business objects*, they are often called *business classes*.

One advantage of developing apps with a layered architecture is that it allows application development to be spread among members of a development team. For example, one group of developers might work on the database layer, another group on the middle layer, and still another group on the presentation layer.

Another advantage is that it allows classes to be shared among apps. In particular, the classes that make up the database and middle layers can be placed in *class libraries* that can be used by more than one project. You'll learn how to work with class libraries in chapter 16.

The architecture of a three-layered app

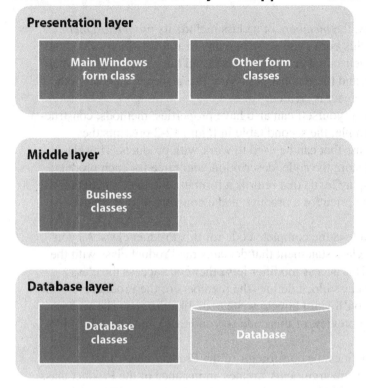

Description

- To simplify development and maintenance, many apps use a *three-layered architecture* to separate the app's user interface, business rules, and database processing. Classes are used to implement the functions performed at each layer of the architecture.

- The classes in the *presentation layer* control the app's user interface. For a Windows Forms app, the user interface consists of the various forms that make up the app.

- The classes in the *database layer* handle all the app's data processing.

- The classes in the *middle layer*, sometimes called the *business layer* or *domain layer*, act as an interface between the classes in the presentation and database layers. These classes can represent business entities, such as customers or products, or they can implement business rules, such as discount or credit policies.

- When the classes in the middle layer represent business entities, the classes can be referred to as *business classes*, and the objects that are created from these classes can be referred to as *business objects*.

- Often, the classes that make up the database layer and the middle layer are implemented in *class libraries* that can be shared among apps.

Figure 12-1   How classes can be used to structure an app

How to define a class

As you already know, the *members* of a class include its *properties*, *methods*, and *events*. Throughout this book, you've seen many examples of apps that work with .NET classes and their members. You've also used the *constructors* of these classes to create objects, and these constructors are just a special type of method that's executed when an object is created.

The classes you design yourself can also have properties, methods, constructors, and events. For example, the second table in figure 12-2 presents the members of a Product class that can be used to work with products. This class has three properties that store the code, description, and price for each product; a method named GetDisplayText() that returns a formatted string that contains the code, description, and price for a product; and a constructor that creates instances of the class.

Below the second table is the complete code for this Product class. As you can see, it begins with a class statement that declares the Product class with the public access modifier. This access modifier lets other code access the class.

The code within the class block defines the members of the Product class. In the rest of this chapter, you'll learn how to write code like the code shown here. For now, you'll just get a preview of this code so you have a general idea of how it works.

The first statement defines the constructor of the Product class. This constructor, which accepts no arguments, creates an instance of the Product class and initializes its fields to default values. Later in this chapter, you'll learn how to code constructors that initialize fields with values passed via parameters.

Next, three properties of the Product class are defined. These properties provide access to the data associated with a product.

Finally, the GetDisplayText() method is defined. This method accepts a string parameter named sep and returns a string that concatenates the code, description, and price values, separated by the value passed via the sep parameter.

Notice that all these members use the public access modifier to identify the properties and methods that can be accessed by other code. By contrast, you use the private access modifier to declare members that you don't want to be accessed by other code.

This figure also reviews the basic concepts of object-oriented programming that were first introduced in chapter 3. In addition, it presents a fundamental concept of object-oriented programming called *encapsulation*.

Encapsulation lets the programmer hide, or encapsulate, some of the data and operations of a class while exposing others. For example, although a property or method of a class can be called by other code, its implementation is hidden within the class. That way, users of the class can think of it as a black box that provides useful properties and methods. This also means that you can change the code within a class without affecting the other code that uses it. This makes it easier to enhance or change an app because you only need to change the classes that need changing.

Three common class members

Member	Description
Property	Represents a data value associated with an object instance.
Method	An operation that can be performed by an object.
Constructor	A special type of method that's executed when an object is instantiated.

The members of the Product class

Properties	Description
`Code`	A string that contains a code that uniquely identifies each product.
`Description`	A string that contains a description of the product.
`Price`	A decimal that contains the product's price.

Method	Description
`GetDisplayText(sep)`	Returns a string that contains the code, description, and price in a displayable format. The *sep* parameter is a string that's used to separate the elements. It's typically set to a tab or new line character.

Constructor	Description
`()`	Creates a Product object with default values.

The code for the Product class

```
namespace ProductMaintenance
{
    public class Product
    {
        // a constructor
        public Product() { }

        // three public properties
        public string Code { get; set; } = "";
        public string Description { get; set; } = "";
        public decimal Price { get; set; }

        // a public method
        public string GetDisplayText(string sep) =>
            $"{Code}{sep}{Price.ToString("c")}{sep}{Description}";
    }
}
```

Class and object concepts

- An *object* is a self-contained unit that has *properties*, *methods*, and other *members*. A *class* contains the code that defines the members of an object.

- An object is an *instance* of a class, and the process of creating an object is called *instantiation*.

- *Encapsulation* is one of the fundamental concepts of object-oriented programming. It lets you control the data and operations within a class that are exposed to other classes.

- The data of a class is typically encapsulated within a class using *data hiding*. In addition, the code that performs operations within the class is encapsulated so it can be changed without changing the way other classes use it.

Figure 12-2   How to define a class

How to create objects from a class

The process of creating an object from a class is called *instantiation*. Figure 12-3 describes how instantiation works.

To start, you can see three ways to declare and create an object. The first syntax explicitly declares the class name on the left side of the assignment statement. The second syntax uses the var keyword to let the compiler determine the type of the variable. This is called implicit typing, and it can make your code shorter. The third syntax shows that, with C# 9.0 and later, you don't need to code the class name after the new keyword if the compiler can determine the class type from the surrounding code. You do still need to code the set of parentheses, though. This can also make your code shorter.

Next, you can see two *instances* of the Product class. Each instance represents a different Product object. Because both objects were created from the same class, they both have the same properties. However, the objects have distinct values for each property. For example, the value of the Code property for the product1 object is C#, but the value of the Code property for the product2 object is ASPMVC.

The first code example in this figure shows how you can create these two objects. Here, the first line of code declares a variable named product1 that has a type of Product. To do that, it uses the new keyword followed by the name of the class and a set of parentheses to call the default constructor. Then, the next three lines assign values to the object's properties.

The last four lines of code repeat the process to declare a second variable that has a type of Product named product2 and assign values to its properties. The only difference is that the class name isn't coded after the new keyword. That's because the compiler can determine the class type from the class name that's declared on the left side of the assignment statement.

The second code example shows how to use an *object initializer* to create an object and assign values to it. To do that with C# 9.0 and later, you can code the new keyword and a set of parentheses, followed by a list enclosed in braces. This list specifies the names of the properties you want to initialize and their values. Prior to C# 9.0, you had to include the class name following the new keyword like this:

```
Product product1 = new Product { ... };
```

The use of object initializers improves your code by making it more concise.

If you're working with existing code that doesn't use object initializers and you're using Visual Studio 2017 or later, you can use refactoring to modify the code so it does use object initializers. To do that, place the cursor in the statement that creates the object, press Ctrl + period (.), and select "Object Initialization can be Simplified" from the Quick Actions menu.

At this point, it's important to realize that a class defines a *reference type*. That means that the variable that's used to access an object contains the address of the memory location where the object is stored, not the object itself. In other words, the product1 variable holds a *reference* to a Product object, not an actual Product object.

Three ways to declare and create an object

```
ClassName variableName = new ClassName();    // explicitly typed
var variableName = new ClassName();           // implicitly typed
ClassName variableName = new();               // with C# 9.0 and later
```

Two Product objects that have been instantiated from the Product class

product1
Code=C#
Description=Murach's C#
Price=59.50

product2
Code=ASPMVC
Description=Murach's ASP.NET MVC
Price=61.50

Code that declares and creates these two objects

```
Product product1 = new Product();
product1.Code = "C#";
product1.Description = "Murach's C#";
product1.Price = 59.50m;

Product product2 = new();             // C# 9.0 and later
product2.Code = "ASPMVC";
product2.Description = "Murach's ASP.NET MVC";
product2.Price = 61.50m;
```

Code that declares and creates an object with an object initializer

```
Product product1 = new() {            // C# 9.0 and later
    Code = "C#",
    Description = "Murach's C#",
    Price = 59.50m
};
```

Description

- When an object is instantiated, a *constructor* is executed to initialize the data that makes up the object. If a class doesn't provide a constructor, a default constructor is executed. The default constructor initializes all the data to default values.

- The data that makes up an object is sometimes referred to as the object's *state*. Once an object has been instantiated, its state can change.

- The state of an object changes whenever you change the value of one of the object's properties. The state can also change when you call a method that affects the data stored within an object.

- An app can create two or more instances of the same class. Each instance is a separate entity with its own state. If you change the state of one object, the state of other objects created from the same class is not affected.

- *Object initializers* let you create an object and assign values to that object in a single statement.

- A class defines a *reference type*. That means that the variable that's used to access an object instantiated from a class contains the address of the object, not the actual object.

Figure 12-3   How to create objects from a class

Basic skills for creating a class

Now that you've learned about some of the members that make up a class and you've seen the code for the Product class, you're ready to learn the basic skills for creating and using your own classes. The topics that follow present these skills.

How to add a class file to a project

To create a user-defined class, you start by adding a *class file* to your project. To do that, you use the dialog shown in figure 12-4. When you complete this dialog, the class file will appear in the Solution Explorer with the extension *cs*.

When you add a class to a project, Visual Studio automatically generates the class declaration. Then, you can complete the class by adding constructors, properties, methods, and whatever other members the class may require.

Note that, by default, the class declaration that Visual Studio generates has an access modifier of internal. You'll learn about the internal access modifier in chapter 14. For now, you'll want to change the class declaration so it uses the public access modifier. That way, you can be sure that it's accessible by all other code in your project.

Visual Studio also generates several using directives by default. If you want, you can leave those using directives in your class file. Or, when you're done coding the class, you can delete the using directives that it doesn't need. Visual Studio makes this easy to do by graying out any using directive that isn't used by the code in your class.

The dialog for adding a class

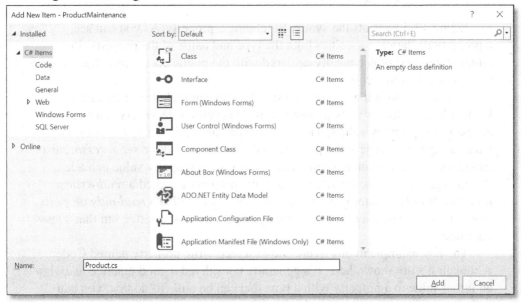

How to add a new class to a project

1. Use the Project→Add Class command to display the Add New Item dialog. Or, right-click the project name and select the Add→Class command to open this dialog.

2. Enter the name you want for the new class and click the Add button.

The starting code for the new class

```csharp
using System;
using System.Collections.Generic;
using System.Linq;
using System.Text;
using System.Threading.Tasks;

namespace ProductMaintenance
{
    internal class Product
    {
    }
}
```

Description

- When you complete the Add New Item dialog, a *class file* is added to the project. This class file will appear in the Solution Explorer window with the extension *cs*.

- The namespace and class blocks are automatically added to the class. Then, you can enter the code for the class within the class block.

- By default, the class block that Visual Studio generates has an access modifier of internal, which is similar to private. Usually, you'll want to change this modifier to public.

Figure 12-4   How to add a class file to a project

How to code properties

Figure 12-5 presents the syntax for coding a property. As you can see, a property declaration specifies both the type and name of the property. In addition, a property is typically declared with the public access modifier so it can be accessed by other code.

Within the block that defines a property, you can include the get and set keywords, each followed by a semi-colon. This defines *accessors* that provide access to the property values. The *get accessor*, also called a *getter*, is executed when a request to retrieve the property value is made, and the *set accessor*, also called a *setter*, is executed when a request to set the property value is made. If both a getter and a setter are included, the property is called a *read/write property*. If only a getter is included, the property is called a *read-only property*. You can also create a *write-only property*, which has just a setter, but that's less common.

The first example in this figure shows a read/write property named Code. Although it's not shown here, it's generally considered a good practice to assign an initial value to a property with a type that can be null. To do that, you can code an assignment statement, like this:

```
public string Code { get; set; } = "";
```

The second and third examples show how to work with the Code property. Specifically, the second example sets the property's value, and the third example gets the property's value.

The fourth and fifth examples show how to code a read-only property that's assigned an initial value. To do that, the fourth example uses an assignment statement. By contrast, the fifth example uses an *expression-bodied property*. To code an expression-bodied property, you code an access modifier, a return type, and the property name just like you do for any other property. Then, you code a *lambda operator* (=>, read as "goes to"), followed by the expression to be returned. This simplifies the read-only property by eliminating the need for the braces and the get keyword.

With C# 9.0 and later, you can use the init keyword instead of the set keyword to create an init-only setter. This is illustrated by the sixth example. When you use an init-only setter, you can only assign a value to the property when the object is being initialized by a constructor or an object initializer. The seventh example shows how to use an object initializer to set the value of the Code property. However, you could also use a constructor as described in figure 12-7.

You should know that the properties presented in this figure are *auto-implemented properties*, which provide a concise way to code a simple property. When you use an auto-implemented property, the compiler creates a private instance variable behind the scenes to store the value of the property. Most of the time, auto-implemented properties are all you need. However, sometimes you need direct access to the instance variable that stores the value of a property. Later in this chapter, you'll learn how to do that.

The syntax for coding a property

```
public type PropertyName { [get;] [set;] } [= value;]
```

A read/write property with both a getter and a setter

```
public string Code { get; set; }
```

A statement that sets the value of a property

```
product.Code = txtProductCode.Text;
```

A statement that gets the value of a property

```
string code = product.Code;
```

A read-only property with a getter and an initial value

```
public string Code { get; } = "C#";
```

The same read-only property coded with an expression body

```
public string Code => "C#";
```

A property with an init-only setter (C# 9.0 and later)

```
public string Code { get; init; };
```

A statement that uses an object-initializer to set the init-only property

```
Product product2 = new() { Code = "C#" };
```

Description

- You use a *property* to get and set data values associated with an object.
- You can code a *get accessor*, or *getter*, to retrieve the value of the property.
- You can code a *set accessor*, or *setter*, to set the value of the property.
- A property that has both a getter and a setter is called a *read/write property*. A property that has just a getter is called a *read-only property*. And a property that has just a setter is called a *write-only property*.
- You can also use an *expression body* to code a read-only property. To do that, you code the access modifier, return type, and property name, followed by the *lambda operator* (=>) and the expression to be returned.
- You can initialize the value of a property by coding an equal sign, the value, and a semicolon following the closing brace for the property.
- With C# 9.0 and later, you can use the init keyword instead of the set keyword to create an init-only setter. Then, you can only set the value of the property when the object is being initialized by a constructor or by an object initializer.
- The properties shown here are *auto-implemented* properties. An auto-implemented property stores its value in a corresponding instance variable that's accessible only via the property. Later in this chapter, you'll learn how to code properties so you can access the corresponding instance variable directly.

Figure 12-5   How to code properties

How to code methods

Figure 12-6 shows you how to code the methods for a class. Because the basics of coding methods were presented in chapter 6, most of the information in this figure should be review for you. The main difference is that the methods presented here use the public access modifier, which makes them available to other classes.

For instance, the first example presents a version of the GetDisplayText() method that you saw earlier in this chapter. This method uses a return statement to return a string with the values of three properties separated by the string that's passed to the sep parameter. The second example shows how to code this same method as an *expression-bodied method*. To do that, you code the method signature just like you do for any other method, followed by the lambda operator and the expression to be returned or the statement to be executed.

Expression-bodied methods don't provide as much simplification of code as expression-bodied properties do. Even so, you should consider using them for consistency when you use the lambda operator for other purposes in your code. In chapter 5, for example, you learned how to use the lambda operator with switch expressions. And in chapter 13, you'll learn how to use the lambda operator to code expression-bodied indexers and operators as well as lambda expressions, which are frequently used with LINQ as shown in chapter 18.

The syntax for coding a public method

```
public returnType MethodName([parameterList])
{
    statements
}
```

A method that accepts parameters

```
public string GetDisplayText(string sep)
{
    return $"{Code}{sep}{Price.ToString("c")}{sep}{Description}";
}
```

The same method coded with an expression body

```
public string GetDisplayText(string sep) =>
    $"{Code}{sep}{Price.ToString("c")}{sep}{Description}";
```

Description

- To provide other classes with access to a method, you declare it using the public access modifier. To prevent other classes from accessing a method, you declare it using the private access modifier.

- The name of a method combined with its parameters form the method's *signature*.

- If a method simply returns an expression or executes a single statement, you can code it as an *expression-bodied method*.

- To code an expression-bodied method, you code the method signature, followed by the lambda operator (=>) and an expression or executable statement.

Figure 12-6   How to code methods

How to code constructors

By default, when you use the new keyword to create an instance of a user-defined class, C# assigns default values to all the properties in the new object. If that's not what you want, you can code a special method called a *constructor* that's executed when an object is created from the class. Figure 12-7 shows you how to do that.

To create a constructor, you declare a public method with the same name as the class. For example, a constructor for the Product class must be named Product. Within the constructor, you initialize the properties, and you include any additional statements you want to be executed when an object is created from the class. Note that a constructor must not be declared with a return type.

The first example in this figure shows a constructor that doesn't provide for any parameters. Because this constructor has no executable statements, it simply initializes all the properties to their default values (excluding read-only properties and properties that were initialized when they were declared). The default values for the various data types are listed in this figure.

In some cases, you might not define any constructors for a class. In that case, the C# compiler generates a *default constructor* that's equivalent to the constructor shown in the first example.

The second example shows a constructor that accepts three parameters. This constructor uses the values passed to the parameters to initialize the properties. This technique is often used to set initial property values for an object.

Notice that the second constructor uses the this keyword to refer to the properties whose values are being initialized. Although this isn't required, it makes it clear that the property that's being referred to is defined in the current class and not in another class.

If you code a constructor with parameters, the compiler won't generate a default constructor. That means you must pass the expected arguments when you call the constructor. It also means you can't use an object initializer to create an instance of the class. If that's not what you want, you need to code a constructor like the one in the first example in addition to any other constructors. Then, your class will have overloaded constructors, which you'll learn more about later.

After the two constructors, this figure presents statements that execute these constructors. The first two execute the constructor with no parameters, and the second two execute the constructor with three parameters. Note that the second and fourth statements omit the class name after the new keyword, which you can do with C# 9.0 and later. Although you've seen statements like these before, you should now have a better understanding of how they work.

With C# 7.0 and later, you can also use expression bodies with constructors. This is illustrated by the last two examples in this figure. The first of these is a constructor that consists of a single statement that initializes a property.

The last example shows how to use a tuple like the ones you learned about in chapter 6 to initialize two or more properties. Here, a tuple is created from the three parameters that are passed to the constructor. Then, the tuple is deconstructed and its values are assigned to the corresponding properties.

A constructor with no parameters

```
public Product()
{
}
```

A constructor with three parameters

```
public Product(string code, string description, decimal price)
{
    this.Code = code;
    this.Description = description;
    this.Price = price;
}
```

Statements that call these constructors

```
Product product1 = new Product();
Product product2 = new();                                // C# 9.0 and later
Product product3 = new Product("C#", "Murach's C#", 59.50m);
Product product4 = new("C#", "Murach's C#", 59.50m);  // C# 9.0 and later
```

A constructor with an expression body (C# 7.0 and later)

```
public Product(string code) => this.Code = code;
```

A constructor with an expression body and a tuple (C# 7.0 and later)

```
public Product(string code, string description, decimal price) =>
    (this.Code, this.Description, this.Price) = (code, description, price);
```

Default values for instance variables

Data type	Default value
All numeric types	0
Boolean	false
Char	null
Object	null
Date	12:00 a.m. on January 1, 0001

Description

- The name of a constructor must be the same as the name of the class. In addition, it must be declared with the public access modifier, and it can't specify a return type.

- To code a constructor that has parameters, code a data type and name for each parameter within the parentheses that follow the class name.

- If a constructor doesn't set a property and the property wasn't initialized when it was declared, the property will be assigned a default value as shown above.

- With C# 7.0 and later, if a constructor contains a single statement, you can code it as an *expression-bodied constructor* using the lambda operator.

- If a constructor contains two or more statements that initialize properties, you can use an expression-bodied constructor with a tuple to initialize those properties.

Figure 12-7   How to code constructors

How to code static members

As figure 12-8 shows, *static members* are members that can be accessed without creating an instance of a class. The idea of static members shouldn't be new to you because you've seen them used in several chapters in this book. In chapter 4, for example, you learned how to use static methods of the Math and Convert classes. And in chapter 9, you learned how to use static members of the DateTime structure and the String class. This figure shows how to create static members in your own classes.

To create a static member, you simply include the *static* keyword on its declaration. The class shown in this figure, for example, provides static members that can be used to perform data validation. This class has a static property named LineEnd and a static method named IsPresent().

The static IsPresent() method validates the value that's passed to it to make sure it isn't an empty string. If it is an empty string, this method assigns an error message to the msg variable that's declared at the beginning of the method. Then, it returns the value of that variable.

The second example in this figure shows how you might call the static IsPresent() method to validate two text boxes. Here, the value of the Text property of each text box and the name of the property that's being validated are passed to the IsPresent() method. To get the name of the property, these statements use the nameof operator. Then, the string that's returned by each call is appended to a variable named errorMessage. If this variable doesn't contain an empty string, it means that one or both of the values are invalid. In that case, the error message is displayed.

Since the Validator class shown in this figure contains only static members, the static keyword is used to declare the entire class as a *static class*. This prevents you from accidentally coding any non-static members for this class or from creating an object from this class. If you attempt to write such code, it won't compile.

However, a class that isn't declared as a static class can include static members and non-static members. Then, when you create an instance of that class, all the instances share the static members. Because of that, you can't access a static member from the variable that refers to the instance of the class. Instead, you can access it only by coding the name of the class.

Keep in mind, too, that a static property or method can only refer to other static members. For example, because the methods shown in this figure are declared as static, the LineEnd property that they use to build the message string must be declared as static too.

You can also refer to a static member of a class without naming the class. To do that, you code a using directive like the one shown in this figure that includes the static keyword. With this using directive, you could refer to the IsPresent() method of the Validator class like this:

```
IsPresent(txtCode)
```

Although this simplifies the code, it's best to use this technique only if it's clear what class contains the static member. Note that you can also use this technique with static members of the .NET classes.

A class that contains static members

```
public static class Validator
{
    public static string LineEnd { get; set; } = "\n";

    public static string IsPresent(string value, string name)
    {
        string msg = "";
        if (value == "")
        {
            msg = $"{name} is a required field.{LineEnd}";
        }
        return msg;
    }
}
```

Code that uses static members

```
string errorMessage = "";
errorMessage += Validator.IsPresent(txtCode.Text, nameof(Product.Code));
errorMessage += Validator.IsPresent(txtDescription.Text,
                                nameof(Product.Description));
if (errorMessage != "")
{
    MessageBox.Show(errorMessage, "Entry Error");
}
```

A using directive for the static Validator class

```
using static ProductMaintenance.Validator;
```

Description

- A *static member* is a property, method, or other member that can be accessed without creating an instance of the class. To define a static member, you use the *static* keyword.

- Static properties and methods can refer only to other static members or to variables declared within the property or method.

- A constant that's declared with the public keyword is implicitly static. You can't code the static keyword on a constant declaration.

- If you create an object from a class, you can't refer to a static member through the variable for the object. You can refer to a static member only through the name of the class.

- If a class only contains static members, you can use the static keyword in the class declaration to declare the class as a *static class*. This prevents programmers from accidentally adding a non-static member to the class or from creating an object from the class.

- The using static directive lets you refer to static members of a type without naming the type.

Figure 12-8   How to code static members

The Product Maintenance app

Now that you've learned the basic skills for creating classes, the topics that follow present a Product Maintenance app that maintains a simple file of products. As you'll see, this app uses three user-defined classes in addition to the two form classes and the Program class that starts the program by running the first form.

The operation of the Product Maintenance app

Figure 12-9 describes the operation of the Product Maintenance app. As you can see, this app uses two forms and a dialog. The main form retrieves a list of products from a file and displays those products in a list box. The user can use this form to add or delete a product.

If the user clicks the Add Product button, the New Product form is displayed as a modal form. Then, the user can enter the data for a new product and click the Save button to add the product to the file. If the user enters incorrect data, the app displays meaningful error messages in a dialog.

After the product is saved, the list box in the Product Maintenance form is refreshed so it includes the new product. The user can also click the Cancel button on the New Product form to cancel the add operation.

To delete a product, the user selects the product in the list box and clicks the Delete Product button. Then, a dialog is displayed to confirm the operation. If the operation is confirmed, the product is deleted and the list box is refreshed so it no longer includes the deleted product.

The Product Maintenance form

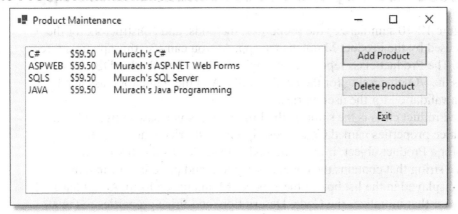

The New Product form

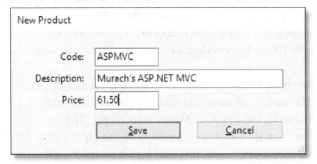

The Confirm Delete dialog

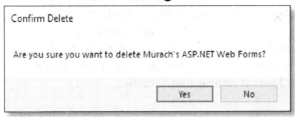

Description

- The Product Maintenance app retrieves product information from a file, displays it in a list box, and lets the user add or delete products.

- To add a product, the user clicks the Add Product button to display the New Product form. Then, the user can enter the data for the new product and click the Save button. Alternatively, the user can click the Cancel button to cancel the add operation. In either case, the user is returned to the Product Maintenance form.

- To delete a product, the user selects the product to be deleted and then clicks the Delete Product button. Then, the Confirm Delete dialog is display to confirm the deletion.

Figure 12-9   The operation of the Product Maintenance app

The classes used by the Product Maintenance app

Figure 12-10 summarizes the properties, methods, and constructors for the classes used by the Product Maintenance app. As you can see, this app uses three classes. The Product class represents a single product. The ProductDB class handles the I/O processing for the Products file. And the Validator class handles the data validation for the user entries.

The Product class is the same as the Product class you saw in figure 12-2. It has three properties named Code, Description, and Price that define the values for a Product object. It has a method named GetDisplayText() that returns a string that contains the code, description, and price in a format that can be displayed in the list box of the Product Maintenance form. And it has a constructor that initializes the Code, Description, and Price properties to their default values.

The ProductDB class contains two methods. The first one, GetProducts(), retrieves all of the products from the Products file and returns them in a List<Product> object. The second one, SaveProducts(), accepts a List<Product> object and writes the products in the list to the Products file, overwriting the previous contents of the file.

Note that the specifications for these methods don't indicate the format of the Products file. That's because the details of how this class saves and retrieves product information are of no concern to the Product Maintenance app. That's one of the benefits of encapsulation: You don't have to know how the class works. You just have to know what members it contains and how you refer to them.

The Validator class contains four static methods that provide for different types of data validation. For example, the IsPresent() method checks if the value that's passed to it is an empty string, and the IsDecimal() method checks if the value that's passed to it is a valid decimal value. If one of these methods determines that the data is invalid, it assigns an error message to a string variable that's initialized to an empty string. Then, it returns that variable.

The Product class

Property	Description
`Code`	A string that contains a code that uniquely identifies the product.
`Description`	A string that contains a description of the product.
`Price`	A decimal that contains the product's price.

Method	Description
`GetDisplayText(sep)`	Returns a string that contains the code, description, and price separated by the sep string.

Constructor	Description
`()`	Creates a Product object with default values.

The ProductDB class

Method	Description
`GetProducts()`	A static method that returns a List<Product> object from the Products file.
`SaveProducts(list)`	A static method that writes the products in the specified List<Product> object to the Products file.

The Validator class

Property	Description
`LineEnd`	A static string that contains the delimiter that's added to the end of an error message. The default is "\n".

Method	Description
`IsPresent(value, name)`	A static method that returns a string with an error message if the value that's passed to it is an empty string.
`IsInt32(value, name)`	A static method that returns a string with an error message if the value that's passed to it isn't an integer.
`IsDecimal(value, name)`	A static method that returns a string with an error message if the value that's passed to it isn't a decimal.
`IsWithinRange(value, name, min, max)`	A static method that returns a string with an error message if the value that's passed to it isn't within the specified range.

Note

* Because you don't need to know how the ProductDB class works, its code isn't shown in this chapter. Please refer to chapter 17 for two different versions of this class.

Figure 12-10   The classes used by the Product Maintenance app

The code for the Product Maintenance app

Figures 12-11 through 12-13 show the code for the Product Maintenance form, the New Product form, and the Validator class. Since you saw the code for the Product class in figure 12-2, the class code isn't shown again here.

Also, because you don't need to know how the ProductDB class is implemented to understand how this app works, the code for that class isn't presented here either. If you're interested, however, you'll find two different implementations of this class in chapter 17.

The code for the Product Maintenance form, shown in figure 12-11, begins by declaring a class variable named products of the List<Product> type. Next, in the Load event handler for the form, the GetProducts() method of the ProductsDB class is called to fill this list with Product objects created from the data in the Products file. Then, the FillProductListBox() method is called. This method uses a foreach loop to add the string returned by each product's GetDisplayText() method to the list box. Notice that a tab character is passed to this method so the products appear as shown in figure 12-9.

If the user clicks the Add Product button, an instance of the New Product form is created, and the GetNewProduct() method of that form is called. If the Product object returned by this method isn't null, the product is added to the products list. Then, the SaveProducts() method of the ProductDB class is called to update the Products file, and the FillProductListBox() method is called to refresh the list box so the new product is included.

If the user selects a product in the list and clicks the Delete Product button, a confirmation dialog is displayed. Then, if the user confirms the deletion, the product is removed from the products list, the Products file is updated, and the list box is refreshed.

The code for the New Product form is shown in figure 12-12. It declares a private Product object named product. Then, the GetNewProduct() method that's called from the Product Maintenance form starts by displaying the New Product form as a dialog. If the user clicks the Save button in this dialog, the IsValidData() method is called to validate the data. This method calls the IsPresent() method of the Validator class for the Code and Description text boxes, and it calls the IsDecimal() method for the Price text box.

If all the values are valid, a new Product object is created with the values entered by the user, the dialog is closed, and the Product object is returned to the Product Maintenance form. By contrast, if the user clicks the Cancel button, the dialog is closed and the product variable, which is initialized to null, is returned to the Product Maintenance form.

The code for the Validator class, shown in figure 12-13, should present no surprises. In fact, you saw code similar to this code back in figure 12-8. The only difference is that, in addition to the IsPresent() method, this version of the Validator class includes an IsDecimal() method, an IsInt32() method, and an IsWithinRange() method.

The code for the Product Maintenance form

```
public partial class frmProductMain : Form
{
    public frmProductMain()
    {
        InitializeComponent();
    }

    private List<Product> products = null!;

    private void frmProductMain_Load(object sender, EventArgs e)
    {
        products = ProductDB.GetProducts();
        FillProductListBox();
    }

    private void FillProductListBox()
    {
        lstProducts.Items.Clear();
        foreach (Product p in products)
        {
            lstProducts.Items.Add(p.GetDisplayText("\t"));
        }
    }

    private void btnAdd_Click(object sender, EventArgs e)
    {
        frmNewProduct newProductForm = new();
        Product product = newProductForm.GetNewProduct();
        if (product != null)
        {
            products.Add(product);
            ProductDB.SaveProducts(products);
            FillProductListBox();
        }
    }

    private void btnDelete_Click(object sender, EventArgs e)
    {
        int i = lstProducts.SelectedIndex;
        if (i != -1)
        {
            Product product = products[i];
            string message = "Are you sure you want to delete "
                + product.Description + "?";
            DialogResult button =
                MessageBox.Show(message, "Confirm Delete",
                MessageBoxButtons.YesNo);
            if (button == DialogResult.Yes)
            {
                products.Remove(product);
                ProductDB.SaveProducts(products);
                FillProductListBox();
            }
        }
    }

    private void btnExit_Click(object sender, EventArgs e)
    {
        this.Close();
    }
}
```

Figure 12-11   The code for the Product Maintenance form

The code for the New Product form

```
public partial class frmNewProduct : Form
{
    public frmNewProduct()
    {
        InitializeComponent();
    }

    private Product product = null!;

    public Product GetNewProduct()
    {
        this.ShowDialog();
        return product;
    }

    private void btnSave_Click(object sender, EventArgs e)
    {
        if (IsValidData())
        {
            product = new()
            {
                Code = txtCode.Text,
                Description = txtDescription.Text,
                Price = Convert.ToDecimal(txtPrice.Text)
            };
            this.Close();
        }
    }

    private bool IsValidData()
    {
        bool success = true;
        string errorMessage = "";

        errorMessage += Validator.IsPresent(txtCode.Text,
                                         nameof(Product.Code));
        errorMessage += Validator.IsPresent(txtDescription.Text,
                                         nameof(Product.Description));
        errorMessage += Validator.IsDecimal(txtPrice.Text,
                                         nameof(Product.Price));

        if (errorMessage != "")
        {
            success = false;
            MessageBox.Show(errorMessage, "Entry Error");
        }
        return success;
    }

    private void btnCancel_Click(object sender, EventArgs e)
    {
        this.Close();
    }
}
```

Figure 12-12   The code for the New Product form

The code for the Validator class

```
public static class Validator
{
    public static string LineEnd { get; set; } = "\n";

    public static string IsPresent(string value, string name)
    {
        string msg = "";
        if (value == "")
        {
            msg = $"{name} is a required field.{LineEnd}";
        }
        return msg;
    }

    public static string IsDecimal(string value, string name)
    {
        string msg = "";
        if (!Decimal.TryParse(value, out _))
        {
            msg = $"{name} must be a valid decimal value.{LineEnd}";
        }
        return msg;
    }

    public static string IsInt32(string value, string name)
    {
        string msg = "";
        if (!Int32.TryParse(value, out _))
        {
            msg = $"{name} must be a valid integer value.{LineEnd}";
        }
        return msg;
    }

    public static string IsWithinRange(string value, string name,
                                       decimal min, decimal max)
    {
        string msg = "";
        if (Decimal.TryParse(value, out decimal number))
        {
            if (number < min || number > max)
            {
                msg = $"{name} must be between {min} and {max}.{LineEnd}";
            }
        }
        return msg;
    }
}
```

Figure 12-13   The code for the Validator class

More skills for creating and using classes

In addition to the skills you've already learned in this chapter for creating classes, the topics that follow present some additional skills that you should know about.

How to code properties with fields

Figure 12-14 shows the syntax for a public property that uses a private *field* to store the value of the property. Fields work like regular variables, but they must be declared at the class level, not within properties, methods, or constructors. That way, they're accessible throughout the entire class.

A class can contain two types of fields: *instance variables* and *static variables*. An instance variable is initialized when an instance of a class is created, so each instance has its own copy. By contrast, a static variable uses the static keyword and can be accessed without creating an instance of a class. The fields shown in this figure are instance variables.

Although the fields in this figure use the private access modifier, you can also declare a field as public. Then, the field is accessible outside the class. However, public fields are generally considered a bad practice. Instead, you should use properties to access private variables most of the time.

The syntax at the top of this figure shows that, after you declare a private field to store the property value, you then declare a property with a getter, a setter, or both. Unlike an auto-implemented property, however, you must code the body of the getter and setter. Specifically, you must code the getter to retrieve the value of the field, and you must code the setter to assign a value to the field.

The public property should be declared with the same data type as the private field. It's also common to use the same name for the property and the field, but to use Camel notation for the field name (first word starts with a lowercase character, all words after that start with uppercase characters) and to use Pascal notation for the property name (each word starts with an uppercase character). In the examples in this figure, for instance, the name of the field for the Code property is code.

The main reason to code a public property that uses a private field is to process the property value in some way. In the first example in this figure, for instance, the getter checks the value of the field and returns a default value if the value of the field is null or empty. The setter, by contrast, only needs to set the value of the field. To do that, it uses an implicit parameter named value to access the value to be assigned to the field. With C# 7.0 and later, you can use an *expression-bodied accessor* for a setter that only sets the field value, as shown here.

In the second example, the getter uses an expression-bodied accessor to return the value of the field. Then, the setter checks if the value parameter is null or empty. If so, a value of "N/A" is assigned to the parameter. Then, the original or modified value is assigned to the field.

The syntax for coding a public property with a private field

```
private type fieldName[= value];

public type PropertyName
{
    [get { code to return field value }]
    [set { code to assign value to field }]
}
```

A property with a getter that processes the field value before returning it

```
private string code;

public string Code
{
    get
    {
        if (String.IsNullOrEmpty(code))
            return "N/A";
        else
            return code;
    }
    set => code = value;                    // expression-bodied set accessor
}
```

A property with a setter that processes the field value before setting it

```
private string code;

public string Code
{
    get => code;                            // expression-bodied get accessor
    set
    {
        if (String.IsNullOrEmpty(value))
            value = "N/A";
        code = value;
    }
}
```

Description

- A variable that's defined at the class level within a class is called a *field*.

- If your property simply sets and returns a value, you can use an auto-implemented property that automatically creates a field behind the scenes to store the property value.

- When you need to process a value before you set or return it, you can code the field yourself. Then, you can work with that field in the code for the getter or setter.

- It's common to use the same name for the property and the field, but to begin the property name with an uppercase letter and the field name with a lowercase letter.

- If the getter or setter for a property simply returns or sets the field value, you can code *expression-bodied accessors*, which were introduced with C# 7.0. To do that, you code the get or set keyword, the lambda operator, and the return expression or assignment statement.

Figure 12-14   How to code properties with fields

How to code overloaded methods and constructors

Figure 12-15 presents the concept of overloading. When you *overload* a method, you code two or more methods with the same name, but with unique combinations of parameters. In other words, you code methods with unique *signatures*.

For a method signature to be unique, the method must have a different number of parameters than the other methods with the same name, or at least one of the parameters must have a different data type. Note that the names of the parameters aren't part of the signature. So, using different names isn't enough to make the signatures unique. Also, the return type isn't part of the signature. As a result, you can't create two methods with the same name and parameters but different return types.

The purpose of overloading is to provide more than one way to invoke a given method. For example, this figure shows two versions of the GetDisplayText() method. The first one is the one you saw in figure 12-2 that accepts a parameter named sep. The second one doesn't accept this parameter. Instead, it calls the first version of the GetDisplayText() method and passes a comma and a space as the argument. This causes the method to return the code, price, and description separated by a comma and a space. This provides a default value for the parameter.

When you refer to an overloaded method, the number of arguments you specify and their types determine which version of the method is executed. The two statements in this figure that call the GetDisplayText() method illustrate how this works. Because the first statement specifies an argument, it will cause the version of the GetDisplayText() method that accepts a parameter to be executed. By contrast, the second statement doesn't specify an argument, so it will cause the version of the GetDisplayText() method that doesn't accept a parameter to be executed.

In chapter 3, you learned that if you type the name of a method followed by a left parenthesis into the Code Editor, Visual Studio's IntelliSense feature displays a list of the method's parameters. You may not have realized, though, that if the method is overloaded, up and down arrows appear to the left of the argument list. Then, you can click the up and down arrows or press the up and down arrow keys to move from one overloaded method to another.

This works with overloaded methods in user-defined classes as well. For example, the illustration in this figure shows how the IntelliSense feature displays the overloaded GetDisplayText() methods. In this case, the method that accepts a parameter is displayed.

Since constructors are methods, you can overload them too. This is useful when you want users of your class to have several ways to instantiate an object. The first constructor in this figure, for example, has no parameters, and the second constructor has three parameters. Because of that, a user of this class can create an object by calling the constructor with no parameters, calling the constructor with three parameters, or using an object initializer.

How to code overloaded methods

The GetDisplayText() method of the Product class
```
public string GetDisplayText(string sep) =>
    $"{Code}{sep}{Price.ToString("c")}{sep}{Description}";
```

An overloaded version of the GetDisplayText() method
```
public string GetDisplayText() => GetDisplayText(", ");
```

Two statements that call the GetDisplayText() method
```
lblProduct.Text = product.GetDisplayText("\t");
lblProduct.Text = product.GetDisplayText();
```

How the IntelliSense feature lists overloaded methods
```
Product product = newProductForm.GetNewProduct();
Console.WriteLine(product.GetDisplayText()
                  ▲ 2 of 2 ▼ string Product.GetDisplayText(string sep)
```

How to code overloaded constructors

A constructor of the Product class with no parameters
```
public Product() { }
```

A constructor of the Product class with three parameters
```
public Product(string code, string description, decimal price)
{
    this.Code = code;
    this.Description = description;
    this.Price = price;
}
```

Description

- The name of a method combined with its parameters form the method's *signature*. More than one method can use the same name, but each method must have a unique signature.

- Methods with the same name but different signatures are *overloaded*. It's common to use overloaded methods to provide two or more versions of a method that work with different data types or that supply default values for omitted parameters.

- When you type a method name followed by a left parenthesis, the IntelliSense feature adds the right parenthesis and displays the parameters expected by the method. If up and down arrows are displayed as shown above, you can click these arrows or press the up and down arrow keys to display each of the method's overloaded parameter lists.

- Since constructors are methods, you can overload them too. The signature of a constructor is the name of the class combined with the parameter list. Each constructor must have a unique signature.

Note

- Instead of using overloaded methods to supply default values for omitted parameters, you can use optional parameters. See chapter 6 for more information.

Figure 12-15   How to code overloaded methods and constructors

How to code required properties

Sometimes, you want to require that a user of a class provides values for some or all of its properties when they create an instance of the class. One way to do that is to code the class with a constructor that accepts parameters. Then, the constructor uses the values it receives to initialize the required properties.

For this to work, you need to make sure that the class doesn't include an overloaded parameterless constructor. That way, a user of the class can only use the constructor with parameters to create an instance of the class. This ensures that values are provided for the required properties.

C# 11.0 introduced another way to code required properties. To do that, you include the *required* keyword on the declaration for each required property. You can see this in the first example in figure 12-16. Here, all three properties of the Product class are required.

When you code a property with the required keyword, a value must be provided for that property when an instance is created. This is shown in the second example, where an instance of the Product class is created with an object initializer that provides a value for the required Code and Description properties but not for the required Price property. As you can see, this causes a syntax error that indicates that the Price property is required.

The use of the required keyword provides two main benefits over coding a constructor for required properties. First, there's less code because you don't need to code a constructor that accepts values and initializes properties. Second, you can use an object initializer to create a new object, which you can't do with a class that only has a constructor with parameters.

Even though the required keyword eliminates the need to code a constructor with parameters, you may still want to provide one for your class. If you do, you need to *decorate* that constructor with the SetsRequiredMembers attribute, as shown in the last example in this figure. An *attribute* gives the compiler information about the code that it decorates. In this case, it tells the compiler that the constructor initializes all required properties and fields.

It's important to understand that when you use the SetsRequiredMembers attribute, the compiler doesn't actually check that the constructor assigns a value to each required member. Rather, the compiler just assumes that it does. So, you need to make sure that a constructor that's decorated with this attribute really does initialize all the required members in your class.

The SetsRequiredMembers attribute is in the System.Diagnostics.Code-Analysis namespace. So, to make it easy to use, you should add a using directive for that namespace as shown here.

When you code a required property that stores a string, you should realize that Visual Studio won't generate a null reference warning if you don't assign an initial value to the property. For example, unlike the Code and Description properties shown in figure 12-2, the required Code and Description properties in this figure aren't initialized to empty strings. That's because the code won't run if an initial value isn't provided, so there's no danger of the value being null.

A Product class with three required properties

```
public class Product
{
    public required string Code { get; set; }
    public required string Description { get; set; }
    public required decimal Price { get; set; }
        . . .
}
```

The compile-time error Visual Studio displays
when a required property isn't set in an object initializer

```
Product p = new() { Code = "C#", Description = "Murach's C#" };

     Product.Product()

     CS9035: Required member 'Product.Price' must be set in the object initializer or attribute constructor.
```

How to use the SetsRequiredMembers attribute

```
using System.Diagnostics.CodeAnalysis;
...
public class Product
{
    public Product() { }

    [SetsRequiredMembers]
    public Product(string code, string description, decimal price)
    {
        Code = code;
        Description = description;
        Price = price;
    }

    public required string Code { get; set; }
    public required string Description { get; set; }
    public required decimal Price { get; set; }
    ...
}
```

Description

- Starting with C# 11.0, you can use the required keyword to specify properties or public fields that must be initialized when an instance of a class is created.

- If your class has a constructor that sets the required members, you must mark that constructor with the SetsRequiredMembers attribute of the System.Diagnostics. CodeAnalysis namespace. This tells the compiler that the required members are set. Without this attribute, you'll get errors when you try to call the constructor.

- Visual Studio doesn't display null reference warnings if a required property or field doesn't have a default value. That's because the code won't run if the required member isn't set when an instance is created, so the property or field can't be null.

Figure 12-16   How to code required properties

How to use property patterns

In chapter 5, you learned how to use pattern matching to test for various characteristics in the match expressions of switch statements and expressions, as well as in is expressions of if statements. When you work with objects, you can use type patterns as described in that chapter to determine if an object is of a given type. In addition, you can use *property patterns* to match the properties of an object.

To help you see how property patterns simplify the way you test property values, figure 12-17 presents three versions of a GetDiscountPercent() method. This method tests the type of an object that's passed to the method, as well as the value of one of its properties. Then, if it's a Product object, it sets the value of the discountPercent variable depending on the value of the Category property. These methods accept a parameter of the Object type so they can work with any type of object.

The first method uses an if statement with an is expression that uses a declaration pattern to assign the object to a variable named p if it's of the Product type. Then, a nested if statement is used to test the value of the Category property. Although this example tests for a single object type, you should know that it could be expanded to test for additional types. To do that, you would add else if clauses to the outer if statement. You could also expand the nested if statement to test additional property values.

The second method uses a switch statement whose case labels use declaration patterns to assign the object to a variable named p if it's of the Product type. When you use a switch statement, you can also code a *when* clause on each case label to test the value of a property or public field. In this example, both case labels test the value of the Category property of the Product object just as in the first example. Notice that these case labels don't include break statements. That's because the return statements return control immediately to the calling code.

Like the first method, this method could also be expanded to test for different types of objects. To do that, you would code additional case labels that test for different object types. In addition, you could expand the when clauses to test additional property values.

The third method uses a switch expression with a property pattern that tests the values of a property. Here, each case starts with the name of the type you want to test for, in this case, Product. Note that you can also use this technique with .NET data types like int and decimal. In that case, the parameter for the method would be declared using the var keyword.

After the object type, you code the property pattern. This pattern includes the property name followed by a colon, the value that's being tested for, and the enclosing braces. In this method, the property patterns test the Category property of the Product object for specific values as in the first two methods. If you compare this method with the first two methods, though, you'll see that this method is considerably simpler.

One more thing you should notice about this switch expression is that it ends with a discard. This is required when you use a switch expression with a property pattern because property patterns must return a non-null value.

The syntax of a property pattern

```
{ property: value[, property: value]... }
```

Methods that test an object's type and property value

With nested if statements

```
private static decimal GetDiscountPercent(Object o) {
    decimal discountPercent = .0m;
    if (o is Product p) {
        if (p.Category == ".NET")
            discountPercent = .1m;
        else if (p.Category == "Java")
            discountPercent = .2m;
    }
    return discountPercent;
}
```

With a switch statement

```
private static decimal GetDiscountPercent(Object o) {
    switch (o) {
        case Product p when p.Category == ".NET":
            return .1m;
        case Product p when p.Category == "Java":
            return .2m;
        default:
            return .0m;
    }
}
```

With a switch expression that uses a property pattern

```
private static decimal GetDiscountPercent(Object o) => o switch
{
    Product { Category: ".NET" } => .1m,
    Product { Category: "Java" } => .2m,
    _ => .0m
};
```

Description

- Prior to C# 8, you had to use an if or switch statement to test if a property or public field of an object has a particular value. With C# 8 and later, you can use *property patterns* with switch expressions to do that.

- A property pattern consists of the name of a property or public field, followed by a colon and the value for the pattern, all enclosed in braces. To test the values of two or more properties or public fields, you separate them with commas.

- To test the type of the object that's passed to a method, you use a type pattern by preceding the property pattern with the name of the type.

- To test the type of an object using a switch statement, you code the object type and the variable you want to assign it to. You can also code a *when* clause to test if a property or field of the object has a particular value.

Figure 12-17   How to use property patterns (part 1 of 2)

The first example in part 2 of figure 12-17 shows that you can use a switch expression to test for more than one type of object. Here, the first four cases test for Product objects, and the next two cases test for Vendor objects. Although you haven't seen Vendor objects used in any of the examples up to now, all you need to know is that these objects are created from a Vendor class that includes properties, methods, and constructors similar to the ones defined by the Product class.

Notice in this example that the property patterns for the cases that test for a Vendor object test a different property than the cases that test for a Product object. You can also test different properties of the same object, and you can test two or more properties of the same object using a single property pattern as shown in the second case for a Vendor object. In other words, you can use a switch expression with property patterns to test any property of any object. That's true regardless of whether the objects are related.

The second example is similar to the first example, except that the method accepts a Product object rather than a generic object. As a result, it isn't necessary to test the object type. However, it can only be used with Product objects.

The last example shows how to use property patterns to refer to nested properties. For example, suppose that a Vendor object includes a property named State that is a State object, and the State object includes a property named StateCode. Then, you can use one of the techniques shown here to refer to the StateCode property. Prior to C# 10, you had to nest two property patterns to do that as shown in the first method. If you're using C# 10 or later, though, you can use dot notation to refer to a nested property as shown in the second method.

A method that tests two types of objects

```
private static decimal GetDiscountPercent(Object o) => o switch
{
    Product { Category: ".NET" } => .1m,
    Product { Category: "Java" } => .2m,
    Product { Category: "Web" } => .3m,
    Product { Category: "Mainframe"} => .4m,
    Vendor  { DiscountType: "Quantity"} => .2m,
    Vendor  { DiscountType: "Terms", Terms: 30 } => .3m,
    _ => .0m
};
```

A method that tests a specific type of object

```
private static decimal GetDiscountPercent(Product p) => p switch
{
    { Category: ".NET" } => .1m,
    { Category: "Java" } => .2m,
    _ => .0m
};
```

How to refer to a nested property in a property pattern

Prior to C# 10.0

```
private static decimal GetTaxPercent(Object o) => o switch
{
    Vendor { State: { StateCode: "CA" } } => 7.5m,
    Vendor { State: { StateCode: "NY" } } => 6m,
    ...
    _ => .0m
};
```

C# 10.0 and later

```
private static decimal GetTaxPercent(Object o) => o switch
{
    Vendor { State.StateCode: "CA" } => 7.5m,
    Vendor { State.StateCode: "NY" } => 6m,
    ...
    _ => .0m
};
```

Description

- You can test two or more types of objects in the same switch expression.
- If you pass a specific type of object to a method, you don't need to test for the type in the switch expression.
- Prior to C# 10, you had to code nested property patterns to refer to nested properties. With C# 10 and later, you can use dot notation to refer to nested properties.

Figure 12-17   How to use property patterns (part 2 of 2)

How to create and use structures, records, and record structs

Now that you've learned how to create and use classes, you're ready to learn how to create and use three additional features of .NET that provide functionality that's similar to the functionality of a class. Those features are structures, records, and record structs.

How to create a structure

A *structure* is similar to a class, but it defines a *value type* rather than a reference type. Although structures require less memory and instantiate faster than classes, it's generally considered a good programming practice to use them only for objects that contain a small amount of data and for objects that you want to work like the .NET value types, such as the int, decimal, and DateTime types.

Figure 12-18 shows how to create a structure. To do that, you can use the procedure described in figure 12-4 to create a class file and then change the code to a struct statement that names the structure. In the body of the structure, you can create members just as you can for classes. In fact, a structure can have all the same types of members that a class can have, including fields, properties, methods, and events. Structures can also have static members. Structures don't support inheritance, though, which you'll learn about in chapter 14.

To illustrate, consider the Product structure shown in the first example in this figure. It includes three read/write properties, a constructor that initializes those properties, and a public method named GetDisplayText() that formats the properties for display. This code is similar to code you would find in a class.

Note, however, that this structure doesn't contain a parameterless constructor. That's because, unlike a class, C# will generate a default constructor even if the structure contains constructors that accept parameters. With C# 10 and later, you can also code your own parameterless constructor if you want to initialize one or more properties to values other than their defaults. Then, only the properties that the constructor doesn't initialize are set to default values.

Another difference between structures and classes is that, prior to C# 11, if a structure contained a constructor that accepts parameters, the constructor had to initialize all the structure's properties. With C# 11 and later, though, a constructor that accepts parameters can initialize just some of the properties. Then, the remaining properties are set to their default values.

Also prior to C# 11, if a structure used properties with fields, the constructor had to refer directly to those fields, not to the associated properties. With C# 11 and later, though, this restriction no longer applies.

In some cases, you won't want the values of a structure to be changed as a program executes. To make sure that doesn't happen, you can create a *read-only structure* as shown in the second example in this figure. Then, the properties of the structure can only contain getters or, in C# 9 or later, init-only setters. Although it's not shown here, you should know that if you don't use auto-

The syntax for creating a structure

```
public [readonly] struct StructureName
{
    structure members...
}
```

A Product structure

```
public struct Product
{
    public Product(string code, string description, decimal price)
    {
        this.Code = code;
        this.Description = description;
        this.Price = price;
    }
    public string Code { get; set; }
    public string Description { get; set; }
    public decimal Price { get; set; }

    public string GetDisplayText(string sep) =>
        $"{Code}{sep}{Price.ToString("c")}{sep}{Description}";
}
```

A read-only Product structure (C# 7.2 and later)

```
public readonly struct Product
{
    public Product(string code, string description, decimal price) {...}

    public string Code { get; }
    public string Description { get; }
    public decimal Price { get; }

    public string GetDisplayText(string sep) =>
        $"{Code}{sep}{Price.ToString("c")}{sep}{Description}";
}
```

Description

- A *structure* is similar to a class, but it represents a *value type*, not a reference type.

- A structure can contain the same types of members as a class, including fields, properties, methods, constructors, and events.

- Prior to C#10, a structure couldn't include a parameterless constructor because the compiler always generated one that initialized all properties to their default values.

- With C# 10 and later, you can code a parameterless constructor that initializes one or more properties. Then, only the properties that aren't initialized are set to default values.

- Prior to C# 11, a constructor that accepted parameters had to initialize all properties and fields to their default values. With C# 11 and later, a constructor that accepts parameters can initialize selected properties and fields and the rest are set to default values.

- If the value of a structure can't be changed, it should be declared as a *read-only structure*. Any private fields in a read-only structure must also be declared read-only.

- Prior to C# 11, if a structure had properties that used private fields, a constructor had to refer to those fields during initialization, not to the associated properties.

Figure 12-18   How to create a structure

implemented properties in a read-only structure, the private fields for the properties must also include the readonly keyword.

How to use a structure

Figure 12-19 shows you how to use a structure. In the first example, the code declares a variable with the structure type and then calls the default constructor. This sets the Code and Description properties to null and the Price property to 0. Note that if you're using C# 9.0 or later, you can omit the object type on the right side of the assignment statement if it's specified on the left side of the assignment statement. That's true of records and record structs as well, as you'll see in the figures that follow. After the structure is created, the code assigns values other than the defaults to its properties and then calls the GetDisplayText() method of the structure.

The second example shows how to call the constructor of the Product structure that accepts three parameters. Then, the third example shows how to use an object initializer to create an instance of a structure and set its properties.

The fourth example shows how to compare two structures. To do that, you use the Equals() method. Here, two structures whose properties contain the same values are created and stored in variables named p1 and p2. As a result, when the first Equals() method compares the two variables, it returns true. However, when the code changes the Price property of the p2 structure, all the properties of the two structures no longer match. As a result, when the second Equals() method compares the two variables, it returns false.

When comparing two variables, this is usually the behavior that you want. However, this isn't the default behavior for classes, as you'll see in the next chapter. For now, you just need to know that, by default, the Equals() method of a structure works differently than the Equals() method of a class. In addition, you should be aware that you can't use the equality operator (==) with structures.

The fifth example shows how to make a copy of a structure. Because a structure is a value type, this example makes a copy of the structure in the variable named product by assigning it to a new variable named copy. Then, it changes the Price property of the structure in the copy variable without affecting the Price property of the structure in the product variable. This is intuitive because it works like making a copy of any other value type.

Code that works with an instance of a structure type

```
// Create an instance of the Product structure using the default constructor
Product p = new();

// Assign values to each property
p.Code = "C#";
p.Description = "Murach's C#";
p.Price = 59.50m;

// Call a method
string msg = p.GetDisplayText("\n");
```

Code that uses a constructor to initialize the properties

```
Product p = new("C#", "Murach's C#", 59.50m);
```

Code that uses an object initializer to initialize the properties

```
Product p = new() {Code = "C#", Description= "Murach's C#",
    Price = 59.50m};
```

Code that creates and compares two structures

```
Product p1 = new("C#", "Murach's C#", 59.50m);
Product p2 = new("C#", "Murach's C#", 59.50m);
bool isEqual = p1.Equals(p2);      // isEqual is true

p2.Price = 61.50m;
isEqual = p1.Equals(p2);           // isEqual is false
```

Code that copies a structure and changes a value

```
Product product = new("C#", "Murach's C#", 59.50m);
Product copy = product;
copy.Price = 61.50m;
```

Description

- To create an instance of a structure and initialize its instance variables to default values, you use the default constructor with the new keyword.

- To create an instance of a structure and initialize its instance variables to values that you specify, you can use an object initializer or, if the structure provides one, a constructor that accepts parameters.

- When you use the Equals() method to compare two instances of a structure type, it will return true if the properties of the instances contain the same values. This is different from how instances of a class work, as you'll learn in chapter 13.

- You can use the assignment operator (=) to create a copy of a structure, just as you would create a copy of any value type.

- Unlike classes, structures can't be inherited. For more information about how inheritance works, please see chapter 14.

Figure 12-19   How to use a structure

How to create and use a record

A *record* works much like a structure, but it defines a *reference type* like a class does. Records are available with C# 9 and later.

Figure 12-20 shows the syntax for creating a record. This syntax is similar to the syntax for creating a class or a structure. Note, however, that with C# 10 and later, you can include the class keyword on a record declaration if you want to make it clear that it's a reference type.

A record can have all the same types of members as a class or structure, including fields, properties, methods, and events. Like classes but unlike structures, records support inheritance and don't generate a default constructor if they have constructors that accept parameters.

The first example in this figure shows a Product record. This is similar to the Product class and Product structure examples presented earlier in this chapter. It has three properties, a constructor that sets the values of the properties, and a method named GetDisplayText()

Although records are reference types, equality comparisons work like they do for structures. This is illustrated by the second code example in this figure. Here, two records whose properties contain the same values are stored in variables named p1 and p2. As a result, a comparison of the variables returns true. However, when the code changes the Price property of the p2 record, the values stored in the properties of the two variables no longer match and the comparison returns false. Note that, unlike structures, you can use either the Equals() method or the equality operator (==) to compare records.

You can also create a record that contains only read-only properties, as shown by the second syntax in this figure. Here, the record is declared with a list of properties that must be passed to the record when an instance is created. Note that because this is a statement, it ends with a semicolon.

Although it's not shown here, you can also include methods or other members in a read-only record. To do that, you replace the semicolon with a pair of braces, and then code the members within the braces.

Since a record is a reference type, you can't make a copy of it by assigning it to a new variable. That's because the variable for a reference type stores a reference to the object, not the object itself. So, if you copy the variable to another variable, both variables refer to the same object. Then, if you use one variable to change a property, that change is reflected in the other variable too.

To copy a record, then, you need to create a new instance of the record and then assign the property values of the original object to the new object. The last example in this figure shows two ways to do that.

First, you can assign the original object's values or new values to the copy. This works with classes, structures, or records, but it's most often used with records. Second, you can use the *with* keyword and a set of braces that includes the values for any properties you want to change. Here, the last statement creates a copy of the Product object but changes the value of the Price property. Or, if you want to copy an object without changing any properties, you can leave the braces empty. This works with records and, with C# 10 and later, structures. However, the with keyword doesn't work with classes.

The syntax for creating a record (C# 9.0 and later)

```
public record [class] RecordName       // optional class keyword (C# 10+)
{
    record members...
}
```

A Product record

```
public record Product
{
    public Product(string code, string description, decimal price) {...}

    public string Code { get; set; }
    public string Description { get; set; }
    public decimal Price { get; set; }

    public string GetDisplayText(string sep) =>
        $"{Code}{sep}{Price.ToString("c")}{sep}{Description}";
}
```

Code that creates and compares two record instances

```
Product p1 = new("C#", "Murach's C#", 59.50m);
Product p2 = new("C#", "Murach's C#", 59.50m);
bool isEqual = p1.Equals(p2);       // Equals() method: isEqual is true

p2.Price = 61.50m;
isEqual = p1 == p2;                  // equality operator(==): isEqual is false
```

The syntax for creating a record with read-only properties

```
public record [class] RecordName(propertyList);
```

A read-only Product record

```
public record Product(string Code, string Description, decimal Price);
```

Code that copies an instance of a read-only record and changes a value

```
Product product = new("C#", "Murach's C#", 59.50m);
```

By passing the values of the original to the constructor of the copy

```
Product copy1 = new(product.Code, product.Description, 61.50m);
```

By using the with keyword

```
Product copy2 = product with { Price = 61.50m };
```

Description

- A *record* is a reference type like a class, but a record's Equals() method and equality operator (==) compare the values of it properties.

- A record can contain the same types of members as a class and it can be inherited.

- You can create a record that only contains read-only properties by passing a list of properties to the record. You can't use an object initializer with this type of record.

- You can use the *with* keyword to copy a record and change one or more property values. With C# 10 and later, you can also use the with keyword to copy structures.

Figure 12-20   How to create and use a record

How to create and use a record struct

A *record struct* also works much like a structure. And, like a structure, it defines a *value type*. However, it provides better equality comparison than a structure. Record structs are available with C# 10 and later.

Figure 12-21 shows the syntax for creating a record struct. This syntax is similar to the syntax for a class, structure, or record. It can have all the same types of members, including fields, properties, methods, and events. Like structures, record structs don't support inheritance. They also generate a default constructor if they have constructors that accept parameters unless a parameterless constructor is coded.

In fact, a record struct is basically the same as a structure, with one important difference. With a structure, you can only use the Equals() method to compare two instances for equality. With a record struct, you can also use the equality operator (==). In addition, equality comparisons between instances of record structs are generally more efficient than equality comparisons between instances of structures.

The first code example in this figure shows a Product record struct. This is similar to the Product class, Product structure, and Product record examples presented earlier in this chapter.

The first statement in the second example creates an instance of the Product record struct named p1, and the second statement uses the assignment operator to make a copy of it. This works because a record struct is a value type. Then, the remaining statements use both the Equals() method and the equality operator to compare p1 and p2.

Like a record, you can declare a record struct that accepts a list of properties as shown by the second syntax in this figure. Unlike a record, however, this doesn't create read-only properties. If you want the properties to be read-only, you need to include the readonly keyword as shown here. You can also code the readonly keyword when you use the first syntax for creating a record struct.

When to use classes, structures, records, and record structs

Since classes, structures, records, and record structs are so similar to each other, it can be hard to determine when you would use each one. To help clarify this, the table at the end of figure 12-21 provides some guidance.

In general, you use a class for objects that are complex, have lots of methods, or need to be part of a class hierarchy. You use a structure for objects that primarily store data, are small enough to copy efficiently, and do equality comparisons based on the values of the data. You use a record for objects that primarily store data, should be a reference type rather than a value type (because, for instance, the data is too large to copy efficiently), and do equality comparisons based on the values of the data. And you use a record struct for objects that could be structures, but for which you want better equality comparison functionality, such as the ability to use the equality operator.

The syntax for creating a record struct (C# 10.0 and later)

```
public [readonly] record struct RecordName
{
    record members...
}
```

A Product record struct

```
public record struct Product
{
    public Product(string code, string description, decimal price) {...}

    public string Code { get; set; }
    public string Description { get; set; }
    public decimal Price { get; set; }

    public string GetDisplayText(string sep) =>
        $"{Code}{sep}{Price.ToString("c")}{sep}{Description}";
}
```

Code that creates and compares two record struct instances

```
Product p1 = new("C#", "Murach's C#", 59.50m);
Product p2 = p1;                       // makes a copy
bool isEqual = p1.Equals(p2);          // Equals() method: isEqual is true

p2.Price = 61.50m;                     // changes p2 but doesn't change p1
isEqual = p1 == p2;                    // equality operator(==): isEqual is false
```

The syntax for creating a record struct with read-only properties

```
public readonly record struct RecordName(propertyList);
```

A read-only Product record struct

```
public readonly record struct Product(string Code, string Description,
decimal Price);
```

When to use classes, structures, records, and record structs

Use a ...	When...
class	your object is complex, has many methods, or you need to create a hierarchy.
structure	your object primarily stores data and is small enough to copy efficiently.
record	your object primarily stores data, you want a reference type rather than one that you can copy, and you want to compare objects based on values.
record struct	your object primarily stores data, is small enough to copy efficiently, and you want improved equality comparison features and performance.

Description

- A *record struct* is a value type that has most of the same functionality as a structure.

- A record struct provides an equality operator (==) as well as the Equals() method. An equality comparison between two record structs is more efficient than between two structures.

- You can make a record struct read-only by including the readonly keyword. Unlike a read-only record, you can use an object initializer with a read-only record struct.

Figure 12-21   How to create and use a record struct; when to use records and structs

The Product Maintenance app updated to use a record

Figure 12-22 presents another version of the Product Maintenance app that you saw earlier in the chapter. This version has been updated to use a Product record rather than a Product class. Since most of the code in this version of the app is the same as it was before, only the code that's changed is shown here.

The first example shows the Product record, which uses the constructor-like syntax to create a read-only record. However, this record also includes an overloaded GetDisplayText() method. To do that, the declaration ends with a pair of braces rather than a semicolon. Then, the overloaded methods are coded within those braces.

The second example shows the event handler for the Save button of the New Product form. This code creates a new Product object by calling the constructor and passing it values for the code, description, and price. In the version of this app that uses a class, this code used an object initializer to create a new Product object. However, that won't work with the Product record shown here because of the way it's declared.

The third example shows the event handler for the Add button of the main form. This code didn't actually need to be changed to accommodate the change from a class to a record. However, this code is updated to take advantage of the fact that a record, unlike a class, compares two instances for equality by comparing the values of the properties. This makes it easy to add functionality that checks whether a product with the specified code, description, and price is already in the list of products.

To do that, this code calls the Contains() method of the List<Product> class and passes it the current Product object. The Contains() method then compares the values of the Product object it receives to the values of the Product objects in the list. If the Contains() method finds a Product object with the same values, it returns true and the user is notified. Otherwise, the new Product object is added to the list and the list box is updated.

The Product record

```
public record Product(string Code, string Description, decimal Price)
{
    public string GetDisplayText() => GetDisplayText(", ");

    public string GetDisplayText(string sep) =>
        $"{Code}{sep}{Price.ToString("c")}{sep}{Description}";
}
```

The Save button event handler in the frmNewProduct code behind

```
private void btnSave_Click(object sender, EventArgs e)
{
    if (IsValidData())
    {
        product = new(txtCode.Text, txtDescription.Text,
                    Convert.ToDecimal(txtPrice.Text));
        this.Close();
    }
}
```

The Add button event handler in the frmProductMain code behind

```
private void btnAdd_Click(object sender, EventArgs e)
{
    frmNewProduct newProductForm = new();
    Product product = newProductForm.GetNewProduct();
    if (product != null)
    {
        if (products.Contains(product))  // check if already in list
        {
            MessageBox.Show(
                "A product with values " + product.GetDisplayText() +
                " is already in the list.", "Unable to add");
        }
        else
        {
            products.Add(product);
            ProductDB.SaveProducts(products);
            FillProductListBox();
        }
    }
}
```

Description

- This version of the Product Maintenance app uses a record rather than a class. This code uses the constructor-like syntax to create a read-only record, but it adds an overloaded GetDisplayText() method within braces.

- To accommodate this change, the event handler for the Save button creates a new Product object by calling its constructor. The earlier version used an object initializer, but that won't work with the Product record shown here.

- Since a record compares the values in an object's properties, it's easy to add functionality to the Add button event handler that checks to see if the product is already in the list.

Figure 12-22   The Product Maintenance app updated to use a record

Perspective

At this point, you may be wondering why you should go to the extra effort of dividing an app into classes. The answer is twofold. First, dividing the code into classes makes it easier to use the code in two or more apps. For example, any app that needs to work with the data in the Products file can use the Product and ProductDB classes. Second, using classes helps you separate the business logic and database processing of an app from the user interface. That can simplify the development of the app and make it easier to maintain and enhance later on.

Now that you've had this introduction to the use of classes, you can continue in two different ways. If you already feel comfortable with the use of classes, you can read the next four chapters in this section to learn more about object-oriented programming. That will give you the background you need for understanding how the .NET classes work and for creating complex classes of your own.

On the other hand, if you're new to programming and the use of classes, you may want to skip to section 4 or 5 where you'll see how business classes are used in other apps. As you will see in the chapters in those sections, this chapter has already given you the skills that you need for developing most business classes and apps. Then, when you're more comfortable with the use of classes, you can return to the last four chapters in this section.

Terms

multi-layered architecture	instance	expression-bodied constructor
three-layered architecture	object initializer	static member
presentation layer	constructor	static class
database layer	state	field
middle layer	reference type	instance variable
business layer	class file	static variable
domain layer	get accessor	expression-bodied accessor
business class	getter	overloaded method
business object	set accessor	method signature
three-tiered architecture	setter	required property
object	read/write property	decorate a constructor
property	read-only property	attribute
method	write-only property	property pattern
member	expression-bodied property	structure
class	lambda operator	value type
encapsulation	auto-implemented property	read-only structure
data hiding	expression-bodied method	record
instantiation	default constructor	record struct

Exercise 12-1   Create a Customer Maintenance app that uses classes

In this exercise, you'll create a Customer Maintenance app that uses three classes. To make this app easier to develop, we'll give you the starting forms, a complete Validator class, and a complete CustomerDB class for working with the data in a file of customers. Note that the CustomerDB class assumes that the file of customers (Customers.txt) is in the C:\C#\Files directory. If you placed this file in a different directory after downloading and installing the files for this book, you will need to change the path specification in the CustomerDB class.

Open the project and add a Customer class

1. Open the app in the C:\C#\Ch12\CustomerMaintenance directory. Then, review both forms in the Form Designer window so you get an idea of how this project should work.

2. Add a class named Customer to this project, and add the properties, method, and constructors that are shown in the table below. Code the properties as auto-implemented properties, code the method as an expression-bodied method, and code the constructor that accepts parameters as an expression-bodied constructor that uses a tuple.

Property	Description
FirstName	Gets or sets a string that contains the customer's first name.
LastName	Gets or sets a string that contains the customer's last name.
Email	Gets or sets a string that contains the customer's email address.

Method	Description
GetDisplayText()	Returns a string that contains the customer's name and email address formatted like this: Joanne Smith, jsmith@armaco.com.

Constructor	Description
()	Creates a Customer object with default values.
(firstName, lastName, email)	Creates a Customer object using the specified values.

3. When you complete the Customer class, review the Validator class. Note that one of its methods is IsValidEmail(), which you can use to validate email addresses.

Add code to implement the Add Customer form

4. Display the code for the Add Customer form, and declare a class variable named customer of type Customer with an initial value of null.

5. Add a public method named GetNewCustomer() that displays the form as a dialog and returns a Customer object.

6. Add an event handler for the Click event of the Save button that validates the data on the form using the methods of the Validator class (all three fields are required and the email field must be a valid email address), and then creates a new Customer object and closes the form if the data is valid.

7. Add an event handler for the Click event of the Cancel button that simply closes the form.

Add code to implement the Customer Maintenance form

8. Display the code for the Customer Maintenance form, and declare a class variable named customers of type List<Customer> with an initial value of null.

9. Add an event handler for the Load event of the form that uses the GetCustomers() method of the CustomerDB class to load the customers list and then adds the customers to the Customers list box. Use the GetDisplayText() method of the Customer class to format the customer data.

10. Add an event handler for the Click event of the Add button that creates a new instance of the Add Customer form and executes the GetNewCustomer() method of that form. If the customer object that's returned by this method is not null, this event handler should add the new customer to the list, call the SaveCustomers() method of the CustomerDB class to save the list, and then refresh the Customers list box.

11. Add an event handler for the Click event of the Delete button that removes the selected customer from the list, calls the SaveCustomers() method of the CustomerDB class to save the list, and refreshes the Customers list box. Be sure to confirm the delete operation.

12. Add an event handler for the Click event of the Exit button that closes the form.

Run and test the app

13. Run the app and test it to be sure that it works properly. When you're done, end the app, but leave the solution open if you're going to continue with the next exercise.

Exercise 12-2   Use a structure or record struct

In this exercise, you'll modify your solution to exercise 12-1 by converting the Customer class to a structure or a record struct.

1. If it isn't open already, open the project in the C:\C#\Ch12\Customer-Maintenance directory.

2. Modify the Customer class so it defines a structure or a record struct.

3. Run the app, and debug any errors that you encounter. Note that you can't assign a null value to a Customer object anymore as it is now a value type. However, you can check if any of the properties of the Customer object are null or empty as those properties are of the String type.

4. Update the code to check if a customer is already in the list before adding it.

13

How to work with indexers, delegates, events, and operators

In the last chapter, you learned some basic skills for creating and working with classes. Now, this chapter will teach you some additional skills that you can use to create more complex classes. That includes creating indexers, throwing argument exceptions, defining delegates, raising events, and overloading operators.

An introduction to the ProductList class

As you may recall, the Product Maintenance app in chapter 12 used a variable of type List<Product> to store Product objects. To demonstrate the techniques that you're about to learn, the Product Maintenance app in this chapter uses a new class named ProductList. As you'll see, this class represents a collection of Product objects.

The code for a simple ProductList class

Figure 13-1 shows a simple version of the ProductList class. This class only uses coding techniques described in chapter 12. As a result, you shouldn't have any trouble understanding how this class works.

To start, the ProductList class defines a private List<Product> variable named products to store the product list. Then, it provides a constructor with no parameters that instantiates a new list, followed by a Count property that indicates how many products are in the product list.

Next, this class includes an overloaded Add() method. The first version of this method accepts a single parameter: a Product object that's added to the product list. The second version accepts three parameters: code, description, and price. The Add() method uses these parameters to create a Product object, which is then added to the list.

After that, the ProductList class provides a GetProductByIndex() method that returns a Product object from the list based on the specified index, and a Remove() method that removes a specified product from the list. The last two methods in this class are a Fill() method that fills the product list with the data from a file, and a Save() method that saves the product list to a file. Both of these methods call static methods in the ProductDB class, and both are coded as expression-bodied methods. Although the first Add() method and the Remove() method could also have been coded as expression-bodied methods, additional code will be added to these methods in this chapter. Then, they'll no longer be able to be coded as expression-bodied methods. To help you see the changes more easily, then, they're coded in the standard format here.

Of the methods in this class, only the Fill() and Save() methods provide functionality that isn't available from the List<T> class itself. In fact, the ProductList class actually limits the functionality of the List<T> class. For example, the ProductList class doesn't provide many of the properties and methods that are available from the List<T> class (such as the Insert() method).

Often, limiting functionality like this is what you want. For instance, you may not want users of the ProductList class to be able to insert items anywhere but at the end of the list. If that's not what you want, though, you'll learn an easy way to code a ProductList class in the next chapter that provides access to all the functionality of the List<T> class.

The code for a simple ProductList class

```
public class ProductList
{
    private List<Product> products;

    public ProductList() => products = new();

    public int Count => products.Count;

    public void Add(Product product)
    {
        products.Add(product);
    }

    public void Add(string code, string description, decimal price)
    {
        Product p = new Product(code, description, price);
        products.Add(p);
    }

    public Product GetProductByIndex(int i) =>  products[i];

    public void Remove(Product product)
    {
        products.Remove(product);
    }

    public void Fill() => products = ProductDB.GetProducts();

    public void Save() => ProductDB.SaveProducts(products);

}
```

Figure 13-1   The code for a simple ProductList class

The specifications
for the enhanced ProductList class

Figure 13-2 shows the specifications for an enhanced version of the ProductList class. To start, this class provides two indexers that let you access a product based on its index or product code (instead of using the GetProductByIndex() method). Besides these indexers, the enhanced ProductList class includes a + operator that adds a product to the list and a – operator that removes a product from the list.

Finally, this class includes a delegate named ChangeHandler, and an event named Changed. The delegate is designed to wire event handlers to the Changed event of the ProductList class. The ProductList class raises this event whenever the contents of the product list change due to a product being added to, updated in, or removed from the list. As you'll see, the Product Maintenance app uses this event to determine when it should save the product list and refresh the list box that displays the products.

The ProductList class

Constructor	Description
()	Creates a new product list.

Indexer	Description
[index]	Provides access to the product at the specified position.
[code]	Provides access to the product with the specified code.

Property	Description
Count	An integer that indicates how many Product objects are in the list.

Method	Description
Add(product)	Adds the specified Product object to the list.
Add(code, description, price)	Creates a Product object with the specified code, description, and price values, and then adds the Product object to the list.
Remove(product)	Removes the specified Product object from the list.
Fill()	Fills the list with product data from a file.
Save()	Saves the products to a file.

Operator	Description
+	Adds a Product object to the list.
-	Removes a Product object from the list.

Delegate	Description
ChangeHandler	Can be used to register the method that's used to handle the Changed event.

Event	Description
Changed	Raised whenever a Product object is added to, updated in, or removed from the list.

Figure 13-2   The specifications for the enhanced ProductList class

How to work with indexers

In the topics that follow, you'll learn two skills for working with indexers. First, you'll learn how to code an indexer both without and with expression bodies. Then, you'll learn how to throw an argument exception if the argument that's passed to the indexer isn't valid.

How to create an indexer

As figure 13-3 shows, an *indexer* is a special type of property that's used with classes that represent collections of objects. An indexer allows other code to access a specific item in the collection by specifying an index value.

The first example in this figure shows an indexer for the ProductList class. First, the class declares a private List<Product> field named products, which is used to store products within a ProductList object. Then, an indexer with the type Product is declared. Notice that this indexer is not given a name. Instead, it uses the this keyword to refer to the current object. Because of that, indexers can't be static. The this keyword is followed by a parameter that identifies the index used by the indexer. Unlike most parameters, which are coded within parentheses, the parameter for an indexer is coded within brackets.

Like any other property, an indexer can provide a getter and a setter. For example, the getter in the first example uses an integer index to return a Product object from the products list based on its position in the list. Conversely, the setter in this example allows you to assign a Product object to the products list at the specified integer index. Note that the index you specify must already exist in the list.

A class can have any number of indexers, as long as the parameter lists are different. This is called *indexer overloading* because all the indexers have the same name (the this keyword).

The second example in this figure shows another indexer for the ProductList class, which varies from the first one in two ways. First, it doesn't include a setter, so it provides read-only access to the products list. Second, it uses a string index that provides for getting a product by product code. To do that, this getter uses a foreach loop to search the product list, and it returns the first product whose Code property matches the index. If no match is found, null is returned.

If you have null reference types enabled in Visual Studio, you may get a warning when you return null from an indexer. To remove that warning, this indexer uses the null-forgiving operator (!). You can also remove this warning by declaring the indexer with a nullable type, like this:

```
public Product? this[string code] {...}
```

Or, you can throw an argument exception, which you'll learn to do shortly.

The third example in this figure shows how you can use these indexers. The first two statements create a new ProductList object and add a product to it using the Add() method. Then, the next two statements use the two indexers in this figure to retrieve the product from the list by index and by product code. Finally,

An indexer that uses an integer as an index

```
private List<Product> products;

public Product this[int i]
{
    get { return products[i]; }
    set { products[i] = value; }
}
```

A read-only indexer that uses a string as an index

```
public Product this[string code]
{
    get
    {
        foreach (Product p in products)
        {
            if (p.Code == code)
                return p;
        }
        return null!;
    }
}
```

Code that uses these indexers

```
ProductList products = new();
products.Add("C#", "Murach's C#", 59.50m);
Product p1 = products[0];
Product p2 = products["C#"];
products[i] = new(code, description, price);
```

Description

- An *indexer* is a special type of property that lets a user of the class access individual items within the class by specifying an index value. Indexers are used for classes that represent collections of objects.

- Before you add an indexer to a class, you should create an array or a collection as a private instance variable to hold the objects that will be accessed by the indexer.

- The declaration for an indexer includes the type of object it indexes, the this keyword, and a parameter that defines the index to be used, enclosed in brackets. Because indexers refer to the current object, they can't be declared static.

- The indexer's getter should return the object specified by the index value that's passed to it from the underlying collection. The indexer's setter should set the object in the underlying collection that's specified by the index that's passed to it to the object passed via the value keyword.

- Although the index used by an indexer is typically an int, it doesn't have to be.

- You can code two or more indexers with different parameter lists. This is called *indexer overloading*.

Figure 13-3   How to create an indexer

the last statement in this group uses the setter in the first indexer to assign a new product to the list at the index specified by the variable i.

How to code expression-bodied indexers and accessors

In chapter 12, you saw that you can code read-only properties that simply return the value of an expression using an expression body. This applies to indexers as well, as shown in the first example in figure 13-4. This example starts by showing a read-only indexer that doesn't use an expression body. Then, the statement that follows shows an *expression-bodied indexer* that performs the same function.

You can also use expression-bodied accessors with indexers just like you can with properties. For this to work, the getter must simply return an expression and the setter must execute a single statement. Expression-bodied accessors with indexers were introduced with C# 7.0, and they're illustrated by the second example in this figure.

The indexer in this example performs the same function as the first indexer in the previous figure. If you compare these two indexers, you'll see that the one that uses expression-bodied accessors doesn't provide much simplification. Even so, you should consider using expression-bodied accessors whenever you use the lambda operator for other purposes.

The third example in this figure shows how you can use the expression-bodied indexer and the indexer with expression-bodied accessors. Here, the first two statements create a new ProductList object and add a product to the list using the Add() method just as in the previous figure. Then, the next statement retrieves a product from the list by index. This statement will work with either the expression-bodied indexer in the first example or the indexer with expression-bodied accessors in the second example. Finally, the last statement assigns a new product to the list at the index specified by the variable i. This statement will work with the indexer with expression-bodied accessors in the second example.

A read-only indexer that uses an integer as an index

```
private List<Product> products;

public Product this[int i]
{
    get { return products[i]; }
}
```

The same indexer using an expression body
```
public Product this[int i] => products[i];
```

An indexer with expression-bodied getters and setters

```
public Product this[int i]
{
    get => products[i];
    set => products[i] = value;
}
```

Code that uses these indexers

```
ProductList products = new();
products.Add("C#", "Murach's C#", 59.50m);
Product p1 = products[0];
products[i] = new(code, description, price);
```

Description

- If an indexer is read-only and simply returns the value of an expression, you can code it as an *expression-bodied indexer*.

- To code an expression-bodied indexer, you code the access modifier, return type, and the this keyword, followed by the lambda operator and the expression to be returned.

- If the getter for an indexer simply returns an expression or the setter executes a single statement, they can be coded as expression-bodied accessors. Expression-bodied accessors were introduced with C# 7.0.

- To code an expression-bodied getter, you code the get keyword, followed by the lambda operator and the expression to be returned.

- To code an expression-bodied setter, you code the set keyword, followed by the lambda operator and the statement to be executed.

Figure 13-4   How to code expression-bodied indexers and accessors

How to throw an argument exception

When you code properties and methods, it's often a good idea to check the arguments that are passed to them to make sure that they are valid. Then, if an argument isn't valid, you can throw an exception to notify the user of the class that an error has occurred. For example, when you code indexers, you may want to check that the index argument falls within a valid range.

Figure 13-5 shows how argument exceptions should be handled. Here, the getter for the first indexer checks that the int value that's passed to it falls within a valid range. If the int value is less than zero or if it's greater than or equal to the number of products in the list, the indexer throws an exception. Otherwise, the int value is used to return the specified Product object from the product list.

The second indexer works similarly to the first indexer, but it accepts a string that specifies the product's code. To start, the getter uses the ThrowIfNull() method of the ArgumentNullException class to throw a null argument exception if the code is null. This method was introduced with C# 10.0, and it makes it easier to check for null and throw an exception.

Next, the getter checks if the code contains more than eight characters. If so, the getter throws an argument exception. Otherwise, a foreach loop compares the code with the product code for each product in the list. If the codes match, the getter returns the Product object from the list. If the product with the specified code isn't found in the list, though, the getter returns a null value.

As you learned in chapter 7, the throw statement and throw expression specify an exception object to be thrown. .NET defines the exception classes listed in this figure as standard exceptions that you can use when validating arguments. If an argument is outside the range of values that are acceptable for a property, for example, you should throw an ArgumentOutOfRangeException. If an attempt is made to set a property to a null value and the property requires a value, you should throw an ArgumentNullException. For any other argument errors, you should throw an ArgumentException.

Notice that all three of these exceptions have a constructor that accepts a message parameter. You can use this parameter to provide an error message that indicates what's wrong with the data. However, since the ArgumentOutOfRangeException already contains an error message that describes the problem, you can just specify the name of the parameter that's out of range.

When you code a statement that uses a property or method that throws an argument exception, you might think that you should enclose the statement in a try-catch statement so you can catch any exception when it occurs. Rather than do that, though, it's better to validate the data before passing it to the property or method. The if statement shown in this figure, for example, checks the length of the product code that the user enters before it passes this product code to the second indexer. That way, the exception should never occur.

So why include the validation code in the class at all? Because if you design your classes so they're reusable, you can't always ensure that other programmers will validate the data they pass to the class. By including this validation code, you make the class completely self-contained.

An indexer that checks the range and throws an argument exception

```
public Product this[int i]
{
    get
    {
        if (i < 0 || i >= products.Count)
            throw new ArgumentOutOfRangeException(i.ToString());

        return products[i];
    }
    set => products[i] = value;
}
```

An indexer that validates data and throws an argument exception

```
public Product this[string code]
{
    get
    {
        ArgumentNullException.ThrowIfNull(code);    // C# 10.0 or later

        if (code.Length > 8)
            throw new ArgumentException(
                "Maximum length of Code is 8 characters.");

        foreach (Product p in products)
        {
            if (p.Code == code)
                return p;
        }
        return null!;
    }
}
```

Three argument exceptions

Exception	Use when...
ArgumentOutOfRangeException(message)	the value is outside the acceptable range of values.
ArgumentNullException(message)	the value is null and a null value is not allowed.
ArgumentException(message)	the value is invalid for any other reason.

An if statement that validates data before using an indexer

```
Product p = null;
if (txtCode.Text.Length <= 8)
    p = products[txtCode.Text];
```

Description

- If a class detects an invalid argument, it should throw one of the three argument exceptions with a message that describes the error. All of the argument exceptions are part of the System namespace.

- With C# 10.0 and later, you can use the ThrowIfNull() method of the ArgumentNullException class to throw a null argument exception.

Figure 13-5   How to throw an argument exception

How to work with delegates and events

In addition to fields, properties, indexers, methods, and constructors, a class can also define delegates and events.

How to define and use a delegate

Figure 13-6 shows how to define and use a *delegate*. A delegate is created from a class and can refer to methods with a specific return type and parameter list, which form the signature of the delegate. Because of that, you can think of a delegate as a pointer to a method with the given signature. As such, a method can be called indirectly through the delegate.

In many cases, you'll use delegates to wire event handlers to events. However, you can also use delegates without events. The example shown in this figure will help you understand how this works.

To define a delegate, you start by coding the public and delegate keywords followed by the return type, the name of the delegate, and the parameter list. In this figure, for example, a delegate named ChangeHandler is defined in the ProductList class with a void return type and a single ProductList parameter. Then, you can use that delegate with any method that has the same return type and parameter, which forms the *signature* of the delegate.

In this figure, the PrintToDebug() method has the same signature as the ChangeHandler delegate. As you can see, this method is coded in the main form for the app. Then, it's called from the Load event handler for the form after the ProductList object is created and products are added to it.

To use the ChangeHandler delegate, you start by creating an instance of the delegate. This works the same as instantiating any type of object. In this case, though, because the delegate is declared in the ProductList class, the name of the delegate is qualified with that class. You also specify the method that's used by the delegate when you instantiate it. In this figure, that's the PrintToDebug() method. Note that the statement that creates the delegate object is coded at the class level so it can be accessed from anywhere in the class. Because of that, the method it uses is declared as static.

After you instantiate the delegate, you can call it and pass all arguments required by the method it refers to. In this example, the last statement in the Load event handler for the form calls the delegate and passes the ProductList object that's required by the PrintToDebug() method. This causes all the products in the product list to be printed to the Debug portion of the Output window, along with a message that indicates that the product list has changed.

Although the example that's presented in this figure isn't realistic, it should give you an idea of how delegates work. For example, instead of adding products and calling the delegate in the Load event handler for the form, you might have an event handler for the Click event of a button that adds the product the user enters on the form and then calls the delegate. More likely, though, you'll use delegates to wire event handlers to events as shown in the next figure.

The syntax for declaring a delegate

```
public delegate returnType DelegateName([parameterList]);
```

Code that declares a delegate in the ProductList class

```
public delegate void ChangeHandler(ProductList products);
```

Code in a form that uses an instance of the delegate

```
public partial class frmProducts : Form
{
    // create an instance of the delegate and identify the method it uses
    ProductList.ChangeHandler myDelegate = new(PrintToDebug);

    // a method with the same signature as the delegate
    private static void PrintToDebug(ProductList products) {
        Debug.WriteLine("The products list has changed!");
        for (int i = 0; i < products.Count; i++) {
            Product p = products[i];
            Debug.WriteLine(p.GetDisplayText("\t"));
        }
    }

    private void frmProducts_Load(object sender, EventArgs e) {
        // create the argument that's required by the delegate
        ProductList products = new();

        // add products to the product list
        products.Add("JAVA", "Murach's Java Programming", 59.50m);
        products.Add("C#", "Murach's C#", 59.50m);

        // call the delegate and pass the required argument
        myDelegate(products);
    }
}
```

Description

- A *delegate* is a type that can refer to methods with a specific return type and parameter list (the *signature* of the delegate). You define the return type and parameters when you declare the delegate.

- To use a delegate, you start by creating an instance of the delegate and identifying the method it will use. This statement is typically coded at the class level so all the members of the class can use it. Then, you call the delegate and pass any arguments required by the method.

- Delegates allow you to indirectly call the method that they refer to. You can change the method that a delegate refers to at runtime.

- A common use of delegates is to wire an event handler to an event so the event handler is called when the event is raised. For more information, see figure 13-7.

Figure 13-6   How to define and use a delegate

How to define and use events

An *event* is a signal that a particular action has occurred on an object that's an instance of a class. Then, any code that uses that object can respond to the event by wiring an event handler to it. Figure 13-7 illustrates how this works using a delegate like the one in the last figure.

To define an event, you start by declaring a delegate that will be used to refer to the event handler for the event. This is done by the first statement in the ProductList class. Then, you code an event declaration as shown by the second statement. This declaration names the delegate followed by an event name. In this case, the event declaration specifies the ChangeHandler delegate and the Changed event.

Finally, the event declaration initializes the event to null. It also suppresses any warnings you may get when nullable reference types are enabled in Visual Studio. To do that, it uses the null-forgiving operator (!).

Once you've declared an event, you can raise it by referring to it by name as shown in the Add() method of the ProductList class. This method raises the Changed event after it adds a product to the list. Here, the this keyword is used as the parameter, which causes the ProductList object that raised the event to be passed to the event handler.

Before you raise an event, it's a good practice to check that the event isn't null. One way to do that is to use an if statement as shown in this figure. Another way is to use the null-conditional operator (?). When you use this operator, you must explicitly call the Invoke() method like this:

```
Changed?.Invoke(this);
```

Although the if statement is easy to read and understand, the null-conditional operator with the Invoke() method is more concise. The technique you use is mostly a matter of personal preference.

To respond to an event that's raised by a class, you use code like that shown in the second example. This code includes a method named PrintToDebug() that will handle the event. Notice that this event handler accepts the ProductList parameter that will be passed by the Changed event.

To use this event handler, you start by creating an instance of the class that raises the event. In this case, an instance of the ProductList class named products is created. Then, you wire the event handler to the event. Here, the ChangeHandler delegate is used to wire the PrintToDebug() event handler to the Changed event of the products list when the form is loaded. As a result, the PrintToDebug() method will be called whenever the Changed event is raised for this object.

In most cases, you'll code the statement that wires the event handler in the Load event of the form that uses it as shown here. However, you can also wire an event handler in the constructor of a class. The only restriction is that this statement must be executed before the event is raised. If the event is raised before you've wired the event handler to it, the event handler won't execute.

The syntax for declaring an event

```
public event Delegate EventName;
```

Code that declares and raises an event in the ProductList class

```
public class ProductList
{
    public delegate void ChangeHandler(ProductList products);

    // declare the event and initialize it to null
    public event ChangeHandler Changed = null!;

    public void Add(Product product)
    {
        products.Add(product);
        if (Changed != null)
            Changed(this);        // raise the event after checking for null
    }
    ...
}
```

Code in a form that wires the event handler and handles the event

```
ProductList products = new();

private void frmProducts_Load(object sender, EventArgs e)
{
    // wire the event to the method that handles the event
    products.Changed += new ProductList.ChangeHandler(PrintToDebug);
    ...
}

// the method that handles the event
private void PrintToDebug(ProductList products)
{
    Debug.WriteLine("The products list has changed!");
    for (int i = 0; i < products.Count; i++) {
        Product p = products[i];
        Debug.WriteLine(p.GetDisplayText("\t"));
    }
}
```

Description

- An *event* is a signal that an action has occurred on an object that was created from the class. To be used by other classes, the event must be declared with public access at the class level. Then, the event can be raised by any property or method of the class.

- An event declaration specifies a delegate that will handle the event along with an event name.

- To raise the event, call it by its name and pass the arguments required by the delegate.

- To handle an event from another class, create an instance of the class that raises the event and assign it to a class variable. Then, declare an event handler with a signature that matches the delegate's signature. Finally, wire the event handler to the event in the class constructor or, if the class is a form, in the Load event handler.

Figure 13-7   How to define and use events

How to use anonymous methods and lambda expressions with delegates and events

When working with delegates, you can sometimes shorten and simplify your code by using an *anonymous method*, which is simply a method that doesn't have a name. This is particularly true if the method is short and it's only called from one place. Figure 13-8 shows how anonymous methods work.

The anonymous method in the first example in this figure creates an instance of the ChangeHandler delegate that you saw in figure 13-6. To do that, it uses the delegate keyword followed by the parameter list for the delegate and the anonymous method. This anonymous method performs the same task as the PrintToDebug() method. Because it doesn't require a method signature, though, it doesn't take as many lines of code.

If the anonymous method doesn't require a parameter, you can also omit the parameter declaration. If the ChangeHandler delegate was defined without any parameters, for example, you could create the delegate like this:

```
ProductList.ChangeHandler myDelegate =
    delegate
    {
        MessageBox.Show("The products list has changed!");
    };
```

C# also includes a feature similar to anonymous methods called *lambda expressions*. When you code a lambda expression, you omit the delegate keyword and include the lambda operator. This is illustrated by the lambda expression in the first example. This code performs the same function as the anonymous method.

The rules for coding the parameter list for a lambda expression also differ from the rules for coding the parameter list for an anonymous method. If the method requires a single parameter, for example, you can omit the parentheses as shown here. If no parameters are required, though, or if two or more parameters are required, you must include the parentheses.

Notice in this example that no data type is coded for the parameter. That's because in most cases, the type can be inferred from its use. If you code a data type, note that you must enclose the parameter list in parentheses even if the list consists of a single parameter.

You can also use anonymous methods and lambda expressions in statements that wire events. The second example in this figure shows how this works. As you can see, you use the delegate keyword to wire an anonymous function to an event, and you use the lambda operator to wire a lambda expression to an event. Once you do that, you can use a statement like the one you saw in the last figure to raise the event.

How to create an instance of a delegate

Using an anonymous method

```
ProductList.ChangeHandler myDelegate =
    delegate (ProductList products)
    {
        Debug.WriteLine("The products list has changed!");
        for (int i = 0; i < products.Count; i++) { ... }
    };
myDelegate(products);
```

Using a lambda expression

```
ProductList.ChangeHandler myDelegate = products =>
{
    Debug.WriteLine("The products list has changed!");
    for (int i = 0; i < products.Count; i++) { ... }
};
myDelegate(products);
```

How to wire an event

Using an anonymous method

```
products.Changed += delegate (ProductList products)
{
    Debug.WriteLine("The products list has changed!");
    for (int i = 0; i < products.Count; i++) { ... }
};
```

Using a lambda expression

```
products.Changed += products =>
{
    Debug.WriteLine("The products list has changed!");
    for (int i = 0; i < products.Count; i++) { ... }
};
```

Description

- An *anonymous method* is a method without a name. You can use an anonymous method when you create a delegate instead of specifying a named method. If the method is only called from one place, this can help simplify your code.

- A *lambda expression* is similar to an anonymous method, but it uses the lambda operator instead of the delegate keyword.

- You can also wire an anonymous method or lambda expression to an event. When you do that, you should place the code in the class constructor or, if the class is a form, the Load event handler.

Figure 13-8   How to use anonymous methods and lambda expressions

How to overload operators

The ProductList class in figure 13-2 uses overloaded operators. Specifically, this class overloads the + and - operators so you can add products to and remove products from the product list using these operators rather than using the Add() and Remove() methods. The following topics explain how you implement overloaded operators like these.

An introduction to operator overloading

Figure 13-9 presents some basic information about *operator overloading*. First, you should know that you can overload both unary and binary operators. The most common operators you can overload are listed in this figure.

C# defines the meanings of these operators for built-in types such as decimal, int, string, and DateTime. However, for user-defined types such as the Product class presented in the last chapter or the ProductList class presented in this chapter, these operators are either undefined or are defined in ways that may not be appropriate for the class. For example, the + operator isn't defined for user-defined types, but the == operator is. By default, if you compare two object variables using the == operator, they're considered equal if they refer to the same object.

With operator overloading, you can create your own implementations of C# operators that are appropriate for your classes. For example, a more appropriate definition of the == operator for the Product class would be to consider two Product variables equal if they refer to objects that contain the same data for the Code, Description, and Price properties. As you learned in the last chapter, this is how the == operator works for records and record structs.

As the syntax at the top of this figure shows, you use the operator keyword to declare an operator. In the operator declaration, you specify the return type, which indicates the type of object that's returned by the operation. In most cases, the return type is the same as the class that contains the declaration (for example, Product in the Product class). Then, you specify the operator you want to define, followed by one or two operands depending on whether the operator is a unary or a binary operator.

Notice that operators are always declared as static. That way, they can deal with null operands properly. That will make more sense when you see the code for the overloaded == operator.

Overloaded operators often depend on methods that are defined by the class. In figure 13-10, for example, you'll see that the + operator for the ProductList class uses the Add() method of the class to add a product to the list. Then, in figure 13-11, you'll see that the == and != operators for the Product class are implemented by overriding the Equals() and GetHashCode() methods of the Object class, which is inherited by all other classes.

The syntax for overloading unary operators

```
public static returnType operator unary-operator(type operand)
```

The syntax for overloading binary operators

```
public static returnType operator
    binary-operator(type-1 operand-1, type-2 operand-2)
```

Common operators you can overload

Unary operators
```
+ - ! ++ -- true false
```

Binary operators
```
+ - * / % & | == != > < >= <=
```

The Equals() method of the Object class

Method	Description
Equals(object)	Returns a Boolean value that indicates whether the current object refers to the same instance as the specified object. If that's not what you want, you can override this method.
Equals(object1, object2)	A static version of the Equals() method that compares two objects to determine if they refer to the same instance.

The GetHashCode() method of the Object class

Method	Description
GetHashCode()	Returns an integer value that's used to identify objects in a hash table. If you override the Equals() method, you must also override the GetHashCode() method.

Description

- You use the *operator* keyword to *overload an operator* within a class. For example, you might overload the + operator in the ProductList class so it can be used to add products to the list. You might also overload the == and != operators in the Product class so you can compare two Product objects to see if they contain identical data rather than whether they refer to the same instance.

- You can overload all of the unary and binary operators shown above, as well as some that aren't presented in this book. When you overload a binary operator, *operand-1* is the operand that appears to the left of the operator, and *operand-2* is the operand that appears to the right of the operator.

- *Overloaded operators* are always static so they can deal with null operands properly.

- When you overload relational operators like == and !=, you need to provide your own versions of the Equals() and GetHashCode() methods. See figure 13-11 for details.

Figure 13-9   An introduction to operator overloading

How to overload arithmetic operators

Figure 13-10 shows how to overload arithmetic operators such as + and -. For instance, the code at the top of this figure shows an implementation of the + operator for the ProductList class. This operator is used to add a Product object to the product list. As you can see, the declaration for the + operator specifies ProductList as the return type, which means that it will return a ProductList object. In addition, this operator accepts two parameters: a ProductList object named list and a Product object named p. Then, the code for the + operator calls the Add() method of the list operand, passing the p object as the argument. This method adds the p object to the products list that's stored in the list object. Then, the + operator returns the list object.

The second code example shows how you might use the + operator in an app to add a Product object to a product list. First, a new ProductList object named products is created. Then, a new Product object named p is created. Finally, the + operator is used in an assignment statement to add the product to the product list.

The third example in this figure shows another way that you can use the overloaded + operator of the ProductList class to add a Product object to a product list. As you can see, this statement uses the += shortcut assignment operator. You may remember from chapter 4 that you can use shortcut operators like these in place of the assignment operator when the expression that's being assigned involves an arithmetic operation. You can use these shortcut operators with overloaded operators as well. Note that you don't need to provide any special code to use a shortcut operator. That's because when you use a shortcut operator, the compiler automatically converts it to an equivalent assignment statement that uses the assignment operator (=) and an arithmetic operator.

As you learned earlier in this chapter, C# also uses the += operator to wire event handlers to events. However, this is not an example of overloading operators. Instead, the use of the += operator for wiring events is a language feature that's built in to the C# compiler.

If an operator simply returns an expression or executes a single statement, you can code it as an *expression-bodied operator*. This is illustrated by the last example in this figure. Here, the declaration for the + operator of the ProductList class is followed by the lambda operator and the statement that calls the Add() method to add the product that's passed to the second parameter to the product list that's passed to the first parameter. Notice that for this to work, the Add() method was changed so it returns the new product list.

Part of a ProductList class that overloads the + operator

```
public class ProductList
{
    private List<Product> products;

    public void Add(Product p)
    {
        products.Add(p);
    }

    public static ProductList operator + (ProductList list, Product p)
    {
        list.Add(p);
        return list;
    }
    ...
}
```

Code that uses the + operator of the ProductList class

```
ProductList products = new();
Product p = new("C#", "Murach's C#", 59.50m);
products = products + p;
```

Another way to use the + operator

```
products += p;
```

Code that uses an expression-bodied operator

```
public ProductList Add(Product p)
{
    products.Add(p);
    return this;
}

public static ProductList operator + (ProductList list, Product p) =>
    list.Add(p);
```

Description

- You can overload the built-in arithmetic operators so they perform customized functions on objects created from the class that defines them.

- You should overload only those arithmetic operators that make sense for a class. For example, it's reasonable to overload the + operator for the ProductList class as a way to add products to a product list. But it doesn't make sense to overload the * or / operators for this class.

- You don't overload the += or -= operators separately. Instead, these operators are handled automatically by the overloaded + and - operators.

- An operator that simply returns an expression or executes a single statement can be coded as an *expression-bodied operator*.

Figure 13-10   How to overload arithmetic operators

How to overload relational operators

Figure 13-11 shows that relational operators are often more difficult to overload than arithmetic operators. Here, the first example shows how to implement the == operator for the Product class so you can compare products based on their values rather than on object references. The two objects that will be compared are passed as arguments to this operator.

Remember that with C# 9.0 and later, you can use a record if you just need a reference type that primarily stores values. Then, you don't have to override the == operator because records compare objects based on their values. If you need a reference type with more functionality, though, it's useful to know how to implement the == operator in a class.

The operator presented here starts by using the static Equals() method of the Object class to check both objects to see if they are null. This works because the implementation of the Equals() method is based on reference, not value. As a result, it lets you test an object to see if it's null. This testing is necessary to prevent the overloaded == operator from throwing an exception if one of the operands is null.

If both operands are null, the == operator returns true. If the first operand is null but the second one isn't, it returns false. And if the first operand isn't null, the == operator calls the Equals() method of the first operand to compare it with the second operand, and then returns the result of the comparison.

You can also see the overloaded Equals() method in this figure. This method overrides the Equals() method defined by the Object class that every class inherits. You'll learn more about inheritance and overriding in the next chapter.

The Equals() method shown here starts by setting a Boolean isEquals flag to false. Then, it uses pattern matching to test if the object that's passed to it is a Product object. If so, the code compares its own Code, Description, and Price values with the Code, Description, and Price values of the object it received. If all three properties are equal, it changes the isEqual flag to true. The last statement of the Equals() method returns the value of the isEqual flag.

When you overload a comparison operator, you must also overload the operator that performs the opposite operation. If, for example, you overload the == operator, you must also overload the != operator. Similarly, if you overload the < operator, you must also overload the > operator. The code that's used to implement the != operator in the Product class is also shown in this figure. As you can see, this operator defines itself in terms of the == operator. That way, you can be sure that these operators return consistent results.

The last method that's required when you overload the == operator is the GetHashCode() method. Like the Equals() method, this method overrides the GetHashCode() method that's defined by the Object class. The main requirement for the GetHashCode() method is that it return the same value for any two objects that are considered equal by the Equals() method. The easiest way to accomplish that is to combine the values that are used for comparison in the Equals() method to create a string, and then return the *hash code* of that string.

The second example in this figure shows how you can use the == operator to compare two Product objects. First, two object variables named p1 and p2

Code that overloads the == operator for a Product class

```
public static bool operator == (Product p1, Product p2)
{
    if (Object.Equals(p1, null))
        if (Object.Equals(p2, null))
            return true;
        else
            return false;
    else
        return p1.Equals(p2);
}

public static bool operator != (Product p1, Product p2)
{
    return !(p1 == p2);
}

public override bool Equals(Object? obj)
{
    bool isEquals = false;
    if (obj is Product p)
    {
        if (this.Code == p.Code &&
            this.Description == p.Description &&
            this.Price == p.Price)
            isEquals = true;
    }
    return isEquals;
}

public override int GetHashCode()
{
    string hashString = this.Code + this.Description + this.Price;
    return hashString.GetHashCode();
}
```

Code that uses the == operator of the Product class

```
Product p1 = new("C#", "Murach's C#", 59.50m);
Product p2 = new("C#", "Murach's C#", 59.50m);
if (p1 == p2)          // This evaluates to true. Without the overloaded
                       // == operator, it would evaluate to false.
```

Description

- If you overload the == operator, you must also override the non-static Equals() method. Then, the == operator should use this Equals() method for its equality test.

- Before it calls the Equals() method, the overloaded == operator should test the operands for null values. If both operands are null, they should be considered equal. If only the first operand is null, the operands should be considered unequal.

- Relational operators must always be implemented in pairs. For example, if you overload the == operator, you must also overload the != operator.

- When you override the Equals() method, you must also override the GetHashCode() method. That's because the GetHashCode() method must return the same hash code for any two instances that are considered equal by the Equals() method.

Figure 13-11   How to overload the relational operators

are created from the Product class with identical values. Then, the products are compared in an if statement using the == operator. Because both products have the same Code, Description, and Price values, this comparison returns true. If the Product class didn't override the == operator, however, this comparison would return false because the p1 and p2 variables refer to different instances of the Product class, even though they both have the same values.

At this point, you might wonder why it's necessary for the == operator to be static. The answer is that, if it weren't, you would have to call it from an instance of the Product class, for example, p1. But what if p1 was null? In other words, what if p1 didn't refer to an instance of the Product class? In that case, you couldn't use the == operator. To work with null operands, then, overloaded operators must be declared as static.

An enhanced version of the Product Maintenance application

Now that you've learned the techniques for enhancing your classes, the topics that follow present an enhanced version of the Product Maintenance app that uses those enhancements. From the user's standpoint, this app operates exactly like the one that was presented in chapter 12. The only difference is that the classes in this version of the app are implemented differently. Specifically, the app uses a ProductList class that includes the additional members that are shown in figure 13-2.

Because the code for the Product class is the same as the Product class presented in chapter 12, it's not repeated here. Similarly, the New Product form that's used in this version of the Product Maintenance app is identical to the code shown in chapter 12. As a result, that code isn't repeated either. Finally, like the app in chapter 12, you should know that this app will work with either of the versions of the ProductDB class that are presented in chapter 17.

The code for the ProductList class

Figure 13-12 shows the code for the ProductList class, which stores a collection of Product objects. As you can see, this class begins by declaring a List<Product> object named products. This instance variable is used to store the product list. Next, the ProductList class declares a delegate named ChangeHandler and an event named Changed that uses this delegate. This event is raised whenever the contents of the products list are changed.

The two indexers for this class let users of the class access a specific product in the list by specifying an integer value or a product code. Since these indexers are similar to ones you saw earlier in this chapter, you shouldn't have any trouble understanding how they work. The main difference is that the set accessor for the first indexer raises the Changed event to indicate that the contents of the products list have been changed.

The code for the ProductList class

```csharp
public class ProductList
{
    private List<Product> products;

    public delegate void ChangeHandler(ProductList products);
    public event ChangeHandler Changed = null!;

    public ProductList() => products = new();

    public int Count => products.Count;

    public Product this[int i]
    {
        get
        {
            if (i < 0 || i >= products.Count)
            {
                throw new ArgumentOutOfRangeException(i.ToString());
            }
            return products[i];
        }
        set
        {
            products[i] = value;
            if (Changed != null)
                Changed(this);
        }
    }

    public Product this[string code]
    {
        get
        {
            ArgumentNullException.ThrowIfNull(code);

            foreach (Product p in products)
            {
                if (p.Code == code)
                    return p;
            }
            return null!;
        }
    }
```

Figure 13-12   The code for the enhanced ProductList class (part 1 of 2)

The Fill() method of the ProductList class, shown on page 2 of this listing, calls the GetProducts() method of the ProductDB class to get the products from a file. Similarly, the Save() method calls the SaveProducts() method of this class to save the products to a file.

The ProductList class also provides two overloads for the Add() method: one that accepts a Product object and one that accepts a code, description, and price. It also includes a Remove() method that removes the specified Product object. As you can see, all three of these methods raise the Changed event.

Finally, this class provides an overloaded + operator and an overloaded - operator. The overloaded + operator calls the first Add() method to add the specified object to the product list and then returns the updated product list. Similarly, the - operator calls the Remove() method to remove the specified product from the product list and then returns the updated product list.

The code for the ProductList class   Page 2

```csharp
public void Fill() => products = ProductDB.GetProducts();

public void Save() => ProductDB.SaveProducts(products);

public void Add(Product product)
{
    products.Add(product);
    if (Changed != null)
        Changed(this);
}

public void Add(string code, string description, decimal price)
{
    Product p = new(code, description, price);
    products.Add(p);
    if (Changed != null)
        Changed(this);
}

public void Remove(Product product)
{
    products.Remove(product);
    if (Changed != null)
        Changed(this);
}

public static ProductList operator + (ProductList list, Product p)
{
    list.Add(p);
    return list;
}

public static ProductList operator - (ProductList list, Product p)
{
    list.Remove(p);
    return list;
}
}
```

Figure 13-12   The code for the enhanced ProductList class (part 2 of 2)

The code for the Product Maintenance form

Figure 13-13 shows the code for the enhanced version of the Product Maintenance form. Because most of this code is the same as in chapter 12, the key differences are highlighted here.

First, the products variable that's used by the class to store Product objects is a ProductList object, not a List<Product> object. As a result, this version of the app can use the features of the ProductList class, such as the indexer, the Fill() and Save() methods, the overloaded + and - operators, and the Changed event.

In the Load event handler for the form, the ChangeHandler delegate is used to wire the HandleChange() method (which appears after the Load event handler) to the Changed event of the products object. As you have seen in the ProductList class, this event is raised any time a product is added to, removed from, or changed in the product list. Then, the HandleChange() method calls the Save() method of the products object to save the new list, and it calls the FillProductListBox() method to refresh the list box.

After it wires the Changed event, the Load event handler calls the Fill() method of the products object to fill the product list. Then, it calls the FillProductListBox() method to fill the list box. Notice that this method uses a for loop to retrieve each product in the product list by its index.

The Click event handler for the Add button calls the GetNewProduct() method of the New Product form to get a new product. Then, if the Product object that's returned by this method isn't null, the += operator is used to add the product to the product list.

The Click event handler for the Delete button uses an indexer of the ProductList class to retrieve the selected product from the product list. Then, assuming the user confirms that the product should be deleted, it uses the -= operator to remove the product from the list.

The code for the Product Maintenance form

```csharp
private ProductList products = new();

private void frmProductMain_Load(object sender, EventArgs e)
{
    products.Changed += new ProductList.ChangeHandler(HandleChange);
    products.Fill();
    FillProductListBox();
}

private void HandleChange(ProductList products)
{
    products.Save();
    FillProductListBox();
}

private void FillProductListBox()
{
    Product p;
    lstProducts.Items.Clear();
    for (int i = 0; i < products.Count; i++)
    {
        p = products[i];
        lstProducts.Items.Add(p.GetDisplayText("\t"));
    }
}

private void btnAdd_Click(object sender, EventArgs e)
{
    frmNewProduct newForm = new();
    Product product = newForm.GetNewProduct();
    if (product != null)
    {
        products += product;
    }
}

private void btnDelete_Click(object sender, EventArgs e)
{
    int i = lstProducts.SelectedIndex;
    if (i != -1)
    {
        Product product = products[i];

        string message = "Are you sure you want to delete "
            + product.Description + "?";
        DialogResult button = MessageBox.Show(message, "Confirm Delete",
            MessageBoxButtons.YesNo);
        if (button == DialogResult.Yes)
        {
            products -= product;
        }
    }
}

private void btnExit_Click(object sender, EventArgs e)
{
    this.Close();
}
```

Figure 13-13   The code for the Product Maintenance form

Perspective

In this chapter, you've learned about a variety of features that you can include in the classes you create. You should keep in mind, however, that not all classes require these features. In fact, most classes require just the features you learned about in chapter 12. Nevertheless, it's important that you know about the features presented in this chapter so you can use them when that's appropriate.

Now that you've read this chapter, you should begin to appreciate the power and complexity of C# classes. Still, there's much more to learn about coding C# classes than what's presented here. In the next chapter, then, you'll learn about one of the most important and potentially confusing aspects of object-oriented programming in C#: inheritance.

Terms

indexer	anonymous method
indexer overloading	lambda expression
expression-bodied indexer	overload an operator
delegate	operator overloading
signature of a delegate	expression-bodied operator
event	hash code

Exercise 13-1   Create a Customer Maintenance app that uses classes

In this exercise, you'll create a Customer Maintenance app that uses classes with the features presented in this chapter. To make this app easier to develop, we'll give you the starting forms and classes.

Open the project and add validation code to the Customer class

1. Open the app in the C:\C#\Ch13\CustomerMaintenance directory.

2. Open the Customer class and note how the constructor for this class sets the properties to the appropriate parameters.

3. Update the FirstName, LastName, and Email properties to use private fields and getters and setters with bodies instead of auto-implemented properties. Then, add code to the setters that throws an exception if the value is longer than 30 characters.

4. Test the class by trying to add a new customer with an email address that's longer than 30 characters. When you do, an exception should be thrown. Then, end the app.

5. Set the MaxLength properties of the First Name, Last Name, and Email text boxes to 30. Then, run the app again and try to add a new customer with an email address that's longer than 30 characters. This shows one way to avoid the exceptions, but your classes should still throw them in case they are used by other apps that don't avoid them.

Add a CustomerList class

6.   Add a class named CustomerList to the project, and declare a private variable that can store a list of Customer objects.

7.   Add the following members to the CustomerList class:

Constructor	Description
`()`	Creates a new list of Customer objects.

Indexer	Description
`[index]`	Provides access to the Customer at the specified position.

Property	Description
`Count`	An integer that indicates how many Customer objects are in the list.

Method	Description
`Add(customer)`	Adds the specified Customer object to the list.
`Remove(customer)`	Removes the specified Customer object from the list.
`Fill()`	Fills the list with customer data from a file using the GetCustomers() method of the CustomerDB class.
`Save()`	Saves the customers to a file using the SaveCustomers() method of the CustomerDB class.

8.   Modify the Customer Maintenance form to use this class. To do that, you'll need to use the Fill() and Save() methods of the CustomerList object instead of the methods of the CustomerDB class. In addition, you'll need to use a for loop instead of a foreach loop when you fill the list box.

9.   Run the app and test it to be sure it works properly.

Exercise 13-2   Use overloaded operators

In this exercise, you'll enhance the Customer Maintenance app from exercise 13-1 so it uses overloaded operators to add and remove customers from the customer list.

1.   If it isn't open already, open the app in the C:\C#\Ch13\ CustomerMaintenance directory

2.   Add overloaded + and – operators to the CustomerList class that add and remove a customer from the customer list.

3.   Modify the Customer Maintenance form to use these operators instead of the Add() and Remove() methods.

4.   Run and test the app to make sure it works correctly.

Exercise 13-3 Use delegates and events

In this exercise, you'll enhance the Customer Maintenance app from exercise 13-2 so it uses a delegate and an event to handle changes to the customer list.

1. If it isn't open already, open the app in the C:\C#\Ch13\Customer-Maintenance directory.

2. Add a delegate named ChangeHandler to the CustomerList class. This delegate should specify a method with a void return type and a CustomerList parameter as described in figure 13-6.

3. Add an event named Changed to the CustomerList class. This event should use the ChangeHandler delegate and should be raised any time the customer list changes as described in figure 13-7. If you coded the CustomerList class with expression-bodied accessors and methods, you'll need to change some of those to standard accessors and methods to accommodate this.

4. Modify the Customer Maintenance form to use the Changed event to save the customers and refresh the list box any time the list changes. To do that, you'll need to code an event handler that has the signature specified by the delegate, you'll need to wire the event handler to the event, and you'll need to remove any unnecessary code from the event handlers for the Add and Delete buttons.

5. Run and test the app.

6. Modify the statement that wires an event handler to the event so it uses a lambda expression as shown in figure 13-8. The lambda expression should execute the same two statements as the named method that you created for the event handler in step 4.

7. Run and test the app one more time. If this works, delete the named method that was used previously for the event handler.

14

How to work with inheritance

Inheritance is one of the key concepts of object-oriented programming. It lets you create a class that's based on another class. As you'll see in this chapter, inheritance is used throughout the .NET classes. In addition, you can use it in the classes that you create.

An introduction to inheritance

Inheritance allows you to create a class that's based on another class. When used correctly, inheritance can simplify the overall design of an app. The following topics present an introduction to the basic concepts of inheritance. You need to understand these concepts before you learn how to write the code needed to implement classes that use inheritance.

How inheritance works

Figure 14-1 illustrates how inheritance works. When inheritance is used, a *derived class* inherits the properties, methods, and other members of a *base class*. Then, the objects that are created from the derived class can use these inherited members. The derived class can also provide its own members that extend the base class. In addition, the derived class can *override* properties and methods of the base class by providing replacement definitions for them.

The two classes shown in this figure illustrate how this works. Here, the base class is System.Windows.Forms.Form, the .NET class that all Windows forms inherit. As this figure shows, this class has several public properties and methods, such as the Text property and the Close() method. (This class has many more properties and methods. Just a few representative ones are included here.)

The derived class in this figure is the class for the New Product form in the Product Maintenance app (ProductMaintenance.frmNewProduct). As you can see, two groups of members are listed for this class. The first group includes the properties and methods that the class inherits from its base class. The second group includes the members that have been added to the derived class. In this case, the derived class includes five new properties (the text box and button controls) and one new method (GetNewProduct()).

How inheritance works

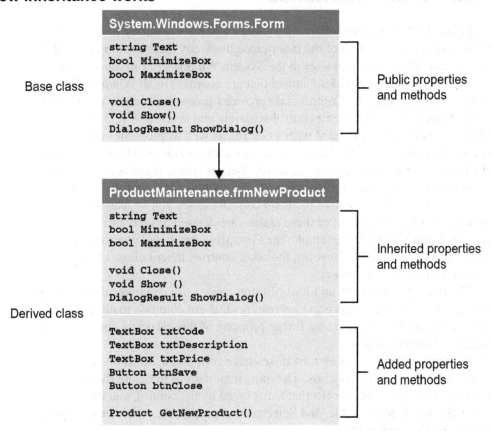

Base class

System.Windows.Forms.Form

```
string Text
bool MinimizeBox
bool MaximizeBox

void Close()
void Show()
DialogResult ShowDialog()
```

Public properties and methods

Derived class

ProductMaintenance.frmNewProduct

```
string Text
bool MinimizeBox
bool MaximizeBox

void Close()
void Show ()
DialogResult ShowDialog()
```

Inherited properties and methods

```
TextBox txtCode
TextBox txtDescription
TextBox txtPrice
Button btnSave
Button btnClose

Product GetNewProduct()
```

Added properties and methods

Description

- *Inheritance* lets you create a new class based on an existing class. Then, the new class *inherits* the properties, methods, and other members of the existing class.

- A class that inherits from an existing class is called a *derived class, child class,* or *subclass*. A class that another class inherits is called a *base class, parent class*, or *superclass*.

- A derived class can *extend* the base class by adding new properties, methods, or other members to the base class. It can also replace a member from the base class with its own version of the member. Depending on how that's done, this is called *hiding* or *overriding*.

- When you create a new form in C#, the form inherits the .NET class named System.Windows.Forms.Form. As a result, all C# forms inherit the members defined by this base class. Then, as you add controls and code to the form, you extend the base class by creating new properties and methods.

Figure 14-1   How inheritance works

How .NET uses inheritance

Figure 14-2 shows that inheritance is used extensively throughout .NET. This figure shows a portion of the inheritance hierarchy that's used by several of the Windows form control classes in the System.Windows.Forms namespace.

The Control class provides features that are common to all Windows form controls. For example, the Control class provides properties such as Visible and Enabled that indicate whether a control is visible and enabled, a Text property that specifies the text associated with a control, as well as properties that specify a control's display location. The Control class also provides the Focus() method, which lets you move the focus to a control. Because these features are provided by the Control class, they are available to all Windows form controls.

This figure includes nine of the form control classes you've learned about so far in this book. Note that all of these classes are derived directly or indirectly from the Control class. For example, the GroupBox and Label controls inherit the Control class directly. However, the other controls inherit classes that are derived from the Control class.

The Button, CheckBox, and RadioButton classes, for example, all inherit the ButtonBase class. This class provides features that are common to all types of button controls. For example, the Image property of this class lets you display an image on a button control.

Similarly, combo boxes and list boxes have common features that are provided by the ListControl class. The most important of these are the Items property, which provides the list that's displayed by the control, and the SelectedIndex, SelectedValue, and SelectedItem properties, which let you access the item that's selected in the list.

Likewise, the TextBoxBase class provides some features that are common to text box controls. That includes the MultiLine property that lets you display multiple lines and the ReadOnly property that lets you create read-only text boxes. By the way, if you're wondering why an intermediate TextBoxBase class is used in the TextBox hierarchy, it's because .NET provides two additional types of text boxes, called the RichTextBox and MaskedTextBox, that also inherit TextBoxBase. Because the RichTextBox and MaskedTextBox controls aren't covered in this book, however, they're not included in this figure.

You may be surprised to learn that the Form class itself is also derived from the Control class by way of two other classes: ContainerControl and ScrollableControl. A form's ability to contain other controls is provided by the ContainerControl class. And a form's ability to display scroll bars if its controls can't all be displayed at once is provided by the ScrollableControl class.

Don't be dismayed by the amount of detail presented in this figure. In fact, the actual inheritance hierarchy for the classes in the System.Windows.Forms namespace is far more complicated than indicated here. The intent of this figure is simply to illustrate that inheritance is a feature that's used extensively within .NET.

The inheritance hierarchy for form control classes

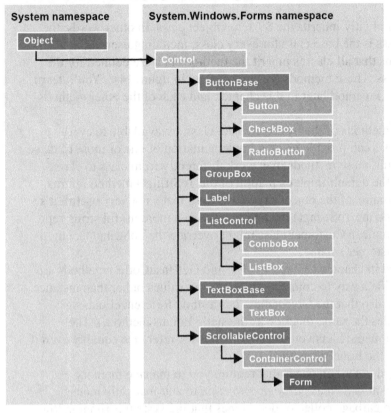

Description

- .NET uses inheritance extensively in its own classes. For example, inheritance is used throughout the System.Windows.Forms namespace.

- All of the control classes are derived from a base Control class. This class provides properties and methods that all controls have in common, such as Name and Text. Like all classes, the Control class is ultimately derived from System.Object.

- Some controls have an additional layer of inheritance. For example, the ListControl class provides features common to ListBox and ComboBox controls, such as the SelectedValue property.

- The *fully qualified name* of a class includes the name of the namespace that the class belongs to. For example, the fully qualified name for the ComboBox control is System.Windows.Forms.ComboBox.

Figure 14-2   How .NET uses inheritance

Methods inherited from the System.Object class

Every class implicitly inherits the System.Object class. In other words, the System.Object class is the base class for every class, including user-defined classes. This means that all classes inherit the methods that are defined for the System.Object class. These methods are summarized in figure 14-3. You'll learn about the GetType() method later in this chapter, and each of the other methods now.

Although the methods of the System.Object class are available to every class, a derived class can provide its own implementation of one or more of these methods. As a result, these methods may work differently from class to class.

For example, the default implementation of the ToString() method returns the fully qualified name of the object's type. Because that's not very useful, it's common to override the ToString() method to provide a more useful string representation. For example, a Customer class might override the ToString() method so it returns the customer's name.

As you learned in chapter 13, the Equals() and GetHashCode() methods are often used to provide a way to compare objects using values rather than instance references. Notice also that the Object class has a static ReferenceEquals() method that provides the same function as the static Equals method(). The ReferenceEquals() method lets you test two objects for reference equality even if the class overrides the Equals() method.

Unlike C++ and other languages that require you to manage memory, C# uses a mechanism known as *garbage collection* to automatically manage memory. When the garbage collector determines that the system is running low on memory and that the system is idle, it frees the memory for any objects that don't have any more references to them. Before it does that, though, it calls the Finalize() method for each of those objects, even though the default implementation of this method doesn't do anything. Although you can override the Finalize() method to provide specific finalization code for an object, you rarely need to do that.

The last method shown in this figure is MemberwiseClone(). You can use this method to create a simple copy of an object that doesn't expose other objects as properties or fields. You'll learn more about cloning objects in the next chapter.

Methods of the System.Object class

Method	Description
`ToString()`	Returns a string that contains the fully qualified name of the object's type.
`Equals(object)`	Returns true if this object refers to the same instance as the specified object. Otherwise, it returns false, even if both objects contain the same data.
`Equals(object1, object2)`	A static version of the Equals() method that compares two objects to determine if they refer to the same instance.
`ReferenceEquals(object1, object2)`	A static method that determines whether two object references refer to the same instance. This method is typically not overridden, so it can be used to test for reference equality in classes that override the Equals() method.
`GetType()`	Returns a Type object that represents the type of an object.
`GetHashCode()`	Returns the integer hash code for an object.
`Finalize()`	Frees resources used by an object. This method is called by the garbage collector when it determines that there are no more references to the object.
`MemberwiseClone()`	Creates a shallow copy of an object. For more information, refer to chapter 15.

Description

- System.Object is the root base class for all classes. In other words, every class inherits either System.Object or some other class that ultimately inherits System.Object. As a result, the methods defined by System.Object are available to all classes.

- When creating classes, it's a common practice to override the ToString() and Equals() methods so they work appropriately for each class. For example, the ToString() method might return a value that uniquely identifies an object. And the Equals() method might compare two objects to see if their values are equal.

- The *hash code* for an object is an integer that uniquely identifies the object. Object instances that are considered equal should return the same hash code. A common way to implement the GetHashCode() method is to return ToString().GetHashCode(). This returns the hash code of the string that's returned by the object's ToString() method.

- In general, you don't need to override the Finalize() method for an object, even though its default implementation doesn't do anything. That's because the .NET *garbage collector* automatically reclaims the memory used by an object whenever it needs to. Before it does that, though, it calls the Finalize() method of the object.

Figure 14-3   Methods inherited from the System.Object class

How to use inheritance in your apps

Figure 14-4 describes the two main ways inheritance is used in business apps. First, it can be used to simplify the task of creating classes that represent similar types of objects. For example, the first inheritance hierarchy in this figure shows how you might use inheritance to create classes for two types of products: books and software products. As you can see, the Product class is used as the base class for the Book and Software classes. These subclasses inherit the Code, Description, and Price properties, as well as the GetDisplayText() method, from the Product class. In addition, each class adds a property that's unique to the class: the Book class adds an Author property, and the Software class adds a Version property.

The second inheritance hierarchy in this figure shows how you can use the .NET classes as base classes for your own classes. Here, a ProductList class inherits the System.Collections.Generic.List<Product> class. That way, the ProductList class has all the features of a List<Product> object (such as an indexer and a Remove() method). However, the ProductList class provides its own Add() method that is used instead of the Add() method that's available from the List<Product> class. This lets you change any members in the base class that don't work the way you want them to. You'll learn more about how this works in figure 14-6. Finally, the ProductList class provides two more methods (the Fill() and Save() methods) that don't exist in the base class. These methods allow you to read and write the list to a data store.

An important aspect of inheritance is that you can use a subclass as an argument or return value for any method that is designed to work with the base class. For example, the Add() method of the ProductList class accepts a parameter of type Product. However, because both the Book and Software classes are subclasses of the Product class, you can pass either a Book or a Software object to the Add() method to add a book or software product to the product list. You'll learn more about how this works in figure 14-7.

Business classes for a Product Maintenance app

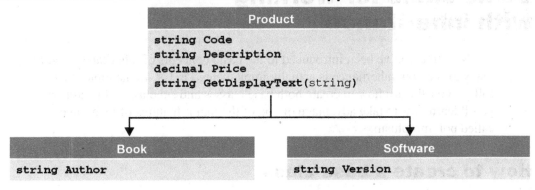

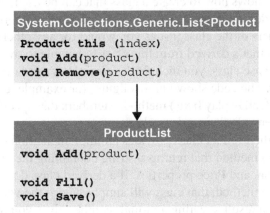

Description

- You can use inheritance in your apps to create generic base classes that implement common elements of related subclasses. For example, if you need separate classes to represent distinct types of products, you can create a Product base class and then use it to create a separate subclass for each type of product.

- It's also common to create classes that inherit classes that are defined by .NET. For example, you might create a ProductList class that inherits the List<Product> class.

- When you inherit a class, you can use the derived class whenever an instance of the base class is called for. For example, a ProductList object based on a class that inherits List<Product> can be used whenever a List<Product> object is called for.

Figure 14-4   How to use inheritance in your apps

Basic skills for working with inheritance

Now that you've been introduced to the basic concepts of inheritance, you're ready to see how inheritance is actually implemented in C#. In the topics that follow, you'll learn how to create both base classes and subclasses. In addition, you'll learn how to take advantage of one of the major features of inheritance, called polymorphism.

How to create a base class

Figure 14-5 shows how to create a class that can be used as a base class for one or more derived classes. To start, you define the properties, methods, and other members of the class just as you would for any other class. Then, if you want a class that's derived from this class to be able to override one of the members of the base class, you include the *virtual* keyword on the declaration for that member. The code shown in this figure, for example, uses the virtual keyword on the GetDisplayText() method. Members that specify the virtual keyword are often called *virtual members*.

Notice that the Product class provides an implementation of the GetDisplayText() method that returns a string containing the values for the Code, Description, and Price properties. If a derived class doesn't override the GetDisplayText() method, that class will simply inherit the version implemented by this class. As a result, creating a virtual member gives you the option of overriding the member in the derived class or allowing the derived class to defer to the version of the member defined by the base class.

The table in this figure lists several *access modifiers* you can use to indicate whether members of a base class are accessible to other code. You already know how to use the private and public modifiers to create private and public members. When you work with inheritance, you also need to know about the protected modifier. A *protected member* is a member that can be accessed within the defining class and within any class that's derived from the defining class, but not by any other class. A *private protected member* is similar, but a class that's derived from the defining class can access the member only if it's declared within the same project. Protected and private protected members let derived classes access certain parts of the base class without exposing those parts to other code.

The internal and protected internal access modifiers are sometimes useful when you work with class libraries or with solutions that have more than one project. To understand how they work, remember that when you build a project, all the classes that make up the project are compiled into a single assembly. Members that use the internal keyword alone are accessible to all the classes within that assembly, but not to classes in other assemblies. Members that specify protected internal are also accessible to derived classes that are a part of the same assembly. In addition, members that specify protected internal are accessible to derived classes in other assemblies.

The code for the Product base class

```
public class Product
{
    public Product(string code, string description, decimal price) =>
        (this.Code, this.Description, this.Price) =
            (code, description, price);

    public string Code { get; set; } = "";
    public string Description { get; set; } = "";
    public decimal Price { get; set; }

    public virtual string GetDisplayText(string sep) =>
        $"{Code}{sep}{Price.ToString("c")}{sep}{Description}";
}
```

Access modifiers

Keyword	Description
public	Available to all classes.
protected	Available only to the current class or to derived classes.
internal	Available only to classes in the current assembly.
protected internal	Available to the current class, derived classes in the current assembly, or derived classes in other assemblies.
private protected	Available to the current class or to derived classes in the current assembly.
private	Available only to the current class.

Description

- You create a base class the same way you create any other class: by defining its properties, methods, events, and other members.

- *Access modifiers* specify the accessibility of the members declared by a class. Public members are accessible to code outside the class, while private members are accessible only to the class in which they're defined.

- *Protected members* are accessible within the class in which they're declared. They can also be used by any class that inherits the class in which they're declared.

- A derived class can access the public and protected members of its base class, but not the private members.

- *Internal members* are accessible by other classes in the same assembly, but not by classes in other assemblies. This can sometimes be useful to control access to members declared by classes in a class library. For more information about class libraries, see chapter 16.

- If you want to be able to override a member in a derived class, you must include the *virtual* keyword on the member declaration.

- If you don't code an access modifier, the default access is private.

Figure 14-5   How to create a base class

How to create a subclass

Figure 14-6 shows how to create a subclass. To indicate that a class is a subclass, you follow the class name on the class declaration with a colon and the name of the base class that the subclass inherits. For example, the code for the Book class shown in this figure specifies that the Book class is a subclass of the Product class.

After you identify the base class, you can extend its functionality by coding additional properties, methods, or other members. In this figure, for example, the Book class adds a new constructor and a new property named Author. In addition, it overrides the GetDisplayText() method defined by the Product class.

The constructor for the Book subclass accepts four parameters: code, description, price, and author. The colon, base keyword, and parameter list that follow indicate that this constructor should call the constructor from the base class using the specified parameters. In this case, the base class constructor is called using the code, description, and price parameters. Then, the base class constructor initializes the Code, Description, and Price properties with these values. After the base class constructor is called, the code in the Book subclass constructor is executed. This code initializes the Author property with the value passed to the author parameter. Note that this constructor could also be coded with an expression body, since it consists of a single statement.

To override the GetDisplayText() method, the method declaration includes the *override* keyword. Note that when you override a method, the override must have the same signature as the method it's overriding. In this case, the method must have a single string parameter that can be used as a separator for the formatted string. In this case, the separator is used to separate the Code, Description, and Price properties. Although it could also be used to separate the Author property, this method uses different formatting for that.

An easy way to generate the signature for a method you want to override is to use refactoring. To do that, place the cursor in the derived class where you want to put the code for the overridden method, press Ctrl + period (.), and select Generate Overrides from the Quick Actions menu that's displayed. Then select the member you'd like to override and click OK.

Notice that the GetDisplayText() method shown here provides its own complete implementation. By contrast, the GetDisplayText() method in the second code example builds on the implementation of this method in the Product class. To do that, it starts by calling the GetDisplayText() method of the base class, which returns a formatted string that contains the Code, Description, and Price properties. Then, it adds the Author property to the end of this string.

This figure also introduces the concept of *hiding*. When you use the *new* keyword on a subclass member, the member *hides* the corresponding base class member. As a result, the subclass doesn't inherit the original version of the member, but uses the new version instead. Hiding is similar to overriding, but it can be used only with non-virtual methods or properties. Because hiding doesn't provide for polymorphism as described in the next topic, you should avoid hiding if possible. Instead, you should use virtual methods and properties whenever you expect to provide a different implementation of those members in a subclass.

The syntax for creating subclasses

To declare a subclass
```
public class SubclassName : BaseClassName
```

To create a constructor that calls a base class constructor
```
public ClassName(parameterlist) : base(parameterlist)
```

To call a base class method or property
```
base.MethodName(parameterlist)
base.PropertyName
```

To hide a non-virtual method or property
```
public new type name
```

To override a virtual method or property
```
public override type name
```

The code for a Book class
```
public class Book : Product
{
    public string Author { get; set; } = "";    // A new property

    public Book(string code, string description, decimal price,
        string author) : base(code, description, price)
    {
        this.Author = author;    // Initializes the Author field after
    }                            // the base class constructor is called.

    public override string GetDisplayText(string sep) =>
        $"{Code}{sep}{Description}{sep}{Price.ToString("c")} ({Author})";
}
```

Another way to override a method
```
public override string GetDisplayText(string sep) =>
    $"{base.GetDisplayText(sep)} ({Author})";
```

Description
- A constructor of a derived class automatically calls the default constructor of the base class before the derived class constructor executes. If you want to call a non-default base class constructor, you can specify the constructor to call when you declare the constructor of the derived class. Then, you can pass parameters to the base class constructor.

- You use the *base* keyword to refer to a member of the base class.

- You use the *override* keyword to override a virtual member of the base class. To automatically generate the signature for a base class method you want to override, you can use refactoring.

- You can use the *new* keyword to provide a new implementation for a non-virtual method or property of the base class. This is called *hiding*. In most cases, it's better to use virtual and overridden methods and properties so you can benefit from polymorphism.

Figure 14-6   How to create a subclass

How polymorphism works

Polymorphism is one of the most important features of object-oriented programming and inheritance. As figure 14-7 shows, polymorphism lets you treat objects of different types as if they were the same type by referring to a base class that's common to both objects. For example, consider the Book and Software classes that were presented in figure 14-4. Because both of these classes inherit the Product class, objects created from these classes can be treated as if they were Product objects.

One benefit of polymorphism is that you can write generic code that's designed to work with a base class. Then, you can use that code with instances of any class that's derived from the base class. For example, the Add() method for the List<Product> class described in figure 14-4 accepts a Product object as a parameter. Since the ProductList class inherits the List<Product> class, this method is also available to the ProductList class. And since the Book and Software classes are derived from the Product class, this Add() method will accept Book or Software objects.

The code examples in this figure illustrate a confusing but useful aspect of polymorphism. The first example shows a virtual method named GetDisplayText() that's defined in the Product base class. This method returns a string that includes the Code, Description, and Price properties. The next two examples show overridden versions of the GetDisplayText() method for the Book and Software classes. The Book version of this method calls the GetDisplayText() method of the base class and then adds the author's name to the end of the string that's returned by that method. Similarly, the Software version calls the GetDisplayText() method of the base class and then adds the software version to the end of the string that's returned.

The last code example in this figure shows how you can use polymorphism with these classes. This code begins by creating an instance of the Book class and assigning it to a variable named b. Then, it creates an instance of the Software class and assigns it to a variable named s.

Next, a variable named p of type Product is declared, and the Book object is assigned to it. Then, the GetDisplayText() method of the Product class is called. When .NET sees that the GetDisplayText() method of the Product class is a virtual method, however, it checks to see what type of object the p variable refers to. In this case, the p variable refers to a Book object, so it calls the overridden version of the GetDisplayText() method that's defined by the Book class.

The example then does the same thing with the Software object. First, this object is assigned to the p variable. Then, the GetDisplayText() method defined by the Product class is called. This time, .NET determines that the product is a Software object, so it calls the overridden version of the GetDisplayText() method that's defined by the Software class.

Note that to use this type of polymorphism, you must code the virtual keyword on the base class member. Otherwise, you can't override the member in the derived classes. Then, any call to the base class member executes that member regardless of the object type.

Three versions of the GetDisplayText() method

A virtual GetDisplayText() method in the Product base class

```
public virtual string GetDisplayText(string sep) =>
    $"{Code}{sep}{Price.ToString("c")}{sep}{Description}";
```

An overridden GetDisplayText() method in the Book class

```
public override string GetDisplayText(string sep) =>
    $"{base.GetDisplayText(sep)} ({Author})";
```

An overridden GetDisplayText() method in the Software class

```
public override string GetDisplayText(string sep) =>
    $"{base.GetDisplayText(sep)}, Version {Version}";
```

Code that uses the overridden methods

```
Book b = new("C#", "Murach's C#", 59.50m, "Anne Boehm");
Software s = new("NPTK", ".NET Programmer's Toolkit", 179.99m, "4.5");
Product p;
p = b;
MessageBox.Show(p.GetDisplayText("\n"));   // Calls Book.GetDisplayText()
p = s;
MessageBox.Show(p.GetDisplayText("\n"));   // Calls Software.GetDisplayText()
```

Description

- *Polymorphism* is a feature of inheritance that lets you treat objects of different subclasses that are derived from the same base class as if they had the type of the base class. If, for example, Book is a subclass of Product, you can treat a Book object as if it were a Product object.

- If you access a virtual member of a base class object and the member is overridden in the subclasses of that class, polymorphism determines the member that's executed based on the object's type. For example, if you call the GetDisplayText() method of a Product object, the GetDisplayText() method of the Book class is executed if the object is a Book object.

- Polymorphism is most useful when you have two or more derived classes that use the same base class. It allows you to write generic code that targets the base class rather than having to write specific code for each object type.

Figure 14-7   How polymorphism works

An inheritance version of the Product Maintenance app

Now that you've learned how to create base classes and subclasses, the following topics present a version of the Product Maintenance app that uses inheritance. This version of the app uses the classes that were described in figure 14-4. It works with a Products file that can hold two distinct types of products: books and software.

Note that this version of the Product Maintenance app won't work with the ProductDB classes that are presented in chapter 17, since those classes are designed to work only with Product objects. Instead, this version of the app requires a ProductDB class that can save and retrieve data for both Book and Software objects. Although this class isn't presented here, you shouldn't have any trouble figuring out how to implement it after you read chapter 17.

The operation of the Product Maintenance app

Figure 14-8 shows the operation of this version of the Product Maintenance app. As you can see, the Product Maintenance form looks just like the one you saw in chapter 12. From this form, you can click the Add Product button to display the New Product form, or you can select a product in the list and then click the Delete Product button to delete a product.

The main difference between this app and the app presented in chapter 12 is that the New Product form includes two radio buttons. These buttons let the user choose whether a book or a software product is added to the file. Note that the label that's displayed for the last text box changes depending on which of these buttons is selected. If the Book button is selected, this label is set to Author. If the Software button is selected, it's set to Version.

The Product Maintenance form

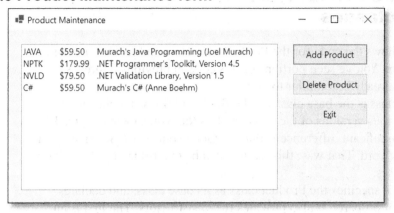

Two versions of the New Product form

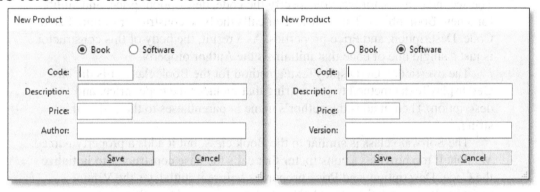

Description

- This version of the Product Maintenance app handles two types of products: books and software.

- The New Product form has a radio button that lets the user choose to create a book or a software product. The label for the last text box changes depending on which option is selected.

Figure 14-8   The operation of the Product Maintenance app

The code for the Product, Book, and Software classes

Figure 14-9 shows the code for the Product base class and its two subclasses, Book and Software. You've seen portions of this code in previous figures, so most of it should already be familiar to you.

The Product class is the base class for the Book and Software classes. It's similar to the previous versions of the Product class that you saw in chapter 12. In fact, the only significant difference is that the GetDisplayText() method specifies the virtual keyword. That way, this method can be overridden by the Book and Software classes.

The Book class specifies the Product class as its base class, and declares a read/write Author property. It also provides two constructors. The first is an empty constructor that lets you create a new Book object with default values. The second constructor lets you specify the code, description, price, and author for a new Book object. This constructor calls the base constructor to initialize the Code, Description, and Price properties. As a result, the body of this constructor is just a single line of code that initializes the Author property.

The overridden GetDisplayText() method for the Book class calls the base GetDisplayText() method to get a string that includes the code, price, and description. Then, it adds the author's name in parentheses to the end of this string.

The Software class is similar to the Book class, but it adds a property named Version. It too provides a constructor that calls the base constructor to initialize the Code, Description, and Price properties before it initializes the Version property. It also overrides the GetDisplayText() method by calling the base GetDisplayText() method and then adding the version information to the end of the string that's returned.

The code for the Product class

```
public class Product
{
    public Product() { }

    public Product(string code, string description, decimal price) =>
        (Code, Description, Price) = (code, description, price);

    public string Code { get; set; } = "";
    public string Description { get; set; } = "";
    public decimal Price { get; set; }

    public virtual string GetDisplayText(string sep) =>
        $"{Code}{sep}{Price.ToString("c")}{sep}{Description}";
}
```

The code for the Book class

```
public class Book : Product
{
    public Book() { }

    public Book(string code, string description, decimal price,
        string author) : base(code, description, price) => Author = author;

    public string Author { get; set; } = "";

    public override string GetDisplayText(string sep) =>
        $"{base.GetDisplayText(sep)} ({Author})";
}
```

The code for the Software class

```
public class Software : Product
{
    public Software() { }

    public Software(string code, string description, decimal price,
        string version) : base(code, description, price) => Version = version;

    public string Version { get; set; } = "";

    public override string GetDisplayText(string sep) =>
        $"{base.GetDisplayText(sep)}, Version {Version}";
}
```

Figure 14-9   The code for the Product, Book, and Software classes

The code for the ProductList class

Figure 14-10 shows the code for the ProductList class, which is used to hold the Book and Software objects that are maintained by the Product Maintenance app. This class inherits the List<Product> class. As a result, the basic functions of the ProductList class, such as its ability to hold multiple Product objects, are provided by the base class. For example, even though the ProductList class doesn't provide code for an indexer or a Remove() method, both of these members are available from the ProductList class because they are available from the base class.

However, the ProductList class does provide an implementation of an Add() method that hides the Add() method that's available from the List<Product> class. To start, the declaration for this Add() method uses the new keyword to indicate that it hides rather than overrides the Add() method from the base class. Since this method isn't declared as virtual in the base class, this is the only way to modify this method. Then, the body of this method uses the base keyword to call the Insert() method of the List<Product> class to insert the Product object that's passed to the method at the beginning of the list. As a result, the Add() method for this version of the ProductList class adds products to the beginning of the list instead of adding them to the end of the list. Although this might not be the behavior you would want for most lists, it does show how you can change the functionality of a subclass by hiding a method from the base class.

The last two methods of the ProductList class, Fill() and Save(), aren't available from the base class. These methods can be used to read or write the list of products to a data store. For example, the Fill() method calls the GetProducts() method of the ProductDB class to load the products in the Products file into a list of products. Then, it uses a foreach loop to add each product in the list to the base list by calling the Add() method of the base class. (Although the Add() method of the ProductList class hides the Add() method of the base class, you can still refer to the method of the base class using the base keyword.) Conversely, the Save() method calls the SaveProducts() method of the ProductDB class to save the current instance of the ProductList class to the Products file.

The code for the ProductList class

```
public class ProductList : List<Product>
{
    // Modify the behavior of the Add method of the List<Product> class
    public new void Add(Product p) => base.Insert(0, p);

    // Provide two additional methods
    public void Fill()
    {
        List<Product> products = ProductDB.GetProducts();
        foreach (Product product in products)
            base.Add(product);
    }

    public void Save() => ProductDB.SaveProducts(this);
}
```

Description

- This version of the ProductList class inherits the .NET List<Product> class. As a result, it doesn't need to define a List<Product> instance variable because the class is itself a type of List<Product> class.

Figure 14-10   The code for the ProductList class

The code for the Product Maintenance form

Figure 14-11 shows the code for this version of the Product Maintenance form. The first thing you should notice here is the code for the FillProductListBox() method. You may remember that the code for this method in the Product Maintenance form in chapter 13 had to use a for loop along with the indexer of the ProductList class to process the product list. By contrast, because the ProductList class in this chapter inherits the List<Product> class, it can use a foreach loop to process the product list. You'll learn more about the features that make it possible to process a collection this way in the next chapter.

You can also see polymorphism at work in this foreach loop. Here, the statement that adds the text to the Items collection of the list box calls the GetDisplayText() method for each product. Because GetDisplayText() is a virtual method that's overridden by both the Book and Software classes, this code calls the GetDisplayText() method of the Book class for Book objects and the GetDisplayText() method of the Software class for Software objects. To confirm that's what's happening, you can look back to figure 14-9 to see the differences between these two methods, and you can look back to figure 14-8 to see the differences in the resulting display.

The code for the Product Maintenance form

```
public partial class frmProductMain : Form
{
    public frmProductMain()
    {
        InitializeComponent();
    }

    private ProductList products = new();

    private void frmProductMain_Load(object sender, EventArgs e)
    {
        products.Fill();
        FillProductListBox();
    }

    private void FillProductListBox()
    {
        lstProducts.Items.Clear();
        foreach (Product p in products)
            lstProducts.Items.Add(p.GetDisplayText("\t"));
    }

    private void btnAdd_Click(object sender, EventArgs e)
    {
        frmNewProduct newForm = new();
        Product product = newForm.GetNewProduct();
        if (product != null)
        {
            products.Add(product);
            products.Save();
            FillProductListBox();
        }
    }

    private void btnDelete_Click(object sender, EventArgs e)
    {
        int i = lstProducts.SelectedIndex;
        if (i != -1)
        {
            Product product = products[i];
            string message = "Are you sure you want to delete "
                + product.Description + "?";
            DialogResult button =
                MessageBox.Show(message, "Confirm Delete",
                MessageBoxButtons.YesNo);
            if (button == DialogResult.Yes)
            {
                products.Remove(product);
                products.Save();
                FillProductListBox();
            }
        }
    }

    private void btnExit_Click(object sender, EventArgs e)
    {
        this.Close();
    }
}
```

Figure 14-11   The code for the Product Maintenance form

The code for the New Product form

Figure 14-12 shows some of the code for the New Product form. Here, you can see that an event handler for the CheckedChanged event of the Book radio button is used to set the Text property of the fourth label control to reflect the radio button that's selected. This works because the Checked property of the Book radio button changes regardless of whether the user selects the Book or Software option. Then, within the CheckedChanged event handler, the Checked property of the Book radio button is tested to determine which option is selected. The Checked property of the Book radio button is also tested in the event handler for the Click event of the Save button to determine whether it should create a Book or Software object. Last, the IsValidData() method in this form uses the IsPresent() method of the Validator class to validate the author or version that the user enters.

Some of the code for the New Product form

```
public partial class frmNewProduct : Form
{
    ...
    private Product product = null!;

    public Product GetNewProduct()
    {
        this.ShowDialog();
        return product;
    }

    private void rbBook_CheckedChanged(object sender, EventArgs e)
    {
        if (rbBook.Checked)
            lblAuthorOrVersion.Text = "Author: ";
        else
            lblAuthorOrVersion.Text = "Version: ";
        txtCode.Focus();
    }

    private void btnSave_Click(object sender, EventArgs e)
    {
        if (IsValidData())
        {
            if (rbBook.Checked)
                product = new Book(txtCode.Text, txtDescription.Text,
                    Convert.ToDecimal(txtPrice.Text),
                    txtAuthorOrVersion.Text);
            else
                product = new Software(txtCode.Text, txtDescription.Text,
                    Convert.ToDecimal(txtPrice.Text),
                    txtAuthorOrVersion.Text);
            this.Close();
        }
    }

    private bool IsValidData()
    {
        bool success = true;
        string errorMessage = "";

        errorMessage += Validator.IsPresent(txtCode.Text,
                            nameof(Product.Code));
        errorMessage += Validator.IsPresent(txtDescription.Text,
                            nameof(Product.Description));
        errorMessage += Validator.IsDecimal(txtPrice.Text,
                            nameof(Product.Price));
        if (rbBook.Checked)
            errorMessage += Validator.IsPresent(txtAuthorOrVersion.Text,
                                nameof(Book.Author));
        else
            errorMessage += Validator.IsPresent(txtAuthorOrVersion.Text,
                                nameof(Software.Version));

        if (errorMessage != "")
        {
            success = false;
            MessageBox.Show(errorMessage, "Entry Error");
        }
        return success;
    }
    ...
}
```

Figure 14-12   Some of the code for the New Product form

Object types and casting

Now that you've learned the basics of inheritance and you've seen an example of an app that uses it, you're ready to learn some additional techniques that are often required when you work with inheritance. That includes casting objects and getting information about an object's type.

How to use the Type class to get information about an object's type

As you know, the System.Object class includes a GetType() method that you can use to get a Type object that represents the type of a .NET object. Figure 14-13 lists some of the members of the Type class that you can use to get information about an object. For example, you can use the Name property to get the name of a type, such as "Product" or "Book"; you can use the Namespace property to get the name of the namespace that contains a type, such as "ProductMaintenance"; and you can use the FullName property to get the fully qualified name of a type, such as "ProductMaintenance.Book". In addition, you can use the BaseType property to get a Type object that represents the type of the class that a type inherits.

The first example in this figure shows how you can use these properties to display information about an object. Here, the GetType() method is used to get information about a Book object that's accessed through a variable of type Product. Notice that even though the variable has a type of Product, the Type object that's returned by the GetType() method represents a Book object.

The second example shows two ways you can code an if statement to test an object's type. The first way is to use the *typeof operator* to get a Type object for the Book class. Then, you compare this Type object to the Type object that's returned by the GetType() method of the Product object. This way of testing an object's type was common before C# 7.0, and it's still often found in online examples and legacy code.

Another way to test an object's type is to use pattern matching. Specifically, you can use a declaration pattern to test an object's type and assign that object to a variable if it has that type. You saw how this worked in chapter 12. The advantages of using pattern matching are that it's more concise, and you don't have to cast the object being tested. If you need to get information about a type, though, you'll need to use the members of the Type class as shown in this figure.

The Type class

Property	Description
Name	Returns a string that contains the name of a type.
FullName	Returns a string that contains the fully qualified name of a type, which includes the namespace name and the type name.
BaseType	Returns a Type object that represents the class that a type inherits.
Namespace	Returns a string that contains the name of the namespace that contains a type.

Method	Description
GetType()	Returns a Type object that represents the type of an object.

Code that uses the Type class to get information about an object

```
Product product = new Book("C#", "Murach's C#", 59.50m, "Anne Boehm");
Type t = product.GetType();
Console.WriteLine("Name: " + t.Name);
Console.WriteLine("Namespace: " + t.Namespace);
Console.WriteLine("FullName: " + t.FullName);
Console.WriteLine("BaseType: " + t.BaseType.Name);
```

The result that's displayed on the console

```
Name: Book
Namespace: ProductMaintenance
FullName: ProductMaintenance.Book
BaseType: Product
```

How to test an object's type

Using the GetType() method

```
if (product.GetType() == typeof(Book)) {
    // need to cast product object to type Book
}
```

Using pattern matching (C# 7.0 and later)

```
if (product is Book b) {
    // no cast needed to work with Book object b
}
```

Description

- Every object has a GetType() method that returns a Type object that corresponds to the object's type.

- You can use the properties of the Type class to obtain information about the type of any object, such as the type's name and the name of its base class.

- The properties and methods shown above are only some of the more than 90 properties and methods of the Type class.

- One way to test an object's type is by comparing the Type object that's returned by the GetType() method of the object with the Type object that's returned by the *typeof operator* of a type. With C# 7.0 and later, you can use pattern matching instead.

Figure 14-13   How to use the Type class to get information about an object's type

How to use casting with inheritance

Another potentially confusing aspect of using inheritance is knowing when to cast inherited objects explicitly. The basic rule is that C# can implicitly cast a subclass to its base class, but you must use explicit casting if you want to treat a base class object as one of its subclasses. Figure 14-14 illustrates how this works.

The two methods at the top of this figure both call the GetDisplayText() method to get data in a displayable format. The first method, named DisplayProduct(), accepts a Product object and executes the GetDisplayText() method of the Product class, so it can be used with either a Book or a Software object. By contrast, the second method, named DisplayBook(), accepts a Book object and calls the GetDisplayText() method of the Book class, so it can only be used with Book objects.

The second example shows code that doesn't require casting. Here, the first statement creates a new Book object and assigns it to a variable of type Book. Then, the DisplayProduct() method is called to display the Book object that this variable refers to. Although the DisplayProduct() method expects a Product object, it can cast the Book object to a Product object since Book is a subclass of the Product class.

The third example is similar, but it assigns the new Book object to a variable of type Product. Then, it calls the DisplayBook() method. Because this method expects a Book object, however, the Product object must be explicitly cast to a Book object. If it isn't, the C# compiler will display a compiler error indicating that it can't convert a Product object to a Book object.

The fourth example shows code that results in a casting exception. Here, a Software object is assigned to a variable of type Product. Then, the DisplayBook() method is called to display the object that this variable refers to. Notice that this variable is explicitly cast to a Book object since that's what the DisplayBook() method expects. Because the p variable holds a Software object rather than a Book object, however, this cast results in a casting exception.

The last example shows how you can use the *as operator* to avoid throwing an exception if a cast is invalid. The as operator is similar to a cast, but it returns null if the object can't be converted to the specified type. In the example, a null value will be passed to the DisplaySoftware() method because the object referenced by the p variable is a Book object, which can't be cast to a Software object. Note that Visual Studio might generate a null reference warning about the statement that uses the as operator in this example.

Two methods that display product information

```
public void DisplayProduct(Product p) =>
    MessageBox.Show(p.GetDisplayText());

public void DisplayBook(Book b) =>
    MessageBox.Show(b.GetDisplayText());
```

Code that doesn't require casting

```
Book b = new Book("C#", "Murach's C#", 59.50m, "Anne Boehm");
DisplayProduct(b);        // Casting is not required because Book
                          // is a subclass of Product.
```

Code that requires casting

```
Product p = new Book("C#", "Murach's C#", 59.50m, "Anne Boehm");
DisplayBook((Book)p);     // Casting is required because Product
                          // is the base class for Book.
```

Code that throws a casting exception

```
Product p = new Software("NPTK", ".NET Programmer's Toolkit",
                          179.99m, "4.5");
DisplayBook((Book)p);     // Will throw a casting exception because p is a
                          // Software object, not a Book object.
```

Code that uses the as operator

```
Product p = new Book("C#", "Murach's C#", 59.50m, "Anne Boehm");
DisplaySoftware(p as Software);  // Passes null because p isn't
                                 // a Software object
```

Description

- C# can implicitly cast a subclass to its base class. As a result, you can use a subclass whenever a reference to its base class is called for. For example, you can specify a Book object whenever a Product object is expected because Book is a subclass of Product.

- You must explicitly cast a base class object when a reference to one of its subclasses is required. For example, you must explicitly cast a Product object to Book if a Book object is expected.

- If you attempt to cast a base class object to a subclass, an InvalidCastException will be thrown if the object is not of the correct type. For example, if you store a Software object in a variable of type Product and then try to cast the Product variable to a Book, a casting exception will be thrown.

- You can use the *as operator* to cast an object to another type without throwing a casting exception if the cast is invalid. The as operator simply returns null if the cast is invalid.

Figure 14-14   How to use casting with inheritance

How to work with abstract and sealed classes

The last two topics of this chapter show how you can require or restrict the use of inheritance in the classes you create by using abstract and sealed classes.

How to work with abstract classes

An *abstract class* is a class that can't be instantiated. In other words, it can be used only as a base class that other classes can inherit. Figure 14-15 shows how to work with abstract classes.

To declare an abstract class, you include the *abstract* keyword in the class declaration as shown in the Product class at the top of this figure. Then, you can code any members you want within this class. In addition, you can code *abstract methods* and *abstract properties*. For example, the Product class shown here includes an abstract read-only property named IsValid and an abstract method named GetDisplayText(). As you can see, the declarations for this property and this method include the abstract keyword, and no bodies are coded.

When you include abstract properties and methods in an abstract class, you must override them in any non-abstract class that inherits the abstract class. This is illustrated in the second example in this figure. Here, you can see that a class named Book that inherits the Product class overrides the abstract IsValid property and the GetDisplayText() method that are defined by that class.

Although you must override abstract properties and methods, you should notice that they're not declared with the virtual keyword. That's because abstract properties and methods are implicitly virtual.

At this point, you may be wondering why you would use abstract classes. To help you understand, consider the Product Maintenance app that's presented in this chapter. This app uses two types of product objects: Book objects and Software objects. However, there's nothing to stop you from creating instances of the Product class as well. As a result, the Product class hierarchy actually allows for three types of objects: Book objects, Software objects, and Product objects.

If that's not what you want, you can declare the Product class as an abstract class. Then, you can't create instances of the Product class itself. Instead, the Product class can only be used as the base class for other classes.

Note that this doesn't mean that you can't declare variables of an abstract type. It simply means that you can't use the new keyword with an abstract type to create an instance of the type. For example, if you declared the Product class as an abstract class, you could still declare a Product variable that could hold Book or Software objects like this:

```
Product p = new Book("C#", "Murach's C#", 59.50m, "Anne Boehm");
```

However, you wouldn't be able to use the new keyword with the Product class to create a Product object.

An abstract Product class with an abstract read-only property and an abstract method

```
public abstract class Product
{
    public string Code { get; set; } = "";
    public string Description { get; set; } = "";
    public decimal Price { get; set; }

    public abstract bool IsValid
    {
        get;        // No body is coded for the getter
    }

    public abstract string GetDisplayText(string sep);
    // No method body is coded.
}
```

A class that inherits the abstract Product class

```
public class Book : Product
{
    public string Author { get; set; } = "";

    public override bool IsValid =>
        !String.IsNullOrEmpty(Code) && !String.IsNullOrEmpty(Description) &&
        Price > 0 && !String.IsNullOrEmpty(Author);

    public override string GetDisplayText(string sep) =>
        $"{Code}{sep}{Description}({Author}){sep}{Price.ToString("c")}";
}
```

Description

- An *abstract class* is a class that can be inherited by other classes but that you can't use to create an object. To declare an abstract class, code the *abstract* keyword in the class declaration.

- An abstract class can contain properties, methods, and other members just like other base classes. In addition, an abstract class can contain abstract methods and properties.

- To create an *abstract method*, you code the abstract keyword in the method declaration and you omit the method body.

- To create an *abstract property*, you code the abstract keyword in the property declaration. Then, you code a get accessor, a set accessor, or both get and set accessors with no bodies.

- Abstract methods and properties are implicitly virtual, and you can't code the virtual keyword on an abstract method or property.

- When a subclass inherits an abstract class, all abstract methods and properties in the abstract class must be overridden in the subclass. The exception is if the subclass is also an abstract class.

- An abstract class doesn't have to contain abstract methods or properties. However, any class that contains an abstract method or property must be declared as abstract.

Figure 14-15   How to work with abstract classes

How to work with sealed classes

In contrast to an abstract class that must be inherited, a *sealed class* is a class that can't be inherited. Because C# doesn't have to generate code that provides for inheritance and polymorphism when it compiles sealed classes, using them can result in a minor performance benefit. If you know that a class won't be used as a base class, then, you should consider creating a sealed class.

Figure 14-16 shows how to create and work with sealed classes, as well as sealed properties and methods. To create a sealed class, you include the *sealed* keyword in the class declaration as shown in the example at the top of this figure. Then, you add the members that are required by the class just as you do for any other class.

You can also seal selected properties and methods of a class by omitting the sealed keyword from the class declaration and coding it on just the properties and methods you want to seal. Then, you can use the class as a base class for other classes, but you can't override the sealed members. This is illustrated by the example in this figure.

This example uses three classes named A, B, and C. Class A is a base class that declares a virtual method named ShowMessage(). Class B inherits class A and overrides the ShowMessage() method. In addition, class B seals this method. Then, class C inherits class B and attempts to override the ShowMessage() method. Because class B sealed the ShowMessage() method, however, this results in a compiler error.

In most cases, an entire class will be sealed rather than specific methods or properties. Because of that, you won't have to worry about whether individual properties and methods of a class are sealed. If you ever encounter sealed properties or methods, however, you should now understand how they work.

Keep in mind too that it's often hard to know when someone else might want to inherit a class that you create. So you shouldn't seal a class unless you're certain that no one else will benefit by extending it.

The class declaration for a sealed Book class

```
public sealed class Book : Product
```

How sealed methods work

A base class named A that declares a virtual method

```
public class A
{
    public virtual void ShowMessage() =>
        MessageBox.Show("Hello from class A");
}
```

A class named B that inherits class A and overrides and seals its method

```
public class B : A
{
    public sealed override void ShowMessage() =>
        MessageBox.Show("Hello from class B");
}
```

A class named C that inherits class B and tries to override its sealed method

```
public class C : B
{
    public override void ShowMessage() =>        // Not allowed
        MessageBox.Show("Hello from class C");
}
```

Description

- A *sealed class* is a class that can't be inherited. To create a sealed class, you code the *sealed* keyword in the class declaration.

- Sealing a class can result in a minor performance improvement for your app because the C# compiler doesn't have to allow for inheritance and polymorphism. As a result, it can generate more efficient code.

- You can also seal individual properties and methods. To create a *sealed property* or a *sealed method*, code the sealed keyword in the property or method declaration.

- You can only seal a property or method if the property or method overrides a member of the base class. This allows you to create a virtual member in a base class, and then seal it in a derived class so that any subclasses derived from that class can't override the member.

Figure 14-16   How to work with sealed classes

Perspective

Conceptually, this is probably the most difficult chapter in this book. Although the basic idea of inheritance isn't that difficult to understand, the complications of virtual members, overridden members, casting, and abstract and sealed classes are enough to make inheritance a difficult topic. So if you find yourself a bit confused right now, don't be disheartened. It will become clearer as you actually use the techniques you've learned here.

The good news is that you don't have to understand every nuance of how inheritance works to use it. In fact, you've used inheritance in every C# app you've written without even knowing it. Now that you've completed this chapter, though, you should have a better understanding of how the .NET classes work, and you should have a greater appreciation for how much .NET does on your behalf. In addition, you should have a better idea of how you can use inheritance to improve the design of your own classes.

In addition to using inheritance to add functionality to a type, you can use a feature of C# called extension methods. .NET includes some extension methods, such as the ones that provide for the LINQ query operators you'll learn about in chapter 18. Although you can also code your own extension methods, that's beyond the scope of this book.

Terms

inheritance	protected member
derived class	internal member
child class	hiding
subclass	polymorphism
base class	typeof operator
parent class	as operator
superclass	abstract class
overriding	abstract method
fully qualified name	abstract property
hash code	sealed class
garbage collector	sealed property
virtual member	sealed method
access modifier	

Exercise 14-1   Create a Customer Maintenance app that uses inheritance

In this exercise, you'll create a Customer Maintenance app that uses classes with inheritance. This app works with two types of customers: retail and wholesale. Both customer types are derived from a Customer base class. To make this app easier to develop, we'll give you the starting forms and classes.

The Customer Maintenance form

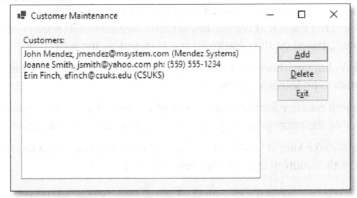

The updated Add Customer form

Open the project and create the derived classes

1. Open the app in the C:\C#\Ch14\CustomerMaintenance directory.

2. Modify the GetDisplayText() method of the Customer class so it's overridable.

3. Add a class named WholesaleCustomer that inherits the Customer class. This new class should add a string property named Company. It should also provide a default constructor and a constructor that accepts four parameters (first name, last name, email, and company) to initialize the class properties. This constructor should call the base class constructor to initialize the properties defined by that class. Finally, this class should override the GetDisplayText() method to add the company name in parentheses to the end of the display string, as in this example:

John Mendez, jmendez@msystem.com (Mendez Systems)

4. Add another class named RetailCustomer that inherits the Customer class and adds a string property named HomePhone. Like the WholesaleCustomer class, the RetailCustomer class should provide a default constructor and a constructor that accepts four parameters, and it should override the GetDisplayText() method so the phone number is added to the end of the string like this:

   Joanne Smith, jsmith@armaco.com ph: (559) 555-1234

Update the code for the Add Customer form

5. Add an event handler for the CheckedChanged event of one of the radio buttons that sets the label text for the last textbox to either "Company:" or "Home Phone:", based on the customer type selected by the user.

6. Update the IsValid() method to validate the company or home phone, based on the customer type selected by the user.

7. Update the event handler for the Click event of the Save button so it creates a new customer of the appropriate type using the data entered by the user.

8. Run the app to make sure it works. If you're going to continue with the next exercise, leave the solution open. Otherwise, close it.

Exercise 14-2   Modify the CustomerList class to inherit the List<Customer> class

This exercise builds on the Customer Maintenance app you created in exercise 14-1 by modifying the CustomerList class so it inherits the .NET List<Customer> class.

1. If it isn't already open, open the app in the C:\C#\Ch14\CustomerMaintenance directory.

2. Modify the CustomerList class so it inherits the List<Customer> class instead of using a private List<Customer> variable to hold the customer list. To do that, you can delete the Count() method because it's provided by the base class. You can use the new keyword to hide some of the methods in the base class so you can use the ones that are already in this CustomerList class. And you can use the base keyword to refer to the base class whenever that's necessary. As you do this step, you may want to use figure 14-10 as a guide.

3. Modify the FillCustomerListBox() method of the Customer Maintenance form so it gets the list of customers using the GetCustomers() method of the CustomerDB class, and then fills the list box using a foreach statement instead of a for statement.

4. Run the app and test it to be sure it works properly.

15

How to work with interfaces and generics

This chapter starts by showing you how to use interfaces. Interfaces are similar to abstract classes, but they have some advantages that make them easier to create and more flexible to use. Then, this chapter shows you how to use generics so you can code your own collections that work like the generic .NET collections presented in chapter 8. Along the way, you'll learn how to work with the generic interfaces that are used with generic collections.

How to work with interfaces

In some object-oriented programming languages, such as C++ and Perl, a class can inherit more than one class. This is known as *multiple inheritance*. In C#, however, a class can inherit only one class.

Although C# doesn't support multiple inheritance, it does support a special type of coding element known as an *interface*. An interface provides many of the advantages of multiple inheritance without some of the problems that are associated with it. In the topics that follow, you'll learn how to work with interfaces.

An introduction to interfaces

In some ways, an interface is similar to an abstract class. That's why figure 15-1 compares interfaces to abstract classes. To start, abstract classes and interfaces can both include one or more members that aren't implemented. In the case of an abstract class, the implementation for these members must be provided by any subclass that inherits the abstract class. Similarly, the implementation for the members of an interface must be included in any class that *implements* the interface.

Prior to C# 8.0, an interface couldn't include the implementation for any of its members like an abstract class can. With C# 8.0 and later, though, an interface can provide implementation for its *default interface members*. Then, a class that implements the interface can override those members or use the default implementations. You'll learn more about how one type of default interface member, default methods, works later in this chapter.

An important difference between abstract classes and interfaces is that a C# class can inherit only one class (abstract or not), but it can implement more than one interface. This is how C# interfaces can be used to provide some of the features of multiple inheritance.

The examples in this figure show how a simple interface is declared and implemented by a class. The first example shows the declaration for a custom interface named IDisplayable. This interface includes a single method named GetDisplayText() that allows an object to return a string that can be used to display the object. Any class that implements the IDisplayable interface must provide an implementation of the GetDisplayText() method.

The second example shows a version of a Product class that implements the IDisplayable interface. Here, you can see that the class statement for the Product class lists IDisplayable as an interface that's implemented by the class. Then, the class provides an implementation of the GetDisplayText() method that returns a string that contains all three properties of the Product class.

The third example shows that a Product object that implements the IDisplayable interface can be stored in a variable of the IDisplayable type. In other words, an object created from a Product class that implements the IDisplayable interface is both a Product object and an IDisplayable object. As a result, you can use this object anywhere an IDisplayable object is expected.

A comparison of interfaces and abstract classes

- Both interfaces and abstract classes can provide signatures for properties and methods that a class must implement.
- Both interfaces and abstract classes can implement some or all of their properties and methods.
- An abstract class can use instance variables and constants as well as static variables and constants. An interface can only use static variables and constants.
- A class can inherit only one class (including abstract classes), but a class can implement more than one interface.

The IDisplayable interface

```
public interface IDisplayable
{
    string GetDisplayText(string sep);
}
```

A Product class that implements the IDisplayable interface

```
public class Product : IDisplayable
{
    public Product() { }

    public Product(string code, string description, decimal price) =>
        (Code, Description, Price) = (code, description, price);

    public string Code { get; set; } = "";
    public string Description { get; set; } = "";
    public decimal Price { get; set; }

    public string GetDisplayText(string sep) =>
        $"{Code}{sep}{Description}{sep}{Price.ToString("c")}";
}
```

Code that uses the IDisplayable interface

```
IDisplayable product = new Product("C#", "Murach's C#", 59.50m);
Debug.WriteLine(product.GetDisplayText("\n"));
```

Description

- An *interface* consists of a set of signatures for one or more methods, properties, indexers, or events.
- With C# 8.0 and later, an interface can provide implementation for its *default interface members*. Default interface members may be overridden by any class that *implements* the interface, and all non-default interface members must be defined by those classes.
- By convention, interface names begin with the letter I to distinguish them from classes.
- To implement an interface, a class must name the interface on the class declaration, and it must provide an implementation for every non-default member of the interface.

Figure 15-1   An introduction to interfaces

In figure 15-1, the interface name begins with the capital letter I. Although that's not a requirement, it's a coding convention that's followed by all the .NET interfaces, and it helps you distinguish between interfaces and classes. So when you create your own interfaces, we recommend that you follow this coding convention.

Some of the interfaces defined by .NET

.NET defines hundreds of interfaces. Fortunately, most of them are intended for use by other .NET classes. As a result, you don't need to learn them all. To give you an idea of what some of these interfaces do, though, figure 15-2 lists some of them.

The table in this figure lists four general purpose .NET interfaces: ICloneable, IComparable, IConvertible, and IDisposable. Of these four, the one you're most likely to implement is ICloneable. This interface lets you create objects that can produce copies of themselves. It consists of a single method named Clone() that returns a copy of the object. You'll see an example of a Product class that implements this interface in figure 15-6.

The other three interfaces are commonly used by .NET interfaces, but you may occasionally need to implement them for the classes that you code as well. For example, the IComparable interface provides a standard way for an object to compare itself with another object. You might want to implement this interface so it compares objects based on the values of one of their properties. You'll see an example of that later in this chapter.

The interfaces in this figure were used by .NET prior to the introduction of generics. However, many .NET interfaces have generic versions as well. For instance, the IComparable interface presented here also has a generic version. In addition, there are many generic interfaces that are used with generic collections. You'll learn about generic interfaces later in this chapter.

Commonly used .NET interfaces

Interface	Members	Description
ICloneable	object Clone()	Creates a duplicate copy of an object.
IComparable	int CompareTo(object)	Compares objects.
IConvertible	TypeCode GetTypeCode() decimal ToDecimal() int ToInt32() ...	Converts an object to one of the common language runtime types, such as Int32, Decimal, or Boolean.
IDisposable	void Dispose()	Frees unmanaged resources.

Description

- .NET defines many interfaces that you can implement in your classes.
- This table only lists the most important members of each interface. For a complete description of these interfaces and a list of their members, see the online documentation.

Figure 15-2   Some of the interfaces defined by .NET

How to create an interface

Figure 15-3 shows how to create an interface. As you can see in the syntax at the top of this figure, you declare an interface using the *interface* keyword. This keyword is followed by the interface name.

Within the body of an interface, you can declare one or more methods, properties, and events. Although these declarations are similar to the declarations for a class, there is one important difference. Because an interface doesn't provide the implementation for its non-default members, non-default method declarations and the get and set accessors for non-default properties always end in a semicolon.

With C# 8.0 and later, you can also code access modifiers on member declarations. If you don't, all members are considered to be public by default. By contrast, prior to C# 8.0, you couldn't code access modifiers on member declarations. Instead, all members were considered to be public and abstract.

To begin coding an interface, you can add a new interface to your project by selecting the Project→Add New Item command and then selecting the Interface item from the resulting dialog. This will generate the code for the beginning of the interface. Then, you can modify the generated code and add members to the interface.

In the first example, the IDisplayable interface has been declared as public, so it's available to all classes in the current namespace. In addition, a GetDisplayText() method has been declared. The signature for this method specifies that the method accepts a separator string as a parameter and returns a string that contains the display text for the object.

In the second example, the IPersistable interface defines two methods and a property. Here, the Read() and Save() methods can be used to read and write the object, and the HasChanges property can be used to determine if the object contains any unsaved changes.

If an interface inherits other interfaces, the interface name is followed by a colon and a list of the inherited interfaces. In the last example, for instance, the IDataAccessObject interface inherits the IDisplayable and IPersistable interfaces. As a result, any class that implements IDataAccessObject must implement all three of the methods and the one property defined by IDisplayable and IPersistable. Although it isn't shown in this figure, IDataAccessObject could also add additional members.

The syntax for creating an interface

```
public interface InterfaceName
{
    modifier type MethodName(parameters);      // Declares a method

    modifier type PropertyName                 // Declares a property
    {
        [get;]                         // Declares a get accessor
        [set;]                         // Declares a set accessor
    }
    ...
}
```

An interface that defines one method

```
public interface IDisplayable
{
    string GetDisplayText(string sep);
}
```

An interface that defines two methods and a property

```
public interface IPersistable
{
    object Read(string id);
    bool Save(object o);
    bool HasChanges { get; set; }
}
```

The syntax for creating an interface that inherits other interfaces

```
public interface InterfaceName : InterfaceName1[, InterfaceName2]...
{
    interface members...
}
```

An interface that inherits two interfaces

```
public interface IDataAccessObject : IDisplayable, IPersistable
{
    // add additional members here
}
```

Description

- The declaration for an interface is similar to the declaration for a class. The only difference is that you use the *interface* keyword instead of the class keyword.

- The non-default methods and properties that are declared within an interface can't include implementation. As a result, non-default method declarations and non-default get and set accessors always end with a semicolon.

- Prior to C# 8.0, all members of an interface were considered to be public and abstract, and static members weren't allowed. With C# 8.0 and later, you can include any access modifier on an interface member, except that a non-default member can't be private.

Figure 15-3   How to create an interface

How to work with default methods

Prior to C# 8.0, interfaces could only contain abstract methods and any class that implemented an interface had to implement all the methods of that interface. This was a significant problem because if you changed an interface by adding or modifying a method, you also had to update any class that implemented the interface so it implemented the new or modified method.

Fortunately, C# 8.0 provides a new feature that allows you to include regular (non-abstract) methods in interfaces, known as *default methods*. Now, if a class implements an interface, it doesn't have to override the default methods of the interface. Instead, it can use these default methods. However, whenever necessary, a class can override a default method to change its functionality.

The first example in figure 15-4 shows an interface that declares a default method named GetDisplayText() that accepts a string parameter named sep. This method calls the ToString() method from the object that implements the interface to get a String object that represents the object. Then it returns that String object with the value of the sep parameter appended to it.

Next, this example shows a class that implements this interface and uses the default GetDisplayText() method. Since this method is included in the interface, this class doesn't need to implement the GetDisplayText() method. Instead, it can use the functionality that's provided by the default method in the interface. This works as if the class has inherited the method from another class.

Finally, this example shows a class that implements the interface in the first example and overrides the GetDisplayText() method. This allows the class to change the functionality that's provided by the default method. Note that you don't use the override keyword when overriding a default method of an interface. If you do, you'll get a compiler error.

How to work with static methods and fields

With C# 8.0 and later, you can also code static methods and fields in interfaces, as shown in the second example in figure 15-4. Here, an interface named IPrintable contains a static field named terminator and a static method named Print() that accepts a parameter of the IDisplayable type. This method contains a single line of code that calls the GetDisplayText() method of the IDisplayable object.

Next, this example shows code that uses the IPrintable interface. To start, the first statement creates an IDisplayable object named product. Then, the second statement passes this object to the static Print() method of the IPrintable interface. As you can see, this works much like calling a static method from a class.

The syntax for declaring a default method (C# 8.0 or later)

```
accessModifier returnType MethodName([parameterlist]) { ... }
```

An interface that defines a default method

```
public interface IDisplayable
{
    string GetDisplayText(string sep) => ToString() + sep;
}
```

A class that uses the default method

```
public class Product : IDisplayable
{
    // This class doesn't override the GetDisplayText() method.
    // As a result, it uses the GetDisplayText() method defined
    // by the interface.
}
```

A class that overrides the default method

```
public class Product : IDisplayable
{
    ...
    public string GetDisplayText(string sep) =>
        $"{Code}{sep}{Description}{sep}{Price.ToString("c")}";
}
```

An interface that defines a static method and a static field

```
public interface IPrintable
{
    static string terminator = "\r\n";
    static string Print(IDisplayable d) => d.GetDisplayText(terminator);
}
```

Code that calls a static method from an interface

```
IDisplayable product = new Product("C#", "Murach's C#", 59.50m);
string printString = IPrintable.Print(product);
```

Description

- With C# 8.0 and later, you can add regular (non-abstract) methods to an interface. These methods are known as *default methods*, and they have the same syntax as a method in a class.

- When you code a class that implements an interface, you don't need to implement its default methods. Instead, you can use the default methods defined in the interface in your class. However, if you want to change the functionality of a default method, you can override it.

- With C# 8.0 or later, you can include static methods and fields in interfaces. To call a static method or to refer to a static field in an interface, prefix the method or field with the name of the interface.

Figure 15-4   How to work with default methods and static methods and fields

How to implement an interface

Figure 15-5 shows how to code a class that implements one or more interfaces. To do that, you code the class name, followed by a colon and a list of the interfaces on the class declaration. Note that if the class also inherits another class, you must list the class before the interfaces.

The three class declarations in this figure illustrate how this works. The first class declaration is for a Product class that implements the ICloneable interface. The second class declaration is for a Product class that implements two interfaces: ICloneable and IDisplayable. And the third class declaration is for a Book class that inherits the Product class and implements the ICloneable and IDisplayable interfaces.

When you enter the name of an interface on a class declaration, you can use Visual Studio to automatically generate stubs for each member of the interface. To do that, you can click in the line that contains the name of the interface so a light bulb appears in the margin. Then, you can click on the light bulb to display a Quick Actions menu that contains two commands. If you select the Implement Interface command, code that's similar to the code in the second to last example in this figure is inserted into the class. At this point, you can begin entering the code that's needed to implement each member of the interface.

Code is also inserted into the class if you select the Implement All Members Explicitly command instead of the Implement Interface command. However, the code that's inserted doesn't use the public keyword, and it fully qualifies each member of the interface. In this figure, for example, it specifies ICloneable. Clone instead of just specifying the Clone() method. Although this can help to avoid naming conflicts in some situations, you typically won't need to use this command.

The syntax for implementing an interface

```
public class ClassName : [BaseClassName,] InterfaceName1
                    [, InterfaceName2]...
```

A Product class that implements ICloneable

```
public class Product : ICloneable
```

A Product class that implements two interfaces

```
public class Product : ICloneable, IDisplayable
```

A class that inherits a class and implements two interfaces

```
public class Book : Product, ICloneable, IDisplayable
```

The Quick Actions menu for an interface name

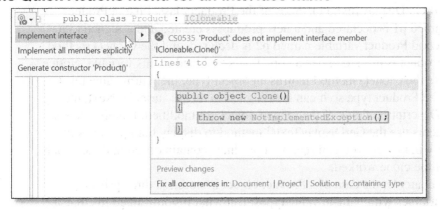

The code that's generated when you implement the interface

```
public object Clone()
{
    throw new NotImplementedException();
}
```

The code that's generated when you explicitly implement the interface

```
object ICloneable.Clone()
{
    throw new NotImplementedException();
}
```

Description

- To declare a class that implements one or more interfaces, type a colon after the class name, then list the interfaces that the class implements.
- If a class inherits another class, you must include the name of the inherited class before the names of any interfaces the class implements.
- To automatically generate stubs for the members of an interface in Visual Studio, click on the light bulb that appears in the left margin and select the Implement Interface command from the resulting menu. Then, you can add the code required to implement the members.

Figure 15-5　How to implement an interface

A Product class that implements the ICloneable interface

Now that you've seen the basic skills for creating and implementing interfaces, figure 15-6 presents an example of a Product class that implements the IDisplayable and ICloneable interfaces. This example is similar to the example that was shown in figure 15-1.

The Product class begins by declaring two constructors and three properties named Code, Description, and Price. Then, the GetDisplayText() method provides the implementation for the IDisplayable interface. Finally, the Clone() method creates a new product using the Code, Description, and Price values from the current product and returns the new product.

The second code example in this figure illustrates how you can use the Clone() and GetDisplayText() methods of the Product class. First, a Product variable named p1 is declared and a new product is created and assigned to it. Then, a second Product variable named p2 is declared, and the Clone() method of the p1 product is used to create a copy that's assigned to this variable. Notice that because the Clone() method returns an object type, the return value must be cast to the Product type so it can be assigned to the p2 variable. Next, the Code and Description fields of the second object are modified. Finally, the last two statements use the GetDisplayText() method to display both products in the Output window. As you can see, both products contain different data, which proves that the clone worked.

In this example, the data of a Product object is stored in three private instance variables with built-in value types. But what if you wanted to clone a more complicated object with fields that represent other objects? For example, consider an Invoice class with a Customer property that returns a Customer object that's stored in a private instance variable. In that case, you can clone the Invoice object using either a shallow copy or a deep copy.

If you use a *shallow copy*, the Customer property of the cloned Invoice object would refer to the same Customer object as the original Invoice object. By contrast, if you use a *deep copy*, the Customer property of the cloned Invoice object would refer to a clone of the Customer object. The easiest way to accomplish that would be to implement the ICloneable interface in the Customer class and then call the Clone() method of this class from the Invoice object. However, you could also clone the Customer object within the Clone() method of the Invoice class.

As defined by the ICloneable interface, the Clone() method doesn't specify whether the returned value should be a deep copy or a shallow copy. So, you can implement whichever type of copy you think is most appropriate for a class. Just be sure to specify whether the Clone() method returns a deep copy or a shallow copy in the class documentation so users of the class will know what to expect when they use this method. You'll learn how to provide documentation for a class in chapter 16.

The code for the cloneable Product class

```
public class Product : IDisplayable, ICloneable
{
    public Product() { }

    public Product(string code, string description, decimal price) =>
        (Code, Description, Price) = (code, description, price);

    public string Code { get; set; } = "";
    public string Description { get; set; } = "";
    public decimal Price { get; set; }

    public string GetDisplayText(string sep) =>
        $"{Code}{sep}{Description}{sep}{Price.ToString("c")}";

    public object Clone() => new Product(Code, Description, Price);
}
```

Code that creates and clones a Product object

```
Product p1 = new("RDA", "Murach's R for Data Analysis", 59.50m);
Product p2 = (Product)p1.Clone();

p2.Code = "PDA";
p2.Description = "Murach's Python for Data Analysis";

Debug.WriteLine(p1.GetDisplayText("\n") + "\n");
Debug.WriteLine(p2.GetDisplayText("\n") + "\n");
```

The output that's displayed by the code shown above

```
RDA
Murach's R for Data Analysis
$59.50

PDA
Murach's Python for Data Analysis
$59.50
```

Figure 15-6   A Product class that implements the ICloneable interface

How to use an interface as a parameter

Figure 15-7 shows how to use an interface as a parameter of a method. To do that, you code the name of the interface as the parameter type as shown in the first example. Here, a method named CreateList() accepts two parameters: an object that implements ICloneable and an integer. This method returns a list that's filled with copies of the object specified by the first parameter. The number of copies to be included in the list is specified by the second parameter. To generate the copies, the CreateList() method uses the Clone() method of the object that's passed to it.

The second example shows how to code a method named WriteToDebug() that accepts the IDisplayable interface as a parameter. This method uses the GetDisplayText() method of the IDisplayable interface to return the display text for the object. Then, it uses the WriteLine() method of the Debug class to write this text to the Output window.

When you declare a method that accepts an interface as a parameter, you can pass any object that implements that interface to the method. This is illustrated by the third code example in this figure. Here, a new Product object is created and stored in a variable named product. Then, the CreateList() method is used to create three copies of the Product object. Finally, the WriteToDebug() method is used to write each Product object to the Output window. You can see the result in the last example in this figure.

The key point here is that the CreateList() method doesn't know what type of object it's cloning. All it knows is that the object implements the ICloneable interface, which means that it has a Clone() method. Similarly, the WriteToDebug() method doesn't know what type of object it's writing to the Output window. All it knows is that the object implements the IDisplayable interface. Both of these methods work for the Product object because the Product class implements ICloneable and IDisplayable.

This example illustrates an even larger point. In short, a Product object can be thought of as an ICloneable or IDisplayable object. As a result, you can supply a Product object anywhere an ICloneable or IDisplayable object is expected. In this figure, interfaces are used to specify the type for a parameter of a method. However, interfaces can be used to specify a type in other places too. For example, an interface can be used as a return type for a method. Similarly, an interface can be used to specify the type of a property. And anywhere an interface is used to specify a type, you can supply any object that implements that interface.

A CreateList() method that uses an interface as a parameter

```
public static List<object> CreateList(ICloneable obj, int count)
{
    List<object> objects = new();
    for (int i = 0; i < count; i++)
    {
        object o = obj.Clone();
        objects.Add(o);
    }
    return objects;
}
```

A WriteToDebug() method that uses an interface as a parameter

```
public static void WriteToDebug(IDisplayable d) =>
    Debug.WriteLine(d.GetDisplayText("\n") + "\n");
```

Code that uses these methods

```
Product product = new("C#", "Murach's C#", 59.50m);
List<object> products = CreateList(product, 3);
foreach (Product p in products)
{
    WriteToDebug(p);
}
```

The output that's displayed by the code shown above

```
C#
Murach's C#
$59.50

C#
Murach's C#
$59.50

C#
Murach's C#
$59.50
```

Description

- You can declare a parameter that's used by a method as an interface type. Then, you can pass any object that implements the interface to the parameter.

- Since the Product class implements both the ICloneable and IDisplayable interfaces, it can be passed as an argument to a method that accepts an object of the ICloneable or IDisplayable type.

Figure 15-7   How to use an interface as a parameter

How to work with generics

In chapter 8, you learned how to work with generic collections such as ones defined by the List<T>, SortedList<T>, Stack<T>, and Queue<T> classes. Most of the time, you can use these or other collections from .NET whenever you need to work with a collection of objects. Sometimes, though, you may need to use *generics* to define your own generic collection. For instance, you may need to add some functionality that isn't available from the generic collections provided by .NET. Or, you may need to limit some of the functionality of a generic collection, such as not allowing items to be removed. If so, the topics that follow show you how to do that. In addition, they shed some light on the inner workings of the generic collections available from .NET.

How to code a class that defines a generic collection

Part 1 of figure 15-8 shows a class named CustomList<T> that defines a generic collection that limits the functionality of the List<T> class to adding and retrieving items, getting a count of the items, and producing a string that represents the items. This class illustrates all of the basic principles that are needed to define a generic collection.

To start, a data type variable named T is declared within the angle brackets immediately after the class name. This variable represents the data type that's specified for the class when an object is created from the class. For example, if you create a custom list class like this

```
CustomList<Product> products = new();
```

the compiler substitutes the Product type wherever the T variable is coded. As a result, when you code the CustomList class, you can use the T variable to represent the data type that's specified for the class.

Then, this class declares a private List<T> variable. As a result, this private list can store any data type. Then, the Add() method adds an object of type T to the private list. Next, the read-only indexer for this class returns an object of type T at the specified index, and the Count property returns the number of items in the list. Finally, this class declares a standard ToString() method that returns a string that represents the objects of type T that are stored in the list.

Although this CustomList class uses T as the name of the type parameter for the class, you can use any parameter name here. For example, you could use a longer name such as DocumentType. However, most generic classes use T as the name of the type parameter. The main exception to this rule is the generic collections that work with dictionaries that contain keys and values. These typically use K for the key type and V for the value type like this:

```
public class CustomDictionary<K, V>
```

Incidentally, this shows how to define a generic class that accepts two type parameters, which is possible but rare.

A CustomList<T> class that uses generics

```
public class CustomList<T>
{
    private List<T> list = new();

    // an Add() method
    public void Add(T item) => list.Add(item);

    // a read-only indexer
    public T this[int i] => list[i];

    // a read-only property
    public int Count => list.Count;

    // the ToString() method
    public override string ToString()
    {
        string listString = "";
        foreach (T item in list)
        {
            listString += item?.ToString() + "\n";
        }
        return listString;
    }
}
```

Description

- You can use *generics* to define a type-safe collection that can accept elements of any type.

- To define a class for a generic collection, you code angle brackets after the name of the class, and you specify the type parameter within these brackets. Then, within the class, you can use the type parameter anywhere a data type might be used. For example, you can use it as a return type or a parameter type for a method.

- By convention, most programmers use the letter T as the name for the type parameter for most classes. However, you can use any parameter name here.

Figure 15-8   How to code a class that uses generics (part 1 of 2)

Part 2 of figure 15-8 shows some code that uses the CustomList<T> class defined in part 1. To start, the first test creates a CustomList<int> class that can store int types, adds two int values to the list, and writes these values to the Output window. Then, the second test creates a CustomList<Product> class that can store Product types, adds two Product objects to the list, and writes these objects to the Output window.

This example shows that the CustomList<T> class can store value types (such as int types) or reference types (such as Product types). More importantly, it shows that the CustomList<T> class works like the other generic classes defined by .NET, although it doesn't provide as much functionality as any of those classes. Note that the output for this example assumes that the Product class contains a ToString() method that returns a string that includes the product's code, description, and price separated by tabs.

Code that uses the CustomList<T> class

```
// Test 1
Debug.WriteLine("List 1 - ints");
CustomList<int> list1 = new();
int int1 = 11;
int int2 = 7;
list1.Add(int1);
list1.Add(int2);
Debug.WriteLine(list1.ToString());

// Test 2
Debug.WriteLine("List 2 - Products");
CustomList<Product> list2 = new();
Product p1 = new("JAVA", "Murach's Java Programming", 59.50m);
Product p2 = new("C#", "Murach's C#", 59.50m);
list2.Add(p1);
list2.Add(p2);
Debug.Write(list2.ToString());
```

Resulting output

```
List 1 - ints
11
7

List 2 - Products
JAVA        Murach's Java Programming  $59.50
C#          Murach's C#                $59.50
```

Description

- The generic CustomList<T> class works like the generic .NET collection classes described in chapter 8.

- The resulting output shown above assumes that the Product class includes a ToString() method that displays the product code, description, and price separated by tabs.

Figure 15-8   How to code a class that uses generics (part 2 of 2)

Some of the generic interfaces defined by .NET

The generic collections of .NET work with the generic interfaces described in figure 15-9. Most of these generic interfaces also have corresponding regular interfaces, such as IEnumerable and ICollection. These regular interfaces were used by .NET prior to the introduction of generics and are rarely used today.

The generic interfaces use angle brackets to specify the data type for the interface, just as generic classes use angle brackets to specify the data type for the class. In addition, the generic interfaces are stored in the System.Collections. Generic namespace and were designed to work with the generic collections stored in that namespace.

If you decide to define your own generic collection, such as the CustomList<T> class shown in the previous figure, you may want to implement some of these interfaces. For example, if you want to be able to use a foreach loop to iterate through your generic collection, you'll need to implement the IEnumerable<T> interface. You'll learn how to do that in figure 15-12. But first, you'll learn how to implement the IComparable<T> interface in the next figure.

A commonly used generic .NET interface

Interface	Member	Description
`IComparable<T>`	`int CompareTo(T)`	Compares objects of type T.

Commonly used .NET interfaces for generic collections

Interface	Members	Description
`IEnumerable<T>`	`IEnumerator<T>` `GetEnumerator()`	Gets an enumerator of type T for the collection.

`ICollection<T>`	`int Count`
	`bool IsReadOnly`
	`T SyncRoot`
	`Add(T)`
	`void Clear()`
	`bool Contains(T)`
	`void CopyTo(array, int)`
	`bool Remove(T)`
		Provides basic properties for an enumerable collection. This interface inherits IEnumerable<T>.

`IList<T>`	`[int]`
	`int IndexOf(T)`
	`void Insert(int, T)`
	`void RemoveAt(int)`
		Manages a basic list of objects. This interface inherits ICollection<T> and IEnumerable<T>.

`IDictionary<T>`	`[int]`
	`ICollection<K> Keys`
	`ICollection<V> Values`
	`bool Remove(K)`
	`bool TryGetValue(K, V)`
		Manages a collection of key/value pairs. This interface inherits ICollection<T> and IEnumerable<T>.

Description

- .NET defines many generic interfaces. These interfaces are particularly useful for working with classes that define generic collections.

- The ICollection<T> interface inherits the IEnumerable<T> interface, which means that any class that implements ICollection<T> must also implement IEnumerable<T>. Similarly, the IList<T> and IDictionary<T> interfaces inherit ICollection<T> and IEnumerable<T>.

- The interfaces for working with generic collections are stored in the System.Collections.Generic namespace.

- This table only lists the most important members of each interface. For a complete description of these interfaces and a list of their members, see the online documentation.

Figure 15-9   Some of the generic interfaces defined by .NET

How to implement the IComparable<T> interface

Figure 15-10 shows a Product class that implements the IComparable<T> interface. To start, the declaration for this class indicates that it implements the IComparable interface for the Product type. Since you would typically want to compare one Product object to another Product object, this makes sense.

Then, this class implements the IComparable<T> interface's only member, the CompareTo() method. Since the class specifies an IComparable interface for a Product type, this method compares a parameter of the Product type against the current Product object and returns an int value. For this method to work properly, this int value should be greater than zero if the current product is greater than the compared product, less than zero if the current product is less than the compared product, and zero if the two products are equal.

To accomplish this task, this method uses the CompareTo() method of the String class to compare the Code property for the two Product objects. The CompareTo() method of the String class compares the two strings alphabetically and returns a 1 when the current string comes later in the alphabet than the compared string. Conversely, this method typically returns -1 when the current string comes earlier in the alphabet than the compared element. And it returns a 0 when the two strings are the same. As a result, the CompareTo() method of the Product class allows you to define a generic collection of Product objects that are sorted alphabetically by their Code fields. You'll see an example of this in the next figure.

Notice that the Product parameter of the CompareTo() method of the Product object in this example is declared as a nullable type. In addition, the parameter of the CompareTo() method of the String class uses a null-conditional operator to prevent the Code property of the Product object from being retrieved if the Product object is null. In that case, a null value is returned and the current object is compared to that value. Then, because a null value is considered to be less than any other value, the CompareTo() method returns a negative value. When you compare objects, then, you'll want to be sure to handle null values appropriately.

The second example shows some code that uses the CompareTo() method of the Product class. To start, this code creates two Product objects. The first has a Code field of "JAVA", and the second has a Code field of "C#". Then, this example uses the CompareTo() method to compare these two objects. Since the Code field for the first object comes later in the alphabet, the CompareTo() method returns an int value of 1. As a result, the if statement in this example writes a message to the Output window that indicates that the first Product object is greater than the second one.

A class that implements the IComparable<T> interface

```
public class Product : IComparable<Product>
{
    public string Code { get; set; } = "";
    public string Description { get; set; } = "";
    public decimal Price { get; set; }

    // other members

    public int CompareTo(Product? other) =>
        this.Code.CompareTo(other?.Code);
}
```

Code that uses the class

```
Product p1 = new("JAVA", "Murach's Java Programming", 59.50m);
Product p2 = new("C#", "Murach's C#", 59.50m);
int compareValue = p1.CompareTo(p2);
if (compareValue > 0)
    Debug.WriteLine("p1 is greater than p2");
else if (compareValue < 0)
    Debug.WriteLine("p1 is less than p2");
else if (compareValue == 0)
    Debug.WriteLine("p1 is equal to p2");
```

Values that can be returned by the CompareTo() method

Value	Meaning
-1	The current element is less than the compare element.
0	The current element is equal to the compare element.
1	The current element is greater than the compare element.

Description

- Since the IComparable<T> interface is a generic interface, you can use angle brackets after the IComparable<T> interface to identify the type of the objects that are being compared.

- To implement the IComparable<T> interface, you must implement the CompareTo() method. This method returns an int value that determines if the current element is less than, equal to, or greater than the element that's passed as a parameter of the method.

Figure 15-10   How to implement the IComparable<T> interface

How to use constraints

As you work with generic classes, you may occasionally encounter situations where you need to restrict the possible data types that a generic class can accept. For example, you may need to make sure that a generic class only accepts reference types, not value types. Or, you may need to make sure that a generic class inherits another class or implements an interface. To do that, you can code a *constraint* as shown in figure 15-11.

The example at the top of the figure shows the beginning of a CustomList<T> class that uses the CompareTo() method of an object to insert the object at a point in the list so the list is always sorted. In other words, it implements a sorted list. To accomplish this task, this class restricts the types that can be accepted by the CustomList<T> class to classes (which define reference types) that implement the IComparable<T> interface.

Since the T variable must implement the IComparable<T> interface, the Add() method can call the CompareTo() method from that variable. Without the constraint, this wouldn't be possible, as there would be no guarantee that the T variable would implement the IComparable<T> interface.

To declare a constraint, you begin by coding the *where* keyword after the class declaration. Then, you code the generic type parameter (usually T) followed by a colon. Finally, you code a list of the constraints, separating each constraint with a comma.

When you code these constraints, you must code them in a specific order. To start, if you want to constrain the generic type to a class, record, structure, or record struct, you must code the class or struct keyword first. Similarly, if you want to constrain the generic type to a subclass of a particular class, you must code the name of that class first and you can't use the class or struct keywords.

After that, you can code a list of the interfaces that the type must implement. Then, if you want to constrain the generic type to a class that has a default constructor, you can code the new() keyword at the end of the list. If you want to constrain the generic type to an enum, you can code System.Enum at the end of the list. Or if you want to constrain the generic type to a delegate, you can code System.Delegate at the end of the list.

A class that uses constraints

```
public class CustomList<T> where T: class, IComparable<T>
{
    private List<T> list = new();

    // an Add() method that keeps the list sorted
    public void Add(T newitem)
    {
        for (int i = 0; i < list.Count; i++)
        {
            var item = list[i];
            int compare = newitem.CompareTo(item);
            if (compare <= 0)      // the new item is less than or equal
            {                      // to the current item
                list.Insert(i, newitem);
                return;
            }
        }

        // if the list is empty or the new item is greater than the
        // current item, add the new item to the end of the list
        list.Add(newitem);
    }
    ...
}
```

Keywords that can be used to define constraints

Keyword	Description
class	The type argument must be a class or a record.
struct	The type argument must be a struct or record struct other than one that defines a nullable type.
new()	The type argument must have a default constructor. You can't use this keyword when the type argument must be a structure.
System.Enum	The type argument must be of the System.Enum type.
System.Delegate	The type argument must be of the System.Delegate type.

A class that's constrained to value types

```
public class StructList<T> where T: struct
```

Another class that uses constraints

```
public class ProductList<T> where T: Product, IComparable<T>, new()
```

Description

*   When you define a generic class, you can use *constraints* to restrict the data types that your generic class accepts.

Figure 15-11   How to use constraints

How to implement the IEnumerable<T> interface

The foreach loop only works on generic collections that implement the IEnumerable<T> interface. As a result, if you want to use the foreach loop on a generic collection that you've defined, you must implement the IEnumerable<T> interface. For example, to be able to use a foreach loop on the generic collection defined by the CustomList<T> class presented in this chapter, you must implement the IEnumerable<T> interface for this class as shown in figure 15-12.

To start, you can generate the method stubs for the IEnumerable<T> interface. This includes stubs for the GetEnumerator() method for both the regular IEnumerable interface and the generic IEnumerable<T> interface. However, you only need to implement the GetEnumerator() method for the generic IEnumerable<T> interface.

The easiest way to do that is to code a foreach loop that loops through each item in the list. Then, you can use the *yield* keyword together with the return keyword to return the current item to the enumerator object and to yield control.

In this figure, the enumerator object is a CustomList<Product> object named list. With each execution of the foreach loop that's shown at the end of the figure, the enumerator object (the list) returns a Product object and yields control to the foreach loop. This allows the foreach loop to call the ToString() method of the Product object before yielding control back to the enumerator object. In short, this allows the two loops shown in this figure to be synchronized.

A class that implements the IEnumerable<T> interface

```
public class CustomList<T> : IEnumerable<T>
{
    private List<T> list = new();

    // other members

    public IEnumerator<T> GetEnumerator()
    {
        foreach (T item in list)
        {
            yield return item;
        }
    }

    System.Collections.IEnumerator
        System.Collections.IEnumerable.GetEnumerator()
    {
        throw new NotImplementedException();
    }

}
```

Code that uses the class

```
Product p1 = new("JAVA", "Murach's Java Programming", 59.50m);
Product p2 = new("C#", "Murach's C#", 59.50m);
CustomList<Product> list = new();
list.Add(p1);
list.Add(p2);
foreach (Product p in list)
{
    Debug.WriteLine(p.ToString());
}
```

Description

- The foreach loop only works on generic collections that implement the IEnumerable<T> interface. As a result, if you want to use the foreach loop on a generic collection that you've defined, you must implement the IEnumerable<T> interface.

- When implementing the GetEnumerator() method, you can use the *yield* keyword with the return keyword to return the current element to the object that implements the IEnumerable<T> interface and yield control.

Figure 15-12   How to implement the IEnumerable<T> interface

How to code an interface that uses generics

Figure 15-13 shows how to define a generic interface. In particular, it shows how to define a generic interface named IPersistable<T>. The code for this interface provides a standard way for a business object to read itself from or write itself to a data source such as a database.

To give you an idea of how the IPersistable<T> interface might be used, this figure also shows part of a Customer class that implements this interface. Here, you can see the stubs that have been generated for the members of the interface. As a result, the Read() method must return a Customer object based on the id that's passed to it. The Save() method must accept a Customer object as a parameter and return a Boolean value that indicates whether the save was successful. And the HasChanges property must have accessors that get and set the property to indicate whether the Customer object has been changed since the last time it was saved.

An interface named IPersistable<T> that uses generics

```
public interface IPersistable<T>
{
    T Read(string id);
    bool Save(T obj);
    bool HasChanges { get; set; }
}
```

A class that implements the IPersistable<T> interface

```
public class Customer : IPersistable<Customer>
{
    // other members

    public bool HasChanges {
        get => throw new NotImplementedException();
        set => throw new NotImplementedException();
    }

    public Customer Read(string id)
    {
        throw new NotImplementedException();
    }

    public bool Save(Customer obj)
    {
        throw new NotImplementedException();
    }
}
```

Description

- When defining an interface, you can use generics just as you do when defining a class that uses generics.

- When implementing a generic interface that you defined, you can specify the type argument just as you do when implementing generic .NET interfaces.

Figure 15-13   How to code an interface that uses generics

Perspective

In this chapter, you learned how to work with interfaces. Depending on the type of programming that you're doing, you may or may not need to define your own interfaces. However, understanding interfaces is critical to working with .NET and to using an object-oriented language like C#.

You also learned how to define classes and interfaces that use generics. This allows you to create collection classes and interfaces that can accept any data type and still be type-safe. Again, depending on the type of programming that you're doing, you may never need to create these types of custom collection classes. However, understanding generics helps you understand the inner workings of the generic .NET collection classes.

Now that you've completed this chapter, you have all of the critical skills you need for developing object-oriented programs. In the next chapter, though, you'll learn some new skills for documenting and organizing these classes. This will make it easier for you to share the classes that you develop with other programmers.

Terms

interface
implement an interface
multiple inheritance
default interface member
shallow copy
deep copy
default method
generics
constraint

Exercise 15-1   Implement the ICloneable interface

In this exercise, you'll create an app that includes a Customer class that implements the ICloneable interface. This app creates a List<Customer> object that contains clones of a pre-defined Customer object and displays the cloned customers in a list box as shown below. To make this app easier to develop, we'll give you the starting form and classes.

The design of the Clone Customer form

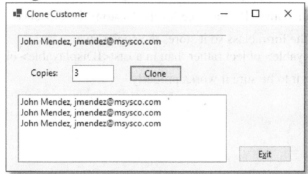

Development procedure

1. Open the app in the C:\C#\Ch15\CloneCustomer directory.

2. Display the code for the form, and notice that the Load event handler creates a Customer object, stores it in a variable named customer, and displays the customer in the label at the top of the form.

3. Create an IDisplayable interface that has a non-default GetDisplayText() method that has no parameters and returns a string.

4. Modify the Customer class so it implements the ICloneable interface and the IDisplayable interface.

5. In the form class, add a private method named MakeCopiesForDisplay() that accepts an ICloneable object and an int and returns a List<IDisplayable> object. This method should use the Clone() method of the ICloneable object to create and return the required number of copies as indicated by the int parameter.

6. Add an event handler for the Click event of the Clone button. This event handler should use the methods in the Validator class to check the value in the Copies text box to be sure it's an integer. Then, it should create a List<IDisplayable> object to hold the objects returned by the MakeCopies-ForDisplay() method. Finally, it should display those objects in the list box.

7. Run the app and test it to make sure it works properly.

Exercise 15-2   Implement an enumerator

In this exercise, you'll modify your solution to exercise 15-1 so the copies are stored in a CustomList<T> object that implements an enumerator.

1. If it isn't already open, open the app in the C:\C#\Ch15\CloneCustomer directory.

2. Add a CustomList<T> class that has a private List<T> field, a public Add() method, a read-only Count property, and a read-only indexer.

3. Implement the IEnumerable<T> interface for the CustomList<T> class.

4. Modify the code in the form class so it stores the copies in a CustomList<IDisplayable> object rather than in a List<IDisplayable> object.

5. Run the app and test it to be sure it works properly.

16

How to organize, document, and test your classes

In the last four chapters, you learned how to develop object-oriented programs that use classes. Now, you'll learn how to organize, document, and test your classes, and you'll learn how to store your classes in class libraries. This makes it easier for other programmers to use your classes.

How to organize your classes

In this topic, you'll learn how to organize apps that use multiple classes by coding more than one class per file, by splitting a single class across multiple files, and by working with namespaces.

How to code multiple classes in a single file

In most cases, you'll code each class that's required by an app in a separate file. If two or more classes are closely related, however, you might want to consider storing them in the same file. Figure 16-1 shows two ways you can do that.

First, you can simply code the class declarations one after the other as shown in the first example in this figure. The advantage of doing that is it makes it easier to manage the files that make up the app. If the classes are large, however, you should place them in separate files even if they are closely related. Otherwise, it may be difficult to locate the code for a specific class.

You can also code two or more classes in a single file by nesting one class within another class. *Nested classes* are useful when one class only makes sense within the context of the other class. The second example in this figure illustrates how to nest two classes. Here, the class named InnerClass is nested within a class named OuterClass.

If you want to refer to the inner class from a class other than the outer class, you have to qualify it with the name of the outer class, as shown in the third example. However, if you only need to refer to the inner class from the outer class, you can do that without qualifying the name of the inner class.

A file with two classes coded one after the other

```
public class Class1
{
    // Body of Class1
}

public class Class2
{
    // Body of Class2
}
```

A file with nested classes

```
public class OuterClass
{
    InnerClass ic = new InnerClass();    // code that uses the inner class
    // Body of OuterClass

    public class InnerClass
    {
        // Body of InnerClass
    }
}
```

Code that refers to the nested class from another class

```
OuterClass.InnerClass inner = new();
```

Description

- When two classes are closely related, it sometimes makes sense to code them in the same file, especially if the classes are small. That way, the project consists of fewer files.

- One way to code two classes in a single file is to code them one after the other.

- Another way to code two classes in a single file is to *nest* one class within the other. This is useful when one class is used only within the context of another class.

- To refer to a nested class from another class, you must qualify it with the name of the class it's nested within.

Figure 16-1   How to code multiple classes in a single file

How to split a single class across multiple files

Figure 16-2 shows how to use *partial classes* to split a single class across multiple files. To do that, you just code the *partial* keyword before the class keyword to indicate that the members of the class may (or may not) be split across multiple source files. Then, when you build the solution, the compiler combines all of the files that it finds for the partial classes to create the class. The resulting intermediate language produced by the compiler is the same as it would be if the entire class was coded in the same source file. One limitation is that all of the partial classes must be in the same namespace and assembly.

If a class that you're working on becomes very large, or if you want to have different programmers work on different parts of a class, you can use partial classes to split the class across two or more files. In this figure, for instance, the first code example shows how to split a Customer class across two files. In most cases, it probably makes more sense to store all of the code for a class that defines a customer in a single source file. However, if necessary, you could split a Customer class across two or more source files.

Visual Studio uses partial classes to separate the code that's generated for a Form class from the code that's entered by the programmer. In this figure, for example, the second example shows the files that Visual Studio uses for a Form class.

Here, the Form1.cs file contains the code that's added to the form by the programmer. The class declaration for this file does three things. First, it marks the Form1 class with the public access modifier. Second, it marks the class as a partial class. Third, it shows that the Form1 class inherits the Form class.

By contrast, the Form1.Designer.cs file contains the code that's generated by Visual Studio. The class declaration for this file marks the class as a partial class. However, since the declaration in the Form1.cs file has already declared the class as public and as a subclass of the Form class, that information isn't duplicated.

Finally, you should realize that a solution won't compile if partial classes contain contradictory information. For example, if one partial class is declared as public and the other as private, you'll get a compile-time error.

C# also lets you code *partial methods* within partial classes. Partial methods are used to implement methods that are similar to events. To code a partial method, you code the signature of the method in one part of the partial class, and you code the implementation of the method in another part of the class. Partial methods are typically used by developers of code generation tools to allow users of those tools to "hook in" to the generated code. Because of that, you won't learn how to code partial methods in this book.

A Customer class that's split into two files

The first file

```
public partial class Customer
{
    // Some members of the Customer class
}
```

The second file

```
public partial class Customer
{
    // The rest of the members of the Customer class
}
```

A Form class that's split into two files

The Form1.cs file

```
public partial class Form1 : Form
{
    // The code for the Form1 class that's added
    // by the programmer
}
```

The Form1.designer.cs file

```
partial class Form1
{
    // The code for the Form1 class that's generated
    // by Visual Studio
}
```

Description

- *Partial classes* can be used to split the code for a class across several files.
- To code a partial class, enter the *partial* keyword before the class keyword.
- All partial classes must belong to the same namespace and the same assembly.
- If a class that you're working on becomes very large, or if you want to have different programmers work on different parts of a class, you can use partial classes to split the class across two or more files.
- Visual Studio uses partial classes to separate the code that's generated for a Form class from the code that's entered by the programmer.

Figure 16-2   How to split a class across multiple files

How to work with namespaces

As you know, a *namespace* is a container that is used to group related classes. For example, all of the .NET classes that are used for creating Windows forms are grouped in the System.Windows.Forms namespace, and all of the classes for working with generic collections are grouped in the System. Collections.Generic namespace.

Every C# class you create must also belong to a namespace. This namespace is identified by a namespace statement that appears near the beginning of the C# source file. This is illustrated in all three of the examples in figure 16-3.

When you create a C# app, Visual Studio creates a namespace that has the same name as the project. Then, it stores all of the classes you create for that project in that namespace. For example, the default form for the Product Maintenance app is stored in a namespace named ProductMaintenance as shown in the first example in this figure. In addition, any other class you create as part of this project is stored in the same namespace.

You can also nest namespaces. In fact, most of the .NET namespaces are nested. For example, System.Collections.Generic is actually a namespace named Generic that's nested within a namespace named Collections that's nested within a namespace named System. As this figure shows, you can create nested namespaces using one of two techniques. First, you can code a namespace statement within another namespace as shown in the second example. This example creates a namespace named Murach.Validation. The more common technique, however, is to simply name all of the nested namespaces on a single namespace statement as shown in the third example.

Although all of the classes of a project are typically stored in the same namespace, those classes use classes that are stored in other namespaces. For example, all C# apps use classes that are defined by .NET. To use a class in another namespace, you typically include a using directive for that namespace at the beginning of the class. Alternatively, you can qualify any reference to the class with the name of the namespace.

For simple C# projects, you don't need to worry about namespaces because Visual Studio takes care of them for you. However, namespaces may become an issue in two situations. The first situation occurs if you copy a class from one project into another project. When you do that, you may need to change the name of the namespace in the class file to the name of the namespace for the project you copied the class into.

The second situation occurs if you want to share a class among several projects by creating a class library. In that case, you should create a separate namespace for the classes in the library. You'll learn how to do that later in this chapter.

Code that declares a namespace

```
namespace ProductMaintenance
{
    public partial class Form1 : Form
    {
        // Body of Form1 class
    }

}
```

Code that declares nested namespaces

```
namespace Murach
{
    namespace Validation
    {
        // Body of Validation namespace
    }
}
```

Another way to nest namespaces

```
namespace Murach.Validation
{
    // Body of Validation namespace
}
```

A using directive that specifies a namespace

```
using Murach.Validation;
```

Description

- A *namespace* is a container that can be used to group related classes. In most cases, all of the classes that make up a C# project are part of the same namespace.

- The namespace statement that appears near the beginning of a source file identifies the namespace that classes defined in that file belong to. By default, when you add a class to a project, it's added to a namespace with the same name as the project.

- Namespaces can be nested. One way to nest namespaces is to include a namespace statement within the body of another namespace. Another way is to code the fully-qualified name of the nested namespace in a namespace statement.

- To use a class in a namespace other than the current namespace, you must either provide a using directive that names the other namespace, or you must qualify the class with the name of the namespace.

Figure 16-3   How to work with namespaces

How to work with file scoped namespaces

In the last figure, you learned how to use namespaces to group related classes. Now, figure 16-4 shows how to use *file scoped* namespaces, which were introduced with C# 10.0. When you use a file scoped namespace, you end the namespace declaration with a semicolon rather than a pair of braces. This removes the indentation required by a traditional, or *block scoped*, namespace. In other words, the body of the namespace is coded at the same level of indentation as the namespace declaration rather than being indented one level. This can save space and make your code easier to read and maintain.

To nest namespaces using a file scoped namespace, you name all the nested namespaces in the namespace declaration as shown in the second example. This is similar to the example you saw in the last figure except this code doesn't use braces or indentation.

This figure also presents the rules for using file scoped namespaces. First, you can only declare one file scoped namespace per file. Second, except for using directives, the file scoped namespace must be declared before all other code in the file. Third, you can't code block scoped namespaces in a file that has a file scoped namespace.

When you use Visual Studio to create a new class, it creates the class within a block scoped namespace by default. You can replace the block scoped namespace with a file scoped namespace simply by typing a semicolon at the end of the namespace name. You can also change the Visual Studio default so class files are generated with file scoped namespaces using the procedure in this figure.

Code that declares a file scoped namespace

```
namespace ProductMaintenance;

public partial class Form1 : Form
{
    // Body of Form1 class
}
```

Code that declares nested namespaces

```
namespace Murach.Validation;
// Body of Validation namespace
```

Rules for file scoped namespaces

- Each file can declare only one file scoped namespace.
- Only using directives can precede the declaration of a file scoped namespace in a file.
- A file cannot declare both a file scoped namespace and block scoped namespaces.

The Options dialog in Visual Studio

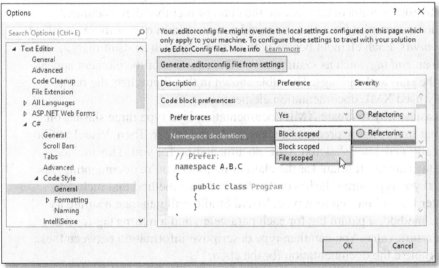

How to configure Visual Studio to generate file scoped namespaces

1. Select Tools→Options to open the Options dialog.
2. In the left pane, expand the Text Editor, C#, and Code Style groups, and then select the General category.
3. In the right pane, scroll to the Code Block Preferences section in the first box, select File Scoped from the Namespace Declarations drop-down list, and click OK.

Description

- C# 10.0 introduced *file scoped namespaces*, which eliminates the need for braces and indentation.

Figure 16-4   How to work with file scoped namespaces

How to document your classes

In this topic, you'll learn how to add documentation to your classes. This can make it easier for other programmers to use your classes.

How to add XML documentation to a class

As you already know, you can add general comments to any C# program by using comment statements that begin with a pair of slashes. You can also use a documentation feature called *XML documentation* to create documentation for the classes and class members you create. XML documentation can make your classes easier for other programmers to use by providing information about the function of the class and its members. Then, this information appears in screen tips that are displayed when you work with the class in Visual Studio.

Figure 16-5 shows how to add XML documentation to a class. Although XML documentation is based on XML syntax, you don't have to know much about XML to use it. As you can see, XML documentation lines begin with three slashes and appear immediately before the class or member they document.

The documentation for a class or member can contain one or more *documentation elements*. Each element begins with a *start tag*, such as <summary>, and ends with an *end tag*, such as </summary>. The contents of the element appear between the start and end tags. The table shown in this figure lists the most commonly used XML documentation elements.

The easiest way to create XML documentation is to type three slashes on the line that immediately precedes a class or class member. Then, Visual Studio automatically generates skeleton XML documentation for you. This includes whatever tags are appropriate for the class or member you're documenting. For example, if you type three slashes on the line before a method that includes a parameter list and has a return type, Visual Studio will generate a summary tag for the method, a param tag for each parameter, and a returns tag for the method's return value. You can then type descriptive information between these tags to complete the documentation for the class.

Part of a Validator class that includes XML documentation

```
/// <summary>
/// Provides static methods for validating data.
/// </summary>
public static class Validator
{
    /// <summary>
    /// The character sequence to terminate each line
    /// in the validation message.
    /// </summary>
    public static string LineEnd { get; set; } = "\n";

    /// <summary>
    /// Checks whether the user entered a value.
    /// </summary>
    /// <param name="value">The value to be validated.</param>
    /// <param name="name">A name that identifies the value
    /// to be validated.</param>
    /// <returns>An error message if the user didn't enter
    /// a value.</returns>
    public static string IsPresent(string value, string name)
    {
        string msg = "";
        if (value == "")
        {
            msg = $"{name} is a required field.{LineEnd}";
        }
        return msg;
    }
    .
    .
    .
}
```

XML elements you can use for class documentation

Element	Description
`<summary>`	Provides a general description of a class, property, method, or other element.
`<value>`	Describes the value of a property.
`<returns>`	Describes the return value of a method.
`<param name="name">`	Describes a parameter of a method.

Description

- You can use special *XML tags* in C# source code to provide class documentation.
- An *XML documentation* line begins with three slashes. Each *documentation element* begins with a *start tag*, such as <summary>, and ends with an *end tag*, such as </summary>. You code the description of the element between these tags.
- If you type three slashes on the line immediately preceding a class or member declaration, Visual Studio automatically generates empty elements for you. Then, you just fill in the text that's appropriate for each element.

Figure 16-5   How to add XML documentation to a class

How to view the XML documentation

Once you add XML documentation, Visual Studio will use that documentation when it displays the screen tips that appear in the Visual Studio Code Editor window. This is illustrated by figure 16-6.

The first example shows that if you type the Validator class and a period, the IntelliSense feature displays a list of the members of the Validator class. Then, you can use the arrow keys to select the IsPresent() method that's shown in the previous figure. When you do, Visual Studio displays a screen tip that includes the signature of the IsPresent() method along with the summary that's provided by the XML documentation.

The second example shows what happens if you enter the IsPresent() method and type its opening parenthesis. Then, Visual Studio displays a screen tip that includes the description of the value parameter that's provided by the XML documentation that's shown in the previous figure.

A screen tip that displays the documentation for a method

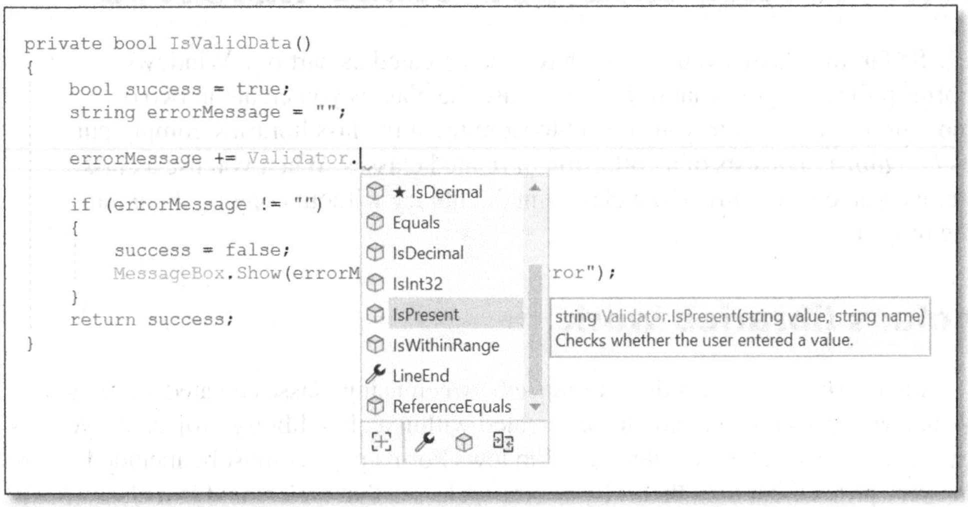

```
private bool IsValidData()
{
    bool success = true;
    string errorMessage = "";

    errorMessage += Validator.|

    if (errorMessage != "")              ★ IsDecimal
    {                                      Equals
        success = false;                   IsDecimal
        MessageBox.Show(errorM             IsInt32          ror");
    }                                      IsPresent
    return success;                        IsWithinRange      string Validator.IsPresent(string value, string name)
}                                          LineEnd            Checks whether the user entered a value.
                                           ReferenceEquals
```

A screen tip that displays the documentation for a parameter

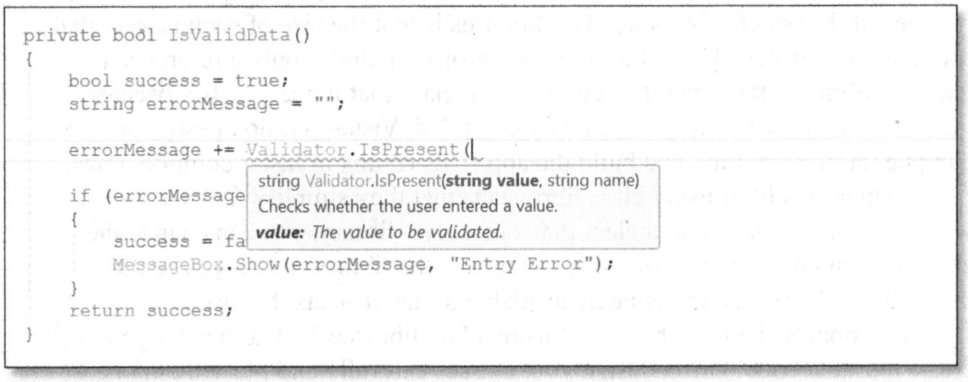

```
private bool IsValidData()
{
    bool success = true;
    string errorMessage = "";

    errorMessage += Validator.IsPresent (|

    if (errorMessage        string Validator.IsPresent(string value, string name)
    {                       Checks whether the user entered a value.
        success = fa        value: The value to be validated.
        MessageBox.Show(errorMessage, "Entry Error");
    }
    return success;
}
```

Description

- The XML documentation that you add to a class is also visible in the screen tips that are displayed in the Code Editor.

Figure 16-6   How to view the XML documentation

How to create and use class libraries

So far, the classes you've seen have been created as part of a Windows Forms project. If you want to be able to use the classes you create in two or more projects, however, you'll want to store them in class libraries. Simply put, a *class library* consists of a collection of related classes. When you use a class library, you can use any of the classes in the library without copying them into the project.

How class libraries work

Figure 16-7 illustrates the difference between using classes created within a Windows Forms project and classes created within a class library project. As you can see, classes that are created in a Windows Forms project must be included in every project that uses them. By contrast, classes that are created in a class library project exist separately from any project that uses them. Because of that, they are available to any project that has access to the class library.

One of the benefits of using class libraries is that the size of each project that uses them is reduced. That's because each project includes only a reference to the class library rather than the code for each class that it needs. Also, because the classes in a class library are already compiled, Visual Studio doesn't have to compile them every time you build the app. This results in faster compile times.

Another benefit of using class libraries is that they simplify maintenance. If you must make a change to a class that's in a class library, you can change the class without changing any of the apps that use the library. When you're done, the modified library is immediately available to the projects that use it.

But probably the main benefit of using class libraries is that they let you create reusable code. If you design your classes carefully and place them in a library, you can reuse them in other projects that require similar functions. In most cases, you'll use the classes directly. However, you can also use them as base classes for the new classes that you add to your projects.

Two projects that use the Validator class

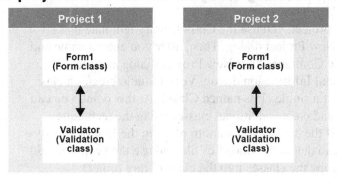

Two projects that access the Validator class via a class library

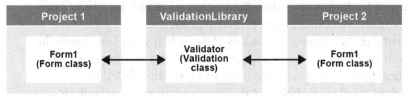

Description

- *Class libraries* provide a central location for storing classes that are used by two or more apps.

- When you store a class in a class library, you don't have to include the class in each app that uses it. Instead, you include a reference to the class library in those apps.

- When you modify a class in a class library, the changes are immediately available to all apps that use the library.

- To create a class library, you develop a class library project. Then, when you build the project, Visual Studio creates a *DLL file* for the class library. It's this *DLL* that you refer to from any app that needs to use the class library.

Figure 16-7   How class libraries work

How to create a class library project

To create a class library project, you use the Class Library template that's available from the Create a New Project dialog. Then, after you enter a name and location for the project in the Configure Your New Project dialog and select a framework from the Additional Information dialog, Visual Studio creates a class library project that consists of a single class named Class1. At this point, you can enter the code for this class and create additional classes using the techniques you've already learned. Or, if the classes you want to place in the library already exist in other projects, you can delete the Class1.cs file and use the Project→Add Existing Item command to copy the classes into the class library project.

Figure 16-8 shows a class library project named ValidationLibrary that includes a class named Validator. This is the same Validator class that was presented in chapter 12. In this case, though, the class is stored in a class library project instead of in the Windows Forms project that uses it.

Notice the name of the namespace for this class. When you place classes in a class library, you should create a namespace that indicates the purpose of the classes in the namespace. In this case, the namespace is Murach.Validation.

Also notice that this class includes XML documentation. By default, this documentation isn't visible to code that uses the class library. To generate a file that contains this documentation so it is visible to code that uses the class library, you can configure the project as described in this figure.

When you're done designing a class library, you build it to create an assembly. The assembly for a class library is a *DLL file*, or just *DLL*. This is a file with the *dll* extension that contains the executable code for the class library. By default, this file includes debugging information and is stored in a subfolder of the bin\Debug folder beneath the project folder for the project. The name of the subfolder reflects the version of .NET you're using. If you're using .NET 7.0, for example, the subfolder is named net7.0.

Because you don't want the final version of a class library to include debugging information, you'll want to create a DLL file without this information when you're done testing the class library. To do that, you change the solution configuration from Debug to Release as shown in this figure before you build the class library. Then, the DLL file is stored in a subfolder of the bin\Release folder, and you can include a reference to this file in other projects as described in the next topic.

As you're developing a class library, it's often useful to create the class library as a project in a solution that contains a project that uses it. That way, you can use the project to test the class library. To add a new class library project to an existing solution, right-click the solution in the Solution Explorer, then choose Add→New Project. You can also add an existing class library project to a solution by choosing Add→Existing Project. If you do that, though, keep in mind that you're working with the original class library project, not a copy of it. So any changes you make affect the original class library.

A class library project

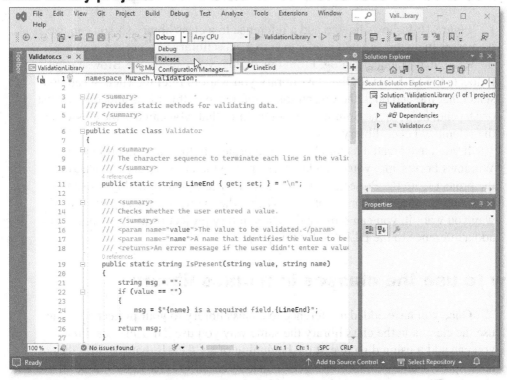

Description

- To create a class library project, display the Create a New Project dialog. Then, select the Class Library template and click the Next button; enter a name and location for the project and click the Next button; and select the framework for the project and click the Create button.

- By default, a class library project includes a single class named Class1. You can modify this class any way you want or delete it from the project. You can also add new classes using the Project→Add Class command, and you can add classes from another project using the Project→Add Existing Item command.

- You should create a namespace for your class library that indicates the purpose of the classes contained in the library. In this example, the namespace is Murach.Validation.

- If you add XML documentation to a class in a class library, you will need to generate a file that contains this documentation before it is visible to code that uses the class. To do that, right-click the project in the Solution Explorer and select the Properties command to display the Properties window. Then, expand the Build group, select the Output category, and check the "Generate a file containing API documentation" check box.

- To compile a class library project, select the Release option from the Solution Configurations combo box in the Standard toolbar as shown above. Then, select the Build→Build Solution command. The class library is compiled into a DLL file that's stored in a folder for the project with a name like bin\Release\net7.0

Figure 16-8   How to create a class library project

How to add a reference to a class library

Figure 16-9 shows how to add a reference to a class library so you can use its classes in an app. To add a reference to a class library in a project, you use the Reference Manager dialog. From this dialog, you can use the Browse page to locate the DLL file for the class library you want to refer to. Then, when you select that file and click the OK button, a reference to this file is added to the list of Dependencies in the Solution Explorer. After that, you can use the classes in the referenced class library.

If you have created a class library as a project in the same solution with a Windows Forms app, you can add a reference to the class library by selecting the project from the Projects page of the Reference Manager dialog instead of browsing for the DLL for the project. Then, when you have the app working the way you want it, you can remove the class library project from the solution and add a reference to the DLL file for this project.

How to use the classes in a class library

Once you have added a reference to a class library to your project, you can use the classes in the class library the same way you use .NET classes. First, you can add a using directive at the beginning of a C# class that specifies the namespace used by the class library to make it easier to refer to the classes it contains. The code example in figure 16-9, for instance, shows a using directive for the Murach.Validation namespace.

After you add the using directive, you can use the classes in the library as if they were part of the same project. A complication arises, however, if the class you want to refer to in the class library has the same name as a class in another namespace in the project or has the same name as the namespace that contains the project (which is usually the same as the project name). In that case, you have to qualify the name of the class so C# knows where to look for it.

A project that includes a reference to a class library

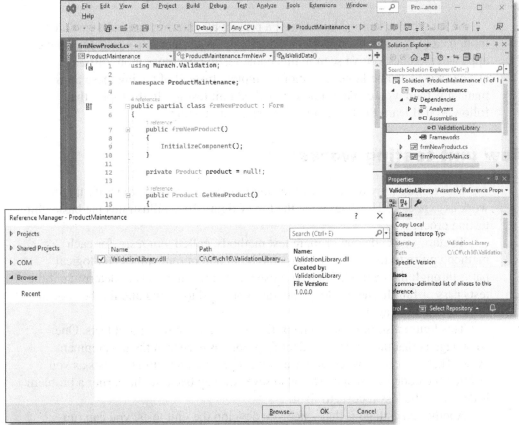

A using directive that simplifies access to the validation class library

```
using Murach.Validation;
```

How to use a class library

- Add a reference to the class library to your project by right-clicking Dependencies in the Solution Explorer and selecting the Add Project Reference command. In the Reference Manager dialog, display the Browse page, click the Browse button, locate the DLL for the class library, select it, and click the OK button.

- If the class library project is included in the same solution as the client project, that project will appear in the list on the Projects page. Then, you can add a reference for the class library by selecting the project name and clicking the OK button.

- Once you have added a reference to the class library, you can include a using directive for the class library's namespace in any class that uses it. You can then use the classes in the class library without qualification. Alternatively, you can qualify the class names with the namespace name you assigned to the library.

Figure 16-9   How to use a class library

How to implement unit testing

So far, you've learned how to test a project by entering valid and invalid input data to be sure that it works in every case. Although this works for simple apps like the ones you've seen in this book, testing becomes more difficult as your apps become larger and more complex. Instead of testing these apps manually, then, you can use a process called unit testing. In the topics that follow, you'll learn the basic skills for using unit testing.

How unit testing works

Unit testing provides a way of testing individual methods to verify that they work as expected. The diagram at the top of figure 16-10 illustrates the basic unit testing process.

To start, you code one or more test methods, called *unit tests*, for each method you're testing to test all possible input and output values and logical paths through the method. Then, you execute the test methods to determine if the tests pass or fail. If one or more tests fail, you need to debug and fix the code and then run the tests again.

This figure also presents some of the advantages of using unit tests. One advantage is that they help you identify problems earlier in the development cycle. That's because, when you use unit testing, you develop the tests as you develop the code for an app. This also saves money because the earlier a problem is detected, the less it costs to fix it.

Another advantage is that, once you develop the unit tests, you can run them anytime you make a change to the code. That helps you quickly detect any problems that were introduced by the new code. It also makes debugging easier because you know that if a test fails, the problem occurred because of the new code. In addition, you don't have to run the program and retest it each time you change the code like you do with traditional testing.

Before you learn how to create unit tests, you should know that, by default, Visual Studio provides support for three unit testing frameworks for .NET projects: MSTest, xUnit, and NUnit. Although other unit testing frameworks are available, the required extensions must be installed before they can be used with Visual Studio. In this chapter, you'll learn how to use MSTest, the framework that was developed by Microsoft.

The unit testing process

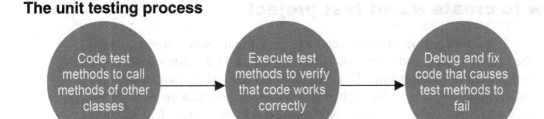

Advantages of using unit tests

- Unit testing helps you find problems earlier in the development cycle than would be possible if you tested all your methods manually.

- You can run the unit tests for a class each time you change it to quickly detect any problems that were introduced.

- You can develop and test an app more quickly because you don't have to run the app and retest it each time you change the code. Instead, you can use unit tests to test just the code that was changed without running the app.

- Unit testing makes debugging easier because when a test fails, you only need to debug the most recent code changes.

Description

- *Unit testing* provides a way to write code that automatically tests individual methods, called *units*, to verify that they work properly in isolation.

- You can use *unit tests* to test the methods in any type of class, including business classes, database classes, and form classes.

- You code unit tests within a separate project that's part of the solution that contains the classes to be tested.

- By default, Visual Studio provides for creating three types of test projects for .NET apps: MSTest, xUnit, and NUnit. In this chapter, you'll learn how to use MSTest.

Figure 16-10   How unit testing works

How to create a unit test project

To use unit testing, you add a unit test project to the solution that contains the project with the code you want to test. Figure 16-11 describes how to do that. Here, a unit test project named ValidationLibraryTests has been added to the solution that contains the ValidationLibrary project. Note that the name of the unit test project clearly indicates the project that contains the code it will test. This is a best practice when creating unit test projects.

When you first create a unit test project, it contains a single class named UnitTest1. In most cases, you'll want to change the name of this class and the file that contains it so they identify the class to be tested. For example, because this unit test class will be used to test the class named Validator in the ValidationLibrary project, an appropriate name for this class would be ValidatorTests.

In most cases, each class in a unit test project will test one class in another project. If the project you're testing contains more than one class, then, you'll want to add additional classes to the unit test project. You can do that using the technique you learned in chapter 12. Note, however, that the new class will contain the default code shown in that chapter. In other words, it won't contain the code that's generated for the default class in a unit test project. Because of that, you'll have to add the required code as shown in the next figure.

By default, the unit test class contains a single method named TestMethod1(). You can add code to this method to perform a specific test, and you can change the name of the method to indicate the test that's being performed. You can also add test methods to the class. You'll learn more about coding test methods in the next figure.

Before you can execute the tests in a unit test project, you must include a reference to the project it will test. Because the project is in the same solution, you can use the Projects page of the Reference Manager dialog you learned about in figure 16-9 to add this reference.

A Visual Studio solution with a unit test project

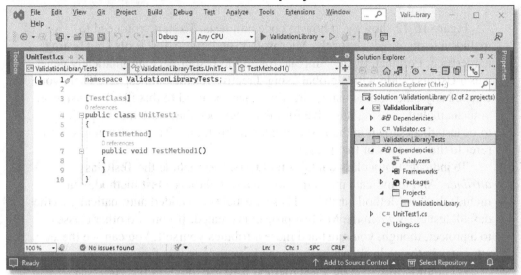

How to add a unit test project to a solution

1. Right-click on the solution in the Solution Explorer and select Add→New Project to display the Create a New Project dialog.

2. Select the MSTest Test Project template, and click the Next button to display the Configure Your New Project dialog.

3. Enter a name for the project. The location will default to the folder for the current solution, which is usually what you want.

4. Click the Next button, select a framework from the Additional Information dialog, and click the Create button.

Description

- The name for a unit test project should indicate the project that's being tested. In addition, the names of the classes within the unit test project should indicate the specific classes being tested.

- By default, a test project includes a single class named UnitTest1 with a single method named TestMethod1(). You can modify this class any way you want, and you can add new classes using the Project→Add Class command.

- Each class in a unit test project should test one class in the project being tested. Each method in a unit test class should test one aspect of a method in the associated class. You can use as many methods as you need to test all aspects of all the methods in the class.

- To test the code in a project, a unit test class must include a reference to that project. You can add this reference using the Projects page of the Reference Manager dialog as described in figure 16-9.

Figure 16-11   How to create a unit test project

How to code unit tests

Figure 16-12 shows you how to code unit tests. To start, you need to include a using directive for the Microsoft.VisualStudio.TestTools.UnitTesting namespace. Fortunately, the template for an MSTest project automatically generates a Usings.cs file with a global using directive for this namespace. Then, you can add any other global using directives that you need to this file. For instance, you can include a using directive for the namespace that contains the project to be tested, as shown in the first example in this figure. This makes it easier to refer to the methods of that project.

To indicate that a class contains unit tests, you include the TestClass *attribute*. And to indicate that a method in a test class is a test method, you include the TestMethod attribute. These attributes are added automatically to the default test class when the MSTest project is created. If you add other classes to a project, though, you must add these attributes yourself. You can see these attributes in the code shown in the second example in this figure.

A common way to code a test method is to use the *Arrange, Act, Assert (AAA) pattern*. With this pattern, you start by creating instances of any objects and initializing any variables that will be passed as arguments to the method being tested. Then, you call the method with those arguments. Finally, you test the result of the method to be sure it's what you expected. To do that, you typically use methods of the Assert class like the ones listed at the top of this figure.

The test methods in this figure illustrate how this works. Here, the first method tests that the IsDecimal() method returns an empty string if a valid decimal is passed to it. To do that, it uses the AreEqual() method of the Assert class. The second method is similar, except it tests whether the error message that's returned by the IsDecimal() method contains the field name that's passed to it.

Notice that each of these methods tests a single aspect of the IsDecimal() method. This is a best practice when coding test methods. In this case, the first method tests that a valid value is handled correctly, and the second method tests that an invalid value is handled correctly. This makes sure that the logic of the method works correctly. Of course, more complex methods would require many more methods to test them. That's particularly true if a method interacts with external data, such as a file or database.

Finally, notice that each method returns void and doesn't accept any parameters. This is a requirement for all test methods.

To keep your unit tests organized, it's a good idea to name them consistently. The names of the test methods shown here, for example, consist of the name of the method being tested, followed by an underscore and a description of the test being performed. When you use names like these, it's easy to identify the method that's being tested and the test that's being performed.

Commonly used static methods of the Assert class

Method	Description
AreEqual(expected, actual)	Tests whether the actual object is equal to the expected object and throws an exception if the two objects are not equal.
AreNotEqual(expected, actual)	Tests whether the actual object is not equal to the expected object and throws an exception if the two objects are equal.
IsFalse(booleanExpression)	Tests whether the Boolean expression is false and throws an exception if it is true.
IsTrue(booleanExpression)	Tests whether the Boolean expression is true and throws an exception if it is false.

The Usings.cs file

```
global using Microsoft.VisualStudio.TestTools.UnitTesting;
global using Murach.Validation;
```

Unit tests for the Validator class

```
[TestClass]
public class ValidatorTests
{
    [TestMethod]
    public void IsDecimal_ValidValueReturnsEmptyString()
    {
        string expected = "";                                  // arrange
        var result = Validator.IsDecimal("3.14", "Name");      // act
        Assert.AreEqual(expected, result);                     // assert
    }

    [TestMethod]
    public void IsDecimal_InvalidValueContainsFieldName()
    {
        string name = "Test field";                            // arrange
        var result = Validator.IsDecimal("three", name);       // act
        Assert.IsTrue(result.Contains(name));                  // assert
    }
    ...
}
```

Description

- You can store global using directives for your project in the Usings.cs file that's generated when you create an MSTest project.

- You must include a TestClass *attribute* before each test class declaration to indicate that the class contains unit tests. You must also include the TestMethod attribute before each method in a test class to indicate that it's a test method.

- Each unit test class should include as many methods as necessary to test all possible aspects of the methods in the class being tested.

- A common way to code a test method is to use the *Arrange, Act, Assert (AAA) pattern*. First, you create the objects and initialize the variables to be passed to the method being tested (Arrange). Then, you call the method with the arranged arguments (Act). Finally, you use methods of the Assert class to test that the result is as expected (Assert).

Figure 16-12　How to code unit tests

How to run unit tests

When you're done coding your unit tests, you need to build the project that contains them. Then, you can run the unit tests. To do that, you use the Test Explorer window shown in figure 16-13.

The first four buttons in the toolbar at the top of this window let you run all tests in the project, run selected tests, repeat the last test run, and run any tests that failed in the previous run. If you click the arrowhead to the right of the second button, you can use the menu that's displayed to select the tests that are run. You can see this menu in the first screen in this figure. Note that before you use the Run command, you must select the tests you want to run. You can do that using standard Windows techniques.

You can also use this menu to debug tests and the methods they're testing as they're run. To do that, set one or more breakpoints in the tests you want to debug, and then select one of the Debug commands. Then, when a test enters break mode, you can use the skills you learned in chapter 11 to debug the test and the method it's testing.

Once a test run is complete, you can click on any of the nodes in the left pane of the Test Explorer to display a summary of the test run in the right pane. In the second screen in this figure, for example, you can see the summary for the IsDecimal_ValidValueReturnsEmptyString unit test. The Test Explorer also shows how long it took to run each unit test. If a unit test is taking too long to run, you may want to consider modifying its code so it runs more quickly.

If any of your unit tests fail, it means that either the method you're testing isn't working properly or the unit test itself isn't coded properly. In either case, you'll need to debug and fix your code until the unit tests pass.

When you use unit testing, you should re-run your unit tests often. In fact, many programmers run their unit tests every time they change the code for a project. To make that easier to do, you can configure the Test Explorer to run the unit tests automatically each time a project is built. To do that, just click the arrowhead to the right of the Settings icon and select the Run Tests After Build option from the menu that's displayed.

The Test Explorer window before the tests are run

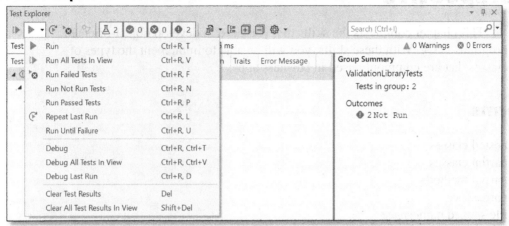

The Test Explorer window with the results of a test run

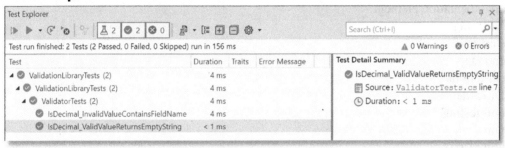

Description

- To run and view the results of unit tests in Visual Studio, you use the Test Explorer. To display the Test Explorer window, use the Test→Test Explorer command.

- The left pane of the Test Explorer window displays a hierarchy of the unit test project, its namespace, the classes it contains, and the methods in those classes.

- The right pane of the Test Explorer window displays the results of the group or individual test you select in the left pane.

- The buttons at the left side of the toolbar let you run all tests, run selected tests, repeat the last test, and run failed tests.

- You can use the menu that appears when you click the arrowhead to the right of the Run button to determine what tests are run. If you select one of the Debug commands, you can set breakpoints and debug the test and the method it's testing using the debugging features presented in chapter 11.

- The numbers to the right of the Run buttons show how many tests are in the class, how many tests passed, how many tests failed, and how many tests haven't been run.

- If a test method fails, you need to check that the test method and the method it's testing are coded properly.

Figure 16-13   How to run unit tests

Perspective

This chapter completes the skills that you need to develop object-oriented programs in C#. With these skills, you will be able to implement the types of classes that are commonly used in business apps.

Terms

nested classes
partial classes
partial methods
namespace
file scoped namespace
block scoped namespace
XML documentation
documentation element
XML tag
start tag
end tag
class library
DLL file
unit testing
unit
unit test
attribute
Arrange, Act, Assert (AAA) pattern

Exercise 16-1 Add XML documentation to a class

1. Open the app in the C:\C#\Ch16\CustomerMaintenance directory. Then, add XML documentation for each member of the Customer class.

2. Open the Add Customer form, and activate IntelliSense for each constructor, property, and method of the Customer class. Note how Visual Studio automatically displays the XML documentation in the screen tip.

3. Continue experimenting until you're comfortable with how XML documentation works. Then, close the solution.

Exercise 16-2   Create and use a class library

In this exercise, you'll create a class library that contains the Validator class. Then, you'll use that class library with the CustomerMaintenance app.

1. Create a new Class Library project named ValidationLib. Then, delete the empty Class1.cs file, and add the Validator.cs file from the CustomerMaintenance project that you worked on in the previous exercise.

2. Change the namespace in the Validator class to Murach.Validation. Then, change the solution configuration to Release, use the Build→Build Solution command to build the class library, and close the solution.

3. Open the app that you used in the previous exercise, delete the Validator.cs file, and add a reference to the ValidationLib assembly you created in step 2. Then, open the Add Customer form and add a using directive for the Murach.Validation namespace.

4. Run the project and test it to make sure the validation works correctly.

Exercise 16-3   Create and run unit tests

In this exercise, you'll create a unit test project that tests one of the methods of the Validator class in the class library you worked on in exercise 16-2.

1. Open the app in the C:\C#\Ch16\ValidationLib directory.

2. Add a new MSTest Test Project to the solution called ValidationLibTests. In the MSTest project, add a reference to the ValidationLib project so you can test the methods in the ValidationLib project.

3. Add a global using directive for the Murach.Validation namespace to the Usings.cs file in the MSTest project.

4. Rename the default class file in the MSTest project to ValidatorTests.

5. Rename the default test method to indicate that it will test that the IsWithinRange() method returns an empty string when it receives a valid value. Then, add code to this method that uses the AreEqual() method of the Assert class to test that the IsWithinRange() method works properly when a valid value is passed to it. As you do that, be sure to use the AAA pattern as described in figure 16-12.

6. Add a test method to the ValidatorTests class to test what happens if the value that's passed to the IsWithinRange() method is smaller than the minimum value. To do that, use the IsTrue() method of the Assert class to test that the method returns the expected error message.

7. Add another test method to test what happens if the value that's passed to the IsWithinRange() method is larger than the maximum value. The easiest way to do that is to copy the method you added in step 6, and then change the method name and the value that's passed to the IsWithinRange() method.

8. Build the project and correct any errors that are detected.

9. Display the Test Explorer window. Then, point to the first four buttons in the toolbar to see what they do, and display the menu for the second button to see what it includes. In addition, point to the next four buttons to see what information they display.

10. Expand the nodes in the left pane of the Test Explorer window until you can see the test methods, and select the first method. Click the Run button to execute the selected method. When it's done, review the information in the right pane of the Test Explorer window.

11. If the test fails, try to determine the cause of the problem. If necessary, set a breakpoint in the test method and then select the Debug Selected Tests command from the Run drop-down menu. When the breakpoint is reached, notice that you can use the debugging features you learned about in chapter 11, including displaying data tips, stepping through the code, and using the debugging windows. If you determine the cause of the error, fix it and then run the test again by clicking the Repeat Last Run button.

12. Click the Run All Tests button to execute all three test methods to be sure they pass. If any of the tests fail, you can debug them as described in step 11 and then run them again until they all pass.

Section 4

Basic skills for working with data

In the previous section of this book, you learned how to create and work with classes. When a class corresponds to a business entity, it's used to create objects that store the data for that type of entity. The Product class used by the apps in the previous section, for example, was used to create Product objects that stored product data. If you looked at the code for the ProductDB class for those apps, you saw that the product data was stored in a text file.

To help you understand how the code in this class works, chapter 17 teaches you the basic skills for working with file I/O. That includes reading and writing data in two of the file types that are supported by .NET: text files and binary files. Since you won't need to use files in all your apps, you may want to just give this chapter a quick first reading. Then, you can return to it for reference whenever you need the skills that it presents.

In chapter 18, you'll learn how to use a feature of C# called LINQ to query the data in a data source. Although you're most likely to use LINQ to work with Entity objects as shown in chapter 20, chapter 18 will introduce you to many of the basic skills by showing you how to use LINQ with arrays and collections.

17

How to work with file I/O

In this chapter, you'll learn how to work with file input and output, or file I/O, for two type of files: text files and binary files. Although binary files are required for some apps, text files are preferred whenever possible because they are more portable and less platform dependent. Because of that, you'll learn how to work with text files before learning how to work with binary files. But first, you'll learn about the classes you use for working with both types of files.

An introduction to the System.IO classes

The System.IO namespace provides a variety of classes for working with files and for managing directories, files, and paths. You'll be introduced to those classes in the topics that follow. In addition, you'll learn about the types of files and streams supported by the System.IO classes and how they're used to perform file I/O.

The classes for managing directories, files, and paths

Figure 17-1 summarizes the classes in the System.IO namespace that you can use to manage directories, files, and paths. As you can see, you can use the methods of the Directory class to create or delete a directory or determine if a directory exists. And you can use the methods of the File class to copy, delete, or move a file, or to determine if a file exists. Since the methods for both of these classes are static methods, you call them directly from the class.

The first example in this figure shows how to use some of the methods of the Directory class. This code starts by declaring a string that holds the path to a directory that contains a file to be processed. Then, an if statement uses the Exists() method of the Directory class to determine if this directory exists. If it doesn't, it uses the CreateDirectory() method to create it.

The second example shows how to use some of the methods of the File class. This code declares a string that will hold the path to a file named Products. txt. Then, the if statement that follows uses the Exists() method of the File class to determine if this file exists. If it does, it uses the Delete() method to delete it.

Note that you do not have to code a using directive for the System.IO namespace before working with any of its classes. In addition, you do not have to qualify each reference to a class with the namespace. That's because, as you learned in chapter 10, Visual Studio generates global using directives for several commonly used namespaces when you create a Windows Forms app, and one of those namespaces is System.IO.

You should know that the Directory and File classes have corresponding DirectoryInfo and FileInfo classes that let you create an instance of an object that represents a directory or a file. This is useful if you're going to access a directory or file multiple times. The DirectoryInfo and FileInfo classes are beyond the scope of this book, but you can refer to the online documentation for more information.

System.IO classes used to work with files and directories

Class	Description
Directory	Used to create, edit, delete, or get information on directories (folders).
File	Used to create, edit, delete, or get information on files.
Path	Used to get path information from a variety of platforms.

Common methods of the Directory class

Method	Description
Exists(path)	Returns a Boolean value indicating whether a directory exists.
CreateDirectory(path)	Creates the directories in a specified path.
Delete(path)	Deletes the directory at the specified path. The directory must be empty.
Delete(path, recursive)	Deletes the directory at the specified path. If true is specified for the recursive argument, any subdirectories and files in the directory are deleted. If false is specified, the directory must be empty.

Common methods of the File class

Method	Description
Exists(path)	Returns a Boolean value indicating whether a file exists.
Delete(path)	Deletes a file.
Copy(source, dest)	Copies a file from a source path to a destination path.
Move(source, dest)	Moves a file from a source path to a destination path.

Code that uses some of the Directory methods

```
string dir = @"C:\C#\Files\";
if (!Directory.Exists(dir))
    Directory.CreateDirectory(dir);
```

Code that uses some of the File methods

```
string path = dir + "Products.txt";
if (File.Exists(path))
    File.Delete(path);
```

Description

- The classes for managing directories, files, and paths are stored in the System. IO namespace. Visual Studio 2022 generates a global using directive for this namespace by default when you create a new project. See chapter 10 for details.
- All of the methods of the Directory, File, and Path classes are static methods.

Figure 17-1   The classes for managing directories, files, and paths

How files and streams work

When you use the System.IO classes to do *I/O operations* (or *file I/O*), you can use two different kinds of files: *text files* or *binary files*. To illustrate, figure 17-2 shows the contents of a text file and a binary file as they look when displayed in a text editor. Although both of these files contain the same data, they look quite different.

In a *text file*, all of the data is stored as text characters (or strings). Often, the *fields* in this type of file are separated by delimiters like tab or pipe characters, and the *records* are separated by end of line characters. Although you can't see the end of line characters in this figure, you know they're there because each record starts at the beginning of a new line.

By contrast, the data in a *binary file* can include text characters as well as data types. Because of that, the data isn't always displayed properly within a text editor. For example, you can't tell what the value of the Price field is in each of these records because this field has a decimal data type. Also, since the records in a binary file don't end with end of line characters, one record isn't displayed on each line in a text editor.

To handle I/O operations with text and binary files, .NET uses *streams*. You can think of a stream as the flow of data from one location to another. For instance, an *output stream* can flow from the internal memory of an app to a disk file, and an *input stream* can flow from a disk file to internal memory. When you work with a text file, you use a *text stream*. When you work with a binary file, you use a *binary stream*.

To work with streams and files using the System.IO namespace, you use the classes summarized in this figure. To create a stream that connects to a file, for example, you use the FileStream class. Then, to read data from a text stream, you use the StreamReader class. And to read data from a binary stream, you use the BinaryReader class. You'll learn how to use all of these classes later in this chapter.

Since you can store all the built-in numeric data types in a binary file, this type of file is more efficient for apps that work with numeric data. By contrast, the numeric data in a text file is stored as characters, so each field must be converted to a numeric data type before it can be used in arithmetic operations.

When you save a text or binary file, you can use any extension you want for the file name. In this book, though, *txt* is used as the extension for all text files, and *dat* is used for all binary files. For instance, the text file in this figure is named Products.txt, and the binary file is named Products.dat.

A text file displayed in a text editor

A binary file displayed in a text editor

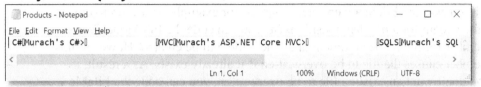

Two types of files

Type	Description
Text	A file that contains text (string) characters. The *fields* in each record are typically delimited by special characters like tab or pipe characters, and the *records* are typically delimited by new line characters.
Binary	A file that can contain a variety of data types.

Two types of streams

Stream	Description
Text	Used to transfer text data.
Binary	Used to transfer binary data.

System.IO classes used to work with files and streams

Class	Description
FileStream	Provides access to input and output files.
StreamReader	Used to read a stream of characters.
StreamWriter	Used to write a stream of characters.
BinaryReader	Used to read a stream of binary data.
BinaryWriter	Used to write a stream of binary data.

Description

- An *input file* is a file that is read by a program; an *output file* is a file that is written by a program. Input and output operations are often referred to as *I/O operations* or *file I/O*.

- A *stream* is the flow of data from one location to another. To write data, you use an *output stream*. To read data, you use an *input stream*. A single stream can also be used for both input and output.

- To read and write text files, you use *text streams*. To read and write binary files, you use *binary streams*.

Figure 17-2   How files and streams work

How to use the FileStream class

To create a stream that connects to a file, you use the FileStream class as shown in figure 17-3. In the syntax at the top of this figure, you can see its arguments. The first two, which specify the path for the file and the mode in which it will be opened, are required. The last two, which specify how the file can be accessed and shared, are optional.

To code the mode, access, and share arguments, you use the FileMode, FileAccess, and FileShare enumerations. If, for example, you want to create a file stream for a file that doesn't exist, you can code the FileMode.Create member for the mode argument and a new file will be created. However, this member causes the file to be overwritten if it already exists. As a result, if you don't want an existing file to be overwritten, you can code the FileMode. CreateNew member for this argument. Then, if the file already exists, an exception is thrown as explained in the next figure.

For the access argument, you can code members that let you read records from the file, write records to the file, or both read and write records. If you omit this argument, the default is to allow both reading and writing of records.

For the share argument, you can code members that let other users read records, write records, or both read and write records at the same time that the first user is accessing the file. Or, you can code the None member to prevent sharing of the file. What you're trying to avoid is two users writing to a file at the same time, which could lead to errors. So if you code the access argument as ReadWrite or Write, you can code the share argument as Read or None. On the other hand, if you code the access argument as Read, you may want to code the share argument as Read or ReadWrite. Then, other apps may be able to write new data to the file while you're using it. However, when you set the share argument, additional permissions may be needed to share this file while it's being used by the current process. In that case, you can use the Close() method to close the file when you're done with it to allow other processes to access the file. Or, you can declare the FileStream object on a using statement or using declaration as shown later in this chapter. Then, the object will be closed automatically when it goes out of scope.

The first example shows how to open a file stream for writing. Since this example uses the Write member to specify file access, this file stream can only be used to write to the file, not to read from it. And since this example uses the Create member for the mode argument, this code will create a new file if the file doesn't exist, or it will overwrite the existing file if the file does exist. However, if the directory for this file doesn't exist, a DirectoryNotFoundException will be thrown as described in the next figure.

The second example shows how to open a file stream for reading. This works similarly to opening a file stream for writing. However, the Open member is used to specify the mode argument. As a result, if the file doesn't exist, a FileNotFoundException will be thrown as described in the next figure.

The syntax for creating a FileStream object

```
new FileStream(path, mode[, access[, share]])
```

Members in the FileMode enumeration

Member	Description
Append	Opens the file if it exists and seeks to the end of the file. If the file doesn't exist, it's created. This member can only be used with Write file access.
Create	Creates a new file. If the file already exists, it's overwritten.
CreateNew	Creates a new file. If the file already exists, an exception is thrown.
Open	Opens an existing file. If the file doesn't exist, an exception is thrown.
OpenOrCreate	Opens a file if it exists, or creates a new file if it doesn't exist.
Truncate	Opens an existing file and truncates it so its size is zero bytes.

Members in the FileAccess enumeration

Member	Description
Read	Data can be read from the file but not written to it.
ReadWrite	Data can be read from and written to the file. This is the default.
Write	Data can be written to the file but not read from it.

Members in the FileShare enumeration

Member	Description
None	The file cannot be opened by other apps.
Read	Allows other apps to open the file for reading only. This is the default.
ReadWrite	Allows other apps to open the file for both reading and writing.
Write	Allows other apps to open the file for writing only.

Common method of the FileStream class

Method	Description
Close()	Closes the file stream and releases any resources associated with it.

Code that creates a FileStream object for writing

```
string path = @"C:\C#\Files\Products.txt";
FileStream fs = new FileStream(path, FileMode.Create, FileAccess.Write);
```

Code that creates a new FileStream object for reading

```
string path = @"C:\C#\Files\Products.txt";
FileStream fs = new FileStream(path, FileMode.Open, FileAccess.Read);
```

Note

- Operating system level permissions may limit which file access and file share options you can use.

Figure 17-3   How to use the FileStream class

How to use the exception classes for file I/O

In chapter 7, you learned the basic skills for handling exceptions. Now, figure 17-4 summarizes some of the exceptions that can occur when you perform I/O operations. Most of the time, you can write code so these exceptions are avoided. For example, you can avoid a DirectoryNotFoundException by using the Exists() method of the Directory class to be sure that the directory exists before you try to use it in the file path for a new file stream. Similarly, you can avoid a FileNotFoundException by using the Exists() method of the File class.

However, I/O exceptions are often serious problems like hardware problems that an app can't do anything about. For example, if an app needs to open a file that's on a network drive that isn't available, an exception will be thrown. In that case, it's common to handle the exception by displaying an error message.

When handling I/O exceptions, it's common to use a finally block. In this block, it's common to use the stream's Close() method to close all streams that are open. This frees the resources that are used to access the file. Another way to do this is to declare the stream on a using statement or using declaration. You'll learn how to do this later in this chapter when you learn how to read and write data.

The code example shows how to handle some of the most common I/O exceptions. To start, the statement just before the try block declares a variable for the stream. That way, this variable is available to the catch blocks and the finally block. In this case, the stream is a FileStream object, but you'll learn how to work with other types of streams later in this chapter.

Within the try block, the first statement creates an instance of the stream. After this statement, the try block will contain more code that uses the stream to read and write data. You'll learn how to write this type of code later in this chapter. For now, you can assume that this code, as well as the statement that creates an instance of the stream, may throw I/O exceptions. For example, code that reads from the stream may throw an EndOfStreamException when it attempts to read beyond the end of the stream.

After the try block, the catch blocks are coded starting with the most specific type of exception and moving up the inheritance hierarchy towards the most general type of exception. In this case, both the DirectoryNotFoundException and FileNotFoundException classes inherit the IOException class. As a result, they must be coded before the catch block for the IOException. All three of these catch blocks display a message box that describes the type of exception to the user. This is a common way to handle I/O exceptions. However, in some cases, you may want to create a directory or file or allow the user to search for a directory or file.

The statement within the finally block calls the Close() method of the stream to free the resources used by the stream. However, this statement uses the null-conditional operator (?) to make sure the Close() method isn't called if the stream variable is null. That can happen if an exception is thrown before the stream is opened.

Four exception classes for file I/O

Class	Description
IOException	The base class for exceptions that are thrown during the processing of a stream, file, or directory.
DirectoryNotFoundException	Occurs when part of a directory or file path can't be found.
FileNotFoundException	Occurs when a file can't be found.
EndOfStreamException	Occurs when an app attempts to read beyond the end of a stream.

Code that uses exception classes

```
string dirPath = @"C:\C#\Files\";
string filePath = dirPath + "Products.txt";
FileStream fs = null!;
try
{
    fs = new FileStream(filePath, FileMode.Open);
    // code that uses the file stream
    // to read and write data from the file
}
catch (FileNotFoundException)
{
    MessageBox.Show(filePath + " not found.", "File Not Found");
}
catch (DirectoryNotFoundException)
{
    MessageBox.Show(dirPath + " not found.", "Directory Not Found");
}
catch (IOException ex)
{
    MessageBox.Show(ex.Message, "IOException");
}
finally
{
    fs?.Close();
}
```

Description

- To catch any I/O exception, you can use the IOException class.
- To catch specific I/O exceptions, you can use the exception classes that inherit the IOException class such as the three shown in this figure.

Figure 17-4   How to use the exception classes for file I/O

How to work with text files

To read and write characters in a text file, you use the StreamReader and StreamWriter classes. When working with text files, you often need to use the techniques you learned in chapters 4 and 9 to build and parse strings.

How to write a text file

Figure 17-5 shows how to use the StreamWriter class to write data to a text file. To do that, you specify a stream when you create the StreamWriter object. Then, you can write data to the text file by using the Write() and WriteLine() methods. When you use the WriteLine() method, a line terminator is automatically added. Typically, a line terminator is used to end each record. However, the fields in a record are typically separated by special characters, such as tab characters or pipe characters, and you have to add those characters through code.

The SaveProducts() method in the example shows how this works. This method accepts a List<Product> object named products. Then, the code for this method creates a FileStream object for a file with write-only access, and it creates a StreamWriter object for that file stream. Although you could also declare the FileStream object separately as shown in the previous two figures and then name the variable that stores the stream when you create the StreamWriter object, you don't usually need to do that. That's because a file stream is typically used to read from or write to a single file.

After the FileStream object is created, this code uses a foreach loop to write the three properties for each Product object in the products collection to the file with pipe characters as separators. (The pipe character is available from the same key as the backslash key on your keyboard.) For the last property, the WriteLine() method is used to end the record with a line terminator. That way, each record will start on a new line. Finally, after all of the records have been written to the file by the foreach loop, the stream writer and file stream are closed.

Both the Write() and WriteLine() methods of the StreamWriter class are overloaded to accept any type of data. As a result, if you pass a non-string data type to either of these methods, the method converts the data type to a string that represents the data type and then it writes that string to the stream. To do that, these methods automatically call the ToString() method of the data type. In other words, you can write the decimal value that's stored in the Price property of a product to a text file like this:

```
textOut.WriteLine(product.Price);
```

This has the same effect as coding the statement like this:

```
textOut.WriteLine(product.Price.ToString());
```

The basic syntax for creating a StreamWriter object

```
new StreamWriter(stream)
```

Common methods of the StreamWriter class

Method	Description
Write(data)	Writes the data to the output stream.
WriteLine(data)	Writes the data to the output stream and appends a line terminator (usually a carriage return and a line feed).
Close()	Closes the StreamWriter object and the associated FileStream object.

A method that writes data from a collection of Product objects to a text file

```
public static void SaveProducts(List<Product> products)
{
    StreamWriter textOut = new(
        new FileStream(path, FileMode.Create, FileAccess.Write));

    foreach (Product product in products)
    {
        textOut.Write(product.Code + "|");
        textOut.Write(product.Description + "|");
        textOut.WriteLine(product.Price);
    }

    textOut.Close();
}
```

Description

- You can use the Write() and WriteLine() methods of a StreamWriter object to write data to a text file. If the data type that's passed to these methods isn't already a string, these methods will call the ToString() method of the data type to convert it to a string before they write the data.

- If the fields that make up a record are stored in individual variables, you need to concatenate these variables to construct each record and you need to add special characters to delimit each field. However, since the WriteLine() method adds the line terminator automatically, you can use it to end each record.

Figure 17-5   How to write a text file

How to read a text file

Figure 17-6 shows how to use the StreamReader class to read data from a text file. To create a StreamReader object, you can use a FileStream object as the argument. Then, you can use the methods shown in this figure to work with the StreamReader object.

The three Read methods let you read a single character, a single line of data (a record), or all of the data from the current position to the end of the file. In most cases, you'll use the ReadLine() method to read one record at a time. You can also use the Peek() method to see if there is additional data in the file before you read from it, and you can use the Close() method to close the stream reader and file stream when you're done with them.

The GetProducts() method in the example shows how you can use a stream reader to read the data in a file one record at a time. After it creates the file stream and stream reader, this method uses a while loop to read the records in the file. The condition on this loop uses the Peek() method to check that there is at least one more character. If there is, the ReadLine() method reads the next record in the file into a string variable. Note that because the string that the ReadLine() method returns is nullable, this statement uses a null-coalescing operator (??) to assign an empty string to the variable if the string is null. Next, the string is parsed into the individual fields. Then, each field is stored in one of the properties of a Product object, and each Product object is added to a List<Product> collection. When all of the records have been read, the Close() method of the stream reader is used to close the StreamReader and FileStream objects, and the list of products is returned to the calling method.

Note in this example that the FileStream object is instantiated in OpenOrCreate mode. Then, if the file exists, it is opened. Otherwise, a new file is created with no records in it. In either case, the code that follows works because it peeks into the file before it tries to read the data. If the file is empty, no records are read.

The basic syntax for creating a StreamReader object

```
new StreamReader(stream)
```

Common methods of the StreamReader class

Method	Description
Peek()	Returns the next available character in the input stream without advancing to the next position. If no more characters are available, this method returns -1.
Read()	Reads the next character from the input stream.
ReadLine()	Reads the next line of characters from the input stream and returns it as a string.
ReadToEnd()	Reads the data from the current position in the input stream to the end of the stream and returns it as a string. This is typically used to read the contents of an entire file.
Close()	Closes both the StreamReader object and the associated FileStream object.

A method that reads data from a text file into a collection of Product objects

```csharp
public static List<Product> GetProducts()
{
    StreamReader textIn = new(
        new FileStream(path, FileMode.OpenOrCreate, FileAccess.Read));

    List<Product> products = new();

    while (textIn.Peek() != -1)
    {
        string row = textIn.ReadLine() ?? "";
        string[] columns = row.Split('|');
        if (columns.Length == 3)
        {
            Product product = new() {
                Code = columns[0],
                Description = columns[1],
                Price = Convert.ToDecimal(columns[2])
            };
            products.Add(product);
        }
    }
    textIn.Close();
    return products;
}
```

Description

- You use a StreamReader object to read data from a text file. Because the records in most text files end with a line terminator (usually a carriage return and a line feed), you'll typically use the ReadLine() method to read one record at a time.

- If the fields in a record are delimited by special characters, you need to parse the fields using the techniques of chapter 9.

- You can use the Peek() method to determine if you are at the end of the stream.

Figure 17-6   How to read a text file

How to use the using statement and the using declaration

In previous examples, you saw how to explicitly close FileStream, StreamReader, and StreamWriter objects using the Close() method. When you call the Close() method, these objects are closed and any resources associated with the objects are released from memory. If you forget to close objects like these, the resources they use aren't released until the .NET garbage collector releases them. As you can imagine, that can cause inefficient code.

One way to prevent this is to use the *using statement* shown in the first example in figure 17-7. This example shows the SaveProducts() method that you saw in figure 17-5. This time, though, it uses a using statement to declare the StreamWriter and FileStream objects. That causes these objects to be closed and the resources they use to be released after the block of code that uses them is executed. Because of that, it isn't necessary to explicitly close these objects.

Another way to prevent resources from being retained unnecessarily is to use the *using declaration*. The using declaration was introduced with C# 8.0 and works similarly to the using statement, as illustrated by the second example in this figure. When you use this declaration, though, the objects that it declares aren't closed and the resources they use aren't released until the block that contains the declaration ends. In this case, that happens when the SaveProducts() method ends.

Although the StreamWriter and FileStream objects in these examples will be closed at the same time, that's not always the case. For example, suppose the SaveProducts() method contained additional code after the foreach statement. Then, if you used a using declaration for the StreamWriter and FileStream objects, these objects wouldn't be closed until after that code was executed. By contrast, if the using statement is used, the StreamWriter and FileStream objects would still be closed after the block that contains the foreach statement is executed. Because of that, you'll want to use the using statement when it will have a significant effect on when objects are closed. Otherwise, we recommend using the using declaration because it's more concise and requires less indentation.

Note that you can use the using statement and using declaration with objects other than those used to process a file. For example, you'll also want to use them with objects that are used to access a database. You'll see examples of that in chapter 21.

A method that uses the using statement

```
public static void SaveProducts(List<Product> products)
{
    using (StreamWriter textOut = new(
        new FileStream(path, FileMode.Create, FileAccess.Write)))
    {
        foreach (Product product in products)
        {
            textOut.Write(product.Code + "|");
            textOut.Write(product.Description + "|");
            textOut.WriteLine(product.Price);
        }
    }
}
```

The same method with a using declaration

```
public static void SaveProducts(List<Product> products)
{
    using StreamWriter textOut = new(
        new FileStream(path, FileMode.Create, FileAccess.Write));

    foreach (Product product in products)
    {
        textOut.Write(product.Code + "|");
        textOut.Write(product.Description + "|");
        textOut.WriteLine(product.Price);
    }
}
```

Description

- The *using statement* causes any resources used by an object to be released from memory when the object goes out of scope. In addition, before the resources are released, the object is closed if necessary.

- To use the using statement, you code the using keyword, followed by the object declaration enclosed in parentheses and the block of code that uses the object. Then, the resources used by the object will be released when the block ends.

- C# 8.0 introduced the *using declaration*, which can be used to release the resources used by an object at the end of the scope in which it's declared.

- To use a using declaration, you simply code the using keyword at the beginning of an object declaration.

- An object that is declared with a using statement or using declaration is read-only and can't be modified.

Figure 17-7   How to use the using statement and the using declaration

A class that works with a text file

In chapter 12, you learned how to develop an app that used a business class named Product. You also learned how to use two static methods in a database class named ProductDB to get the data for Product objects and to save the data for Product objects. However, you didn't learn how to code those methods.

Now, in figure 17-8, you can see a ProductDB class that implements those methods using a text file. To start, this class provides three constants. The first two specify the path for the directory and the path for the text file, and the last one specifies the delimiter that's used to separate the fields in a record. These constants are available to all of the methods in the class, and they make it easy to change the directory path, file path, or delimiter.

The GetProducts() method reads the product data from the file, stores that data in a List<Product> object, and returns that collection. Here, a using declaration is used to declare the StreamReader object so the StreamReader and FileStream objects are closed when the GetProducts() method ends. Then, after the List<Product> object is created, the while loop reads the data in the file and stores the Product objects in the List<Product> collection as described in figure17-6. When the loop ends, the method returns the List<Product> object. At least that's the way this method works if the file already exists.

Note, however, that the GetProducts() method also works if the directory or file doesn't exist when the method is executed. This situation could occur the first time an app is run. In that case, the method creates the directory if the directory doesn't exist, and it creates an empty file if the file doesn't exist. Then, the code that follows will still work, but it won't read any records.

The SaveProducts() method writes the data in the Product objects that are stored in the List<Product> collection to the file. To start, this method accepts a List<Product> collection. Then, this method writes each Product object to the file. Because the FileStream object is instantiated in Create mode, the Product objects will be written to a new file if the file doesn't already exist and they will overwrite the old file if it does exist.

To keep the emphasis on the code for file I/O, this class doesn't include exception handling. In a production app, though, you would probably add exception handling to a class like this. That way, the exceptions can be caught and handled close to their source, which often helps to reduce the amount of exception handling code that's necessary for an app.

A class that works with a text file

```
namespace ProductMaintenance;

public class ProductDB
{
    private const string Dir = @"C:\C#\Files\";
    private const string Path = Dir + "Products.txt";
    private const string Sep = "|";

    public static List<Product> GetProducts()
    {
        if (!Directory.Exists(Dir))
            Directory.CreateDirectory(Dir);

        using StreamReader textIn = new(
            new FileStream(Path, FileMode.OpenOrCreate, FileAccess.Read));

        List<Product> products = new();

        while (textIn.Peek() != -1)
        {
            string row = textIn.ReadLine() ?? "";
            string[] columns = row.Split(Sep);

            if (columns.Length == 3)
            {
                Product product = new()
                {
                    Code = columns[0],
                    Description = columns[1],
                    Price = Convert.ToDecimal(columns[2])
                };
                products.Add(product);
            }
        }

        return products;
    }

    public static void SaveProducts(List<Product> products)
    {
        using StreamWriter textOut = new(
            new FileStream(Path, FileMode.Create, FileAccess.Write));

        foreach (Product product in products)
        {
            textOut.Write(product.Code + Sep);
            textOut.Write(product.Description + Sep);
            textOut.WriteLine(product.Price);
        }
    }
}
```

Figure 17-8 A class that works with a text file

How to work with binary files

To read and write data in a binary file, you use the BinaryReader and BinaryWriter classes. You'll learn how to use these classes in the figures that follow, and you'll see a class that can be used to read and write a binary file.

How to write a binary file

Figure 17-9 shows how to use the BinaryWriter class to write data to a binary file. To start, you create a BinaryWriter object using the syntax at the top of this figure. To do that, you must supply a FileStream object as the argument for the constructor of the BinaryWriter class. This links the stream to the BinaryWriter object so it can be used to write to the file.

Once you create a BinaryWriter object, you can use its Write() method to write all types of data. This method begins by figuring out what type of data has been passed to it. Then, it writes that type of data to the file. For example, if you pass a variable that contains a decimal value to the Write() method, this method won't convert the decimal value to a string. Instead, it will write the decimal value to the file.

The SaveProducts() method in the example shows how this works. Here, a binary writer is created for a file stream that specifies a file that has write-only access. Since the mode argument has been set to Create, this will create the file if it doesn't exist, and it will overwrite the file if it does exist. Then, a foreach loop is used to write the elements in the List<Product> collection named products that's passed to the method to the file. Since each element in the List<Product> collection is an object of the Product class, each property of the Product object is written to the file separately using the Write() method. After all of the elements in the List<Product> collection have been written to the file, the Close() method is used to close both the BinaryWriter and the FileStream objects. However, you can also use a using statement or using declaration to close the objects and release the resources they use when they go out of scope.

The basic syntax for creating a BinaryWriter object

```
new BinaryWriter(stream)
```

Common methods of the BinaryWriter class

Method	Description
Write(data)	Writes the specified data to the output stream.
Close()	Closes the BinaryWriter object and the associated FileStream object.

A method that writes data from a collection of Product objects to a binary file

```
public static void SaveProducts(List<Product> products)
{
    BinaryWriter binaryOut = new(
        new FileStream(path, FileMode.Create, FileAccess.Write));

    foreach (Product product in products)
    {
        binaryOut.Write(product.Code);
        binaryOut.Write(product.Description);
        binaryOut.Write(product.Price);
    }
    binaryOut.Close();
}
```

Description

- You use a BinaryWriter object to write data to a binary file. In most cases, you'll write one field at a time in a prescribed sequence.

- The BinaryWriter class provides a single Write() method for writing data to a file. This method determines the type of data being written based on the data type of the argument.

Figure 17-9   How to write a binary file

How to read a binary file

Figure 17-10 shows you how to use the BinaryReader class to read data from a binary file. Like the BinaryWriter class, the argument that you pass to the constructor of the BinaryReader class is a FileStream object that connects the stream to a file.

In a binary file, there's no termination character to indicate where one record ends and another begins. Because of that, you can't read an entire record at once. Instead, you have to read one character or one field at a time. To do that, you use the Read methods of the BinaryReader class that are shown in this figure. When you do, you must use the appropriate method for the data type of the field that you want to read. To read a Boolean field, for example, you use the ReadBoolean() method. To read a Decimal field, you use the ReadDecimal() method.

The BinaryReader class provides methods to read most of the data types provided by .NET. However, this figure only shows the most common of these methods. For a complete list of methods, see the online documentation for the BinaryReader class.

Before you read the next character or field, you want to be sure that you aren't at the end of the file. To do that, you use the PeekChar() method. Then, if there's at least one more character to be read, this method returns that character without advancing to the next position in the file. If there isn't another character, the PeekChar() method returns a value of -1. Then, you can use the Close() method to close the binary reader and the associated file stream.

The GetProducts() method in the example shows how you can use some of these methods. Here, a FileStream object is created for a file that will have read-only access. Since the mode argument for the file stream specifies OpenOrCreate, this opens an existing file if one exists or creates a new file that's empty and opens it. Then, a new BinaryReader object is created for that file stream. Finally, the while loop that follows is executed until the PeekChar() method returns a value of -1, which means the end of the file has been reached.

Within the while loop, the three fields in each record are read and assigned to the properties of the Product object. Because the first two fields in each record contain string data, the ReadString() method is used to retrieve their contents. Because the third field contains decimal data, the ReadDecimal() method is used to retrieve its contents. Then, the Product object is added to the List<Product> collection. When the while loop ends, the Close() method of the BinaryReader object is used to close both the BinaryReader and the FileStream objects, and the list of products is returned to the calling method. Once again, you can use a using statement or using declaration instead of a Close() method to close these objects and release the resources they use when they go out of scope.

The basic syntax for creating a BinaryReader object

```
new BinaryReader(stream)
```

Common methods of the BinaryReader class

Method	Description
PeekChar()	Returns the next available character in the input stream without advancing to the next position. If no more characters are available, this method returns -1.
Read()	Returns the next available character from the input stream and advances to the next position in the file.
ReadBoolean()	Returns a Boolean value from the input stream and advances the current position of the stream by one byte.
ReadByte()	Returns a byte from the input stream and advances the current position of the stream accordingly.
ReadChar()	Returns a character from the input stream and advances the current position of the stream accordingly.
ReadDecimal()	Returns a decimal value from the input stream and advances the current position of the stream by 16 bytes.
ReadInt32()	Returns a 4-byte signed integer from the input stream and advances the current position of the stream by 4 bytes.
ReadString()	Returns a string from the input stream and advances the current position of the stream by the number of characters in the string.
Close()	Closes the BinaryReader object and the associated FileStream object.

A method that reads data from a binary file into a collection of Product objects

```
public static List<Product> GetProducts()
{
    BinaryReader binaryIn = new(
        new FileStream(path, FileMode.OpenOrCreate, FileAccess.Read));

    List<Product> products = new();

    while (binaryIn.PeekChar() != -1)
    {
        Product product = new() {
            Code = binaryIn.ReadString(),
            Description = binaryIn.ReadString(),
            Price = binaryIn.ReadDecimal()
        };
        products.Add(product);
    }
    binaryIn.Close();
    return products;
}
```

Description

- You use a BinaryReader object to read a single character or an entire field from a binary file. To read a single character, you use the Read() method. And to read a field, you use the method that indicates the type of data the field contains.

- You can use the PeekChar() method to determine if you are at the end of the stream.

Figure 17-10   How to read a binary file

A class that works with a binary file

Figure 17-11 presents the code for the ProductDB class that you saw in figure 17-8, but this time it uses a binary file instead of a text file. Because the methods in this class are similar to the ones for the text file, you shouldn't have any trouble understanding how they work.

Note, however, that the signatures for the two methods in this class are the same as the signatures for the methods in the ProductDB class in figure 17-8. As a result, the Product Maintenance app presented in chapter 12 can use either of these classes. This clearly illustrates the benefit of encapsulation: the calling method doesn't know or care how the method is implemented. As a result, the programmer can change the way these methods are implemented without changing the rest of the app.

A class that works with a binary file

```
namespace ProductMaintenance;

public class ProductDB
{
    private const string Dir = @"C:\C#\Files\";
    private const string Path = Dir + "Products.dat";

    public static List<Product> GetProducts()
    {
        if (!Directory.Exists(Dir))
            Directory.CreateDirectory(Dir);

        using BinaryReader binaryIn = new(
            new FileStream(Path, FileMode.OpenOrCreate, FileAccess.Read));

        List<Product> products = new();

        while (binaryIn.PeekChar() != -1)
        {
            Product product = new()
            {
                Code = binaryIn.ReadString(),
                Description = binaryIn.ReadString(),
                Price = binaryIn.ReadDecimal()
            };
            products.Add(product);
        }

        return products;
    }

    public static void SaveProducts(List<Product> products)
    {
        using BinaryWriter binaryOut = new(
            new FileStream(Path, FileMode.Create, FileAccess.Write));

        foreach (Product product in products)
        {
            binaryOut.Write(product.Code);
            binaryOut.Write(product.Description);
            binaryOut.Write(product.Price);
        }
    }
}
```

Figure 17-11   A class that works with a binary file

Perspective

In this chapter, you learned how to read and write the data in text and binary files. These files can be used when you need a relatively easy way to store a limited number of records with a limited number of fields. However, when the data requirements for an app are more complex, it usually makes sense to use a database instead of text or binary files.

Terms

input file	stream
output file	output stream
I/O operations	input stream
file I/O	text stream
text file	binary stream
field	using statement
record	using declaration
binary file	

Exercise 17-1   Work with a text file

1. Open the project in the C:\C#\Ch17\CustomerText directory. This is the Customer Maintenance app that you developed for exercise 12-1, but it doesn't save or retrieve the data. Test it to see that you can add a customer but the data doesn't remain when you stop the app and run it again.

2. In the CustomerDB class, add code to the GetCustomers() and SaveCustomers() methods so they use a text file to read and write a List<Customer> collection of Customer objects. Unless you moved it after downloading and installing the files for this book, the path for this file should be C:\C#\Files\Customers.txt.

3. Test the app by adding and deleting customers. To verify that the data is now being saved to disk, stop the app and run it again. Or, use a text editor like NotePad to open the file after a test run.

Exercise 17-2   Work with a binary file

1. Use Windows Explorer to copy the directory named CustomerText from the previous exercise within the ch17 directory. Then, rename that directory CustomerBinary, and open the project in that directory.

2. Modify the CustomerDB class so it uses a binary file named Customers.dat instead of a text file. Also, leave the signatures of the GetCustomers() and SaveCustomers() methods as they are so you won't need to modify the code in the form class that calls these methods. Then, test the app by adding and deleting customers.

18

How to use LINQ

In this chapter, you'll learn the basic skills for using a feature of C# called LINQ. LINQ provides a way for you to query a data source using constructs that are built into the C# language. That way, you can use the same language to access a variety of data sources.

This chapter will focus on using LINQ with in-memory data structures such as arrays and generic lists. Keep in mind as you read this chapter, though, that you can also use the same skills with other types of data sources. In chapter 20, for example, you'll learn how to use LINQ with Entity Framework Core.

Basic concepts for working with LINQ

As its name implies, *LINQ*, or *Language-Integrated Query*, lets you query a data source using the C# language. Before you learn how to code LINQ queries, you need to learn some concepts related to LINQ, such as how LINQ is implemented and what the three stages of a query operation are. In addition, you'll want to know the advantages you'll get from using LINQ.

How LINQ is implemented

LINQ is implemented as a set of *extension methods* that are defined by the Enumerable and Queryable classes. Because these methods can only be used in a query operation, they're referred to as *query operators*. Although you can call the query operators directly by coding a *method-based query*, you can also use the clauses C# provides that give you access to the operators. When you use C# clauses to code a LINQ query, the result is called a *query expression*.

Figure 18-1 presents the C# clauses you're most likely to use in a query expression. If you've ever coded a query using SQL, you shouldn't have any trouble understanding what each of these clauses does. For example, you use the *from* clause to identify the data source for the query. You use the *where* clause to filter the data that's returned by the query. And you use the *select* clause to identify the fields you want to be returned by the query. You'll learn how to code queries that use all of these clauses later in this chapter.

Advantages of using LINQ

Figure 18-1 also lists several advantages of LINQ. Probably the biggest advantage is that it lets you query different types of data sources using the same language. As you'll see in this chapter, for example, you can use the same language to query an array and a generic list of objects. Keep in mind as you read this chapter, though, that you can use these same skills to query more sophisticated data sources such as databases and entity objects defined by Entity Framework Core.

The key to making this work is that the query language is integrated into C#. Because of that, you don't have to learn a different query language for each type of data source. In addition, as you enter your queries, you can take advantage of the IntelliSense features that are provided for the C# language. The compiler can catch errors in the query, such as a field that doesn't exist in the data source, so you don't get errors at runtime. And when a runtime error does occur, you can use the Visual Studio debugging features to determine its cause.

Finally, if you're working with a relational data source such as a SQL Server database, you can use an *object relational mapping (ORM)* framework like Entity Framework Core to develop a data model that maps to the data source. Then, you can use LINQ to query the objects in the data model, and the query will be converted to the form required by the data source. This can make it significantly easier to work with relational data sources.

Some of the C# clauses for working with LINQ

Clause	Description
from	Identifies the source of data for the query.
where	Provides a condition that specifies which elements are retrieved from the data source.
orderby	Indicates how the elements that are returned by the query are sorted.
select	Specifies the content of the returned elements.
join	Combines data from two data sources.

Advantages of using LINQ

- Makes it easier for you to query a data source by integrating the query language with C#.

- Makes it easier to develop applications that query a data source by providing IntelliSense, compile-time syntax checking, and debugging support.

- Makes it easier for you to query different types of data sources because you use the same basic syntax for each type.

- Makes it easier for you to use objects to work with relational data sources by using an *object relational mapping* framework.

Description

- *Language-Integrated Query* (*LINQ*) provides a set of *query operators* that are implemented using *extension methods*. These methods are static members of the Enumerable and Queryable classes.

- You can work with LINQ by calling the extension methods directly or by using C# clauses that are converted to calls to the methods at compile time.

- A query that calls LINQ methods directly is called a *method-based query*. A query that uses C# clauses is called a *query expression*. You use a method-based query or query expression to identify the data you want to retrieve from the data source.

- To use LINQ with a data source, the data source must implement the IEnumerable<T> interface or another interface that implements IEnumerable<T> such as IQueryable<T>. For more information on interfaces, see chapter 15.

- A data source such as an array or an array list that supports the non-generic IEnumerable interface can also be used with LINQ.

Figure 18-1   An introduction to LINQ

The three stages of a query operation

Figure 18-2 presents the three stages of a query operation and illustrates these stages using an array. The first stage is to get the data source. How you do that depends on the type of data source you're working with. For the array shown here, getting the data source means defining an array named numbers and assigning values to its elements. In this case, the array contains five integers with the values 0, 1, 2, 3, and 4.

The second stage is to define the query. This query identifies the data source and the data to be retrieved from that data source. In this figure, for example, a query expression is used to retrieve the even integers from the numbers array. It also sorts those integers in descending sequence. (Don't worry if you don't understand the syntax of this query expression. You'll learn how to code query expressions in the topics that follow.)

Notice here that the query expression is stored in a *query variable*. That's necessary because this query isn't executed when it's defined. Also notice that the query variable isn't declared with an explicit type. Instead, it's given a type implicitly based on the type of elements returned by the query. In this case, because the query returns integers, the query variable is implicitly given a type of IEnumerable<int>.

For this to work, the data source must implement the IEnumerable or IEnumerable<T> interface. In case you're not familiar with interfaces, they consist of a set of declarations for one or more properties, methods, and events, but they don't provide implementation for those properties, methods, and events. If you want to learn more about interfaces, you can read chapter 15. For the example in this figure, however, all you need to know is that an array implements the IEnumerable interface.

The third stage of a query operation is to execute the query. To do that, you can use a foreach statement like the one shown in this figure. Here, each element that's returned by the query expression is added to a string variable. Then, after all the elements have been processed, the string is displayed in a message box. As you can see, this message box lists the even numbers from 4 to 0 as defined by the query expression.

By the way, you may have noticed the two tab characters that are included in each line of the display in this example. They're needed to make the dialog wide enough to accommodate the entire title. Without these characters, the title would be cut off.

When a query is defined and executed separately as shown here, the process is referred to as *deferred execution*. By contrast, queries that are executed when they're defined use *immediate execution*. Immediate execution typically occurs when a method that requires access to the individual elements returned by the query is executed on the query expression. For example, to get a count of the number of elements returned by a query, you can execute the Count() method on the query expression. Then, the query will be executed immediately so the count can be calculated.

The three stages of a query operation

1. Get the data source. If the data source is an array, for example, you must declare the array and then assign values to its elements.

2. Define the query.

3. Execute the query to return the results.

A LINQ query that retrieves data from an array

Code that defines the array

```
int[] numbers = new int[] { 0, 1, 2, 3, 4 };
```

A statement that defines the query expression

```
var numberList = from number in numbers
                 where number % 2 == 0
                 orderby number descending
                 select number;
```

Code that executes the query

```
string numberDisplay = "";
foreach (var number in numberList)
    numberDisplay += number + "\t\t\n";
MessageBox.Show(numberDisplay, "Sorted Even Numbers");
```

Description

- The process described above is called *deferred execution* because the query isn't executed when it's defined. Instead, it's executed when the application tries to access the individual elements returned by the query, such as when the query is used in a foreach statement.

- If a query isn't executed when it's defined, it's stored in a *query variable*. In that case, the query variable is implicitly typed as IEnumerable<T> where T is the type of each element. In the example above, the numberList variable is assigned the type IEnumerable<int> since the numbers array contains integers.

- If a query requires access to the individual elements identified by the query expression, *immediate execution* occurs. In that case, the query expression isn't saved in a query variable.

Figure 18-2   The three stages of a query operation

How to code query expressions

Now that you have a basic understanding of what a LINQ query is, you need to learn the syntax for coding query expressions. That's what you'll learn in the topics that follow.

How to identify the data source for a query

To identify the source of data for a query, you use the *from* clause shown in figure 18-3. As you can see, this clause declares a *range variable* that will be used to represent each element of the data source, and it names the data source, which must be a collection that implements the IEnumerable or IEnumerable<T> interface. It can also declare a type for the range variable, although the type is usually omitted. If it is omitted, it's determined by the type of elements in the data source.

The first example in this figure shows how to use the from clause with an array of decimals named salesTotals. The first statement in this example declares the array and assigns values to its elements. Then, the second statement defines the query expression, which consists of just the from clause and a select clause. This expression is stored in a query variable named salesList. Finally, a foreach statement loops through the values returned by the query and calculates a sum of those values.

At this point, you should realize that a query expression must always start with a from clause that identifies the data source. That way, the compiler knows what the source of data for the query is, and it can help you construct the rest of the query based on that data source. In addition, a query expression must end with either a *select* clause or a *group* clause. In the example in this figure, the select clause simply indicates that array elements should be returned by the query. Later in this chapter, however, you'll see that you can use the select clause to return just the fields you want from each element of a data source.

The second example in this figure shows how to use the from clause with a generic list of invoices. Here, you can see that the Invoice class consists of a set of auto-implemented properties. Then, the statement that follows creates a list that's based on this class and loads invoices into it using the GetInvoices() method of the InvoiceDB class. Note that it's not important for you to know how this method works. All you need to know is that it returns a List<Invoice> object. This object is then assigned to a variable named invoiceList.

The next statement defines the query expression, which includes a from clause that identifies invoiceList as the data source. This expression is assigned to a query variable named invoices. Then, this variable is used in a foreach statement to calculate a sum of the InvoiceTotal fields in the invoices.

You may have noticed in both of the examples in this figure that the variable that's used in the query expression and the variable that's used in the foreach loop have the same name. That makes sense because they both refer to an element in the data source. However, you should know that you don't have to use the same names for these variables. In fact, when you code more sophisticated query expressions, you'll want to use different variable names to indicate the difference

The syntax of the from clause

```
from [type] elementName in collectionName
```

An example that uses an array of decimals as the data source

A statement that gets the data source

```
decimal[] salesTotals =
    new decimal[] { 1286.45m, 2433.49m, 2893.85m, 2094.53m };
```

A statement that defines the query expression

```
var salesList = from sales in salesTotals
                select sales;
```

Code that executes the query

```
decimal sum = 0;
foreach (var sales in salesList)
    sum += sales;
```

An example that uses a generic list of invoices as the data source

The Invoice class

```
public class Invoice
{
    public int InvoiceID { get; set; }
    public int CustomerID { get; set; }
    public DateTime InvoiceDate { get; set; }
    public decimal ProductTotal { get; set; }
    public decimal SalesTax { get; set; }
    public decimal Shipping { get; set; }
    public decimal InvoiceTotal { get; set; }
}
```

A statement that gets the data source

```
List<Invoice> invoiceList = InvoiceDB.GetInvoices();
```

A statement that defines the query expression

```
var invoices = from invoice in invoiceList
               select invoice;
```

Code that executes the query

```
decimal sum = 0;
foreach (var invoice in invoices)
    sum += invoice.InvoiceTotal;
```

Description

- The *from* clause identifies the source of data for a query and declares a *range variable* that's used to represent each element of the data source.

- If the range variable you use in a query expression and the iteration variable you use in the foreach statement that executes the query refer to the same type of elements, you should give them the same name for clarity. Otherwise, you should give them different names to indicate the type of elements they refer to.

- The from clause must be the first clause in a query expression. In addition, a query expression must end with a *select* clause or a *group* clause.

Figure 18-3   How to identify the data source for a query

between the elements they refer to. That will make more sense when you see the select clause later in this chapter.

How to filter the results of a query

To filter the results of a query, you use the *where* clause shown in figure 18-4. On this clause, you specify a condition that an element must meet to be returned by the query. The condition is coded as a Boolean expression like the ones you learned about in chapter 5. The two examples in this figure illustrate how this works.

The where clause in the first example specifies that for an element to be returned from the salesTotals array, its value must be greater than 2000. Notice here that the range variable that's declared by the from clause is used in the where clause to refer to the elements that are returned by the query. Then, the code that executes the query adds the returned values to a string, and the string is then displayed in a message box. If you compare the values that are listed in this message box to the values in the array shown in figure 18-3, you'll see that the value that is less than 2000 has been omitted.

The second example is similar, but it uses the generic list of invoices. Here, the where clause indicates that only those invoices with invoice totals greater than 150 should be returned by the query. Notice again that the range variable that's declared by the from clause is used to refer to the elements that are returned by the query. This time, though, because each element is an Invoice object, the condition on the where clause can refer to a member of that object.

The syntax of the where clause

```
where condition
```

An example that filters the salesTotals array

A query expression that returns only sales greater than $2000

```
var salesList = from sales in salesTotals
                where sales > 2000
                select sales;
```

Code that executes the query

```
string salesDisplay = "";
foreach (var sales in salesList)
    salesDisplay += sales.ToString("c") + "\t\t\n";
MessageBox.Show(salesDisplay, "Sales Over $2000");
```

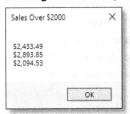

An example that filters the generic list of invoices

A query expression that returns invoices with totals over $150

```
var invoices = from invoice in invoiceList
               where invoice.InvoiceTotal > 150
               select invoice;
```

Code that executes the query

```
string invoiceDisplay = "";
foreach (var invoice in invoices)
    invoiceDisplay += invoice.InvoiceTotal.ToString("c") + "\t\t\n";
MessageBox.Show(invoiceDisplay, "Invoices Over $150");
```

Description

- The *where* clause lets you filter the data in a data source by specifying a condition that the elements of the data source must meet to be returned by the query.
- The condition is coded as a Boolean expression that can contain one or more relational and logical operators.

Figure 18-4   How to filter the results of a query

How to sort the results of a query

If you want the results of a query to be returned in a particular sequence, you can include the *orderby* clause in the query expression. The syntax of this clause is shown at the top of figure 18-5. This syntax indicates that you can sort by one or more expressions in either ascending or descending sequence.

To understand how this works, the first example in this figure shows how you might sort the salesTotals array. Here, the query expression includes an orderby clause that sorts the elements in this array in ascending sequence (the default). To do that, it names the range variable that is declared by the from clause. If you compare the results of this query with the results shown in the previous figure, you'll see how the sequence has changed.

The second example shows how you can sort query results by two expressions. In this case, the query will return invoices from the generic invoice list in descending invoice total sequence within customer ID sequence. If you look at the results of this query, you can see that the customer IDs are in ascending sequence. You can also see that the second and third invoices are for the same customer, and the invoice with the largest total is listed first.

The syntax of the orderby clause

```
orderby expression1 [ascending|descending]
        [, expression2 [ascending|descending]]...
```

An example that sorts the salesTotals array

A query expression that sorts the sales in ascending sequence

```
var salesList = from sales in salesTotals
                where sales > 2000
                orderby sales
                select sales;
```

Code that executes the query

```
string salesDisplay = "";
foreach (var sales in salesList)
    salesDisplay += sales.ToString("c") + "\t\t\t\n";
MessageBox.Show(salesDisplay, "Sorted Sales Over $2000");
```

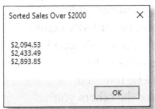

An example that sorts the generic list of invoices

A query expression that sorts the invoices by customer ID and invoice total

```
var invoices = from invoice in invoiceList
               where invoice.InvoiceTotal > 150
               orderby invoice.CustomerID, invoice.InvoiceTotal descending
               select invoice;
```

Code that executes the query

```
string invoiceDisplay = "Cust ID\tInvoice amount\n";
foreach (var invoice in invoices)
    invoiceDisplay += invoice.CustomerID + "\t"
                    + invoice.InvoiceTotal.ToString("c") + "\n";
MessageBox.Show(invoiceDisplay, "Sorted Invoices Over $150");
```

Description

- The *orderby* clause lets you specify how the results of the query are sorted. You can specify one or more expressions on this clause.

Figure 18-5   How to sort the results of a query

How to select fields from a query

So far, the queries you've seen in this chapter have returned entire elements of a data source. To do that, the select clause simply named the range variable that represents those elements. But you can also return selected fields of the elements. To do that, you code the select clause as shown in figure 18-6. As you can see, the select clause lets you identify one or more fields to be included in the query results. A query that returns something other than entire source elements is called a *projection*.

To illustrate how this works, the first example in this figure uses a sorted list named employeeSales. The keys for this list are employee names, and the values are sales totals. You can see the definition of this list and the data it contains at the beginning of this example.

The query expression that uses this list includes the from, where, and orderby clauses. The where clause indicates that only those elements with values (sales totals) greater than 2000 should be returned, and the orderby clause indicates that the returned elements should be sorted by the values in descending sequence. In addition, this query expression includes a select clause that indicates that only the key field (the employee name) should be returned.

The foreach statement that executes this query works like the others you've seen in this chapter. It creates a string that includes a list of the employee names. Notice, however, that the name of the iteration variable that's used in this statement is different from the name of the range variable used in the query expression. That's because the variable in the query expression refers to an element in the sorted list, but the variable in the foreach statement refers only to the employee names returned from the list by the query.

The second example shows a query expression that returns selected fields from the Invoice objects. Specifically, it returns the CustomerID and InvoiceTotal fields. If you look back at the example in the previous figure, you'll see that these are the only two fields that are used when the query is executed. Because of that, these are the only two fields that need to be retrieved.

Notice that the select clause in this example uses an object initializer to create the objects that are returned by the query. In this case, each object includes a CustomerID property and an InvoiceTotal property. Unlike the object intializers you saw in chapter 12, however, the object initializer shown here doesn't specify a type. That's because a type that includes just CustomerID and InvoiceTotal properties doesn't exist. In that case, an *anonymous type* is created. Note that because the name of an anonymous type is generated by the compiler, you can't refer to it directly. If that's a problem, you can define the type you want to use and then name it on the object initializer. Many programmers use a simple type called a data transfer object (DTO) for this, as you'll see in chapter 22.

In addition to the type, the names of the properties have been omitted from the object initializer. Because of that, the properties are given the same names as the fields that are listed in the initializer. If that's not what you want, you can specify the names in the initializer. For example, to name the two properties of the type shown here ID and Total, you'd code the initializer like this:

```
new { ID = invoice.CustomerID, Total = invoice.InvoiceTotal }
```

Two ways to code the select clause

```
select columnExpression
select new [type] { [PropertyName1 =] columnExpression1
                 [, [PropertyName2 =] columnExpression2]... }
```

An example that selects key values from a sorted list

The employee sales sorted list

```
SortedList<string, decimal> employeeSales = new()
    { ["Anderson"] = 1286.45m, ["Menendez"] = 2433.49m,
      ["Thompson"] = 2893.85m, ["Wilkinson"] = 2094.53m };
```

A query expression that selects the employee names from the list

```
var employeeList = from sales in employeeSales
                   where sales.Value > 2000
                   orderby sales.Value descending
                   select sales.Key;
```

Code that executes the query

```
string employeeDisplay = "";
foreach (var employee in employeeList)
    employeeDisplay += employee + "\t\t\t\n";
MessageBox.Show(employeeDisplay, "Sorted Employees With Sales Over $2000");
```

A query expression that creates an anonymous type from the list of invoices

```
var invoices = from invoice in invoiceList
               where invoice.InvoiceTotal > 150
               orderby invoice.CustomerID, invoice.InvoiceTotal descending
               select new { invoice.CustomerID, invoice.InvoiceTotal };
```

Description

- The *select* clause indicates the data you want to return from each element of the query results.

- A query that returns anything other than entire source elements is called a *projection*. Both examples above illustrate projections.

- To return two or more fields from each element, you code an object initializer within the select clause. If the object initializer doesn't specify a type, an *anonymous type* that contains the specified fields as its properties is created.

Figure 18-6   How to select fields from a query

How to join data from two or more data sources

Figure 18-7 shows how you can include data from two or more data sources in a query. To do that, you use the *join* clause shown at the top of this figure. To start, this clause declares a range variable and names a data source just like the from clause does. Then, it indicates how the two data sources are related.

To illustrate, the example in this figure joins data from the list of Invoice objects you've seen in the previous figures with a list of Customer objects. You can see the definition of the Customer class at the beginning of this example, along with the statements that declare and load the two lists. Like the invoice list, the customer list is loaded by calling a method of a database class.

The query expression that follows joins the data in these two lists. To do that, it names the invoice list on the from clause, and it names the customer list on the join clause. Then, the on condition indicates that only customers in the customer list with customer IDs that match customer IDs in the invoice list should be included in the results.

Because both the invoice and customer lists are included as data sources in this query expression, the rest of the query can refer to fields in either data source. For example, the orderby clause in this query expression sorts the results by the InvoiceTotal field in the invoice list within the Name field in the customer list. Similarly, the select clause selects the Name field from the customer list and the InvoiceTotal field from the invoice list.

The remaining code in this example executes the query and creates a list that includes the customer names and invoice totals. This is similar to the list you saw in figure 18-5. Because the list in figure 18-7 includes the customer names instead of the customer IDs, however, it provides more useful information.

Although this figure only shows how to join data from two data sources, you can extend this syntax to join data from additional data sources. For example, suppose you have three data sources named invoiceList, lineItemList, and productList. Then, you could join the data in these lists using code like this:

```
from invoice in invoiceList
join lineItem in lineItemList
    on invoice.InvoiceID equals lineItem.InvoiceID
join product in productList
    on lineItem.ProductCode equals product.ProductCode
```

Once the three tables are joined, you can refer to fields from any of these tables in the query expression.

The basic syntax of the join clause

```
join elementName in collectionName on keyName1 equals keyName2
```

An example that joins data from two generic lists

The Customer class

```
public class Customer
{
    public int CustomerID { get; set; }
    public string Name { get; set; } = "";
}
```

Code that gets the two data sources

```
List<Invoice> invoiceList = InvoiceDB.GetInvoices();
List<Customer> customerList = CustomerDB.GetCustomers();
```

A query expression that joins data from the two data sources

```
var invoices = from invoice in invoiceList
               join customer in customerList
               on invoice.CustomerID equals customer.CustomerID
               where invoice.InvoiceTotal > 150
               orderby customer.Name, invoice.InvoiceTotal descending
               select new { customer.Name, invoice.InvoiceTotal };
```

Code that executes the query

```
string invoiceDisplay = "Customer Name\t\tInvoice amount\n";
foreach (var invoice in invoices)
{
    invoiceDisplay += invoice.Name + "\t\t";
    invoiceDisplay += invoice.InvoiceTotal.ToString("c") + "\n";
}
MessageBox.Show(invoiceDisplay, "Joined Customer and Invoice Data");
```

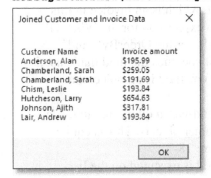

Description

- The *join* clause lets you combine data from two or more data sources based on matching key values. The query results will include only those elements that meet the condition specified by the equals operator.

- You can extend the syntax shown above to join data from additional data sources.

Figure 18-7   How to join data from two or more data sources

How to code method-based queries

Earlier in this chapter, you learned that the query operators provided by LINQ are implemented as extension methods and that you can call these methods directly rather than use the C# clauses for LINQ. In the topics that follow, you'll learn how to use these extension methods to implement LINQ functionality.

How to use the LINQ methods for query operations

To code method-based queries, you use LINQ *extension methods*. Extension methods provide for adding methods to a data type from outside the definition of that data type. Fortunately, you don't need to understand how that works to use them. Instead, you can just use an extension method like any other method.

The table at the top of figure 18-8 lists the extension methods that are used to implement common C# clauses for LINQ. These extension methods define one or more parameters that represent *delegates* that accept *lambda expressions*. If you've read chapter 13, you're already familiar with lambda expressions and delegates. To review, a delegate specifies the signature of a function, and a lambda expression is an unnamed function that evaluates an expression and returns a value.

The first example in this figure illustrates how this works. Here, the query uses four extension methods. This method-based query is equivalent to the query expression you saw in figure 18-6 that creates an anonymous type from the list of invoices. Each of the methods used by this query accepts a single lambda expression. For each lambda expression, the parameter list contains a single parameter that represents the source element, which is an invoice in this example. Then, the expression body for the lambda expression for the Where() method is a Boolean expression, the expression body for the OrderBy() and ThenByDescending() methods is an expression that specifies the field that's used for sorting, and the expression body for the Select() method is an object that identifies the values to be returned by the query.

The second example in this figure is for a method-based query that joins data from the list of Invoice objects and the list of Customer objects. This is equivalent to the second query expression you saw in figure 18-7.

To join data from the two lists, the Join() method is executed on the list of Invoice objects. Then, four arguments are passed to this method. The first argument is the list of Customer objects that the list of Invoice objects will be joined with. The second and third arguments are lambda expressions that identify the fields of the Invoice and Customer objects that will be used to join the objects. In this case, an Invoice object will be joined with a Customer object if their CustomerID fields match. Finally, the fourth argument is a lambda expression that specifies the values to be included from the two objects. Note that for this to work, the lambda expression includes two parameters that identify the two objects.

The result of a join is an anonymous type that includes the fields specified by the fourth parameter. Then, any extension methods that follow are executed on this anonymous type. In this case, that includes the Where(), OrderBy(), and

Extension methods used to implement common C# clauses for LINQ

Clause	Method
where	Where()
orderby	OrderBy(), OrderByDescending(), ThenBy(), ThenByDescending()
select	Select()
join	Join()

The basic syntax of a lambda expression

```
[()parameterList[]] => expression
```

A method-based query that filters and sorts the results and selects fields

```
var invoices = invoiceList
            .Where(i => i.InvoiceTotal > 150)
            .OrderBy(i => i.CustomerID)
            .ThenByDescending(i => i.InvoiceTotal)
            .Select(i => new { i.CustomerID, i.InvoiceTotal });
```

A method-based query that joins data from two data sources

```
var invoices =
    invoiceList.Join(customerList,
        i => i.CustomerID,
        c => c.CustomerID,
        (i, c) => new { c.Name, i.InvoiceTotal })
    .Where(ci => ci.InvoiceTotal > 150)
    .OrderBy(ci => ci.Name)
    .ThenByDescending(ci => ci.InvoiceTotal);
```

A method-based query that joins data and selects fields

```
var invoices =
    invoiceList.Join(customerList,
        i => i.CustomerID,
        c => c.CustomerID,
        (i, c) => new { c.Name, i.InvoiceDate, i.InvoiceTotal })
    .Where(ci => ci.InvoiceTotal > 150)
    .OrderBy(ci => ci.Name)
    .ThenBy(ci => ci.InvoiceDate)
    .Select(ci => new { ci.Name, ci.InvoiceTotal });
```

Description

- C# uses *extension methods* to implement the standard query operators provided by LINQ. These methods are defined for the Enumerable and Queryable classes.

- To code a method-based query, you use *lambda expressions* like the ones shown above. A lambda expression consists of an unnamed function that evaluates a single expression and returns its value.

- When you join two or more data sources, you create an anonymous type that incudes the fields required by the query. Then, any extension methods that follow refer to that type.

- If you don't need to include all of the fields of an anonymous type that's created by a join, you can code a Select() method to create a new anonymous type with just the fields you need.

Figure 18-8   How to use the LINQ methods for query operations

ThenByDescending() methods. Note that a different parameter name is used in the lambda expressions for these methods to indicate that they refer to the anonymous type and not the Customer or Invoice objects.

Note also that this query doesn't include a Select() method. That's because the anonymous type that's created by the join includes all of the fields needed by the methods that follow and all of the fields to be included in the results. If you needed to use additional fields in the query, though, and you didn't want to include those fields in the results, you could include a Select() method that creates another anonymous type with just the fields you want. This is illustrated by the third example. Here, the InvoiceDate field is included in the anonymous type that's created by the join so it can be used by the ThenBy() method. Then, a Select() method is included to create an anonymous type that doesn't include this field.

How to use additional LINQ methods

LINQ provides a number of other methods in addition to the ones that are used to implement the C# clauses for LINQ. Some of these methods, many of which are extension methods, are summarized in figure 18-9.

The first five methods shown here can be referred to as aggregate methods because they perform a calculation on all of the elements in the results of a query. For instance, the first example shows how to use the Count() method to get a count of the number of elements in the results, and the second example shows how to use the Sum() method to get the total of invoice totals in the results. When you use these methods, the query is executed immediately to get the resulting value.

The last example shows how to use two additional methods, Skip() and Take(). The Skip() method lets you skip over a specified number of elements before starting to retrieve elements, and the Take() method lets you retrieve a specified number of elements. In this example, ten elements are retrieved from the list of Invoice objects after skipping over the first 20 elements. Because these methods use deferred execution, this query is stored in a query variable.

Although this chapter doesn't present examples of the rest of the LINQ methods, you shouldn't have any trouble understanding what they do. Then, if you ever need to use any of these methods, you can use the online documentation for the Enumerable and Queryable classes to find out more about how they work.

Additional LINQ methods

Method	Description
Count()	Gets the number of elements in the results of a query.
Average()	Calculates the average of an expression in the results of a query.
Sum()	Calculates the sum of an expression in the results of a query.
Max()	Gets the maximum value of an expression in the results of a query.
Min()	Gets the minimum value of an expression in the results of a query.
First()	Gets the first element from the results of a query.
FirstOrDefault()	Gets the first element from the results of a query or a default value if no element exists.
Single()	Gets the only element from the results of a query. Throws an exception if the results don't contain exactly one element.
SingleOrDefault()	Gets the only element from the results of a query or a default value if no element exists. Throws an exception if the results contain more than one element.
Skip()	Skips over the specified number of elements in the results of a query and then returns the remaining elements.
Take()	Gets the specified number of elements from the beginning of the results of a query.
ToList()	Creates a List<T> object from the results of a query.

A query that gets a count of the items in the results

```
int invoiceCount = invoiceList
    .Where(i => i.InvoiceTotal > 150)
    .Count();
```

A query that gets the invoice total for the items in the results

```
decimal invoiceTotal = invoiceList
    .Where(i => i.InvoiceDate >= DateTime.Parse("01/01/2023")
              & i.InvoiceDate <= DateTime.Parse("06/30/2023"))
    .Sum(i => i.InvoiceTotal);
```

A query that gets a subset of the results

```
int skipCount = 20;
int takeCount = 10;
var invoices = invoiceList
    .Skip(skipCount)
    .Take(takeCount);
```

Description

- LINQ provides other methods in addition to those that are used to implement the query operators. For a complete list of LINQ methods, see the online documentation for the Enumerable and Queryable classes.

Figure 18-9 How to use additional LINQ methods

A Customer Invoice application that uses generic lists

The next two topics of this chapter present a simple application that uses a query to display customer and invoice information on a form. This will help you see how you can use a query from within a C# application.

The user interface

Figure 18-10 shows the user interface for the Customer Invoice application. As you can see, this interface consists of a single form that lists invoices by customer. This list is sorted by invoice total in descending sequence within customer name.

The list in this form is displayed in a ListView control. If you aren't familiar with this control, you may want to refer to the online documentation to find out how it works. For the purposes of this application, though, you just need to set the View property of this control to Details, and you need to define the column headings as described in this figure. In addition, you need to know how to load data into the control as shown in the next figure.

Note that the columns in a ListView control may be displayed at different widths than what's shown here. That depends on the resolution of your screen display, which is measured in dots per inch (DPI). For example, a display with a higher resolution will display narrower columns, and you may not be able to see all of the data in each column.

To prevent this problem, you can add the code shown in this figure anywhere in the code for the form to scale the columns depending on the DPI. Although you don't need to understand how this code works, you should know that the ScaleControl() method is called when the ListView control is initialized. Because of that, you don't need to call it explicitly. You should also know that the DPI can affect the height of the rows in a ListView control. However, that isn't usually a problem.

The Customer Invoice form

A window titled "Customer Invoices By Invoice Total" showing a ListView with columns: Customer, Invoice ID, Invoice Date, Invoice Total.

Customer	Invoice ID	Invoice Date	Invoice Total
Anderson, Alan	102	2/9/2023	$188.46
Anderson, Jeff	105	2/22/2023	$126.48
Anderson, Randy	117	5/7/2023	$122.18
Bommareddy, Richard	118	6/13/2023	$64.49
Browning, Albert	45	1/13/2023	$64.49
Chamberland, Sarah	46	1/13/2023	$239.16
	18	1/13/2023	$172.88
	50	1/14/2023	$64.49
Chism, Leslie	106	2/23/2023	$188.46
Czarnik, Mark	49	1/14/2023	$110.89
De la fuente, Cathy	48	1/14/2023	$64.49
	104	2/22/2023	$64.49
Galloway, Mariola	43	1/13/2023	$64.49
Howell, Kim	116	4/26/2023	$64.49
Hutcheson, Larry	59	1/19/2023	$622.38
Kittendorf, Joe	111	4/19/2023	$126.48
Lair, Andrew	33	1/13/2023	$181.48

Description

- The Customer Invoice form uses a ListView control to display a list of invoices for each customer. The list is sorted by invoice total in descending sequence within customer name.

- To make this work, the View property of the ListView control is set to Details, which causes the data items to be displayed in columns. In addition, the column headers for the control were added using the ColumnHeader Collection Editor. To display this editor, you can select Edit Columns from the smart tag menu that's displayed when you click the arrowhead icon near the upper right of the control. Then, you can set the Text, TextAlign, and Width properties for each column as necessary.

Note

- The resolution of your screen display, which is measured in dots per inch (DPI), can affect the widths of the columns in a ListView control. To correct this problem, you can add this code to scale the columns depending on the DPI:

```
protected override void ScaleControl(SizeF factor,
BoundsSpecified specified)
{
    base.ScaleControl(factor, specified);
    ScaleListViewColumns(lvInvoices, factor);
}

private void ScaleListViewColumns(ListView listview, SizeF factor)
{
    foreach (ColumnHeader column in listview.Columns)
    {
        column.Width = (int)Math.Round(column.Width * factor.Width);
    }
}
```

Figure 18-10   The user interface for the Customer Invoice application

The code for the form

Figure 18-11 shows the code for the Customer Invoice form. To start, you should know that the Customer and Invoice classes used by this code are the same as the classes shown earlier in this chapter, so they aren't repeated here. The database classes that contain the methods for getting the customer and invoice data also aren't presented here. That's because it doesn't matter where these methods get the data from or how they work. The only thing that matters is that the InvoiceDB class contains a method named GetInvoices() that returns a List<Invoice> object, and the CustomerDB class contains a method named GetCustomers() that returns a List<Customer> object.

All of the code for this form is placed within the Load event handler for the form so the list is displayed when the form is loaded. To start, this code uses the methods of the InvoiceDB and CustomerDB classes to load the invoice and customer lists. Then, the next statement defines the query expression. This expression is similar to others you've seen in this chapter.

First, notice that the query expression joins data from the invoice and customer lists. That's necessary because the customer name will be displayed on the form along with the invoice information. Second, notice that the query expression doesn't include a where clause. Because of that, all of the invoices will be included in the results. Third, the results are sorted by invoice total within customer name so the invoices can be displayed as shown in the previous figure. And fourth, only the fields that are required by the form are included in the results.

To load data into the ListView control, this code uses a foreach statement that loops through the query results. But first, this code initializes two variables. The first one, customerName, will store the name of the current customer. This variable will be used to determine if the customer name is displayed for an invoice. The second variable, i, will be used as an index for the items that are added to the ListView control.

For each element in the query results, the foreach loop starts by checking if the Name field is equal to the customerName variable. If not, the Name field is added to the Items collection of the ListView control, which causes the name to be displayed in the first column of the control. In addition, the customerName variable is set to the Name field so the next element will be processed correctly. On the other hand, if the Name field and the customerName variable are equal, an empty string is added to the Items collection of the ListView control so the name isn't repeated.

The next three statements add the InvoiceID, InvoiceDate, and InvoiceTotal fields as subitems of the item that was just added. This causes these values to be displayed in the columns following the customer name column. Notice that these statements refer to the item by its index. Then, the last statement in the loop increments the index variable.

The code for the Customer Invoice form

```
private void frmCustomerInvoices_Load(object sender, EventArgs e)
{
    List<Customer> customerList = CustomerDB.GetCustomers();
    List<Invoice> invoiceList = InvoiceDB.GetInvoices();

    var invoices = from invoice in invoiceList
                   join customer in customerList
                   on invoice.CustomerID equals customer.CustomerID
                   orderby customer.Name, invoice.InvoiceTotal descending
                   select new { customer.Name,
                                invoice.InvoiceID,
                                invoice.InvoiceDate,
                                invoice.InvoiceTotal };

    string customerName = "";
    int i = 0;
    foreach (var invoice in invoices)
    {
        if (invoice.Name != customerName)
        {
            lvInvoices.Items.Add(invoice.Name);
            customerName = invoice.Name;
        }
        else
        {
            lvInvoices.Items.Add("");
        }
        lvInvoices.Items[i].SubItems.Add(invoice.InvoiceID.ToString());
        lvInvoices.Items[i].SubItems.Add(
            Convert.ToDateTime(invoice.InvoiceDate).ToShortDateString());
        lvInvoices.Items[i].SubItems.Add(invoice.InvoiceTotal.ToString("c"));
        i += 1;
    }
}
```

Description

- The LINQ query used by this application makes it easy to include data from two generic lists. Without LINQ, you'd have to code your own procedure to get the customer name from the customer list.

- The LINQ query used by this application also makes it easy to sort the results based on two fields. Although you could sort a list by a single field in ascending sequence by implementing the IComparable<T> interface in the class that defines the objects in the list, it would be much more difficult to sort by two fields in one or more lists.

Notes

- The code for the Invoice and Customer classes is the same as shown earlier in this chapter.

- The invoice and customer data for this application is stored in text files. However, it could have been stored in any other type of data source, such as a binary file or a database.

Figure 18-11   The code for the Customer Invoice form that uses generic lists

Perspective

Now that you've seen an application that uses LINQ with generic lists, you might want to consider how you would accomplish the same thing without using LINQ. If you do, you'll see that LINQ makes it quick and easy to select the data you need.

To join data from two generic lists without using LINQ, for example, you could include code that loops through one list looking for the object that's related to the object in the other list. By contrast, to join two generic lists using LINQ, you can simply code a join clause or Join() method.

Similarly, to sort the data in a generic list without using LINQ, you'd have to write code to implement the sort yourself. If you just needed to sort by a single field in ascending sequence, that would be manageable. If you needed to sort by more than one field, however, or you needed to sort by a field in descending sequence, it would be much more difficult. And if you needed to sort by fields in more than one generic list, it would be extremely difficult. By contrast, to sort by one or more fields using LINQ, you can simply code an orderby clause or an OrderBy(), OrderByDescending(), ThenBy() or ThenByDescending() method.

The bottom line is that LINQ provides concise language for querying data. So, you should consider using it whenever you need to select data from one or more data sources. In chapter 20, for example, you'll learn how to use LINQ with an application that uses Entity Framework Core to work with the data in a database. This is a common use of LINQ.

Terms

Language-Integrated Query (LINQ)
object relational mapping (ORM)
    framework
query operator
extension method
method-based query
query expression
deferred execution

query variable
immediate execution
range variable
projection
anonymous type
delegate
lambda expression

Exercise 18-1   Create the Customer Invoice application

In this exercise, you'll develop and test the Customer Invoice application that was presented in this chapter.

Design the form

1. Open the project that's in the C:\C#\Ch18\CustomerInvoices directory. In addition to the Customer Invoice form, this project contains the business and database classes needed by the application.

2. Add a ListView control to the Customer Invoice form, and set the View property of this control to Details.

3. Display the smart tag menu for the ListView control and click on Edit Columns to display the ColumnHeader Collection Editor. Then, define the column headings for this control so they appear like the columns shown in figure 18-10.

Add code to display the invoice data

4. Open the Invoice and InvoiceDB classes and review the code that they contain. In particular, notice that the GetInvoices() method in the InvoiceDB class gets invoices from a text file named Invoices.txt and returns them in a List<Invoice> object.

5. Add an event handler for the Load event of the form. Then, use the GetInvoices() method to get the list of invoices, and store this list in a variable.

6. Define a query expression that returns all the invoices from the invoice list and sorts them by invoice total in descending sequence. Include a select clause in this query expression that selects entire invoices.

7. Use a foreach statement to execute the query and load the results into the ListView control. For now, load the CustomerID property of the Invoice class into the Customer column. Don't worry about repeating customer IDs.

8. Run the application to see how it works. Make any necessary corrections, and then end the application.

9. Modify the select clause in the query expression so the query returns only the fields needed by the form. Then, run the application again to be sure it still works.

Enhance the application to include customer information

10. Open the Customer and CustomerDB classes and review the code they contain. Note that the GetCustomers() method in the CustomerDB class gets customers from a text file named Customers18.txt and returns them in a List<Customer> object.

11. Add a statement to the Load event handler of the form that uses the GetCustomers() method of the CustomerDB class to get a list of customers, and store the list in a variable.

12. Modify the query expression so it joins the data in the customer list with the data in the invoice list, so it sorts the results by invoice total within customer name, so it returns the customer name instead of the customer ID, and so only the fields that are needed by the form are returned by the query.

13. Modify the foreach statement so it adds the customer name rather than the customer ID to the ListView control. Don't worry about not repeating the customer name.

14. Run the application to make sure it works correctly.

15. If you're going to continue with the next exercise, leave the solution open. Otherwise, close the solution.

Exercise 18-2   Use a method-based query

In this exercise, you'll modify the solution to exercise 18-1 so it uses a method-based query instead of a query expression.

1. If it's not already open, open your solution for exercise 18-1 and display the code for the form.

2. Comment out the query expression in the event handler for the Load event of the form. Then, code a method-based query to replace the query expression. As you do that, you may want to add one method at a time, testing as you go.

3. When you have the query working, close the solution.

Section 5

Database programming

Most real-world apps store their data in databases. As a result, this section is devoted to teaching you the essentials of database programming in C#. When you complete the four chapters in this section, you should be able to develop substantial database apps.

To start, chapter 19 introduces you to the concepts and terms you need to know when you develop database apps. Then, chapter 20 shows you how to use an ORM (Object Relational Mapper) called Entity Framework (EF) Core to work with the data in a relational database. EF Core uses a data provider called ADO.NET under the hood to access the database. This eliminates the need to write your own data access code.

Occasionally, though, you may still want to write your own data access code. To do that, you can write code that works with ADO.NET directly. You'll learn how to write code like this in chapter 21.

Finally, in chapter 22, you'll learn how to use the DataGridView control to display rows of data. In addition, you'll learn how to add, modify, and delete specific rows that the control displays.

19

An introduction to database programming

Before you can develop a database app, you need to be familiar with the concepts and terms that apply to database apps. In particular, you need to understand what a relational database is and how you work with it. This chapter illustrates these concepts and terms using the Microsoft SQL Server database.

An introduction to client/server systems

In case you aren't familiar with client/server systems, this topic introduces you to their essential hardware and software components. Then, the rest of this chapter presents additional information on these components and on how you can use them in database apps.

The hardware components of a client/server system

Figure 19-1 presents the three hardware components of a *client/server system*: the clients, the network, and the server. The *clients* are usually personal computers or mobile devices.

The *network* is the cabling, communication lines, network interface cards, hubs, routers, and other components that connect the clients and the server. Because you don't need to understand how it works to use it, most diagrams use a cloud symbol to represent the network.

The *server* is a computer that has enough processor speed, memory, and disk storage to store the files and databases of the system and provide services to the clients of the system. When its primary purpose is to store databases, the server is often referred to as a *database server*.

In a simple client/server system, the clients and the server are part of a *local area network* (LAN) that connects computers that are near each other. However, two or more LANs that reside at separate geographical locations may be connected as part of a larger network such as a *wide area network (WAN)*. In addition, individual systems or networks can be connected over the internet. When a client/server system consists of private networks and servers, often spread throughout the country or world, it is commonly referred to as an *enterprise system*.

A simple client/server system

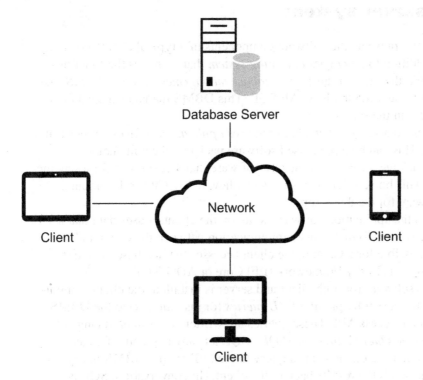

The three hardware components of a client/server system

- The *clients* are the personal computers or mobile devices of the system.
- The *server* is a computer that stores the files and databases of the system and provides services to the clients. When it stores databases, it's often referred to as a *database server*.
- The *network* consists of the cabling, communication lines, and other components that connect the clients and the servers of the system.

Client/server system implementations

- In a simple *client/server system*, the server communicates with the clients over a *local area network (LAN)*.
- LANs can be connected and share data over larger private networks such as a *wide area network (WAN)* or a public network like the internet.
- When a system consists of a private network and servers over a wide area, it is commonly called an *enterprise system*.

Figure 19-1   The hardware components of a client/server system

The software components
of a client/server system

Figure 19-2 presents the software components of a typical client/server system. In addition to a *network operating system* that manages the functions of the network, the server requires a *database management system* (*DBMS*) like Microsoft SQL Server, Oracle, or MySQL. This DBMS manages the databases that are stored on the server.

In contrast to a server, each client requires *application software* to perform useful work. This can be a purchased software package like a financial accounting package, or it can be custom software that's developed for a specific application. This book, of course, shows you how to use C# for developing custom software for database apps.

Although the application software is run on the client, it uses data that's stored on the server. To make this communication between the client and the data source possible for a C# app, the client accesses the database via a *data access API* such as Entity Framework (EF) Core or ADO.NET.

Once the software for both client and server is installed, the client communicates with the server by passing *SQL queries* (or just *queries*) to the DBMS through the data access API. These queries are written in a standard language called *Structured Query Language* (*SQL*). SQL lets any app communicate with any DBMS. After the client sends a query to the DBMS, the DBMS interprets the query and sends the results back to the client. (In conversation, SQL is pronounced as either *S-Q-L* or *sequel*.)

As you can see in this figure, the processing done by a client/server system is divided between the clients and the server. In this case, the DBMS on the server is processing requests made by the app running on the client. Theoretically, at least, this balances the workload between the clients and the server so the system works more efficiently.

Client software, server software, and the SQL interface

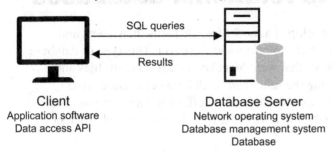

Server software

- To manage the network, the server runs a *network operating system* such as Windows Server.
- To store and manage the databases of the client/server system, each server requires a *database management system* (*DBMS*) such as Microsoft SQL Server.
- The processing that's done by the DBMS is typically referred to as *back-end processing*, and the database server is referred to as the *back end*.

Client software

- The *application software* does the work that the user wants to do. This type of software can be purchased or developed.
- The *data access API* (*application programming interface*) provides the interface between the app and the DBMS. Microsoft's data access APIs are Entity Framework (EF) Core and ADO.NET.
- The processing that's done by the client software is typically referred to as *front-end processing*, and the client is typically referred to as the *front end*.

The SQL interface

- The application software communicates with the DBMS by sending *SQL queries* through the data access API. When the DBMS receives a query, it provides a service like returning the requested data (the *query results*) to the client.
- *SQL,* which stands for *Structured Query Language*, is the standard language for working with a relational database.

Figure 19-2   The software components of a client/server system

An introduction to relational databases

In 1970, Dr. E. F. Codd developed a model for what was then a new and revolutionary type of database called a *relational database*. This type of database eliminated some of the problems that were associated with standard files and other database designs. By using the relational model, you can reduce data redundancy, which saves disk storage and leads to efficient data retrieval. You can also view and manipulate data in a way that is both intuitive and efficient.

How a table is organized

The model for a relational database states that data is stored in one or more *tables*. It also states that each table can be viewed as a two-dimensional matrix consisting of *rows* and *columns*. This is illustrated by the relational table in figure 19-3. Each row in this table contains information about a single product.

In practice, the rows and columns of a relational database table are sometimes referred to by the more traditional terms, *records* and *fields*. In fact, some software packages use one set of terms, some use the other, and some use a combination.

If a table contains one or more columns that uniquely identify each row in the table, you can define these columns as the *primary key* of the table. For instance, the primary key of the Products table in this figure is the ProductCode column.

In this example, the primary key consists of a single column. However, a primary key can also consist of two or more columns, in which case it's called a *composite primary key*.

In addition to primary keys, some database management systems let you define additional keys that uniquely identify each row in a table, called *non-primary keys*. In SQL Server, these keys are also called *unique keys*, and they're implemented by defining *unique key constraints* (also known simply as *unique constraints*). The only difference between a unique key and a primary key is that a unique key can be null and a primary key can't.

Indexes provide an efficient way to access the rows in a table based on the values in one or more columns. Because apps typically access the rows in a table by referring to their key values, an index is automatically created for each key you define. However, you can define indexes for other columns as well. If, for example, you frequently need to sort the rows in the Products table by the Description column, you can set up an index for that column. Like a key, an index can include one or more columns.

The Products table in the MMABooks database

ProductCode	Description	UnitPrice	OnHandQuantity
ANDROID	Murach's Android Programming	57.5000	3756
ASPMVC	Murach's ASP.NET Core MVC	59.5000	3974
C#	Murach's C#	59.5000	4347
C++	Murach's C++ Programming	59.5000	3874
HTML	Murach's HTML and CSS	59.5000	4637
JAVA	Murach's Java Programming	59.5000	4683
JQ	Murach's jQuery	54.5000	677
JS	Murach's JavaScript	54.5000	2136
JSJQ	Murach's JavaScript and jQuery	59.5000	2791
JSP	Murach's Java Servlets and JSP	57.5000	2161
MYSQL	Murach's MySQL	57.5000	3455
ORACLE	Murach's Oracle SQL and PL/SQL	54.5000	4999
PHP	Murach's PHP and MySQL	59.5000	2381
PYTHON	Murach's Python Programming	59.5000	3684
SQLS	Murach's SQL Server for Developers	59.5000	2465
VB	Murach's Visual Basic	57.5000	2193

Concepts

- A *relational database* uses *tables* to store and manipulate data. Each table consists of one or more *records*, or *rows*, that contain the data for a single entry. Each row contains one or more *fields*, or *columns*, with each column representing a single item of data.

- Most tables contain a *primary key* that uniquely identifies each row in the table. The primary key often consists of a single column, but it can also consist of two or more columns. If a primary key uses two or more columns, it's called a *composite primary key*.

- In addition to primary keys, some database management systems let you define one or more *non-primary keys*. In SQL Server, these keys are called *unique keys*, and they're implemented using *unique key constraints*. Like a primary key, a non-primary key uniquely identifies each row in the table.

- A table can also be defined with one or more *indexes*. An index provides an efficient way to access data from a table based on the values in specific columns. An index is automatically created for a table's primary and non-primary keys.

Figure 19-3   How a table is organized

How the tables in a database are related

The tables in a relational database can be related to other tables by values in specific columns. The two tables shown in figure 19-4 illustrate this concept. Here, each row in an Invoices table is related to one or more rows in an InvoiceLineItems table. This is called a *one-to-many relationship*.

Typically, relationships exist between the primary key in one table and the *foreign key* in another table. The foreign key is simply one or more columns in a table that refer to a primary key in another table. In SQL Server, relationships can also exist between a unique key in one table and a foreign key in another table. For simplicity, though, this book only presents relationships that are based on primary keys.

Although it isn't apparent in this figure, the InvoiceLineItems table has a composite primary key that consists of two columns: InvoiceID and ProductCode. As a result, any row in the InvoiceLineItems table can be uniquely identified by a combination of its invoice ID and product code. However, the InvoiceLineItems table can have more than one row for a given invoice ID and more than one row for a given product code.

One-to-many relationships are the most common type of database relationships. However, two tables can also have a one-to-one or many-to-many relationship. If a table has a *one-to-one relationship* with another table, the data in the two tables could be stored in a single table. Because of that, one-to-one relationships are used infrequently.

By contrast, a *many-to-many relationship* is usually implemented by using an intermediate table, called a *linking table*, that has a one-to-many relationship with the two tables in the many-to-many relationship. In other words, a many-to-many relationship can usually be broken down into two one-to-many relationships.

The relationship between the Invoices and InvoiceLineItems tables

Primary key

InvoiceID	CustomerID	InvoiceDate	ProductTotal	SalesTax	Shipping	InvoiceTotal
41	333	10/13/2022 12:...	57.5000	4.3125	3.7500	65.5625
42	666	10/13/2022 12:...	59.5000	4.4625	3.7500	67.7125
43	332	10/13/2022 12:...	54.5000	4.0875	3.7500	62.3375
44	555	10/13/2022 12:...	57.5000	4.3125	3.7500	65.5625
45	213	10/13/2022 12:...	57.5000	4.3125	3.7500	65.5625
46	20	10/13/2022 12:...	234.0000	17.5500	7.5000	259.0500
47	10	10/13/2022 12:...	287.5000	21.5625	8.7500	317.8125

Foreign key

InvoiceID	ProductCode	UnitPrice	Quantity	ItemTotal
41	ANDROID	57.5000	1	57.5000
42	ASPMVC	59.5000	1	59.5000
43	MYSQL	54.5000	1	54.5000
44	PYTHON	57.5000	1	57.5000
45	PYTHON	57.5000	1	57.5000
46	ASPMVC	59.5000	1	59.5000
46	C#	57.5000	1	57.5000
46	HTML	59.5000	1	59.5000
46	SQLS	57.5000	1	57.5000
47	ASPMVC	57.5000	1	57.5000
47	C#	57.5000	4	230.0000

Concepts

- The tables in a relational database are related to each other through their key columns. For example, the InvoiceID column is used to relate the Invoices and InvoiceLineItems tables above. The InvoiceID column in the InvoiceLineItems table is called a *foreign key* because it identifies a related row in the Invoices table.

- Usually, a foreign key corresponds to the primary key in the related table. In SQL Server, however, a foreign key can also correspond to a unique key in the related table.

- When two tables are related via a foreign key, the table with the foreign key is referred to as the *foreign key table* and the table with the primary key is referred to as the *primary key table*.

- The relationships between the tables in a database correspond to the relationships between the entities they represent. The most common type of relationship is a *one-to-many relationship* as illustrated by the Invoices and InvoiceLineItems tables. A table can also have a *one-to-one relationship* or a *many-to-many relationship* with another table.

Figure 19-4   How the tables in a database are related

How the columns in a table are defined

When you define a column in a table, you assign properties to it as indicated by the design of the Products table in figure 19-5. The two most important properties for a column are Name, which provides an identifying name for the column, and Data Type, which specifies the type of information that can be stored in the column. With SQL Server, you can choose from *system data types* like the ones in this figure, and you can define your own data types that are based on the system data types. As you define each column in a table, you generally try to assign the data type that will minimize the use of disk storage because that will improve the performance of the queries later.

In addition to a data type, you must indicate whether the column can be *null*. Null represents a value that's unknown, unavailable, or not applicable. It isn't the same as an empty string or a zero numeric value. Columns that allow nulls often require additional programming, so many database designers avoid these columns unless they're absolutely necessary.

You can also assign a *default value* to each column. Then, that value is assigned to the column if another value isn't provided. If a column doesn't allow nulls and doesn't have a default value, you must supply a value for the column when you add a new row to the table. Otherwise, an error will occur.

Each table can also contain a numeric column whose value is generated automatically by the DBMS. In SQL Server, a column like this is called an *identity column*. Identity columns are often used as the primary key for a table.

A *check constraint* defines the acceptable values for a column. For example, you can define a check constraint for the Invoices table in this figure to make sure that the ProductTotal column is greater than zero. A check constraint like this can be defined at the column level because it refers only to the column it constrains. If the check constraint for a column needs to refer to other columns in the table, however, it can be defined at the table level.

After you define the constraints for a database, they're managed by the DBMS. If, for example, a user tries to add a row with data that violates a constraint, the DBMS sends an appropriate error code back to the app without adding the row to the database. The app can then respond to the error code.

An alternative to constraints is to validate the data that is going to be added to a database before the program tries to add it. That way, the constraints shouldn't be needed and the program should run more efficiently. In many cases, both data validation and constraints are used. That way, the programs run more efficiently if the data validation routines work, but the constraints are there in case the data validation routines don't work or aren't coded.

The SQL Server Object Explorer design view window for the Invoices table

	Name	Data Type	Allow Nulls	Default
⚷	InvoiceID	int	☐	
	CustomerID	int	☐	
	InvoiceDate	datetime2(7)	☐	
	ProductTotal	money	☐	
	SalesTax	money	☐	
	Shipping	money	☐	
	InvoiceTotal	money	☐	
			☐	

▲ **Keys** (1)
　　PK_Invoices   (Primary Key, Clustered: InvoiceID)
Check Constraints (0)
Indexes (0)
▲ **Foreign Keys** (1)
　　FK_Invoices_Customers   (CustomerID)
Triggers (0)

Common SQL Server data types

Type	Description
bit	A value of 1 or 0 that represents a true or false value.
char, varchar, nchar, nvarchar	Any combination of letters, symbols, and numbers.
date, time, datetime2	A date, a time, or a date and time. Various formats are acceptable.
decimal, numeric	Numeric data that is accurate to the least significant digit. The data can contain an integer and a fractional portion.
float, real	Floating-point values that contain an approximation of a decimal value.
bigint, int, smallint, tinyint	Numeric data that contains only an integer portion.
money, smallmoney	Monetary values that are accurate to four decimal places.

Description

- The *data type* that's assigned to a column determines the type of information that can be stored in the column. Depending on the data type, the column definition can also include its length, precision, and scale.
- Each column definition also indicates whether or not the column can contain *null values*. A null value indicates that the value of the column is not known.
- A column can be defined with a *default value*. Then, that value is used for the column if another value isn't provided when a row is added to the table.
- A column can also be defined as an *identity column*. An identity column is a numeric column whose value is generated automatically when a row is added to the table.
- To restrict the values that a column can hold, you define *check constraints*. Check constraints can be defined at either the column level or the table level.

Note

- When you select a column in design view, its properties are displayed in the Properties window. Then, you can use this window to change any of the properties of the column, including those that aren't displayed in design view.

Figure 19-5   How the columns in a table are defined

The design of the MMABooks database

Now that you've seen how the basic elements of a relational database work, figure 19-6 shows the design of the MMABooks database that'll be used in the programming examples throughout this section. Although this database may seem complicated, its design is actually much simpler than most databases you'll encounter when you work on actual database apps.

The purpose of the MMABooks database is to track invoices for a small book publisher. The top-level table in this database is the Customers table, which contains one row for each of the customers who have purchased books. This table records the name and address for each customer. The primary key for the Customers table is the CustomerID column. This column is an identity column, so SQL Server automatically generates its value whenever a new customer is created.

Information for each invoice is stored in the Invoices table. Like the Customers table, the primary key for this table, InvoiceID, is an identity column. To relate each invoice to a customer, the Invoices table includes a CustomerID column. A *foreign key constraint* is used to enforce this relationship and maintain *referential integrity*. When SQL Server enforces referential integrity, it makes sure that any change to the data in the database doesn't create invalid relationships between tables. For example, it won't allow an invoice to be added for a customer that doesn't exist. In addition, if a customer is deleted, this foreign key constraint causes the delete operation to be cascaded from the Customers table to the Invoices table. In other words, any related rows in the Invoices table will also be deleted. That way, you won't run into any problems if you try to delete a customer using any of the versions of the Customer Maintenance app presented in this book.

The InvoiceLineItems table contains the line item details for each invoice. The primary key for this table is a combination of the InvoiceID and ProductCode columns. The InvoiceID column relates each line item to an invoice, and a foreign key constraint that cascades updates and deletes from the Invoices table is defined to enforce this relationship. The ProductCode column relates each line item to a product in the Products table and gives each line item a unique primary key value.

The Products table records information about the company's products. The primary key for this table is the ProductCode column, which can contain a 10-character code. In addition to the product code, each product row contains a description of the product, the unit price, and the number of units currently on hand.

The Customers table is also related to the States table through its State column. The States table contains the state name and the 2-letter state code for each state. Its primary key is the StateCode column.

The final table in the MMABooks database, OrderOptions, contains information that's used to calculate the sales tax and shipping charges that are applied to each invoice. Although this table consists of a single row, it still includes a primary key. This isn't required, but it's a good practice to always include a primary key in case the table is enhanced in the future.

The tables that make up the MMABooks database

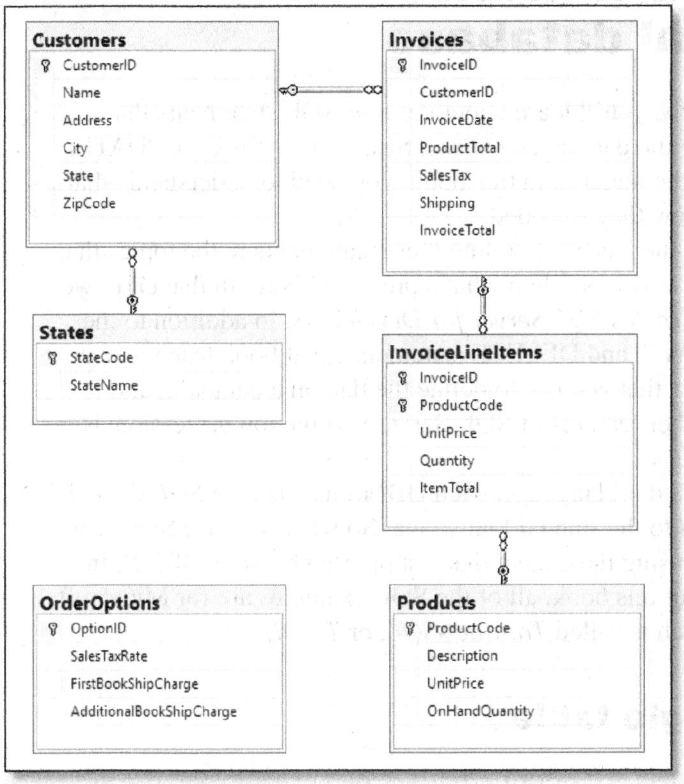

Description

- The Customers table contains a row for each customer. Its primary key is CustomerID, an identity column that's generated automatically when a new customer is created. State is a foreign key that relates each customer to a row in the States table.
- The Invoices table contains a row for each invoice. Its primary key is InvoiceID, an identity column that's generated automatically when a new invoice is created. CustomerID is a foreign key that relates each invoice to a customer.
- The InvoiceLineItems table contains one row for each line item of each invoice. Its primary key is a combination of InvoiceID and ProductCode. InvoiceID is a foreign key that relates each line item to an invoice, and ProductCode is a foreign key that relates each line item to a product.
- The Products table contains a row for each product. Its primary key is ProductCode, a 10-character code that identifies each product.
- The States table contains a row for each state. Its primary key is StateCode.
- The OrderOptions table contains a single row that stores the sales tax and shipping charges used by the app. Its primary key is OptionID.
- The relationships between the tables in this diagram appear as links, where the endpoints indicate the type of relationship. A key indicates the "one" side of a relationship, and the infinity symbol (∞) indicates the "many" side.

Figure 19-6   The design of the MMABooks database

How to use SQL to work with a relational database

In the topics that follow, you'll learn about the four SQL statements that you can use to manipulate the data in a database: SELECT, INSERT, UPDATE, and DELETE. To master the material in this book, you need to understand what these statements do and how they're coded.

Although you'll learn the basics of coding these statements in the topics that follow, you may want to know more than what's presented here. In that case, we recommend our book, *Murach's SQL Server for Developers*. In addition to the SELECT, INSERT, UPDATE, and DELETE statements, that book teaches you how to code the statements that you use to define the data in a database, and it teaches you how to use other features of SQL Server that the top professionals use.

Although SQL is a standard language, each DBMS has its own *SQL dialect*, which includes extensions to the standard language. So when you use SQL, you need to make sure you're using the dialect that's supported by your DBMS. In this chapter and throughout this book, all of the SQL examples are for Microsoft SQL Server's dialect, which is called *Transact-SQL*, or *T-SQL*.

How to query a single table

Figure 19-7 shows how to use a SELECT statement to query a single table in a database. In the syntax summary at the top of this figure, you can see that the SELECT clause names the columns to be retrieved and the FROM clause names the table that contains the columns. You can also code a WHERE clause that gives criteria for the rows to be selected. And you can code an ORDER BY clause that names one or more columns that the results should be sorted by and indicates whether each column should be sorted in ascending or descending sequence.

If you study the SELECT statement below the syntax summary, you can see how this works. Here, the SELECT statement retrieves two columns from the Customers table for all customers who live in the state of Washington. It sorts the returned rows by the Name column.

This figure also shows the *result table*, or *result set*, that's returned by the SELECT statement. A result set is a logical table that's created temporarily within the database. When an app requests data from a database, it receives a result set.

This figure also shows how to code an asterisk in place of the column names to select all the columns in a table. This is a useful technique during development and testing, but you shouldn't include `SELECT *` statements in a production app. That's because they can degrade performance by causing excess data to be retrieved, sent across the network, and stored in memory. An explicit column list makes your code more readable and maintainable.

Simplified syntax of the SELECT statement

```
SELECT column-1 [, column-2]...
FROM table-1
[WHERE selection-criteria]
[ORDER BY column-1 [ASC|DESC] [, column-2 [ASC|DESC]]...]
```

A SELECT statement that retrieves and sorts selected columns and rows from the Customers table

```
SELECT Name, City
FROM Customers
WHERE State = 'WA'
ORDER BY Name
```

The result set defined by the SELECT statement

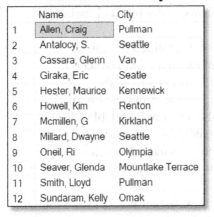

	Name	City
1	Allen, Craig	Pullman
2	Antalocy, S.	Seattle
3	Cassara, Glenn	Van
4	Giraka, Eric	Seatle
5	Hester, Maurice	Kennewick
6	Howell, Kim	Renton
7	Mcmillen, G	Kirkland
8	Millard, Dwayne	Seattle
9	Oneil, Ri	Olympia
10	Seaver, Glenda	Mountlake Terrace
11	Smith, Lloyd	Pullman
12	Sundaram, Kelly	Omak

Concepts

- The result of a SELECT statement is a *result table*, or *result set*, like the one shown above. A result set is a logical set of rows that consists of all the columns and rows requested by the SELECT statement.
- The SELECT clause lists the columns to be included in the result set. This list can include *calculated columns* that are calculated from other columns.
- The FROM clause names the table the data will be retrieved from.
- The WHERE clause provides a condition that specifies which rows should be retrieved. To retrieve all rows from a table, omit the WHERE clause.
- The ORDER BY clause lists the columns that the results are sorted by and indicates whether each column is sorted in ascending or descending sequence.
- To select all of the columns in a table, you can code an asterisk (*) in place of the column names. For example, this statement will select all the columns from the Customers table:

```
SELECT * FROM Customers
```

Figure 19-7   How to query a single table

How to join data from two or more tables

Figure 19-8 presents the syntax of the SELECT statement for retrieving data from two tables. This type of operation is called a *join* because the data from the two tables is joined together into a single result set. For example, the SELECT statement in this figure joins data from the InvoiceLineItems and Products tables into a single result set.

An *inner join* is the most common type of join. When you use an inner join, rows from the two tables in the join are included in the result set only if their related columns match. These matching columns are specified in the FROM clause of the SELECT statement. In the first SELECT statement in this figure, for example, rows from the InvoiceLineItems and Products tables are included only if the value of the ProductCode column in the Products table matches the value of the ProductCode column in one or more rows in the InvoiceLineItems table.

Notice that each column in the SELECT clause is qualified to indicate which table the column is to be retrieved from. For example, the InvoiceID, ProductCode, UnitPrice, and Quantity columns are retrieved from the InvoiceLineItems table, but the Description column comes from the Products table. Qualification is only required for columns that exist in both tables. In this case, only the ProductCode column requires qualification because both the InvoiceLineItems and the Products tables have a column named ProductCode. However, we recommend that you qualify all of the columns just to make it clear which table each column is being retrieved from.

One way to make it easier to qualify your columns is to use *aliases* for your table names. To do that, you code the AS keyword after the table name, followed by the alias. Note that you can omit the AS keyword and just code the alias, but including the AS keyword makes your code more clear.

In the second SELECT statement in this figure, the first SELECT statement is re-written to use an alias of 'li' for the InvoiceLineItems table and an alias of 'p' for the Products table. Then, these aliases are used instead of the full table names to qualify the columns. As you can see, this makes the SQL shorter and easier to read.

Although this figure shows how to join data from two tables, you should know that you can extend this syntax to join data from additional tables. If, for example, you want to include data from the Invoices table along with the InvoiceLineItems and Products data, you could code a FROM clause like this:

```
FROM Invoices AS i
    INNER JOIN InvoiceLineItems AS li
    ON i.InvoiceID = li.InvoiceID
    INNER JOIN Products AS p
    ON li.ProductCode = p.ProductCode
```

Then, in the column list of the SELECT statement, you can include any of the columns in the Invoices, InvoiceLineItems, and Products tables.

The syntax of the SELECT statement for joining two tables

```
SELECT column-list
FROM table-1 [AS alias-1]
    [INNER] JOIN table-2 [AS alias-2]
    ON table-1.column-1 {=|<|>|<=|>=|<>} table-2.column-2
[WHERE selection-criteria]
[ORDER BY column-list]
```

A SELECT statement that joins data from the InvoiceLineItems and Products tables

```
SELECT InvoiceLineItems.InvoiceID, InvoiceLineItems.ProductCode,
    Products.Description, InvoiceLineItems.UnitPrice,
    InvoiceLineItems.Quantity
FROM InvoiceLineItems
    INNER JOIN Products
    ON InvoiceLineItems.ProductCode = Products.ProductCode
WHERE InvoiceLineItems.InvoiceID = 46
```

The result set defined by the SELECT statement

	InvoiceID	ProductCode	Description	UnitPrice	Quantity
1	46	ASPMVC	Murach's ASP.NET Core MVC	59.50	1
2	46	C#	Murach's C#	57.50	1
3	46	HTML	Murach's HTML and CSS	59.50	1
4	46	SQLS	Murach's SQL Server for Developers	57.50	1

A SELECT statement that uses aliases for table names

```
SELECT li.InvoiceID, li.ProductCode, p.Description,
    li.UnitPrice, li.Quantity
FROM InvoiceLineItems AS li
    INNER JOIN Products AS p
    ON li.ProductCode = p.ProductCode
WHERE li.InvoiceID = 46
```

Concepts

- A *join* lets you combine data from two or more tables into a single result set.
- The most common type of join is an *inner join*. This type of join returns rows from both tables only if their related columns match.
- You can make your SQL statements more readable by using *aliases* for table names.

Figure 19-8   How to join data from two or more tables

How to add, update, and delete data in a table

Figure 19-9 presents the basic syntax of the SQL INSERT, UPDATE, and DELETE statements. You use these statements to add new rows to a table, to update the data in existing rows, and to delete existing rows.

To add a single row to a table, you specify the name of the table you want to add the row to, the names of the columns you're supplying data for, and the values for those columns. The statement in this figure, for example, adds a row to the Products table. If you're going to supply values for all the columns in a table, you can omit the column names. If you do that, though, you must be sure to specify the values in the same order as the columns appear in the table. To avoid errors, we recommend you always code the column list.

Note that if a table includes an identity column, you shouldn't provide a value for that column in an INSERT statement. Instead, SQL Server will generate a value for the identity column when it inserts the row.

Also note that you can use single quotes to identify strings. For example, the string for the ProductCode column is enclosed in single quotes. However, if a string value contains a single quote, you can code two single quotes. For example, the string for the Description column uses two single quotes to identify the single quote in *Murach's*.

To change the values of one or more columns in a table, you use the UPDATE statement. On this statement, you specify the name of the table you want to update, along with expressions that indicate the columns you want to change and how you want to change them. You can also specify a condition that identifies the rows you want to change. In the example in this figure, the UPDATE statement changes the UnitPrice column for the product identified by product code MYSQL to 54.00.

To delete rows from a table, you use the DELETE statement. On this statement, you specify the table you want to delete rows from and, in most cases, a condition that indicates the rows you want to delete. The DELETE statement in this figure deletes all the rows from the Customers table for customer 558. It's important to note that if you omit the WHERE clause, all of the rows in the table will be deleted, which is almost never what you want.

How to add a single row

The syntax of the INSERT statement for adding a single row

```
INSERT [INTO] table-name [(column-list)]
    VALUES (value-list)
```

A statement that adds a single row to the Products table

```
INSERT INTO Products (ProductCode, Description, UnitPrice, OnHandQuantity)
    VALUES ('R', 'Murach''s R for Data Analysis', 59.50, 3000)
```

How to update rows

The syntax of the UPDATE statement

```
UPDATE table-name
    SET column-name-1 = expression-1 [, column-name-2 = expression-2]...
    [WHERE selection-criteria]
```

A statement that updates the UnitPrice column for a specified product

```
UPDATE Products
    SET UnitPrice = 54.00
    WHERE ProductCode = 'MYSQL'
```

How to delete rows

The syntax of the DELETE statement

```
DELETE [FROM] table-name
    [WHERE selection-criteria]
```

A statement that deletes a specified customer

```
DELETE FROM Customers
    WHERE CustomerID = 558
```

Description

- You use the INSERT, UPDATE, and DELETE statements to maintain the data in a database table.

- The INSERT statement can be used to add one or more rows to a table. Although the syntax shown above is for adding just one row, there is another syntax for adding more than one row.

- The UPDATE and DELETE statements can be used to update or delete one or more rows in a table using the syntax shown above.

Figure 19-9   How to add, update, and delete data in a table

Perspective

This chapter has introduced you to the hardware and software components of a multi-user system and described how you use SQL to work with the data in a relational database. With that as background, you're now ready to develop a database app with C#.

Terms

client	non-primary key
server	unique key
database server	unique key constraint
network	index
client/server system	foreign key
enterprise system	foreign key table
local area network (LAN)	primary key table
wide area network (WAN)	one-to-many relationship
network operating system	one-to-one relationship
database management system	many-to-many relationship
(DBMS)	linking table
back-end processing	data type
application software	system data type
data source	null value
data access API	default value
application programming interface	identity column
front-end processing	check constraint
SQL query	foreign key constraint
query	referential integrity
Structured Query Language (SQL)	SQL dialect
query results	Transact-SQL
relational database	T-SQL
table	result table
record	result set
row	calculated column
field	join
column	inner join
primary key	alias
composite primary key	

20

How to use Entity Framework Core

In this chapter, you'll learn how to use Entity Framework (EF) Core to work with the data in a database. To use EF Core, you create a data model that maps the objects of an app to the database. Then, you can work with those objects instead of the database.

How to create a data model

In the topics that follow, you'll learn how to create a data model for an app that uses Entity Framework Core. But first, you need to know how Entity Framework Core works and where the data model fits into that framework.

How Entity Framework Core works

Entity Framework (EF) Core is an *Object Relational Mapping (ORM)* framework that allows you to map the objects of an app to a database. Its goal is to address the mismatch that often exists between the tabular structure of a relational database and the objects used in an app. To resolve this problem, EF Core uses a data model that maps the objects used by the app to the relational model of the database.

Figure 20-1 shows how EF Core works. As you can see, the data model consists of the *DbContext class* and *entity classes*. EF Core manages the transfer of data to and from the database using the DbContext object, which stores database connection information as well as collections of entity objects. Note that EF Core uses an ADO.NET data provider to access the database.

When you use EF Core, you use queries to retrieve data from a database. Then, EF Core translates the queries into a form that the database understands, and it translates the data that's returned from the database into the objects that can be used by the app. It also tracks any changes that are made to those objects and provides for submitting those changes to the database.

When you work with EF Core, you can query the data in two ways. The most common way is to use LINQ, and that's what you'll learn in this chapter. However, you can also use the FromSql() method to execute SQL statements directly. Since writing your own SQL statements can be error prone, you won't use this technique very often. However, it can come in handy in some situations.

It's important to understand that because EF Core has abstracted away the details of the underlying data source, you query the objects in the DbContext, not the database itself. In fact, once the entity and DbContext classes have been set up, you don't need to consider how the underlying data source is configured. Instead, you work with the objects and properties that represent the tables and columns of the database.

How Entity Framework Core works

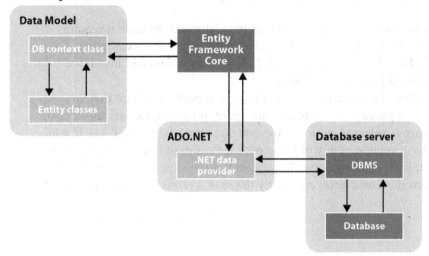

Two ways to query a database

Technique	Description
LINQ	Execute LINQ query expressions or method-based queries.
SQL	Execute SQL statements using the FromSql() method.

Description

- *Entity Framework (EF) Core* provides a layer between the database for an app and the objects for an app. The purpose of this layer is to provide an interface that allows the data in the database to be presented to the app as objects.

- To provide the interface between the objects and the database, EF Core uses a *DbContext class* and *entity classes* that define the entities used by the app and the relationships between those entities.

- When you execute a query with LINQ, EF Core translates the query to one that can be executed by the database. Then, it sends the query to the data provider, which then sends it to the database. When the results are returned from the database, EF Core translates them to the objects defined by the entity classes.

- EF Core also provides for tracking changes and submitting those changes to the database.

Figure 20-1   An introduction to Entity Framework Core

How to add EF Core to your project

Before you can use EF Core, you must manually add the code it requires to your project. This code is stored in packages that you can access using the *NuGet Package Manager*. Figure 20-2 shows how to find and install the packages you need from Visual Studio.

As you follow the procedure in this figure, you need to be sure that you install the correct package versions. In this figure, for example, version 7.0.2 of the first package is selected, which is the one that works with .NET 7.0. If you install the wrong version of any of these packages, almost none of the EF code in this chapter will work correctly. To prevent that, be sure to carefully follow the instructions presented here, especially the search terms described in steps 2 and 6.

How to open the NuGet Package Manager

- Select Tools→NuGet Package Manager→Manage NuGet Packages for Solution.

The NuGet Package Manager with the EF Core package selected

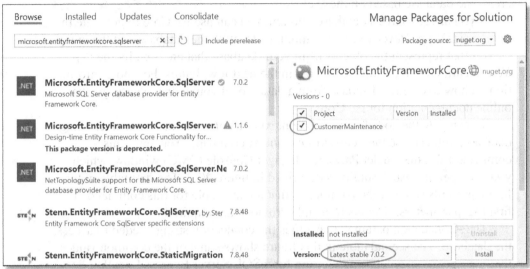

How to install the EF Core packages

1. Click on the Browse link in the upper left corner.
2. Type "Microsoft.EntityFrameworkCore.SqlServer" in the search box.
3. Click on the appropriate package from the list that appears in the left-hand panel.
4. In the right-hand panel, check the project name, select the version that matches the version of .NET you're running, and click Install.
5. Review the License Acceptance dialog that comes up and click I Accept.
6. Type "Microsoft.EntityFrameworkCore.Tools" in the search box.
7. Repeat steps 3 through 5.

Description

- With .NET Core 3.0 and later, you must manually add EF Core and EF Core Tools to your project using the *NuGet Package Manager*.

Figure 20-2   How to add EF Core to your project

How to generate DB context and entity classes

EF Core provides two different development techniques. First, you can start by defining the data model using C# classes. Then, you can use EF Core to create the database based on those classes.

If you already have a database, though, you can use EF Core to generate the *database (DB) context class* that communicates with the database and the *entity classes* that represent the objects from your database that are used by the app. You'll learn how to use this technique in the next few figures. For more information on how to create a database from a data model you define, please see the online documentation for EF Core.

To generate the code for the DB context and entity classes from an existing database, you can use the Scaffold-DbContext command. You enter this command from the NuGet Package Manager Console (PMC) window, which you can open in Visual Studio as described in figure 20-3. The first table in this figure presents some of the parameters that are available for this command. The first two parameters, -Connection and -Provider, are required.

The -Connection parameter specifies the connection string needed to access the database. The second table in this figure shows some of the common values that you specify in a connection string for a SQL Server Express LocalDB database. For example, the two connection strings for the MMABooks database shown in this figure use (LocalDB)\MSSQLLocalDB for the server name. In addition, they specify the name and location of the .mdf file for the database and the type of security to be used.

The -Provider parameter specifies the database provider you'll use to access the database. This value is typically the name of a NuGet package. In this figure, the examples specify the Microsoft.EntityFrameworkCore.SqlServer package.

The -OutputDir parameter specifies the folder where the generated files are stored. If you don't include this parameter, the files are stored in the root folder for the project. In most cases, you'll want to store the generated files in a subfolder of the root folder. In this figure, the examples store the files in the Models\DataLayer subfolder.

The -Context parameter specifies the name you want to use for the generated DB context file. If you don't include this parameter, Visual Studio generates a name that's often long and unwieldy. In most cases, then, you'll include the -Context parameter so you can control the name of your DB context file.

The last three parameters change some of the defaults used by EF Core. If you don't include the -DataAnnotations parameter, for example, the generated entity classes are configured using the Fluent API. When you use the Fluent API, all configuration information is included in the DB context class. By contrast, if you include the -DataAnnotations parameter, the generated code uses data annotation attributes whenever possible. These attributes are included in the entity classes and typically make these classes easier to understand. This chapter presents examples of both the Fluent API and data annotation attributes.

If you don't include the -UseDatabaseNames parameter, EF Core changes the names of the tables and columns in the database so they conform to C# conventions when it generates the entity classes. In particular, it changes names

Parameters for the Scaffold-DbContext command

Parameter	Description
-Connection	The connection string for the database. This parameter is required.
-Provider	The provider, often a NuGet package name. This parameter is required.
-OutputDir	The folder where the generated files are stored. The default is the root folder for the project.
-Context	The name for the generated DB context file.
-DataAnnotations	Specifies that attributes are used to configure the entity classes whenever possible. Otherwise, EF Core uses the Fluent API for all configuration.
-UseDatabaseNames	Specifies that entity classes and properties are given the same names as the tables and columns in the database. Otherwise, EF Core uses names that conform to C# conventions.
-Force	Specifies that existing files can be overwritten. Otherwise, existing files can't be overwritten.

Common values used in a connection string for SQL Server Express LocalDB

Name	Description
Data Source/Server	The name of the instance of SQL Server you want to connect to.
AttachDbFilename	The path and file name for the database's .mdf file.
Integrated Security	Determines whether the connection is secure. Valid values are True, False, and SSPI. SSPI uses Windows integrated security and is equivalent to True.

A Scaffold-DbContext command for a Sql Server Express LocalDB database

```
PM> Scaffold-DbContext -Connection "Data Source=(LocalDB)\MSSQLLocalDB;
AttachDBFilename=C:\C#\Database\MMABooks.mdf;Integrated security=True"
-Provider Microsoft.EntityFrameworkCore.SqlServer -OutputDir Models\DataLayer
-Context MMABooksContext -DataAnnotations -Force
```

The same command with the flags for the required parameters omitted

```
PM> Scaffold-DbContext "Data Source=(LocalDB)\MSSQLLocalDB;
AttachDBFilename=C:\C#\Database\MMABooks.mdf;Integrated security=True"
Microsoft.EntityFrameworkCore.SqlServer -OutputDir Models\DataLayer -Context
MMABooksContext -DataAnnotations -Force
```

Description

- To generate *database (DB) context* and *entity classes* from an existing database, you can use the Scaffold-DbContext command.
- The *DB context class* is used to communicate with the database, and the entity classes represent the objects used by the app.
- You enter the Scaffold-DbContext command in the NuGet Package Manager Console (PMC) window. To display this window from Visual Studio, select Tools→NuGet Package Manager→Package Manager Console.
- When you use the Scaffold-DbContext command, you can omit the parameter flags for required parameters. If you do that, you need to code the value for the -Connection parameter first, followed by the value for the -Provider parameter.

Figure 20-3 How to generate the DB context and entity classes

so they use Pascal notation. So, for example, a column named CustomerID is changed to a property named CustomerId. If that's not what you want, you can include the -UseDatabaseNames parameter.

If you don't include the -Force parameter, you'll get an error if you execute the Scaffold-DbContext command and the files that would be generated already exist. That way, you can't unintentionally overwrite existing files. In some cases, though, you'll need to regenerate the DB context and entity classes after making changes to the databases. To do that, you can use the -Force parameter to allow the overwriting of existing files.

When you use the Scaffold-DbContext command, you can code the flags for all parameters as shown in the first example. Alternatively, you can omit the flags for the two required parameters, -Connection and -Provider. If you do that, though, you need to be sure to code the value for the -Connection parameter first, followed by the value for the -Provider parameter.

The data model for the MMABooks database

If the Scaffold-DbContext command runs without error, the data model is created and displayed in the Solution Explorer as shown in figure 20-4. Here, the model is stored in the Models\DataLayer folder as specified by the Scaffold-DbContext command. This folder includes a DB context file named MMABooksContext.cs, as well as an entity class for each of the tables in the MMABooks database.

With EF Core 3.1 and earlier, the entity classes are given the same names as the database tables, which in this case are pluralized. By contrast, when you create your own objects, you typically use singular names. Unfortunately, these early versions of EF don't provide a way to change the generated names from plural to singular. However, with EF Core 5.0 and later, entity classes are given singular names, even if the names of the database tables are pluralized.

By the way, if you run the Scaffold-DbContext command and get a "Build failed" message, it's because the source code for your app has syntax errors. Because of that, you'll typically want to generate the data model before you start coding an app.

When the Scaffold-DbContext command is running, you will likely see a couple of warnings highlighted in yellow. The first warning is about not storing the database connection string in the generated code, and the DB context class will contain a similar warning. To address this warning, you can store the connection string outside the DB context class and then modify the code for that class to get the connection string. You'll learn how to do that later in this chapter.

The second warning is about the user not having VIEW DEFINITION rights. If the user hasn't been granted VIEW DEFINITION rights, EF Core can't scaffold advanced features in the database. You can ignore this warning when working with databases that don't use advanced features, such as the MMABooks database presented in this chapter.

A Visual Studio project with a data model

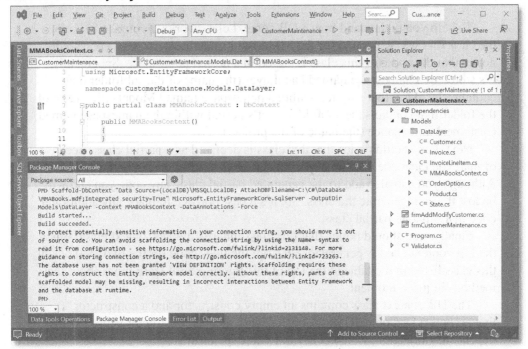

Description

- When the Scaffold-DbContext command completes, the generated files for the data model are displayed in the Solution Explorer.

- Because Models\DataLayer was specified for the -OutputDir parameter, the generated files are stored in a folder with that name.

- Because MMABooksContext was specified for the -Context parameter, the DB context class is stored in a file named MMABooksContext.cs.

- When the Scaffold-DbContext command completes, the Package Manager Console may display two warnings. The first one is about not storing the connection string in your source code, and the second is about the user not having VIEW DEFINITION rights. You'll learn how to address the connection string warning later in this chapter, but you don't typically need to worry about the VIEW DEFINITION rights warning.

Figure 20-4   The data model for the MMABooks database

The code for the DB context class

To help you understand how a DB context class works, figure 20-5 shows the class that was generated for the MMABooks database. To start, you should notice that the code for this class is stored in a nested namespace. Specifically, it's stored in a namespace named DataLayer (the name of the subfolder that contains the class) that's nested within a namespace named Models (the name of the folder that contains the subfolder) that's nested within the namespace named CustomerMaintenance (the name of the project).

Next, you should notice that this class is declared as a partial class. Because of that, you can code additional partial classes that add to the generated class. Although you can also add to the generated partial class, any code you add will be lost if you regenerate the class. So, it's a best practice to place any additional code in a separate partial class.

Finally, you should notice that this class inherits the DbContext class. When the DB context class is generated, EF Core includes code for the two methods of this class listed in the table at the top of this figure. You'll learn more about these methods in just a moment.

The DB context class contains an empty constructor and a constructor that accepts a DbContextOptions object. This second constructor is used with dependency injection, which is beyond the scope of this book.

The constructors are followed by properties that define collections of DbSet<Entity> objects for each of the entity classes. For example, the DbSet<Customer> object represents all of the Customer entities in the context. The DbSet<Entity> class can be used to retrieve, add, update, and delete data.

The first method of the DB context class overrides the OnConfiguring() method of the DbContext class it inherits. This method receives a DbContextOptionsBuilder object that includes configuration information, such as the connection string for the database to be used. Then, an extension method of this object is used to configure the connection for the context. In this case, the UseSqlServer() method is used since the context will use a SQL Server database.

The second method of the DB context class overrides the OnModelCreating() method of the DbContext class. This method accepts a ModelBuilder object that provides the Fluent API that's used to perform some of the configuration for the context and entity classes.

For example, the first two statements that configure the Customer entity use the IsFixedLength() method to indicate that the State and ZipCode properties contain a fixed number of characters. Then, the next statement uses *method chaining* to configure the *navigation properties* between the Customer and State entities. This method chaining is possible because each method returns an object that the next method in the chain can operate on.

The navigation properties define relationships between entities in a way that makes sense in an object-oriented programming language. Navigation properties are convenient because they allow you to traverse related entities in code. EF Core creates a navigation property for each foreign key that's defined for a table.

Two methods of the DbContext class

Method	Description
OnConfiguring(DbContextOptionsBuilder)	Called by the framework for each instance of the context that is created to configure the database used by this context.
OnModelCreating(ModelBuilder)	Called by the framework when the context is created to configure the context.

The DB context class generated by the Scaffold-DbContext command

```
using Microsoft.EntityFrameworkCore;

namespace CustomerMaintenance.Models.DataLayer;

public partial class MMABooksContext : DbContext
{
    public MMABooksContext() {}

    public MMABooksContext(DbContextOptions<MMABooksContext> options)
        : base(options) {}

    public virtual DbSet<Customer> Customers { get; set; }
    public virtual DbSet<Invoice> Invoices { get; set; }
    public virtual DbSet<InvoiceLineItem> InvoiceLineItems { get; set; }
    public virtual DbSet<OrderOption> OrderOptions { get; set; }
    public virtual DbSet<Product> Products { get; set; }
    public virtual DbSet<State> States { get; set; }

    protected override void OnConfiguring(
        DbContextOptionsBuilder optionsBuilder) =>
            optionsBuilder.UseSqlServer(
                "Data Source=(LocalDB)\\MSSQLLocalDB; " +
                "AttachDBFilename=C:\\C#\\Database\\MMABooks.mdf;" +
                "Integrated security=True");

    protected override void OnModelCreating(ModelBuilder modelBuilder)
    {
        modelBuilder.Entity<Customer>(entity =>
        {
            entity.Property(e => e.State).IsFixedLength();
            entity.Property(e => e.ZipCode).IsFixedLength();

            entity.HasOne(d => d.StateNavigation)
                .WithMany(p => p.Customers)
                .OnDelete(DeleteBehavior.ClientSetNull)
                .HasConstraintName("FK_Customers_States");
        });

        modelBuilder.Entity<Invoice>(entity =>
        {
            entity.HasOne(d => d.Customer)
                .WithMany(p => p.Invoices)
                .HasConstraintName("FK_Invoices_Customers");
        });
```

Figure 20-5   The code for the DB context class (part 1 of 2)

To illustrate, the third statement in the code in part 2 of figure 20-5 that configures the InvoiceLineItem entity defines a navigation property named ProductCodeNavigation. The HasOne() method indicates that each invoice line item is related to one product, and the WithMany() method indicates that each product can be related to many invoice line items. In other words, the Product entity has a one-to-many relationship with the InvoiceLineItem entity.

The next two methods provide more information about that relationship. The OnDelete() method indicates what happens when a product is deleted, and the HasConstraintName() method identifies the name of the foreign key constraint. Because the database doesn't indicate what happens when a row is deleted from the Products table, the value that's passed to the OnDelete() method (DeleteBehavior.ClientSetNull) indicates that EF Core will try to set the value of the ProductCode property to null. Because the ProductCode property can't contain a null value, though, an exception is thrown. The same is true of the foreign key that's defined for the relationship between the State and Customer entities shown in part 1 of this figure.

By contrast, the foreign keys that are defined for the relationships between the InvoiceLineItem and Invoice entities here and the Invoice and Customer entities in part 1 don't include the OnDelete() method. That's because the database provides for cascading the deletes for these relationships. With *cascading deletes,* if a row in a table on the one side of a relationship is deleted, all of the related rows in the table on the many side of the relationship are deleted. Because of that, it isn't necessary to specify a delete behavior.

The last statement in the OnModelCreating() method calls the OnModelCreatingPartial() method that follows and passes the ModelBuilder object to it. Note that only the signature for the OnModelCreatingPartial() method is provided. You can use this method to customize the OnModelCreating() method. To do that, you create a partial class with the same name as the DB context class. Then, you can add a partial method to this class named OnModelCreatingPartial(), and you can add your custom code to this method. If you add your custom code to the OnModelCreating() method in the generated DB context class instead, it will be overwritten if you regenerate the model.

The DB context class (continued)

```
        modelBuilder.Entity<InvoiceLineItem>(entity =>
        {
            entity.Property(e => e.ProductCode).IsFixedLength();

            entity.HasOne(d => d.Invoice)
                .WithMany(p => p.InvoiceLineItems)
                .HasConstraintName("FK_InvoiceLineItems_Invoices");

            entity.HasOne(d => d.ProductCodeNavigation)
                .WithMany(p => p.InvoiceLineItems)
                .OnDelete(DeleteBehavior.ClientSetNull)
                .HasConstraintName("FK_InvoiceLineItems_Products");
        });

        modelBuilder.Entity<Product>(entity =>
        {
            entity.Property(e => e.ProductCode).IsFixedLength();
        });

        modelBuilder.Entity<State>(entity =>
        {
            entity.Property(e => e.StateCode).IsFixedLength();
        });

        OnModelCreatingPartial(modelBuilder);
    }

    partial void OnModelCreatingPartial(ModelBuilder modelBuilder);
}
```

Description

- The DbContext class that's inherited by the generated context class provides for communicating with a database.
- The DbSet<Entity> properties represent the collections of entities in the context and map to the database tables.
- A *navigation property* provides a way to define the relationship between two entity types and is based on the foreign key for two related tables.

Figure 20-5   The code for the DB context class (part 2 of 2)

The code for the Customer entity class

Figure 20-6 presents the code for the Customer entity class that was generated by EF Core. You should notice two important things about this class. First, it's a partial class. Second, it's stored in a nested namespace just like the DB context class.

The Customer class has several properties that correspond to the columns of the Customers table in the database. Because the -DataAnnotations parameter was included on the Scaffold-DbContext command that generated the model that contains this entity class, each property contains data annotation attributes that describe that property. The table at the top of this figure lists the attributes used by the properties in the Customer entity. For example, the CustomerId property includes the Key attribute, which indicates that it's the primary key, and the Column attribute, which indicates the name of the column in the corresponding table. Note that this attribute is included only if the property name is different from the column name. In this case, EF Core changed the name of the property so it uses Pascal notation.

Each of the remaining properties that correspond to columns in the Customers table includes the StringLength and Unicode attributes. The StringLength property specifies the maximum length of a string that's allowed by the database column. The Unicode attribute indicates whether the database column allows Unicode values. In SQL Server, the data type nvarchar(n) allows Unicode, while the data type varchar(n) does not.

To save space, the City, State, and ZipCode properties aren't shown here. However, they are also string properties that include the StringLength and Unicode attributes.

After the properties that correspond to database columns are two navigation properties. The Invoices property defines a collection of Invoice entities that provides for navigating to the invoices for a customer. This property includes an InverseProperty attribute that identifies the property on the other end of the relationship. In this case, it's the Customer property of the Invoice entity.

The StateNavigation property provides for navigating to the related State entity. This property includes a ForeignKey attribute that identifies the property of the Customer entity that contains the foreign key value. In this case, that's the State property. Like the Invoices property, the StateNavigation property includes the InverseProperty attribute that identifies the property on the other end of the relationship. In this case, it's the Customers property of the State entity.

Notice that the name of this *foreign key property* consists of the related entity, State, appended with "Navigation". In most cases, though, the name of a foreign key property is just the related entity. But because the Customer entity already includes a property named State, the Scaffold-DbContext command changed the foreign key property name to StateNavigation to make it unique.

Some of the data annotation attributes for configuration

Attribute	Description
`Key`	The database column that's the primary key.
`Column`	The name of the column in the database if it's different from the property name.
`Unicode`	Specifies whether the database column allows Unicode strings.
`StringLength`	Specifies the maximum string length allowed by the database column.
`ForeignKey`	Specifies the property that's used as a foreign key in a relationship.
`InverseProperty`	Specifies the navigation property on the other end of a relationship.

The generated Customer partial class

```
using System.ComponentModel.DataAnnotations;
using System.ComponentModel.DataAnnotations.Schema;
using Microsoft.EntityFrameworkCore;

namespace CustomerMaintenance.Models.DataLayer;

public partial class Customer
{
    [Key]
    [Column("CustomerID")]
    public int CustomerId { get; set; }

    [StringLength(100)]
    [Unicode(false)]
    public string Name { get; set; } = null!;

    [StringLength(50)]
    [Unicode(false)]
    public string Address { get; set; } = null!;

    // City, State, and ZipCode properties go here

    [InverseProperty("Customer")]
    public virtual ICollection<Invoice> Invoices { get; } =
        new List<Invoice>();

    [ForeignKey("State")]
    [InverseProperty("Customers")]
    public virtual State StateNavigation { get; set; } = null!;
}
```

Description

- A *foreign key property* identifies the property that's the primary key in the related class. This works much like a foreign key constraint in a relational database.
- EF Core creates partial classes for the entity classes it generates. That way, if you want to add code to a class, you can store it in another partial class and it won't be overwritten if you have to generate the DB context again. For more information, see figure 20-7.

Figure 20-6   The code for the generated Customer entity class

How to modify the generated code

When EF Core generates a DB context class, it includes the connection string for the database in the OnConfiguring() method as you saw in part 1 of figure 20-5. However, this can cause security vulnerabilities. In addition, if the connection string ever changes, you'll have to recompile the app. Because of that, connection strings are often stored in an App.config file. An App.config file is an XML file that contains settings that are specific to a particular app. And when you change the settings in the App.config file, you don't have to recompile your app.

To add an App.config file to a project, you select the Application Configuration File template from the Add New Item dialog. Then, you can add any configuration items you need to the starting code for this file. The first example in figure 20-7, for instance, shows an App.config file after a connection string for the MMABooks database has been added.

After you add the connection string to the App.config file, you can change the OnConfiguring() method in the DB context file so it gets the connection string from this file. The second example in this figure shows how to use the ConfigurationManager.ConnectionStrings property to do that. Note that for this to work, you have to include a using directive for the System.Configuration namespace.

This figure also shows how to enhance the code that's generated for an entity class. You might want to do that, for example, to add properties that indicate the state of the entity. Although you might be tempted to add this code directly to the generated classes, it's a best practice to create partial classes instead. Then, the code in the custom partial class won't be overwritten if you regenerate the model.

To illustrate, the third example presents another partial class named Customer that adds to the generated partial class. It adds a read-only property named HasAddress that returns a Boolean value that indicates whether the Address property has a value. For this to work, this class must be in the same namespace as the generated class, as shown here. However, if the file that contains your partial class has the same name as the file for the generated partial class, you'll need to store it in a different folder than the generated class. For example, you might store it in a folder named Models\DataLayer\PartialClasses or Models\DataLayer\CustomClasses.

An App.config file that includes a database connection string

```xml
<?xml version="1.0" encoding="utf-8" ?>
<configuration>
  <connectionStrings>
    <add name="MMABooks"
         connectionString="Data Source=(LocalDB)\MSSQLLocalDB;
         AttachDBFilename=C:\C#\Database\MMABooks.mdf;
         Integrated Security=True"/>
  </connectionStrings>
</configuration>
```

The updated OnConfiguring() method in the DB context file

```csharp
using Microsoft.EntityFrameworkCore;
using System.Configuration;
...
protected override void OnConfiguring(
    DbContextOptionsBuilder optionsBuilder)
{
    if (!optionsBuilder.IsConfigured)
    {
        optionsBuilder
            .UseSqlServer(ConfigurationManager.ConnectionStrings["MMABooks"]
            .ConnectionString);
    }
}
```

A partial class that adds a read-only property

```csharp
namespace CustomerMaintenance.Models.DataLayer;

public partial class Customer
{
    public bool HasAddress => !string.IsNullOrEmpty(Address);
}
```

Description

- By default, the OnConfiguring() method of the DB context class includes the connection string to the database. However, it's considered a best practice to change this method so it gets the connection string from an App.config file.

- To add an App.config file to a project, select the Application Configuration File template from the Add New Item dialog (Project→Add New Item). Then, you can add a named connection string to this file and refer to it from the OnConfiguring() method.

- If you add custom code to a generated entity class, those additions will be lost if you regenerate the model. To avoid that, you should store custom code in a separate partial class that's in the same namespace as the generated class.

- If you want to use the same file name for a custom partial class as the generated partial class, you have to store the custom partial class in a different subfolder.

Figure 20-7   How to modify the generated code

How to use LINQ with EF Core

To get data from a database when you use EF Core, you can use LINQ. In the topics that follow, you'll learn the basic skills for using LINQ with EF Core.

How to retrieve data

To use LINQ to retrieve data from a single table, you first create an instance of the DB context for the data model. This is illustrated by the first example in figure 20-8. This statement creates an instance of the MMABooksContext class and stores it in a variable named context.

Once you've done that, you can use the properties of this object to refer to the entity collections in the data model that correspond to tables in the database. To illustrate, the query in the second example retrieves all of the rows from the table that corresponds to the Invoices entity collection. To do that, it uses the Invoices property of the context object. Because this query ends with the ToList() method, it's executed immediately and the list of invoices is stored in the invoices variable. When you use LINQ with EF Core, you often use immediate execution like this.

The third example shows a query that returns a single invoice. To do that, it includes a Where() method with a lambda expression that specifies the invoice ID for the invoice to be retrieved. Then, it calls the FirstOrDefault() method to retrieve the invoice. This gets the first invoice with the specified ID. If an invoice with that ID isn't found, a default value is returned.

Note that you can also use the First(), Single(), or SingleOrDefault() method to retrieve a single invoice. If you use the First() method, however, an exception will be thrown if the invoice isn't found. If you use the Single() or SingleOrDefault() method, an exception is thrown if there is more than one invoice with the specified value. In addition, if you use the Single() method, an exception is thrown if the invoice isn't found. When you use LINQ with EF Core, you can only use the Single() or SingleOrDefault() method if you're retrieving a row by its primary key. Finally, you should know that the First() and FirstOrDefault() methods are more efficient because they stop searching when they find the first invoice with the specified ID.

The fourth example shows another way to retrieve a row by its primary key. To do that, you use the Find() method. Because this method results in more concise code than the Where() method, you'll typically use it when you're retrieving a row by primary key.

The fifth example shows a query with Where() and Select() methods that retrieves data from the Invoices table. This time, though, it only selects three properties of each invoice. This limits the amount of data that's retrieved, which makes your app more efficient.

The last example shows a query that uses the Join(), OrderBy(), and ThenByDescending() methods. This also works like the example you saw in chapter 18, except that it queries entity collections. In addition, it ends with the ToList() method so it's executed immediately.

A statement that creates an instance of the DB context

```
MMABooksContext context = new();
```

A query that stores all the invoices in a variable

```
var invoices = context.Invoices.ToList();
```

A query that gets a single invoice by ID

```
var selectedInvoice = context.Invoices.Where(i => i.InvoiceId == 33)
                                       .FirstOrDefault();
```

Another way to get a single invoice by ID

```
var selectedInvoice = context.Invoices.Find(33);
```

A query that gets selected invoices

```
var invoices = context.Invoices.Where(i => i.InvoiceTotal > 250)
                               .Select(i => new { i.CustomerId,
                                                  i.InvoiceDate,
                                                  i.InvoiceTotal })
                               .ToList();
```

A query that joins customer and invoice data

```
var customerInvoices = context.Customers
    .Join(context.Invoices,
          c => c.CustomerId,
          i => i.CustomerId,
          (c, i) => new { c.Name, i.InvoiceDate, i.InvoiceTotal })
    .OrderBy(ci => ci.Name)
    .ThenByDescending(ci => ci.InvoiceTotal)
    .ToList();
```

Description

- To work with the entities in a data model, you create an instance of the DB context for the model.

- After you create an instance of the DB context, you can use LINQ to query the entity collections in the data model as shown above. This works just like it does for any data source as shown in chapter 18.

- When you query entity collections, data is retrieved from the database tables that the entities are mapped to.

- To execute a query that retrieves a single entity object, you can use the First(), FirstOrDefault(), Single(), or SingleOrDefault() method. For a description of these methods, see figure 18-9 in chapter 18.

- To retrieve an entity object with a specific primary key value, you can use the Find() method of the object collection. This is more concise than using the Where() method.

- To execute a query that can retrieve two or more entity objects and store those objects in a List<T> object, you can use the ToList() method.

Figure 20-8   How to use LINQ to retrieve data

How to load related objects

In addition to retrieving selected columns from two tables using a join, you may want to return all of the columns from two related tables. For example, suppose an app lets the user retrieve the data for a selected customer and then displays the customer data along with the invoices for that customer. To do that, the app must load the invoice data as well as the customer data. Figure 20-9 shows two ways you can do that.

The first example in this figure shows how to use a technique called *eager loading*. To do that, you use the Include() method to load related entities. As you can see, you code this method on the data source for the query, in this case, the Customers entity collection. Then, you code a lambda expression that identifies the entity collection to include. Note that you can also code a string known as a *query path* as the argument. In most cases, the query path is the name of the navigation property that identifies the related entities to be loaded, such as "Invoices".

You can also load related entities explicitly using the Load() method. This is referred to as *explicit loading*. The technique you use to load entities explicitly depends on whether you want to load the objects on the one side of a relationship or on the many side of a relationship.

The second example in this figure shows how to load the objects on the many side of a relationship. Here, the query that retrieves the Customer entity is executed. Then, the IsLoaded property of the collection of Invoice entities that are related to the Customer entity checks that the invoices for that customer aren't already loaded. To do that, the Entry() method is used to access the Customer entity, and the Collection property is used to access the collection of related Invoice entities. The use of the IsLoaded property ensures that any existing data isn't overwritten, and it improves the efficiency of the app. If the invoices haven't been loaded, the Load() method is then used to load them.

The third example shows how to use the Load() method to load the related entity on the one side of a relationship. In this example, the Customer entity for an Invoice entity is being loaded. To do that, you use code similar to the code in the second example. The only difference is that you use the Reference property instead of the Collection property to refer to the entity on the one side of the relationship.

Note that because the queries in the second and third examples retrieve a row by its primary key, they could use the Find() method instead of the Where() and Single() methods. However, the use of the Where() and Single() methods makes it easier to compare these two examples with the first example.

You can also load data from a related table using a technique called *lazy loading*. However, because lazy loading isn't enabled in EF Core by default, and because it can cause performance issues, this book doesn't present it. If you'd like to know more about lazy loading, you can consult the online documentation.

A query that uses eager loading to load related entities

```
var selectedCustomer = context.Customers
    .Include(c => c.Invoices)
    .Where(c => c.CustomerId == customerID)
    .Single();
```

Code that explicitly loads the entities on the many side of a relationship

```
var selectedCustomer = context.Customers
    .Where(c => c.CustomerId == customerID)
    .Single();

if (!context.Entry(selectedCustomer).Collection("Invoices").IsLoaded)
    context.Entry(selectedCustomer).Collection("Invoices").Load();
```

Code that explicitly loads the entity on the one side of a relationship

```
var selectedInvoice = context.Invoices
    .Where(i => i.InvoiceId == invoiceID)
    .Single();

if (!context.Entry(selectedInvoice).Reference("Customer").IsLoaded)
    context.Entry(selectedInvoice).Reference("Customer").Load();
```

Description

- By default, only the entity objects that are specifically requested by a query are loaded into the DB context. To load related objects, you can use eager loading or explicit loading.
- For *eager loading*, you use the Include() method with a lambda expression or *query path* that specifies the related objects to include in the query results.
- For *explicit loading*, you use the Load() method to load the related objects.
- To load the related objects on the many side of an association using the Load() method, you use the Entry() method of the DB context to get the entity on the one side of the relationship. Then, you use the Collection() method of that object to get the entities on the many side of the association.
- To load the related object on the one side of an association using the Load() method, you use the Entry() method of the DB context to get the entity on the many side of the association. Then, you use the Reference() method of that object to get the entity on the one side of the association.
- Before you load related entities explicitly, you should use the IsLoaded property to check that the entities aren't already loaded. Otherwise, the current data will be overwritten, which may not be what you want.
- To use the Include() or Load() method, the query must return an entity type.
- To use the Include() method, you must import the Microsoft.EntityFrameworkCore namespace.
- You can also use *lazy loading* to load related data, although it isn't enable in EF Core by default. For more information, you can consult the online documentation.

Figure 20-9   How to load related objects

How to use EF Core to modify a database

So far, this chapter has shown how to use LINQ to query data. When you use EF Core, however, you also need to know how to insert, update, and delete data, and you need to know how to handle the errors that can occur when you do that. That's what you'll learn in the topics that follow.

How to insert, update, and delete data

The two tables at the top of figure 20-10 present the methods of the DbSet and DbContext classes that you use to add, modify, and delete data in a database. When you use the Add(), Update(), and Remove() methods of the DbSet class, you should know that they don't actually communicate with the database. Instead, they update the state of an entity in the DbSet collection to Added, Modified, or Deleted. These states are defined by the EntityState enumeration. In addition, the Add() method adds the entity to the DbSet collection so it can be tracked.

The first example in this figure shows how to add an entity to an entity collection. To do that, you create an entity object, assign values to its properties, and then call the Add() method to add it to the entity collection.

The second example shows how to modify an existing entity. To do that, you start by retrieving the entity and storing it in an entity object. Then, you change the values of one or more properties of the object.

At this point, in an environment like a WinForms app, you don't need to call the Update() method. That's because a WinForms app tracks the state of its variables. So, the act of changing an entity's property automatically causes the entity to be marked as Modified. Then, when the database is updated, only those fields that have changed are updated.

By contrast, when you call the Update() method, every field in the table is updated, whether the corresponding property value has changed or not. For this reason, it's better not to call the Update() method unless you need to. Typically, that would be in an environment like a web app, which loses the state of its variables between trips to the web server.

The third example shows how to delete an existing entity. To do that, you retrieve the entity and store it in an entity object just as you do when you modify an object. Then, you call the Remove() method to mark the object as deleted.

After you add, update, or remove one or more entities, you can call the SaveChanges() method of the DB context class to save the changes to the database as shown in the last example. When you call this method, it checks the state of all the entities in the context and then executes an INSERT, UPDATE, or DELETE statement at the database for each entity marked as Added, Modified, or Deleted. It also resets the state of the objects in the context to Unchanged and returns a value that indicates how many entities were affected.

Note that it's more efficient to call the SaveChanges() method once after all changes have been made rather than after each change is made. However, that

Three of the methods of the DbSet class

Method	Description
Add(entity)	Sets the state of the specified entity to Added. Also adds the entity to the DbSet<entity> property of the context.
Update(entity)	Sets the state of the specified entity to Modified.
Remove(entity)	Sets the state of the specified entity to Deleted.

One of the methods of the DbContext class

Method	Description
SaveChanges()	Saves all pending changes to the underlying database, sets the state of the entities to Unchanged, and returns the number of entities that were affected.

Code that adds a new entity

```
var customer = new() { Name="Nick Taggart", Address="123 Main St",
                       City="Fresno", State="CA", ZipCode="93650" };
context.Customers.Add(customer);
```

Code that modifies an existing entity

```
var customer = context.Customers.Find(1);
customer.ZipCode = "93651";
context.Customers.Update(customer);      // optional - usually not needed
```

Code that marks an entity for deletion

```
var customer = context.Customers.Find(1);
context.Customers.Remove(customer);
```

A statement that saves the changes to the database

```
int rowsAffected = context.SaveChanges();
```

Description

- The Add(), Update(), and Delete() methods of the DbSet class change the state of the specified entity to Added, Modified, or Deleted. That is, it marks the entity as having pending changes, but doesn't actually make any changes to the database.

- The SaveChanges() method of the DB context object saves the pending changes to the database. That is, it generates the appropriate SQL statements and passes them to the database for processing.

- If you delete a row and a foreign key relationship in the database provides for *cascading deletes*, related rows are deleted automatically. Otherwise, you have to load the related objects and delete them explicitly.

- If you update a row and a foreign key relationship in the database provides for *cascading updates*, primary key values in related rows are updated automatically. Otherwise, you have to load the related objects for the primary keys to be updated.

Figure 20-10　How to insert, update, and delete data

can cause problems if the data in the database is likely to change between the time you retrieve the data and update or delete the data. Because of that, you'll need to decide what technique works best for each app.

As you learned earlier in this chapter, if a foreign key in a database provides for cascading deletes, all of the related rows in the table on the many side of a relationship will be deleted if a row on the one side of the relationship is deleted. However, if cascading deletes aren't defined, you'll need to load and delete the related rows first. Otherwise, EF Core will throw an exception. Similarly, if a foreign key provides for *cascading updates*, primary key values in related rows are updated automatically. Otherwise, you have to load the related rows for the primary keys to be updated.

How to handle database exceptions

When you use the SaveChanges() method to save changes to the database, the DB context throws a DbUpdateException if it encounters any errors. That can happen, for example, if you try to add a row to a table with a primary key that already exists or you don't provide a value for a required column. Then, you can use this exception to display information to the user or write information to an error log. To do that, you code the SaveChanges() method within the try block of a try-catch statement, and you use a catch block to catch the exception.

Figure 20-11 shows one way to work with a DbUpdateException object. This example starts with a using directive for the Microsoft.EntityFrameworkCore namespace, which stores the DbUpdateException class, and a using directive for the Microsoft.Data.SqlClient namespace, which stores the SqlException class. Note that before you can use the Microsoft.Data.SqlClient namespace, you must load its NuGet package using the procedure shown in figure 20-2.

Next, the method in this example attempts to delete a customer. If a DbUpdateException is thrown, the code in the catch block casts it to the SqlException type, which is the appropriate exception type for the database this app uses. Then, it uses the Errors property of the InnerException property of that type to get the details of the exception. This Errors property contains a collection of the errors that occurred. Often, this collection will contain just a single error. To handle situations where it can contain two or more errors, though, you can iterate over the collection and display a message for each error.

In this figure, the catch block code uses a foreach statement to iterate over the Errors collection. Then, the code within the foreach loop formats a message that uses the Number property of each error to get the error code and the Message property to get the description. When all of the errors have been processed, the results are displayed in a dialog.

Another way to work with a DbUpdateException object is to test for specific errors. To do that, you can check for specific error codes and then display your own custom error messages. For example, an error code of 2601 indicates that a row being added contains a duplicate primary key, and an error code of 2627 indicates that an add or update operation violates a unique key constraint. Although this technique requires more work, it can make it easier for the users of the app to understand what caused the problem.

Code that handles database exceptions

```
using Microsoft.EntityFrameworkCore;
using Microsoft.Data.SqlClient;
...
private void btnDelete_Click(object sender, EventArgs e)
{
    DialogResult result =
        MessageBox.Show($"Delete {selectedCustomer.Name}?",
        "Confirm Delete", MessageBoxButtons.YesNo, MessageBoxIcon.Question);
    if (result == DialogResult.Yes)
    {
        try
        {
            context.Customers.Remove(selectedCustomer);
            context.SaveChanges();
            ClearControls();
        }
        catch (DbUpdateException ex)
        {
            string msg = "";
            var sqlException = (SqlException)ex.InnerException!;
            foreach (SqlError error in sqlException.Errors)
            {
                msg += $"ERROR CODE {error.Number}: {error.Message}\n";
            }
            MessageBox.Show(msg, "Database Error");
        }
    }
}
```

Description

- The DbUpdateException is thrown by the DB context when changes can't be saved to the database.

- When you catch the DbUpdateException, you must cast it to the appropriate exception type for the database you're using, such as SqlException. Then, you can use the InnerException property of that type to get the actual exception that occurred.

- The InnerException property contains a collection of one or more errors. You can refer to this collection using the Errors property, and you can get a count of the errors using the Count property of the Errors property.

- One way to handle the DbUpdateException is to iterate through the collection of errors and display information about each error. To do that, you can use properties of each error like the Number and Message properties shown above.

- Another way to handle the DbUpdateException is to check for specific error numbers. Although this is more cumbersome, it allows you to display your own custom messages.

- The SqlException class is in the Microsoft.Data.Sqlclient namespace, which is available as a NuGet package. Before you can use this package, you must search for and install it as shown in figure 20-2.

Figure 20-11   How to handle database exceptions

How concurrency affects insert, update, and delete operations

When using EF Core, a common problem is the conflict that can occur when two or more users retrieve data in the same row of a table and then try to update that row. This is called a *concurrency conflict*. It's possible because once an app retrieves data from a database, the connection to that database is dropped. As a result, the database management system can't manage the update process.

To illustrate, consider the diagram shown in figure 20-12. Here, two users have retrieved the Products table from a database, so a copy of the Products table is stored on each user's computer. These users could be using the same program or two different programs. Now, suppose that user 1 modifies the unit price in the row for product CPLS and updates the Products table in the database. Then, suppose that user 2 modifies the description in the row for the same product and attempts to update the Products table in the database. What will happen? That depends on the *concurrency control* that's used by the programs.

When you use EF Core, you have two main choices for concurrency control. By default, EF Core uses the *last in wins* technique, which works the way its name implies. Since no checking is done with this technique, the row that's updated by the last user overwrites any changes made to the row by a previous user. For the example above, the row updated by user 2 overwrites changes made by user 1, which means that the description is right but the unit price is wrong.

To prevent data errors like this, many programs use a technique known as *optimistic concurrency* that checks whether a row has been changed since it was retrieved. If so, it doesn't save the data. Instead, it throws a concurrency exception. Then, the program can handle the concurrency exception.

If you know that concurrency conflicts will be a problem, you can use a couple of programming techniques to limit concurrency exceptions. One technique is to update the database frequently so other users can retrieve the correct data. The program should also refresh its entity collections frequently so it contains the recent changes made by other users. To do that, you simply create a new instance of the DB context. Then, the next time you retrieve rows, they'll be retrieved from the database.

Another way to avoid concurrency exceptions is to retrieve and work with just one row at a time. That way, it's less likely that two users will update the same row at the same time. By contrast, if two users retrieve the same table, they will of course retrieve the same rows. Then, if they both update the same row in the table, even though it may not be at the same time, a concurrency exception will occur when they try to update the database.

Because most database apps are multi-user apps, you have to add code to them to deal with concurrency conflicts. In the topics that follow, then, you'll learn how to configure entities so they use optimistic concurrency. Then, you'll learn how to handle concurrency exceptions when they occur.

You should also be aware of a third technique, *pessimistic concurrency*, that assumes conflicts will happen (it's pessimistic about them) and locks the database to avoid them. Since pessimistic concurrency is rarely used, this book only shows how to work with optimistic concurrency.

Two users who are working with copies of the same data

What happens when two users try to update the same row?

- When two or more users retrieve the data in the same row of a database table at the same time, it is called a *concurrency conflict*. Because EF Core uses a disconnected data architecture, the database management system can't prevent this from happening.

- If two users try to update the same row in a database table at the same time, the second user's changes could overwrite the changes made by the first user. Whether or not that happens, though, depends on the *concurrency control* that the programs use.

- By default, EF Core uses *last in wins*. This means that the program doesn't check whether a row has been changed before an update or delete operation takes place. Instead, the operation proceeds without throwing an exception. This can lead to errors in the database.

- With *optimistic concurrency*, the program checks whether the database row that's going to be updated or deleted has been changed since it was retrieved. If it has, a *concurrency exception* occurs and the update or delete operation is refused. Then, the calling program should handle the exception.

How to avoid concurrency conflicts

- Use optimistic concurrency for apps where concurrency conflicts are likely to be rare. Then, code the app to handle any concurrency exceptions that occur.

- Design a program so it updates the database and refreshes the entity collections frequently. That way, concurrency errors are less likely to occur.

- Design a program so it retrieves and updates just one row at a time. That way, there's less chance that two users will retrieve and update the same row at the same time.

- Use *pessimistic concurrency*, which assumes that concurrency conflicts will happen and avoids them by locking a database record while it's being updated. Since locking database records creates its own problems, most apps don't use pessimistic concurrency.

Figure 20-12   How concurrency effects insert, update and delete operations

How to check for concurrency conflicts

You can use two techniques to enable optimistic concurrency with EF Core. First, you can check individual properties of an entity for changes. To do that, you can configure those properties with a *concurrency token* like the one shown in the first example in figure 20-13. Here, the ConcurrencyCheck attribute is included on the Address property. Then, if you try to modify or delete a customer and the address you originally retrieved has changed, a concurrency exception is thrown.

In most cases, you'll want to check an entire entity for changes instead of individual properties. To do that for a SQL Server database, you can add a column to the corresponding table with the rowversion data type. This data type is used to store unique numbers that are generated by SQL Server to indicate when a row was last changed. Then, you can re-run the Scaffold-DbContext command to add a *rowversion property* to the entity class as shown in the second example.

Once you've updated the database table and the entity class, EF Core gets the value of the rowversion column every time you query the database. Then, when your app attempts to update or delete a row, EF Core compares the rowversion value that was retrieved with the initial query to its current value in the database. If these values match, EF Core performs the operation and the rowversion property in the database is updated. If these values don't match, though, it means that the row has changed since it was retrieved. In that case, EF Core refuses the action and throws a concurrency exception.

The third example in this figure shows a technique you can use to simulate a concurrency conflict. That way, you can test your exception handling code to be sure it works the way you want. As you can see, this example starts by retrieving a row. Then, it uses the ExecuteSqlRaw() method to modify that same row in the database. This method is available through the Database property of the DB context.

After executing the raw SQL, this code modifies a property of the entity and attempts to save the change to the database. However, the corresponding row in the database has been changed since it was retrieved. As a result, EF Core throws a concurrency exception.

How to configure a concurrency token with attributes

```
public partial class Customer {
    [Key]
    [Column("CustomerID")]
    public int CustomerId { get; set; }
    .
    .
    [StringLength(50)]
    [Unicode(false)]
    [ConcurrencyCheck]
    public string Address {get; set; }
    .
    .
}
```

How to configure a rowversion property

```
public partial class Customer {
    [Key]
    [Column("CustomerID")]
    public int CustomerId { get; set; }
    .
    .
    public byte[] Rowversion { get; set; }
}
```

How to simulate a concurrency conflict

```
var c = context.Customers.Find(1)!;        // get a customer from the database

context.Database.ExecuteSqlRaw(             // change the address in the database
    "UPDATE Customers " +
    "SET Address = '123 Main St' " +
    "WHERE CustomerId = 1");

c.Address = "26 Duffie Drive";             // change the address in the entity
context.SaveChanges();                     // save entity to the database
```

Description

- To check an individual property for a concurrency conflict, you configure the property with a *concurrency token* by adding the ConcurrencyCheck attribute to the property.

- To check all the properties in an entity for conflicts, you use a *rowversion property*. To use a rowversion property with a SQL Server database, you must first add a column with the rowversion data type to the corresponding database table. Then, the rowversion property is generated for you when you generate the DB context.

- To simulate a concurrency conflict to test your exception handling code, you can use the ExecuteSqlRaw() method of the Database property of the DbContext class. This method lets you execute a query against the database. You can use it to update or delete a row that you've retrieved into the DB context. Then, when you update that row or mark it for deletion and save the changes to the database, a concurrency exception will occur.

Figure 20-13   How to check for concurrency conflicts

How to handle concurrency exceptions

If you've enabled optimistic concurrency and an update or delete operation fails because of a concurrency conflict, EF Core throws a DbUpdateConcurrencyException. To handle this exception, you include a catch block that catches it. Because this exception is a subclass of the DbUpdateException class, it must be caught before the DbUpdateException.

Figure 20-14 shows how to work with a DbUpdateConcurrencyException object. Once again, this example starts with a using directive for the Microsoft.EntityFrameworkCore namespace, which stores the DbUpdateConcurrencyException and DbUpdateException classes.

Next, the method in this example shows an event handler that catches a concurrency exception. This event handler is called each time the user updates a Customer entity. Here, the catch block for the concurrency exception starts by using the Entries property of the exception to get a collection of the EntityEntry objects that caused the exception. Because changes are saved to the database each time an entity is updated, though, the Single() method is used here to get the only EntityEntry object. If the app saved two or more changes at once, you could use a loop to process the entries one at a time instead.

Once the EntityEntry object is retrieved, the Reload() method is called to load the current database values into the entity. Then, the code checks if the State property of the entity is equal to EntityState.Detached, which indicates that the row has been deleted from the database. In that case, the code displays an appropriate error message and clears the controls of the form.

If the State property isn't equal to EntityState.Detached, the database row has been updated. In that case, the code displays an error message notifying the user that the data has changed and displays the new values in the form. That way, the user can decide if any of those values need to be changed.

Note that this is just one way that you can handle concurrency exceptions. If you design your apps so concurrency conflicts aren't likely to occur, this technique is acceptable. In some cases, though, you'll want to code more sophisticated routines to handle concurrency conflicts.

For example, you can use the OriginalValues property of the EntityEntry object to get the original values that were retrieved from the database. Then, you can compare them against the current database values to determine which values changed. If any of the values have changed, you can notify the user, update the original values so they match what's in the database, and then let the user decide whether to cancel the changes or submit them again. The technique you choose depends mostly on how often concurrency conflicts are likely to occur and how much control you want users to have over what happens when they do.

A method that handles a concurrency exception

```
using Microsoft.EntityFrameworkCore;

private void btnModify_Click(object sender, EventArgs e)
{
    // code that updates a Customer object
    try
    {
        context.SaveChanges();
        DisplayCustomer();
    }
    catch (DbUpdateConcurrencyException ex)
    {
        ex.Entries.Single().Reload();
        if (context.Entry(customer).State == EntityState.Detached)
        {
            MessageBox.Show("Another user has deleted that customer.",
                "Concurrency Error");
            ClearControls();
        }
        else
        {
            string message = "Another user has updated that customer.\n" +
                "The current database values will be displayed.";
            MessageBox.Show(message, "Concurrency Error");
            DisplayCustomer();
        }
    }
    catch (DbUpdateException ex) {...}
}
```

Description

- The DbUpdateConcurrencyException is thrown when a concurrency conflict occurs.

- To get a collection of the entities that caused the concurrency exception, you use the Entries property of the DbUpdateConcurrencyException class.

- You can use a loop to iterate over the Entries collection. Or, if you're updating or deleting a single entity, you can use the Single() method to get an EntityEntry object for that entity.

- You can use the Reload() method of the EntityEntry object to load the current database values into the entity.

- You can use the Entry() method of the DB context to check whether the entity is detached. If it is, you know that row has been deleted in the database.

- Because DbUpdateConcurrencyException is a subclass of DbUpdateException, you must catch this exception before you catch DbUpdateException.

Figure 20-14   How to handle concurrency exceptions

How to bind controls

When you use Entity Framework Core, you can bind controls to an entity collection or to the results of a query. That's what you'll learn next.

How to bind controls to a collection

Figure 20-15 shows how to bind controls when you use Entity Framework Core. To start, you can bind a control to a collection of entity objects as shown in the first example. Here, the first statement sets the DataSource property of a combo box to the collection returned by the ToList() method of the Customers collection in the DB context object. Notice that the ToList() method of the Customers collection is called so the customer data is retrieved from the database. Then, the second statement sets the ValueMember property of the combo box so the value of the CustomerId property of the entity will be used when a name is selected. Finally, the third statement sets the DisplayMember property of the combo box so the Name property of the entity will be displayed in the combo box list.

How to bind controls to the results of a query

In the first example in figure 20-15, all the rows and columns that the entity is mapped to in the database are retrieved into the DB context when the ToList() method is called. If that's not what you want, you can bind the control to the results of a query instead as illustrated in the second example. Here, only the CustomerId and Name columns are retrieved from the database since these are the only two columns that are used by the combo box. Once again, it's the call to the ToList() method that actually retrieves the data from the database.

The first two examples in this figure use string literals to assign property names from the entity to the ValueMember and DisplayMember properties of the control. However, using string literals in this way can be error prone, because it's easy to mistype the property name. The third example in this figure shows how to use a nameof expression to get the entity's property names. This reduces the chance that you'll introduce errors into your code.

Combo box properties for binding

Property	Description
DataSource	The collection that contains the data displayed in the list.
DisplayMember	The name of the data column whose data is displayed in the list.
ValueMember	The name of the data column whose value is stored in the list. This value is returned by the SelectedValue property of the control.

Code that binds a combo box to an entity collection

```
cboCustomers.DataSource = context.Customers.ToList();
cboCustomers.ValueMember = "CustomerId";
cboCustomers.DisplayMember = "Name";
```

Code that binds a combo box to the results of a query

```
var customers = context.Customers
                .OrderBy(c => c.Name)
                .Select(c => new { c.CustomerId, c.Name });

cboCustomers.DataSource = customers.ToList();
cboCustomers.ValueMember = "CustomerId";
cboCustomers.DisplayMember = "Name";
```

How to assign the entity property names without using string literals

```
cboCustomers.ValueMember = nameof(Customer.CustomerId);
cboCustomers.DisplayMember = nameof(Customer.Name);
```

Description

- You can bind a control such as a combo box or a DataGridView control to an entity collection or to the results of a query by setting the DataSource property of the control to the collection or results. For more information on using the DataGridView control, see chapter 22.

- You can use bound controls to display, add, modify, and delete data. To save any changes you make to the database, you can use the SaveChanges() method of the DB context.

- When you assign the name of an entity property while binding a control, you can code the property name as a string literal. Or, you can use a nameof expression to get the property name from the entity. This can reduce the chances of typos that lead to errors.

Figure 20-15   How to bind controls

How to code a data access class

So far, this chapter has shown how to use EF Core from the code in a form. If you ever decide to use an ORM other than EF Core, however, or you decide to use ADO.NET to write your own data access code as shown in the next chapter, you'll need to change the code in every form that accesses the database. A better practice is to encapsulate your EF Core code within a separate data access class. That way, if you ever change how your app accesses data, you only need to change the code in the data access class.

A simple data access class

Figure 20-16 presents a data access class named MMABooksDataAccess. This class has a private MMABooksContext object that it uses to access the database. Note that many data access classes use dependency injection to get the DB context object used by the class, but that's beyond the scope of this book.

The FindCustomer() method returns a Customer object. It accepts a customer ID that's an integer value and uses it to get the selected customer from the database. You should notice three things about this code. First, it uses the Include() method to load the related State object for the selected customer. Second, because it uses the Include() method, the class has a using directive for the Microsoft.EntityFrameworkCore namespace. And third, since the FirstOrDefault() method returns null if there's no customer in the database with the specified customer ID, the return type of this method is nullable.

The GetStates() method returns a collection of State objects. You should notice three things about this code too. First, because it doesn't use the Where() method, it returns all the states in the States table of the database. Second, it uses the OrderBy() method to sort the states alphabetically by name. And third, since the ToList() method returns an empty collection if there are no records in the database, the return type of this method doesn't need to be nullable.

The AddCustomer(), UpdateCustomer(), and RemoveCustomer() methods all receive a Customer object, and they all call the SaveChanges() method of the DB context object to save changes to the database. Before calling this method, though, the AddCustomer() method adds the Customer object to the Customer collection of the DB context, and the RemoveCustomer() method removes it from that collection. By contrast, the UpdateCustomer() method only calls the SaveChanges() method. That's because the state of the customer entity is automatically set to modified when the entity is changed, so it isn't necessary to call the Update() method of the Customer collection.

Although the data access class presented here calls the SaveChanges() method after each add, update, or delete operation, you could also code the call to SaveChanges() in a separate method. That way, you could perform several add, update, and delete operations before saving the changes to the database. This would result in fewer database calls, but it would also increase the chances of a concurrency conflict.

When you code a data access class, you'll want to store it in a folder that's subordinate to the folder that contains the classes for the data model. That way,

The MMABooksDataAccess class

```
using Microsoft.EntityFrameworkCore;

namespace CustomerMaintenance.Models.DataLayer;

public class MMABooksDataAccess
{
    private MMABooksContext context = new();

    public Customer? FindCustomer(int customerId) =>
        context.Customers
            .Where(c => c.CustomerId == customerId)
            .Include(c => c.StateNavigation)
            .FirstOrDefault();

    public List<State> GetStates() =>
        context.States.OrderBy(s => s.StateName).ToList();

    public void AddCustomer(Customer customer)
    {
        context.Customers.Add(customer);
        context.SaveChanges();
    }

    public void UpdateCustomer(Customer customer)
    {
        context.SaveChanges();
    }

    public void RemoveCustomer(Customer customer)
    {
        context.Customers.Remove(customer);
        context.SaveChanges();
    }
}
```

A form that uses the data access class

```
using CustomerMaintenance.Models.DataLayer;
...
public partial class frmCustomerMaintenance : Form
{
    private MMABooksDataAccess data = new();

    private void btnGetCustomer_Click(object sender, EventArgs e)
    {
        if (IsValidData())
        {
            int customerID = Convert.ToInt32(txtCustomerID.Text);
            var selectedCustomer = data.FindCustomer(customerID);
            DisplayCustomer();
        }
    }
    ...
}
```

Figure 20-16   A simple data access class

the data access class won't be lost if you have to regenerate the data model. In the Product Maintenance app you'll see later in this chapter, for example, the data access class is stored in a folder named DataAccessClasses that's subordinate to the Models\DataLayer folder.

A data access class that handles exceptions

It's generally considered a best practice to place code that accesses a database within the try block of a try-catch statement. However, this can cause problems with a data access class, because different types of exceptions can be thrown for different data access strategies. For instance, a data access class that uses EF Core might throw a Microsoft.EntityFrameworkCore.DbUpdateException, where a class that uses ADO.NET would throw a Microsoft.Data.SqlClient.SqlException. Unfortunately, this once again means you need to change the code in your forms when you change how you access data.

One way to address this issue is to use a custom exception class with your data access class. That way, the form code can catch the custom exception, which will remain the same no matter how the data access code works with the database.

Figure 20-17 shows an example of a data access class that uses a custom exception class named DataAccessException. You'll see this class in a moment. For now, just notice that the data access class starts with directives for the namespaces that contain the exception objects the class uses. Then, it uses try-catch statements to catch any errors when the code accesses the database and then creates and throws a custom exception.

The FindCustomer() method uses a single catch block for the SqlException object of the Microsoft.Data.SqlClient namespace. This exception is thrown for database errors such as permission issues or the database not being found. By contrast, the UpdateCustomer() method uses three catch blocks for concurrency exceptions, update exceptions, and SQL exceptions.

Although the GetStates(), AddCustomer(), and RemoveCustomer() methods aren't shown here, you should know that they include try-catch statements just like the FindCustomer() and UpdateCustomer() methods. Like the FindCustomer() method, the GetStates() method only handles SQL exceptions. The AddCustomer() method handles update and SQL exceptions but not concurrency exceptions. And the RemoveCustomer() method handles all three exceptions just like the UpdateCustomer() method.

All the catch blocks call helper methods to get an exception object to throw, and all of these helper methods return a DataAccessException. In addition, before it throws an exception, the catch block for a concurrency exception reloads the values from the database and gets an EntityState object.

The CreateConcurrencyException() method accepts an EntityState object and uses it to determine the error message for the exception. If the entity state is Detached, the message indicates that the row has been deleted. Otherwise, it indicates that the row has been updated. Then, this method creates a new DataAccessException object, passing the error message and the string "Concurrency Error" as parameters to the constructor, and it returns that object.

The MMABooksDataAccess class updated to handle database exceptions

```
using Microsoft.Data.SqlClient;
using Microsoft.EntityFrameworkCore;

namespace CustomerMaintenance.Models.DataLayer;

public class MMABooksDataAccess
{
    private MMABooksContext context = new();

    public Customer? FindCustomer(int customerId)
    {
        try {
            // same as figure 20-16
        }
        catch (SqlException ex) {
            throw CreateDataAccessException(ex);
        }
    }

    // GetStates() and AddCustomer() methods with exception handling

    public void UpdateCustomer(Customer customer)
    {
        try {
            // same as figure 20-16
        }
        catch (DbUpdateConcurrencyException ex) {
            ex.Entries.Single().Reload();
            var state = context.Entry(customer).State;
            throw CreateConcurrencyException(state);
        }
        catch (DbUpdateException ex) {
            throw CreateUpdateException(ex);
        }
        catch (SqlException ex) {
            throw CreateDataAccessException(ex);
        }
    }

    // RemoveCustomer() method with exception handling

    private DataAccessException CreateConcurrencyException(
        EntityState state)
    {
        string msg = "";
        if (state == EntityState.Detached)
            msg = "Another user has deleted that record.";
        else
            msg = "Another user has updated that record.\n" +
            "The current database values will be displayed.";

        return new DataAccessException(msg, "Concurrency Error");
    }
```

Figure 20-17   A data access class that handles database exceptions (part 1 of 2)

The CreateUpdateException() method shown in part 2 accepts a DbUpdateException object and casts it to a SqlException object. Then, it passes the SqlException object to the CreateDataAccessException() helper method. That method loops through the SqlError objects in the Errors property of the SqlException class to build an error message. When the loop ends, this method creates a new DataAccessException object using the error message and the string "Database Error" as parameters, and it returns that object to the CreateUpdateException() method. That method in turn returns the DataAcessException object.

Note that the CreateDataAccessException() method is also called when a SQL exception is thrown. That can happen anytime the code in the data access class accesses the database.

The DataAccessException class is also shown in part 2. This class is typically stored in the same folder as the data access class. It inherits and extends the Exception class. It has a property named ErrorType and a constructor that initializes this property and calls the base constructor to initialize the inherited Message property. It also has two read-only properties named IsConcurrencyError and IsDeleted. The IsConcurrencyError property looks for the word "concurrency" in the ErrorType to determine if a concurrency error has occurred. The IsDeleted property looks for the occurrence of the word "deleted" in the Message property to see if a row has been deleted. These properties are used when a method handles an exception thrown by the data access class.

This figure ends with an example of an event handler in a form that uses the custom DataAccessException class with the data access class. This event handler is executed after the user makes changes to the data for a customer and then clicks a button to apply the changes. It starts by getting the updated Customer object. Although this code isn't shown here, you can see this code in the complete listing for the Customer Maintenance app that's presented in figure 20-19. After it gets the updated Customer object, this code calls the UpdateCustomer() method of the data access class within the try block of a try-catch statement.

Because the UpdateCustomer() method can throw concurrency exceptions, update exceptions, and database exceptions, and because the methods that are called when these exceptions occur all return a DataAccessException object, the catch block catches this exception. Then, it checks the IsConcurrency property of the exception to see if it's a concurrency exception. If it is, the catch block then checks the IsDeleted property of the exception to see if the concurrency exception occurred because the row was deleted. If so, the code clears the controls on the form. Otherwise, it means that the concurrency exception occurred because the row was updated. In that case, the code displays the current customer data that was loaded when the concurrency exception occurred. Finally, the code in the catch block displays the Message property of the exception in a dialog with the ErrorType property of the exception as the title.

The MMABooksDataAccess class (continued)

```
        private DataAccessException CreateUpdateException(
            DbUpdateException ex)
        {
            var sqlException = (SqlException)ex.InnerException!;
            return CreateDataAccessException(sqlException);
        }

        private DataAccessException CreateDataAccessException(SqlException ex)
        {
            string msg = "";
            foreach (SqlError error in ex.Errors) {
                msg += $"ERROR CODE {error.Number}: {error.Message}\n";
            }

            return new DataAccessException(msg, "Database Error");
        }
    }
```

The DataAccessException class

```
    namespace CustomerMaintenance.Models.DataLayer;

    public class DataAccessException : Exception
    {
        public DataAccessException(string msg, string type) : base(msg) =>
            ErrorType = type;

        public string ErrorType { get; init; }

        public bool IsConcurrencyError =>
            ErrorType.ToLower().Contains("concurrency");

        public bool IsDeleted => Message.ToLower().Contains("deleted");
    }
```

A method that handles an exception thrown by the data access class

```
    private void btnModify_Click(object sender, EventArgs e)
    {
        // code that gets an updated Customer object

        try {
            data.UpdateCustomer(selectedCustomer);
            DisplayCustomer();
        }
        catch (DataAccessException ex) {
            if (ex.IsConcurrencyError)
            {
                if (ex.IsDeleted)
                    ClearControls();
                else
                    DisplayCustomer();
            }

            MessageBox.Show(ex.Message, ex.ErrorType);
        }
    }
```

Figure 20-17   A data access class that handles database exceptions (part 2 of 2)

The Customer Maintenance app

Now that you've learned the basic skills for using EF Core to work with a database, including encapsulating your EF Core code in a data access class, you're ready to see a complete app that uses EF Core. This will help you see how all the coding skills you've learned work together.

The user interface

Figure 20-18 presents the user interface for the Customer Maintenance app. This app consists of two forms. The Customer Maintenance form lets the user select an existing customer and then displays the information for that customer on the form. Then, the user can click the Modify button to modify the information for the customer or the Delete button to delete the customer. The user can also click the Add button to add a new customer.

If the user clicks the Add or Modify button, the Add/Modify Customer form is displayed. The title of this form changes depending on whether a customer is being added or modified. In this case, the user that was selected in the Customer Maintenance form is being modified.

After entering the appropriate values on the Add/Modify Customer form, the user can click the Accept button or press the Enter key to accept the new or modified customer. Or, the user can click the Cancel button or press the Esc key to cancel the operation.

If the user clicks the Delete button, a dialog like the one shown in this figure is displayed to confirm the delete operation. Then, if the user confirms the operation, the customer is deleted and the form is cleared.

At this point, you may be wondering why the Customer Maintenance app uses two forms. The answer is that most maintenance apps in the real world aren't this simple. In many cases, in fact, the maintenance of a table will be combined with other functions. Even if the table maintenance is provided by a separate app, however, it can be easier to implement the app using two forms because it simplifies the program logic.

The Customer Maintenance form

Customer Maintenance — □ ×

Customer ID: 9 [Get Customer]

Name: Rascano, Darrell

Address: 16 Remington Dr. E

City: Rancho Cordova

State: California   Zip code: 95760

[Add]   [Modify]   [Delete]   [Exit]

The Add/Modify Customer form

Modify Customer

Name: Rascano, Darrell

Address: 16 Remington Dr. E

City: Rancho Cordova

State: California   ⌄   Zip code: 95760

[Accept]   [Cancel]

The dialog that's displayed to confirm a delete operation

Confirm Delete   ×

? Delete Rascano, Darrell?

[Yes]   [No]

Description

- To add a new customer, the user clicks the Add button on the Customer Maintenance form to display a blank Add Customer form. Then, the user enters the data for the new customer and clicks the Accept button to return to the Customer Maintenance form.

- To modify the data for an existing customer, the user enters the customer ID and clicks the Get Customer button to display the information for that customer. Then, the user clicks the Modify button to display the Modify Customer form, makes the appropriate modifications, and clicks the Accept button to return to the Customer Maintenance form.

- To delete an existing customer, the user enters the customer ID and clicks the Get Customer button to display the information for that customer. Then, the user clicks the Delete button and responds to the dialog that's displayed to confirm the delete operation.

Figure 20-18   The user interface for the Customer Maintenance app

The code for the Customer Maintenance form

Figure 20-19 shows the code for the Customer Maintenance form. It starts by importing the CustomerMaintenance.Models.DataLayer namespace. Then, it declares the CustomerMaintenance namespace using a file scoped namespace declaration.

The form class starts with the default constructor that's generated by Visual Studio. After that, it declares two class variables. The first stores an instance of the data access class you saw earlier in this chapter, and the second stores the customer that's currently displayed on the form.

Since no data is displayed when the form is first loaded, this form doesn't contain a Load event handler. Instead, after the form loads, the user can enter a customer ID and click the Get Customer button to retrieve the data for a customer, or the user can click the Add button to add a new customer.

The event handler for the Click event of the Get Customer button starts by calling the IsValidData() method. This method, in turn, calls the IsInt32() method in a class named Validator to check that the user entered an integer for the customer ID. This class contains methods like the ones in the Validator class from chapter 12.

If the customer ID entered by the user is an integer, it's used to get the customer with that ID from the database. To do that, the code calls the FindCustomer() method of the data access class. This method will return a Customer object if the customer with the specified ID is found, or null if it isn't.

The statement that calls the FindCustomer() method is coded within the try block of a try-catch statement. That's because, as you saw in the previous figure, the FindCustomer() method throws a DataAccessException if there's a problem accessing the database. To handle this exception, the catch block passes the DataAccessException to the HandleDataAccessException() method shown on page 2 of this code listing.

After it executes the FindCustomer() method, the event handler checks if the Customer object contains a null value. If it does, a message is displayed indicating that the customer wasn't found, and the ClearControls() method is called. This method, which is presented on page 2, clears the data from the controls on the form and moves the focus to the Customer ID text box so the user can enter another ID.

If the Customer object isn't null, the event handler calls the DisplayCustomer() method. This method, which is also presented on page 2, displays the data retrieved from the database on the form.

The code for the Customer Maintenance form   Page 1

```
using CustomerMaintenance.Models.DataLayer;

namespace CustomerMaintenance;

public partial class frmCustomerMaintenance : Form
{
    public frmCustomerMaintenance()
    {
        InitializeComponent();
    }

    private MMABooksDataAccess data = new();
    private Customer selectedCustomer = null!;

    private void btnGetCustomer_Click(object sender, EventArgs e)
    {
        if (IsValidData())
        {
            int customerID = Convert.ToInt32(txtCustomerID.Text);
            try {
                selectedCustomer = data.FindCustomer(customerID)!;
                if (selectedCustomer == null)
                {
                    MessageBox.Show("No customer found with this ID. " +
                        "Please try again.", "Customer Not Found");
                    ClearControls();
                }
                else
                {
                    DisplayCustomer();
                }
            }
            catch (DataAccessException ex) {
                HandleDataAccessException(ex);
            }
        }
    }

    private bool IsValidData()
    {
        bool success = true;
        string errorMessage = "";
        errorMessage = Validator.IsInt32(txtCustomerID.Text, "CustomerID");

        if (errorMessage != "")
        {
            success = false;
            MessageBox.Show(errorMessage, "Entry Error");
            txtCustomerID.Focus();
        }
        return success;
    }
```

Figure 20-19   The code for the Customer Maintenance form (part 1 of 3)

The ClearControls() method at the top of page 2 of figure 20-19 assigns empty strings to the text boxes on the form and disables the Modify and Delete buttons. Finally, it moves the focus to the Customer ID text box so the user can enter another ID.

The DisplayCustomer() method assigns the appropriate properties of the selectedCustomer object to the Text properties of the text boxes. For the State text box, the value is retrieved from the related State object using the StateNavigation property of the selectedCustomer object. This works because the FindCustomer() method loads the related State object. Then, the StateNavigation property can be used to access the State object to get the StateName property. Finally, the method enables the Modify and Delete buttons so the user can choose to update or delete the selected customer.

The HandleDataAccessException() method accepts a DataAccessException object. This is the exception that the data access class throws when it encounters any type of error accessing the database. Because the code in this method is identical to the code you saw in the catch block of the event handler you saw in part 2 of figure 20-17, you shouldn't have any trouble understanding how it works. To review, it starts by checking if a concurrency error has occurred. If so, it checks if the row has been deleted or updated and then either clears the controls or displays the updated customer data. Finally, for any error, it displays an error message.

The Click event handler for the Add button displays the Add/Modify Customer form as a dialog. But first, it creates an instance of that form and assigns a collection of State objects to its public States property. To do that, it calls the GetStates() method of the data access class, which returns a collection of State objects sorted by name.

If a customer is created successfully, the new customer is retrieved from the Customer property of the Add/Modify Customer form. Then, the AddCustomer() method of the data access class is called within a try block to add the customer to the database. If the add operation is successful, the customer data is displayed on the Customer Maintenance form. If any exceptions occur, however, the catch block catches the DataAccessException that's thrown by the data access class. Then, the exception object is passed to the HandleDataAccessException() method to handle the exception.

The code for the Customer Maintenance form   Page 2

```
private void ClearControls()
{
    txtCustomerID.Text = "";
    txtName.Text = "";
    txtAddress.Text = "";
    txtCity.Text = "";
    txtState.Text = "";
    txtZipCode.Text = "";
    btnModify.Enabled = false;
    btnDelete.Enabled = false;
    txtCustomerID.Focus();
}

private void DisplayCustomer()
{
    txtCustomerID.Text = selectedCustomer.CustomerId.ToString();
    txtName.Text = selectedCustomer.Name;
    txtAddress.Text = selectedCustomer.Address;
    txtCity.Text = selectedCustomer.City;
    txtState.Text = selectedCustomer.StateNavigation.StateName;
    txtZipCode.Text = selectedCustomer.ZipCode;
    btnModify.Enabled = true;
    btnDelete.Enabled = true;
}

private void HandleDataAccessException(DataAccessException ex)
{
    if (ex.IsConcurrencyError)
    {
        if (ex.IsDeleted)
            ClearControls();
        else
            DisplayCustomer();
    }
    MessageBox.Show(ex.Message, ex.ErrorType);
}

private void btnAdd_Click(object sender, EventArgs e)
{
    var addModifyForm = new frmAddModifyCustomer {
        States = data.GetStates()
    };
    DialogResult result = addModifyForm.ShowDialog();
    if (result == DialogResult.OK)
    {
        selectedCustomer = addModifyForm.Customer;
        try {
            data.AddCustomer(selectedCustomer);
            DisplayCustomer();
        }
        catch (DataAccessException ex) {
            HandleDataAccessException(ex);
        }
    }
}
```

Figure 20-19   The code for the Customer Maintenance form (part 2 of 3)

The Click event handler for the Modify button at the top of page 3 of figure 20-19 is similar to the event handler for the Add button on page 2. However, it assigns the selectedCustomer object to the public Customer property of the Add/Modify Customer form. That way, the form can display this data without having to retrieve it from the database again.

If the customer data is updated successfully, the modified customer is retrieved from the Customer property of the Add/Modify Customer form. Then, the UpdateCustomer() method of the data access class is called within the try block of a try-catch statement to update the customer data in the database. If the update operation is successful, the updated data is displayed on the form. Otherwise, the catch block handles the DataAccessException that's thrown by the data access class by passing the exception object to the HandleDataAccessException() method.

The Click event handler for the Delete button is similar to the Click event handler for the Modify button, but instead of displaying the Add/Modify form, it displays a dialog to confirm the delete operation. If the user confirms the deletion, the code in the try block calls the RemoveCustomer() method of the data access class to delete the customer from the database, and it clears the controls on the form. If the data access class throws a DataAccessException, the catch block catches and handles the exception.

The Click event handler for the Exit button calls the Close() method of the form. This closes the form and ends the app.

The code for the Customer Maintenance form   **Page 3**

```
private void btnModify_Click(object sender, EventArgs e)
{
    var addModifyForm = new frmAddModifyCustomer {
        Customer = selectedCustomer,
        States = data.GetStates()
    };
    DialogResult result = addModifyForm.ShowDialog();
    if (result == DialogResult.OK)
    {
        selectedCustomer = addModifyForm.Customer;
        try {
            data.UpdateCustomer(selectedCustomer);
            DisplayCustomer();
        }
        catch (DataAccessException ex) {
            HandleDataAccessException(ex);
        }
    }
}

private void btnDelete_Click(object sender, EventArgs e)
{
    DialogResult result =
        MessageBox.Show($"Delete {selectedCustomer.Name}?",
        "Confirm Delete", MessageBoxButtons.YesNo,
        MessageBoxIcon.Question);

    if (result == DialogResult.Yes)
    {
        try {
            data.RemoveCustomer(selectedCustomer);
            ClearControls();
        }
        catch (DataAccessException ex) {
            HandleDataAccessException(ex);
        }
    }
}

private void btnExit_Click(object sender, EventArgs e)
{
    this.Close();
}
}
```

Figure 20-19   The code for the Customer Maintenance form (part 3 of 3)

The code for the Add/Modify Customer form

Figure 20-20 shows the code for the Add/Modify Customer form. This form starts by importing the CustomerMaintenance.Models.DataLayer namespace and declaring the CustomerMaintenance namespace.

After the default constructor for the form, this code declares the two public properties that get data from and provide data to the Customer Maintenance form. You'll see how these properties are used in a minute.

When this form is first loaded, the Load event handler calls the LoadStatesComboBox() method to bind the State combo box to the collection of State objects. Next, the load event handler checks if the Customer property is null. If it is, a new customer is being added. In that case, the Load event handler sets the Text property of the form to "Add Customer", sets the value of the State combo box so that no state is selected, and initializes the Customer property to a new Customer object.

If the Customer property isn't null, it means that a Customer object was assigned to this property by the Customer Maintenance form. Remember, that only happens when an existing customer is being modified. In that case, the code sets the Text property of the form to "Modify Customer" and calls the DisplayCustomerData() method to display the data for the customer on the form. When the Load() method is complete, the user can enter the data for a new customer or modify the data for an existing customer.

The LoadStatesComboBox() method binds the States combo box to the collection of State objects that the Customer Maintenance form assigns to the States property of this form. Then it sets the DisplayMember property of the combo box to the StateName property of the State class, and the ValueMember property of the combo box to the StateCode property of the State class.

The DisplayCustomerData() method sets the values of the text box and combo box controls of the form. To do that, it uses the data in the Customer property of the form.

The Click event handler for the Accept button calls the IsValidData() method presented on page 2 to determine if the data on the form is valid. If it is, the LoadCustomerData() method, also presented on page 2, is called to update the Customer property with the new or modified customer data. Then, the DialogResult property of the form is set to DialogResult.OK and the Add/Modify form closes. If the data entered by the user isn't valid, the user is notified and the Add/Modify form stays open so the user can correct their entries.

The code for the Add/Modify Customer form

```csharp
using CustomerMaintenance.Models.DataLayer;

namespace CustomerMaintenance;

public partial class frmAddModifyCustomer : Form
{
    public frmAddModifyCustomer()
    {
        InitializeComponent();
    }

    public Customer Customer { get; set; } = null!;
    public List<State> States { get; set; } = null!;

    private void frmAddModifyCustomer_Load(object sender, EventArgs e)
    {
        LoadStatesComboBox();
        if (Customer == null)
        {
            Text = "Add Customer";
            cboStates.SelectedIndex = -1;
            Customer = new();
        }
        else
        {
            Text = "Modify Customer";
            DisplayCustomerData();
        }
    }

    private void LoadStatesComboBox()
    {
        cboStates.DataSource = States;
        cboStates.DisplayMember = nameof(State.StateName);
        cboStates.ValueMember = nameof(State.StateCode);
    }

    private void DisplayCustomerData()
    {
        txtName.Text = Customer.Name;
        txtAddress.Text = Customer.Address;
        txtCity.Text = Customer.City;
        cboStates.SelectedValue = Customer.State;
        txtZipCode.Text = Customer.ZipCode;
    }

    private void btnAccept_Click(object sender, EventArgs e)
    {
        if (IsValidData())
        {
            LoadCustomerData();
            DialogResult = DialogResult.OK;
        }
    }
```

Figure 20-20   The code for the Add/Modify Customer form (part 1 of 2)

The IsValidData() method at the top of page 2 of figure 20-20 tests that the user has entered a name, address, city, state, and zip code. If the user has entered this data, the method returns a true value. Otherwise, it displays an appropriate error message and returns a false value.

The LoadCustomerData() method assigns the values that the user entered into the text boxes and combo box to the appropriate properties of the Customer property of the form. Here, the SelectedValue property is used to get the value of the State combo box. Then, the ToString() method is called to convert the object that's returned by that property to a string.

The Click event handler for the Cancel button works much like the Click event handler for the Exit button in the Customer Maintenance form. It contains a single statement that calls the Close() method to close the form. However, this doesn't exit the app. Instead, it closes the Add/Modify form and returns the focus to the Customer Maintenance form.

The code for the Add/Modify Customer form   **Page 2**

```csharp
        private bool IsValidData()
        {
            bool success = true;
            string errorMessage = "";

            errorMessage += Validator.IsPresent(txtName.Text, "Name");
            errorMessage += Validator.IsPresent(txtAddress.Text, "Address");
            errorMessage += Validator.IsPresent(txtCity.Text, "City");
            errorMessage += Validator.IsPresent(cboStates.Text, "State");
            errorMessage += Validator.IsPresent(txtZipCode.Text, "Zip Code");

            if (errorMessage != "")
            {
                success = false;
                MessageBox.Show(errorMessage, "Entry Error");
            }
            return success;
        }

        private void LoadCustomerData()
        {
            Customer.Name = txtName.Text;
            Customer.Address = txtAddress.Text;
            Customer.City = txtCity.Text;
            Customer.State = cboStates.SelectedValue?.ToString() ?? "";
            Customer.ZipCode = txtZipCode.Text;
        }

        private void btnCancel_Click(object sender, EventArgs e)
        {
            this.Close();
        }
    }
```

Figure 20-20   The code for the Add/Modify Customer form (part 2 of 2)

Perspective

In this chapter, you learned how to use EF Core to create a data model from an existing database. You also learned how to use LINQ to query the model, how to use EF Core to insert, update, and delete data and check for exceptions, and how to code a data access class to encapsulate your data access code. With these skills, you should be able to develop apps that let the user display and maintain data.

Keep in mind, though, that there's a lot more to learn about EF Core than what's presented here. In particular, if the database that an app will work with doesn't already exist, you can code your own data model and then use it to create the database. For more information on how to do that, you can refer to the online documentation or get a separate book on EF Core.

Terms

Entity Framework (EF) Core	query path
Object Relational Mapping (ORM)	explicit loading
framework	cascading updates
NuGet Package Manager	concurrency conflict
database (DB) context class	concurrency control
entity class	last in wins
method chaining	optimistic concurrency
navigation property	pessimistic concurrency
cascading deletes	concurrency exception
foreign key property	concurrency token
lazy loading	rowversion property
eager loading	

Exercise 20-1   Build a Product Maintenance app

For this exercise, you'll develop an app to display, modify, insert, and delete products. To make that easier for you to do, we'll give you the forms and some of the code for the project.

Review the code and run the app

1. Open the app in the C:\C#\Ch20\ProductMaintenance directory.

2. Review the two forms in the designer, and then display the code for each form and review that code.

3. Run the app and click some of the buttons. Note that they don't do much yet, though the Add and Modify buttons do display the Add/Modify form. Note also that the Product Code field is read-only when you click the Modify button. That's because you shouldn't be able to change an existing product code. When you're done, click the Exit button to close the app.

Add EF Core and create the data model

4. Use the procedure in figure 20-2 to install the NuGet packages required to use EF Core in your project.

5. Use the Scaffold-DbContext command as shown in figure 20-3 to generate the DB context and entity classes for the MMABooks database. After you open the NuGet PMC window and enter the command as shown in figure 20-3, make sure to provide a value for the AttachDBFilename parameter that corresponds to a location on your hard disk that contains the MMABooks.mdf file. Also, use Models\DataLayer for the -OutputDir parameter.

6. Review the code of the context class and entity classes in the Models\ DataLayer directory to get an idea how it works. Note the names it uses for entities and properties.

Create an App.config file to store the database connection

7. Add an App.config file to the project as described in figure 20-7.

8. Add a connectionStrings node under the configuration node as shown in the first example of figure 20-7, and add a key for MMABooks that refers to your local database.

9. Modify the code in the OnConfiguring() method of the DB context class to use the ConfigurationManager to retrieve the MMABooks key from the App.config file as shown in figure 20-7 instead of hard-coding the connection string. To do that, you need to add a using directive for System.Configuration to the top of the DB Context class file.

Write the code to retrieve a product

10. Display the code for the Product Maintenance form, and add code to create a class variable for an MMABooksContext object. Also, create a class variable for a Product object named selectedProduct. You can use quick actions and refactoring to include the correct using directive.

11. In the Click event handler for the Get Product button, find the code that retrieves the value entered in the Product Code text box. In the try block below that code, add code that retrieves the data for that product code and assigns the result to the selectedProduct class variable.

12. Add code that calls the DisplayProduct() method if the product is found. If the product isn't found, display a friendly message to the user and call the ClearControls() method.

13. Add code to the DisplayProduct() method that displays the details of the selectedProduct object in the form.

14. Run the app, enter "PHP" for the product code, and click the Get Product button. After the product information is displayed in the form, click the Exit button to close the app.

Write the code to modify a product

15. In the code for the Add/Modify Product form, add a public property named Product that can store a Product object. You can use quick actions and refactoring to include the correct using directive.

16. Add code to the DisplayProduct() method that updates the form's controls with data from the Product property.

17. Add code to the LoadProductData() method that updates the Product property with data from the form's controls.

18. In the Product Maintenance form, find the Click event handler for the Modify button. Review the code that creates a new Add/Modify Product form, sets the form's IsAdd property to false, and displays the form as a dialog. Update this code to assign the selectedProduct class variable to the Product property of the Add/Modify form.

19. In the try block, add code that stores the updated Product object from the Add/Modify form in the selectedProduct class variable. Then, add code that saves the changes to the database and calls the DisplayProduct() method.

20. Run the app, retrieve the data for product code "PHP", and click the Modify button to display the Add/Modify Product form. Make one or more changes to the product's price or quantity on hand, accept the changes, and make sure the changes are reflected on the Product Maintenance form.

Write the code to add a new product

21. In the Add/Modify Product form, find the event handler for the Load event. Add code that initializes the Product property with a new Product object if the IsAdd property is true.

22. In the Product Maintenance form, find the Click event handler for the Add button. Review the code that creates a new Add/Modify Product form, sets the form's IsAdd property to true, and displays the form as a dialog.

23. In the try block, add code that stores the new Product object from the Add/Modify form in the selectedProduct class variable. Then, add code that adds the new product to the context, saves the context changes to the database, and calls the DisplayProduct() method.

24. Run the app and click the Add button on the Product Maintenance form to display the Add Product form.

25. Enter the data for a new product and then click the Accept button to return to the Product Maintenance form. Make a note of the product code for the new product and then end the app.

Write the code to delete a product

26. In the Product Maintenance form, add code to the Click event handler for the Delete button that gets the description for the selected product and assigns it to the desc variable. Then, add code to the try block to delete the product, save the changes to the database, and clear the controls on the form.

27. Run the app, enter the code for the product you just added, and click the Get Product button.

28. Click the Delete button and then click Yes when you're asked to confirm the operation. The data for the product should be cleared from the form.

29. Enter the same product code and click the Get Product button to confirm that the product has been deleted.

Add a data access class and update the form to use it

30. Use figure 20-16 as a guide to add a data access class with methods that add a new product and get, update, and delete an existing product.

31. Update the code for the form to use the data access class instead of the DB context object.

32. Test the app to make sure it works as expected.

Write the code to handle database and concurrency exceptions in the data access class

33. Use part 2 of figure 20-17 as a guide to add a custom exception class that handles data access errors.

34. Update the methods of the data access class so the code that accesses the database is coded within the try block of a try-catch statement. The method that retrieves a product should catch and handle the SqlException object. The method that adds a product should catch and handle the DbUpdateException and SqlException objects. And the methods that update and delete a product should handle the DbUpdateConcurrencyException, DbUpdateException, and SqlException objects. Be sure to code these exceptions in the correct order.

35. Add helper methods to the data access class that handle the exceptions for concurrency errors, update errors, and database errors.

36. Use part 2 of figure 21-19 as a guide to update the HandleDataAccessError() method in the Product Maintenance form so it accepts and handles a DataAccessException object.

37. Update the catch blocks in the Product Maintenance form so they catch a DataAccessException object instead of an Exception object.

38. Test the app again to make sure it works as expected.

21

How to use ADO.NET to write your own data access code

In the previous chapter, you learned how to use Entity Framework (EF) Core to develop database apps. When you do that, EF Core uses ADO.NET under the hood to access the database. EF Core lets you develop database apps with less code than writing the code for working with ADO.NET yourself.

In some cases, though, you may want more control over how the data for an app is being processed. In those cases, you can create and work with ADO.NET objects through code. That's what you'll learn to do in this chapter.

An introduction to ADO.NET

ADO.NET (*ActiveX Data Objects .NET*) is the primary data access API for .NET. It provides classes to develop database apps with C# as well as other .NET languages. In the topics that follow, you'll be introduced to the .NET data provider for SQL Server and the objects it provides for accessing databases.

The .NET data provider for SQL Server

A *.NET data provider* is a set of classes that enables you to access data that's managed by a particular database server. All .NET data providers must include core classes for creating the three types of objects listed in the table in figure 21-1. This table also lists the names of the classes you use to create objects using the SQL Server data provider.

Although there are many data providers for .NET, only the two industry standard providers are included with .NET: OLE DB and ODBC. These data providers can access any database that supports these standards, including SQL Server. However, the SQL Server data provider is designed to provide efficient access to a Microsoft SQL Server database, and it's the one you'll learn about in this chapter.

To use the SQL Server data provider, you must start by installing the Microsoft.Data.SqlClient package. To do that, you can use the NuGet Package Manager as described in figure 20-2. Then, you can add a using directive like the one shown in this figure at the beginning of each source file that uses those classes. That way, you won't have to qualify the references to these classes.

How the connection, command, and data reader objects work

Figure 21-1 shows how you work with the data in a database directly using ADO.NET. To do that, you execute a *command* object that contains a SQL statement. Then, the command object uses a *connection* object to connect to the database.

When you access a database directly, you have to provide code to handle the result of the command. If you issue a command that contains an INSERT, UPDATE, or DELETE statement, for example, the result is an integer that indicates the number of rows that were affected by the operation. You can use that information to determine if the operation was successful.

If you execute a command that contains a SELECT statement, the result is a result set that contains the rows you requested. To read through the rows in the result set, you use a *data reader* object. Although a data reader provides an efficient way of reading the rows in a result set, you can't use it to modify those rows. In addition, it only lets you read rows in a forward direction. Once you read the next row, the previous row is unavailable.

.NET data provider core objects for SQL Server

Object	Class Name	Description
Connection	**SqlConnection**	Establishes a connection to a database.
Command	**SqlCommand**	Represents an individual SQL statement that can be executed against the database.
Data reader	**SqlDataReader**	Provides read-only, forward-only access to the data in a database.

A using directive for the SQL Server data provider namespace

```
using Microsoft.Data.SqlClient;
```

ADO.NET components for accessing a database directly

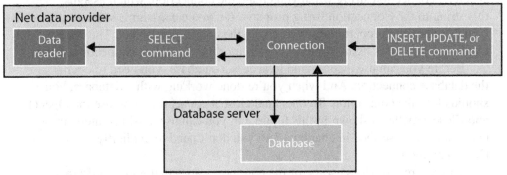

Description

- The *.NET data providers* provide the ADO.NET classes that are responsible for working directly with a database.

- The SQL Server data provider is optimized for working with a SQL Server database. As a result, you should use that data provider if you're using a SQL Server database.

- To use the Microsoft.Data.SqlClient namespace, you must install its NuGet package. To do that, you can use the procedure presented in figure 20-2 to search for and install the Microsoft.Data.SqlClient NuGet package.

- To retrieve data from a database, you execute a *command* object that contains a SELECT statement. This command object uses a *connection* object to connect to the database and retrieve the data. Then, you can read the results one row at a time using a *data reader* object.

- To insert, update, or delete data in a database, you execute a command object that contains an INSERT, UPDATE, or DELETE statement. This command object uses a connection to connect to the database and update the data. Then, you can check the value that's returned to determine if the operation was successful.

- If an app maintains the data in a database, you typically work with a single row at a time so the chance of a concurrency conflict is reduced.

Figure 21-1   An introduction to ADO.NET

How to work with connections and commands

Before you can access the data in a database, you must create a connection object. Then, you must create one or more command objects that contain the SQL statements you want to execute against the database.

How to create and work with connections

Figure 21-2 shows how you create and use a connection to access a SQL Server database. As the syntax at the top of this figure shows, you can specify a connection string when you create the connection, which assigns this string to the ConnectionString property. Or, you can assign a value to the ConnectionString property after you create the connection object. The code example later in this figure uses the constructor that accepts a connection string.

Before you can use a command to access a database, you need to open the database connection. And when you're done working with a database, you should close the connection. To open and close a connection, you use the Open() and Close() methods shown in this figure. Or, you can use a using statement or declaration as described in chapter 17 so you don't need to explicitly call the Close() method.

This figure also shows some of the common values that you specify in a connection string for a SQL Server database. Then, the first two examples show connection strings for SQL Server Express LocalDB and SQL Server Express databases. The connection string for the LocalDB database uses (LocalDB)\MSSQLLocalDB for the server name. In addition, it specifies the name and location of the .mdf file for the database and the type of security to be used.

The connection string for the SQL Server Express database specifies the name of the server where the database resides, the name of the database, and the type of security to be used. Here, the localhost keyword indicates that the SqlExpress database server is running on the same machine as the app. However, if you're accessing a SQL Server database that resides on a remote server, you'll need to modify this connection string to point to that server.

If you're using a different provider, you should consult the documentation for that provider to determine what values to specify. That's because the requirements for each provider differ.

The code example at the bottom of this figure starts by using the ConfigurationManager object to retrieve a connection string from the App.config file. This works like the example presented in figure 20-7. Then, it creates a new SqlConnection object, calls the Open() method, and executes some database code (not shown). Since this example uses a using declaration, the connection automatically closes and its resources are released when the block that contains the declaration ends and the connection goes out of scope. If you don't use a using statement or declaration, you should call the Close() method to close the connection when you're done with the connection.

Two constructors for the SqlConnection class

```
new SqlConnection()
new SqlConnection(connectionString)
```

Common properties and methods of the SqlConnection class

Property	Description
ConnectionString	Provides information for accessing a SQL Server database.

Method	Description
Open()	Opens the connection using the specified connection string.
Close()	Closes the connection.

Common values used in the ConnectionString property for SQL Server

Name	Description
Data Source/Server	The name of the instance of SQL Server you want to connect to.
Initial Catalog/Database	The name of the database you want to access.
AttachDbFilename	The path and file name for the database's .mdf file.
Integrated Security	Determines whether the connection is secure.
User ID	The user ID that's used to log in to SQL Server.
Password/Pwd	The password that's used to log in to SQL Server.

Two connection strings for the SQL Server provider

A connection string for a SQL Server Express LocalDB database

```
Data Source=(LocalDB)\MSSQLLocalDB;AttachDbFilename=C:\C#\Database\
MMABooks.mdf;Integrated Security=True
```

A connection string for a SQL Server Express database

```
Data Source=localhost\SqlExpress;Initial Catalog=MMABooks;Integrated
Security=True
```

Code that creates, opens, and closes a connection

```csharp
// get the connection string from the App.config file
string connectionString = ConfigurationManager.ConnectionStrings["MMABooks"]
    .ConnectionString;

// create the connection and open it
using SqlConnection connection = new(connectionString);
connection.Open();

// code that uses the connection goes here

// the connection is closed automatically when it goes out of scope
```

Description

- You can store the connection string in the App.config file as described in the previous chapter in figure 20-7.

Figure 21-2   How to create and work with connections

A connection object should be closed as soon as you're done with it. For this reason, if your method needs to do a lot of processing after it retrieves data from the database, it's best to use a using statement rather than the using declaration shown here. That way, you can use braces to specify the end of the scope for the connection object.

How to create and work with commands

After you define the connection to the database, you create the command objects that contain the SQL statements you want to execute against the database. Figure 21-3 shows three constructors for the SqlCommand class. The first one doesn't require arguments. When you use this constructor, you must set the Connection property to the connection and the CommandText property to the text of the SQL statement before you execute the command.

The second constructor accepts the SQL command text as an argument. Then, you just have to set the Connection property before you can execute the command. The third constructor accepts both the connection and the command text as arguments. The code example in the figure uses this constructor.

Another property you may need to set is the CommandType property. This property determines how the value of the CommandText property is interpreted. The values you can specify for this property are members of the CommandType enumeration that's shown in this figure. The default value is Text, which causes the value of the CommandText property to be interpreted as a SQL statement. If the CommandText property contains the name of a stored procedure, however, you'll need to set this property to StoredProcedure. (In case you're not familiar with stored procedures, they consist of one or more SQL statements that have been compiled and stored with the database.) And if the CommandText property contains the name of a table, you'll need to set this property to TableDirect. Then, all the rows and columns will be retrieved from the table. Note that this setting is only available for the OLE DB data provider.

The last property that's shown in this figure, Parameters, lets you work with the collection of parameters for a command. You'll see how to use this property in the next two topics.

To execute the query that a command contains, you use the Execute methods of the command shown in this figure. To execute a command that returns a result set, you use the ExecuteReader() method of the command. By contrast, you use the ExecuteScalar() method to execute a query that returns a single value, and you use the ExecuteNonQuery() method to execute an action query. You'll learn how to use all three of these methods later in this chapter.

The code example here shows how to work with a SqlCommand object. It starts by creating a SQL statement and a connection object. Then, it creates a new command object and passes the SQL statement and connection to it. Next, it opens the connection and executes the command (not shown). Then, since both objects are coded with using declarations, the connection is closed and the resources for both objects are released when they go out of scope.

Three constructors for the SqlCommand class

```
new SqlCommand()
new SqlCommand(commandText)
new SqlCommand(commandText, connection)
```

Common properties and methods of the SqlCommand class

Property	Description
Connection	The connection used to connect to the database.
CommandText	A SQL statement or the name of a stored procedure.
CommandType	A member of the CommandType enumeration that determines how the value in the CommandText property is interpreted.
Parameters	The collection of parameters for the command.

Method	Description
ExecuteReader()	Executes the query identified by the CommandText property and returns the result as a SqlDataReader object.
ExecuteNonQuery()	Executes the query identified by the CommandText property and returns an integer that indicates the number of rows that were affected.
ExecuteScalar()	Executes the query identified by the CommandText property and returns the first column of the first row of the result set.

CommandType enumeration members

Member	Description
Text	The CommandText property contains a SQL statement. This is the default.
StoredProcedure	The CommandText property contains the name of a stored procedure.
TableDirect	The CommandText property contains the name of a table (OLE DB only).

Code that creates a SqlCommand object
that executes a SELECT statement

```
string select =
    "SELECT CustomerID, Name, Address, City, State, ZipCode " +
    "FROM Customers";
using SqlConnection connection = new(connectionString);
using SqlCommand command = new(select, connection);
connection.Open();

// code that executes the command

// the connection and command are closed when they go out of scope
```

Figure 21-3   How to create and work with commands

How to work with parameters

A *parameter* is a variable that's used in a SQL statement. When you work with commands, you have to create the parameters for the command yourself. You'll learn how to do that in just a minute. But first, you need to know how to use parameters in the SQL statements you code.

How to use parameters in SQL statements

Parameters let you create statements that retrieve or update database data based on variable information. For example, an app that maintains the Customers table can use a parameter in the WHERE clause of a SELECT statement to retrieve a specific row from the Customers table based on the value of the CustomerID column. A SELECT statement that uses parameters in the WHERE clause is called a *parameterized query*. You can also use parameters in other types of SQL statements, including INSERT, UPDATE, and DELETE statements.

To use parameters in a SQL statement, you use placeholders as shown in figure 21-4. These placeholders indicate where the parameters should be inserted when the statement is executed.

The first example in this figure shows a SELECT statement for SQL Server. As you can see, you use a *named variable* to identify a parameter. Note that the name of the variable must begin with an at sign (@) and is usually given the same name as the column it's associated with.

The second example shows how to use parameters in an INSERT statement. Here, a row is being inserted into the Customers table. To do that, a variable is included in the VALUES clause for each required column in the table.

The third and fourth examples show how you can use a parameter to provide for concurrency. In the third example, the Name column in a row of the Customers table is being updated. To do that, the @Name parameter contains the new name for the customer, and the @CustomerID parameter identifies the customer to be updated. Then, the @Rowversion parameter contains the data that was retrieved from the rowversion column. This parameter will keep the statement from being executed if any of the customer's data has been changed since the customer was retrieved.

The fourth example is similar, but it deletes a row from the Customers table. To do that, the @CustomerID parameter identifies the customer to be deleted. Then, the @Rowversion parameter provides for concurrency just as in the third example.

You should know that database management systems don't use a standard syntax for coding placeholders. For example, the placeholder for an OLE DB or ODBC parameter is a question mark rather than a named variable. So, if you're using a different provider, you should consult the documentation for that provider.

A SQL Server SELECT statement that uses a parameter

```
SELECT CustomerID, Name, Address, City, State, ZipCode
FROM Customers
WHERE CustomerID = @CustomerID
```

A SQL Server INSERT statement that uses parameters

```
INSERT INTO Customers (Name, Address, City, State, ZipCode)
VALUES (@Name, @Address, @City, @State, @ZipCode)
```

A SQL Server UPDATE statement that uses parameters

```
UPDATE Customers
SET Name = @Name
WHERE CustomerID = @CustomerID
AND Rowversion = @Rowversion
```

A SQL Server DELETE statement that uses parameters

```
DELETE FROM Customers
WHERE CustomerID = @CustomerID
AND Rowversion = @Rowversion
```

Description

- A *parameter* lets you place variable information into a SQL statement.
- When you use a parameter in the WHERE clause of a SELECT statement, the resulting query is often called a *parameterized query* because the results of the query depend on the values of the parameters.
- You can also use parameters in INSERT or UPDATE statements to provide the values for the database row or rows to be inserted or updated. Likewise, you can use parameters in a DELETE statement to indicate which row or rows should be deleted.
- You can also use parameters in UPDATE and DELETE statements to provide for concurrency.
- To use parameters, you code a SQL statement with placeholders for the parameters. Then, you create a parameter object that defines each parameter, and you add it to the Parameters collection of the command object that contains the SQL statement.
- The placeholder for a parameter in a SQL Server command is a *named variable* whose name begins with an at sign (@). In most cases, you'll give the variable the same name as the column it's associated with.

Figure 21-4   How to use parameters in SQL statements

How to create and work with the parameters for a command

After you define a SQL statement that contains parameters, you create the parameter objects and add them to the Parameters collection of the command. Figure 21-5 shows you how to do that.

The first example in this figure creates a SqlCommand object that is used by the rest of the examples. Then, the second example shows how to use the Add() method to create a parameter object and add it to the Parameters collection. Here, the Parameters property of the command is used to refer to the Parameters collection. Then, the Add() method of that collection adds a parameter named @CustomerID, and it uses the SqlDbType enumeration to specify the data type of the parameter.

Once you've added a parameter object to the Parameters collection, you can refer to it through that collection using either the parameter's name or its position as an indexer. This is illustrated by the third example. Here, the value of the @CustomerID parameter is set to the value of a variable named customerID.

Another way to create a parameter and add it to the Parameters collection is to use the AddWithValue() method as shown by the fourth example. This is often the easiest way to create a parameter. When you use this method, you don't need to specify the data type or size because they're inferred from the value of the parameter.

Because ADO.NET refers to SQL Server parameters by name, you can add parameters to the Parameters collection in any sequence. However, for this to work, you need to make sure that the name you assign to a parameter is the same as the name of the placeholder that's specified in the SQL statement. For instance, if the SQL statement uses a placeholder named @CustomerID, you need to assign that same name to the parameter that you add to the Parameters collection.

If you're using a different provider, you should consult the documentation for that provider to determine what order you need to add parameters to the Parameters collection. That's because some providers refer to the parameters by position, so they must be added in the same order that they appear in the SQL statement.

Common members of the Parameters collection of the SqlCommand class

Indexer	Description
[name]	Gets the parameter with the specified name from the collection.
[index]	Gets the parameter at the specified position from the collection.

Method	Description
Add(name, type)	Creates a parameter with the specified name and type and adds it to the collection. Uses the SqlDbType enumeration.
Add(name, type, size)	Creates a parameter with the specified name, type, and size and adds it to the collection. Uses the SqlDbType enumeration.
AddWithValue(name, value)	Creates a parameter with the specified name and value and adds it to the collection. The type is inferred from the type of the value.

A statement that creates a SqlCommand object

```
using SqlCommand command = new(select, connection);
```

A statement that adds a parameter to the Parameters collection

```
command.Parameters.Add("@CustomerID", SqlDbType.Int);
```

A statement that sets the value of the parameter

```
command.Parameters["@CustomerID"].Value = customerID;
```

A statement that adds a parameter and sets its value

```
command.Parameters.AddWithValue("@CustomerID", customerID);
```

Description

- To work with the parameters for a command, you use the Parameters property of the command. This property returns a SqlParameterCollection object that contains all the parameters for the command.

- You can use the Add() methods of the Parameters collection to create a parameter with the specified name and type or name, type, and size and add that parameter to the Parameters collection. You use the SqlDbType enumeration to indicate the type.

- You can use the AddWithValue() method of the Parameters collection to create a parameter with the specified name and value and add that parameter to the collection. You don't need to indicate the type or size because they're inferred from the value that's passed to the method.

- You can add SQL Server parameters to the Parameters collection in any order you want since ADO.NET refers to the parameters by name. For this to work, the parameter name needs to match the name of the placeholder in the SQL statement.

Figure 21-5   How to create and work with the parameters for a command

How to execute commands

The method you use to execute the SQL statement a command object contains depends on what the SQL statement does. You can use ExecuteReader() to retrieve a result set using a SELECT statement. You can use ExecuteScalar() to retrieve a single value using a SELECT statement. And you can use ExecuteNonQuery() to execute an INSERT, UPDATE, or DELETE statement.

How to create and work with a data reader

To execute a command that contains a SELECT statement and returns a result set, you use the ExecuteReader() method as shown in figure 21-6. This method executes the SELECT statement and creates a data reader object. Then, you can use the data reader to work with that result set.

When you execute the ExecuteReader() method, you can use the CommandBehavior enumeration of the System.Data namespace to specify a behavior. The most commonly used members of this enumeration are listed in this figure. To combine two or more command behavior members, you can use the And (&) operator.

When you first create a data reader, it's opened automatically and the cursor is positioned before the first row in the result set. To retrieve the first row, you can execute the Read() method. While a data reader is open, no other data readers can be opened on the same connection.

To access a column from the most recently retrieved row, you can use the column name as an indexer. You can also specify a column by its position in the row by using an integer indexer. For example, since the first column retrieved from the States table is named StateCode, you can supply "StateCode" as the name or 0 as the indexer for a reader to retrieve the data for that column.

The code example in this figure shows how to use a data reader. First, the code creates a List<State> object. Then, it opens a connection for the SqlCommand object. Although it's not shown here, this command contains a SELECT statement that retrieves all the rows from the States table. Then, the ExecuteReader() method retrieves that data and creates a data reader that can process the state rows. Because the CloseConnection behavior is specified for this method, the connection will be closed automatically when the data reader is closed. The ExecuteReader() method also opens the data reader and positions the cursor before the first row in the result set.

After creating the data reader, a while statement loops through the rows in the result set. To do that, the condition on the while statement calls the Read() method of the data reader. This method returns a Boolean value that indicates whether the result set contains additional rows. As a result, the code within the loop processes the row that was retrieved. In this case, the program creates a State object for each row in the States table and adds it to the List<State> object.

Because this code uses a using declaration for the data reader, it's closed automatically when it goes out of scope. However, if you don't use a using statement or declaration, you should use the Close() method to close the data reader.

Two ways to create a SqlDataReader object

```
sqlCommand.ExecuteReader()
sqlCommand.ExecuteReader(behavior)
```

Common CommandBehavior enumeration members

Member	Description
CloseConnection	Closes the connection when the data reader is closed.
Default	Equivalent to specifying no command behavior.
SingleRow	Only a single row is returned.

Common members of the SqlDataReader class

Indexer	Description
[name]	Gets the value of the column with the specified name.
[index]	Gets the value of the column at the specified position.

Property	Description
IsClosed	Gets a value that indicates if the data reader is closed.

Method	Description
Close()	Closes the data reader.
Read()	Retrieves the next row and returns a Boolean value that indicates whether there are additional rows.

Code that uses a data reader to read a list of State objects

```
using System.Data;  // namespace for the CommandBehavior enumeration
...
// code that defines the connection and command goes here
List<State> states = new();
connection.Open();
using SqlDataReader reader =
    command.ExecuteReader(CommandBehavior.CloseConnection);
while (reader.Read())
{
    State state = new() {
        StateCode = reader["StateCode"].ToString(),
        StateName = reader["StateName"].ToString()
    };
    states.Add(state);
}
// reader closes automatically when it goes out of scope
```

Description

- The data reader is opened automatically when it's created. While it's open, no other data readers can be opened on the same connection.
- When you first create a data reader, it's positioned before the first row in the result set.
- You can combine two or more command behavior members using the And (&) operator.

Figure 21-6   How to create and work with a data reader

How to execute queries that return a single value

The first example in figure 21-7 shows you how to execute a command that returns a single value, called a *scalar value*. To do that, you use the ExecuteScalar() method of the command. In this case, the command contains a SELECT statement that retrieves a sum of the invoice totals in the Invoices table. This type of summary value is often called an *aggregate value*. A scalar value can also be the value of a single column, a calculated value, or any other value that can be retrieved from the database.

Since the ExecuteScalar() method returns an Object type, you must cast that object to an appropriate data type to get its value. In this example, the object is cast to a decimal value.

If you want, you can use the ExecuteScalar() method with a SELECT statement that retrieves more than one value. In that case, though, the ExecuteScalar() method returns only the first value and discards the others.

How to execute action queries

As you know, you can use an INSERT, UPDATE, or DELETE statement to perform actions against a database. These statements are sometimes referred to as *action queries*. To execute an action query, you use the ExecuteNonQuery() method of a command as shown in the second example of figure 21-7.

This example executes a command that contains an INSERT statement that adds a row to the Products table. Here, the ExecuteNonQuery() method returns an integer that indicates the number of rows in the database that were affected by the operation. You can use this value to check that the operation was successful as shown by the Customer Maintenance app presented next.

You can also use the ExecuteNonQuery() method to execute statements that affect the structure of a database object. For more information, see the documentation for your database management system.

Code that executes a command that returns a single value

```
string select = "SELECT SUM(InvoiceTotal) FROM Invoices";
using SqlConnection connection = new(connectionString);
using SqlCommand command = new(select, connection);
connection.Open();
decimal invoiceTotal = (decimal)command.ExecuteScalar;
```

Code that executes a command that inserts a row

```
string insert =
    "INSERT Products (ProductCode, Description, UnitPrice) " +
    "VALUES (@ProductCode, @Description, @UnitPrice)";
using SqlConnection connection = new(connectionString);
using SqlCommand command = new(insert, connection);
command.Parameters.AddWithValue("@ProductCode", product.Code);
command.Parameters.AddWithValue("@Description", product.Description);
command.Parameters.AddWithValue("@UnitPrice", product.Price);
try
{
    connection.Open();
    int productCount = command.ExecuteNonQuery();
}
catch (SqlException ex)
{
    MessageBox.Show(ex.Message);
}
```

How to execute queries that return a single value

- You use the ExecuteScalar() method of a command object to retrieve a single value, called a *scalar value*.
- If the SELECT statement returns more than one column or row, only the value in the first column and row is retrieved by the ExecuteScalar() method.

How to execute action queries

- The INSERT, UPDATE, and DELETE statements are sometimes called *action queries*.
- You use the ExecuteNonQuery() method of a command object to execute an INSERT, UPDATE, or DELETE statement.
- The ExecuteNonQuery() method returns an integer that indicates the number of rows that were affected by the query.

Figure 21-7   How to execute queries that don't return a result set

The Customer Maintenance app

In the topics that follow, you'll see another version of the Customer Maintenance app that was first presented in chapter 20. Unlike the app shown in that chapter, this version doesn't use EF Core. Instead, it uses ADO.NET commands to retrieve, insert, update, and delete rows from the Customers table. This app should give you a thorough understanding of how you can build apps with ADO.NET.

Because the Customer Maintenance app in chapter 20 uses a data access class, this version of the app only needs to change the code in that class. So, only the code for the updated data access class is presented here. This shows the benefit of encapsulating your data access code in a separate class.

The user interface

Figure 21-8 presents the user interface for the Customer Maintenance app. This user interface consists of two forms and works just like the app presented in chapter 20.

To review, the Customer Maintenance form lets the user add a new customer by clicking the Add button to display the Add Customer form. Or, the user can enter a customer ID into the text box and click the Get Customer button to retrieve the data for an existing customer. Then, the user can modify the data for that customer by clicking the Modify button to display the Modify Customer form. Or, the user can delete that customer by clicking the Delete button.

The Customer Maintenance form

Customer Maintenance	— □ ✕

Customer ID: `35`   Get Customer

Name: `Morgan, Robert`

Address: `48289 Fremont Blvd`

City: `Carrollton`

State: `Texas`   Zip code: `75006`

| Add | Modify | Delete | | Exit |

The Add/Modify Customer form

Modify Customer

Name: `Morgan, Robert`

Address: `48289 Fremont Blvd`

City: `Carrollton`

State: `Texas`   ∨   Zip code: `75006`

Accept   Cancel

The dialog that's displayed to confirm a delete operation

Confirm Delete

? Delete Morgan, Robert?

Yes   No

Description

- To add a customer, the user clicks the Add button on the Customer Maintenance form to display a blank Add Customer form. Then, the user enters the data for the new customer and clicks the Accept button to return to the Customer Maintenance form.

- To modify the data for an existing customer, the user enters the customer ID and clicks the Get Customer button to display the information for that customer. Then, the user clicks the Modify button to display the Modify Customer form, makes the appropriate modifications, and clicks the Accept button to return to the Customer Maintenance form.

- To delete a customer, the user enters the customer ID and clicks the Get Customer button to display the information for that customer. Then, the user clicks the Delete button and responds to the dialog that's displayed to confirm the delete operation.

Figure 21-8   The user interface for the Customer Maintenance app

The code for the data access class

Figure 21-9 presents the code for the MMABooksDataAccess class that you saw in chapter 20, updated to use ADO.NET. This class starts with a private read-only property named ConnectionString that retrieves and returns a connection string for the MMABooks database from the App.config file.

Next, the FindCustomer() method returns a Customer object that contains the data for the customer row specified by the customer ID that's passed to it. This method creates a SqlCommand object with a parameterized query that contains a placeholder for the customer ID. Then, it creates the parameter, sets its value to the customerID that was passed to the method, and adds the parameter to the Parameters collection of the command.

After the command is ready, this code opens the connection and executes the command to create a data reader object. Notice that the ExecuteReader() method specifies the SingleRow command behavior in addition to the CloseConnection behavior. That's because the query will return just one row. Then, the Read() method of the data reader is used to retrieve that row, the values of that row are assigned to a new Customer object, and the Customer object is returned to the calling method. However, if the reader doesn't contain a row, the code returns the default null value to indicate that the customer wasn't found.

If a SQL Server exception occurs, a SqlException object is thrown. Because of that, the ExecuteReader() method is coded within the try block of a try-catch statement that catches the SqlException object. That exception object is passed to a helper method named CreateDataAccessException(), which you'll see in part 4 of this figure. That method returns an instance of the DataAccessException object you saw in chapter 20. The catch block then throws that exception object. As you'll see, the other methods in this class are also coded to catch SqlException objects and throw DataAccessException objects.

In this method, the statements that create the connection, command, and data reader objects are coded with using declarations. Because of that, the connection, command, and data reader objects are closed when the method ends, and the resources for all three objects are released. As you'll see, the other methods in this class are also coded with using declarations like these.

The code for the MMABooksDataAccess class   Page 1

```
using System.Data;
using Microsoft.Data.SqlClient;
using System.Configuration;
...
public class MMABooksDataAccess
{
    private string ConnectionString =>
        ConfigurationManager.ConnectionStrings["MMABooks"].ConnectionString;

    public Customer? FindCustomer(int customerId)
    {
        try {
            Customer customer = null!;      // default return value

            string selectStatement =
                "SELECT c.CustomerID, c.Name, c.Address, c.City, c.State, " +
                    " s.StateName, c.ZipCode, c.Rowversion " +
                "FROM Customers AS c " +
                "JOIN States AS s " +
                "ON c.State = s.StateCode " +
                "WHERE c.CustomerID = @CustomerID";

            using SqlConnection connection = new(ConnectionString);
            using SqlCommand command = new(selectStatement, connection);
            command.Parameters.AddWithValue("@CustomerID", customerId);
            connection.Open();

            using SqlDataReader reader = command.ExecuteReader(
                CommandBehavior.SingleRow & CommandBehavior.CloseConnection);

            if (reader.Read())
            {
                customer = new() {
                    CustomerId = (int)reader["CustomerID"],
                    Name = reader["Name"].ToString()!,
                    Address = reader["Address"].ToString()!,
                    City = reader["City"].ToString()!,
                    State = reader["State"].ToString()!,
                    ZipCode = reader["ZipCode"].ToString()!,
                    StateNavigation = new() {
                        StateCode = reader["State"].ToString()!,
                        StateName = reader["StateName"].ToString()!,
                    },
                    Rowversion = (byte[])reader["Rowversion"]
                };
            }
            return customer;
        }
        catch (SqlException ex) {
            throw CreateDataAccessException(ex);
        }
    }
```

Figure 21-9   The code for the data access class (part 1 of 4)

The GetStates() method returns a List<State> object that contains one State object for each row in the States table, sorted by state name. To get this list, it creates a command with a SELECT statement that retrieves the appropriate data. Then, it executes this command to create a data reader that can be used to read each state. Next, this method uses this reader to read each row in the table, create a State object for each row, and add each State object to the List<State> object. Finally, the method returns the list of State objects.

The AddCustomer() method adds a new row to the Customers table. This method receives a Customer object that contains the data for the new row. Then, it creates a command object that contains an INSERT statement.

After that, this code adds the parameters to the Parameters collection of the command. Then, it opens the connection and uses the ExecuteNonQuery() method of the command object to execute the INSERT statement

After executing the command, this code checks the value that's returned to determine if any rows in the database were affected. If so, the insert was successful. In that case, the code assigns a SELECT statement to the CommandText property that retrieves the ID of the customer that was just added. Then, the code executes this new statement using the ExecuteScalar() method of the existing command.

Next, the code assigns this customer ID to the CustomerId property of the Customer object that was passed to the method. Then, it passes that Customer object to a helper method named Reload(), which you'll see in part 3 of this figure. This gets the rowversion column and the related state data for the new customer from the database.

The code for the MMABooksDataAccess class   Page 2

```
public List<State> GetStates()
{
    try {
        List<State> states = new();
        string selectStatement = "SELECT StateCode, StateName " +
            "FROM States ORDER BY StateName";

        using SqlConnection connection = new(ConnectionString);
        using SqlCommand command = new(selectStatement, connection);
        connection.Open();
        using SqlDataReader reader = command.ExecuteReader(
            CommandBehavior.CloseConnection);
        while (reader.Read()) {
            State state = new() {
                StateCode = reader["StateCode"].ToString()!,
                StateName = reader["StateName"].ToString()!
            };
            states.Add(state);
        }
        return states;
    }
    catch (SqlException ex) {
        throw CreateDataAccessException(ex);
    }
}

public void AddCustomer(Customer customer)
{
    try {
        string insertStatement =
            "INSERT Customers (Name, Address, City, State, ZipCode) " +
            "VALUES (@Name, @Address, @City, @State, @ZipCode)";

        using SqlConnection connection = new(ConnectionString);
        using SqlCommand command = new(insertStatement, connection);
        command.Parameters.AddWithValue("@Name", customer.Name);
        command.Parameters.AddWithValue("@Address", customer.Address);
        command.Parameters.AddWithValue("@City", customer.City);
        command.Parameters.AddWithValue("@State", customer.State);
        command.Parameters.AddWithValue("@ZipCode", customer.ZipCode);
        connection.Open();
        int count = command.ExecuteNonQuery();

        if (count > 0) {  // get newly created CustomerId from database
            command.CommandText =
                "SELECT IDENT_CURRENT('Customers') FROM Customers";
            customer.CustomerId =
                Convert.ToInt32(command.ExecuteScalar());
            Reload(customer);  // to get rowversion and State values
        }
    }
    catch (SqlException ex) {
        throw CreateDataAccessException(ex);
    }
}
```

Figure 21-9   The code for the data access class (part 2 of 4)

The Reload() method receives a Customer object and uses it to get the current data for the customer from the database. To do that, it calls the FindCustomer() method presented in part 1 of this figure.

Next, the code checks to see if the call to FindCustomer() returned null. If it did, then the selected customer is no longer in the database. In that case, the method returns the string "Deleted". Otherwise, it uses the data it retrieved from the database to update the properties in the customer object it receives. Then, it returns the string "Updated".

As you saw in part 2 of this figure, the AddCustomer() method calls the Reload() method to get the rowversion column and the related state data for the new customer from the database. Since that's all the AddCustomer() method needs to do, it doesn't use the string value that the Reload() method returns. As you'll see in a moment, though, the UpdateCustomer() and RemoveCustomer() methods use this return value to handle concurrency conflicts.

The UpdateCustomer() method updates an existing row in the Customers table. This method receives a Customer object that contains the updated data. Then, it creates a command object that contains an UPDATE statement. Notice that the WHERE clause of the UPDATE statement queries the Customers table by the CustomerID column and by the Rowversion column. Remember that if the row associated with the CustomerID has changed since the customer data was retrieved, the value of the Rowversion column will be different. Because of that, this UPDATE statement will update the row only if the customer is still in the database and none of the columns have been changed since the customer was retrieved.

After the parameter values are set, the UpdateCustomer() method uses the ExecuteNonQuery() method to execute the UPDATE statement and stores its return value in a variable named count. As you recall, this return value indicates the number of rows affected by the update. The method uses this value to determine whether the update succeeded.

First, though, the method passes the Customer object to the Reload() method and stores the string that method returns in a variable named status. It does this before checking the return value of the ExecuteNonQuery() method because it needs to update the customer data regardless of whether the update succeeded. If it did succeed, the app needs the updated rowversion and state data. And if it didn't succeed, the app needs the current database values to display to the user.

Finally, the code checks the number of rows affected by the update. If no rows were affected, it means that the customer data in the database has been changed since the customer was retrieved. In this case, the status returned by the Reload() method is passed to a helper method named CreateConcurrencyException(), which you'll see in part 4 of this figure. That method returns a DataAccessException object, which the code then throws.

The code for the MMABooksDataAccess class

```csharp
private string Reload(Customer customer)
{
    Customer current = FindCustomer(customer.CustomerId)!;
    if (current == null) {
        return "Deleted";
    }
    else {
        customer.Name = current.Name;
        customer.Address = current.Address;
        customer.City = current.City;
        customer.State = current.State;
        customer.ZipCode = current.ZipCode;
        customer.Rowversion = current.Rowversion;
        customer.StateNavigation = new() {
            StateCode = current.State,
            StateName = current.StateNavigation.StateName
        };
        return "Updated";
    }
}

public void UpdateCustomer(Customer customer)
{
    try {
        string updateStatement =
          "UPDATE Customers SET " +
            "Name = @Name, Address = @Address, City = @City, " +
            "State = @State, ZipCode = @ZipCode " +
          "WHERE CustomerID = @CustomerID " +
          "AND Rowversion = @Rowversion";

        using SqlConnection connection = new(ConnectionString);
        using SqlCommand command = new(updateStatement, connection);
        command.Parameters.AddWithValue("@Name", customer.Name);
        command.Parameters.AddWithValue("@Address", customer.Address);
        command.Parameters.AddWithValue("@City", customer.City);
        command.Parameters.AddWithValue("@State", customer.State);
        command.Parameters.AddWithValue("@ZipCode", customer.ZipCode);
        command.Parameters.AddWithValue("@CustomerID",
            customer.CustomerId);
        command.Parameters.AddWithValue("@Rowversion",
            customer.Rowversion);
        connection.Open();
        int count = command.ExecuteNonQuery();

        string status = Reload(customer);
        if (count == 0) {
            throw CreateConcurrencyException(status);
        }
    }
    catch (SqlException ex) {
        throw CreateDataAccessException(ex);
    }
}
```

Figure 21-9   The code for the data access class (part 3 of 4)

The RemoveCustomer() method deletes an existing row from the Customers table. This method receives a Customer object that contains the customer to delete. Then, it creates a command object that contains a DELETE statement and executes that DELETE statement.

This method implements concurrency checking using the same technique as the UpdateCustomer() method. That is, it includes the Rowversion column in the WHERE clause of the DELETE statement. Then, if the delete operation is unsuccessful due to a concurrency conflict, the method reloads the data, calls the CreateConcurrencyException() method, and then throws the DataAccessException object that's returned by that method. Notice that, unlike the UpdateCustomer() method, this method only calls the Reload() method if there's a concurrency conflict. That's because the Customer object doesn't need to be updated if the delete succeeds.

The private CreateConcurrencyException() helper method accepts a string parameter named status that it uses to create the appropriate error message. If the status is deleted, the error message indicates that another user has deleted the selected row. Otherwise, it indicates that another user has updated the selected row. Then, the method creates a new DataAccessException object with this error message and an error type of "Concurrency Error", and it returns that DataAccessException object.

The private CreateDataAccessException() helper method accepts a SqlException parameter that it uses to create the appropriate error message. To do that, it loops though the SqlError objects in the Errors collection and adds the error number and error message for each SqlError object to its error message. Then, the method creates a new DataAccessException object with this error message and an error type of "Database Error", and it returns that DataAccessException object.

The code for the MMABooksDataAccess class   Page 4

```csharp
public void RemoveCustomer(Customer customer)
{
    try {
        string deleteStatement =
            "DELETE FROM Customers " +
            "WHERE CustomerID = @CustomerID " +
            "AND Rowversion = @Rowversion";

        using SqlConnection connection = new(ConnectionString);
        using SqlCommand command = new(deleteStatement, connection);
        command.Parameters.AddWithValue("@CustomerID",
            customer.CustomerId);
        command.Parameters.AddWithValue("@Rowversion",
            customer.Rowversion);
        connection.Open();
        int count = command.ExecuteNonQuery();

        if (count == 0) {
            string status = Reload(customer);
            throw CreateConcurrencyException(status);
        }
    }
    catch (SqlException ex) {
        throw CreateDataAccessException(ex);
    }
}

private DataAccessException CreateConcurrencyException(string status)
{
    string msg = "";
    if (status.ToLower() == "deleted")
        msg = "Another user has deleted that record.";
    else
        msg = "Another user has updated that record.\n" +
                "The current database values will be displayed.";

    return new DataAccessException(msg, "Concurrency Error");
}

private DataAccessException CreateDataAccessException(SqlException ex)
{
    string msg = "";
    foreach (SqlError error in ex.Errors)
    {
        msg += $"ERROR CODE {error.Number}: {error.Message}\n";
    }

    return new DataAccessException(msg, "Database Error");
}
}
```

Figure 21-9   The code for the data access class (part 4 of 4)

Perspective

In this chapter, you learned another technique for developing database apps. Instead of using Entity Framework (EF) Core, you learned how to use ADO.NET to create and work with connections, commands, and data readers. When you work this way, you have to write code to perform many of the tasks that are handled automatically by EF Core. As a result, you have to write more code. However, you also gain control over how the data is processed.

Terms

ADO.NET (ActiveX Data Objects .NET)	parameter
.NET data provider	parameterized query
command	named variable
connection	scalar value
data reader	aggregate value
	action query

Exercise 21-1   Update the Product Maintenance app

For this exercise, you'll update the Product Maintenance app from the exercise for chapter 20 to use ADO.NET for database access instead of EF Core. To make that easier for you to do, all the EF Core code has been removed from the app.

Review the app

1. Open the app in the C:\C#\Ch21\ProductMaintenance directory and review the code for the Product Maintenance form. Notice that it has an MMABooksDataAccess class variable, a Product class variable, and calls several methods of the MMABooksDataAccess class.

2. Review the class files in the Models/DataLayer directory. Notice that the Product class is complete, as is the DataAccessException class in the DataAccess subdirectory. However, the MMABooksDataAccess class just contains some helper methods and stubs for the find, add, update, and remove methods. These stubs are where you'll add database access code.

Write the code to retrieve the connection string

3. Open the App.config file and review the connection string setting. If you're using SQL Server Express, or you're using SQL Server Express LocalDB but you've changed the location of the .mdf file, modify the connection string as needed.

4. In the data access class, add a private read-only property named ConnectionString. Code this property so it uses the ConfigurationManager object to return the connection string from the App.config file. Be sure to add a using directive for the System.Configuration namespace. You can use the code in figure 21-9 (part 1) as a guide.

Write the code to retrieve a product

5. Review the FindProduct() method in the data access class, and note that the try block starts by declaring a Product object that's initialized to null and ends by return the Product object. Update this method to query the database using the product code it receives. This method should use a data reader object to load the product data into a Product object. You can use the code in figure 21-9 (part 1) as a guide. The SELECT statement should include the Product-Code, Description, UnitPrice, OnHandQuantity, and Rowversion columns.

6. In the Product Maintenance form, find the event handler for the Click event of the Get Product button, and review the code that calls the FindProduct() method of the data access class. Then, run the app and try to display the data for product code PHP. If this doesn't work, modify your code until it does.

Write the code to add a product

7. In the data access class, update the AddProduct() method so the code in the try block adds the data in the Product object it receives to the database. You can use the code in figure 21-9 (part 2) as a guide. Note that, because the ProductCode primary key isn't generated by the database, you don't need to retrieve it after the product is added. But you do still need to reload the product to get the rowversion value for the new row.

8. In the Product Maintenance form, find the event handler for the Click event of the Add button, and review the code that calls the AddProduct() method of the data access class. Then, run the app and click the Add button to display the Add Product form.

9. Enter the data for a new product, making a note of the product code so you can find it again later. Then, click the Accept button to add the product to the database and display the product data on the Product Maintenance form. When you have this working correctly, end the app.

Write the code to modify a product

10. In the data access class, update the UpdateProduct() method so the code in the try block updates the database with the product data it receives. Be sure to include the rowversion column in the WHERE clause of your UPDATE statement to provide for optimistic concurrency. Also, be sure to reload the product data after the update. And be sure to check for a concurrency conflict and throw a concurrency exception if the row wasn't updated. You can use the code in figure 21-9 (part 3) as a guide.

11. In the Product Maintenance form, find the event handler for the Click event of the Modify button, and review the code that calls the UpdateProduct() method of the data access class.

12. Run the app and get the product that you added earlier in this exercise. Then, click the Modify button to display that product in the Modify Product form.

13. Make a change to the product description, price, or quantity and then click the Accept button. If you coded the UpdateProduct() method correctly, the updated data should now be displayed on the Product Maintenance form. Otherwise, you'll need to correct the code.

Write the code to delete a customer

14. In the data access class, update the RemoveProduct() method so the code in the try block deletes the data in the Product object it receives from the database. This method should implement optimistic concurrency, and it should reload the product data and throw a concurrency exception if a concurrency conflict occurs. You can use the code in figure 21-9 (part 4) as a guide.

15. In the Product Maintenance form, find the event handler for the Click event of the Delete button, and review the code that calls the RemoveProduct() method of the data access class.

16. Run the app and get the product that you added earlier in this exercise. Then, click the Delete button and confirm the deletion. If this worked correctly, the data should be cleared from the Product Maintenance form. When you have this working correctly, end the app.

Test the code that handles concurrency conflicts

17. In the data access class, add a method named SimulateConcurrentUpdate() that receives a string parameter for the product code and doesn't return a value.

18. Within this method, write an UPDATE statement that sets the value of the OnHandQuantity field to -1 for the specified product code. Then, write database access code that executes the UPDATE statement in the database. Don't worry about using a try-catch statement for this code.

19. Find the event handler for the Click event of the Modify button. In the try block, add code that calls the SimulateConcurrentUpdate() method and passes it the value of the ProductCode property of the Product object. This method should be called just before the UpdateProduct() method.

20. Run the app and display the data for product code PHP. Then, click the Modify button, make a change to the product's price, and click Accept. You should get a message that the data has been changed by another user. Click OK on the dialog and review the updated data that's displayed.

21. Stop the app and comment out the call to the SimulateConcurrentUpdate() method. Then, run the app, display the product again, click Modify, change the on hand quantity to a value other than -1, and click Accept. This time, the update should work. End the app and close the project.

22

How to use the DataGridView control

Windows Forms apps that work with databases frequently use the DataGridView control. This control lets you display multiple rows of data quickly and easily. Although you can also add, modify, and delete rows directly in a DataGridView control, that isn't common in real-world apps. Because of that, this chapter presents another technique for performing these operations when you use a DataGridView control.

How to display data in a DataGridView control

In the topics that follow, you'll learn the skills for displaying data in a DataGridView control and for formatting the grid. First, though, you'll learn the basics of how the control works, including how to set its basic functionality.

An introduction to the DataGridView control

The *DataGridView control* displays data in a row and column format. To illustrate, figure 22-1 shows a DataGridView control that displays data from the Products table of the MMABooks database. As you can see, the grid starts with a *header row* that identifies the columns. Then, each of the remaining rows displays the data for one product. Here, the intersection of a column and row is a *cell* that displays the data for a single column in a single row of the table. In addition, each row starts with a *header column*, and the current row is identified by an arrowhead. To select a row, you can click on its header column.

The grid in this figure has also been formatted so the data is easy to read. For example, the width of each column has been set so you can view all of the data in the column for each row. The foreground and background colors and the font for the column headers have been changed. And the background color of every other row has been changed.

Although the grid in this figure only displays data, you can also use a DataGridView control to add, update, and delete data. However, most production programs are designed so this functionality isn't provided directly from the grid. Instead, it can be provided using buttons like the ones shown in this figure. You'll see how that works later in this chapter.

This figure also lists some of the properties and a method of the DataGridView class. You use the Rows and Columns properties to get a collection of the rows and columns in the grid, and you use the DataSource property to set the data that's displayed in the grid. To size the columns of a grid, you can use the AutoResizeColumns() method. Then, the width of each column is set so the contents of each row in that column, including the header row, fits in the column. In most cases, though, you'll want to set the width of each column explicitly so it's the same width each time the grid is displayed.

Before going on, you should notice the vertical scrollbar that's displayed at the right side of the grid. This scrollbar is displayed automatically if the grid contains more rows than can be displayed at one time. Similarly, if a grid contains more columns than can be displayed at one time, a horizontal scrollbar is displayed. If that's not what you want, you can adjust the height and width of the DataGridView control.

A DataGridView control that displays a list of products

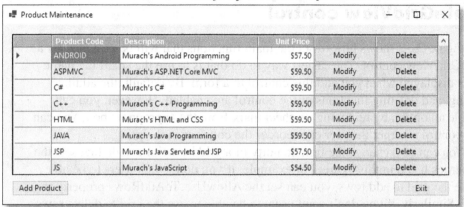

Common properties of the DataGridView class

Property	Description
Rows	A collection that contains all the rows in the control.
Columns	A collection that contains all the columns in the control.
DataSource	The data source for the control.

Common method of the DataGridView class

Method	Description
AutoResizeColumns()	Causes the widths of all columns to be adjusted to fit the contents of their cells, including the header cells.

Description

- You can use a *DataGridView control* to display data in a row and column format. The intersection of a row and column is called a *cell*.

- You can also use a DataGridView control to add, update, and delete data.

- If the data source for a DataGridView control contains more rows and columns than can be displayed at one time, scrollbars are displayed.

- You use the Rows and Columns properties to access the collections of rows and columns in a DataGridView control. Then, you can use an index to access a specific column or row.

- The DataSource property determines what data is displayed in the grid. See figure 22-3 for more information on setting this property.

- Instead of using the AutoResizeColumns() method, you can set the width of each column explicitly so it's the same size each time it's displayed. See figure 22-5 for more information.

Figure 22-1   An introduction to the DataGridView control

How to set the functions provided by a DataGridView control

Figure 22-2 shows how to set the main functions that will be provided by a DataGridView control. The easiest way to do that is to use the smart tag menu that's displayed when you add this control to a form. By default, the adding, editing, and deleting functions of the control are enabled. However, you can disable an option by removing its checkmark from the appropriate box. You can also control whether the user can reorder the columns in the grid.

You can also change the functionality of a grid by writing code that sets the properties listed in this figure. For example, if you don't want users to be able to use the grid to add rows, you can set the AllowUserToAddRows property to false. Similarly, if you don't want users to be able to use the grid to delete rows, you can set the AllowUserToDeleteRows property to false. However, to determine whether users can use the grid to edit data, you use the ReadOnly property. For example, if you don't want users to be able to use the grid to edit its data, you set the ReadOnly property to true.

Note that the smart tag menu contains other options for working with a DataGridView control. For example, it lets you choose the data source for the control, and it lets you edit and add columns. However, you can't use these options when you use code to specify the data source for the grid like you do when you use Entity Framework Core and ADO.NET as shown in this book. Instead, you have to perform these functions in code.

A DataGridView control after it's added to a form

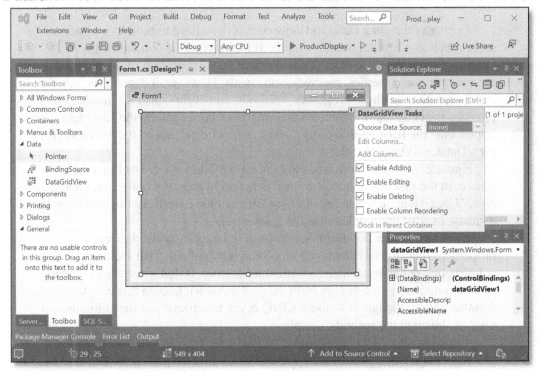

Properties that you can set from the smart tag menu

Property	Description
`AllowUserToAddRows`	If set to true, users can add rows directly to the grid. Otherwise, they can't. The default is true.
`AllowUserToDeleteRows`	If set to true, users can delete rows directly from the grid. Otherwise, they can't. The default is true.
`AllowUsersToOrderColumns`	If set to true, users can manually reposition columns. Otherwise, they can't. The default is false.
`ReadOnly`	If set to true, users can't edit data directly in the grid. Otherwise, they can. The default is false.

Description

- When you first add a DataGridView control to a form, its smart tag menu is displayed. You can use the options in this menu to determine if users can add, edit, and delete data directly in the control and if they can reorder columns.
- You can also determine the functions provided by the DataGridView control by using code to set the properties shown above.
- When you set the data source for a DataGridView control in code as shown in this chapter, you can't choose the data source from the smart tag menu. In addition, you can't edit or add columns using the commands available from this menu.

Figure 22-2   How to set the functions provided by a DataGridView control

How to bind to a data source

To display data in a DataGridView control, you have to bind it to a data source such as a list that implements the IList interface. If you haven't read chapter 15, you should know that an interface consists of a set of declarations for one or more properties, methods, and events. However, it doesn't include the implementation for those properties, methods, and events. Instead, another class provides the code that implements that interface. For example, the List class implements the IList interface. As a result, a List object can be the data source for a DataGridView control.

Figure 22-3 shows three ways to bind a DataGridView control to a data source. In the first example, the control is bound to an entity collection created by EF Core. Here, the code uses the ToList() method to retrieve the data from the database in a list that implements the IList interface.

When you bind a DataGridView control to an entity collection, each property of that entity is displayed in a column by default. That includes columns that define relationships with other entities. If that's not what you want, you can remove those columns from the grid as shown later in this chapter. Another option, though, is to use a LINQ query to retrieve just the columns you need as shown in the second example.

If you're using ADO.NET instead of EF Core, you can call a method that gets a collection of objects. Then, you can bind the DataGridView control to that collection as shown by the third example. Here, the code calls a method named GetAllProducts() that returns a List<Product> object. Then, it binds the grid to this list.

The DataGridView control at this top of this figure shows the default formatting that's applied when you bind the control. Later in this chapter, you'll learn ways to format the control to improve its appearance.

A DataGridView control that's bound to a data source

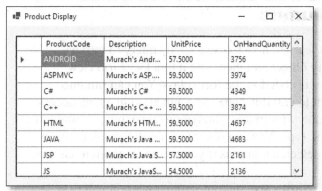

How to bind a DataGridView control to an entity collection

```
MMABooksContext context = new();
dgvProducts.DataSource = context.Products.ToList();
```

How to bind a DataGridView control to the results of a query

```
MMABooksContext context = new();
var products = context.Products
    .OrderBy(p => p.Description)
    .Select(p => new { p.ProductCode, p.Description, p.UnitPrice,
                       p.OnHandQuantity })
    .ToList();
dgvProducts.DataSource = products;
```

How to bind a DataGridView control to a list of objects created in code

```
List<Product> products = GetAllProducts();
dgvProducts.DataSource = products;
```

Description

- A DataGridView control can be bound to any class that implements the IList interface, including an array.

- To bind a DataGridView control, you set its DataSource property. Then, the data in the data source is displayed in the grid.

- When you bind the DataGridView to a list of objects, each property of that object becomes a column in the grid.

- If you're using EF Core and you bind a DataGridView control to an entity collection whose entities contain one or more properties for related entities, a column will be included for each relationship. If that's not what you want, you can use a LINQ query to get just the properties you want to include in the data source. Or, you can remove the relationship columns from the grid as shown later in this chapter.

- If you're using ADO.NET code, you can call a method that gets a collection of objects and then bind the DataGridView control to that collection.

Figure 22-3   How to bind to a data source

How to code a method in a data access class that gets selected columns

In the previous figure, you learned how to use a LINQ query to retrieve selected columns from an entity object and then bind it to a DataGridView control. This works if the query is coded in the form class. You can run into problems, however, if you want to call this code from a method in a data access class. That's because a LINQ query returns an anonymous type, but a method in a class needs to return a specific type. You can run into a similar problem when you use ADO.NET to retrieve selected columns if you create an anonymous type to store those columns.

Figure 22-4 shows how to return a specific type from a method in a data access class that gets selected columns. To do that, you can use a *data transfer object (DTO)* like the one in the first example. This DTO includes a property for each column that will be selected by a method in the data access class. In this case, the DTO is a record, but it could be a class, structure, or record struct as well. Since this DTO will store product data, it's named ProductDTO.

The second example shows how you can use this DTO in a method that uses EF Core and retrieves data using a LINQ query. Here, the GetAllProducts() method returns a List<ProductDTO> object. Then, to create this list, the Select() method of the query uses the constructor of the ProductDTO record. When the query is complete, the list is returned to the calling code.

The third example shows how to accomplish the same thing using ADO.NET. Like the example that uses EF Core and LINQ, the GetAllProducts() method in this example returns a List<ProductDTO> object. This method starts by creating a new List<ProductDTO> object. Then, the code that reads each row creates a new ProductDTO object and adds that object to the list. Finally, the list is returned to the calling code.

The fourth example shows a DataGridView control that's bound to the list that's returned by the GetAllProducts() method of the data access class. This works with either of the methods shown in this figure.

A data transfer object that includes properties for the selected columns

```
public record ProductDTO(string ProductCode, string Description,
    decimal UnitPrice);
```

A data access class that uses EF Core to return a list of DTO objects

```
public class MMABooksDataAccess
{
    private MMABooksContext context = new();

    public List<ProductDTO> GetAllProducts() =>
        context.Products
            .OrderBy(p => p.Description)
            .Select(p => new ProductDTO(p.ProductCode, p.Description,
                p.UnitPrice))
            .ToList();
}
```

A data access class that uses ADO.NET to return a list of DTO objects

```
public class MMABooksDataAccess
{
    // get connection string

    public List<ProductDTO> GetAllProducts()
    {
        List<ProductDTO> products = new();

        string selectStatement =
            "SELECT ProductCode, Description, UnitPrice " +
            "FROM Products ORDER BY Description";

        // create connection and command and open connection
        // create and open data reader

        while (reader.Read())
        {
            products.add(new ProductDTO(
                reader["ProductCode"].ToString()!,
                reader["Description"].ToString()!,
                (decimal)reader["UnitPrice"]));
        }
        return products;
    }
}
```

Code that calls the method to get the data for DataGridView controls

```
dgvProducts.DataSource = data.GetAllProducts();
```

Description

- A method in a data access class must return a specific type. To do that when the method gets selected columns, you can use a *data transfer object* (*DTO*).

- A DTO is a simple class, record, structure, or record struct that holds the data you want to return.

Figure 22-4   How to code a method in a data access class that gets selected columns

How to format the columns

The first table in figure 22-5 lists three of the properties of the DataGridViewColumn class that you can use to format the columns of a grid. This class represents a single column in a grid. The first property, HeaderText, lets you set the text you want displayed in a column's header. The second property, Width, lets you set the width of a column in pixels. By default, each column is set to a width of 100 pixels.

The third property, DefaultCellStyle, lets you set the default styles for all the cells in a column. The second table in this figure lists some of the properties of the DefaultCellStyle object that you can use to set styles. For example, you can use the Format property to format the data in a column, and you can use the Alignment property to align the data in a column.

The code example in this figure shows how you can change some of these column styles. Here, the first statement starts by using the Columns property to get the collection of columns in the grid. Then, it uses an index of 0 to get the first column in the collection, and it sets the header text for that column to "Product Code". The second statement sets the width of the second column to 300. The third statement applies currency formatting to the third column. And the fourth statement right-aligns the third column. To do that, the Alignment property is set to a member of the DataGridViewContentAlignment enumeration. After these and similar styles are applied, the grid looks as shown at the top of this figure.

Before going on, you should know that the way the data appears in the columns of a DataGridView control depends on the DPI of your monitor. For example, if the grid shown in this figure is displayed on a monitor with a lower DPI than the one it was developed on, some of the data will run past the ends of the columns. If possible, then, you should adjust the column widths to the DPI that you're targeting. Otherwise, it's best to do your development on a lower DPI monitor.

A DataGridView control after its columns are formatted

Product Code	Description	Unit Price	On Hand
ANDROID	Murach's Android Programming	$57.50	3756
ASPMVC	Murach's ASP.NET Core MVC	$59.50	3974
C#	Murach's C#	$59.50	4349
C++	Murach's C++ Programming	$59.50	3874
HTML	Murach's HTML and CSS	$59.50	4637
JAVA	Murach's Java Programming	$59.50	4683
JSP	Murach's Java Servlets and JSP	$57.50	2161
JS	Murach's JavaScript	$54.50	2136

Common properties of the DataGridViewColumn class for formatting

Property	Description
HeaderText	The text displayed in the header cell of a column.
Width	The width of a column in pixels. The default is 100.
DefaultCellStyle	The default cell style for a column.

Common properties used for cell styles

Property	Description
Format	The format string that's applied to the text content of a cell.
BackColor	A member of the Color structure that specifies the background color of a cell.
ForeColor	A member of the Color structure that specifies the foreground color of a cell.
Alignment	A member of the DataGridViewContentAlignment enumeration that specifies the alignment of the content within a cell.
Font	The font that's used to display the text content of a cell.

Code that changes some of the formatting for the columns in a grid

```
dgvProducts.Columns[0].HeaderText = "Product Code";
dgvProducts.Columns[1].Width = 300;
dgvProducts.Columns[2].DefaultCellStyle.Format = "c";
dgvProducts.Columns[2].DefaultCellStyle.Alignment =
    DataGridViewContentAlignment.MiddleRight;
```

Description

- To set the font for a cell, you create a font object by passing the appropriate arguments to its constructor and then assign the font to the Font property. For an example, see the next figure.

- In addition to formatting columns, you can also format rows using properties of the DataGridViewRow class. For more information, see the online documentation.

Note

- If an app with a DataGridView control is displayed on a screen with a higher DPI than the one it was developed on, the data may not fit in the columns correctly.

Figure 22-5   How to format the columns

How to format the headers and alternating rows

In addition to formatting the columns of a grid, you can format the column headers and alternating rows. The first table in figure 22-6 lists three properties of the DataGridView class that you can use to do that.

Before you can change the default cell styles for the headers of a grid, you have to turn off the default theme for the headers. To do that, you set the EnableHeadersVisualStyles property to false as shown by the first statement in the example in this figure.

Then, you can use the ColumnHeadersDefaultCellStyle property to set the default cell styles for the column headers. You do that using the cell style properties listed in the second table in figure 22-5. For example, the second statement in this figure uses the Font property to set the font for the headers. To do that, it creates a Font object using the arguments that are passed to its constructor and then assigns this object to the Font property.

The third and fourth statements in this figure show how to use the ColumnHeadersDefaultCellStyle property set the background and text colors of the row header. Here, the statement uses the BackColor and ForeColor properties to set the colors to members of the Color structure.

The fifth statement in this figure shows how to set the background color of the odd numbered rows using the AlternatingRowsDefaultCellStyle property. Like the ColumnHeadersDefaultCellStyle property, you set the styles for the alternating rows using the cell style properties listed in figure 22-5. Here, the statement uses the BackColor property to set the color to a member of the Color structure.

To change the styles for the header cells in individual columns, you use the HeaderCell property of the column to get a HeaderCell object. Then, you can use the Style property of that object to set any of the cell styles shown in the previous figure. For example, the last statement in this figure right-aligns the text in the header for the third column.

Before the header text is aligned, this code sets the SortMode property of the cell to the NotSortable member of the DataGridViewColumnSortMode enumeration. That's because, by default, space is allotted at the right side of each column header for the glyph that's displayed if the column provides for sorting. However, if you indicate that the column won't be sortable, no space is reserved for this glyph. That way, the header will be properly aligned.

Note that although all columns with text boxes provide for sorting by default, sorting isn't available if the grid is bound to a data source. That's why you don't see the sort glyph in any of the column headers in the grid shown here. However, space is still allotted for the glyph unless you set the SortMode property to NotSortable.

A DataGridView control after its headers and rows are formatted

Common properties of the DataGridView class for formatting

Property	Description
EnableHeadersVisualStyles	If set to false, turns off the default theme for the header styles. If set to true, the default theme is used and can't be overridden. The default is true.
ColumnHeadersDefaultCellStyle	The default style for the column headers.
AlternatingRowsDefaultCellStyle	The default style for the odd numbered rows.

Common properties of the DataGridViewColumn class for formatting headers

Property	Description
SortMode	A member of the DataGridViewColumnSortMode enumeration that determines if and how a column can be sorted. If set to NotSortable, the sort glyph that's displayed at the right side of the column header isn't display and no space is allotted for it.
HeaderCell	The header cell for the column.

Common property of the DataGridViewCell class for formatting

Property	Description
Style	The style for the cell.

Code that changes some of the formatting for a grid

```
dgvProducts.EnableHeadersVisualStyles = false;
dgvProducts.ColumnHeadersDefaultCellStyle.Font =
    new Font("Arial", 9, FontStyle.Bold);
dgvProducts.ColumnHeadersDefaultCellStyle.BackColor = Color.Goldenrod;
dgvProducts.ColumnHeadersDefaultCellStyle.ForeColor = Color.White;
dgvProducts.AlternatingRowsDefaultCellStyle.BackColor = Color.PaleGoldenrod;
dgvProducts.Columns[2].HeaderCell.Style.Alignment =
    DataGridViewContentAlignment.MiddleRight;
```

Description

- Before you can change the default cell styles for the headers of a grid, you have to set the EnableHeadersVisualStyles property of the grid to false so you can override the default theme for the headers.

Figure 22-6   How to format the headers and alternating rows

How to work with columns and events

As mentioned earlier in this chapter, the DataGridView controls in most production apps don't provide for adding, modifying, and deleting data directly in the grid. However, you can add columns that contain buttons for modifying and deleting rows. Then, when a user clicks on one of these buttons, you can handle the event that occurs to execute custom code that performs the modify or delete operation. You can also provide a button outside of the DataGridView control that lets the user add new rows.

How to add and remove columns

Figure 22-7 shows how to add a button column to a DataGridView control. To start, you use the constructor for the DataGridViewButtonColumn class to create a column that contains a button. Then, you can use the properties of this class to determine how the column is formatted. Finally, you can use the Add() method to add the column to the end of the Columns collection. Alternatively, you can use the Insert() method to insert the column at a specific index.

The first example in this figure shows how this works. Here, the first statement uses an object initializer to create the column. This sets the HeaderText property to an empty string so nothing is displayed in the column header. It sets the UseColumnTextForButtonValue to true so the value of the Text property is displayed on each button in the column. And it sets the Text property to "Delete". Then, the Add() method adds the column to the end of the Columns collection. The column that's created by this code is shown in the grid at the top of this figure. This grid also includes a button column with Modify buttons that's created using similar code.In addition to adding button columns, you can add columns that provide other types of controls including text boxes, checkboxes, and images. For more information on how to use these types of columns, see the online documentation.

This figure also shows how to delete a column from a grid. You might want to that, for example, if the grid is bound to an entity collection and the entity contains one or more properties that define relationships with other tables. Then, you can use the Remove() or RemoveAt() method to delete those columns.

A DataGridView control with two button columns

Common properties of the DataGridViewButtonColumn class

Property	Description
HeaderText	The text displayed in the header cell of a column.
Text	The default text that's displayed on a button.
UseColumnTextForButtonValue	If set to true, the value of the Text property is displayed on the button in each cell of the column. If set to false, the value of the FormattedValue property for each cell in the column is displayed on the button in that column. The default is false.

Common methods of the DataGridViewColumnCollection class

Method	Description
Add(column)	Adds the column to the end of the collection.
Insert(index, column)	Inserts a column at the specified index in the collection.
Remove(column)	Removes the specified column from the collection.
RemoveAt(index)	Removes the column at the specified index from the collection.

Code that adds a button column to a DataGridView control

```
DataGridViewButtonColumn deleteColumn = new() {
    HeaderText = "";
    UseColumnTextForButtonValue = true;
    Text = "Delete";
}
dgvProducts.Columns.Add(deleteColumn);
```

A statement that deletes a column from a DataGridView control

```
dgvProducts.Columns.RemoveAt(4);
```

Description

- In addition to displaying bound data, you can add columns to a DataGridView control that display a number of items, including buttons, checkboxes, and images.

- You can also delete columns from a DataGridView control. You might want to do that if the data source for the control includes columns that you don't want to display.

Figure 22-7   How to add and remove columns

How to work with the object that's passed to an event handler

If you add button columns to a DataGridView control, you'll need to code an event handler that's executed if a user clicks in one of those columns. In most cases, you'll code an event handler for the CellClick event as shown in figure 22-8. This event occurs when the user clicks on any part of the cell that contains the button. You can also code an event handler for the CellContentClick event, which occurs when the user clicks directly on the button.

When one of these events occurs, a DataGridViewCellEventArgs object is passed to the event handler. You can use the RowIndex and ColumnIndex properties of this object to get the indexes of the row and column that were clicked. The example in this figure shows how this works.

This example shows an event handler for the CellClick event of a DataGridView control that contains two button columns. This event handler starts by storing the index values of the button columns in constants named ModifyIndex and DeleteIndex. If you have several methods or event handlers that need to work with the index values of the button columns, you can use class constants, or you can move the constants to a separate utility class. Using constants like this makes your code easier to understand. In addition, this technique makes it so you only have to change the index values in one place if you add or remove columns from the control.

Next, this event handler checks that the row that was clicked isn't the header row. To do that, it makes sure that the RowIndex property is greater than -1.

If the header row wasn't clicked, this event handler uses the ColumnIndex property to check if the index for the column that was clicked matches the index for one of the button columns. If so, this code uses the RowIndex property to get the first cell of the row that was clicked. This cell contains the product code. Then, if the product code isn't null, the code gets the value of the cell, converts that value to a string, and trims any spaces from the beginning and end of the string. If the product code is null, however, it's set to an empty string.

After the product code is retrieved, it's used to get the Product object for that product. To do that, this code calls the FindProduct() method of the data access class. Then, the product is assigned to a class variable named selectedProduct.

This event handler ends by checking if the column that contains the Modify button was clicked. If so, it calls the ModifyProduct() method. Otherwise, it checks if the column that contains the Delete button was clicked. If so, it calls the DeleteProduct() method.

Properties of the DataGridViewCellEventArgs class

Property	Description
RowIndex	The index of the row that was clicked. Value is -1 if header row was clicked.
ColumnIndex	The index of the column that was clicked. Value is -1 if header column was clicked.

A property of the DataGridViewRow class

Property	Description
Cells	A collection that contains all the cells in a row.

A property of the DataGridViewCell class

Property	Description
Value	The value that's associated with the cell.

Code that handles the CellClick event of a DataGridView control

```
private MMABooksDataAccess data = new();
private Product selectedProduct = null!;

private void dgvProducts_CellClick(object sender,
DataGridViewCellEventArgs e)
{
    const int ModifyIndex = 4; // index for the Modify button column
    const int DeleteIndex = 5; // index for the Delete button column

    if (e.RowIndex > -1)          // make sure header row wasn't clicked
    {
        if (e.ColumnIndex == ModifyIndex || e.ColumnIndex == DeleteIndex)
        {
            DataGridViewCell cell = dgvProducts.Rows[e.RowIndex].Cells[0];
            string productCode = cell.Value?.ToString()?.Trim() ?? "";
            selectedProduct = data.FindProduct(productCode)!;
        }
        if (e.ColumnIndex == ModifyIndex)
            ModifyProduct();
        else if (e.ColumnIndex == DeleteIndex)
            DeleteProduct();
    }
}
```

Description

- When a user clicks on any part of a cell in a DataGridView control, the CellClick event occurs. When the user clicks on the content of a cell, the CellContentClick event occurs.

- When one of these events occurs, a DataGridViewCellEventArgs object is passed to the event handler for that event. You can use the RowIndex and ColumnIndex properties of that object to determine which row and column were clicked.

- You can use the Cells property of the DataGridViewRow class to get the collection of cells in a row. Then, you can use an index to get a DataGridViewCell object for a specific cell, and you can use the Value property of that object to get the value of the cell.

Figure 22-8   How to work with the object that's passed to an event handler

A Product Maintenance app

Now that you've learned the basic skills for working with a DataGridView control, you're ready to see a complete app that uses this control. This app uses EF Core to display, add, modify, and delete rows in the Products table. Of course, you could also use ADO.NET to implement this app. If you're interested, the download for this book includes an ADO.NET version of this app.

The user interface

Figure 22-9 presents the user interface for the Product Maintenance app. As you can see, this app consists of two forms. The Product Maintenance form includes a DataGridView control that lists all the products. Then, the user can click the Modify button for a product to modify the data for that product or the Delete button to delete that product. The user can also click the Add Product button below the grid to add a product.

If the user clicks the Add Product button or one of the Modify buttons, the Add/Modify Product form is displayed. This form works like the Add/Modify Customer form presented in the last two chapters. In the form shown here, the Modify button for the fourth Product was clicked, and the data for that product is displayed in the form.

After the user enters the appropriate values on the Add/Modify Product form and clicks the Accept button, the Product Maintenance form is redisplayed. Then, if a product was modified, the grid displays the new values for that product. Or, if a product was added, the grid includes that product.

If the user clicks one of the Delete buttons, a dialog like the one shown in this figure is displayed to confirm the delete operation. Then, if the user confirms the operation, the product is deleted from the grid, the Product Maintenance form is redisplayed, and the updated product data is displayed in the grid.

The Product Maintenance form

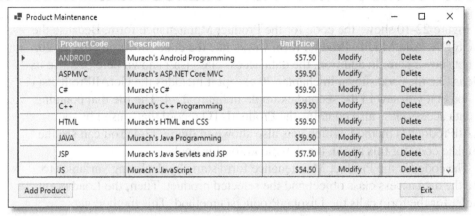

The Add/Modify Product form

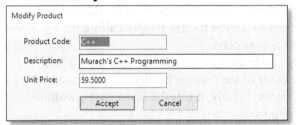

The dialog that's displayed to confirm a delete operation

Description

- To modify a product, the user clicks the Modify button for the product to display it in the Modify Product form. Then, the user can edit the product and click the Accept button.

- To delete a product, the user clicks the Delete button for the product. Then, the user responds to the dialog that's displayed to confirm the delete operation.

- To add a product, the user clicks the Add Product button below the DataGridView control to display a blank Add Product form. Then, the user enters the data for the new product and clicks the Accept button.

Figure 22-9   The user interface for the Product Maintenance app

The code for the Product Maintenance form

Figure 22-10 shows the code for the Product Maintenance form. Because the code for the Add/Modify Product form works like the code shown in chapter 20, it's not shown here. In addition, the data access class isn't shown here because its code is like the code shown in chapter 20 except it includes the GetAllProducts() method that you saw in the second example in figure 22-4. The file that contains the data access class also contains the ProductDTO record that's used by the GetAllProducts() method, which was also shown in figure 22-4. You can see the complete code for this app in the download for this book.

The code for the Product Maintenance form starts by declaring variables to store the data access class object and the selected product. Then, the Load event handler for the form calls the DisplayProducts() method. This method gets the data source for the grid and then formats the grid.

To do that, the DisplayProducts() method starts by clearing the grid. That's because the products need to be redisplayed each time a product is added, modified, or deleted. Then, it sets the data source for the grid by calling the GetAllProducts() method of the data access class.

After setting the data source, this code adds the two button columns. Then, it sets the font, back color, and fore color of the column headers. Next, it sets the back color of the odd numbered rows. Finally, it sets the header text, widths, alignment, and formatting of the columns.

Page 2 of this listing presents the event handler for the CellClick event of the grid. This event handler is similar to the one shown in figure 22-8, so you shouldn't have much trouble understanding how it works.

If the user clicks a Modify button, the ModifyProduct() method is executed. This method displays the Add/Modify Product form with the data for the selected product. Then, if the updated product data is valid (DialogResult.OK), this code gets the data from the form, stores it in the selectedProduct variable, saves the changes to the database, and displays the updated list of products in the grid.

Page 3 of this listing presents the DeleteProduct() method. This method is executed if the user clicks a Delete button. It begins by displaying a dialog that confirms the delete operation. If the operation is confirmed, this code deletes the product from the database and displays the updated list of products in the grid.

If the user clicks the Add Product button, this code displays a blank Add/Modify Product form. Then, if the product data is valid (DialogResult.OK), this code retrieves the data from the form and stores it in the selectedProduct variable. Then, it adds the new product to the database and displays an updated list of products in the grid.

The methods that edit, delete, and add products use a try-catch statement to handle any database errors that might occur. In the catch block for each method, the HandleDataAccessError() helper method is called. This method accepts a DataAccessException object and checks it to see if the error was caused by a concurrency conflict. If so, the products are redisplayed to show the current database values for the selected product. Then, for all errors, the code displays the error message to the user.

The code for the Product Maintenance form

Page 1

```
private MMABooksDataAccess data = new();
private Product selectedProduct = null!;

private void frmProductMaintenance_Load(object sender, EventArgs e)
{
    DisplayProducts();
}

private void DisplayProducts()
{
    dgvProducts.Columns.Clear();
    dgvProducts.DataSource = data.GetAllProducts();

    // add column for modify button
    DataGridViewButtonColumn modifyColumn = new() {
        UseColumnTextForButtonValue = true,
        HeaderText = "",
        Text = "Modify"
    };
    dgvProducts.Columns.Add(modifyColumn);

    // add column for delete button
    DataGridViewButtonColumn deleteColumn = new() {
        UseColumnTextForButtonValue = true,
        HeaderText = "",
        Text = "Delete"
    };
    dgvProducts.Columns.Add(deleteColumn);

    // format the column headers
    dgvProducts.EnableHeadersVisualStyles = false;
    dgvProducts.ColumnHeadersDefaultCellStyle.Font =
        new Font("Arial", 9, FontStyle.Bold);
    dgvProducts.ColumnHeadersDefaultCellStyle.BackColor = Color.Goldenrod;
    dgvProducts.ColumnHeadersDefaultCellStyle.ForeColor = Color.White;

    // format the odd numbered rows
    dgvProducts.AlternatingRowsDefaultCellStyle.BackColor =
        Color.PaleGoldenrod;

    // format the first column
    dgvProducts.Columns[0].HeaderText = "Product Code";
    dgvProducts.Columns[0].Width = 200;

    // format the second column
    dgvProducts.Columns[1].Width = 350;
```

Figure 22-10   The code for the Product Maintenance form (part 1 of 3)

The code for the Product Maintenance form

```
        // format the third column
        dgvProducts.Columns[2].HeaderText = "Unit Price";
        dgvProducts.Columns[2].HeaderCell.Style.Alignment =
            DataGridViewContentAlignment.MiddleRight;
        dgvProducts.Columns[2].Width = 135;
        dgvProducts.Columns[2].DefaultCellStyle.Format = "c";
        dgvProducts.Columns[2].DefaultCellStyle.Alignment =
            DataGridViewContentAlignment.MiddleRight;
    }

    private void dgvProducts_CellClick(object sender,
    DataGridViewCellEventArgs e)
    {
        // store index values for Modify and Delete button columns
        const int ModifyIndex = 3;
        const int DeleteIndex = 4;

        if (e.RowIndex > -1)  // make sure header row wasn't clicked
        {
            if (e.ColumnIndex == ModifyIndex || e.ColumnIndex == DeleteIndex)
            {
                string productCode = dgvProducts.Rows[e.RowIndex]
                    .Cells[0].Value?.ToString()?.Trim() ?? "";
                selectedProduct = data.FindProduct(productCode)!;
            }

            if (selectedProduct != null)
            {
                if (e.ColumnIndex == ModifyIndex)
                    ModifyProduct();
                else if (e.ColumnIndex == DeleteIndex)
                    DeleteProduct();
            }
        }
    }

    private void ModifyProduct()
    {
        frmAddModify addModifyForm = new() {
            Product = selectedProduct
        };
        DialogResult result = addModifyProductForm.ShowDialog();
        if (result == DialogResult.OK)
        {
            try {
                selectedProduct = addModifyForm.Product;
                data.UpdateProduct(selectedProduct);
                DisplayProducts();
            }
            catch (DataAccessException ex)
            {
                HandleDataAccessError(ex);
            }
        }
    }
```

Figure 22-10   The code for the Product Maintenance form (part 2 of 3)

The code for the Product Maintenance form   Page 3

```csharp
private void DeleteProduct()
{
    DialogResult result =
        MessageBox.Show($"Delete {selectedProduct.ProductCode.Trim()}?",
        "Confirm Delete", MessageBoxButtons.YesNo, MessageBoxIcon.Question);
    if (result == DialogResult.Yes)
    {
        try
        {
            data.RemoveProduct(selectedProduct);
            DisplayProducts();
        }
        catch (DataAccessException ex)
        {
            HandleDataAccessError(ex);
        }
    }
}

private void btnAdd_Click(object sender, EventArgs e)
{
    frmAddModify addModifyForm = new();
    DialogResult result = addModifyProductForm.ShowDialog();
    if (result == DialogResult.OK)
    {
        try
        {
            selectedProduct = addModifyForm.Product;
            data.AddProduct(selectedProduct);
            DisplayProducts();
        }
        catch (DataAccessException ex)
        {
            HandleDataAccessError(ex);
        }
    }
}

private void HandleDataAccessError(DataAccessException ex)
{
    if (ex.IsConcurrencyError)
    {
        DisplayProducts();
    }

    MessageBox.Show(ex.Message, ex.ErrorType);
}

private void btnExit_Click(object sender, EventArgs e)
{
    this.Close();
}
```

Figure 22-10   The code for the Product Maintenance form (part 3 of 3)

How to provide paging for a DataGridView control

If the data source for a DataGridView control contains a large number of rows, you may want to let the user display those rows page by page rather than by using a scroll bar. This allows the app to work more efficiently because it only retrieves the rows for one page at a time.

The user interface for a form that provides for paging

Figure 22-11 shows the user interface for a Customer Display app that uses paging. Here, the four paging controls are included below the grid on its left side. These controls let the user move to the first, previous, next, and last pages. In this case, the first page is displayed so the First and Previous buttons are disabled.

In most cases, you'll also want to include controls that let users jump to a specific page. To display a customer whose name is near the middle of the alphabet, for example, a user can enter the middle page number in the text box below the grid and click the Go To Page button. Then, if necessary, the user can click the Previous or Next button to locate the customer. This can be more efficient than clicking the Next button multiple times to get to the same page.

A Customer Display form that provides for paging

Customer Display					− □ ×

	Name	Address	City	State	Zip Code
▶	Abeyatunge, Derek	1414 S. Dairy Ashford	North Chili	NY	14514
	Abueg, Don	901 N. Lake Destiny	Montvale	NJ	07645
	Agarwala, Troy	2308 Fair St.	Wapakoneta	OH	45895
	Agrawal, Weining	1435 Chrome Hill Road	Chickasha	OK	73018
	Aguimba, Edward	444 Propsect St	Streamwood	IL	60107
	Ahmed, Uma	110 Jay Dr.	Polk City	IA	50226
	Akkiraju, Mike	3811 N. Bell	Hazlet	NJ	07730
	Alderman, James	6405 N Mokane Ct	Columbia	MD	21046
	Alexander, Skip	15 Gettysburg Square 187	West Hartford	CT	06107
	Allen, Craig	P.O. Box 50016	Pullman	WA	99164

| << | < | > | >> | 1 of 70 | Go To Page | Exit |

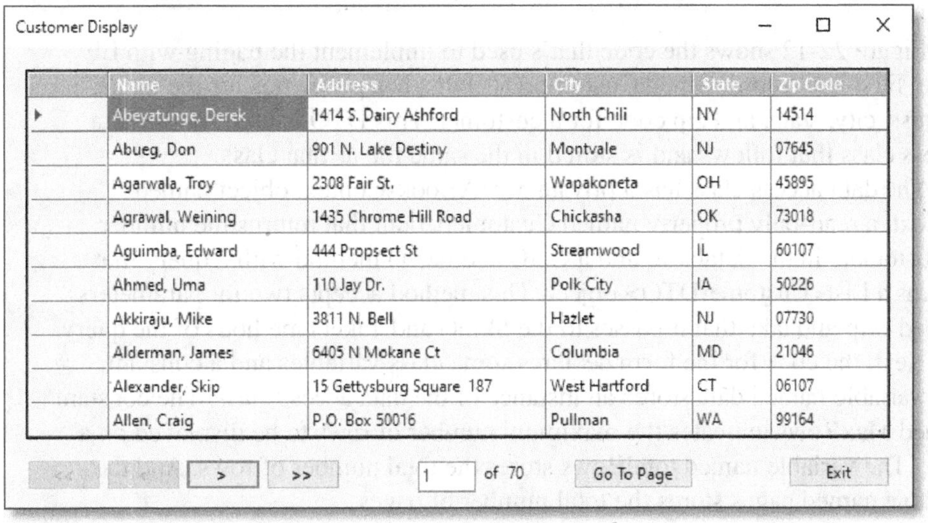

Description

- The Customer Display app provides for displaying data for all of the customers in the Customers table, with ten customers displayed per page. To do that, it uses Entity Framework Core and LINQ queries in a data access class.

- The user can click the four buttons below the left side of the grid to display the first, previous, next, or last page. These buttons are enabled and disabled depending on what page is displayed.

- The text box below the grid indicates the current page that's displayed, and the label to the right of the text box indicates the total number of pages. The user can jump to a specific page by entering the page number in the text box and then clicking the Go To Page button.

Figure 22-11   The user interface for a form that provides for paging

The code that implements the paging

Figure 22-12 shows the code that's used to implement the paging with EF Core. First is a record named CustomerDTO that has properties for the name, address, city, state, and zip code for a customer. This DTO is used by the data access class that follows and is stored in the same file as that class.

The data access class has a private MMABooksContext object named context, a read-only property named CustomerCount that returns the number of customers in the database, and a GetCustomers() method with a query that returns a List<CustomerDTO> object. This method accepts two int parameters named skip and take that it passes to the Skip() and Take() methods of the query.

Next, the code for the form declares some class variables and a constant. The variable named data stores an instance of the data access class. The constant named MaxRows indicates the maximum number of rows to be displayed on a page. The variable named totalRows stores the total number of rows. And the variable named pages stores the total number of pages.

The Load event handler for the form starts by using the CustomerCount property of the data access class to get the total number of rows. Then, it calculates the number of pages. To do that, it divides the total number of rows by the maximum number of rows per page. Then, it uses the modulus operator to check whether there are any remaining rows after the division operation. If so, it adds one to the number of pages.

After these calculations, this code displays the total number of pages in the label to the right of the text box. Then, the code calls the DisplayCustomers() method and passes it a value of 1 to display the first page of customer rows.

The DisplayCustomers() method begins by displaying the current page number in the text box on the form. Then, it calculates the values for the variables named skip and take. The skip variable stores the number of rows to be skipped before rows are retrieved, and the take variable stores the number of rows to be retrieved for a specific page.

To calculate the take variable, the code begins by setting it equal to the MaxRows constant. In most cases, this is what you want because it displays a full page of rows. However, if the page number is equal to the total number of pages, the code sets the take variable equal to the total number of rows minus the skip variable. That's because the last page might not have a full page of rows. Similarly, if the total number of rows is less than or equal to the maximum number of rows for a page, it means that the first page doesn't display a full page of rows. In that case, this code sets the take variable to the totalRows variable.

After calculating the take variable, this code calls the GetCustomers() method of the data access class, passing the skip and take variables to that method. Then, it uses the list that's returned by the method as the data source for the grid.

After setting the data source for the grid, this code formats the grid so it appears as shown in the previous figure. To do that, it uses the same techniques used by the Product Maintenance app presented in figure 22-10.

The DisplayCustomers() method finishes by passing its pageNumber parameter to the EnableDisableButtons() helper method. This method enables or

The DTO and data access class

```
public record CustomerDTO(string Name, string Address,
    string City, string State, string ZipCode);

public class MMABooksDataAccess
{
    private MMABooksContext context = new();

    public int CustomerCount => context.Customers.Count();

    public List<CustomerDTO> GetCustomers(int skip, int take) =>
        context.Customers
            .OrderBy(c => c.Name)
            .Select(c => new CustomerDTO(c.Name, c.Address, c.City,
                c.State, c.ZipCode))
            .Skip(skip)
            .Take(take)
            .ToList();
}
```

The code in the form that implements the paging

```
private MMABooksDataAccess data = new();
private const int MaxRows = 10;
private int totalRows = 0;
private int pages = 0;

private void frmCustDisplay_Load(object sender, EventArgs e)
{
    totalRows = data.CustomerCount;
    pages = totalRows / MaxRows;
    if (totalRows % MaxRows != 0) {
        pages += 1;
    }
    lblPages.Text = pages.ToString();

    DisplayCustomers(1);
}

private void DisplayCustomers(int pageNumber)
{
    txtPage.Text = pageNumber.ToString();
    int skip = MaxRows * (pageNumber - 1);
    int take = MaxRows;

    if (pageNumber == pages) {
        take = totalRows - skip;
    }
    if (totalRows <= MaxRows) {
        take = totalRows;
    }
    dgvCustomers.DataSource = data.GetCustomers(skip, take);

    // Code that formats the DataGridView control goes here

    EnableDisableButtons(pageNumber);
}
```

Figure 22-12   The code that implements the paging (part 1 of 2)

disables the buttons on the form depending on the page number, as shown in part 2 of this figure.

The EnableDisableButtons() method first checks whether the page number equals 1. If so, the app is displaying the first page of customers, and the code disables the First and Previous buttons. Otherwise, the app is displaying a page other than the first one, so this code enables the First and Previous buttons.

Then, this method checks whether the page number equals the total number of pages. If so, the app is displaying the last page of customers, and the code disables the Next and Last buttons. Otherwise, the app is displaying a page other than the last page, so this code enables the Next and Last buttons.

Finally, this method checks whether the total number of rows is less than or equal to the maximum number of rows for a page. If so, there's only one page of customer rows. In that case, the previous if statements have already disabled the First, Previous, Next, and Last buttons. As a result, the third if statement just disables the Go To Page button.

If the user clicks the First, Previous, Next, or Last button, the corresponding event handler is executed. Each of these event handlers passes a page number to the DisplayCustomers() method to display the appropriate page. If the user clicks the First button, for example, its event handler passes a value of 1 to the DisplayCustomers() method to display the first page of customers. Similarly, if the user clicks the Last button, its event handler passes the total number of pages to the DisplayCustomers() method to display the last page of customers.

If the user clicks the Previous or Next button, the event handler starts by determining the page number to display. To do that, these event handlers start by getting the current page number from the form and converting it to an int value. Then, the event handler for the Previous button decreases the page number by 1, and the event handler for the Next button increases the page number by 1. Then, the event handlers call the DisplayCustomer() method with the new page number to display the previous or next page.

If the user enters a page number in the text box and clicks the Go To Page button, the event handler for this button first calls the IsValidData() method to make sure the user entered a valid page number. Although the code for this method isn't shown here, it works like the code you've seen throughout this book to check that the user entered a valid integer that's within the range of pages.

If the page number is valid, this event handler gets the page number from the text box on the form. Then, it passes the page number to the DisplayCustomers() method. This displays the specified page of customer rows.

Although this figure shows how to use EF Core to implement paging, you can use ADO.NET if you prefer. To do that with a SQL Server database, you can use a SELECT statement something like this:

```
SELECT Name, Address, City, State, ZipCode
FROM Customers
ORDER BY Name
    OFFSET @Skip ROWS
    FETCH NEXT @Take ROWS ONLY
```

Then, you can set the values of the @Skip and @Take parameters before executing the statement.

The code that implements the paging (continued)

```csharp
private void EnableDisableButtons(int pageNumber)
{
    if (pageNumber == 1) {              // if it's the first page,
        btnFirst.Enabled = false;      // disable the first and
        btnPrev.Enabled = false;       // previous buttons
    } else {
        btnFirst.Enabled = true;
        btnPrev.Enabled = true;
    }

    if (pageNumber == pages) {          // if it's the last page,
        btnNext.Enabled = false;       // disable the last and
        btnLast.Enabled = false;       // next buttons
    } else {
        btnNext.Enabled = true;
        btnLast.Enabled = true;
    }

    if (totalRows <= MaxRows) {         // if there's only one page,
        btnGoTo.Enabled = false;       // disable the GoTo button
    }
}

private void btnFirst_Click(object sender, EventArgs e)
{
    DisplayCustomers(1);
}

private void btnPrev_Click(object sender, EventArgs e)
{
    int pageNumber = Convert.ToInt32(txtPage.Text);
    pageNumber -= 1;
    DisplayCustomers(pageNumber);
}

private void btnNext_Click(object sender, EventArgs e)
{
    int pageNumber = Convert.ToInt32(txtPage.Text);
    pageNumber += 1;
    DisplayCustomers(pageNumber);
}

private void btnLast_Click(object sender, EventArgs e)
{
    DisplayCustomers(pages);
}

private void btnGoTo_Click(object sender, EventArgs e)
{
    if (IsValidData()) {
        int pageNumber = Convert.ToInt32(txtPage.Text);
        DisplayCustomers(pageNumber);
    }
}
```

Figure 22-12   The code that implements the paging (part 2 of 2)

How to create a Master/Detail form

You can also use DataGridView controls to display data in related tables of a database. To do that, you can use one grid to display the rows on the one side of the relationship and another to display the rows on the many side of the relationship.

The user interface for a Master/Detail form

Figure 22-13 presents the user interface for a *Master/Detail form* that uses two DataGridView controls. This form lets users select a customer from the Customers grid. Then, it displays the invoices for that customer in the Invoices grid.

In addition, the Customers grid provides paging controls. Then, each time a different page is displayed, the first customer on that page is selected by default and any invoices for that customer are displayed in the Invoices grid. To display the invoices for another customer on the page, the user can click on the row header for that customer. In this figure, for example, the user clicked on the row header for the customer named Sarah Chamberland. Then, the Invoices grid displayed the three invoices for that customer.

A Master/Detail form that displays customers and invoices

Customer Invoice Display   —   □   ×

Name	Address	City	State	Zip Code
Castle, Kenneth	1536 Chicago Blvd	Clearwater	FL	33756
Cate, Kim	123 Wild Lilac Court	San Mateo	CA	94402-5009
Cefalu, George	19 Winchester St #207	Milwaukee	WI	53212
Chamberland, Sarah	1942 S. Gaydon Avenue	Doraville	CA	30340
Chandrasekhar, Yagnaraju	2149 West Dunlap Avenue	Bethalto	IL	62010
Chanduri, Walter c	1331 Jefferson Avenue	Delray Beach	FL	33445
Chang, Simon	8317 Cabin Creek Drive	Oshkosh	WI	54901
Chansa, Tom	123 Sfsdfsdfsdf	Sacramento	CA	95820-4617
Chavan, Rhonda	518 Commanche Tr.	Greensboro	NC	27410
Chavez, Gregory	6472 Mll Ct	Frederick	MD	21703

[<<] [<] [>] [>>]   [13] of 70   [Go To Page]

Invoice ID	Invoice Date	Product Total	Sales Tax	Shipping	Invoice Total
18	10/13/2022	$172.50	$12.94	$6.25	$191.69
46	10/13/2022	$234.00	$17.55	$7.50	$259.05
50	10/14/2022	$59.50	$4.46	$3.75	$67.71

[Exit]

Description

- The Customer Invoice Display app displays data about customers and their related invoices. To do that, it uses two DataGridView controls.

- Paging is provided for the DataGridView control that displays the customer data. This works the same as for the Customer Display app shown in figures 22-11 and 22-12.

- When a page of customers is first displayed, the first customer is selected and any invoices for that customer are displayed in the second DataGridView control.

- To display the invoices for another customer, the user clicks the row header for that customer.

Figure 22-13   The user interface for a Master/Detail form

The code for the DTOs, data access class, and form

Figure 22-14 shows the code that's needed to implement the Master/Detail form used by the Customer Invoice Display app. To start, this app uses two DTOs. The CustomerDTO record is similar to the one for the Customer Display app you saw in figure 22-12, but it includes a property for the customer id. That's because this app needs the customer id to get the related invoices for a customer. The second DTO is implemented using a record named InvoiceDTO that holds the values from the Invoices table to be displayed in the second grid.

The GetCustomers() method of the data access class is also similar to the one for the Customer Display app. However, because the CustomerDTO record includes a CustomerId property, this property is included in the constructor of the CustomerDTO record.

This data access class also includes a method named GetCustomerInvoices(). This method accepts a customer id and returns a List<InvoiceDTO> object that includes all the invoices for that customer, sorted by invoice id.

The DisplayCustomers() method in the code for the form is mostly the same as in the Customer Display app. One difference is that the DisplayCustomers() method now includes code that selects the first customer on the page and displays that customer's invoices. To do that, it uses one statement to select the first row of the Customers grid, which has an index of 0. Then, it uses a second statement to pass a value of 0 to the DisplayInvoices() method. This displays the invoices for the first row of the Customers grid.

Another difference is that the DisplayCustomers() method now sets the Visible property of the first column to false. That's the column for the customer id that the GetCustomers() method now returns. Although the app needs the customer id value in this column to get the invoices for a customer, the id does not need to be displayed in the grid. So, this code hides it.

When the user clicks the row header for a customer, the event handler for the RowHeaderMouseClick event is executed. This event handler calls the DisplayInvoices() method and passes the RowIndex property of the DataGridViewCellMouseEventArgs parameter to it. This provides the index of the row that was clicked.

The code for the DisplayInvoices() method starts by getting the row that the user clicked. Then, it gets the value of the first cell in that row, which contains the customer id. Next, it calls the GetCustomerInvoices() method of the data access class and passes it the customer id. This method returns a List<InvoiceDTO> object that contains the invoices with that customer id, which the code then assigns to the DataSource property of the Invoices grid. This displays the invoices in that grid.

The DTOs and data access class

```
public record CustomerDTO(int CustomerId, string Name, string Address,
    string City, string State, string ZipCode);

public record InvoiceDTO(int InvoiceId, DateTime InvoiceDate,
    decimal ProductTotal, decimal SalesTax, decimal Shipping,
    decimal InvoiceTotal);

public class MMABooksDataAccess
{
    private MMABooksContext context = new();
    public int CustomerCount => context.Customers.Count();

    public List<CustomerDTO> GetCustomers(int skip, int take) =>
        context.Customers.OrderBy(c => c.Name)
            .Select(c => new CustomerDTO(c.CustomerId, c.Name, c.Address,
                c.City, c.State, c.ZipCode))
            .Skip(skip).Take(take).ToList();

    public List<InvoiceDTO> GetCustomerInvoices(int customerID) =>
        context.Invoices
            .Where(i => i.CustomerId == customerID)
            .OrderBy(i => i.InvoiceId)
            .Select(i => new InvoiceDTO(i.InvoiceId, i.InvoiceDate,
                i.ProductTotal, i.SalesTax, i.Shipping, i.InvoiceTotal))
            .ToList();
}
```

The code that implements the Master/Detail form

```
private void DisplayCustomers(int pageNumber)
{
    ...
    dgvCustomers.DataSource = data.GetCustomers(skip, take);

    dgvCustomers.Rows[0].Selected = true;        // select the first row
    DisplayInvoices(0);                          // display its invoices

    // format customer grid
    dgvCustomers.Columns[0].Visible = false;  // hide the customer id column
    ...
}
private void dgvCustomers_RowHeaderMouseClick(object sender,
DataGridViewCellMouseEventArgs e)
{
    DisplayInvoices(e.RowIndex);
}

private void DisplayInvoices(int rowIndex)
{
    DataGridViewRow row = dgvCustomers.Rows[rowIndex];
    int customerID = Convert.ToInt32(row.Cells[0].Value);
    dgvInvoices.DataSource = data.GetCustomerInvoices(customerID);

    // format the invoices grid
}
```

Figure 22-14   The code for the Master/Detail form

Perspective

In this chapter, you learned how to display multiple rows from a database table in a DataGridView control. In addition, you learned how to provide for add, update, and delete operations when you use a DataGridView control, you learned how to provide paging for a DataGridView control, and you learned how to use two DataGridView controls to create a Master/Detail form. These are some of the most important skills for working with this control. At this point, you have the background you need to learn more about this control if you ever need to do that.

Terms

DataGridView control
header row
cell
header column
data transfer object (DTO)
Master/Detail form

Exercise 22-1   Create a Customer Maintenance app that uses a grid

In this exercise, you'll create a Customer Maintenance app that displays customer data in a DataGridView control. This control will also contain button columns that let the user modify and delete customers, and the form will contain an Add button that lets the user add customers. To make this app easier to develop, we'll give you the Entity Data Model and data access class, the Add/Modify Customer form, the Validator class, and some of the code for the Customer Maintenance form.

The design of the Customer Maintenance form

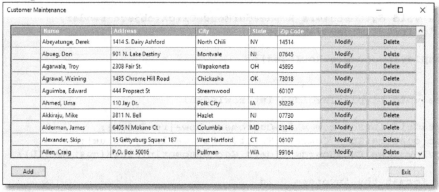

Open the project and create the grid

1.   Open the app in the C:\C#\Ch22\CustomerMaintenance directory.

2. Add a DataGridView control to the Customer Maintenance form. When the smart tag menu is displayed, set the options so the user can't add, edit, or delete data directly in the control.

3. In the MMABooksDataAccess.cs file, immediately after the namespace statement, add a record named CustomerDTO that includes properties for the customer id, name, address, city, state, and zip code. (Since this record is used only by the MMABooksDataAccess class, it makes sense to code this record in the same file as the class.)

4. Add a method to the data access class that uses a LINQ query to get the customer id, name, address, city, state, and zip code for each customer. Sort the customers by name, and return the results in a List<CustomerDTO> object. To keep things simple, don't worry about exception handling.

5. Back in the Customer Maintenance form, bind the DataGridView control to the list that's returned by the new data access method.

6. Set the Visible property of the column that contains the customer id so it isn't displayed. Then, set the widths of the remaining columns so they can display the data they contain. In addition, format the column headers and alternating rows any way you like.

7. Adjust the width of the grid so you can see all the columns as well as the vertical scrollbar. In addition, adjust the height of the grid so you can see 10 customers at a time. You may have to run the app and adjust the width and height multiple times before you get this right.

Add two button columns to the grid

8. Declare a constant that contains the index value for the Modify button column that you'll add to the grid. Then, declare a constant that contains the index value for the Delete button column. Remember, indexes are zero based and the first column isn't visible.

9. Add the button columns to the grid. To do that, use the Insert() method of the Columns collection, and pass in the correct constant for the index argument.

10. Re-adjust the width of the grid so you can see all the columns as well as the vertical scrollbar. Adjust the position of the buttons and the size of the form so it looks as shown on the previous page.

11. Generate an event handler for the CellClick event of the DataGridView control. This event handler should start by using the constant values to check if a cell that contains a Modify or Delete button was clicked. If it was, it should get the customer id from the row that was clicked and then call the FindCustomer() method in the data access class to get the customer with that id and store it in the selectedCustomer variable. Then, if a Modify button was clicked, it should call the ModifyCustomer() helper method, and if a Delete button was clicked, it should call the DeleteCustomer() helper method.

12. Test these changes to be sure they work. To test the delete operation, first add a new customer and then delete that customer.

Exercise 22-2 Add paging to the Customer Maintenance app

In this exercise, you'll provide paging for the DataGridView control used by the Customer Maintenance app you worked on in exercise 22-1.

1. Open the app in the C:\C#\Ch22\CustomerMaintenancePaging directory.

2. Add four buttons between the Add and Exit buttons that will let the user move to the first, previous, next, and last page of customers.

3. Declare a constant with a value that indicates the maximum number of rows per page. Then, declare class variables to store the total number of rows, the total number of pages, and the current page number.

4. Add a read-only property to the data access class that returns the total number of customers in the database.

5. Add code to the event handler for the Load event of the form that assigns the value of this new data access property to the total rows class variable. Then, add code that calculates and sets the total number of pages. Finally, set the current page number class variable to 1 so the DisplayCustomers() method displays the first page of customers.

6. Modify the GetCustomers() method of the data access class so it accepts two int parameters named skip and take. Then, use those parameters in the LINQ query to return the customers for the requested page. If you need help, you can refer to the code in figure 22-12.

7. Modify the DisplayCustomers() method so it calculates the skip and take variables and passes them to the GetCustomers() method. If you need help, you can refer to the code in figure 22-12.

8. Modify the EnableDisableButtons() method so it enables or disables the appropriate buttons depending on the current page.

9. Add an event handler for the Click event of the First button. Then, add code to this event handler that sets the current page to the first page and calls the DisplayCustomers() method.

10. Add event handlers for the remaining paging buttons, and add the code necessary to set the current page number and display that page of customers. If you need help, you can refer to the code in figure 22-12.

11. Run the app to be sure the paging buttons work and are enabled and disabled as appropriate.

Exercise 22-3   Create an Invoice Line Item Display app

In this exercise, you'll create an app that displays a grid with all the invoices in the Invoices table. Then, when the user selects an invoice, all the line items for that invoice are displayed in a second grid. To make this app easier to develop, the starting point provides the design of the form.

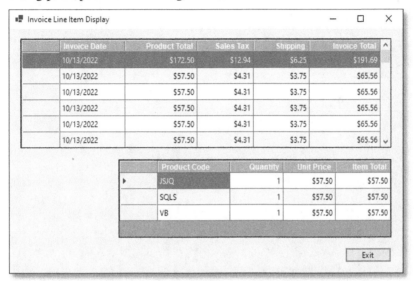

1. Open the app in the C:\C#\Ch22\InvoiceLineItemDisplay directory, and display the form to see that it contains two DataGridView controls.

2. In the file that contains the data access class, add a record for a data transfer object that includes properties for the columns in the grid of invoices shown above plus the invoice id. Then, update the GetInvoices() method so it returns a list of the DTO objects.

3. Add code to the DisplayInvoices() method in the form that binds the Invoices grid to the data returned by the GetInvoices() method.

4. In the file that contains the data access class, add a record for a data transfer object that includes properties for the columns in the grid of line items shown above. Then, update the GetInvoiceLineItems() method so it returns a list of the DTO objects.

5. Add code to the DisplayLineItems() method to get the invoice row that was selected and then the invoice id from that row. Then, use that invoice id to bind the Line Items grid to the data returned by the GetInvoiceLineItems() method.

6. Add code to the Load event handler for the form that calls the DisplayInvoices() method, calls the DisplayLineItems() method to display the line items for the first invoice, and selects the first invoice.

7. Generate an event handler for the RowHeaderMouseClick event of the Invoices grid. Then, add code to display the line items for the invoice that was clicked.

Appendix A

How to set up Windows for this book

To develop the apps presented in this book, you need to have a computer that's running Windows, and you need to install Visual Studio on it. In addition, if you're going to develop apps that use a database as described in chapters 19 through 22, you need to install SQL Server. The easiest way to do that is to install SQL Server Express LocalDB when you install Visual Studio Community.

This appendix describes how to install Visual Studio. In addition, it describes how to make sure your system is set up to use the database that's presented in chapters 19 through 22. But first, it describes how to download the files for this book from our website and install them on your computer.

How to install the files for this book

This book presents complete apps that illustrate the skills that are presented in each chapter. You can download these apps from our website. Then, you can install them as described in figure A-1. This download also includes the starting points and solutions for the exercises that are at the end of each chapter.

After you're done downloading the files, you should run the copy_exercises.bat file as described at the bottom of this figure. This copies the subdirectories of the ExStarts directory into the C:\C# directory (creating this directory if necessary). That way, you can find the exercise start for chapter 1 in the C:\C#\Ch01 directory. In addition, if you make a mistake and want to restore a file to its original state, you can do that by copying it from the ExStarts directory.

The BookApps directory contains all of the Windows Forms apps presented in this book. As a result, you can use Visual Studio to open these apps. Then, you can view the source code for these apps, and you can run them to see how they work.

The ExStarts directory contains the starting points for the exercises presented at the end of each chapter. To do that, it contains one subdirectory for each chapter. In addition, it contains two subdirectories named Database and Files. The Database subdirectory contains the files for the MMABooks database that's used by the exercises in section 5. The Files subdirectory contains the files used by the exercises for the chapters in sections 3 and 4.

The ExSolutions directory contains the source code for the solutions to the exercises. If you have trouble doing an exercise, you can use Visual Studio to open the solution. Then, you can compare the solution to your app to solve any problems that you encountered while attempting to do the exercise.

The Database directory contains another copy of the files for the MMABooks database that's used in section 5. In addition, it contains a SQL script file that you can use to create the MMABooks database if necessary. You'll learn more about that in figure A-3.

The Murach website

www.murach.com

The directory that contains the Visual Studio projects

C:\Murach\C#

The subdirectories

Directory	Description
BookApps	The apps presented throughout this book.
ExStarts	The starting points for the exercises at the end of each chapter.
ExSolutions	The solutions to the exercises.
Database	The database files for the book apps and exercises.

How to download and install the files for this book

1. Go to www.murach.com and find the page for *Murach's C# (8ᵗʰ Edition)*.
2. If necessary, scroll down to the FREE Downloads tab. Then, click on it.
3. Click the DOWNLOAD NOW button for the zip file for Windows. This should download a file named cse8_allfiles.zip.
4. Use File Explorer to find the zip file on your computer.
5. Extract the files stored in this zip file into the C:\Murach directory. If the C:\Murach directory doesn't already exist, create it.

The directory that contains a copy of the exercise starts

C:\C#

How to make a copy of the exercise starts

1. Use File Explorer to find the copy_exercises.bat file in the C:\Murach\C# directory.
2. Double-click the copy_exercises.bat file. This should copy all of the subdirectories of the ExStarts directory to the C:\C# directory.

Description

- We recommend that you store the files for this book in the folders shown above.

Figure A-1   How to install the files for this book

How to install Visual Studio

If you've installed Windows applications before, you shouldn't have any trouble installing Visual Studio. To do that, you download the installer program from the website address shown at the top of figure A-2. Then, you run the executable file that's downloaded as described in the procedure in this figure. This procedure describes how to install Visual Studio 2022 Community. However, you should be able to use this procedure to install other editions and newer versions of Visual Studio too.

When you install Visual Studio, it's important to select the correct workload. This workload determines the components that are installed. To develop Windows Forms apps as described in this book, for example, you need to select the .NET Desktop Development workload as shown in this figure. This installs all required components for .NET desktop development including the C# language as shown by the right side of the installer window.

The Installer program also selects several optional components. In most cases, you can accept these selections. However, if you want to work with databases as shown in section 5, you should make sure to select a version of SQL Server Express LocalDB.

Once you've selected the components you want to install, you click the Install button to start the installation. Then, Visual Studio displays a window that shows the installation progress. When the installation completes, Visual Studio may start automatically, but if it doesn't, you can start it by using the Windows Start menu. Then, you'll be asked to sign in to or create your Microsoft account. You'll also be asked to set the default environment settings for Visual Studio. When you do that, select Visual C# from the Development Settings combo box if you want your menus to match the ones described in this book. These steps are described in more detail in chapters 1 and 2.

If you want to install new components after you've already installed Visual Studio, you can run the Visual Studio Installer program again. To do that, you can select the Tools→Get Tools and Features command from the Visual Studio menus. Then, in the Installer program, click the Individual Components tab, select the component that you want, and click the Modify button. For example, you can use this technique to install other versions of .NET.

Note that you can also download a free trial of the Professional and Enterprise Editions of Visual Studio from the website address shown in this figure. However, these trials are only free for 30 days (90 days if you sign in), and this book only describes features provided by the Community Edition. As a result, we recommend installing the Community Edition.

The download page for Visual Studio

https://visualstudio.microsoft.com/downloads/

The Visual Studio Installer program

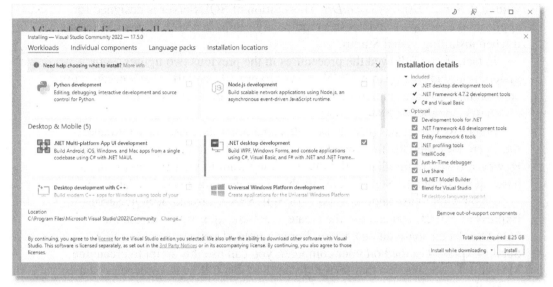

How to install Visual Studio Community

1. Download the Visual Studio Community Installer program from the page shown above.
2. Run the downloaded exe file.
3. Select the .NET Desktop Development workload. Note that this includes support for the C# programming language.
4. In the Optional category, select the SQL Server Express LocalDB item if it isn't already selected.
5. Click the Install button.
6. When the installation is complete, Visual Studio may start automatically. If it doesn't, you can start Visual Studio by using the Windows Start menu. Then, you'll be asked to sign in and set the default environment settings. If you want your menus to match the ones described in this book, select Visual C# from the Development Settings combo box. These settings are described in more detail in chapters 1 and 2.

Description

*   You can use the Visual Studio Installer program to install not only Visual Studio, but also C#, .NET, and SQL Server Express LocalDB.
*   After you install Visual Studio, you can install new components such as new versions of .NET. To do that, start the Visual Studio Installer program by selecting the Get Tools and Features item from the Tools menu of Visual Studio. Then, click the Individual Components tab, select the version of .NET that you want, and click the Modify button.

Figure A-2   How to install Visual Studio

How to set up your system to use the database

Chapters 19 through 22 show how to develop apps that work with a database. These apps use a database named MMABooks and are designed to work with *SQL Server Express LocalDB*. This edition of SQL Server is designed for application developers and doesn't require any setup. In addition, you can install it when installing Visual Studio.

In fact, if you followed the procedures in the previous two figures, your system is already set up to use SQL Server Express LocalDB. That's because the apps in this book are configured to use the database file that's stored here:

`C:\C#\database\MMABooks.mdf`

Figure A-3 describes this file as well as the other database files. Of these files, you only need the first two if you're using SQL Server Express LocalDB. However, if you're familiar with SQL, you may want to view the create_database.sql file to see the SQL statements that were used to create this database.

If you want to use another version of SQL Server instead of SQL Server Express LocalDB, you can use the create_database.sql script to create the MMABooks database on that server. For example, if you already have SQL Server Express installed on your computer, you can use this script to create the MMABooks database on that server. To do that, just follow the procedure shown in this figure.

However, using SQL Server Express requires changing the connection string for each database app presented in chapters 20 through 22. As a result, even if you already have SQL Server Express installed on your computer, you may want to install SQL Server Express LocalDB too. That way, you won't have to change the connection string for each database app presented in this book. Instead, you can just change the connection string for each app that you want to run on SQL Server Express.

The database files for the MMABooks database

Filename	Description
MMABooks.mdf	The main database file for the MMABooks database. This file stores the data for the database.
MMABooks_log.mdf	The log file for the MMABooks database. SQL Server uses this file to keep track of changes that have been made to the database. If it doesn't exist, SQL Server creates it.
create_database.sql	A script file that contains the SQL statements used to create the MMABooks database.

The directory that contains the database files for this book

```
C:\Murach\C#\database
```

The directory that contains a copy of the database files for this book

```
C:\C#\database
```

How to use SQL Server Express LocalDB

- If you followed the procedures described in figures A-1 and A-2, your system is already set up to use SQL Server Express LocalDB.

How to use SQL Server Express instead of SQL Server Express LocalDB

1. Install SQL Server Express and SQL Server Management Studio. To do that, you can download these products for free from Microsoft's website and install them.
2. Start SQL Server Management Studio and connect to SQL Server Express.
3. Use SQL Server Management Studio to open the create_database.sql script and run it. This should create the MMABooks database and fill it with data.
4. Edit the connection strings for the database apps presented in chapters 20 through 22 so they work with SQL Server Express. To do that, you can specify that SQL Server Express is running on your computer like this:

```
Server=localhost\SQLExpress;Database=MMABooks;Integrated Security=True
```

Description

- SQL Server Express LocalDB is an embedded edition of SQL Server that's designed for application developers and requires no setup. Because it's so easy to use, the apps in this book are configured to work with LocalDB.
- SQL Server Express is a scaled down edition of SQL Server that includes the core database engine. Since this requires more setup, we don't recommend using this approach with this book. However, if you want to use SQL Server Express anyway, you can use the procedure shown in this figure to do that.

Figure A-3   How to set up your system to use the MMABooks database

Index

W

XYZ